The
Essential
Dictionary of
Management and
Human Resources

The
Essential
Dictionary of
Management and
Human Resources

Jerry M. Rosenberg

Professor, Rutgers University Business School

**BARNES
& NOBLE
BOOKS**

NEW YORK

To Lauren, Bob, Bess, and Ella
"They make it all worthwhile."

PREFACE

> "Language is a city, to building of which every human being brought a stone."
>
> — Ralph Waldo Emerson

Twenty-five years ago, the first edition of the *Dictionary of Management* (originally published by John Wiley & Sons) appeared. It was planned as a one and only effort. This dictionary, now in its fourth edition, testifies to significant changes in the world of management, in its broadest sense of 40 subdisciplines, with special emphasis on the critical aspects of human resources (called personnel in its early days). Over the past several years, events and new concepts have necessitated the redoing of this lexicon to update its entries and to include terminology only recently coined.

The art and craft of dictionary creation demands patience—patience to track a newly heard or read word, to closely watch whether it can survive the passage of time. Some do, others do not. For example, there is *Reaganomics,* while there is no concept of *Clintonomics.* A lexicographer is obligated to track an evolving phrase, to seek its appearance in print. One appearance does not suffice. With repetition and ultimate longevity, there remains the issue of definition. The same word can be used by different people, at varying times, for differing situations, and thus evolve alternative meanings. All has to be justified, and that's where the lexicographer can be harshly tested.

Since the appearance of the third edition of this work more than a decade ago, numerous new entries have been gathered, followed, and now entered into the millennium of new terminology. With this edition, I have attempted to incorporate those phrases and concepts that are ever present in management, integrating the latest thinking, in order to clarify for the user how the terminology can be translated into comprehension, action, and reward.

A very special thanks to Rick Campbell, publisher at Barnes and Noble, for his initiation of this twenty-fifth anniversary project and for his keen sense of quality lexicography.

A lifetime of pursuing the proper and meaningful usage of business and management words has found support from those individuals that are most important to me. There is my precious wife Ellen, who after 43 years of marriage remains a partner in all of our activities. Sharing my interest in lexicography are others in my family: my daughters Lauren and Liz, respectively married to Bob and Jon, and my three grandchildren, Bess, Ella, and Celia. Only in their presence do I at times find myself lacking in the proper verbal expression of true love.

To my audience and users, I continue to appreciate your efforts communicating with me with suggestions for new entries and/or corrections of definitions found in this volume.

Jerry M. Rosenberg, Ph.D.
January 2004
New York, New York

INTRODUCTION

This *Essential Dictionary of Management and Human Resources* incorporates traditional terms used throughout the world of business, management, and human resources. Issues and practices for worker development—from the hiring to the motivational experience—to enhance satisfaction and productivity have been given proper attention only in the past 100 years. Thus a library of concepts and terms have mushroomed in the past century as this discipline has received its rightful place in the organizational experience.

This work has been prepared with the hope that awareness of the accepted meanings of terms may enhance the process of sharing information and ideas. Though it cannot eliminate the need for the user to determine how an individual writer or speaker treats a word, such a dictionary shows what usages exist. It should assist in stabilizing terminology. Most important, it should aid people in saying and writing precisely what they intend, with greater clarity.

A word can take on different meanings in different contexts. There may be as many meanings as there are areas of specialty. A goal of this lexicon is to be broad and to establish core definitions that represent the variety of individual meanings, to enhance clarity in the communication process.

Many terms are used in different ways. I have tried to unite them without giving one meaning advantage or dominance over another. Whenever possible (without creating a controversy), I have stated the connections among multiple usages.

Commonly used symbols, acronyms, and abbreviations are included. Foreign words and phrases are given only if, considering globalization, they have become an integral part of our English vocabulary.

This work reaches throughout all departments, both private and public, by acknowledging that the sum of an organization is greater than any of its individual parts. The result is an all-inclusive dictionary of business, management, and human resources.

ORGANIZATION & FORMAT

This is a defining work rather than a compilation of facts. This line is not easy to draw, because in the final analysis, meanings are based on facts. Consequently, factual information is used where necessary to make a term more readily understood. All entries are presented in the language of those who use them. The level of complexity needed to define a term will vary with the user; one person's complexity is another's precise and parsimonious statement. Several meanings are sometimes given, both general and specialized entries, to make this dictionary an especially useful reference source.

Alphabetization. Words are presented alphabetically. Compound terms are placed where the reader is most likely to look for them. They are entered under their most distinctive component, usually the noun. Should you fail to locate a word or phrase where you initially searched for it, turn to a variant spelling, a synonym, a shortened form, or a different word of the compound term. Numbers are alphabetized as if they are spelled out.

Entries containing mutual concepts are usually grouped for comparison. They are then given in inverted order; that is, the standard order of words is reversed to allow the major word of the phrase to appear at the beginning of the term. These entries precede those that are given in the standard order. The terms are alphabetized up to the first comma, and then by words following the comma, thus establishing clusters of related terms.

Headings. The current popular term is usually given as the principal entry, with other terms cross-referenced to it. Some terms have been included for historical significance, even though they are no longer in common use.

Cross-References. Cross-references go from the general to the specific. Occasionally, "See" references from the specific to the general are used to inform the user of words related to particular entries. "See" references to currently accepted terminology are made wherever possible. The use of "Cf." suggests words to be "compared with" the original entry.

Synonyms. The phrase "Synonymous with" following a definition does not imply that the term is exactly equivalent to the principal entry under which it appears. Frequently, the synonymous term only approximates the primary sense of the original entry.

Disciplines. Many words are given multiple definitions based on their utilization in various fields of activity. The definition with the widest application is given first, with the remaining definitions listed by area of specialty. Since the areas may overlap, the user should read all multiple definitions.

The
Essential
Dictionary of
Management and
Human Resources

A

A: the total average dollar inventory.

AAA: see *American Accounting Association*.

ABA: see *American Bankers Association*.

abandonment:

(1) **finance:** the elimination from use of a fixed asset; the total retirement of a fixed asset from service following salvage or other reclaiming of removable parts.

(2) **insurance:** a surrender of property by the owner to the insurer in order to claim a total loss when, in fact, the loss may be less than total. This is not permitted under a fire insurance policy, but under proper circumstances the principle is applicable in ocean marine business.

(3) **transportation:** a request by a carrier for permission to stop service over all or part of its route or to give up ownership or control of the cargo or carrier; a refusal to accept delivery of badly damaged items.

(4) **business law:** with a patent, trademark, or copyright, the cession of rights by the owner, whereby the invention, design, or name falls into the public domain.

abandonment stage: the final stage in a product's life cycle, when the profit potential is such that management decides that the best course is to discontinue marketing it.

abatement:

(1) **finance:** cancellation of part or all of an expenditure.

(2) **finance:** cancellation or reduction of an assessed tax.

(3) **business law:** a reduction or pulling down, as with nuisance.

abatement of a nuisance: a court action to terminate acts detrimental to the public welfare.

ABC inventory method: the classification of inventory items, for control purposes, into three categories, according to unit costs and number of items kept on hand.

ability: an individual's capacity to perform the various tasks in a job.

ability tests: tests purporting to measure an individual's capacity to perform the various tasks in a job. Cf. *aptitude tests*.

ability to pay:

(1) **collective bargaining:** the ability of management to meet the financial demands of a union. This capacity depends on the financial condition of the firm and often is disputed.

(2) **finance:** a criterion used to ascertain who shall bear the cost of federal programs; the rationale for taxing individuals in the form of a progressive income tax.

ability to pay basis: in wage and salary administration, a concept in which an employer's ability to pay specific wage rates is a factor.

able-bodied labor: workers who possess the physical strength to perform a variety of manual tasks. The term excludes the very young, the very old, and those who are incapacitated, either physically or mentally.

above-normal loss (ANL): a loss made greater than normal by virtue of weather, delayed alarm, or other conditions not usually expected. See *loss expectancy.* Cf. *consequential loss; extraordinary gain or loss; normal foreseeable loss.*

above par: the price of a stock or bond, that is higher than its face amount.

above the line: the promotional expenses associated with advertising in one of the media.

abreaction channels: ways established by management to give employees opportunities to air dissatisfactions and blow off steam (e.g., attitude surveys, counseling).

abrogation of agreement: the cancellation or setting aside of a contract or any portion of it.

absence: an employee's temporary unavailability for work that lasts for one or more days or shifts.

absence of demand: within a market, when a significant portion of the market finds no possibilities of benefits from a product and is, consequently, entirely disinterested in the item.

absence rate: the ratio of absences to available work days, determined by the total number of man-days missed divided by the total number of man-days worked over a specified time frame.

absentee: a person who is absent, usually referring to a worker who is absent for a particular work day or shift.

absenteeism: failure to report to work.

absolute advantage: an advantage of one nation or area over another in the costs of manufacturing an item in terms of resources used.

absolute cost barriers: barriers to entry into an industry that are not related to economies of scale. These barriers allow established firms to produce at lower cost than potential entrants, and they derive from control of sources of raw materials, patent rights, and established marketing approaches. See *economies of scale.*

absoluteness of responsibility: the concept that managers cannot avoid responsibility for the activities of their subordinates. They may delegate authority, but they cannot delegate all responsibility.

absolute sale: any transaction where no qualifications to completion are imposed by either the buyer or the seller.

absorb:

(1) **accounting:** to merge by transfer all or portions of an account with another account, resulting in the loss of identity of the first account.

(2) **finance:** to include pertinent actual costs in determining a price or standard cost.

absorbed: designating a security no longer in the hands of an underwriter and now with a shareholder. Cf. *outstanding*.

absorption account: see *adjunct account*.

absorption costing: a type of product costing that assigns fixed manufacturing overhead to the units produced as a product cost.

absorption point: the point at which the securities market rejects further offerings that are unaccompanied by price concessions.

abstinence concept: a theory according to which a postponement in the use of an item involves a cost that should be reimbursed by a payment such as interest.

abstract:

(1) **general:** a document that summarizes another document.

(2) **personnel:** a brief summary of a potential employee's background, interests, and other relevant information.

abstract of title: an attorney's prepared statement tracing the history of the ownership of real property to determine the present title. See *encumbrance*.

accelerated depreciation: depreciation at a greater than expected rate. This makes the depreciation allowance, and therefore the tax allowance, available sooner, resulting in a benefit to the owner.

accelerating premium pay: a wage incentive system under which the bonus or premium is progressively higher as the production standard is exceeded.

acceleration principle: exemplified by the direct relationship in which a change in sales at the consumer level results in an even greater change in the sales of goods.

accelerator: synonymous with *marginal propensity to invest*.

accelerator theory of business investment: a concept that investment spending is closely related to changes in consumption. An increase or decrease in consumption spending will induce a change in investment that is proportionally even greater than the change in consumption.

acceptability: an attitude toward money resulting in its acceptance as a medium of exchange in the marketplace.

acceptable quality level: the percent of defects in a lot that would be acceptable most of the time. A concept of quality control whereby managers are willing to accept a certain level of production defects, which are dealt with through repair facilities and service centers.

acceptance:

(1) **banking:** a time draft (bill of exchange) on the face of which the drawee has written "accepted" over his or her signature. The date and place payable are also indicated. The person accepting the draft is known as the acceptor. A bank acceptance is a draft drawn on and accepted by a bank.

(2) **transportation:** the acknowledged receipt by a shipment's consignee, resulting in termination of the common carrier contract.

acceptance for honor: the receipt of a draft or bill of exchange by another party when collection has been rejected by the drawee and protest for nonacceptance has been claimed. Cf. *notice of dishonor.*

acceptance house: an organization that specializes in lending funds on the security of bills of exchange or offers its name as an endorser to a bill drawn on another party.

acceptance line: the maximum limit in monies that a bank commits itself to accept for a single client.

acceptance number: the maximum number of defects allowed in a sample for acceptance of a lot. Cf. *acceptable quality level.*

acceptance supra protest: following a protest, the payment of a bill in order to preserve the reputation or credit of the drawer or endorser.

acceptance theory of authority: a theory suggesting that a subordinate's decision to accept a superior's order is the ultimate source of authority. See *authority.*

acceptor: the drawee of a note for acceptance, who agrees, upon signing the form, to pay a draft or bill when due.

accession:

(1) **personnel:** the hiring of a new employee or the rehiring of a former worker.

(2) **business law:** the doctrine that the property owner is entitled to all that is added or affixed to the property.

(3) **management:** elevation to office.

accession rate: the average number of persons added to a payroll in a given period per 100 employees. See *turnover.* Cf. *dismissal pay; termination pay; separation rate.*

accessory equipment: industrial goods, such as hand tools, office equipment, or forklifts, that usually do not operate directly in the production process and normally have shorter lives and are less costly than installations.

accidental death benefit: an amount payable in addition to the face amount of an insurance policy in the event of the accidental death of the insured.

accident and health insurance: a type of coverage that pays benefits, sometimes including reimbursement for loss of income, in case of sickness, accidental injury, or accidental death. Cf. *health insurance; hospitalization insurance; medical expense insurance; medical payments insurance.*

accident insurance: insurance against the loss of earning power as the result of a disabling accident only. Cf. *health insurance.*

accident severity: a measure of the amount of time lost as the result of an accident.

accommodation: historically, the lending of currency by a person who has it to another who has need of it, without collateral; more popularly, the lending of a person's honor or credit, without any consideration, to enable another to obtain borrowed money.

accommodation desk: an area in a store for providing customer services, including gift wrapping, adjustments, and refunds.

accommodation endorsement: signature or endorsement of a note or draft solely for the purpose of inducing a bank to lend money to a borrower whose personal credit is not substantial enough to warrant a loan.

accommodation line: insurance business accepted by an insurer from an agent, a broker, or the insured (assuming his or her account is otherwise satisfactory), that would be declined if considered strictly on the merits of the individual risk.

accommodation paper: a promissory note, endorsed by an individual(s), allowing the original signer of the note to receive bank credit; thus the second or other signer(s) accepts the guarantee of credit.

accommodation party: one who signs a note as maker, drawer, acceptor, or endorser without receiving value, though remaining totally liable, for the purpose of lending the creditworthiness of his or her name to another person.

accommodative social responsibility strategy: assuming additional responsibilities of the underlying substance to which they relate.

account:

(1) **finance:** a record of all the transactions, and the date of each, affecting a particular phase of a business, expressed in debits and credits, evaluated in money, and showing the current balance, if any.

(2) **advertising:** an advertiser; the client of an advertising agency or an organization that places promotional material directly with the media.

accountability in management: the process of making top corporate leaders responsible for their actions, goals, and so on, utilizing available objective measures.

accountability practices: focuses on treating diverse employees fairly.

accountant: an individual engaged in accounting work. Cf. *certified public accountant.*

account balance: the net debit or net credit amount in a specific account in the ledger. An excess of total debits over total credits results in a debit balance; an excess of total credits over total debits results in a credit balance.

account classification: the evaluation of retail or other buyers according to existing and, in particular, potential business.

account current: the accounting for business produced by an insurance agent for each month, reported by him or her to the company no later than the tenth of the following month.

account debtor: an individual who is obligated on an account, contract right, or general intangible.

account executive:

(1) **advertising:** the member of an agency who supervises the planning and preparation of advertising of clients and is responsible for contacts between the agency and the advertiser.

(2) **securities:** synonymous with *registered representative.*

accounting: the art, science, interpretation, and organized method of recording all the transactions affecting the financial condition of a business or organization.

accounting conventions: synonymous with *accounting principles.*

accounting cycle: see *accounting process.*

accounting principles: broad guidelines that identify the procedures to be used in specific accounting situations. Synonymous with *accounting conventions.*

Accounting Principles Board (APB): the top private-sector regulatory body; existed from 1959 to 1973, when it was succeeded by the Financial Accounting Standards Board. See *Financial Accounting Standards Board.*

accounting procedure: methods that uncover, record, or summarize financial information in the yielding of financial statements.

accounting process: the means of transforming accounting data into accounting reports that can be interpreted and used in decision making; often used interchangeably with *accounting cycle.*

accounting profit: revenue receipts of a firm less explicit costs. See *explicit costs.*

accounting cushion: overstating an expense provision.

accounting rate of return: income for a period divided by the average investment made in that period.

account number: the numeric identification given to an account in an institution or business, such numerical identification being a part of and in direct harmony with the overall system of numerical description given to the accounts that exist in that institution or business.

accounts payable: a current liability representing the amount owed by an individual or a business to a creditor for merchandise or services purchased on an open account or short-term credit.

accounts receivable: money owed a business enterprise for merchandise bought on open account.

accounts receivable financing: short-term financing that involves either the pledge of receivables as collateral for a loan or the outright sale of receivables.

accredited list: a listing of people to whom a public warehouse representative makes issue of merchandise stored without the specific authority in each instance from the merchandise's owner.

accretion account: a record of the increase between the acquisition value and the face value of bonds purchased at a discount.

accruals: items of revenue, expenses, receivables, or payables recorded as a result of the use of the accrual basis of accounting.

accrual system: a method of recording and apportioning expense and income for the period in which each is involved, regardless of the date of payment or collection.

accrue:
  (1) **economics:** to gain or profit by.
  (2) **business law:** to become eligible for a right or claim.

(3) **finance:** to accumulate, grow, or add in an orderly fashion (e.g., interest accrues on invested funds).

accrued assets: interest, commission, services offered, and items of revenue neither received nor past due but earned (e.g., accrued dividends).

accrued charges: as contrasted with payment in advance, charges that, though known, are not yet due (e.g., rent payment to be made at the end of the month).

accrued depreciation: depreciation, or loss in value, that has occurred during a specified period.

accrued dividend: the customary, regular dividend considered to be earned but not declared or payable on legally issued stock or other instruments of part ownership of a legally organized business or financial institution.

accrued expenses: expenses that are recognized by a firm prior to that firm's disbursement of cash. Accrued expenses arise when a company has used goods or services provided before it has paid for them.

accrued interest payable: interest accumulated on an indebtedness (time deposits, borrowed money, etc.) but not yet paid.

accrued interest receivable: interest earned by a bank but not yet collected.

accrued liabilities: liabilities arising from expenses that have been incurred but have not yet been paid. Cf. *prepaid expenses.*

accumulated depreciation: the fixed asset valuation account offsetting the depreciation provisions.

accumulated dividend: a dividend not paid when due. The dividend is expected to be paid at a later time, but it becomes a business liability until payment.

accumulated leave: all unused leave from the previous year that remains to the credit of the employee at the beginning of the first pay period. The taking of such leave is usually subject to administrative control.

accumulated profit tax: a tax penalty directed at corporations that avoid announcing dividends in order to reduce stockholders' declarations of additional income.

accumulation:
(1) **securities:** the deliberate, well-controlled assembling of blocks of stock without necessarily bidding up prices.
(2) **securities:** profits that are not distributed to stockholders as dividends but instead are transferred to a capital account.

(3) **insurance:** the opposite of amortization: a percentage added to policy benefits as a form of reward for continuous renewal.

(4) **business law:** the addition of income from dividends, interest, and other sources to the principal amount of a fund and the treatment of such additions as capital.

ACE: see *Amex Commodities Exchange.*

ACH: see *automated clearinghouse.*

achieved penetration: a marketing measure of the ratio of existing users (or buyers) to current potential users (or buyers) of a product class.

achieved precision: the calculated range within which the true value of the population most likely falls.

achievement motivation theory: a motivation theory that seeks to explain high achievement drive in people.

achievement need: the drive to excel, to achieve in relation to a set of standards, to strive to succeed.

acid-test ratio: a credit barometer used by lending institutions; indicates the ability of a business enterprise to meet its current obligations. The formula used to determine the ratio is

$$\frac{cash + receivables + marketable\ securities}{current\ liabilities}$$

Usually a 1:1 ratio is considered to be satisfactory.

acknowledgment:

(1) **general:** on a document, a signature that has received certification from an authorized person.

(2) **business law:** a statement that a proper document has been submitted.

ACL: see *action-centered leadership.*

acquired-needs theory: theory of motivation which argues that our needs are acquired or learned on the basis of our life experiences.

acquisition: a general term for the takeover of one company by another. See *amalgamation, merger.*

acquisition cost: the cost to a company of securing business; primarily commissions to agents and brokers.

acquittance: a document giving written evidence of the discharge of, or freedom from, a debt or financial obligation.

across the board:

(1) **general:** applying to all, in a uniform fashion.

(2) **advertising:** a broadcast program aired every day of the week at the same time; often also applied to such broadcast activity five or more times per week.

across-the-board increase: a general pay increase equally affecting all or most of the employees covered by a contract; may be in percentage or cents per hour.

action:

(1) **securities:** the performance by a stock with respect to trading volume and price trend.

(2) **business law:** the legal demand for rights, as asked of a court.

(3) **management:** the last step in the communication process, entailing implementation of the communication.

action-centered leadership (ACL): a training approach based on the belief that leaders are made, not born. This concept of training, developed by John Adair, emphasizes that a leader's basic needs are less important than his or her actions as a measure of effectiveness.

action statements: statements that reflect the means by which an organization moves forward to attain its goals.

active account:

(1) **finance:** an account in which bank deposits or withdrawals are made often.

(2) **securities:** an account handled by one broker, who makes frequent purchases and sales.

active employee: an employee who is currently at work.

active income: income generated by active business operations such as production, marketing, and distribution.

active investor: an investor who not only invests equity capital but also packages, builds, or manages a project.

active market: numerous transactions in securities trading.

active money: currency in circulation.

active trade balance: a balance of trade that is favorable.

activity center: pool of costs of two or more activities.

activity charge: a bank service charge imposed on checking account depositors for check or deposit activity, when the average balances maintained are not enough to compensate for the cost of handling the items.

actual cash value: the cost of repairing or replacing damaged property with other property of like kind and quality in the same physical condition; commonly defined as replacement cost less depreciation.

actual costing: the method of allocating costs to products according to actual direct materials consumed, direct labor used, and overhead.

actual investment: expenditures on facilities and equipment, plus adjustments in inventories; includes involuntary adjustments in inventories forced on companies by unexpected shifts in demand for their products.

actual normal system: a means of determining the costs of production by examining the number of units produced, the actual direct material consumed, the actual direct labor used, and a portion of overhead, calculated on the basis of a typical schedule of production for a specified item.

actuals: merchandise and other items available for immediate purchase and subsequent sale.

actual total loss: a loss that occurs when an item is totally destroyed or destroyed sufficiently to become useless.

actual valuation: the true value of a shipment at the time of delivery to the carrier.

actuarial equivalent: equivalent pension rates created after equating such factors as interest, form of pension, and mortality.

actuarial cost method: approach for determining the periodic employer contribution to a plan. Synonymous with *actuarial funding method.*

actuarial funding method: synonymous with *actuarial cost method.*

actuarial reserve retirement system: a comprehensive retirement plan that provides benefits to employees when they retire, become disabled, or die. It consists of contributions made periodically to a fund plus the compounded earnings during each year of active service.

actuary: an individual, often holding a professional degree, whose primary functions include determining rates and rating systems, determining reserves against future liabilities for corporate and rate-making purposes, and designing and interpreting experience systems.

adaptability screening: the process of evaluating how well a family is likely to stand up to the stresses of overseas life.

adaptive management: management that properly relates an organization to its environment by responding to and/or challenging conditions in the environment.

adaptiveness: a criterion of effectiveness that identifies an organization's ability to respond to change due to either internal or external forces.

addback method: the practice of beginning a statement of changes in financial position with net income and then adding or deducting income statement items that do not affect working capital.

added value: the value that is attached to the cost of unprocessed resources.

additional mark-on: an increase in the retail price of merchandise above the price placed on it when it was originally accepted for sale.

ad hoc: "for this" (*Latin*); refers to a specific situation, for one purpose only.

ad idem: "to the same effect" (*Latin*).

adjudication: the resolution of a dispute by a court or tribunal; specifically, the act of a court declaring a person or business bankrupt.

adjunct account: an account that adds to another existing account, represented by transfers from another account (e.g., the balances of related accounts are combined when preparing a financial statement). Synonymous with *absorption account*.

adjustable peg: a system permitting changes in the par rate of foreign exchange after a country has had long-run disequilibrium in its balance of payments. It also allows for short-run variations within a narrow range of a few percentage points around the par value.

adjusted gross income: the gross income of an individual minus business expenses, deductions for income-producing property, some property losses, self-employment expenses, and moving expenses; usually applied in federal income tax returns.

adjuster:
(1) **insurance:** an individual representing the insurer in discussions to reach agreement on the amount of a loss and the company's liability. An adjuster may be a salaried employee of an adjusting organization, an individual operating independently and engaged by an insurance company to adjust a particular loss, or a representative of a company.
(2) **retailing:** an individual who reviews a customer's complaint concerning service, error, or merchandise and who has the authority to offer a refund or find other acceptable remedy.

adjusting entries: entries required at the end of each accounting period to recognize on an accrual basis all revenues and expenses for the period and to report proper amounts for assets, liabilities, and owners' equity accounts.

adjustment:
(1) **insurance:** the process of determining the cause and amount of a loss, the amount of indemnity the insured may recover after all proper allowances and deductions have been made, and the proportion each company (if more than one is involved) is required to pay under its contract.

(2) **accounting:** a change in an account resulting from an incorrect entry.

adjustment board: an agency designed to deal with labor-management problems; may be given authority to adjust or resolve the grievance by majority or unanimous agreement.

adjustment bond: see *bond, adjustment*.

adjustment preferred securities: preferred stock that has resulted from an adjustment of claims in a restructuring of the company.

ad litem: "for purposes of a suit" (*Latin*); for a suit's duration.

administered price: the price established under situations of imbalanced competition wherein one business has some degree of control.

administration:

(1) **general:** designating those who determine purpose and policy in an organization.

(2) **business law:** the management and settling of the estate of an intestate person under a commission from a proper authority.

administrative accounting: the area of the accounting process that is generally associated with management.

administrative action: any act or decision on matters of policy that is made by executives or top management. It is usually associated with discretion and judgment.

administrative control: management's process of influencing organizational forces, activities, or events to make certain that the goals that have been established and the assignments given are carried out according to the requirements of organizational policies, plans, or programs; a continuous job of planning, evaluating, organizing, regulating, restraining, analyzing, verifying, and synchronizing.

administrative culture: a culture typified by the presence of such characteristics as a hierarchical management structure, ownership of enterprise resources, a competitive commitment of resources, and a long-run time perspective.

administrative discretion: the authority, freedom, and power delegated to an executive for discerning and making independent decisions on problems within his or her areas of responsibility.

administrative expenses: expenses chargeable to the managerial and policy-making phases of a business. Cf. *cost*.

administrative hierarchy: the system of reporting relationships in the organization, from the lowest to the highest managerial levels.

administrative officer: a high-level staff officer in charge of personnel, budgeting, training, or other related administrative functions.

administrative planning: a systematic process of looking and thinking ahead to recognize and define future trends, to see the relationships between these trends and organizational objectives, and to take necessary steps to adjust to these trends in terms of the goals and general framework of a firm by feasible, efficient, and economic use of personnel, methods, funds, and other resources.

administrative policy: a statement of a rule, judgment, or decision that, by defining and outlining the objectives of a firm, can guide and regulate organizational policies and methods.

administrative principles perspective: the management perspective in which management principles are proposed in order to streamline administrative procedures.

administrative reorganization: an effort to reform administrative policies and procedures in order to encourage greater efficiency, economy, responsibility, and control through a change in the administrative apparatus of a unit.

administrative unit: any line unit in the chain of command of an organization.

admission by investment: the addition to a partnership of a new partner who contributes more cash to the business, thus increasing the assets and the number of owners of the firm.

admission of partner: when a new partner joins a partnership. Thereby, a new partnership comes into being.

admission temporaire: the free entry of normally dutiable goods for the purpose of processing items for export.

admonition: an advice, warning, or reprimand given orally by a supervisor to a subordinate about his or her area of responsibility. It carries with it an implied penalty or sanction.

adopter: a first-purchase buyer of a new product who continues to buy or use the product.

adoption notice: a statement by a carrier that it is lawfully accepting an obligation (usually the freight tariffs) of a predecessor.

adoption process: a five-stage procedure by which an individual makes a decision to buy a new product. The stages are awareness, interest, evaluation, trial, and adoption.

ADR: see *American Depositary Receipt.*

ad referendum: indicating that, even though a contract has been signed, specific issues remain to be considered.

ad valorem: "according to value" (*Latin*); rates or duty based on a percentage of the invoice value, not on weight or quantity.

ad valorem tariff: a tariff based on a percentage of the value of the goods imported.

advance:
 (1) **banking:** a loan.
 (2) **economics:** a price increase.
 (3) **finance:** a payment on account made prior to due date.
 (4) **finance:** a rise in value or cost.

advance bill: the invoice presented before the items or services itemized have been delivered or carried out. It is usually requested by purchasers for tax reasons.

advance commitment: a commitment by a lender to make or buy a loan for a stated amount on a specified property within a stated period of time to a borrower whose credit will meet the lender's approval.

advance dating: added time allowed by a vendor to pay for goods, enabling the purchaser to receive a cash discount. Such extensions usually are arranged before the goods are shipped.

advance freight: freight paid for in advance.

advance on wages: payment of earnings prior to the regular pay day.

advance refunding: in public debt refinancing, the ability of possessors of a government security that will mature soon to exchange their securities ahead of the due date for others that mature at a later time. By this process, the national debt is extended.

advantage:
 (1) **general:** favorable state or circumstances.
 (2) **business:** superiority over a competitor.
 (3) **salesmanship:** the way an item or service can assist in solving problems or fulfilling needs.

adventure:
 (1) **finance:** a speculative undertaking involving the sale of goods overseas at the best available price.
 (2) **securities:** a security flotation by a syndicate; a joint venture.
 (3) **marine insurance:** a peril.
 (4) see *venture.*

adverse action: suspension, demotion, or separation for reasons other than reduction in labor force.

adverse impact: the effect produced when a job selection rate for a protected group is less than 80 percent of the rate for the majority group.

adverse selection:
  (1) **general:** a ruling "against the company."
  (2) **insurance:** the tendency of less desirable insurance risks to seek or continue insurance to a greater extent than others.
  (3) **insurance:** the tendency of policy owners to take advantage of favorable privileges in insurance contracts, such as renewal and conversion of term life insurance policies.

advertisement (ad): a public announcement or sale offer in a public area or medium, expressed in print, by other visual means, or orally. Major locations of advertisements are in newspapers, magazines, and journals and on signs, billboards, radio, and television. Synonymous with *commercial*.

advertising: a paid form of nonpersonal presentation or promotion of goods, services, and/or ideas. It is usually paid for by an identifiable sponsor. See *promotion*.

advertising allowance: a discount in price or payment given to a store to help meet the expense of the store's advertising of a product. Such allowances are most often granted when new products are being introduced or when manufacturers are attempting to increase promotion of their products. Cf. *promotional allowance*.

advertising campaign: the planned use of varying media and advertising methods to solicit acceptance for an idea or item or to increase the sales of a product or service.

advertising credit: the mention of a store's name in the advertisement of a producer.

advertising media: various publications, devices, and structures that carry messages to intended recipients (e.g., newspapers, television, billboards). See *media*.

advertising specialty: low-cost item (e.g., a ballpoint pen, a key ring) on which the seller's name, address, and telephone number are printed to give visibility and to promote awareness of the seller's name and location.

advice note: a supplier's listing of items that is sent to a customer prior to an invoice, either accompanying the merchandise or preceding it, identifying the nature and quantity of the goods but not giving prices.

advising bank: a bank that gives notification of the issuance of credit by another bank.

affective component of attitude: the emotional or feeling segment of an attitude. See *attitude*.

affiant: owe who swears to an affidavit. See *affidavit*.

affidavit: a written, notarized, dated, and sworn statement of the facts pertaining to a financial transaction or civil event. Such a statement must show the name and address of the affiant, must be signed by that person, and must bear the signature of the attesting official (e.g., a notary public). See *affiant.*

affiliate:

(1) **business:** an organization whose management is connected by contract with that of another organization.

(2) **advertising:** a broadcast station that belongs to or carries the programs of a national network.

affiliation:

(1) **general:** adoption as a member or branch.

(2) **labor relations:** the association of a local or international union with a larger group (e.g., a state, national, or international labor union federation).

affiliation need: the desire for friendly and close interpersonal relationships.

affirmative action: positive steps taken by firms or other organizations to remedy imbalances in their employment of members of minority groups. See *Federal Contract Compliance Office.*

affirmative action plan:

(1) a legislated requirement that employers make an extra effort to hire and promote those in a protected (women or minority) group.

(2) a plan, often demanded by the federal government, to ensure that applicants are employed, and that employees are treated appropriately during employment, without regard to race, creed, color, or national origin.

affordable method: a method of setting marketing budgets based on what a firm can afford to spend.

affreightment: an agreement for chartering a carrier for the movement of goods.

AFL: see *American Federation of Labor.*

a fortiori: "by a stronger reason" (*Latin*). For conclusions that are made from stated and accepted facts, there are other facts that logically follow to make the conclusion even stronger.

after-action review: initially used in the military, a postmortem to analyze business successes and shortcomings. This formalized process does not truly end until the lessons learned are incorporated in and change the behavior of the company.

after charge: a charge assessed against the insured in some fire insurance rating schedules for easily correctable hazards, such as faulty wiring or improper storage of flammable liquids. The purpose of such a charge is to encourage prompt correction of the hazardous conditions.

after date: used in bills of exchange and notes; the stated maturity of the instrument.

aftersight: used in a bill to determine the due date of payment, meaning "after the bill is given to the drawee for acceptance."

against the box: in a short sale of stock, when the seller actually owns the security sold short but prefers not to or cannot deliver the stock to the buyer. The result is that, through a broker, the seller borrows the stock in order to make delivery.

age change: the date halfway between natural birthdays when the age of an individual changes to the next higher age for purposes of life insurance rating.

Age Discrimination in Employment Act of 1967: federal legislation that bans employers of 20 or more workers from firing or refusing to hire an individual 40 to 65 years of age simply because of age-unless age is a bona fide job qualification; forbids employment agencies to refuse to refer a job applicant because of age and to indulge in other discriminatory practices. Violators of the law face penalties. This act was amended in 1978, raising from 65 to 70 the age at which an employer can require workers to retire involuntarily.

agency agreement: a contract between a company and an agency listing all the conditions the company grants the agency upon appointment (credit terms, commission schedule, type of enterprise, etc.).

agency fund: an account for assets received by governmental agencies in the capacity of trustee or agent.

agency of record: the agency, one of many, that coordinates the activity of the advertising campaign.

agency recognition: action by a unit of an advertising medium signifying acceptance under its terms of the qualifications of an organization purporting to be an advertising agency, entitling that organization to receive the agency commission for placed business.

agency shop: the result of a provision in a collective-bargaining agreement stating that nonunion employees in the bargaining unit must pay the union a sum equal to union fees and dues as a condition of continuing employment. Nonunion workers are not required to join the union, however. This is the most commonly encountered union security measure in the public sector. See *union security clauses; union shop*. Cf. *Rand formula*.

agenda: a listing of activities to be carried out during a meeting.

agent:

(1) **insurance:** an individual who represents insurance companies in a sales and service capacity and is wholly or partially paid on a commission basis. An agent is licensed by the state in which he or she operates, and his or her powers are limited by the terms of the agency contract and by the state laws. See *producer*.

(2) **business law:** an individual authorized to act in behalf of another person, the principal.

(3) **marketing:** a middleman who does not take title to the goods he sells.

agent, direct: a salaried or commissioned employee of a single insurance company.

agent, exclusive: an individual representing only one insurance company, usually on a commission basis. An exclusive agent is not an employee of the insurance firm.

agent, independent: an independent business executive who represents two or more insurance companies under contract in a sales and service capacity and is paid on a commission basis.

agent de change: a member of the Paris Bourse (stock exchange).

age reduction: the lowering of insurance payments upon attainment of a specified age. This often occurs when an individual reaches his or her late sixties or early seventies. Age reduction clauses must be identified in the insurance policy.

agglomeration diseconomies: an imbalance of scale occurring when a large number of individuals live close together. See *diseconomies of scale*.

agglomeration economies: benefits occurring when a large number of individuals live close together. See *economies of scale*.

aggregate: any total (e.g., the gross national product; the sum of monthly sales).

aggregate corporation: an incorporated venture that has more than one stockholder.

aggregate demand:

(1) the total spending within the economy.

(2) the total of personal consumption expenditures, business investments, and government spending. See *aggregate real demand*.

aggregate economics: synonymous with *macroeconomics*.

aggregate limit: see *liability limits*.

aggregate real demand: the total in real dollars, expressed in terms of a base year, that all purchasers are willing and able to spend on all goods and services. See *aggregate demand*.

aggregate supply: the capacity of a country's total resources to produce real goods and services.

aggressive portfolio: a portfolio of stocks and bonds usually held for appreciation.

aggressive style: expressive and self-enhancing, but takes unfair advantage of others.

aging of receivables: an accounting check that analyzes the time interval between the date of sale and the current date; used to evaluate the adequacy of a firm's allowance for uncollectable accounts.

agio:

(1) **finance:** a premium paid for the exchange of one nation's currency for that of another. Cf. *disagio*.

(2) **finance:** the sum given above a nominal value, as in the *agio of exchange*.

(3) **international business:** the rate of exchange among differing countries of the world.

agio of exchange: see *agio*.

agreed amount clause: a provision in fire insurance policies covering certain classes of property, whereby the coinsurance clause is suspended if the insured carries an amount of insurance specified by the company, usually 90 percent or more of value.

agreed valuation: the value of a shipment agreed upon in exchange for a reduced liability.

agribusiness: the activity of farming as a major force in the economy. California has the largest agribusiness in the United States.

agricultural economics: a specialty within economics dealing with aspects of production and movement to the market of agricultural items.

agricultural parity: the ratio between the price index numbers for farmers' purchases and sales; reflects an attempt to simulate conditions of a period when farm income standards were about equal to other income standards within the economy.

Agriculture, Department of (U.S): see *Department of Agriculture (U.S.)*.

aided recall: a method to survey the impression made by an advertisement or other media communication whereby an interviewer presents an advertisement or other aid to memory. Cf. *diary method*.

air cargo: in the United States, mail, freight, or express moving by air; in other countries, freight only.

air freight: a service offered by airlines for the movement of goods.

air pocket: noticeably extreme weakness in a specific stock.

air shipment: transportation by air, either within the United States or around the world.

air taxi service: uncertified air delivery service contracts between designated points, exclusively for the movement of mail.

air waybill: a shipping statement used by international air freight carriers.

a/k/a: also known as (e.g., John Doe a/k/a J. Doe).

alienation: the transfer of interest and property title to another person or organization.

alien company: an incorporated company formed and operating under the regulations of a foreign nation.

aliquot: a part of the whole; a subdivision or unit of an entirety.

all-commodity distribution: a method of measuring distribution based on dollar volume. A grocery product that has 90 percent all-commodity distribution would be distributed in stores doing 90 percent of the product's dollar volume.

all-commodity rate: a freight charge applying to shipments regardless of their content.

all-inclusive concept: a form of income statement presentation incorporating all items of revenue and expense in the computation of net income for an accounting period. This concept makes no distinction between items that are related to the current operations of the entity and those that are unusual and infrequent.

allocation: assigning one or more items of cost or revenue to one or more segments of an organization according to benefits received, responsibilities, or other logical measure of use.

allocation models: models used in situations where several possible candidates or activities are competing for limited resources. Such models enable the user to allocate scarce resources in order to maximize some predetermined objective.

allonge: a paper affixed to a bill on which further endorsements are written.

allotment:
    (1) **general:** an assignment of pay for the benefit of dependents.

(2) **accounting:** the separation of anticipated revenues among specific classes of expenditures.

(3) **securities:** the part of a stock issue apportioned or assigned by an investment firm to a purchaser or subscriber.

allowable depreciation: the amount permitted to be deducted annually as an expense, resulting in a decrease in adjusted basis.

allowance:

(1) **transportation:** a deduction from the weight or value of merchandise; a reduction permitted if the carrier does not supply appropriate equipment and the shipper then produces the equipment for use.

(2) **sales:** any price reduction.

(3) **finance:** a reserve, or money set aside, for bad debts or for depreciation.

allowance method: the recording of estimated losses due to uncollectable accounts as expenses during the period in which the sales occurred. Cf. *direct write-off method.*

allowed time: for incentive workers, the time set aside for tool care, fatigue, and personal needs. Cf. *base time.*

all-risks insurance: insurance that protects the insured from direct loss arising from any fortuitous cause other than the perils or causes specifically excluded by name. Synonymous with *floater policy.* Cf. *named-peril insurance.*

all-union shop: see *union shop.*

altered check: a check on which the date, payee, or amount has been changed or erased. A bank is responsible for paying a check only as it is originally drawn; consequently, it may refuse to pay a check that has been altered.

alternate sponsorship: two TV/radio sponsors sharing a program, usually each one taking a week.

alternative budget: a budgetary approach in which budgets are set up on the basis of the level of operations: high, medium, or low.

alternative work schedules: schedules based on adjustments in the normal work schedule, job content or activities.

amalgamation:

(1) **accounting:** a combination under a single title of all or a portion of the assets and liabilities of two orn more business units by either merger or consolidation. It may take the form of a merger, whereby one company absorbs another, or a consolidation, whereby the original companies form a new one.

(2) **economics:** the joining together of businesses for the mutual advantage of all.

amenity: a feature that makes a property more attractive, such as accessibility; good design; proximity to shops, schools, public transportation, and recreation facilities; beautiful scenery; pleasant and congenial neighbors.

American Accounting Association (AAA): the national organization representing accounting educators and practitioners; serves as a forum for the expression of accounting ideas and encourages accounting research.

American agency system: an approach for selling insurance through independent agents, who are compensated on a commission basis, as opposed to the system of selling insurance through employed company representatives (direct agents), who write insurance for only one company. See *agent, direct, National Association of Insurance Agents.*

American Arbitration Association: a private, nonprofit organization formed in 1926 to encourage the use of arbitration in the settlement of disputes.

American Bankers Association (ABA): the national organization of banking formed in 1875 to "promote the general welfare and usefulness of banks and financial institutions"; consists of 35 working groups, four divisions, seven commissions, and a number of councils and committees.

American Bankers Association (ABA) number: a unit in the numerical coding system originated by the American Bankers Association for easy identification of banks and to aid in sorting checks for their proper ultimate destinations. Used principally on checks, the ABA number is usually placed in the upper right-hand corner of the check, after the drawee bank's name.

American Depository Receipt: a form similar to a stock certificate which is registered in the holder's name. The certificate represents a certain number of shares in an alien corporation. Such shares are held by an alien bank that serves as the agent for a domestic commercial bank which has released the depository receipt.

American Federation of Labor (AFL): a federation of craft unions organized in 1881. Originally called the Federation of Organized Trade and Labor Unions of the United States and Canada, the name American Federation of Labor was adopted in 1886. In 1955 the AFL merged with the Congress of Industrial Organizations (CIO), which had been expelled from the AFL in 1937, to form the AFL-CIO.

American Federation of Labor-Congress of Industrial Organizations (AFL-CIO): a federation of craft and industrial unions, as well as unions of mixed structure. Created in 1955 by the merger of the AFL and the CIO, the AFL-CIO is not itself a bargaining agent; its primary functions are education, lobbying and furnishing organizational aid to constituent unions. See *COPE.*

American Marketing Association (AMA): a national professional organization for persons engaged in the practice and teaching of marketing.

American selling price: the price charged by U.S. producers for goods; used to determine the duty to be paid on a similar item brought into the United States, rather than determining the duty on the actual cost of the item to an importer.

American Society for Personnel Administration (ASPA): the major association of professional personnel specialists and administrators.

American Stock Exchange (Amex): once, the second largest securities exchange in the country; called the Little Board or the Curb Exchange, from the market's origin on a street in downtown Manhattan. See *New York Stock Exchange.*

Americans with Disabilities Act: Federal law prohibiting discrimination against the disabled.

Amex: see *American Stock Exchange.*

Amex Commodities Exchange (ACE): a commodities exchange launched by the American Stock Exchange in 1977 to offer its member firms a broader range of products. ACE functions as an independent exchange, sharing facilities and services with the American Stock Exchange by contract.

amoral management: management that is neither moral nor immoral.

amortize:
(1) to discharge a debt in periodic payments until the total, including the interest, has been paid.
(2) to write off a portion or all of the cost of an asset; to retire debt over a period of time.

amortized loan: a loan requiring periodic payments that are used to reduce the principal so that the loan will be repaid in full by a predetermined date.

amount subject: the value that may reasonably be expected to be lost in a single fire or other casualty. It depends on the protection and construction of the insured property and on the distribution or concentration of values.

analysis of performance: a manager's assessment of how well the organization's members, subsystems, and goals interact to function as a unit.

analytical forecasting: an internally consistent forecast of gross national product and its major components for a short period ahead.

ANL: see *above-normal loss.*

annual capital cost: the cost arrived at by a technique of determining and observing the activities of a firm experiencing a constant yearly cash flow that can be compared with an annual capital charge.

annual earnings: the total of all monies received during a year.

annual improvement factor: a condition of a contract clause that provides for annual wage increases of stated amount as a share of increased productivity. See *incentive pay.*

annual percentage rate (APR): on a loan, the basic finance charges, the service charges, and the costs of extras, if any, such as compulsory insurance on the loan.

annual report: a report of financial and organizational conditions prepared by corporate management at yearly intervals. In most cases, the Securities and Exchange Commission requires an annual report for publicly held firms.

annual statement: the annual report, as of each December 31, of an insurer to the state insurance department, showing assets and liabilities, receipts and disbursements, and other information.

annual wage: a guaranteed minimum income and/or total paid hours during a year.

annual wage plan: an approach designed to give continuous income to workers throughout the year.

annuitant: an individual to whom an annuity is payable, usually the person who is to receive the annuity throughout his or her lifetime.

annuity:

(1) **finance:** a series of equal payments at fixed intervals.

(2) **human resources:** a scheduled payment to a retired person. Synonymous with *pension plan.* See *frozen pension.*

annuity accumulation period: the time span during which an annuitant makes a deposit in his or her retirement fund before the annuity payments begin.

annuity accumulation unit: an accounting device used to determine the value of an annuitant's accumulation account before the annuity payments begin. Under a variable annuity contract, the value of an annuitant's account is determined by multiplying the number of units owned by the daily value of one unit.

annuity accumulation value: the monetary value, as of a certain date, of the number of accumulation units credited to the account of a variable annuity contract holder.

annuity commencement date: the day on which annuity payments begin, as determined by the settlement option elected by the annuitant.

annuity period: the period after retirement during which an annuitant receives payments.

antagonistic cooperation: the concept that people work jointly for mutual advantage by suppressing their aggressive and competitive feelings. See *mirror principle.*

antedate: to place on a check a date prior to the current one.

anticipated balance: a savings account balance projected through the end of the interest or dividend period, assuming that no additional deposits or withdrawals occur.

anticipated interest: the amount of interest projected as earnings on savings accounts, assuming that no deposits or withdrawals occur before the end of the current interest period. This figure is updated after each deposit or withdrawal transaction.

anticipation:

(1) **business:** payment of an account before the actual due date, thus permitting a discount.

(2) **accounting:** assigning or making charges against income or profit before such gain is actually realized.

(3) **business law:** a situation in which a claimed invention is known to others, regardless of whether or not the anticipating invention has been patented.

anticipatory breach: the informing of a seller by a buyer before closing of title that the buyer plans to terminate any involvement in the transaction.

antifreeloader argument: argument that holds that since businesses benefit from a better society, they should bear part of the costs by actively working to bring about solutions to social problems.

antitrust: an action of the courts taken to curb monopolistic tendencies or to limit power stemming from monopolies.

A/P: authority to purchase or authority to pay.

APB: see *Accounting Principles Board.*

appeal:

(1) **salesmanship:** the motivation of a sales pitch with the expectation that the potential customer will become favorably disposed toward the product or service.

(2) **business law:** the removal or attempted removal of a case from a lower to a higher court.

appeals subsystem: the deliberately instituted process whereby grievances of managers and workers can be adjudicated before an elected body of representatives. Usually, half the representatives are chosen by management and the other half by the workers.

applicant: a person seeking employment.

application blank: form that requests information, such as education, work history, and hobbies, from a job candidate as a means of quickly collecting verifiable historical data.

applied economics: the use of economic theory to assist in solving economic problems. See *normative economics.*

applied overhead: under a job-order or process costing system, the overhead costs assigned to products (including work in process) on the basis of a predetermined application rate.

applied psychology:

(1) **general:** the use in practical situations of the principles developed in the field of psychology. See *human engineering.* Cf. *industrial psychology.*

(2) **human resources:** an approach to securing desired conduct that deals with physical, psychological, and/ or social conditions as they relate to a person's performance. Cf. *personnel psychology.*

applied research: research concerned with solving practical problems, in which researchers have specific uses for the results of their efforts in relation to organizational issues. Cf. *basic research; descriptive research; operators research; research and development.*

apportion:

(1) **budgeting:** to assign a cost factor to a person, unit, product, or order.

(2) **retail accounting:** to hold inventory and incoming material for specific production orders, unfilled requisitions, or other expected needs.

apportionment:

(1) **general:** dividing a unit into proportionate parts.

(2) **insurance:** determination of how much each of two or more

insurance policies will contribute to the compensation for a loss sustained by a covered risk.

appraise: to determine the cost, quality, or value of an item.

appreciation: the increase in the value of an asset in excess of its depreciable cost that is due to economic and other conditions; the increase of present value over the listed book value.

apprentice: in the skilled trades, a learner who is under supervision in the work experience, often with related classroom studies. Usually, completion of four to five years of apprenticeship training leads to journeyman status. Cf. *executive trainee*.

apprenticeship training: an arrangement whereby an employee enters into an agreement with an employer and a union to learn a skilled trade by work experience and technical instruction. To protect job opportunities for journeymen, unions often restrict the number of apprentices to a certain percentage of practicing journeymen.

approach: the initial contact with a prospect by a salesperson.

approach-approach conflict: a situation in which a person is drawn toward two potentially satisfying goals that are at least partially incompatible. See *role conflict*.

approach phase: the part of a sales presentation that includes the announcement and rapid sales work of the seller, the firm, and the product to gain customer interest.

appropriate unit: as decided by an examiner of the National Labor Relations Board (NLRB) after a hearing, what constitutes (who is to be included in) a unit for purposes of an NLRB representation election and, subsequently, collective bargaining.

appropriation: an authorized sum of money set aside to pay certain known or anticipated costs of a given item or service.

approved bond: see *bond, approved*.

APR: see *annual percentage rate*.

aptitude tests: tests that attempt to measure a person's capacity to learn or acquire skills. Cf. *ability tests*.

arbitrage:

(1) simultaneous purchasing and selling of an identical item in different markets in order to yield profits. The result is that the price of the item becomes equal in all markets.

(2) the purchase of foreign exchange, stocks, bonds, silver, gold, or other commodities in one market for sale in another market at a profit.

arbitrageur: an arbitrage dealer.

arbitration: a method of settling a labor-management dispute whereby an impartial third party renders a decision that is binding on both the union and the employer; most frequently applied when labor and management disagree on the interpretation of contract language that is applicable to a grievance. The procedures are customarily specified in the collective-bargaining agreement. See *compulsory arbitration.* Cf. *conciliation; mediation; negotiation.*

arbitration award: a final and binding award issued by an arbitrator in a labor-management dispute.

arbitrator: an individual who has been designated by disagreeing parties to make a final and binding decision on the basis of the evidence presented to him or her. Synonymous with *umpire.* See *binding arbitration, impartial chairman.* Cf. *mediator.*

area agreement: an agreement between labor and management that covers all or nearly all organizations and workers in a given industry or craft within a geographical area. It is signed individually by each employer involved in the agreement.

arguendo: (*Latin*) referring to a case by way of argument or within an argument.

arm's-length bargaining: open, sincere, purposeful across-the-table negotiations between an employer and a union of his employees. See *good-faith bargaining.* Cf. *collusion.*

arrears: monies due but unpaid; a real or contingent obligation that remains unpaid at the date of maturity; frequently used in connection with installment notes, mortgages, rents, and other obligations that are due and payable on a specified date.

Arthur Andersen: a major world-wide accounting firm that in Spring 2002 went on trial on charges of obstructing justice by deliberately shredding documents about its audit of Enron. Ultimately it collapsed. See *cook the books; Corporate Accountability Act of 2002; Enron; Sarbanes-Oxley Act.*

articles of agreement: any contract between two or more people that is reduced to a written instrument.

articles of association: an instrument similar to a corporate certificate that is usually used for nonstock corporations (e.g., charitable organizations).

articles of incorporation: a document filed with an appropriate state agency by persons establishing a corporation. When it is returned, accompanied by a certificate of incorporation, the document becomes the firm's charter.

artisan's lien: a claim to take possession of property belonging to person for whom a worker has rendered unpaid service until reimbursement is made. Cf. *mechanic's lien; particular lien*. See *quantum meruit*.

ascribed status: a status that a worker has outside the working hierarchy, usually as a result of association or professional reputation or membership. It often affects the worker's relationship with others on the job.

as is: describing items that have no warranty and may be damaged or shopworn.

asked: see *bid and asked*.

asking price:

(1) **general:** the price that is officially offered by a seller.

(2) **securities:** the price at which a stock is offered for sale.

ASPA: see *American Society for Personnel Administration*.

as per advice: words on a bill of exchange indicating that the drawee has been notified that the bill has been drawn.

assailing thieves: a term that appears in marine insurance contracts, referring to coverage of losses due to use of force or violence by thieves.

assembling:

(1) **general:** putting together different parts of an article or machine. Cf. *fabrication*.

(2) **marketing:** the activities involved in gathering supplies or assortments of items or services to assist in sales or purchases.

assembly-line production: a procedure widely used in mass production industries whereby each worker performs a single specialized task. The materials and parts are conveyed on mechanical belts and the worker performs the appropriate task as the material or equipment moves past his or her work station. See *interchangeable parts*.

assented securities: securities whose owners agree to a change in status, usually in cases of corporate restructuring, when an assessment is made or when the amount of securities is reduced according to a logical plan.

assess: to determine the value of something or to fix its value for tax purposes.

assessment:

(1) **finance:** any levy on members of a corporation for the purpose of raising capital.

(2) **labor relations:** a levy by a union on its membership for purposes other than regular dues (e.g., to meet heavy strike expenses or to replenish a depleted defense fund).

(3) **insurance:** a company charge against all policyholders to cover the amounts paid out to sustain major losses.

assessment center: a multidimensional approach to the measurement of performance and potential.

asset:

(1) **general:** anything owned by an individual or business that has commercial or exchange value. Assets may consist of specific property or claims against others, in contrast to obligations due others.

(2) **insurance:** all funds, property, goods, securities, rights of action, or resources of any kind owned by an insurance company, less any items that are declared nonadmissible by state laws, mainly deferred or over-due premiums.

(3) **accounting:** all the entries on a balance sheet that indicate the entire property or resources of a person or organization.

asset approach: a method of accounting for prepaid expenses whereby these expenses are initially debited to an asset account. A year-end adjustment is required to record the asset value used up as an expense of the period and to adjust the related asset account to its proper balance. Cf. *expense approach.*

asset management: an approach that uses manipulation of a group's or organization's strengths, both tangible and intangible, in order to achieve stated objectives.

asset turnover: the ratio of sales to total assets available.

assignability: the capacity of property to be transferred from one person or organization to another.

assigned risk: a risk that underwriters do not wish to insure but, because of state law or regulation, must be insured. It is handled through a pool of insurers and assigned to the several companies in turn. The term is used primarily in connection with automobile and workers' compensation insurance. Cf. *fair plan.*

assignee:

(1) **general:** one to whom an assignment is granted.

(2) **business law:** an individual to whom property or rights have been transferred for the benefit of that individual or others.

assignment:

(1) **administration:** a given task.

(2) **insurance:** the transfer in writing of the legal right in a policy to another party.

(3) **securities:** the transfer of stock title.

assignment of wages: initiated by an employee, a designation that future wages are to be turned over to a creditor or an authorization for management to release a specified amount to charitable institutions or to be applied to dues, etc. The agreement in writing is signed by the employee.

assignor:

(1) **general:** an individual who makes an assignment.

(2) **business law:** an individual who assigns or transfers a claim, right, or property.

assimilation: the completed distribution of new shares of securities to the public by the issue's underwriters and syndicate members.

assistance and subsidies: direct cash assistance payments (e.g., public welfare payments, veterans' bonuses, direct cash grants for tuition, scholarships, aid to nonpublic educational institutions, aid to farmers).

assistant to: a staff assistant to a line manager, who, though normally lacking line authority, often has considerable responsibility and influence.

association: a grouping of people for mutually beneficial purposes or for the furtherance of some goal; an unincorporated group, that is not formed for profit.

assumed bond: see *bond, assumed.*

assumed liability: an obligation for payment that is accepted by another person.

assumpsit:

(1) a common-law action alleging that damages have been incurred.

(2) a common-law action to recover damages for breach of contract.

assumption: bank loan payments that are accepted by a party other than the original maker.

assumption of risk: one of the defenses by employers against claims of employees who have been injured on the job, whereby management claims that the worker was aware of the hazards of the job when he or she accepted employment and therefore assumed the risks incident to the position.

assumptive close: in salesmanship, a close accomplished without the buyer's verbal consent. This becomes presumed when the purchaser fails to protest the salesperson's beginning to write an order, or to wrap the item.

assurance: a term commonly used in England, that is similar to *insurance,* but different in that it does not depend on a possibility. It involves payment of a premium at regular periods for a stated sum that becomes payable at a given time.

astray freight: freight that is destined for a particular location and owner but does not arrive.

Atkinson system: a wage incentive plan allowing for the payment of 1.3 percent on each 1 percent of production, accompanied by a 5 percent step bonus upon achievement of the task, with a base wage or a minimum when production drops below 75 percent of the task.

ATM: see *automated teller machine.*

atomistic economy: an economy characterized by the competition of small, independent manufacturers in each industry.

at or better: in placing a purchase order for securities, buying at the price specified or under; in a selling request, selling at the price given or above.

at par: a term designating a bond or share of preferred stock that is issued or selling at its face amount.

at-risk rules: regulations limiting the loss write-off on an investment to the amount "at risk," usually the cash invested plus borrowed amounts on which the investor is personally liable. See *Tax Reform Act of 1986.*

at sight: used in the body of negotiable instruments, indicating that payment is due upon presentation or demand.

attached account: an account against which a court order has been issued, permitting disbursement of the balance only with the consent of the court. See *frozen account.*

attached ledger: the book or ledger in which attached accounts are kept to separate them from free accounts, since court orders are required to pay out funds.

attachment: the legal proceeding following a court's action whereby a plaintiff acquires a lien on a dependant's property as security for payment of a judgment that the plaintiff can recover.

attainable standard: a guide for judging actual performance, based on efficient but not perfect productivity.

attendance: an employee's availability for being present at work or actual participation in work when so assigned.

attention directing: the function of the accountant's information-supplying task that focuses on problems in the operation of the firm or points out imperfections or inefficiencies in certain areas of the firm's operation.

attestation: the act of bearing witness to or giving authenticity to a document by signing as a witness to the signature of another. Cf. *countersignature.*

attitudes: evaluative statements or judgments concerning objects, people, or events. See *affective component of an attitude; behavioral component of an attitude; behavioral tendency component.*

attitude survey: a method for ascertaining employees' perceptions of their firm, usually by use of questionnaires or interviews.

attorney-at-law: an individual who has a state license to practice law.

attorney-in-fact: an individual who has the written authorization of another person to carry out business for that person out of court.

attorney-of-record: the lawyer whose name is entered in the records of the court as the representative of a party in a legal action or suit.

attribution theory: when individuals observe behavior, they attempt to determine whether it is internally or externally caused. Cf. *attribution theory of leadership.*

attribution theory of leadership: leadership is merely an attribution that people make about other individuals. Cf. *attribution theory.*

attrition: shrinking of employee rolls through death, resignation, or retirement.

auction: a unique trading market in which there is one seller and many potential buyers. See *Dutch auction.*

audience composition: the mix of people, classified by age, sex, or other characteristics, who are reached by an advertising approach.

audience flow: the gain or loss of a broadcast audience during a program or from one program to another. Cf. *share of audience.*

audience study: a form of analysis to determine the characteristics and attitudes of listeners, viewers, or readers of advertising media. See *Hooperating; Nielsen rating; Videodex.* Cf. *media analysis.*

audience turnover: the ratio between the cumulative and average audiences for a specific broadcast.

Audimeter: an electromechanical unit used by A. C. Nielsen Company to record station tuning of radio and television receivers by tapping a sample of home users. See *Nielsen rating; share of audience.* Cf. *coincidental telephone method.*

audit:
   (1) **finance:** periodic or continuous verification of the stated assets

and liabilities of a company or other organization.

(2) **accounting:** inspection of a firm's books.

accounting: a final statement of account.

audited net sales: the total amount of sales for a specified period, computed after returns and allowances have been deducted. These totals are circulated by the auditing department of a store and credited to the book inventory of each department.

auditor: a person who is qualified to conduct an audit. Qualification is defined by each state.

audit trail: a printed record of transaction listings created as a byproduct of data-processing runs or mechanized accounting operations.

augmented skills: skills not critical but helpful in facilitating the efforts of managers.

authentication:

(1) **business law:** verification of a document as truthful, genuine, or valid.

(2) **securities:** the signing of a certificate on a bond by a trustee in order to identify it as having been issued under a specific indenture, thereby validating the bond.

authoritarian leadership: absolute leadership, whereby a person vested with authority sets the goals and sets all policy, assigns functions, prescribes procedures, directs, checks, evaluates, and corrects the work in great detail.

authority:

(1) **administration:** describing the relationship in an organization between positions and expectations of members. It also specifies behavior necessary for company effectiveness and is a cost of organizational membership. See *chain of command*.

(2) **administration:** the power possessed by an individual for making decisions and carrying them out. See *span of control*.

authority bond: see *bond, authority*.

authority boundary: boundary represented by differences in organizational level or status across which communications may be distorted or constrained due to the status difference.

authority of knowledge: the right to command that is held by the person who knows the most about a situation and is therefore put in charge of its operation.

authority of situation: the right to command that is held by a person on the basis of the need for immediate action, as in a crisis in which a leader emerges.

authority relationships: relationships between people and between people and their work.

authority to purchase: used in Far Eastern trade, a substitute for a commercial letter of credit. This instrument permits the bank to which it is directed to purchase drafts drawn on an importer rather than on a bank.

authorization: the amount of insurance coverage an underwriter will accept on a risk of a given class or on specific property. This information is provided to agents as a guide and in response to their requests in specific instances, such as large lines or special-hazard risks.

authorization card: a card signed by a worker in a plant being organized, authorizing the union to be that person's collective-bargaining agent.

authorized dealer: a middleman who has received a franchise to represent or sell a manufacturer's products.

authorized stock: the maximum number of all classes of securities that can be issued by a corporation.

autocratic: referring to management by one-person control, with a minimum of decision making by others in the firm. See *Caesar management; Theory X and Theory Y.* Cf. *decentralization; degree of freedom; delegated strategy; multiple management.*

autocratic leadership: a leadership style characterized by heavy emphasis on a task accomplishment and very little emphasis on the human element.

autogestion: organization and management by a committee of workers, in factories, farms, and so on.

automated clearinghouse (ACH): a computerized facility used by member depository institutions to process (i.e., combine, sort, and distribute) payment orders in machine-readable form (computer tapes or punched cards).

automated teller machine (ATM): a machine that is capable of processing a variety of transactions between a depository institution and its customers. Its functions might include accepting deposits, providing withdrawals, transferring funds between accounts, and accepting instructions to pay third parties in a transaction. An ATM may or may not be on-line to a computer system and may be located on or off the premises of a depository institution. Placement in certain locations may permit customer access seven days a week, 24 hours a day. See *debit card.* Cf. *customer-bank communication terminal.*

automatic check-off: a procedure whereby an employer deducts monies from the pay of employees and turns over these monies to a union or other approved organization.

automatic coverage: insurance coverage for a stated period and limited amount to cover increasing values and interest charges.

automatic fiscal stabilizers: nondiscretionary approaches that automatically cushion recession effects by helping to create a budget deficit and that curb inflation by helping to create a budget surplus.

automatic premium loan option: a life insurance clause that permits paying any premium that is in default at the end of a grace period and charging the payment against the policy as a policy loan, provided that such premium is not in excess of the policy's cash surrender value on the due date of the premium.

automatic progression: automatic pay increases at set time intervals until a maximum rate for the job is reached. Cf. *incentive pay.*

automatic selling: the retail sale of merchandise from money-operated machines that are activated by the buyer.

automatic stabilizer: a tool of economics used to compensate for shifts in the business cycle without the involvement of a government official.

automatic wage adjustment: a wage rate fluctuation determined by a formula that responds to specific changes, such as variations in the cost-of-living index or in prevailing wage rates; sometimes included as part of a collective-bargaining agreement.

automation: conversion to the use of automatic machines or devices that are designed to control various processes. The term was coined in 1935 by D.S. Harder of the Ford Motor Company and was popularized by John Diebold. Cf. *labor-saving equipment; mechanization.*

automatization:
(1) the use of machines as a major replacement for people.
(2) a manufacturing process with minimal human intervention.
(3) often reduced to *automation.*

autonomous change in demand: a change in planned expenditure that is not induced by a change in income.

autonomous consumption: consumption that is independent of income; the part of total consumption that is unrelated to income.

autonomous transactions: transactions among nations that arise from factors unrelated to the balance of payments as such. The primary classes are merchandise trade and services, long-term capital movements, and unilateral transfers.

autonomous work groups: various arrangements that allow employees to decide democratically how to meet their group's work objectives.

autonomy: personal control over one's own work.

auxiliary agency: a coordinative, technical part of a firm that takes care of the financial, accounting, personnel, supply, and maintenance needs of all operating units and controls these divisions.

autonomy and independence anchor: need to be able to work without direction or restraints, often manifested in a departure from traditional jobs.

avail: the amount remaining following a discount or expense deduction.

availability: the broadcast time offered to an advertiser for sponsorship.

availability date: the date on which checks payable at out-of-town banks are considered to be collected and are converted into cash; determined by the geographical location of the drawee bank, in relation to time and distance from the sending bank.

avails: the proceeds from a discounted note.

average:
  (1) **shipping:** the loss or damage of a ship or its freight, or the amount payable by a ship's or cargo's owners to make good such loss or damage
  (2) **securities:** to buy or sell more shares, items, and so on, with the goal of receiving a better average price.

average adjustor: the person who prepares claims made under the average clause in insurance contracts.

average blanket rate: a rate for a blanket policy, determined by multiplying the rate for each location by the value at that location declared by the insured, then dividing the sum of the results by the total value. See *blanket policy*.

average bond: see *bond, average*.

average clause: a clause in an insurance contract stating that, if the insurer fails to insure property for its full value and a loss ensues, the amount to be paid will be limited to a proportion of the loss, namely, the proportion of the value of the policy that is related to the value of the property.

average cost: the sum of all output costs divided by the quantity of production.

average daily balance: the average amount of money that a customer keeps on deposit; determined by adding the daily balances of an account for a given length of time and dividing the total by the number of days covered.

average demurrage agreement: a shipper's and carrier's agreement according to which the shipper is debited for the time vehicles or vessels are held for loading and unloading (beyond a specified time) and is credited for the time they are released by the shipper within a fixed time. Demurrage charges are assessed by the transportation firm, usually at the end of the month, for outstanding debits.

average due date: the average date when several payments that are coming due at different times can be paid.

average fixed costs: production costs that do not depend on the amount produced divided by the quantity produced. Average fixed costs decline as production grows.

average gross sales: the dollar amount of gross sales divided by the number of sales transactions that created the gross sales.

average haul: the average distance in miles one ton is moved, computed by dividing the number of tonmiles by the number of tons moved.

average hourly earnings: the amount of money actually received by an employee per hour of work during a pay period.

average load: the average number of tons of freight per loaded vehicle, obtained by dividing the total number of tons by the number of vehicle loads originated.

average mark-on: the mark-on obtained when the costs and retail prices of several purchases are combined.

average rate: see *composite rate.*

average revenue: the sum of revenues divided by the quantity sold; often presented as an average revenue curve, with quantity plotted on the horizontal axis and average revenue on the vertical.

averages: various ways of measuring the trend of securities prices. One of the most popular is the Dow Jones average of 30 industrial stocks listed on the New York Stock Exchange.

average straight-time hourly earnings: actual earnings per straight-time hour, excluding shift differentials and overtime pay but including incentive and merit payments.

average total cost: see *average cost.*

average variable cost: cost per unit of production of inputs such as labor, materials, and utilities, which are used in increasing amounts as production increases.

average weekly benefits: as prescribed by law, the amount payable per week to compensate for disability or death. It is usually a percentage of the average weekly wage, subject to a minimum and a maximum amount. In workers' compensation insurance, this is referred to a weekly compensation. The benefit is paid by an insurance carrier of the company.

average weekly wage: the average rate of remuneration per week, computed as prescribed by law.

averaging: methods used in attempt to improve the average price paid or received for securities by buying or selling at a variable rate as prices climb or drop.

avoidance-avoidance conflict: a situation in which a person, in moving away from one undesirable path, must move toward another undesirable path. See *role conflict*.

avoidance conflict resolution: a strategy that generally disregards causes of a conflict by allowing the conflict to continue only under controlled conditions.

avoiding: desire to withdraw from or suppress a conflict.

award:

(1) **labor relations:** the final decision of an arbitrator, which is binding on both parties to the dispute.

(2) **finance:** the acceptance of a bid or the assigning of a project on the basis of a made offer.

B

baby bond: see *bond, baby.*

Baby Wagner Acts: state and territorial labor laws, based on the Wagner-Connery Act, that deal with representation procedures and unfair labor and management practices.

back: to finance, sponsor, or endorse (e.g., to back a plan for adding a wing to a plant).

backdoor financing: a practice enabling a government agency to borrow from the U.S. Treasury rather than relying on congressional appropriations. Synonymous with *public debt transaction.*

backer: an individual who supports a project or person with money. Cf. *promoter.*

background investigation: a procedure to determine if an applicant's past work history and experience is related to the qualifications needed for a job.

back pay: wages due an employee because of the employer's violation of minimum wage laws, layoff or discharge in violation of a collective-bargaining agreement, or adjustment of the piece rate following settlement of a grievance.

back-to-work movement: a return of strikers to their jobs before their union has declared that the strike is ended.

backtracking: using seniority rights to displace junior workers when business conditions warrant layoffs. See *bumping.*

bad delivery:
(1) **general:** a delivered item that does not conform to the original terms of agreement.
(2) **securities:** an improperly prepared or transferred security or certificate.

bad faith: the intent to mislead or deceive (*Latin: mala fides*). It does not include misleading by an honest, inadvertent, or uncalled-for misstatement. See *fraud.*

bagged: (slang) discharged from one's job.

bail bond: see *bond, bail.*

bait advertising: advertising exceptional prices or terms for a specified product to attract prospects to a store; potential customers find, however, that it is difficult to buy the product there as advertised.

bait and switch: an unethical approach in which a retailer advertises a product at a particularly low price with the intention of inducing people who ask for the item to purchase a more costly one. Sometimes the switch is made by the salesperson telling the purchaser that the advertised item is not good or has been sold out. See *switch selling.*

Baker Plan: plan developed in 1985 by U.S. Secretary James Baker to solve the international debt crisis; stressed debt rescheduling, tight controls over domestic monetary and fiscal policies, and continued loans to debtor nations. Cf. *Brady Commission.*

balanced budget: a budget in which forward expenditures for a set period are matched by expected revenues for the same period.

balanced economic growth: economic expansion throughout the country at approximately the same geometric rate for all items manufactured.

balanced economy: a condition of national finances in which imports and exports are equal.

balanced growth equilibrium: stable economic expansion over an extensive time period.

balance due: the total amount needed to equalize the debit and credit sum of an account; the amount owed.

balance of account: the net amount of the total debits and total credits posted to a given account. Balances are of three types: zero balance indicating that total debits and total credits are equal; debit balance-indicating an excess of total debits over total credits; and credit balance, indicating an excess of total credits over debits, at a given time.

balance of payments (b.o.p.): a statement identifying all financial transactions of a country and its population with the other nations of the world. Cf. *dollar shortage.*

balance-of-payments deficit: a situation in which a nation is spending more abroad that it earns abroad.

balance of trade: the difference between a country's imports and exports over a set period.

balance sheet: an itemized statement listing the total assets and total liabilities of a business to portray its net worth at a particular moment in time.

balance theory: theory used in the study of communication to explain how people react to change, placing primary attention on the consideration of three relationships: (a) the attitude of the receiver toward the sender, (b) the attitude of the receiver toward the change, and (c) the receiver's perception of the sender's attitude toward the change.

balancing time: shifting the hours of work within a time period without altering the total number of hours worked within that period.

ballooning: price manipulation used to send prices beyond safe or real values.

balloon loan: a loan on which small payments are made during the term of the obligation.

balloon note: a promissory note requiring only a small payment during the initial loan period, offset by larger payments before the date of maturity.

bandwagon: a propaganda technique of appealing to the tendency of workers to identify with, conform to, and follow their own particular group or the ideas that represent the group. It makes use of the concept that it is difficult to stand alone when everybody else is doing the same thing.

bank: defined according to function, organizational setup, or relationship to one another. See *branch banking; commercial bank; correspondent bank; country bank; Federal Reserve Bank; group banking; independent bank; industrial bank; insured bank; investment banking; member bank; mortgage banker; multiple banking; mutual savings bank; national bank; private bank; savings bank; state bank; trust company.*

bank acceptance: see *acceptance.*

bank accommodation: a short-term bank loan to a customer, either on the individual's own note or on the endorsement of another's note owed to him or her.

bank bailout bill: see *Savings Industry Bill.*

bank bill: see *bank note.*

bank call: a request for a bank's balance sheet for a specified date, made by government statement.

bank clearing:
(1) **banking:** bank items sent by member banks to a local clearinghouse for collection.
(2) **finance:** the total volume of dollars on all items that are exchanged among members of a local clearinghouse.

bank credit: credit created by commercial banks through loans and discounts granted with or without collateral. The amount of credit so extended is controlled in part by the rediscount rates established by the Federal Reserve Board.

bank currency: see *bank note.*

bank debits: the sum total of all debits drawn against deposited funds of individuals, partnerships, corporations, and other legal entities during a given period. Usually, debits are reported by banks daily.

bank deregulation: see *Depository Institutions Deregulation Committee.*

bank discount: a bank's charge for discounting a bill of exchange or, at times, a promissory note. It is equal to simple interest on the face value of the note or bill, from the date of discounting to the due date.

bank draft: a check drawn by one bank against funds deposited to its account in another bank.

banker's acceptance: a bill of exchange drawn on or accepted by a bank to pay specific bills for one of its customers when the bills become due.

banker's bank: a central bank. In the United States, it is one of the 12 Federal Reserve district banks.

Bank for International Settlements (BIS): an international institution founded in Basle, Switzerland, in 1930; designed to foster cooperation among world central banks, to seek opportunities for development of financial activity among governments, and to serve as an agent involving the transfer of payments.

banking power: the strength of investing possessed by a bank, as determined by the bank's excess reserves.

banking time off: a reward practice of permitting workers to build up time-off credits for such things as good performance or attendance. Employees then receive the time off in addition to the regular vacation time granted by the organization.

Bank Insurance Fund: see *BIF.*

bank money: funds in demand deposits; that is, checking accounts in banks.

bank note: a promissory note released by an authorized bank that is payable on demand to the bearer and can be used as cash. Such notes, as established by law, are redeemable as money and are considered to be full legal tender. Synonymous with *bank bill; bank currency.*

bank of issue: a bank authorized to issue its own bank notes to circulate freely as currency. Only 12 Federal Reserve banks have the authority to issue bank notes.

bank overdraft: an amount owed to a bank by a customer on his or her account. The bank will make a charge that is calculated on the amount overdrawn on a day-to-day basis, establishing a fixed limit that the customer may withdraw.

bank post remittance: conversion into cash or a money form of a foreign bill of exchange and subsequent mailing to the payee.

bank rate:
 (1) the rate of discount established by the national bank of a country for rediscounting eligible paper.
 (2) the rate charged by the national bank of a country for advances on specified collateral to banks.

bank reconciliation: the process of systematically comparing a company's cash balance as reported by the bank and as recorded on the company's books and explaining any differences.

bank reserve: the stock of money a bank is required to put aside (and not lend) to fulfill the demands of depositors.

bank run: a series of unusually large withdrawals from a bank because of customers' fears that the bank may run out of funds.

bankrupt: a person, corporation, or other legal entity that, being unable to meet its financial obligations, has been declared by a decree of the court to be insolvent and whose property becomes liable to administration under the National Bankruptcy Act. See *insolvent*.

bankruptcy: the conditions under which the financial position of an individual, corporation, or other legal entity is such as to cause actual or legal insolvency. Two types are (1) involuntary bankruptcy, whereby one or more creditors of an insolvent debtor file a petition having the debtor declared a bankrupt; and (2) voluntary bankruptcy, whereby the debtor files a petition claiming inability to meet debts and willingness to be declared a bankrupt. A court adjudges and declares a debtor a bankrupt. See *insolvency; National Bankruptcy Act of 1898*.

Bankruptcy Reform Act of 1978: federal legislation that streamlined bankruptcy cases, permitting them to be settled more rapidly. The major sections of the Act, chapters 7 and 11, allow for liquidations and reorganizations, respectively.

Bank Secrecy Act of 1970: federal legislation compelling banks to keep records of all customer transactions and to report any financial dealings involving more than $10,000 to the Department of the Treasury. The government contends that the records are the bank's business records and are not owned by the depositor.

bank service charge: a bank's fee for servicing an account, usually charged monthly.

bank statement:
 (1) a statement of a customer's account periodically rendered by the bank. It shows all deposits made and all checks paid during the period, usually a month, as well as the current balance; the customer's

canceled checks, or copies of them, are enclosed.

(2) a bank's financial statement.

Bank Wire System: a private, computerized message system administered for and by participating banks through the facilities of Western Union. The system links about 250 banks in about 75 cities. Like the Fed Wire, the Bank Wire system transmits funds and transfers information, but it also relays data concerning loan participations, bond closings, payment for securities, borrowing of federal funds, and balances in company accounts. Cf. *Fed Wire.*

bantam store: a community food market that remains open in the late evening or on weekends or holidays when many supermarkets are closed. Cf. *convenience goods; depot store.*

bare-label: having a label with only a product name but with no brand name or other information.

bargain:

(1) **general:** an item bought at a low or advantageous price; a good buy

(2) **sales:** to arrive at an agreement on the price of goods to be sold.

bargain counter:

(1) **securities:** describing stocks offered for sale at prices below their intrinsic value.

(2) **retailing:** an area for the sale of discounted merchandise.

bargain hunter:

(1) **general:** an individual who seeks out the store that is selling items at the lowest possible price.

(2) **securities:** a speculator or investor who waits until stocks are on the bargain counter.

bargaining: a process in which offers, counteroffers, and concessions are exchanged as conflicting groups search for some mutually acceptable resolution.

bargaining agent: the formally designated agency, usually a labor union, that represents employees seeking or having a collective-bargaining agreement (contract). Its rights and obligations are defined by federal law. See *Wagner-Connery Act.*

bargaining book: a compilation of a negotiation team's plans for collective-bargaining negotiations with labor or management.

bargaining creep: progress in collective bargaining that is slow, with minimal compromise.

bargaining rights:

(1) **general:** the legal rights of workers to bargain collectively with their employers.

(2) **labor relations:** the right of a specific union to represent its members in collective bargaining.

bargaining unit: the group of employees, usually defined by the National Labor Relations Board after a hearing, that a union may seek to represent as bargaining agent on wages, hours, and working conditions. See *collective bargaining*.

bargaining zone: area with which the union and the employer are willing to concede when bargaining.

bargain store: a store that sells merchandise at a sub-market price. Assortments and sizes are often limited, and the merchandise frequently is damaged or seconds. See *seconds*.

bargain theory: the concept according to which wages are determined by demand for and supply of labor and by the relative bargaining strengths of employer and employee.

Barnard's unit concept: the idea, developed by Chester Barnard, that an organization should be made up of small departments, each composed of 10 or fewer members.

barn-burner wizards: (slang) high-power salespeople who skillfully push to achieve their stated goals or sales.

barometric price leader: a firm that interprets best the current economic situation in an industry and is, therefore, followed in the setting of prices for that industry.

barratry:
(1) **transportation:** an intentional act by the master of a ship or its crew to the injury of the owner of the ship or cargo.
(2) **business law:** the practice of exciting and encouraging quarrels and lawsuits.

barren money: currency that does not earn interest or other forms of income.

barriers to change: factors that interfere with employee acceptance and implementation of change.

barriers to entry: obstacles to creating a new company within a particular industry, resulting from legal or economic advantages enjoyed by existing companies.

barter: the direct exchange of one item for another without the transfer of money.

base inventory level: the normal aggregate inventory level composed of the aggregate lot size inventory plus the aggregate safety stock inventory, but not taking into account the anticipation inventory resulting from the production plan. The base inventory level is usually known before the production plan is made.

basement store: the department in a store, where bargain merchandise is consigned.

base pay: the regular rate of pay for an identified time period, excluding overtime, bonuses, and other premiums. See *basic wages.*

base period:

(1) **personnel:** the period during which an employee fulfills the length-of-employment requirement in order to receive state unemployment insurance benefits.

(2) **economics:** a chosen date from the past used in measuring the price index. See *index number.*

base rate: under an incentive system, the amount guaranteed per hour or other time period.

base rate bias: tendency of decision makers to ignore the underlying objective probability, or base rate, that a particular outcome will follow a particular course of action.

base stock method: inventory assessment that assumes that a minimum normal or base stock of items must be retained at all times to ensure effective continuity of activity.

base time: the established time for the normal performance of work by an average employee, excluding time allowed for rest, mechanical failures, and other delays.

basic decisions: long-range decisions, often involving large expenditures of funds and carrying a high degree of importance.

basic piece rate: part of a wage incentive plan allowing for payment to be made in direct proportion to the production yield.

basic rate: the manual or experience rating from which discounts are taken or to which charges are added to compensate for the individual circumstances of the risk.

basic research: research motivated by the search for the advancement of knowledge rather than for momentary economic gain. Cf. *applied research.*

basic stock: merchandise that is in constant demand, thus requiring perpetual inventory throughout the year.

basic wages: payment received by employees for work performed, based on time or output. See *base pay*

basing point pricing: an approach used by an industry whose goal is for all sellers to charge identical prices. The basing point is frequently the location of a plant near the buyer. Such pricing has been declared to be price discrimination in violation of the Clayton Antitrust Act.

basis:

(1) **finance:** the yield to maturity of bonds at a given price, as shown by bond tables.

(2) **taxation:** in calculating capital gains or losses, the value employed as the original property cost, which may or may not be the true cost.

(3) **securities:** the difference between the cash price of a money market instrument that is hedged and a futures contract.

basis point: 1/100 of 1 percent, a minimal measure in finance and trade.

basket purchase: the purchase of a group of assets for one price; so that the items can be recorded individually in the accounts, however, a cost is assigned to each asset.

BATNA: Best Alternative To A Negotiated Agreement. The lowest acceptable value to an individual for a negotiated agreement.

batten:

(1) **packaging:** a wood strip attached to a structure to reinforce it.

(2) **economics:** to grow wealthy at another's expense.

Bayes criterion: see *Laplace criterion.*

BDI: see *behavioral description interview.*

B/E: *bill of exchange.*

beachhead demands: demands the union makes in current negotiations that it does not expect to receive at the time but hopes to receive in future negotiations.

bearer: any person holding a negotiable instrument.

bearer bond: see *bond, bearer.*

bearer certificate: a certificate that is not filled out in the name of a particular person. Since such certificates are negotiable without endorsement, they should be kept in a safe place.

bear hug: (slang) an unnegotiated corporate takeover proposal made privately or publicly to directors. The major goal is to force a board into a quick decision.

bear market: a declining stock market.

bear position: a stance taken by a person who expects the market to fall. Consequently, he or she sells securities short, hoping that the market will move downward.

bears: speculators who anticipate that prices are going to drop. See *hammering the market.*

beat down: (slang) to bargain in order to lower the cost of an item.

beef: see *grievance.*

beggar-my-neighbor policy: an attempt to discourage imports by increasing tariffs or using other effective means.

beginning balance: the balance in an account at the commencement of a fiscal period.

beginning inventory: the valuation of inventory on hand at the beginning of an accounting period.

behavioral approach: approach to leadership that tries to identify behaviors that differentiate effective leaders from nonleaders. See *satisficing* and *suboptimization.*

behavioral component of an attitude: an intention to behave in a certain way toward someone or something. See *attitudes.*

behavioral decision theory: decision models that examine the influence of individual, group, and organizational factors in decision making.

behavioral description interview (BDI): an interview in which an applicant is asked questions about what he or she actually did in a given situation.

behavioral displacement: a reaction to being controlled, in which employees concentrate too narrowly on the company's control standards and thereby miss the firm's more important objectives.

behavioral economics: an approach to economic research which uses behavioral sciences (psychology, sociology, management, and decision theories) and findings in explaining and predicting economic behavior. The pioneering work can be found in the *Handbook of Behavioral Economics,* edited by B. Gilad and S. Kaish (JAI Press, Greenwich, CT, 1986).

behavioral school: a modern school of management theory propounded by those who view management as a psychological process. Advocates of this school are particularly concerned with such topics as needs, drives, motivation, leadership, personality, behavior, work groups, and the management of change.

behavioral science movement: movement stressing the need to conduct systematic and controlled studies of workers and their attitudes and behaviors.

behavioral self-management: modifying one's own behavior by managing cues, cognitive processes, and consequences.

behavioral tendency component: the part of an attitude that identifies how workers intend to behave toward a person, task, or the like. See *attitudes.*

behavioral theories of leadership: theories proposing that specific behaviors differentiate leaders from nonleaders.

behavioral viewpoint: a perspective on management that emphasizes the importance of attempting to understand the various factors that affect human behavior in organizations.

behavior modeling: a training process for helping managers to develop interpersonal skills.

behavior modification: making specific behavior occur more or less often by managing its cues and consequences.

behavior observation scale (BOS): a behavioral approach to performance appraisal that measures the frequency of observed behavior.

bell-ringer: (slang) a door-to-door salesperson.

belongingness needs: needs in Maslow's hierarchy that involve the desire to affiliate with and be accepted by others. See *hierarchy of needs*.

below par: at a discount; less than face amount.

below the line: not expensed but capitalized over a period of time; does not normally affect operating budgets, percentages, or line items.

bench:
(1) **general:** a place where a worker performs his or her tasks.
(2) **business law:** the court or the judges sitting in the court.

benchmarking: process by which a company compares its performance with that of high-performing organizations.

bench scale production: the manufacture of a small number of units before the development of normal production techniques.

beneficiary:
(1) **general:** a person who is beneficially interested in a trust or estate.
(2) **business law:** the person for whose benefit a trust, policy, will, or contract promise is made.
(3) **insurance:** the person(s) to whom the proceeds of a life insurance contract are payable upon the death of the insured.

benefit:
(1) **general:** a gain or advantage received by an individual.
(2) **insurance:** the amount of indemnity to be regularly paid.
(3) **salesmanship:** that which fulfills a need.

benefit year: the period of time specified by law during which an employee fulfills the employment requirements in order to qualify for unemployment compensation.

benevolent-authoritative leadership style: a basic leadership style in which management acts in a condescending manner toward subordinates, and decision making at the lower levels occurs only within a prescribed framework.

Best Alternative to a Negotiated Agreement: see *BATNA*.

Better Business Bureau: a voluntary agency of business executives created to improve business practices and to define fair standards and ethics in the conduct of business activity. The movement to improve conditions began in 1921, when vigilance committees for truth in advertising first appeared in local advertising clubs.

BFOQ: see *bona fide occupational qualification*.

bid: an offering of money in exchange for property (items, goods, etc.) put up for sale. Three types are: *best bid,* not necessarily the lowest or highest but good for the organization seeking a bid; *competitive* bid, secured from a public announcement of the competition; and *sealed bid*, not disclosed until a specified time, when all other bids are revealed and compared (this approach purports to guarantee the independence of bidders).

bid and asked: "bid" is the quotation of a prospective buyer and "asked" is the quotation of a seller for the sale of a trading unit or other specified amount of security (often referred to as a quotation or quote). The bid is the highest price anyone has offered to pay for a security at a given time.

bidding:

(1) **general:** offering money as an exchange for an item or service.

(2) **personnel:** application by an employee for consideration for a job that is open in a plant or office. In most contracts, assuming that all qualifications are equal, first preference is given to the applicant with the most seniority. See *posting*.

bidding up: raising the price bid for a security for fear of not having an order executed before an upswing begins.

BIF: Bank Insurance Fund. The new name for the Federal Deposit Insurance Corporation's fund that insures bank deposits up to $100,000. Its assets are currently $14 billion, considered too low. A new law increases bank premiums to replenish the fund. FDIC cannot commingle BIF and SAIF funds. See *Savings Industry Bill*.

big bath: a write-off of a substantial amount of costs treated previously as assets.

big-bath accounting: a corporate strategy of taking a large write-off or getting rid of an unprofitable line of business in one quarterly period in order to report high earnings for the quarter.

Big Board: the New York Stock Exchange, Inc. Cf. *Little Board.*

big business: a business that is very large or one that controls a substantial portion of the market. Big business often holds monopolistic markets and exercises power over a large segment of the population.

Bigelow plan: a wage incentive approach providing for a step bonus between the minimum wage and the standard wage, with more than 1 percent additional salary for 1 percent additional performance.

big ticket items: frequently refers to merchandise that is large in size and high in price (furniture, appliances, etc.).

bilateral agreement: an agreement between two persons or groups.

bilateral assistance: foreign aid provided by one country directly to another rather than channeled via an international (multilateral) agency such as the United Nations.

bilateral contract: an agreement containing promises, with each party serving as a promisor or promisee.

bilateralism: the practice or system of trade and payments arrangements between two countries with special privileges extended only to each other. Cf. *multilateralism.*

bilateral monopoly: a condition that exists when there is only one purchaser for an item or service and the creation of the supply is controlled by one seller. Cf. *monopoly.*

bill:
    (1) **sales:** an invoice of charges for services or a product.
    (2) **business law:** the instrument of formal issuance of a complaint before a court.
    (3) **business law:** a court's formal statement reporting its findings.
    (4) **finance:** paper currency.

bill check: a payment system in which a debtor, on receipt of an invoice or statement, authorizes the creditor to obtain payment directly from the debtor's deposit account.

bill discounted: a promissory note or bill of exchange from which a bank deducts its interest in advance.

billed escrow: the amount of escrow payment that represents a total of the regular escrow payment plus arrears or minus prepaid escrow amounts.

billed principal: the amount of principal payment that represents a total of the normal principal amount plus any arrears.

billing:
    (1) **advertising:** the total amount of money charged to clients by an

advertising agency. This includes production costs, expenses, media costs, and other service charges.

(2) **accounting:** the process of submitting invoices or bills.

bill of capacity: a document showing how much standard time is needed on each machine to make one finished part in a manufacturing operation.

bill of credit:

(1) **banking:** an individual's written request to a bank asking for the delivery of money to the bearer on the credit or account of the writer.

(2) **finance:** an instrument used as if it were a state's currency. Article 1 of the U.S. Constitution forbids the states to issue their own currency.

bill of exchange: instructions from one party to another party to pay a third party following completion of an assignment. See *commercial set.*

bill of lading: a statement whereby the carrier acknowledges receipt of freight, identifies the freight, and sets forth a contract of carriage. See *commercial set.* Cf. *clean bill of lading; straight bill of lading; through bill of lading; waybill.*

bill of materials: a specification of the quantities of direct materials allowed for manufacturing a given quantity of output.

bill of sale:

(1) a written agreement by whose terms the ownership of goods is transferred or assigned to another person.

(2) a formal written agreement by which one person transfers to another his or her rights, interest, and title in specified property. It is considered to be sufficient warranty of the seller's title to the property and his or her right to sell; it need not be recorded as a deed for real property.

bill of sight: a temporary entry permit authorized by a customs official for imported items, allowing the goods to be unloaded from a carrier to permit examination by a customs agent to identify their true character.

bills payable:

(1) **general:** a comprehensive term that includes the total of notes and trade acceptances that are owed by a business to trade creditors and must be paid by the business at their maturity.

(2) **banking:** the sum of money that a member bank has borrowed on its own collateral note from a Federal Reserve Bank.

bills receivable: a comprehensive term that includes the total of all notes and trade acceptances given by customers, usually in payment of merchandise, that the debtors must pay at maturity.

bimetallism: a double standard of metals used in coins. The ratio of content and weight must be specified in terms of, for example, gold and silver. Cf. *monometallism; parallel standard; real money.*

binder:

(1) **insurance:** a legal agreement issued either by an agent or by a company to provide temporary insurance until a policy can be written. It usually is in writing, contains a definite time limit, and clearly designates the company in which the risk is bound as well as the amount, the perils insured against, and the type of insurance. See *cover note.*

(2) **business law:** any temporary agreement obligating the several parties to the contract.

binding arbitration: process in which both parties are obligated to conform to the findings of an arbitrator. See *arbitrator.*

bird dog (slang):

(1) **administration:** to seek data to assist in studying a firm's position and potential earnings.

(2) **sales:** an individual who is paid to obtain business for a high-powered salesperson.

business law: an individual who is paid to spread fraudulent charges.

B/L: see *bill of lading.*

black book: a brochure prepared to describe a private securities placement. It is not for a public offering and usually excludes data found in a public prospectus and includes information not found in a public prospectus, such as projections of sales.

black box concept: a concept of the inner workings that take place between input and output. As applied to human behavior, the concept may involve, for example, the introduction of a new wage incentive payment scheme (input) and a 10 percent increase in productivity (output). The reason for the increase may be the wage plan, but it may also be something else. The black box, or the transformation process between input and output, is said to contain the answer.

black capitalism: an attempt to increase business ownership among blacks.

blacking: during a union action, the refusal by employees to perform any work that they conclude will hurt their cause. Cf. *sit-down strike; slow-down; soldiering.*

blackleg: (slang) an employee who continues to work during a strike. Cf. *loyal worker.* Synonymous with *scab.*

blacklist: a management roster of persons deemed undesirable as employees. This was declared an unfair labor practice in 1935 by the National Labor Relations Act. Blacklisted workers often were fired or not hired in new jobs when blacklisting was used for antiunion purposes.

black market: buying or selling products and commodities or engaging in exchange of foreign currencies in violation of government restrictions. Cf. *gray market.*

Black Monday: October 19, 1987, when the Dow Jones Industrial Average dropped 508 points, the largest fall in its history. See *Brady Commission.* Cf. *Black Tuesday.*

black money: (slang) income that is not reported for tax purposes because of its illegal origin.

Black Tuesday: name for economic impact of September 11, 2001, attacks on World Trade Towers in New York City and the Pentagon in Washington, D.C. In one week, following the opening of the stock market, the U.S. economy lost more than $1 trillion worth of investments. The Dow dropped 14.3 percent, its largest since the Great Depression. See *September 11, 2001.* Cf. *Black Monday.*

blank check: a bank form that has been signed, although the amount payable or the name of the payee has been left out.

blank-check blind pool: stocks of shell companies that exist only to merge with other unspecified companies. See *penny stocks.*

blank-check buying: the practice of a retailer placing an open order with a supplier, with requests to be made throughout the season as needed.

blanket agreement: a collective bargaining agreement based on an industry-wide negotiation for large geographical areas within an industry, as established by the Norris-LaGuardia Act (the Anti-Injunction Act).

blanket bond: see *bond, blanket.*

blanket injunction: a court order issued during a strike, or to prevent a strike, so broad in its sweep that it encompasses activities that rarely occur in connection with the conditions being enjoined. The Anti-Injunction Act identifies safeguards in the release of labor dispute injunctions.

blanket order: a preseason order to meet expected buyer demand.

blanket policy: an insurance policy that covers several different properties, shipments, or locations under one item rather than under separate items. See *average blanket rate.* Cf. *specific insurance.*

blind ads: help-wanted ads that do not identify the employer.

Blind-alley jobs: (slang) positions accepted by workers that offer little if any chance for advancement.

blind entry: a bookkeeping entry stating only the accounts and the amounts debited and credited but not giving other data or accounting factors essential to an accurate record.

blind selling: (slang) selling merchandise or services without the customer having a chance to examine the item prior to purchase.

block:

(1) **broadcasting:** a group of consecutive time slots, or the same time period from day to day.

(2) **securities:** a large holding or transaction of stock; popularly considered to be 10,000 shares or more. Cf. *lot.*

blockade: the act of preventing commercial exchange with a country or port, usually during wartime, by physically preventing carriers from entering a specific port or nation. See *embargo.* Cf. *preclusive purchasing.*

blocked accounts: in times of war, directives issued by the president of the United States to financial institutions to suspend payment of the accounts of enemy nationals or of individuals inhabiting occupied countries in the sphere of enemy influence. These funds may be released only by executive order or by license under certain conditions. Cf. *frozen accounts.*

block policy: a policy covering all the inventory of the insured against most perils, including transportation. It may also cover property of others held by the insured (a) on consignment, (b) as sold but not delivered, (c) for repairs, or (d) otherwise. It usually applies both on and off the premises of the insured.

blood bath: (slang) a horrendous loss suffered by investors when the stock market declines sharply.

blotter: a book of accounts or a journal used for entering the first or a temporary list of transactions or occurrences. Cf. *daily reports.*

BLS: see *Bureau of Labor Statistics.*

blue chip: stock market term used to describe a corporation that maintains a good dividend return and has sound management and good growth potential. See *bond, gilt-edged, seasoned issues, seasoned security.*

blue-collar workers: production and maintenance workers, as contrasted with office and professional personnel. The force of blue-collar workers is declining numerically.

bluefingers: (slang) workers from one family who attain common goals with efficiency and team spirit; for example, relatives who successfully pursue their objectives while receiving pleasure from their togetherness. Synonymous with *jebble.*

blue sky law: certain laws enacted by various states to regulate the sale and issuance of securities; specifically, attempting to prevent fraud in their sale and disposition. Cf. *SEC.*

board: a standing committee of high rank or importance (e.g., a board of directors).

board lot: the unit of trading for stocks on an exchange. The unit of trading in stocks on the New York Stock Exchange is 100 shares. See *even lots.* Synonymous with *full lot.*

board of directors: people chosen by stockholders of a corporation to manage the enterprise.

Board of Governors: the seven-member governing body of the Federal Reserve System.

board representatives: form of representative participation where employees sit on a company's board of directors and represent the interest of the firm's employees.

bobtail statement: an abbreviated statement prepared for demand deposit accounts.

bod biz: (slang) see *sensitivity training.*

body language: an important part of nonverbal communications that involves the transmittal of thoughts, actions, and feelings through body movements and the interpretation of those movements by other people.

bogey:
(1) **labor relations:** an informal standard that employees exceed, set up as an effort by employees to restrict output.
(2) **salesmanship:** a standard of performance, such as the volume of sales beyond which a bonus is given.

boiler and machinery insurance: coverage for loss arising from the operation of pressure, mechanical, and electrical equipment.

boiler room tactic: (slang) selling of very speculative and often worthless securities through the use of high-pressure, misleading literature. See *dynamiter.*

boll weevil: (slang) any nonunion worker. Synonymous with *scab.*

bona fide: (*Latin*) "in good faith"; with honest intent. Cf. *mala fides; bad faith.*

bona fide occupational qualification (BFOQ): an employer's justified business reason for discriminating against a member of a protected class.

bond:

    (1) **general:** an interest-bearing certificate of debt, usually issued in series, by which the issuer obligates itself to pay the principal amount at a specified time, usually five years or more after date of issue, and to pay interest periodically, usually semiannually. Bonds may be distinguished from promissory notes or other evidences of debt by their formal execution under seal and by the certification by a bank that their issue has been authorized by the board of directors of a corporation or other governing body. Corporate bonds are usually secured by a lien against specified property. Bonds may be issued in bearer form or registered.

    (2) **finance:** a promise under seal (i.e., closed from view by the public) to pay money.

    (3) **finance:** an obligation to answer for the debt of another person.

bond, adjustment: an income bond issued as a result of a firm's reorganization. See *bond, reorganization.*

bond, approved: a bond named in the legal list prepared for fiduciaries in some states. See *legal list.*

bond, assumed: a bond of one corporation whose liability is taken on by another corporation. See *bond, guaranteed.*

bond, authority: a bond payable from the revenues of a specific authority. Since such authorities usually have no revenue other than charges for services, their bonds ordinarily are revenue bonds.

bond, average: a bond given by an individual in receipt of freight, stating that the recipient will contribute to any standard claim.

bond, baby: a bond with a face value that usually is $100 or less.

bond, bail: a bond guaranteeing the appearance in court of the principal named in the bond.

bond, bearer: a bond payable to the holder that does not have the owner's name registered on the books of the issuing company.

bond, blanket: a form of broad-coverage protection carried by financial institutions to cover losses from robbery, burglary, or employee dishonesty.

bond, callable: a bond issue all or part of which may be redeemed before maturity by the issuing corporation under definite conditions.

bond, called: a bond that the debtor has declared to be due and payable on a certain date prior to maturity, in accordance with the provisions of an issue to be redeemed. The bonds to be retired are usually drawn by loss.

bond, city: see *bond, municipal.*

bond, civil: a bond circulated by any government agency.

bond, classified: a debt security that receives a designation, such as Series A or Series B, to differentiate it from another bond of the same debtor. The series differ in maturity date and interest.

bond, clean: a coupon-type bond that has not been changed by any endorsement or rephrasing of the original contract, such as the words *assented* or *extended.*

bond, collateral: further security for a loan.

bond, collateral trust: an issue of bonds for which collateral has been pledged to guarantee repayment of the principal. This type of bond usually arises from intercompany transactions in which the parent company issues bonds for which securities of a subsidiary are the underlying collateral.

bond, combination: a bond issued by a governmental unit that is payable from the revenues of a governmental enterprise but is also backed by the full faith and credit of the governmental unit.

bond, consolidated: a debt instrument issued to replace two or more bonds issued earlier, often done to simplify a debt structure or to benefit from a lower prevailing rate of interest.

bond, continued: a debt instrument that need not be redeemed at maturity but can continue to earn interest.

bond, convertible: a bond that gives its owner the privilege of exchanging it for other securities of the issuing corporation on a preferred basis at some future date or under certain conditions.

bond, corporate: an obligation of a corporation. See *bond, long-term corporate.*

bond, coupon: a bond with interest coupons attached. The coupons are clipped as they come due and are presented by the holder for payment of interest. See *talon.*

bond, court: all bonds and mortgages required of litigants to enable them to pursue certain remedies of the courts.

bond, cushion: a high-interest-rate, top-quality bond that sells at a premium level above par and that usually results in a higher yield to maturity.

bond, customhouse: a bond required by the federal government in connection with the payment of duties or for producing bills of lading.

bond, debenture: a bond for which there is no specific security set aside or allocated for repayment of the principal.

bond, deferred serial: a serial bond in which the first installment does not fall due for two or more years from the date of issue.

bond, definitive: any bond that is issued in final form; used particularly to refer to permanent bonds for which temporary bonds or interim certificates were issued.

bond, depository: a bond guaranteeing payment of funds to depositors in accordance with the terms of a deposit in a bank.

bond, drawn: a bond that has been called for redemption by lot. See *bond, called.*

bond, endorsed: a bond that has been extraneously signed, permitting it to be considered for normal delivery according to the regulations of the exchange, and that therefore must be sold.

bond, escrow: a bond that is held in escrow. See *escrow.*

bond, estate tax: a designated government bond that is redeemable at par less accrued interest for federal estate taxes to the extent that the entire proceeds are applied to such taxes due, provided that the bond was owned by the decedent at the time of death.

bond, extended: a bond that has matured and on which the debtor has not yet paid the principal but has agreed to extend or continue to pay the principal at a later time. Upon the creditor's acceptance of the extension, the bond is stamped to show such agreement.

bond, external: a bond issued by a country or firm for purchase outside that country, usually denominated in the currency of the purchaser. Cf. *bond, internal.*

bond, federal: the promissory note of a central government.

bond, fidelity: insurance for an employer (the insured) for loss sustained as a result of any dishonest act by an employee covered by the insurance. Blanket fidelity bonds cover groups of employees. See *fidelity insurance.*

bond, fiduciary: a bond in behalf of a person appointed by a court to a position of trust (e.g., the executor of an estate).

bond, flower: a U.S. government bond. Until the Tax Reform Act of 1976, flower bonds sold at a substantial premium in relation to other bonds issued at similarly low interest rates because the Treasury accepted them for estate tax payments at 100 cents on the dollar, whatever their costs were at the time of purchase. This benefit is now taxable in part as a capital gain.

bond, forgery: insurance against loss due to forgery or alteration of, on, or in checks or other instruments.

bond, free: an unpledged bond; any bond that is immediately disposable.

bond, funding: a bond issued to retire outstanding floating debt and to eliminate deficits.

bond, gilt-edged: a high-grade bond issued by a company that has demonstrated its ability to earn a comfortable profit over a period of years and to pay its bondholders their interest without interruption. See *blue chip.*

bond, government: an obligation of the U.S. government, regarded as the highest-grade issues in existence. See *Treasury bill, Treasury note.*

bond, guaranteed: a bond on which the principal or income or both are guaranteed by another corporation or a parent company in case of default by the issuing corporation.

bond, high-yield: see *bond, junk.*

bond, honor: a consumer-size certificate of deposit with denominations as low as five dollars. Many banks promoted these bonds and told purchasers that they were merely honor-bound to report the interest on their tax returns. The Internal Revenue Service moved swiftly to eliminate this irregularity. **bond, improvement:** any bond issued by a municipality to finance a public improvement.

bond, improvement mortgage: a bond issued for financing improvements of the debtor's business that are secured by a general mortgage.

bond, inactive: see *inactive stock (bond).*

bond, income: a type of bond on which interest is paid when and only when earned by the issuing corporation.

bond, indemnity: a bond that protects the obligee (the party for whom the applicant for bond, or the principal, has undertaken to perform specified duties) against losses resulting from the principal's failure to fulfill the obligations. Examples of miscellaneous indemnity bonds are warehouse, lost instrument, and lien.

bond, indenture: a written agreement under which bonds are issued, setting forth maturity date, interest rate, and other terms.

bond, installment: see *bond, serial.*

bond, insular: a bond issued by a unit of the United States (e.g., Alaska, New York); synonymous with "territorial bond."

bond, interchangeable: a bond in either a registered or coupon form that can be converted to the other form or its original form at the request of the holder. A service charge is often made for such a conversion.

bond, interim: a bond sometimes used before the issuance of permanent bonds to raise funds that are needed only temporarily.

bond, intermediate: a callable bond bearing no date of maturity. The call aspect usually is not effective until some stated time period has passed.

bond, internal: a bond issued by a country that is payable in its own currency. Cf. *bond, external.*

bond, irredeemable: a bond that contains no provisions for being called or redeemed prior to maturity date.

bond, joint and several: any debt instrument by which the holder seeks payment from more than one corporation up to the full face amount of the security.

bond, joint control: a bond needed before transfer of the assets of an estate to the custody of the principal.

bond, judgment: a bond issued to fund judgments. See *funding.*

bond, junior: a bond that is subordinate or secondary to another issue, which, in the event of liquidation, would have prior claim to the junior bond. Cf. *bond, senior.*

bond, junk: a bond that typically offers interest rates three to four percentage points higher than Treasury issues. This is to compensate for the increased possibility of default. Synonymous with *high-yield bond.*

bond, legal: a bond that federal and state laws identify as an acceptable and legal investment for fiduciary institutions. See *bond, approved.*

bond, limited tax: a bond that is secured by a tax that is limited in amount and rate.

bond, long-term corporate: a debt of industrial corporations, finance companies, utilities, and telephone companies. Maturities range from 10 to 40 years, with intermediates running from four to 10 years. Such bonds are rated AAA and AA for high quality. The face denomination is $1000, but new issues often are marketed above or below par to adjust to current yields. Older bonds with lower-interest coupons sell at discounts.

bond, maintenance: a bond guaranteeing against defects in workmanship or materials for a stated time after the acceptance of the work.

bond, mortgage: a bond that has a mortgage on all properties of the issuing corporation as an underlying security.

bond, municipal: a bond issued by a state or a political subdivision (county, city, town, village, etc.); also, a bond issued by a state agency or authority. In general, interest paid on municipal bonds is exempt from federal income taxes and state and local taxes in the state of issue.

bond, noncallable: a bond that, under the terms of the issue, cannot be called by the obligor (the corporation) for redemption or conversion.

bond, obligation: a bond authorized by a mortgagor that is larger than the original mortgage amount. A personal obligation is created to safeguard the lender against any costs over the amount of the mortgage that may develop.

bond, open-end: a mortgage bond of an issue that has no limit on the number or quantity of bonds that can be issued under the mortgage. Often, however, some relationship is required between the number and quantity of bonds and the value of the property that has been mortgaged.

bond, optional: see *bond, callable.*

bond, overlying: a junior bond, subject to the claim of a senior underlying bond that has priority of claim.

bond, participating: a bond that, following the receipt of a fixed rate of periodic interest, also receives some of the profit held by the issuing business. A form of profit sharing, this bond is rarely used today.

bond, passive: a bond that does not carry any interest. Such bonds are often issued following a reorganization.

bond, penal: a bond given by an accused, or by another in his or her behalf, for the repayment of money in the event that the accused fails to appear in court on a specific day. See *bond, surety.*

bond, performance: a bond supplied by one party to another, protecting the second party against loss in the event of improper performance or completion of the terms of an existing contract.

bond, permit: a bond guaranteeing that the person to whom a permit is issued or is to be issued will comply with the law or ordinance regulating the privilege for which the permit is issued.

bond, plain: any debenture.

bond, preference: any income or adjustment bond.

bond, premium: in the United States, a bond that is selling above its face value; in Europe, a bond that has a lottery feature. When called, as distinguished from regular maturity, a premium bond generally pays substantially more than the face amount; also used for the excess of the price at which a bond is acquired or sold over its face value. The price does not include accrued interest at the date of acquisition or sale.

bond, prior-lien: a bond that holds precedence over other bonds issued by the same corporation.

bond, privileged: convertible bond that has attached warrants.

bond, public: any bond issued by a government agency, domestic or foreign.

bond, real estate: a bond secured by a mortgage or trust conveyance of real estate.

bond, redemption: a refunding bond. See *redemption*.

bond, refunding: a bond issued to retire a bond that is already outstanding. Refunding bonds may be sold for cash and outstanding bonds redeemed in cash, or they may be exchanged for outstanding bonds.

bond, registered: a bond in which the name of the owner is designated and the proceeds are payable only to him or her. Bonds may be registered for both principal and interest or for principal only. Interest on a bond that is registered for both principal and interest is paid to the owner by check as it becomes due. Bonds registered for principal only have coupons attached, which are detached and collected as the interest becomes due.

bond, reorganization: a debt security issued in the re-capitalization of a firm that is in financial difficulty; an adjustment bond.

bond, revenue: a bond whose principal and interest are to be paid solely from earnings. Such bonds are usually issued by a municipally owned utility or other public service enterprise, the revenues and possibly the properties of which are pledged for this purpose.

Bond, Savings (U.S.): Series EE, introduced at the start of 1980, replaced the highly popular Series E bonds. These new bonds are available in face-value denominations of $50, $75, and so on, up to $10,000 and are sold at half their face value. Series EE bonds pay varying interest rates—as much as 1 percent at six-month intervals if market conditions warrant. Currently, the maturity on Series EE bonds is eight years, down from nine years, effectively boosting the rate on those bonds to 9 percent. The rate on Series HH bonds is 8.5 percent. Series HH bonds are bought at face value, pay interest semi-annually, and mature in ten years.

bond, schedule: a bond listing the names and positions of employees included as principals. See *bond, fidelity*.

bond, second-mortgage: a bond is issued on property that already has an outstanding first mortgage.

bond, secured: a bond secured by the pledge of assets (plant or equipment), the title to which is transferred to bondholders in case of fore-closure.

bond, senior: a bond that has prior claim to the assets of the debtor upon liquidation. Cf. *bond, junior.*

bond, serial: an issue of bonds in which a certain proportion of the bonds is retired at regular intervals. Such bonds are issued when the security depreciates through use or obsolescence. These issues usually provide that the outstanding bonds shall not exceed the value of the security.

bond, sinking fund: a bond secured by the deposit of specified amounts. The issuing corporation makes these deposits to secure the principal of the bonds, and it is sometimes required that the funds be invested in other securities.

bond, special assessment: a bond payable from the proceeds of special assessments, which must be levied against the properties presumed to be benefited by the improvements or services for which the special assessment was made.

bond, special lien: a special assessment bond that acts as a lien against a particular piece or pieces of property.

bond, surety: an agreement providing for monetary compensation in the event of failure to perform specified acts within a stated period. The firm that is the surety company becomes responsible for fulfillment of a contract if the contractor defaults. See *bond, penal.*

bond, tax-exempt: any security of a state, city, or other public authority specified under federal law, the interest on which is either wholly or partly exempt from federal income taxes. See *bond, municipal.*

bond, temporary: similar to a definitive bond except that it has been printed rather than engraved. See *bond, definitive.*

bond, term: bonds of the same issue that usually mature at the same time and ordinarily are to be retired from sinking funds. Sometimes a term bond has more than one maturity date (e.g., a serial issue that has postponed maturities in only a few late years of its term).

bond, territorial: see *bond, insular.*

bond, Treasury: a U.S. government long-term security sold to the public that has a maturity longer than five years. See *Treasury bill, Treasury note.*

bond, underlying: a bond that has a senior lien where subsequent claims exist.

bond, unlimited tax: a bond secured by pledge of taxes which may be levied by the issuer in unlimited rate or amount.

bond, zero-coupon: a security sold at a deep discount from its face value and redeemed at the full amount at maturity.

bond discount: the difference between the face value and the sale price of a bond when it is sold below its face value.

bonded:

(1) **general:** a bond posted as security that a tax or tariff will be paid on time.

(2) **warehousing:** describing goods in a government-supervised storage facility where items are stored without payment of duties or taxes until they are removed.

bond indenture: a contract between a bond issuer and a bond buyer that specifies the terms of the bond. **bonding company:** an organization whose business is forming contracts of surety and providing bonds.

bond of indemnity: an indemnity agreement used in filing a claim when the claimant, unable to show the freight bill or bill of lading, is given relief from liability for any action for which a carrier otherwise would have been liable.

bond premium: the difference between the face value and the sale price of a bond when it is sold above its face value.

bond rating: appraising and rating, by a recognized financial organization (e.g., Moody's Investors Service), the worth of a bond as a sound investment. Ratings are based on the reputation of the organization, its record of interest payments, its profitability, and so on. Bonds rated AAA are the most secure, followed by AA, A, B, and so on.

bonification:

(1) **general:** rendering of an advantage or benefit.

(2) **manufacturing:** said to be achieved when certain items that are made for export relieve the manufacturer of paying an excise tax on such items.

(3) **taxation:** the return or exclusion of a tax.

bonus: additional monies paid to workers to supplement their regular salary (e.g., Christmas bonus, end-of-year corporate profit bonus).

book crowd: see *cabinet crowd.*

book inventory: inventory calculated by adding the units and the cost of incoming goods to previous inventory figures and subtracting the units and the cost of outgoing goods. See *inventory; perpetual inventory.*

bookkeeper: a person who makes entries on the general ledger of a business.

bookkeeping: the art, practice, or labor involved in the systematic recording of the transactions affecting a business.

booklet certificate: a pamphlet or booklet that serves both as an explanation of a group insurance plan and as an individual certificate of coverage under the plan.

book value:

(1) **general:** the value of an asset found in the company's records, not necessarily what it could bring in the open market. See *depreciated cost*.

(2) **securities:** a value determined from a company's records by adding all assets and then deducting all debts and other liabilities, plus the liquidation price of any preferred issues. The sum arrived at is divided by the number of common shares outstanding to determine book value per common share.

boom:

(1) **finance:** a time when business expands and the value of commodities and securities increases.

(2) **economics:** a period of rapidly rising prices and increased demand for goods and services, usually accompanied by full employment.

boomerang: (slang) an international program to minimize the practice of goods dumping by returning such items duty free and exempt of quantity restrictions.

bootlegging: illegal movement of items in order to avoid payment of taxes on such items. The items themselves may or may not be prohibited by law.

boot money: (slang) money used as an additional compensation by one of the parties to a bargain.

b.o.p: see *balance of payments.*

bordereau: a special form for transmitting information required in reinsurance transactions, such as reinsuring an entire agency's business.

borrow: to receive something from another, with the understanding that the item is to be returned.

borrower: one who borrows cash or buys something on credit.

BOS: see *behavior observation scale.*

bosshead: (slang) the head of a project (i.e., the foreman, the boss).

bot: abbreviation for *bought*, as used in the securities market.

bottleneck: anything that holds up the normal flow of organizational communications, operations, activities, or processes.

bottom dropped out: a situation of sharply falling prices occurring when the market is well liquidated, thus establishing a panic atmosphere.

bottom line: the figure that reflects company profitability on the income statement.

bottom-up approach: an approach to strategy making whereby the lower levels of the organization push ideas to the top and strategy is then made.

bounceback: a quick recovery, especially from a period of economic slump or decline.

boundaryless organization: an organization that seeks to eliminate the chain of command, to have limitless spans of control, and replaces departments with empowered teams.

boundary-spanning role: the role of a worker who must relate to two different systems, usually an organization and some part of its environment.

bourse: (French) a European stock exchange.

boutique: a shop or part of a store that specializes in merchandise that is new and different.

box store: a retail store that sells a limited assortment of basic grocery items in their original boxes or cartons at much lower prices than available in supermarkets.

boycott:

(1) **labor relations:** collective pressure against an employer to discourage public acceptance of his products or services. Cf. *picketing.* A primary boycott involves one employer and his employees only; a secondary boycott involves a third party. Cf. *situs picketing; strike.* See *unfair list.*

(2) **economics:** an attempt to prevent the carrying on of a business by urging people not to buy from the firm being boycotted; frequently used on the international scene for political or economic reasons; illustrated by appeals, threats, and so on, to secure redress of a grievance.

bracket creep: the process by which inflation lifts wage earners into higher tax brackets.

Brady Commission: a 1988 federal commission to study the impact of Black Monday and to propose ways to minimize the future possibility of stock market crashes. See *Black Monday.* Synonymous with *Presidential Task Force on Market Mechanisms.* Cf. *Baker Plan.*

brainstorming: a process of generating creativity and useful concepts through team or group discussions for solving problems.

branch:

(1) **business:** an offshoot of a major unit of operation (e.g., a branch store).

(2) **mining:** a vein from the main lode.

branch banking: any banking system in which there are few parent institutions, each having branches operating over a large geographical area. Some states have authorized the concept of branch banking under strict regulation. Federal control is maintained by the Board of Governors of the Federal Reserve System and the Office of the Comptroller of the Currency. In the United States there is no nationwide branch banking, whereas in some countries (e.g., Canada, England, France, Germany) the branch system of banking dominates. Cf. *chain banking.*

branch house: a location away from headquarters that is maintained by a manufacturer and used almost exclusively for purposes of stocking, selling, shipping, and servicing the company's products.

branch organization: an overseas office set up by a parent company that is often employed in a firm's operations in other countries.

branch store: a store owned by a parent store. Usually the parent store is located in the center of the city, with branch stores located in suburban areas of the city or other cities. Cf. *regional store.*

branch warehouse: a separate stocking location removed from the primary manufacturing plan typically carrying finished-goods inventory or service parts.

brand: a name, sign, or symbol used to identify items or services of the seller(s) and to differentiate them from goods of competitors. A brand aids consumers in differentiating between items of different manufacturers. Cf. *trademark.*

brand awareness: realization by a buyer of the existence and availability of a branded product. See *determinant attributes; differential advantages.*

branded: carrying the brand or trademark of a manufacturer.

brand extension: a competitive strategy that involves applying a market-accepted brand to other firm products provided doing so will not confuse existing customers or lessen the original image of product or brand.

brand franchise: the extent to which a brand has attracted a substantial and loyal following.

brand leader: an item that is considered best in its field or is marketed with that assumption.

brand loyalty: the strength of a buyer's preference for a particular brand, which suggests a refusal to purchase a substitute. Brand loyalty is usually measured in terms of repeat sales and is also reflected in purchases of other items produced by same company.

brand mark: that part of a brand identification that can be recognized but cannot be verbalized.

brand name:

(1) **marketing:** a word or term that is placed on an item for identification or to be communicated orally.

(2) **business law:** a registered name used to prevent copying.

brand-name bias: a person's tendency to respond to surveys by naming widely advertised brands, often for purposes of giving a good impression, rather than naming the brands that are actually purchased.

brand recognition: the perception by buyers, when confronted with a product, that they have been exposed to that brand name previously.

brand strategy: plans and tactics relating to the use of brand names.

brand-switching model: a model that provides a manager with some idea of the behavior of consumers in terms of their loyalty and the likelihood that they will switch from one brand to another.

brass: (slang) term borrowed from the military to describe key executives in a business.

brazen law of wages: see *iron law of wages.*

breach of contract: not fulfilling one's part in an agreement; breaking a promise to carry out one's contractual responsibility.

bread: (slang) money.

breakage:

(1) **general:** an allowance for losses resulting from damage to merchandise.

(2) **finance:** the fractional cents due either party as a result of rounding percentage calculations (e.g., when the decimal is 0.5 or more, an added point is entered).

break-even model: a model that shows the basic relationships among units produced (output), dollars of sales revenue, and the levels of costs and profits for an entire firm or a product line.

break-even point: the point of activity at which a company earns zero profit. It is reached when total revenue equals total expense. See *margin of safety.*

break-even pricing: pricing at a level that will enable a firm to break even.

breaking away: the first career phase. During this period, individuals begin establishing independence and autonomy from their parents.

breaking bulk:

(1) **finance:** the practice of some middlemen to take a large, economical shipment from a manufacturer and divide it into smaller units to sell for greater profit.

(2) **transportation:** the point when cargo is first unloaded.

break-up value: in an investment fund or an issue of a holding firm, the value of the assets available for the issue, taking all marketable securities at their market price.

bribe: a payment resulting in the payer receiving some right, benefit, or preference to which he has no legal right and which he would not have obtained except by paying the money. A bribe is a criminal offense.

bridges: individuals in a social network who serve as linking pins by belonging to two or more clusters.

broadened collision coverage: a no-fault automobile insurance term combining the coverage afforded under regular as well as limited collision policies.

broad form insurance: a term generally understood to describe the combination, at a special discount, of various real and personal property coverages and comprehensive personal liability. It is sometimes used to describe the more comprehensive of two similar coverages (e.g., ocean marine insurance as opposed to inland insurance).

broad market: a time of considerable volume in the buying and selling of stocks and bonds.

broad tape: the Dow Jones news ticker, displayed in brokerage houses as a large rectangular screen with lines of copy rolling upward.

broken lot: an odd lot of a stock, usually less than 100 shares.

broken time: a work schedule or shift in which an employee works for a certain length of time, then is off duty, then returns for another period of work. Synonymous with *split shift.*

broker:

(1) **business:** a person who prepares contracts with third parties on behalf of a principal.

(2) **insurance:** a specialist who represents buyers of property and liability insurance and deals with either agents or companies in arranging for the coverage required by the customer. The broker is licensed by the state or states in which he or she conducts business. See *producer.* Cf. *reinsurance broker.*

(3) **securities:** a member of a stock exchange firm or any exchange member who handles orders to buy and sell securities and commodities for a commission. Cf. *street broker.* See *floor broker.*

broker's loan: a loan made to a stockbroker and secured by stock exchange collateral.

broker's market: the condition that exists when the investing public is generally inactive while brokers are trading heavily with their own accounts.

broker's ticket: a written statement of all buy and sell orders executed by a broker, giving the date, name, and amount of the security traded, the price, the customer's name, the broker's name, and so on.

brother: (archaic) term used by organized workers when referring to a coworker.

brotherhood: a union, federation, guild, or association. The term derives from the strong fraternal nature of early trade unions and their primary concept of the brotherhood of working men.

brown goods: in retailing, for television sets and radios.

bubble: an unwise business venture in which the price has little or no relationship to the value of the asset.

bubble company: a firm that never had any true business or did not intend to be honest, or a firm created to defraud ,the public.

bucketing: (slang) activity of a broker who executes a customer's order for his or her own account instead of on the market, expecting to profit from a balancing transaction at a future time. This activity is forbidden by the SEC.

bucket shop: (slang)

(1) an institution engaged in securities dealings of doubtful legality.

(2) an unlicensed, dishonest business in which customers place bets on the increase or decrease of stock prices on the regular exchange. No orders are filled, but profits and losses are based on the actual price movement on the exchange, with a commission going to the broker. The SEC has declared such businesses illegal.

buddy system: a method of training whereby a new worker is assigned a partner to help him or her become oriented to the job and fellow workers.

budget:

(1) **general:** an itemized listing, and frequently the allotment, of all estimated revenues a business anticipates receiving and listing, and frequently the segregation of all estimated costs and expenses that will be incurred in obtaining those revenues during a stated period of time. See *cash budget; flexible budget.*

(2) **human resources:** resources or administrative changes that reduce burnout.

budget account: see *charge account.*

budget deficit: an excess of expenditures over revenues.

budgeting: the process of determining and assigning the resources required to reach objectives.

budget surplus: an excess of revenues over expenditures.

budget variance: the difference between budgeted or projected costs and actual costs.

buffer:

(1) **general:** a mechanism that permits the temporary excess supply of one instant to offset the temporary shortage of another instant.

(2) **packaging:** any material or device placed inside a container to absorb the forces of impact. Buffers are usually made of cushioning or compressible material.

buffering: the action of certain positive factors in the person's environment to limit the capacity of other factors to create dissatisfaction and stress.

buffer stock: merchandise kept on hand to prevent a shortage resulting from an unexpected increase in demand for the items.

built-in stabilizer: a fiscal approach that operates automatically, without the need for congressional or presidential impetus, to mitigate the worst effects of a cyclical downturn and to keep the downturn from snowballing.

bulk discount: a reduced charge for quantity or multiple purchases.

bulk freight: liquid or dry freight that is not carried in packages or individual containers.

bulletin board: wall space for the display of union messages or information, made available in conformity to a contract provision.

bulling the market: speculator trading purporting to force the level of prices upward. Techniques include spreading rumors and entering price orders at levels somewhat above the prevailing price.

bullion: usually gold or silver, formed in ingots or bars, for use in coinage.

bull market: an advancing stock market.

bulls: speculators who anticipate that prices will rise.

bumping: application of seniority in the layoff of employees, ordinarily set forth in detail in the collective bargaining agreement. A senior employee laid off from his or her own job may displace (bump) a junior employee from a lessor post. See *backtracking; preferential rehiring; recall*. Cf. *deadheading*.

bundle of benefits concept: where consumers do not purchase things as such, but instead buy the benefits that those items are expected to provide.

bundle of service concept: the argument favoring leasing rather than owning equipment based on the consideration that the purchase of a machine is perceived of as the purchase of the number of yearly services that the unit is expected to last. The costs thus calculated can be compared with the yearly cost of the lease on a present value basis.

burden: a ship's carrying capacity.

burden hour: (slang) an hour of paperwork performed by one person.

bureaucracy:

(1) **general:** concentration of authority in administrative groups.

(2) **administration:** a written statement of the procedures and regulations in an organizational structure.

bureaucratic theory: relating to the characteristic of an organization that maximizes stability and controllability of its members. The ideal bureaucracy is an organization that contains these two elements to a high degree.

bureaucratic control: a method of control that employs strict rules and regulations to help ensure desired behavior by organizational units; often used by multinational enterprises to control subsidiaries.

bureaucratization: the process of organizing and maintaining an administrative hierarchy characterized by bureaucracy; also, the extension of bureaucracy and regimentation into certain areas of social life.

Bureau of Labor Standards: formerly the Division of Labor Standards; an agency of the U.S. Department of Labor that is concerned with developing and establishing better working standards, primarily in the field of labor legislation.

Bureau of Labor Statistics (BLS): a research agency of the U.S. Department of Labor that compiles statistics on hours of work, average hourly earnings, employment and unemployment, consumer prices, and many other variables.

Bureau of Old Age and Survivors Insurance: a service bureau within the Bureau of Employment Security that is responsible for the administration of benefit payments to retired employees or their survivors.

Bureau of the Budget: originally part of the Treasury Department, a federal agency that was responsible for the presentation of the federal budget; now under the Executive Office of the President and called the Office of Management and Budget.

burglary and theft insurance: protection for loss of property due to burglary, robbery, or larceny.

burnout: a condition of emotional, physical, and mental exhaustion resulting from prolonged exposure to intense stress.

business:

(1) **economics:** the buying and selling of goods and services.

(2) **finance:** the activity of an individual, partnership, or organization, involving production, commerce, and/or service.

(3) **human resources:** a person's occupation or employment.

business agent: an elected or appointed representative of one or more local unions, with responsibility for negotiating contracts, administering existing contracts, and adjusting grievances. The agent is usually a full-time unionist, as contrasted with the shop steward or committeeman. The business agent may also have organizing duties. Synonymous with *walking delegate.* Cf. *shop steward.*

business credit: the privilege of deferring payment for purchases, extended to customers by the vendors of items and services.

business cycle: any interval embracing alternating periods of economic prosperity and depression. See *compensatory fiscal policy; contraction; expansion; inflation; recession; recovery; reflation.* Cf. *reference cycle.*

business ethics: socially accepted rules of behavior that place pressure on business executives to maintain a high sense of values and to be honest and fair in their dealings with the public. See *ethics.*

business expenses: expenses paid or incurred in the course of business that are ordinary, necessary, and reasonable in amount.

business game: a simulation that represents an actual business situation. It attempts to duplicate selected aspects of a particular situation, which are then manipulated by the participants.

business interruption insurance: coverage for loss of earnings in case the policyholder's business is shut down by fire, windstorm, explosion, or other insured peril. Cf. *extra expense insurance.* See *boiler and machinery insurance.*

business logistics: a set of activities dealing with the control of incoming and outgoing materials. Its major function is to create "place and time utility" in goods, locating them at the right place at the right time and in the right quantity to meet consumer demand.

business manager:

(1) **business:** the individual responsible for overseeing a firm, department, or other unit, to ensure smooth operations.

(2) **labor relations:** a business agent. See *business agent.*

business necessity: work-related practice that is necessary to the safe and efficient operation of an organization.

business plan: a concise, written document prepared by an entrepreneur, describing the present venture and market situation, future directions, and implementation strategies. The major purposes of the plan are supporting the financing needs for the entrepreneur and guiding the future direction of the venture.

business representative: a paid labor official responsible for negotiating and administering the labor agreement and working to resolve union members' problems.

business transfer payments: transfers from businesses to persons that are charges against business products but for which no services are rendered currently. Major items included are corporate gifts to nonprofit institutions and allowance for consumer bad debts.

business trust: an unincorporated business organization in which title to the property is given to trustees to hold, manage, or sell. This structure is sometimes employed when a parcel of land is divided, improved, or sold. Synonymous with *Massachusetts trust; common law trust.*

bust: a severe decrease in business activity leading to high unemployment, low incomes, and low profits.

butterfly spread: the simultaneous purchase or sale of three futures contracts in the same or different markets—for example, buying 10 soybean futures contracts in January and another 10 for April delivery and at the same moment selling (going short) 20 soybean contracts for May of the same year. Borrowing power and profits may result, and any profits are held until after the tax year ends. See *spread; straddle.*

buy:

(1) **finance:** to acquire ownership of something in exchange for a monetary consideration.

(2) **economics:** the quality of a purchase (e.g., a good buy).

buy-back agreement: a provision in a sales contract stating that the seller will repurchase the property within a specified period of time, usually for the selling price, if the purchaser is transferred from the area.

buy-backs: way of convincing an employee who attempts to resign to stay in the employ of the firm. Normally, the person is bought back with an offer of an increased wage or salary.

buyer:

(1) **general:** an individual who acquires goods for purposes of making a profit, usually as the result of a resale.

(2) **retailing:** an executive responsible for purchasing merchandise to be sold in a store. See *procurement*. Cf. *purchasing agent.*

buyers' market: a market characterized by low or falling prices, occurring when supply is greater than demand and buyers tend to set the prices and terms of sale.

buyers over: a situation of more buyers than sellers. Cf. *overbought.*

buyer's right to route: the purchaser's privilege to determine the route of the shipment when the seller does not pay the freight charges. If the seller goes against the buyer's wishes, the seller is liable for any loss incurred.

buying by specifications: a store submitting specific requests for delivery rather than purchasing standard merchandise available from the manufacturer.

buying committee: a group of buyers, often chain stores, who decide by committee on the items that will and will not be purchased.

buying in: a purchaser obtaining shares wherever he or she can find them when a seller does not hand over securities at the expected time. The seller becomes responsible for all added expenses.

buying off the peg: the purchase of ready-to-wear merchandise, to be taken home or delivered immediately, thus involving no adjustments or alterations.

buying on balance: a situation that occurs when a stockbroker's orders to buy exceed his or her cumulative orders to sell.

buying on margin: purchasing securities without paying the full price immediately. Margin regulations are closely controlled by the SEC. See *margin; marginal trading; margin call.*

buying policy index: an important leading indicator of business conditions that measures the percentage of industrial purchasing agents who report buying commitments 30, 60, or 90 days ahead or longer.

buying power: money available for spending and consumption, consisting of a combination of liquid assets and available credit.

buy-off: the act of purchasing all rights to a product or service.

buy out: to purchase all the assets, stock, and so on, of an ongoing organization; to purchase the interest in a firm that is owned by another.

buy-sell agreement: an agreement designed to handle situations in which one or more of the entrepreneurs wants to sell their interest in the venture.

buzz group (session): a small, informal group (four to 10 people), usually chosen from a larger group, that gathers to consider and discuss informally what they have heard at a lecture or meeting, often with full participation. The discussion, which is aimed at and should ideally develop a group point of view, lasts about 20 minutes. Following the discussion, a chosen representative presents the concepts or questions that the group decided to put to the speaker(s) during the general discussion period.

buzzwords: the language of leadership; words or terms employed for quick communication with group members who are familiar with the terms. Little concern is given to comprehension by persons who are not group members.

by-bidder: a person who makes fictitious bids at an auction, on behalf of the owner or seller of the items, to obtain a higher price or to encourage further bidding.

bylaws: rules accepted by board members of a firm or other organization for governance. Such rules cannot be in opposition to laws imposed by government, and they pertain only to the rights and duties of members of the stated organization.

by-product: a secondary product obtained during the course of manufacturing.

C

CA: see *chartered accountant*.

cabinet crowd: the section of the bond trading unit of the New York Stock Exchange that handles trading in active bonds. Synonymous with *book crowd*. See *inactive stock (bond)*.

cable transfer: use of a cablegram to place funds in the hands of an individual in a foreign country. Funds are deposited with a local (i.e., domestic) bank, which cables instructions to a correspondent bank abroad to make the funds available to the payee.

CAD: see *cash against documents*.

cadillac effect: A licensing strategy that provides high-quality service for high-income consumers, developed because licensing often lowers the quality and quantity of consumer service.

Caesar management: demanding autocratic, power-oriented leadership. Cf. *multiple management; participative-democratic leadership style*.

CAF: see *cost and freight*.

cafeteria benefit programs: programs that allow employees to select the mix of fringe benefits they receive by substituting less desired benefits for more highly desired ones.

calendar spreading: simultaneous purchase and sale of options within the same class that have different expiration dates.

calendar year experience: experience developed on premium and loss transactions occurring during the 12 calendar months beginning January 1, irrespective of the effective dates of the policies on which these transactions took place.

call:
(1) **securities:** to demand payment of an installment of the price of bonds or stocks that have been subscribed. See *puts and calls*.
(2) **finance:** to demand payment of a loan secured by collateral because of failure by a borrower to comply with the terms of the loan.
(3) **business:** the power of a corporation to make an assessment.
(4) **business law:** an assessment for partial or total payment on shares of unpaid stock of a corporation.

callable:
(1) **finance:** that which must be paid on request, as a loan.
(2) **securities:** preferred stock that can readily be called in for payment at a stated price.

callable bond: see *bond, callable*.

callback: the technique used by a sales representative on a second or subsequent effort to induce a potential customer to buy. Cf. *user calls.*

callback pay: premium wage paid to an employee who has been asked to return to work after completing his or her regular work shift. Contract provisions usually provide for a minimum number of hours' pay, regardless of the number of hours actually worked.

call compensation: guaranteed monies for a worker who reports for assignment and is informed that there is no work for him or her.

call credit: credit given for the price of an item when merchandise is picked up from a customer and returned to the store.

called bond: see *bond, called.*

call-in pay: guaranteed minimum payment to an employee called to work for less than a full shift, usually on a day outside his or her regular work schedule. Provisions for call-in pay are usually spelled out in collective agreements. Synonymous with *reporting pay.*

call loan: a loan payable on request. Cf. *day loan.*

call money: currency lent by banks, usually to stockbrokers, for which payment can be demanded at any time.

call of more: the right to call again for the same amount of goods previously bought; used primarily in the purchase of options.

call option: giving the option buyer the right to buy 100 shares of stock at a stated price at any time before a deadline, at which point the option expires.

call pay: a sum of money guaranteed to a worker for reporting to work for only a portion of a day that he or she was not originally scheduled to work.

call price: the price at which a callable bond is redeemable.

call provision: an indenture provision permitting an issuer to repurchase a stock prior to maturity by forcing stock holders to sell at a specified price.

call purchase: the buying of commodities when the seller has some option of pricing at a later date within a given range of the existing price.

call report: the salesperson's communication to a supervisor of calls made to prospective customers during a stated time period or in a given market.

calls: an option contract that entitles the holder to buy a number of shares of the underlying security at a stated price on or before a fixed expiration date. See *puts and calls.*

call sale: the sale of a commodity of known quality under a contract providing for the purchaser to select a future day on which the price in the contract will be fixed on the basis of a stipulated number of points above or below the price of a designated future on that chosen day.

call station: an area at which a pickup and delivery service is available, although there are no dock or warehouse facilities.

call system: in retailing, where the salesperson's compensation is determined in part on the amount of business he or she completed.

cambism (cambistry): engaging in the sale of foreign monies.

cambist:
(1) **finance:** an individual who buys and sells foreign currencies.
(2) **international trade:** a handbook in which foreign currencies are converted into currency tables of the country for which the handbook is issued.

cameralism: see *Kameralism.*

cancellation:
(1) **business law:** the annulment or rendering void of any instrument upon payment.
(2) **securities:** the termination of open doors for the purchase or sale of stock.
(3) **insurance:** the termination of an insurance policy or bond before its expiration, by either the insured or the company. Almost invariably, the contract sales states the type of notice necessary before cancellation becomes effective.

cancellation clause: a provision giving one or both parties the right to cancel the agreement in the event of a specified occurrence.

cancellation evidence: a terminated policy or any legal notice of cancellation.

canned presentation: a prewritten and usually memorized presentation by a sales representative, spoken sentence for sentence, with little or no deviation.

canvass:
(1) **general:** to count or examine.
(2) **salesmanship:** to call on prospective customers in person or by telephone to sell merchandise or services, to determine interest, or to gather information. Cf. *cold canvassing.* See *preapproach.* Synonymous with *territory screening.*

CAO: chief administrative officer.

capacity:

(1) **insurance:** the largest amount of insurance a company will accept on one risk.

(2) **packaging:** the volume of space within a container or other spaces, expressed in units.

(3) **finance:** one of the three elements of *credit*.

(4) **manufacturing:** the ability of a factory to produce at a stated level.

(5) **transportation:** the amount of cargo that can be handled by a freight car, truck, or other carrier.

(6) **business law:** competency or legal authority.

capacity costs: an alternative term for fixed costs, emphasizing that fixed costs are needed to provide operating facilities and an organization ready to produce and sell at a planned volume of activity.

capias ad respondendum: a judicial writ commencing actions at law (e.g., an order directing the sheriff to place a defendant in custody).

capital:

(1) **business:** the amount invested in a venture. See *equity; fixed capital*.

(2) **accounting:** describing a long-term debt plus owners' equity.

(3) **finance:** net assets of a firm, partnership, and the like, including the original investment, all gains and profits.

(4) **economics:** the physical plant and equipment used to produce, transport, and market the output of an economy.

capital account: an account maintained in the name of the owner or owners of a business and indicating his or their equity in that business, usually at the close of the last accounting period.

capital assets: a collective term that includes all fixed assets, consisting of furniture and fixtures, land, buildings, machinery, and so on, as differentiated from property consumed and property that yields income.

capital budget: a budget that itemizes expenditures to be used for building and for purchasing capital goods and which identifies the source of the funds required to meet the expenditures.

capital consumption: that portion of a firm's investment used in part or in its entirety in the process of production.

capital consumption allowance: sums set aside by accountants to recover the initial costs of investments in equipment, buildings, and improvements to land; usually treated as a cost of production and occasionally accumulated in a fund for replacing the asset when necessary. Synonymous with *depreciation*.

capital deepening: increasing the amount of capital for each worker.

capital expenditure: an expenditure to acquire an asset with an expected useful life of more than one year; also referred to as a capital investment because it is expected to yield revenue or reduce expenses. See *capital investments.*

capital flight: a large transfer of money from one nation to another as a hedge against poor economic or political conditions.

capital formation: the development or expansion of capital goods as a result of savings.

capital gain or loss:

(1) **finance:** the difference (gain or loss) between the market or book value at purchase or other acquisition and the value realized from the sale or disposition of a capital asset. See *long-term capital gain; long-term capital loss.*

(2) **finance:** the gain or loss from the sale of a capital asset at above or below cost or appraised value.

capital goods: items ordinarily treated as long-term investment (capitalized) because of substantial value and life (e.g., industrial machinery).

capital improvement program: a plan that coordinates capital improvements and expenses over a specified time period to assure proper timing, location, and financing.

capital intensive: characterized by the need to utilize additional capital to increase productivity or profits.

capital investments: a collective term representing the amounts invested in capital or fixed assets or in long-term securities, as contrasted with funds invested in current assets or short-term securities. Generally, capital investments include all funds invested in assets that are not expected to be returned during the normal course of business in the coming fiscal period. See *capital expenditure.*

capitalism:

(1) an economic system under which the means of production are owned and controlled by the private sector of the population, with a minimum of government involvement.

(2) an economic system based on freedoms of ownership, production, exchange, acquisition, work, movement, and open competition. See *laissez-faire.*

capitalist:

(1) **general:** loosely, a wealthy person.

(2) **economics:** in Marxist terms, an individual who owns or shares in the ownership of the means of production and employs others. Cf. *mixed capitalism; people's capitalism; private enterprise.*

(3) **business:** an individual investor in a business.

capitalization:

(1) **securities:** the total value of all securities in a firm.

(2) **business law:** the act of converting something into capital.

(3) **accounting:** the sum of all monies invested in a firm by the owners; total liabilities.

capitalize:

(1) **accounting:** to classify a cost as a long-term investment item instead of a charge to current operations.

(2) **finance:** to convert into cash that which can be used in production.

(3) **securities:** to issue shares to represent an investment.

(4) **accounting:** to divide income by an interest rate to obtain principal.

capital liability: a fixed liability (e.g., a corporate bond) that is created for acquiring fixed assets or for purposes of funding.

capital loss: see *long-term capital loss.*

capital market: a place or system in which the requirements for capital of a business can be satisfied.

capital outlay: expenditures for the acquisition of or addition to fixed assets; included are amounts for replacements and major alterations but not for repair. Cf. *operating expense.*

capital rating: a rating given by a mercantile organization in appraising the net worth of a firm.

capital rationing: the process of determining which investments offer the highest returns.

capital requirement: the total monetary investment needed to create and operate a business.

capital stock: the specified amount of stock a corporation may sell, as authorized by the state granting the corporate charter. If the stock has a stated value per share, such value is known as par value. Stock without a designated value is referred to as no par value stock. See *common stock.*

capital sum:

(1) **finance:** the original amount of an estate, fund, mortgage, bond, or other financial dealing, together with accrued sums not yet recognized as income.

(2) **insurance:** the amount specified in an accident policy for payment in the event of the loss of a limb or sight or other physical incapacity of the insured.

capital surplus: the excess of assets over liabilities plus the value given to issued capital stock, less amounts in paid-in or earned surplus.

capital turnover: the rate at which an organization's assets are converted into cash.

captive audience:

(1) **advertising:** people exposed to commercial messages while passengers on carriers whose use of media they cannot control.

(2) **labor relations:** a work force assembled on company property and forced to listen to antiunion propaganda on company time. See *employer interference.*

captive insurer: an organization, whose stock is generally owned by one business firm, that undertakes insurance company ownership in an attempt to obtain its business insurance at a lower cost than purchasing coverage from other insurers.

captive market: purchasers who have little latitude in choosing the vendor of a product or service (e.g., people who want to buy hot dogs at a sporting event and must buy from the stadium concessionaire).

captive shop: a manufacturing facility whose production is used solely by the company owners (e.g., an iron ore mine owned by a steel company).

career anchors: distinct patterns of self-perceived talents and abilities, motives and needs, and attitudes and values that guide and stabilize a person's career after several years of real-world experience and feedback.

career concepts: the four basic career patterns—linear, steady state, spiral, and transitory—by which people perceive their careers.

career counseling: process of discussing with employees their current job activities and performance, their personal job and career goals, their personal skills, and suitable career development objectives.

career curves: experience of performance bases for providing salary increases for professional employees.

career path: the sequence of jobs planned for or by a person that leads to a career objective.

career planning: the process of systematically matching an individual's career aspirations with opportunities for achieving them.

career plateau: a stage in one's career from which further advancement is not expected.

career risk: whether or not an entrepreneur will be able to find a job or go back to an old job if his or her venture fails.

career stages: distinct but interrelated steps or phases of a career.

Carey Street: (slang) British term for *bankruptcy.*

carnet: a document of international customs that permits temporary duty-free importation of specific items into certain nations. See *admission temporaire.*

carriage charge: the charge made by a carrier of freight for carrying items from one place to another.

carrier:

(1) **transportation:** an individual or organization, usually without a permit of public franchise, that is engaged in transporting products or people. Cf. *common carrier; franchise.*

(2) **insurance:** an insurance company that writes and fulfills the conditions of an insurance policy.

carrier's lien: the carrier's right to hold the shipper's property as security until the shipping obligation is paid. Cf. *general lien; seller's lien; stoppage in transit.*

carry:

(1) **accounting:** to enter or post.

(2) **finance:** to supply funds to a customer.

(3) **securities:** to hold stocks; to be long of stock. See *long.*

(4) **securities:** the act of a broker in providing money to customers who trade by margin accounts.

carry forward:

(1) **accounting:** transferring the balance of an account from one balance sheet to another.

(2) **federal income taxes:** declaring an item of expense as minimal until a later time period when revenue is received.

carrying charge:

(1) **general:** the continuing cost of owning or holding any property or items.

(2) **securities:** the fee charged by stockbrokers for handling margin accounts.

(3) **merchandising:** a charge added to the price of merchandise to compensate for deferred payment.

carrying costs: costs incurred by carrying an inventory, including taxes and insurance on the goods in inventory, interest on money invested in inventory and storage space, and costs incurred because of obsolescence of the inventory.

carryover clause: a clause to protect a broker for a specified time, usually beyond the expiration date of the property listing.

cartel: a group of separate business organizations that have agreed to institute approaches to altering competition by influencing prices, production, or marketing; rarely as effective as a monopoly. See *monopoly; oligopoly.* Cf. *consortium.*

case study: an attempt to examine numerous characteristics of one person or organization, usually over an extended period of time.

cash: an all-embracing term associated with any business transaction that involves the handling of currency and coins.

cash accounting: an accounting system whereby revenues are accounted for and entered only when money is received, and expenditures are accounted for only when they are actually paid.

cash against documents (CAD): a requirement that a purchaser make payment for items before receipt of the shipping papers that will give him control of the items once they are surrendered to him.

cash and carry wholesaler: a wholesaler who demands that the buyer must pay when he picks up his merchandise, without credit, or the wholesaler will not make delivery.

cash assets: assets described on a financial statement that are represented by actual cash on hand plus the total of bank deposits.

cash audit: an examination of cash transactions during a particular time period to determine whether all received cash has been documented and all other cash accounted for.

cash-basis accounting: a system of accounting in which transactions are recorded and revenues and expenses are recognized only when payments are received or made. See *cash accounting.*

cash-basis method: a method of measuring income whereby income is defined as cash receipts less cash disbursements during an accounting period.

cash before delivery (CBD): a requirement to pay prior to delivery of goods.

cash budget:
   (1) a schedule of expected cash receipts and disbursements.
   (2) the sum of cash receipts and expenditures of an agency, including those of public trust funds (e.g., Social Security).

cash buying: the purchase of securities or commodities outright, for immediate delivery.

cash card: a card given by a retailer or store owner to a customer to guarantee a discount for cash payment. It is a substitute for credit cards. Some merchants give cash-paying customers up to 8 percent discount.

cash discount: a percentage deduction from the selling price permitted by the seller for merchandise sold on credit, to encourage prompt payment of the invoice covering the goods or services purchased. Synonymous with *sales discount.*

cash dividend: declared dividends that are payable in cash; usually paid by check.

cash flow: the reported net income of a corporation, plus amounts charged off for depreciation, depletion, amortization, and extraordinary charges to reserves, which are bookkeeping deductions and are not actually paid out in cash. Knowledge of these factors results in a better understanding of a firm's ability to pay dividends. Cf. *net cash flow.*

cashier's check: a bank's own check signed by a cashier, becoming a direct obligation of the bank. Upon issue to a customer, it becomes a loan and a debit in the cashier's account. It differs from a certified check in that it is drawn against the funds of the bank itself, not against funds in a specific depositor's account. Cf. *certified check; register(ed) check.* Synonymous with *officer's check.*

cash inflows: any current or expected revenues directly associated with an investment.

cash on delivery (COD): describing any purchase made with the expectation that the item(s) will be paid for on delivery. Cf. *franco delivery.*

cash outflows: the initial cost and other expected outlays associated with an investment.

cash over and short: an account used to record overages and shortages in petty cash.

cash position: the ratio of cash to total net assets; the net amount after the deduction of current liabilities.

cash receipts: all sums of money received by an organization.

cash refund annuity: a policy that provides an annual income at retirement for life. Provision is made that, upon death prior to full payment of the annuity, the remainder will go to the beneficiary's estate.

cash reserve:
  (1) **finance:** funds readily available to be converted into cash in an emergency. See *liquid; liquid assets.*
  (2) **banking:** refers to requirements that banks maintain a sufficient portion of deposits, as required by federal law.

cash sale:
   (1) **securities:** a transaction on the floor of an exchange that calls for delivery of the securities the same day. In "regular way" trades, the seller is to deliver on the fifth business day.
   (2) **retailing:** the surrender of cash at the time of sale.
cash surrender value: the sum total of money paid by an insurance company upon cancellation of a policy. See *surrender value.*
cash value: the amount available to the owner of a life insurance policy when the policy is surrendered to the company.
casting up: adding up a total, as "casting up an account." Synonymous with *footing.*
casualty insurance: insurance primarily concerned with the losses caused by injuries to persons and the legal liability imposed on the insured for such injury or for damage to property of others.
catastrophic insurance: a form of insurance that provides benefits that begin where popular major medical coverage leaves off (e.g., coverage given following the total benefits, often after one year, of a major medical plan).
catastrophic success: first used in the military, where corporate executives prepare for a spectrum of possible outcomes, from prolonged competition to a rapid dominance of the industry.
cats and dogs: (slang)
   (1) **securities:** highly speculative stocks.
   (2) **business:** items that do not have satisfactory sales turnover and therefore accumulate in inventory.
caveat:
   (1) **business law:** "let him beware" (*Latin*); a warning; a notice filed by an interested party with a proper legal authority, directing others to cease or refrain from an act until the person filing can be heard from fully.
   (2) **finance:** a notice to cease payment.
caveat emptor: "let the buyer beware" (*Latin*). When merchandise is sold without a warranty by the vendor, the purchaser takes the risk of loss due to defects. See *without recourse.* Cf. *caveat subscriptor.*
caveat subscriptor (venditor): "let the seller beware" (*Latin*). Unless the seller states no responsibility, he or she is liable to the purchaser for any alterations from the written contract. Cf. *caveat emptor.*
CBCT: see *customer-bank communication terminal.*
CBD: see *cash before delivery.*

CD: see *certificate of deposit.*

CEA: see *Council of Economic Advisers.*

cease and desist order:

(1) **labor relations:** directions to management or the union, usually issued by the National Labor Relations Board, to halt an unfair labor practice. See *Taft-Hartley Act.*

(2) **business law:** a demand by court or government agency that a person or firm cease an activity.

CEC: see *Commodities Exchange Center.*

cede: to yield or grant business by agreement (e.g., a company reinsuring liability with another company "cedes" business to that company).

cent: the coin of lowest worth in the United States, equal to one-hundredth of a dollar ($0.01).

central bank:

(1) **banking:** a banker's bank.

(2) **banking:** a bank that holds the main body of bank reserves of a nation and is the prime reservoir of credit (e.g., Bank of England, Bank of France).

central body: a geographical gathering of local unions for political, legislative, and other purposes. A central body, state or local, is the focal point for the common efforts of unions within its area.

central buying: a popular approach in chain stores whereby all purchasing is done through a central or main office. Shipments of merchandise, however, are usually made directly to the branch stores of the chain.

Central Certificate Service (CCS): a privately run depository through which members effect security deliveries among themselves via computerized bookkeeping entries, thereby reducing the physical movement of stock certificates.

centrality: the position of a person or group within the flow of work in an organization.

centralization: the concentration of authority and decision making at the top of an organization; opposite of *decentralization.*

centralized administration: a system in which authority for direction, control, and management has become concentrated in the hands of a few persons or offices.

centralized decision making: when top managers make all key decisions.

centralized purchasing: a system by which a department or unit is authorized to procure, handle, or store all supplies, materials, and equipment required by some or all of the other departments or units of a company.

central labor union: a grouping of local unions in a specific geographical area.

central planning: a type of economic organization whereby resources are allocated by national authorities rather than by local bureaucrats and markets.

cents per cent: usual form of quoting marine rates of insurance ("20 cents per hundred dollars").

CEO: see *chief executive officer.*

certainty: a decision-making condition under which the manager has enough information to know the outcome of the decision before it is made.

certificate:

(1) **securities:** the piece of paper that is evidence of ownership of stock in a corporation. Watermarked paper is finely engraved with delicate etchings to discourage forgery.

(2) **business law:** any written or printed document of truth that can be used as proof of a fact.

certificate of beneficial interest: a statement of a share of a firm's business when such ownership has been deposited with a trustee. The certificate holder receives the income from and holds an interest in the firm's assets but relinquishes management control. This certificate is used when a business is operated as a trust.

certificate of deposit (CD): a negotiable or transferable receipt payable to the depositor, for funds deposited with a bank.

certificate of deposit, demand: a negotiable or transferable receipt issued for funds deposited with a bank and payable on demand to the holder. These receipts do not bear interest and are used principally by contractors and others as a guarantee of performance of a contract or as evidence of good faith when submitting a bid. They may also be used as collateral.

certificate of deposit, time: a negotiable or transferable receipt for funds deposited with a bank, payable to the holder at some specified date (not less than 30 days after issuance) and bearing interest.

certificate of incorporation: the franchise or charter issued by a state to the original petitioners of an approved corporation. Such franchise or charter constitutes the authority granted by the state for the organization to transact business as a corporation.

certificate of indebtedness: a short-term note issued by a government agency, describing the current debt; an unsecured promissory note whereby the holder has a general creditor's recourse against general assets.

certificate of insurance: evidence that an insurance policy has been issued, showing the amount and type of insurance provided. It may be used as evidence of reinsurance between companies, and it is the document that contains specific details of property covered by master or open policies. See *commercial set.*

certificate of origin: a certificate declaring that goods purchased from a foreign country have indeed been produced in that country and not in another.

certificate of ownership: see *proprietorship certificate.*

certificate of public convenience and necessity: permission required of transport, communication, and utility organizations desiring to enter into business. Usually, state or other authority authorization is required.

certification:

(1) **labor relations:** determination by the National Labor Relations Board or an appropriate state agency that a particular union is the majority choice, and hence the exclusive bargaining agent, of all employees in a particular bargaining unit.

(2) **banking:** an assurance by a bank that the drawer of a check has sufficient funds on deposit to cover payment on the check and that monies have been set aside to meet the incoming obligation. "Certification" is usually stamped across the face of the check.

certified check: the check of a depositor drawn on a bank. The face of the check bears the word "accepted" or "certified," with the date and signature of a bank official or authorized clerk. The check then becomes an obligation of the bank, and regulations require that the amount of the check be immediately charged against the depositor's account. Cf. *cashier's check.*

certified public accountant (CPA): an accountant who has been certified by the state as having met that state's requirements of age, education, experience, and technical qualifications. Not all who practice accounting are certified.

cession number: a number assigned by an underwriting office to identify reinsurance premium transactions.

CFO: see *chief financial officer.*

CFTC: see *Commodity Futures Trading Commission.*

chain banking: a form of multiple-office banking under which a minimum of three independently incorporated banks are controlled by one or more individuals. Cf. *branch banking.*

chain of command: the organizational design for the flow of communications, outlining direction toward authority, peers, and subordinates. See *scalar chain principle.* Cf. *unity of command.*

chain picketing: a procedure of marching around a struck company or at entrances to the owner's property so that the line of marchers forms an impenetrable column to prevent comings or goings across the picket line.

chain store: two or more stores, usually in different locations, being operated by the same organization.

chairman of the board: the highest-ranking executive of a corporation. In some cases the firm's president is also the chairman of the board.

chairman of the Office of Savings Associations: the new head regulator of the savings and loan industry, replacing the Federal Home Loan Bank Board.

chamber of commerce: an organization of business executives created to advance the interests of its members.

change: money returned following a purchase, when a larger sum of money was given than was required (e.g., on a sale of $.98, a $1 handout returns $.02 in change).

change advocates: leaders who champion organizational change, often by cajoling, inspiring, and negotiating it.

change agent: a consultant, usually from outside the organization, who aids the organization in a change process.

change form: discrimination complaint filed with the EEOC by employees or job applicants.

change fund: coins and currency issued to cashiers, delivery drivers, and so on.

change in supply: a shift of the entire supply schedule to a new position.

change order: a written agreement, signed by all parties to a contract, formalizing and defining a change in the original contract.

change process: a three-step organizational process entailing the unfreezing of old ways, the introduction of new behaviors, and the refreezing of a resulting new equilibrium.

change sequence: the sequence of events that is needed to bring about change in an organization.

channel of distribution: the route a product follows from an original grower, producer, or importer to the last consumer. Often a middleman is used (e.g., automobile manufacturers sell to car dealers, who then sell to consumers).

Chapter 7: the section of the Federal Bankruptcy Act of 1978 providing for the liquidation of a company that cannot reasonably be expected to return to a viable and profitable operating condition. See *Chapter 11.*

Chapter 11: the section of the Federal Bankruptcy Act of 1978 providing for court-supervised reorganization of a company in order to permit it to return to an improved financial position. See *Chapter 7.*

character classification of expenditures: a classification that reflects the time element involved in expenditures, chiefly the distinction between current operations and capital outlays.

charge:

(1) **finance:** a demanded price.

(2) **accounting:** a cost or expense allocated to a specific account.

(3) **business law:** a judge's instruction to a jury.

(4) **sales:** to purchase for credit without making an immediate payment; usually to pay following billing.

charge account: a means of making sales on credit to retail customers. The various types are as follows:

(a) open (30-day) account: an account in which the store accepts the customer's promise to pay for items bought, usually within 30 days of purchase.

(b) revolving account: an account in which the store sets the maximum amount of money the customer may owe at any one time. The amount is determined at the time the account is opened and is based on individual income and credit rating.

(c) budget or flexible account: an account in which monthly installment payments are based on the size of the customer's account balance, and interest is charged on the unpaid amount.

(d) coupon credit plan: an account in which the customer is given credit coupons that may be used in the store as cash. Payment for the coupons is made over a period of time, usually six months. This plan eliminates the need for a monthly billing.

charge off: to treat as a loss; to designate as an expense an amount originally recorded as an asset. Cf. *write-off.*

charges and miscellaneous revenue: nontax revenue derived chiefly from fees, assessments, and other reimbursements for current services and from rents and sales of commodities or services furnished incident to the performance of particular general government functions.

charges forward: a system whereby the purchaser pays for merchandise and shipping charges only upon receipt of the goods or, following receipt of goods, when a bill arrives.

charismatic leadership: followers make attributions of heroic or extraordinary leadership abilities to others when they observe certain behaviors, considered by them to be attractive.

charter:

(1) **general:** the contract between a private corporation and the state, identifying the articles of association granted to the corporation by authority of the legislative act. Powers and privileges granted are included.

(2) **transportation:** the hiring of a vehicle or other carrier.

chartered accountant (CA): in the United Kingdom, Canada, and Australia, a certified accountant.

Chartered Life Underwriter (CLU): the professional designation awarded by the American College of Life Underwriters to those who have completed the prescribed series of examinations and have satisfied the organization's experience requirement.

Chartered Property & Casualty Underwriter (CPCU): the professional designation awarded by the American Institute for Property and Liability Underwriters to those who have completed the prescribed series of examinations and have satisfied the organization's experience requirement.

charterer: an individual or organization, usually a state agency, that grants a firm the right to incorporate and transact business.

chartist: an individual who interprets stock market activity and predicts future movement, usually over a short period, through a graphic depiction of price and volume on charts. Cf. *Delphi technique; Dow theory.*

chart of accounts: a systematic listing of all accounts used by a firm.

chattel paper: written evidence, of both a monetary obligation and a security interest in or lease of specific goods. When a transaction is evidenced both by a security agreement or a lease and by an instrument or a series of instruments, the group of documents taken together constitutes chattel paper.

cheap jack: (slang) an individual who sells merchandise rapidly by unorthodox approaches, including using unoccupied stores to set up his goods.

cheap money: money that is available at relatively low rates of interest.

cheap stock: heavily discounted stock sold to an underwriter, who will attempt to find an investor.

check:

(1) **general:** a process for determining accuracy.

(2) **banking:** defined by the Federal Reserve Board as follows: "A draft or order upon a bank or banking house purporting to be drawn upon a deposit of funds, for the payment of a certain sum of money to a certain person therein named, or to his order, or to bearer, and payable instantly on demand."

check authorization/verification: an inquiry process undertaken to reduce the risk of accepting a fraudulent check or a check written for an amount that exceeds the account balance. Check authorization systems may be provided and maintained by the party accepting the check, by a financial institution, or by a third party engaged in such a business. These systems may be designed to access bank records directly or may rely on secondary data sources. In some systems check approval is accompanied by a guarantee of payment.

checking account: a demand account subject to withdrawal of funds on deposit by check.

checking copy: copy of a publication delivered to an agency or advertiser to verify the inclusion of an advertisement as requested. See *tear sheet*.

check list: a worker-evaluation approach whereby a supervisor or other person who is familiar with an employee's work checks off statements on a list that he or she believes are characteristic of the worker's performance, attitudes, and behavior on the job.

check-off: withholding of wages by an employer for direct payment of dues and assessments to a union. The Taft-Hartley Act states that union members must give written permission for these sums to be deducted. The check-off cannot exist for longer than one year or until the termination of the union contract, whichever date comes first. A check-off can also be used to deduct assessments for nonunion members.

check trading: selling bank checks to a customer, who is expected to repay the amount of the check plus interest in installments.

cheque: chiefly British variation of *check,* used in Canada and other countries where French or English is spoken.

cherry picking: buyer selection of only a few items from a vendor's line, rather than buying a complete line or classification of merchandise from any one source.

chief: (slang) a superior; the boss. For example, executive director of a major religious organization.

chief executive officer (CEO): the person accountable to the board of directors for the activities and profits of the firm.

chief financial officer (CFO): the person usually accountable to the chief executive officer for the profitability and financial status of the firm.

chief learning officer: the senior most executive responsible for learning and development in the organization; the role increasingly includes many organizational development roles as well, as these executives are responsible for creating a learning culture within the organization.

chief operating officer (COO): the person usually accountable to the chief executive officer for the production and distribution of the firm's output.

chronic unemployment: as defined by the U.S. Department of Labor, unemployment lasting for a minimum of six months. See *unemployment.* Cf. *cyclical unemployment.*

churning: the repetitive buying and selling of securities when such activity has a minimal effect on the market but generates additional commissions to a stock broker.

CID's: see *civil investigative demands.*

CIF: see *cost, insurance, and freight.*

Cincotta-Conklin Bill of 1976: a New York State law permitting state savings banks and savings and loan associations to offer checking accounts like commercial banks, but at no cost.

CIO: see *Congress of Industrial Organizations.*

circle network: where each member communicates with the people on both sides but with no one else.

circuit breakers: in program-trading, a nickname for measures to stop the market from plunging too far too fast. Several moves were taken following the October 1987 crash to coordinate and sometimes deliberately disconnect the stock and futures markets in times of heightened volatility. On the New York Stock Exchange, a "side car" is placed into effect when the S&P futures rise or fall 12 points. The side car routes program trades into a special computer file that scans for imbalances of buy and sell orders. The reforms permit the New York Stock Exchange to cease trading for one hour should the Dow Jones Industrial Average fall 250 points, and for two more hours if the DJ slides an additional 150 points on the same day. On the Chicago Mercantile Exchange, S&P 500 futures are not permitted to drop further than 12 points from the previous day's close for half an hour.

circuitry of action: when a bill of exchange is returned to the person who has already signed it, he or she may renegotiate it, but this person has no claim against individuals who signed the bill between the time he or she initially signed it and its return to him or her.

circulating capital good: any capital good item in use that is consumed by a single use (e.g., gasoline used to make a car engine function).

circulation:

(1) **advertising:** the number of copies of publication that are distributed. Cf. *readership.*

(2) **finance:** the total of all currency in use at a given period. See *velocity of circulation.*

(3) **banking:** the total value of the issued bank notes of a bank that are in use, as distinguished from those being held in the bank's reserve.

circulation rate base: the circulation that a magazine guarantees as a minimum. Should circulation fall below this consistently, the publisher may make a pro rate refund.

city bond: see *bond, municipal.*

civil bond: see *bond, civil.*

civil investigative demands (CIDs): in civil antitrust investigations, instruments analogous to subpoenas issued in criminal investigations; created in legislation signed by President Ford on September 30, 1976, to give the Antitrust Division of the Justice Department added investigative authority. CID's may be issued to a company, its executives, or a third party, such as a competitor, to obtain documents or to require oral testimony.

Civil Rights Act of 1964, Title VII: legislation creating the federal Fair Employment Practice Law, covering all industries that affect interstate commerce. It bars discrimination by employers, unions, and employment agencies based on race, color, sex, religion, or national origin. Employers and unions may not discriminate in regard to apprenticeship, training, or retraining programs. Employers, unions, and employment agencies may not retaliate against any person opposing, making a charge, testifying, or taking part in probes or proceedings regarding any practice deemed to be unlawful under the act, or publishing or printing notices or advertisements indicating discrimination. Employment agencies are forbidden to discriminate by failing or refusing to refer applicants on the basis of race, color, religion, sex, or national origin. The law is administered by the Equal Employment Opportunity Commission, which has five members. See *Civil Rights Act of 1968; fair employment practices.*

Civil Rights Act of 1968: law guaranteeing to all citizens equal treatment in matters pertaining to housing and real estate; prohibits discrimination because of race, color, religion, national origin, or sex against individuals who are trying to obtain financing for a home or property. See *Civil Rights Act of 1964, Title VII.*

CKO: chief knowledge officer.

claim:

(1) **business law:** a demand for payment, reimbursement, or compensation for damages or injury as identified in a contract or under law.

(2) **insurance:** a demand by an individual or a corporation to recover, under a policy of insurance, for loss that is covered by that policy.

clan control: a managerial approach that relies on values, beliefs, traditions, corporate culture, shared norms, and informal relationships to regulate employee behaviors and facilitate the reaching of organizational goals.

class:

(1) **insurance:** a category of employees in a schedule of group insurance, denoting the amounts of coverage for which the members of the class are eligible.

(2) **administration:** to place in ranks or divisions.

class action: a legal action in which one or more persons move against an organization on behalf of themselves as well as an aggrieved group or class of citizens deemed to be affected by the same condition. Cf. *co-optation.*

classical design theory: a collection of literature that evolved from scientific management, classical organization, and bureaucratic theory. The theory emphasizes the design of a preplanned structure for doing work and minimizes the importance of the social system. See *structural principles; unilateral strategy.* Cf. *human relations theory; organic structure.*

classical economics: economic concepts from the late eighteenth cen-

tury until the 1930s, emphasizing human self-interest and the operation of universal economic laws that tend automatically to guide the
economy toward full-employment equilibrium if the government adheres to a policy of laissez-faire.

classical management: the first schools of management thought,
including scientific management, functionalism, and bureaucracy. Cf.
contingency theory of leadership.

classical organization theory: a collection of literature that developed
from writings of managers who proposed organizational principles.
These conclusions were intended to serve as guidelines for other
managers.

classical viewpoint: a perspective on management that emphasizes
finding ways to manage work and organizations more efficiently.

classification:

(1) **merchandising:** an assortment of items, all of which are substi-
tutable for one another to the customer.

(2) **insurance:** the underwriting or rating group into which a particular risk must be placed; pertains to type of business, location and
other factors, not to be confused with *class*. See *class rate*.

classification merchandising: a system of record keeping that assists
inventory control and results in categorization of merchandise.

classification method: a job-evaluation method in which jobs are
grouped in a number of classes or grades. See *job evaluation*.

classified advertising: advertising identified by product or service. Cf.
display advertisement.

classified balance sheet: a balance sheet on which assets, liabilities, and
owners' equity are subdivided by age, use, and source.

classified bond: see *bond, classified*.

class rate: a type of insurance rate applicable to risks that are so similar in character that it is unnecessary to go to the expense of differentiating among them as to varying factors of hazards.

claw-back: a British term for the retrieval of funds spent by the government on added benefits and allowances by a corresponding tax
increase.

clean bill of lading: a bill of lading receipted by the carrier for goods
received in appropriate condition (no damages or missing items); does
not bear the notation "Shippers Load and Count." Cf. *over, short, and
damaged (OS&D)*.

clean bond: see *bond, clean*.

clean up: (slang) to take all available profits in a market; to make a substantial and rapid profit.

clean-up fund: provided as one of the basic services of life insurance, a reserve to cover costs of last illness, burial, legal and administrative expenses, miscellaneous outstanding debts, and so on. Synonymous with *final expense fund*.

clear:

(1) **finance:** free from encumbrance.

(2) **banking:** having passed through or having been collected by a clearinghouse. See *clearing and settlement*.

(3) **business:** to make a profit or gain.

(4) **retailing:** to reduce inventory (e.g., clearing out merchandise).

clearance:

(1) **general:** an act of clearing.

(2) **shipping:** a certificate of authority by a customs official permitting a ship to leave or enter port after having met customs requirements.

(3) **retailing:** a reduction on the price of items; a special sale.

(4) **banking:** the adjustment of debits and credits in a clearinghouse.

clearing account: an account having amounts to be transferred to another account(s) prior to the end of the accounting period.

clearing and settlement: the process whereby checks or other records of financial or point-of-sale transactions are moved (physically or electronically) from the point at which they were originated to the organization (bank, thrift institution, or other agency) that keeps the accounts for and expects to collect from and account to the responsible payer. The settlement process completes the internal financial transactions among the possibly many parties involved in the clearing operation.

clearing corporation: a corporation whose entire capital stock is held by or for a national securities exchange or association registered under a statute of the United States, such as the Securities Exchange Act of 1934.

clearinghouse: an association of banks in a city, created to facilitate the clearing of checks, drafts, notes, or other items among the members. It also formulates policies and rules for the mutual welfare of all members. See *Stock Clearing Corporation*.

clearing union: an international clearinghouse made up of the central banks of member nations, where international payments are settled by means of each nation's trading surplus and/or deficit. It allows countries to concentrate on efficient output, free of worry about exporting to one nation while importing from another.

clear time: time periods reserved by a station for the messages of an advertiser; a check by a network on the availability of time slots with station affiliates.

clerking activities: in a retail operation, work involving direct contact with customers.

client organization: a business firm that produces products and/or services and retains advertising agencies and other suppliers for special services.

cliques: relatively permanent informal groups that involve friendship.

CLOB: see *composite limit order book.*

clock watcher: (slang) an employee who shows little interest in his or her work.

close:

(1) **general:** to finish or wind up.

(2) **finance:** to conclude a sale or agreement.

(3) **salesmanship:** to secure the customer's written or spoken agreement to purchase the item or service being offered.

(4) **securities:** the short period before the end of the trading session when all trades are officially declared to have been confirmed "at or on the close."

(5) **accounting:** to transfer the balances of revenue and expense accounts at the end of an accounting period (e.g., close the books). See *accounting process.*

closed account: an account with equal debits and credits.

closed corporation: a corporation whose shares are held by only a few people, usually in positions of management.

closed shop: an agreement whereby only employees who were union members in good standing before being hired could continue to work. The closed shop was outlawed by the Taft-Hartley Act. Cf. *modified union shop; open shop; union shop.*

closed stock: merchandise sold only in sets (e.g., glassware, china). Individual items from a set cannot be purchased, and there is no certainty that replacements will be available at a future time.

closed structure: characterizing an organization in which there are few chances to affiliate with others, employees have little flexibility to exercise individuality, and company objectives are spelled out by top management.

closed trade: a transaction concluded by selling a security that has been paid for previously, or the conversion of a short sale (i.e., purchasing a security that had been sold short earlier).

closed union: a union that is deliberately made difficult to enter by the setting of high initiation fees, the limiting of admission to those who complete apprenticeship training, the observance of racial and ethnic barriers, or the use of other methods to protect existing members. The Taft-Hartley Act forbids the charging of excessive initiation dues.

close money: term applied when changes in prices between successive stock transactions are fractional or when the last bid and asked quotations hardly differ.

close out:
(1) **business:** an offer by a manufacturer or retailer to clear away his or her inventory.
(2) **finance:** to liquidate; to make a final disposition.

close supervision: a leadership style involving close, hands-on monitoring of subordinates and their work.

closing date: in publishing and advertising, the last day on which advertisements can be accepted for publication in a magazine or other periodical.

closing entries: journal entries made at the end of an accounting period to close (bring to zero balance) all revenue, expense, and other temporary accounts.

closing price: the price of securities quoted at the end of the stock exchange day.

closing purchase: a transaction in which a holder liquidates his or her position by purchasing an option that has the same terms as an option previously written (sold).

closing sale: a transaction in which an investor who had previously purchased an option demonstrates intent to liquidate his or her position as a holder by selling in a closing sale transaction an option that has the same terms as the option previously purchased.

closing title: the formal exchange of money and documents when real estate is transferred from one owner to another. Synonymous with *passing title*. See *quiet title suit*.

clout: the influence that some managers have over decisions. This influence, or "pull," is derived from the manager's location in the formal and informal systems of the organization. Clout enables the manager to deliver valued rewards to subordinates.

CLU: see *Chartered Life Underwriter.*

cluster chain: an informal communication chain in which information is passed on a selective basis.

coalition bargaining: a form of negotiations in which several unions representing different categories of employees of a single employer attempt to coordinate their bargaining.

coalition power: the capacity to exercise a high degree of influence as a result of combining a large number of individuals, groups, and/or organizations.

COB: see *coordination of benefits.*

cobweb chart: a graphic display of the conditions in a market in which sales of a perishable item that needs time to be produced are confined to a brief seasonal demand, although such demand is relatively strong during that season each year.

COD: see *cash on delivery;* terms of sale wherein the invoice is due and before the merchandise is released from shipment. See *collection on delivery.*

code of conduct: a statement of ethical practices and guidelines to which an enterprise adheres.

codetermination: a form of industrial democracy, first popularized in West Germany, that gives employees the right to have their representatives vote on management decisions.

coefficient of cross-elasticity: the arithmetic relationship between a percentage in the price of an item and the actual percentage change in the sales of a substitute or competitive item.

coemption: purchasing the entire supply of any commodity, usually for purposes of gaining a monopoly.

coercive power: influence over others based on fear; for example, a subordinate perceiving that failure to comply with directives would lead to punishment or some other negative act. Cf. *reward power.*

COG: *customer-owned goods.*

cognitive dissonance: any incompatibility between two or more attitudes or between behavior and attitudes.

cognitive evaluation theory: allocating extrinsic rewards for behavior that had been previously intrinsically rewarded tends to decrease the overall level of motivation.

cognitive resource theory: theory of leadership stating that a leader obtains effective group performance by, fit, making effective plans, decisions, and strategies, and then communicating them through directive behavior.

coincidental telephone method: a procedure used by C. E. Hooper in the mid-1930s for ascertaining what radio programs and commercials people listened to. Respondents were called on the telephone and asked whether they were listening to radio and, if so, to name the programs. See *Hooperating.* Cf. *Audimeter; diary method.*

coincident indicator: a measure of activity that traditionally moves in the same direction and during the same time period as total economic movement.

coinsurance:
(1) a provision in a policy that requires that the insured carry additional insurance equal to a certain specified percentage of the value of the property. The inclusion of this provision, whether mandatory or optional, usually gives the insured lower rates than would otherwise apply. See *replacement-cost insurance.*
(2) insurance held jointly with others.

coinsurer: one who shares the loss sustained under an insurance policy or policies; usually applied to an owner of property who fails to carry enough insurance to comply with the coinsurance provision and therefore inevitably suffers part of the loss himself.

COLA: see *cost of living adjustment.*

cold call: contacting a potential customer without prior notice in order to make a sale or arrange for an appointment.

cold canvassing: determining potential investment customers without assistance from others or from references (e.g., selecting every tenth name in the telephone directory within a given location and having a salesman call on these persons). Cf. *territory screening.*

cold storage training: an approach for training workers for advancement or for supervisory positions in advance of any specific openings. The trainee is kept in "cold storage" until such time as he is needed by the firm.

Colgate doctrine: a U.S. Supreme Court decision later incorporated into the Robinson–Patman Act, recognizing the right of a seller to choose his or her own dealers according to his or her criteria and judgment, as well as to announce in advance the circumstances under which he or she refuses to sell to others.

collaboration: in conflict management, seeking true satisfaction of everyone's concerns by working through differences solving problems so everyone wins as a result.

collaborative management: management through power sharing and subordinate participation.

collapse:
  (1) **economics:** a sudden drop in business activity or business prices.
  (2) **business:** failure to ruin of a specific firm.
collateral: security (e.g., a house, an automobile, jewelry) left with a creditor to assure the performance of the obligator. When the obligator has performed, the creditor must return the collateral.
collateral bond: see *bond, collateral.*
collateral businesses: support businesses in the advertising industry, such as package design houses, sales promotion firms, premium shops, media-buying services, marketing research organizations, printing companies, and so forth.
collateral loan: a loan obtained by the pledge of title to personal property. See *hypothecated account.*
collateral trust bond: see *bond, collateral trust.*
collectible: that which can be converted into cash. Synonymous with *liquid.*
collection:
  (1) **general:** presentation for payment of an obligation and the payment thereof.
  (2) **retailing:** an organized gathering of related items.
  (3) **banking:** the gathering of money for presentation of a draft or check for payment at the bank on which it was drawn, or presentation of any item for deposit at the place at which it is payable. See *float; value date.*
collection cycle: the activity that takes place between the extension of credit and the receipt of payment.
collection on delivery (COD): the request that the cost of merchandise and other charges be collected at the time the goods are delivered.
collection service: a system of methods and procedures used to obtain payment of past-due consumer accounts receivable.
collective bargaining: negotiations between an employer or group of employers and a labor union for a contract covering employees in a bargaining unit. First established as a legal right by the National Industrial Recovery Act of 1933 and reconstituted by the Wagner Act and other subsequent legislation, the process is regulated by the National Labor Relations Board. Executive Order 10988 extended limited collective-bargaining rights to federal employees. See *multiemployer bargaining.*
collective entrepreneurship: individual skills integrated into a group

wherein the collective capacity to innovate becomes something greater than the sum of its parts.

collective negotiations: used in the public sector as an alternative to collective bargaining.

collective reserve unit (CRU): an international currency or unit of money for use along with currencies in the reserves of banks around the world.

collect shipment: a shipment for which freight charges and advances are made by the delivering carrier from the consignee.

collegial approach to supervision: an approach whereby decisions are made on the basis of knowledge that individuals hold, regardless of their organizational position. Professionalism and mutual respect are the keys to this sort of relationship. Cf. *custodial approach to supervision; supportive approach to supervision*.

collision insurance: coverage for damage to the insured object caused by collision with any object, stationary or moving.

collusion:
(1) **general:** a secret agreement to defraud.
(2) **labor relations:** a conspiracy between an employer and the certified representative of his or her employees to defraud the employees represented while providing the semblance of a genuine bargaining relationship.

Co. Ltd.: a closed corporation.

comaker: an individual who signs the note of another person as support for the credit of the primary maker. Synonymous with *cosigner*. See *unsecured loan*.

combination bond: see *bond, combination*.

combination policy: an insurance policy, or more often two policies printed on one form, that provides coverage against several hazards under a single document. Sometimes affiliated fire and casualty companies offer insurance under this type of policy.

combination rate: a special rate for advertising in two or more publications owned by a single organization.

command group: a manager and his or her immediate subordinates.

Commerce, Department of (U.S.): see *Department of Commerce, U.S.*

commerce: trade between states and nations.

commercial: see *advertisement*.

commercial account: in general, a checking account; a bank account established for the purpose of enabling the depositor (usually a business person) to draw checks against the balance maintained. See *checking account*.

commercial bank: an organization chartered by the comptroller of the currency and known as a national bank or chartered by the state in which it will conduct the business of banking. A commercial bank generally specializes in demand deposits and commercial loans.

commercial credit: credit extended by firms with which an organization does business.

commercial multiple peril policy: a package type of insurance for commercial establishments that includes a wide range of essential coverages.

commercial paper: any notes, drafts, checks, or deposit certificates used in a business.

commercial property: property to be used for business purposes, as contrasted with residential, agricultural, or industrial functions.

commercial set: the four major documents covering a shipment: the invoice, the bill of lading, the certificate of insurance, and the bill of exchange or draft.

commercial year: a business year. Unlike the calendar year, it consists of 12 months of 30 days each, totaling 360 days.

commission:

(1) **general:** the amount paid to an agent, which may be an individual, a broker, or a financial institution, for consummating a transaction involving sale or purchase of assets or services. Cf. *override*.

(2) **insurance:** compensation for agents and brokers based on a certain percentage of the premiums they produce.

commissioner of insurance: a state official charged with enforcement of the laws pertaining to insurance in his or her state; may be referred to as superintendent or director of insurance.

commission house:

(1) **marketing:** an agent who negotiates the sale of merchandise that he or she handles, with control over prices and terms of sale.

(2) **securities:** a broker who purchases and sells only for customers and does not trade his or her own account.

commitment: an advance agreement by a lender to provide funds for a loan at a later time and upon certain conditions. The commitment is usually limited to a specified period of time and designates a dollar amount and yield.

commitment-based control methods: a category of control tools that rely on the employee's self-control and commitment to doing things right to make sure things stay in control.

committed fixed costs: costs that do not vary in total over a relevant range of activity and that management cannot readily change.

committed principle: the principle that an organization should plan for a period of time in the future sufficient to fulfill the commitments resulting from current decisions.

commodities: see *commodity*.

Commodities Exchange Center (CEC): a facility for the four major New York commodity exchanges, opened in July 1977. Each exchange retains its own autonomy, clears transactions through separate clearing units, and shares in a single computer quotation system. The CEC combines the Commodity Exchange, the New York Coffee and Sugar Exchange, the New York Mercantile Exchange, and the New York Cotton Exchange

commodity: an item of commerce of trade. A basic product, usually but not always agricultural or mineral, which is traded on a commodity exchange. Cf. *spot market*.

commodity agreement: an agreement among producer nations to control the price and/or output of a primary product.

commodity dollar: synonymous with *commodity theory of money*.

Commodity Exchange: formed in 1933 by the merger of the New York Hide Exchange, the National Metal Exchange, the National Raw Silk Exchange, and the New York Rubber Exchange to provide facilities for trading in futures in crude rubber, raw silk, hides, silver, copper, and tin.

Commodity Futures Trading Commission (CFTC): a federal agency established in April 1975, responsible for coordinating the commodities industry in the United States, with primary concern for detecting and prosecuting violators of the Commodity Exchange Act. See *Tax Reform Act of 1976*.

commodity loan: a loan made to a grain producer by the Commodity Credit Corporation.

commodity theory of money: the claim that the value of money is determined by the value of the commodity of which it is composed or which it represents. Synonymous with *commodity dollar*.

common carrier: a carrier that moves people or goods for a price and without partiality.

common cost: a cost that is common to all the segments in question and is not clearly or practically allocable except by some questionable allocation base.

common disaster clause: a clause added to a life insurance policy to instruct the company in paying the proceeds of policies when the insured and the named beneficiary die in the same disaster.

common laborer: synonymous with *unskilled worker.*

common law liability: the responsibility for injuries or damages imposed on a party, because of his or her actions, by that part of the law based on custom and usage as established by the courts, as distinguished from liability under acts passed by a legislative body, which are known as statutory law.

common law trust: synonymous with *business trust.*

Common Market: synonymous with *European Economic Community.*

common stock: securities that represent an ownership interest in a corporation. If the company has also issued preferred stock, both common and preferred have ownership rights. The preferred normally is limited to a fixed dividend but has prior claim on dividends and, in the event of liquidation, assets. Claims of both common and preferred stockholders are junior to claims of bondholders or other creditors of the company. Common stockholders assume the greater risk but generally exercise a greater degree of control and may gain the greater reward in the form of dividends and capital appreciation. Often synonymous with *capital stock.* See *leverage; voting right.*

common stock equivalent: any stock that may be exchanged for common stock, such as options, warrants. This concept is used in determining the number of shares in calculating earnings per share.

common trust fund: a trust fund that provides for the combination of several individual trust funds, such as a number of smaller pension funds.

communication: the transference and understanding of meaning.

communication and decision-making stage: a stage of group development in which members discuss their feelings more openly and agree on group goals and individual roles in the group.

communication channels: the means by which information is transmitted in organizations.

communication competence: ability to effectively use communication behaviors in a given context.

communication distortion: purposely modifying the content of a message.

communication fidelity: the degree of correspondence between the message intended by the source and the message understood by the receiver.

communication networks: the pathways through which messages between and among people in organizations flow.

communication process: the steps between a source and a receiver that results in the transference and understanding of meaning.

communitarian paradigm: the government defines needs and priorities and partners with business in a major way.

community rate of return: the net value of a project to an economy, based on the expected net increase in output that the project, such as a new factory, may bring, directly or indirectly, to the area being developed.

company: an association of people for purposes of carrying on a business activity.

company man: a worker who has greater loyalty to his boss than to his fellow workers.

company mission: a company's overall purpose for existing. It is a major internal factor that affects the tasks of the personnel manager.

company objective: see *company mission.*

company standardization: a management technique for developing and securing optimum utilization of resources and maximum efficiency of operations with the formal creation of the most appropriate predetermined solutions and answers to recurring problems and needs.

company store: a store owned and operated by an organization for the exclusive use of its workers and their families.

company town: a neighborhood or town whose residents are primarily employed by one corporation, which owns most of the property and homes.

company union: an employee organization, usually of a single company, that is dominated or strongly influenced by management. The National Labor Relations Act of 1935 declared such employer domination an unfair labor practice. Synonymous with *inside union.*

comparative advantage: a country's or area's advantage in the manufacture of a particular item when its social cost of production for that item is less than the social cost experienced by other countries or areas for the same item.

comparative advertising: promotional material in which competitors' products are named.

comparative management: study of how organizational behavior and management practices differ across cultures.

comparison shopper: an individual sent to competitors' outlets to determine goods carried and relative prices charged as part of information-gathering activity.

compensating balance: the lowest percentage of a line of credit that the customer of a bank is expected to maintain at all times.

compensating errors: two errors, one on the credit side and the other on the debit side, such that one cancels out the other.

compensation:

(1) **general:** payment for any services or items. See *compensation package; executive compensation.*

(2) **business law:** the settlement of any debt by the debtor's establishment of a counterclaim against the creditor.

(3) **personnel:** an attempt to disguise an undesirable characteristic by exaggerating a desirable one.

compensation award: compensation paid to an injured party for a number of periods, either definite or indefinite, as the nature of the injury requires. Payment is sometimes made in installments.

compensation cafeteria: a compensation strategy whereby firms permit executives to design payment packages by allowing alternate payment streams and deferral periods and at the same time permit senior management to exercise preferences for payment devices. Choices include salary raises, bonuses (paid or deferred), benefits, perquisites, qualified and nonqualified stock options, deferred retirement compensation, added life insurance, and the like.

compensation package: the total array of money (wages, salary, commission), incentives, benefits, perquisites, and awards provided to an employee by an organization.

compensatory fiscal policy: an approach to reversing the direction of the business cycle when it is believed to be becoming inflationary or deflationary. Synonymous with *countercyclical policy.*

competition:

(1) **general:** any rivalry.

(2) **business:** the situation in which a large number of manufacturers serve a large number of consumers, when no manufacturer can demand or offer a quantity sufficiently large to affect the market price. See *invisible hand; monopoly; oligopoly.* Cf. *imperfect competition; nonprice competition; unfair competition.*

competitive bid: the offer to sell, at a price, made by a vendor.

competitive differential: how a company differs from competing companies, making for greater or less acceptance of the organization by the market.

competitive group rewards: group rewards distributed in such a way that members receive equitable rewards in exchange for successful performance as individuals in a group.

Competitive Equality Banking Act, the (1987): allows the Federal Savings and Loan Insurance Corporation, which insures deposits in 3,200 institutions, to borrow up to $10.8 billion over three years to close weak savings and loans or subsidize their takeover by healthier ones. The law also requires banks to clear consumers' checks more quickly, and bans creation of new limited-service banks.

competitive intelligence: systematic techniques used to obtain and interpret public information about competitors. Cf. *competitive strategy.*

competitive price: a price determined in the market by the bargaining of a number of buyers and sellers, each acting separately and without sufficient power to manipulate the market.

competitive strategy: an outline of how a business intends to compete with other firms in the same industry. Cf. *competitive intelligence.*

competitors: in negotiations or conflict management, people whose primary motive is to win to outdo others.

complementary products: items that tent to round out a line of products (e.g., shoes and shoelaces). See *suggestive selling.*

complete audit: an examination of all financial records. See *audit.*

completed transaction: a sale of property that has closed. In such transactions all legal and financial aspects are identified and title to the property is transferred from seller to buyer.

complex organization: any large-scale formal organization.

composite check: a listing of payments to be made from an account, sent by the owner of the account to his or her depository institution with instructions to effect the payments and debit the account for the total amount. The payments are transmitted by the depository institution to the creditors for subsequent deposit by them in their respective accounts.

composite demand: the sum of demands for an item or service, beginning with any number of needs, all of which can be fulfilled by that particular item or service.

composite inventory: data accumulation on customers, including the most pertinent information that can be obtained about them.

composite limit order book (CLOB): a central electronic repository and display that automates all orders to buy and sell securities. It could eliminate the need for any exchanges by allowing buying and selling to be done directly by brokerage offices through a central computer system.

composite rate: a special single rate based on a measure of exposure that will reasonably reflect the variations in the insurable hazards covered for a particular insured. Bases of exposure to which the composite rate is applied include payroll, sales, receipts, and contract cost. This rate is often called an *average rate* in property insurance.

composite supply: an indefinite number and variety of items, each of which is able to satisfy a particular need.

compound: to add interest to principal at time intervals for the purpose of establishing a new basis for subsequent interest computations.

compounded: indicating the frequency with which interest is computed and added to the principal to arrive at a new actual balance.

compound interest: interest created by the periodic addition of simple interest to principal, the new base thus established being the principal for the computation of additional interest. Cf. *simple interest*.

compound period: the period of time for which interest is calculated.

comprehensive: a layout prepared to resemble a completed advertisement as nearly as possible.

comprehensive budgeting: a budgeting process that covers all phases of operations.

comprehensive major medical insurance: a form of major medical insurance written with a low initial deductible in place of separate basic hospital, surgical, and medical benefits.

comprehensive personal liability insurance: a type of insurance that reimburses the policyholder if he or she becomes liable to pay money for damage or injury he or she has caused to others. This coverage does not include automobile liability but includes almost every activity of the insured except his or her business operations.

comprehensive planning: planning that incorporates all levels of the organization, top, middle, and lower.

comprehensive policy: a variety of insurance policies that provide broad protection (e.g., a comprehensive automobile liability policy, a comprehensive personal liability policy).

compressed work week: a work schedule whereby workers spend fewer days on the job but work approximately the same number of hours.

compromise:
   (1) **general:** any agreement between two or more persons, usually in opposition, to settle their differences on areas of controversy without resort to legal action.
   (2) **labor relations:** a settlement of a union-management dispute by an adjustment of differences by both sides, rather than resorting to outside involvement by a mediator or arbitrator.

comptroller: an executive officer whose job embraces the audit functions of the business.

Comptroller of the Currency: a federal office created in 1863 to oversee the chartering and regulation of national banks.

compulsory arbitration: a third-party decision resulting from the order of a judicial body or, in rare instances, agreed to by the parties in a labor-management dispute. Arbitration is a common device for settling disputes that arise under existing contracts but is not considered compulsory in ordinary usage. Cf. *conciliation.*

compulsory insurance: any form of insurance that is required by law (e.g., compulsory automobile liability insurance for all owners of automobiles in Massachusetts).

compulsory retirement: separation from employment at an age specified by union contract or company policy.

compulsory staff consultation: an organizational policy that requires operating (line) managers to confer with appropriate staff personnel before taking action.

concentrated marketing: a form of marketing segmentation in which the marketer concentrates on a single segment of a larger market.

concentration in employment: a situation in which a department or employer has a higher proportion of members of a protected class than is found in the employer's labor market. See *underutilization.*

concentration point: a place where less-than-carload shipments are united to be shipped as a carload.

concentration ratio: in a specific industry, the breakdown of total business that is handled by a specified number of the largest organizations.

concentric diversification: expansion in similar markets, the activity confined to existing structures inside the firm.

concept testing: a marketing strategy whereby members of a psychological test panel conclude whether an idea is acceptable, as contrasted with market research that attempts to determine if an appropriate market exists. Cf. *market research.*

concession:
  (1) **business:** any deviation from regular terms or previous conditions.
  (2) **finance:** a reduction or rebate; an allowance from the initial price or rate.
  (3) **finance:** a right granted to a company to sell its product or services (e.g., to rent chairs at an outdoor party; to check coats and hats in a theater).
concessionaire: the holder of a concession granted by a company, government, or other authorized body.
conciliation: in collective bargaining, the process whereby the parties seek to reconcile their differences. The discussion generated is advisory and participation is not compulsory, but under the Taft-Hartley Act a union must notify the appropriate federal agency of an impending strike. Most conciliation work is conducted by the Federal Mediation and Conciliation Service. Cf. *arbitration; compulsory arbitration; mediation.*
concurrence: duplication of the structure resulting from the joining of marketing elements.
concurrent insurance: two or more insurance policies that provide the same coverage for the same property and the same interests.
concurrent staff authority: an organizational policy requiring that line managers obtain the agreement of appropriate staff personnel on specified types of issues before they take action.
condemnation: taking of private property for public use. Under a condemnation proceeding, the property is taken with or without the consent of the owner but upon payment of just compensation.
condemnation proceedings: court action preceded by legislation to take private property for public use. It reflects the sovereign power of eminent domain.
condition: a contractual clause, implied or expressed, that has the effect of investing or divesting with rights and duties the members of the contract.
conditional sales contract: a sales contract in which ownership of sold items remains with the seller until the goods are paid for in full or until other conditions are met.
conditional value: the value that will insure if a particular event occurs.
conditioning process: the process of shaping material into a usable item. No additional materials are added, but the configuration is altered (e.g., shaping sheet plastic into a tube).

configuration management: the combination of management principles and technological applications in building high-quality products to well-defined requirements; used primarily in the defense and aerospace industry.

confidential risk report: a report, established through investigations, of the physical condition of an insurer or his property, prior to the issuance of a policy.

configuration: an organization's shape, reflecting the division of labor and the means of coordinating the divided tasks.

confirmation:

(1) **purchasing:** a statement from a supplier that he or she will accept a buyer's purchase request.

(2) **business law:** an assurance of title by the conveyance of an estate or right from one to another, by which a voidable estate is made sure or valid or at times increased.

(3) **securities:** a written order or agreement to verify or confirm one previously given verbally, in person or by telephone. Executions of orders to buy or sell securities as substantiated in writing by brokers to their customers. See *dealer.*

confirming bank: a bank that assures either that it will honor a credit already issued by another bank or that such a credit will be honored by the issuer or by a third bank.

conflict: a process that begins when one party perceives that another party has negatively affected, or is about to negatively affect, something that the first party cares about. See *conflict management; conflict process; conflict resolution; conflict stimulation; conflict trigger.*

conflict management: the use of resolution and stimulation techniques to achieve the desired level of conflict.

conflict process: five stages are: potential opposition or incompatibility; cognition and personalization; intentions; behavior; and outcomes.

conflict resolution: occurs when a manager resolves conflict that has become harmful or serious. See *consensus.*

conflict stimulation: the creation and constructive use of conflict by a manager.

conflict trigger: any factor that increases the chances of conflict.

conglomerate: the result of a merging of organizations that produce different items and services to secure a large economic base, to acquire sounder management, and to gain greater potential profit. See *merger.* Cf. *consortium.*

conglomerate merger: a merger of firms that produce unrelated products.

conglomeratize: to gather together varying business units into one massive corporate structure or system. See *conglomerate.*

conglomerchant: a multiline merchandising empire under central ownership, usually combining several styles of retailing with behind-the-scenes observations of some distribution and management functions.

congloperators: (slang) presidents and board chairmen of major worldwide conglomerates; coined by the London-based publication *Economist.*

Congress of Industrial Organizations (CIO): originally organized in 1935 as a committee (Committee for Industrial Organization) within the American Federation of Labor to spur unionization of mass-production industries. Unions organized by the committee were expelled from the AFL in 1937, and the committee reorganized itself to form the Congress of Industrial Organizations in 1938.

conscious parallel action: identical pricing behavior among competing organizations. It has been declared illegal by the courts in antitrust cases. Cf. *price fixing.*

consensus: a form of conflict resolution that presents opinions and gains agreement to support a decision.

consensus management: a management style in which chief executives rely on various committees, groups, and task forces to reach organization-wide agreement on a particular decision.

consent election: voting by employees in a bargaining unit as to their choice of union (or no union), when management and the union or unions have agreed on the terms of the election. See *representation election.*

consequential loss: loss occurring as a consequence of physical damage to property. Standard fire insurance and certain other policies cover only against direct loss resulting from the perils insured against. Cf. *proximate damages.*

conservative groups: groups whose members are scattered throughout an organization, usually at top rungs of the promotional and status ladders of the organization. Members are self-assured and successful, and their work involves individual operations.

consideration:

(1) **insurance:** synonymous with *premium.*

(2) **business law:** a requirement of valid contracts according to which all parties must provide something of value.

consideration behavior: involves being concerned with subordinates' feelings and respecting subordinates' ideas.

consignee: the ultimate recipient of goods.

consignment: the act of entrusting goods to a dealer for sale but retaining ownership of them until sold. The dealer pays only when and if the goods are sold. See *on consignment*.

consignor: the originator of a shipment, a person who delivers goods to an agent.

consol: a bond that will never reach maturity; a bond in perpetuity.

consolidate: to bring together various financial obligations under one agreement, contract, or note.

consolidated balance sheet: a balance sheet that shows the financial condition of a corporation and its subsidiaries.

consolidated bond: see *bond, consolidated*.

consolidation: a combination of two or more organizations into one to form a new entity. Cf. *takeover*.

consortium: a grouping of corporations to fulfill a combined objective or project that usually requires interbusiness cooperation and sharing of resources. Cf. *cartel; conglomerate*.

conspicuous consumption: the purchase and use of items and services primarily for improving an individual's social prestige rather than for the satisfaction of material needs.

conspiracy in restraint of trade: collusion; two or more competitors who conspire to restrain trade in some manner. The conspiracy may be directed at competing firms or may be aimed at customers or suppliers. See *restraint of trade*.

constant-cost industry: industry that experiences no increase in prices or in costs of production during expansion, despite new companies entering it.

constant dollars: the actual prices of a previous year or the average of actual prices of a previous period of years.

constructive delivery: acceptance by buyer and seller that possession and ownership have been transferred from one to another, although the purchased goods may not have been delivered.

constructive mileage: an arbitrary mileage allowed to a carrier in dividing joint rates, or mileage pro rata.

constructive receipt rule: the idea that cash is considered to have been received when the taxpayer can exercise control over it, whether or not the cash has actually been received.

constructive total loss: property so badly damaged that, although not completely destroyed, its condition is such that total loss can be prevented only at an expense greater than the value of the property would be after repair; primarily found in marine insurance. Cf. *incurably depreciated*.

consultant: a specialist in any field of activity (e.g., psychological consultant; Wall Street consultant; engineering consultant), hired by an organization to recommend solutions to a problem.

consumer: any person who uses or consumes goods and services.

consumer analysis: the study of the consumer using marketing research methods to determine as many psychological, sociological, and demographic understandings as possible considering the available time and resources.

consumer behavior research: a technique used to determine what satisfactions people want out of life, how they use products and services to achieve these satisfactions, how they perceive items and various brands, what forms of promotional activities will lead to successful marketing, and how to access the effects of these activities. See *marketing concept*.

consumer convenience goods: low-priced, frequently bought consumer items.

consumer cooperative: a group of consumers who band together to gain buying power; user-owned retail outlets. Such organizations act for the benefit of their consumer-owners.

consumer credit: credit extended by a bank to a borrower for the specific purpose of financing the purchase of a household appliance, alteration, or improvement, or a piece of equipment. Such credit generally is extended to individuals rather than to business executives.

Consumer Credit Protection Act of 1968: see *Truth in Lending Act of 1968*.

consumer deal: a price reduction to a consumer offered by a sale of multiple units at a special price for the package; for example, one-cent-off coupon.

consumer-driven philosophy: a marketing philosophy that relies on research to discover consumer preferences, desires, and needs before production actually begins.

consumer durables: see *consumer goods*.

consumer equilibrium: a situation in which no reallocation of a person's income will improve his or her economic situation.

consumer goods: items bought and used by the final consumer for personal or household purposes.

consumerism: the organized demand that businesses increase their concern for the public in both the manufacture and sale of merchandise. See *Fair Credit Reporting Act of 1971; Federal Equal Credit Opportunity Act of 1977; Occupational Safety and Health Act of 1970; Radiation Control for Health and Safety Act of 1968; Truth in Lending Act of 1968.*

consumerist: an individual or representative who takes a leading position to protect the interests and needs of the consumer. See *consumerism*

consumer market: buyers who purchase for personal needs or family consumption.

consumer package: a container that, because of its construction or design, cannot safely be transported without further packaging, usually in an outer or shipping container.

consumer panel: a group of selected people who serve over a period of time as a sample group for marketing research studies.

consumer picketing: picketing of an establishment to persuade consumers to stop shopping there or to stop buying certain products or services.

Consumer Price Index (CPI): a measurement of the cost of living, determined by the Bureau of Labor Statistics.

Consumer Product Safety Commission: protects the public against unreasonable risks of injury from consumer products; assists consumers in evaluating the comparative safety of consumer products; develops uniform safety standards for consumer products, with the promotion of research and prevention.

consumer sale disclosure statement: a form presented by a dealer giving essential details on financing charges relative to a purchase on an installment plan. This is required under the Consumer Credit Protection (Truth in Lending) Act.

consumer sovereignty: a system wherein consumers decide by their purchasing efforts which items are to be produced.

consumer's surplus: a buyer's payment that is lower than the maximum amount he or she would have been willing to pay for the quantity of the commodity that was purchased.

consumption possibility frontier: the limits of the combination of consumption items that a consumer can afford, thus creating budget constraints. Cf. *optional consumption; production possibility frontier.*

contango:
(1) **finance:** the cost factors used in calculating from a given period to a future point.

(2) **commodities:** a basic pricing system in futures trading; a form of premium or carrying charge; for example, instead of paying for the cost of warehousing silver bullion, paying insurance finance charges and other expenses (silver users prefer to pay more for a futures contract covering later delivery).

contemporaneous reserve accounting: required by the Federal Reserve Board, an accounting method used by all American depository institutions since 1984. It lowers the time for posting the reserves that banks and thrift institutions are required by law to hold against checking account deposits from two weeks to two days.

content theory of motivation: theories of motivation that attempt to explain what motivates people.

contingency fund: assets set aside for use in unpredicted situations. Cf. *sinking fund*.

contingency planning: the process of developing a set of alternative plans to fit a variety of future conditions.

contingency theory of leadership: a leadership concept developed by Fred Fiedler according to which a task-oriented style is more productive when the situation is either quite uncertain or quite well defined, and a considerate style is productive under conditions of moderate certainty. Cf. *classical management*.

contingency theory of management: theory that the success of management is said to depend on such factors as the type of technology used to generate the final service or product and the degree of external environmental uncertainty that will face the company.

contingent asset: an asset that may become actual or unqualified as presently unfulfilled situations are satisfied.

contingent liability: the liability imposed on an individual, corporation, or partnership because of accidents caused by persons (other than employees) for whose acts the first party may be held responsible under the law. See *guaranteed debt; switch (contingent) order*.

contingent reserve: the setting aside of a certain amount of profits to meet unanticipated needs of the business or some unexpected loss, the amount of which cannot be definitely ascertained at the time of budgeting.

contingent time off: rewarding people with early time off when they get the job done.

contingent workers: part-time and other employees who do not have a long-term implicit contract with their ultimate employers.

continued bond: see *bond, continued.*

continuity in advertising: the extended utilization of advertising; in particular, repetition of theme, layout, or commercial format.

continuous audit: an audit performed continuously or at short regular periods during the fiscal year. See *audit.*

continuous budget: a budget that perpetually adds a month in the future as the month just ended is dropped.

continuous production: a production activity that yields a standardized product. Raw materials are continually entered into the production process.

continuum approach to leadership: a representation of styles charted on a scale that suggests that there are an infinite number of leadership approaches a manager might follow.

contra account: a separate offsetting account; e.g., allowance for uncollectable accounts and accumulated depreciation.

contraband: illegal or prohibited goods.

contract: an agreement between two or more persons, as established by law, by which rights are acquired by one or more parties to specific acts or forbearance from acts on the part of others.

contract, breach of: failure by one party to a contract to perform his obligation.

contract bar: a rule followed by the National Labor Relations Board that the NLRB will not disturb a valid, existing contract during its term. Cf. *living document doctrine; no-strike clause; reopener clause.*

contract carrier: a transportation firm that contracts with shippers to transport their goods. The price is negotiated between the carrier and the shipper. The contract carrier cannot accept shipments from the general public.

contract clause: a clause in the Constitution of the United States (Article 1, Section 10) declaring that no state may pass laws diminishing the obligation of a contract. Although corporate franchises are accepted as contracts and protected by this clause, it cannot act a a bar to the regulatory and police powers of the state.

contracting out: subletting certain parts of an operation to subcontractors, rather than having the firm's employees perform the task.

contraction: a decline of economic activity in the business cycle; the opposite of *expansion.*

contract market: one of the 18 commodity exchanges permitted under the Commodity Exchange Act to deal in futures contracts in the commodities.

contract purchasing: a form of purchasing defined in a contract for orders and deliveries, covering a specific time period, usually one year.

contractual channels: a channel system based on a contractual agreement between a producer and other members of the channel of distribution.

contractual liability: liability assumed by contract; an additional coverage for a specific exposure for which the basic liability policy does not provide. It may be obtained for an additional premium.

contrast effects: evaluations of a person's characteristics that are affected by comparisons with other people recently encountered who rank higher or lower on the same characteristics.

contributed capital: that portion of stockholder's equity provided by the owners of a business, usually through the purchase of stock.

contributed value: a measure of efficiency that relates value added to sales or profit.

contribution:

(1) **general:** something given, such as time or money.

(2) **insurance:** an insurance carrier's payment of, or obligation to pay, all or part of a loss

(3) **business law:** the sharing of a common loss or benefit, paid or to be paid by each of

the parties involved.

contribution clause: see *coinsurance*.

contribution margin: the excess of total revenue over total variable cost.

contribution profit: sales revenue less the variable cost of producing the revenue.

contributory negligence: the negligence attributed to the person making a claim against an insured; a defense pleaded by the insured in a lawsuit.

contributory pension plan: a pension plan jointly financed by employer and workers. The employees share in the cost of the plan.

contributory retirement system: a system whereby the responsibility for developing the resources for retirement is shared by the employer and the workers.

control: to meet a situation and handle it capably, physically as well as mentally; to execute procedures in accord with plans and policies established for future policy forming and planning. See *coordination; POSDCORB.*

control account: a summary account in the general ledger that is supported by detailed individual accounts in a subsidiary ledger.

controllable costs: costs whose amounts can be influenced by and which are the direct responsibility of a manager.

controllable marketing activities: those marketing activities over which a firm has control, such as the product itself, the product name, packaging, advertising, pricing, sales promotion, and method of distribution.

controlled company (corporation): a firm whose policies are controlled by another firm that owns 51 percent or more of its voting shares. See *Tax Reform Act of 1969*. Cf. *working control*.

controlled economy: an economy that is regulated and greatly influenced by government. See *statism*. Cf. *laissez-faire*.

controller: see *comptroller*.

controlling function: all managerial activity that is undertaken to assure that operations go according to plan.

controlling interest: any ownership of a business in excess of 50 percent. A smaller percentage of shareholders may control the firm, however, if the remainder of the stock is distributed among many owners and is not active in voting. See *working control*. Cf. *minority interest*.

control process: the process of establishing performance objectives and standards, measuring actual performance, comparing actual performance with objectives and standards, and taking necessary action.

control stock: securities belonging to those who have controlling interest in a company.

control system: a system for ensuring that actions are carried out according to a plan designed within the firm.

convenience goods: products that the public wishes to purchase with a minimum of effort or time (toothpaste, cigarettes, sodas, newspaper, etc.).

convenience store: a small retail outlet that carries a limited line of high-turnover convenience goods and usually operates for extended hours.

conventional career pattern: pattern in which individuals move from an initial job to a trial job to stable employment.

conventional rating scale: a performance appraisal form containing a list of qualities, characteristics, or traits upon which an employee is rated on a scale ranging from poor to outstanding.

conventional warehousing: warehousing in which the primary emphasis is on storage with a minimum of service.

convergence hypothesis: a theoretical assertion that organizations and management practices throughout the world are growing more alike.

convergent marketing: a means of organizing the marketing activity within the company so that all the same resources are used to sell all the products made.

conversion:

(1) **manufacturing:** the process of changing from one type of equipment to another.

(2) **insurance:** a provision whereby a more permanent form of insurance may be elected without a medical examination if the request is made within the specified time and an additional premium is paid.

(3) **business law:** the unauthorized taking of another's goods or property.

conversion costs: the combination of direct labor and factor overhead in the manufacturing process.

convertibility: ease of exchanging one currency for that of another nation or for gold. See *soft currency.*

convertible bond: see *bond, convertible.*

convertibles: interest-paying debentures and dividend-paying preferred shares that can be exchanged for the common stock of the issuing company on a preset basis. The conversion privilege becomes valuable only if the market value of the debenture or preferred stock is below the total value of the common shares into which it can be converted.

conveyance:

(1) **general:** the act of transporting.

(2) **business law:** a written statement, called a deed, whereby ownership of property is passed from one person or organization to another.

COO: see *chief operating officer.*

cook the books: deliberately falsifying the financial statements of a firm; manipulating the profits or losses of a corporation by under or overstating income or by inflating reported earnings. It is both unethical and illegal and a violation of SEC regulations. See *Arthur Anderson; Corporate Accountability Act of 2002; Enron; Sarbanes-Oxley Act.*

cooling-off period:

(1) **labor relations:** suspension of a planned or announced strike in the hope that the dispute can be settled during the term of suspension. If the president of the United States feels that the nation's welfare or security is at stake, he can seek an injunction calling for an 80-day cooling-off period. See *Taft-Hartley Act.*

(2) **finance:** the term for the period, usually 20 days, that must elapse before the filing of a registration for a new security and public sale, as declared by the Securities and Exchange Commission.

cooperative:

(1) **retailing:** an outlet owned and run by the final consumers for purposes of buying and selling items to the members.

(2) **business law:** anything owned jointly to the same end.

cooperative advertising: advertising paid for jointly by the advertiser and its wholesalers or retailers.

cooperative counseling: a mutual counselor-employee relationship that establishes a
cooperative exchange of ideas to help solve an employee's problems. See *directive counseling, nondirective counseling.*

cooperative equilibrium: an oligopoly's equilibrium, derived from a decision of the businesses within the oligopoly to maximize their combined profits.

cooperative group rewards: group rewards distributed in such a way that each member receives an equal reward in exchange for the successful performance of the group.

cooperative marketing: independent manufacturers, wholesalers, retailers, or any combination of them working collectively to buy and/or sell.

cooperative negotiation: a situation where two parties bargain by working with each other to obtain a mutually beneficial solution.

cooperative training: a training program combining practical on-the-job experience with formal educational classes.

cooperators: people whose primary concern in negotiating or managing conflict is to maximize outcomes for themselves and others.

co-optation: a strategy employed by an organization to minimize the uncertainty that it faces (e.g., bringing community members together to discuss the ecological impact of building a new plant before the people have a chance to organize to oppose it). Cf. *class action.*

coordination: the overall management function that integrates planning, organizing, directing, and controlling into a unified total. See *POSDCORB.*

coordination of benefits (COB): a method of integrating benefits payable under more than one group health insurance plan so that an insured's benefits from all sources do not exceed 100 percent of allowable expenses.

coordinative planning: planning done at the middle-management level where the work of different units has to be coordinated.

COPE: the Committee on Political Education, a division of the AFL-CIO whose primary function is to provide support by inducing members to vote for candidates for political office who have received the endorsement of labor unions. See *Hatch Act; Taft-Hartley Act.*

co-plan: a unified staff-line effort of communication, coordination, consultation, analysis, and control.

copy: all words to be included in a written advertisement.

copyright: an exclusive right, guaranteed by federal statute, to reproduce, publish, and sell the matter and form of literary, musical, or artistic works. Any attempt by another person or group to deprive the copyright holder of his or her property is cause for the latter to seek damages. Cf. *patent.*

copy testing: measuring the effectiveness of an advertising campaign. See *aided recall; hidden offer; inquiry test; keying an advertisement; split run.*

core hours: the time periods during the day when, regardless of the flexible work schedules of the various employees, everyone is at work.

core management: the key executives of an organization who are the primary decision makers.

corner the market: to purchase a security on a scale large enough to give the purchaser control over the price.

Corporate Accountability Act of 2002: signed by President George W. Bush on July 30, 2002. Provides for an extensive overhaul of corporate fraud, securities, and accounting laws, and creates a regulatory board with investigative and enforcement powers to oversee the accounting industry and punish corrupt auditors. It also established new standards for prosecuting wrongdoing and gives corporate whistleblowers broad new protections. Executives who deliberately defraud investors would face long prison terms. See *Sarbanes-Oxley Act.*

corporate bond: see *bond, corporate.*

corporate culture: values that set a pattern for a company's activities, opinions and actions.

corporate entrepreneurship: a corporation revolution taking place due to the infusion of entrepreneurial thinking into bureaucratic structures.

corporate income tax: a tax imposed on the net earnings of corporations.

corporate muscle: the ability of an organization to effectively utilize its resources, both financial and human, in meeting its goals and objectives.

corporate profits tax liability: federal and state taxes levied on corporate earnings of a given year; a measurement of taxes for the year in which they are incurred, not necessarily for the year in which they are paid.

corporate state: condition represented by the power of a corporation that is out of control, insensitive to human values, and legalistic; a concept introduced by Charles A. Reich in his book *The Greening of America.*

corporate-level strategy: strategy created by top management to achieve the entire organization's objectives and to provide a framework for strategy and operations at lower levels of the company.

corporate philanthropy: corporate contributions for charitable and social responsibility purposes.

corporate portfolio management: the process through which the top management of a multibusiness company determines the strategic role each of the separate business units will play in the total company's strategy.

corporate response strategies: specific strategies that a corporation may exhibit in response to difficult social situations. These include reaction, defense, accommodation, and proaction.

corporate social audit: a rating system used to evaluate a corporation's performance with regard to meetings its social obligations.

corporate social responsibility: the concept that corporations have an obligation to act for the good of society.

corporate strategy: strategy that defines the domain of an organization and lets its members know which priorities have been set.

corporation:
(1) **business law:** individuals created by law as a legal entity, vested with powers and ability to contract, own, control, and convey property and discharge business within the boundaries of the powers granted. Cf. *firm.*
(2) **administration:** an organization that has purposefulness, declared social benefit, derived powers, legal entity, permanence, and limited liability.

corporation de facto: a legal entity that, despite a minor failure to comply with the regulations for incorporation, thereafter has exercised corporate powers.

corporation de jure: a corporation formed by fulfilling the requirements of the law permitting the formation of the corporation.

corporatize: (slang) to establish a legal corporation as contrasted with an unincorporated system; term coined by Neil H. Jacoby.

corrective discipline: an action that follows a rule infraction and seeks to discourage further infractions so that future actions are in compliance with standards. Cf. *preventive discipline.*

corrective model of control: the process of detecting and correcting deviations from pre-established goals or standards.

correspondent bank: a bank that is the depository for another bank. The correspondent bank accepts all deposits in the form of cash letters and collects items for its bank depositor.

cosigner: synonymous with *comaker.*

cosmopolitans: managers, scientists, and engineers who identify with professional groups outside their organization. They may have different norms and values from those stated by the organization.

cosponsoring:
(1) **general:** joining together in a mutual effort or activity.
(2) **advertising:** sharing by two or more advertisers of the cost of a single broadcast program.

cost: the value given up by an entity in order to receive goods or services. Cost is the value given up to obtain an item in the volume needed, shipped to the desired location. All expenses are costs, but not all costs are expenses.

cost accounting: a branch of accounting that deals with the classification, recording, allocation, summarization, and reporting of current and prospective costs. It provides the means by which management can control manufacturing costs. Synonymous with *costing.*

cost and freight (CAF): shipping term indicating that the seller will pay only freight charges to a location, not insurance. Cf. *cost, insurance, and freight (CIF).*

cost-benefit analysis: a branch of operations research that aids in evaluating the implications of alternative courses of action. This method is primarily concerned with the selection of equipment, products, and so on, before they become available. Synonymous with *cost effectiveness.* See *crossover analysis.*

cost effectiveness: synonymous with *cost-benefit analysis.*

cost inflation: inflation caused when rising costs of labor and production increase prices even though demand has not increased.

costing: synonymous with *cost accounting*.

cost, insurance, and freight (CIF): a quoted price that includes the handling charges, insurance, and freight costs up to delivery, usually up to a port of entry. Cf. *cost and freight*.

cost leadership: a competitive strategy by which a company aims to be the low-cost leader in its industry; promoted by Michael E. Porter.

cost of capital: the weighted-average cost of a firm's debt and equity capital; equals the rate of return that a company must earn to satisfy the demands of its owners and creditors.

cost of distribution: costs involved in the movement of goods from the producer to the consumer.

cost of goods manufactured: all direct material, labor, and overhead transferred from work in process inventory to finished goods inventory.

cost of goods sold: the purchase price of goods sold during a specified period, including transportation costs.

cost of living:
(1) **general:** the average cost to an individual of providing the basics of life. See *price control*.
(2) **economics:** the average of the retail prices of all goods and services required for a reasonable living standard. See *Consumer Price Index*.

cost of living adjustment (COLA): an increase or decrease of wages based on the increase or decrease in the purchasing power of money. Inflation and deflation are primary causes for a cost of living adjustment. See *escalator clause*.

cost plus pricing: the practice of adding a percentage of the cost of goods to the cost before the selling price is established.

cost pool: a group of costs that is allocated to cost objectives in some plausible way.

cost-push inflation: increases in the price level that result from firms passing on increases in costs to purchasers, especially labor costs.

cost-volume profit analysis: a method used for measuring the functional relationships between the major aspects of profits and for identifying the profit structure of an organization.

cosurety: one of a group of surety companies executing a bond. The obligation is joint and several, but common practice provides a stated limit of liability for each surety.

Council of Economic Advisers (CEA): established in the Executive

Office of the President by the Employment Act of 1946. The Council analyzes the national economy and its various segments and advises the President on economic developments.

counseling: process involving a dynamic relationship between two parties in which one is free to discuss needs, feelings, and problems of concern for the purpose of obtaining help.

counter:

(1) **general:** a device for storing a number and allowing the number to be increased or decreased, as determined by instructions.

(2) **retailing:** a bench or table for the display of goods.

counterclaim: a defendant's claim that the defendant is entitled to recover from the plaintiff.

countercyclical (policy): policy of leveling the ups and downs of the business cycle with budget deficits during depression and surpluses during prosperity. Cf. *compensatory fiscal policy.*

counterfeit: imitation or fraudulent money.

countermand: to cancel an order that has not yet been carried out.

counterpurchasing: placing an order with a manufacturer in one country with the expectation that merchandise of equal value and/or quantity will be sold in the opposite direction to the other nation.

countersignature:

(1) **insurance:** the signature of a licensed agent or representative on a policy, which is necessary to validate the contract.

(2) **business law:** a signature added to a document to authenticate it. Cf. *attestation.*

countervailing power: the balancing out of the influence of one economic group with monopolistic power by the influence of another economic group with monopolistic power.

country bank: a national or state bank that is not located in a Federal Reserve city. Country banks' legal reserve requirements are usually less than those of large city banks.

country club billing: a billing system in which the account statement is accompanied by copies of original invoices. Cf. *descriptive billing.*

coupling up: the overlap of workers at the time of shift changes.

coupon:

(1) **securities:** the portion of a bond that is redeemable at a given date for interest payments. Cf. *talon.*

(2) **advertising:** a part of an advertisement that can be used for ordering items or redeeming premiums.

coupon bond: see *bond, coupon.*

coupon credit plan: see *charge account.*

couponing: a means of offering consumers a special, temporary price reduction on an item without actually altering the regular market price. A coupon is used offering a specified cents off on the purchase of the item when mailed to the consumer.

coupon pad: an advertisement attached to a card that is hung on a wall or stood on a counter.

coupon plan: the continuous offering of a variety of premiums for coupons, labels, or other tokens from merchandise.

coupon rate: with a bond, the amount of annual coupons divided by par value.

court bond: see *bond, court.*

coverage:

(1) **advertising:** the number of homes or persons exposed to a specific advertising medium in a controlled location.

(2) **insurance:** synonymous with *protection (1).*

(3) **finance:** the ratio of assets to specific liabilities.

coverage map: a map indicating the prime area of a medium's reach within a market.

coverage ratios: financial ratios that compare a company's fixed obligations to its ability to service them.

covered option: an option in which the seller (or writer) owns the underlying security as opposed to the uncovered (or naked) condition, under which the option is written against cash or other margin. Cf. *option.*

covering:

(1) **securities:** buying a stock that was previously sold short.

(2) **finance:** the act of meeting one's obligation.

cover note: a document similar to a finder, usually issued by a reinsurer as evidence of reinsurance.

CPA: see *certified public accountant.*

CPCU: see *Chartered Property & Casualty Underwriter.*

CPI: see *Consumer Price Index.*

CPM: see *critical path method.*

craft: a manual occupation that requires extensive training, usually including apprenticeship, and a high degree of skill (e.g., carpentry; plumbing; linotype operation).

craft union: a union whose membership is limited to practitioners of a particular craft.

crash: a sudden and disastrous drop in business activity, prices, security values, and so on, as occurred in October of 1929.

crawling peg: a foreign exchange rate that permits the par value of a country's currency to change automatically by small increments, upward or downward, if in actual daily trading on the foreign exchange markets the price in terms of other monies persists on the floor or ceiling of the established range for a given period.

cream: insurance policyholders that pay the lowest premiums, in part because they are the best risks.

creative destruction: a process whereby the attraction of monopoly profits from new products motivates companies to do research and to evolve new products, which then replace products previously available and presumed to be inferior.

credit:

(1) **finance:** sales or purchases that are accompanied by a promise to pay later.

(2) **accounting:** an entry recorded on the right side of an ledger. Cf. *debit*.

(3) **banking:** funds remaining in a bank account. See *bank credit*.

credit application: any form used to secure information relating to consumer credit. Questions often asked deal with a person's present and previous places of residence, work history, present earnings, other credit transactions, and outstanding loans. See *trade reference*.

credit authorization/verification: an inquiry process undertaken to reduce the risk of credit fraud or of extending credit in excess of an imposed credit limit.

credit balance: see *balance of account*.

credit bureau: an agency that holds central files of data on consumers in a given trade area. These bureaus collect personal data, data on paying habits, and so on, and make impartial reports for credit granters.

credit contract: a written statement that shows how, when, and how much the purchaser will pay for goods and services.

credit instrument: a written guarantee to pay, that serves the purpose of money in consummating commercial exchanges, although actual money or bank notes are not used.

credit insurance: an insurance company guarantee to manufacturers, wholesalers, and service organizations that they will be paid for goods shipped or services rendered. It is a guarantee of the part of their working capital represented by accounts receivable.

credit investigation: an inquiry made by a lender to verify data given in a credit application or to investigate other aspects the creditor believes to be relevant to credit worthiness. See *acid test ratio.*

creditism: adopted during President Carter's administrations, the policy of tightened control of credit as a means to combat inflation.

credit life insurance: term life insurance, required by some lenders, that pays off a loan in the event of the borrower's death.

credit line: see *line of credit.*

credit loss: the amount of accounts receivable that is, or is expected to become, uncollectible.

credit memorandum: the document used by a seller to inform a buyer that his or her account receivable is being credited (reduced) because of errors, returns, or allowances.

creditor: one who is due money from another. Synonymous with *lender.* See *guaranty.*

credit rating:

(1) **banking:** the amount, type, and form of credit, if any, that a bank estimates can be extended to an applicant for credit.

(2) **finance:** an estimate of the credit and responsibility assigned to mercantile and other establishments by credit-investigating organizations.

credit report: a confidential report made by an independent individual or organization that has investigated the financial standing, reputation, and record of an applicant for insurance.

credit-reporting agencies: organizations structured to supply to business and industry the information they need to reach credit, sales, financial, and general management decisions.

credit risk: the risk assumed for the possible nonpayment of credit extended.

credit sale: a sale in which the individual is given time to pay for the items purchased. There is an extra charge for this privilege.

credit terms: specification of the terms for payment of a credit obligations.

credit union: a cooperative financial organization established within and listed to a specific group of people. See *Federal Credit Union; share draft.*

credit worthy: receiving a favorable credit rating. An individual is thereby entitled to use the credit facilities of the organization(s) that requested the information. See *open credit.*

creeping inflation: a gradual but continuing increase in the general price level, by as little as 2.5 percent a year. Cf. *flation; inflation.*

critical incident: a management training tool whereby participants in a discussion describe major events in their experience that have caused them difficulty. See *sensitivity training.*

critical contingencies: events, activities, or objects that are required by an organization and its various parts to accomplish organizational goals and to ensure continued survival.

critical path method (CPM): in planning and scheduling a complex series of operations, the sequence of events that are most critical as to timing; the longest path of activities in a system. CPM is based on the network analog principle and was first used in 1957 by E.I. du Pont de Nemours and Co. to improve the planning, scheduling, and coordination of its new-plant construction effort. Cf. *program evaluation and review technique (PERT).*

critical resource factor: that element in the manufacturing process that determines operating capacity by its availability.

critical size: the point at which existing practices and procedures become inadequate to maintain an organization's continuing expansion and growth.

cross-cultural management: understanding and teaching behavior patterns in different cultures.

cross-cultural training: structured experiences to help people adjust to a new culture and/or country.

cross-elasticity: the impact on the demand for one product of price changes in a related product. For example, when the price of butter goes up, the price of margarine, a substitute, usually rises as well. See *coefficient of cross-elasticity; elastic demand.*

crossover analysis: an approach to cost analysis that shows the optimum volume of activity that should be used in alternative means of manufacture.

cross-picketing: see *picketing.*

cross rates of exchange: comparisons of exchange rates between currencies that reveal whether it would be profitable to exchange the first currency for a second, the second for a third, then the third for the first.

CRU: see *collective reserve unit.*

crunch: an economic squeeze; a crisis created by some financial pressure.

cultural artifacts: the obvious signs and symbols of corporate culture, such as organizational structure, policies, and dress codes.

cultural audit: audit of the organizational culture and quality of work life in an organization.

cultural values: values employees need to have and act on in order for the organization to act on strategic values.

culture control: a method of control that emphasizes implicit and informal direction based on a broad company culture.

culture shock: confusion, disorientation, and emotional upheaval caused by being immersed in a new culture.

cum right: the stockholder's right to acquire shares of a new issue of stock in a company in direct proportion to existing holdings. See *rights.*

cumulative dividend: a dividend on cumulative preferred stock payable, under the terms of issue, at intervals and before any distribution is made to holders of common stock.

cumulative mark on: the difference between total delivered cost and total original retail values of merchandise handled within a stated time frame, inclusive of the accumulated inventory.

cumulative preferred (stock): a stock whose holders are entitled, if one or more dividends are omitted, to be paid on the omitted dividends before dividends are paid on the company's common stock.

cumulative quantity discount: a type of rebate given to a store when the total price of all goods purchased is identified. The objective is to encourage the dealer to give seller all his business in that line of trade.

cumulative voting: the right of each share of stock to cast as many votes for one director of the firm as there are directors who seek elected office.

curable depreciation: depreciated property that is still considered economically useful.

Curb Exchange: the name used before 1953 for the American Stock Exchange in New York City. See *American Stock Exchange.*

currency: paper money and coin.

currency appreciation: increase in the relative value of a national currency under a flexible exchange rate system.

currency depreciation: decline in the relative value of a national currency under a flexible exchange rate system. See *depreciation.*

currency leakage: a situation in which demand deposits are converted into cash and leave the banking system. See *demand deposit.*

current account:
　(1) **finance:** a running account between two companies, reflecting the movement of cash, merchandise, and so on.
　(2) **advertising:** customer names taken from a list and ranked in order of past business and potential activity.

current assets: the assets of a company that are reasonably expected to be realized in cash, sold, or consumed during the normal operating cycle of the business. Synonymous with *floating assets*.

current budget: the budget prepared at some level of activity or operation for the following fiscal year.

current cost: what it might cost today to replace an asset or to acquire equivalent productive capacity.

current-dividend preference: the right of preferred shareholders to receive current dividends before common shareholders receive dividends.

current dollars: used to describe the actual prices of goods and services each year.

current earnings distribution: the present distribution of earned income, reflecting earlier discrimination in educational opportunities or employment, or bad judgment. The concept is important because the distribution of earnings in the future may be expected to be different, even without further social changes or new government policies.

current exit value: what a company could sell an asset for (or remove a liability for) in today's market.

current liabilities: money owed and payable by a company, usually within one year.

current operation expenditures: expenditures for salaries and wages, supplies, materials, and contractual services, other than capital outlays.

current ratio: the relationship between total current assets and total current liabilities. It is calculated by dividing current assets by current liabilities.

current value accounting: an accounting approach that requires the measurement of individual assets (e.g., factories, machines, and supplies) in current prices rather than in terms of the actual dollar costs at which they were acquired in earlier years.

cushion bond: see *bond, cushion*.

cushion checking (credit): a check overdraft plan that is also an instant loan. When a check is issued in excess of the customer's account balance or a request is made to transfer from the customer's cash reserve to his checking account, a loan is made for up to 36 months, with a modest interest charge.

custodial approach to supervision: a paternalistic or "parent knows best" approach to dealing with employees. Cf. *collegial approach to supervision; supportive approach to supervision*.

customer: an individual or organization that makes a purchase.

customer-bank communication terminal (CBCT): the name given to a remote (i.e., not on bank premises) electronic device through which customers may withdraw, deposit, or transfer funds from or to their checking or savings accounts. Cf. *automated teller machine*.

customer departmentation: the grouping of jobs into subunits based on the customers to be served, a common practice in retail organizations.

customer-owned goods: for example, suits left at the store after purchase for alterations. Cf. *COG*.

customer's broker (man): synonymous with *registered representative*.

customer's ledger: a ledger that shows accounts receivable of each customer.

customhouse bond: see *bond, customhouse*.

customs: taxes imposed by a government on the import or export of items. Cf. *duty; tariff*.

customs union: an agreement by two or more trading countries to dissolve trade restrictions, such as tariffs and quotas, among themselves, and to develop a common external policy or trade (e.g., a trade agreement).

cutback:
(1) **labor relations:** a layoff of employees caused by a reduction in available work. See *work sharing*.
(2) **manufacturing:** reduction to a former level (e.g., in production).

cutoff date: a specific day chosen for stopping the flow of cash, goods, or other items for closing or audit reasons. Usually such a date is chosen if an inventory is scheduled when sales or purchases are to take place.

cutting a melon: (slang) making an extra distribution of money or stock to shareholders, usually when preceded by an unusually profitable transaction (e.g., the sale of a subsidiary).

cycle billing: matching of alphabetical breakdowns to specific days to assist in customer billing. Each breakdown is a cycle and occurs on the same day every month.

cycle stock: the amount of inventory expected to be used during a particular cycle.

cyclical demand: variations in demand for a product due to factors such as war, elections, economic conditions, and sociological pressures. The cycles are typically greater than one year and less than five years.

cyclical forecast: changes in market demand that are primarily a result of general economic conditions.

cyclical inflation: periodic sudden increases in the general price level. Cf. *secular inflation*.

cyclical stocks: securities that go up and down in value with the trend of business, rising faster in periods of rapidly improving business conditions and sliding very noticeably when business conditions deteriorate.

cyclical unemployment: unemployment caused by fluctuations in the economy due to downward trend in the business cycle. Cyclical unemployment involves many more jobs than seasonal, technological, or frictional unemployment. Cf. *chronic unemployment; frictional unemployment; hard-core unemployed*. See *simultaneous inflation and unemployment*.

cyclic duty: work that is performed periodically.

D

daily effective circulation: in outdoor advertising, the number of people who are expected to observe a message.

daily reports: skeleton copies of insurance policies prepared for the agent and the company, consisting of the declarations page and fill-in endorsements. Cf. *blotter; policy register; scratch daily report.*

Daily Treasury Statement: a listing of transactions that clear through the U.S. Treasurer's account. For each business day it reflects cash deposits, cash withdrawals, and the status of the Treasurer's account.

data administration: involves the establishment and enforcement of policies and procedures for managing data as a strategic corporate resource.

date: the point in time, fixed by the year, month, and day, when an occurrence takes place. See *effective date.*

date of record: the date, selected by a firm's board of directors, on which dividend-receiving shareholders are identified.

dating: a technique of extending credit beyond the time it was originally given; often used as an inducement to dealers to place orders far in advance of the coming season.

daylight trading: making a purchase followed by a sale of a security on the same day, to avoid a holding position in the shares traded overnight or longer.

day loan: a one-day loan, granted for the purchase of stock, for the broker's convenience. Upon delivery, securities are pledged as collateral to secure a regular call loan. Cf. *call loan.*

day order: an order to buy or sell that, if not executed, expires at the end of the trading day on which it was entered.

days of grace: the reasonable length of time allowed, without suffering a loss or penalty, for postponed payment or for the presentment for payment of certain financial documents. See *grace period.*

days sales invested in working capital: an alternative measure of the amount of working capital used in sustaining the sales of a period; computed by dividing 365 days by the working capital turnover.

deadbeat:
    (1) **general:** a person who tries to avoid paying for things.
    (2) **finance:** a person who pays his or her entire charge every billing period, thus avoiding revolving credit charges.

deadheading:
    (1) **transportation:** the movement of empty vehicles or railcars to a

destination point.

(2) **transportation:** the practice of providing free transportation for workers of a transportation firm.

(3) **labor relations:** bypassing seniority regulations and promoting a lower-level employee who is more capable of doing the job. Cf. *bumping.*

(4) **administration:** the moving of workers required to report for assignments far from their homes.

deadline:

(1) **general:** the time, day, or other period on which something is due

(2) **advertising:** the hour or day after which the advertising material will not be accepted to appear in a publication or specific broadcast time period.

dead stock: merchandise that cannot be sold.

dead time: time lost by workers due to lack of materials, machine breakdown, or other causes beyond their control. Cf. *downtime.*

deal: (slang) a large transaction involving a change in ownership.

dealer:

(1) **general:** an individual or firm that divides quantity goods or services into smaller units for resale to customers.

(2) **securities:** an individual or firm in the securities business acting as a principal rather than as an agent. Typically, a dealer buys for his or her own account and sells to a customer from the dealer's inventory. The dealer's profit or loss is the difference between the price he pays and the price he receives for the same security. The dealer's confirmation must disclose to the customer that he has acted as principal. The same individual or firm may function, at different times, both as broker and dealer.

dealer imprint: a dealer's name, address, or other identification, put on material created by an advertiser.

dealer tie-in: a manufacturer's advertisement given at a countrywide rate with a list of local dealers to be included in the ad.

deal stream: (slang) venture capitalist term for a businessman's strategy for finding capital from a venture-financing source. Traditionally, those with ideas who seek money are more numerous than those with money who look for ideas.

dear money:

(1) **banking:** a situation in which interest rates are high. Synonymous with *hard money.*

(2) **finance:** a situation created when loans are difficult to obtain because of the supply and demand for credit.

death benefit: see *principal sum.*

deauthorization: a procedure that permits unionized employees to vote to determine whether they desire an open shop.

debase: to reduce the quality, purity, or content or otherwise alter the accepted intrinsic value of the coinage of a realm.

debenture:

(1) **finance:** used to define indebtedness, usually in long-term obligations, that is unsecured.

(2) **business:** corporate obligations that are sold as investments.

(3) **business law:** a voucher or certificate acknowledging that a debt is owed by the signer.

debenture bond: see *bond, debenture.*

debit:

(1) **accounting:** any amount in dollars and cents that, when posted, will increase the balance of an asset or expense account and decrease the balance of a liability account. All asset and expense accounts normally have debit balances, and all liability, capital, and income accounts normally have credit balances. Cf. *credit.*

(2) **securities:** the portion of the purchase price of stock, bonds, or commodities that is covered by credit extended by a broker to margin customers.

(3) **insurance:** a weekly premium life insurance agent's list of all the premiums he or she is required to collect.

debit balance: see *balance of account.*

debit card: a cash machine automator and a check guarantee; a recent innovation that permits bank customers to withdraw cash at any hour from any affiliated automated teller machine in the country and to make cashless purchases from funds on deposit without incurring revolving finance charges for credit.

debt: money, services, or materials owed to another person as the result of a previous agreement. See *effective debt; funded debt; gross debt; total debt.*

debt capital: funds borrowed to finance the operations of a business.

debtee: a creditor.

debt financing: raising money or capital by borrowing. Cf. *equity financing.*

debt management: managing the sale of new federal securities to repay owners of maturing securities and to cover budget deficits.

debtor: one who owes money to another.

debtor nation: a country whose citizens, companies, and government owe more to foreign creditors than foreign debtors owe them.

debt service: interest payments and capital reduction on government, industrial, or other long-term bonds.

debt to net worth ratio: all liabilities divided by net value.

debureaucratization: a basic approach for shifting and delegating power and authority from a central point to subordinate levels within an organization's hierarchy to promote independence, responsibility, and more rapid decision making in implementing policies and programs to serve the needs of those levels. See *bureaucracy.*

deceased account: a bank deposit account in the name of a deceased person. Upon notification of death, the bank segregates the decedent's account and withholds release of funds until a court of law authorizes payment to the legal heirs. See *frozen account.*

decentralization:

(1) **administration:** placing the decision-making point at the lowest managerial level, involving delegation of decision-making authority. Cf. *autocratic.*

(2) **economics:** the redistribution of population and business from a city to its suburban areas.

decentralized decision-making: lower-level managers are empowered to make important decisions.

decertification: an order by the National Labor Relations Board ending the representation rights of a union, pursuant to a vote of the workers, in an NLRB election. This is done following a petition asserting that the union no longer represents the majority of the employees. See *Taft-Hartley Act.*

deciding to decide: a response in which decision makers accept the challenge of deciding what to do about a problem and follow an effective decision-making process.

decisional roles: the roles of entrepreneur, resource allocator, disturbance handler, and negotiator. A manager who takes on these roles plays a key part in the decision-making system of the organization.

decision maker: a person, usually a member of a group, who either has the authority to make a decision or the ability to influence other members of the group.

decision making: the process of generating and evaluating alternatives and making choices among them.

decision risk: exposure to the possibility that an incorrect decision will have an adverse effect on the organization.

decision rule: a statement that tells a decision maker which alternative to choose based on the characteristics of the decision situation.

decisions: the making of choices from among two or more alternatives.

decision theory model: model that focuses upon certain elements in decision making that are common to all decisions and that provides means to enable a decision maker to better analyze a complex situation containing numerous alternatives and possible consequences. This theory is strongly rooted in the fields of statistics and the behavioral sciences.

decision to participate: according to a proposition developed by J. G. March and H. A. Simon, the decision by an individual to continue to participate in an organization so long as the inducements provided are as great as or greater than the contributions he or she is asked to make. Cf. *dissatisfiers.*

decision to produce: according to a proposition developed by March and Simon, the decision to be a productive member of an organization, depending on the alternatives available to the person, the perceived consequences of adopting a particular production approach, and the person's own objectives.

declaration:

(1) **general:** the full disclosure of items, property, or income (e.g., a customs declaration).

(2) **insurance:** a statement by an applicant for insurance, usually relating to underwriting information. Sometimes, as in most casualty and property policies, this is copied into the policy. See *representation.* Cf. *evidence of insurability.*

(3) **business law:** the first pleading in an action.

declaration date: the date on which payment of a dividend is authorized by a corporation's board of directors.

declared value: the value of merchandise stated by the owner when the goods are delivered to the carrier.

decline stage: the period in a product's life cycle between saturation and abandonment. Since sales are dropping, costs are carefully controlled to minimize added losses.

declining balance depreciation: a depreciation method that charges larger amounts of depreciation expense in earlier years and lesser amounts later.

decommissioning cost: expenses incurred in retiring a plant from service.

decompositional approach: attitude measurement approach in which the utilities of each attribute are obtained from the overall preference judgment for each object.

decomposition product map: a spatial configuration of products developed from judgments about product similarities.

deconglomeration: a form of organization whereby a corporation is split into two or more units, each with a carefully defined product or service and its own common stock, table of organization, and plan for growth. Synonymous with *pluralism.*

deconsolidate: to remove the status of consolidation or of being consolidated from a subsidiary firm.

decouple: to make an adjustment for the cost of living by taking into account as separate factors price inflation and wage inflation, especially in calculating benefit increases for Social Security.

decoupling inventory: the inventory existing between two operations so that the operations can be controlled independently.

decoupling mechanism: a structural approach to managing conflict in which intergroup relations are eliminated, either by buffering or by self-containment.

decreasing costs: costs that decline as output per unit increases.

decrement: a loss in value.

dedomiciling: relocating the headquarters of an international firm to a country where there is less or no taxation of foreign income and few restrictions on foreign investment.

deductible clause: a provision making an insurance company liable only for the excess of a stated amount, to be deducted from any loss. This is used largely on risks for which many small losses may be expected, such as scratches or dents to automobile bodies. Cf. *franchise clause.*

deductible insurance: a method of coverage under which a policyholder agrees to contribute up to a specified sum per claim or per accident toward the total amount of insured loss. Insurance is written on this basis at reduced rates. Cf. *full coverage.*

deduction:

(1) **general:** the logical process of drawing conclusions from a set of assertions or hypotheses.

(2) **accounting:** an item that can be subtracted from income in defining taxable income (e.g., contributions to charities, certain payments of interest, and some taxes).

deductions from gross income: amounts allowed by the Interstate Commerce Commission as deductions in arriving at gross income (e.g., rents, taxes, interest). See *Interstate Commerce Commission; itemized deductions; Tax Reform Act of 1976.*

deductive method: an approach to scientific inquiry in which a premise that has been accepted to be true becomes the basis of additional logical reasoning. Cf. *inductive method.*

deep stock: frequently used merchandise kept in large quantities and in many sizes and colors.

de facto: "in actual fact" (*Latin*); in reality; actually; existing, regardless of legal or moral consideration (e.g., de facto segregation; de facto discrimination in employment). Cf. *de jure.*

defalcation: situation that occurs when an individual in a trust or fiduciary position is unable, by his own fault, to account for funds left in his hands; often interchangeable with embezzlement or misappropriation of funds. Cf. *peculation.*

defamation: words that attribute disreputable conduct or immoral behavior to the person of whom they are spoken.

default: the failure to do that which is required by law or to perform on an obligation previously committed. The term is commonly used when some legally constituted governing body fails to pay the principal or interest on its bond or fails to meet other financial obligations on maturity.

defend-and-hold strategy: investment and marketing efforts designed to maintain sales and profit levels for a particular service or product.

Defense, Department of (U.S.): see *Department of Defense, U.S.*

defense fund: synonymous with *strike fund.*

defensive investment: an investment policy that places its major effort on reducing both the risk of (eventual) loss and the need for special knowledge, skill, and continuous attention. Cf. *speculation.*

deferrals: cash collected before revenue is recognized as being earned or cash disbursed before an expense is recognized as being incurred.

deferred air freight: property received for shipment by an air carrier on a space-available basis after acceptance of all other revenue traffic.

deferred annuity: an annuity contract that provides for the postponement of the start of the annuity until after a specified period or until the annuitant attains a specified age.

deferred charges: expenditures that are written off over a time period.

deferred compensation: the postponement of distribution of a portion of current earnings until a later date, usually at retirement. The object of deferred compensation is to reduce current income taxes by postponing receipt of taxable income until a time when the receiver will likely be in a lower income tax bracket.

deferred credit: a credit that has been delayed in posting for some reason (e.g., a deposit that came into a bank after business hours and is therefore entered on the books in the following day's business).

deferred expense: an asset that has been created through the payment of cash by an entity before it will obtain benefits from that payment. Basically, synonymous with *prepaid expense.*

deferred payment sale:
(1) **retailing:** buying on installment. See *layaway plan.*
(2) **sales:** a sale that is extended beyond a customary credit period.

deferred premium file: an electronic tape file maintained by a company office and used to record and report premium payments when due. Cf. *tickler file.*

deferred revenue: a liability that has been created through the receipt of cash by an entity before its performance of a service or the sale of goods.

deferred sale contract: a contract in which a purchaser pays the owner all or part of the sale price of a property through an obligation other than cash.

deferred serial bond: see *bond, deferred serial.*

deferred stock: stocks whose dividends are not to be paid until the expiration of a stated date or until a specified event has taken place.

deferred tax: a tax liability accrued on income that is reported but not subject to income tax until a later time period.

deferred wage increase: a future increase specified in a union contract (e.g., 10 cents the second year, five cents the third).

deficiency needs: a category of Maslow's hierarchy of needs; includes physiological, security, and belongingness needs.

deficit:
(1) **general:** the amount of obligations and expenditures affecting a given budget period that is in excess of the budget established for the period.
(2) **finance:** obligations or expenditures for items that are in excess of the amount allotted for those items in a financial budget.
(3) **accounting:** the excess of liabilities over assets.
(4) **business:** outgo in excess of income for a fiscal period.

deficit financing: when government expenditures exceed revenues, making up difference by borrowing. The objective is to expand business activity and yield an improvement in general economic conditions. The deficit is covered by release of government bonds. Cf. *deficit spending.*

deficit spending: the spending of public funds raised by borrowing rather than by taxation; a fiscal activity often associated with a government that spends more than it collects from taxes and other revenues. Some fiscal policy experts point out that an increase in the deficit stimulates the economy, whereas a decrease in the deficit has the opposite effect. Cf. *deficit financing.*

defined-benefit plan: benefit plan in which the amount an employee is to receive upon retirement is specifically set forth.

defined-contribution plan: pension plan that establishes the basis on which an employer will contribute to the pension fund.

definitive bond: see *bond, definitive.*

deflation:
(1) **general:** a decline in the general price level, resulting in an increase in the purchasing power of money. Cf. *inflation.*
(2) **economics:** the lessening of the amount of money in circulation.

deflationary gap: the amount by which demand falls short of full employment supply, thus lowering the real value of a nation's output.

defray: to pay; to carry an expense (e.g., a court settlement may include an amount of money to defray the legal costs of the winning party).

defunct company: a firm that has ceased to exist; a dissolved organization.

degree of freedom (d.o.f.): a concept in organizational theory that describes a person's exemption or liberation from the control of some other person or power. Often, within a tightly controlled company where the president dominates, employees are allowed a minimal degree of freedom. Cf. *autocratic.*

degressive taxation: a type of progressive taxation whereby the rates increase as the base amount taxed increases and each addition to the tax rate is lower than the preceding one.

dehire: to discharge from a position.

de jure: "by right" (*Latin*); rightful, legitimate, just; according to law or equity; describing a state of affairs or a condition based on right law, as distinguished from one that exists de facto. Cf. *de facto.*

delayed entry strategy: entering the work force at a later date.

delayed opening: the situation created when buy and sell orders accumulate prior to the opening of a stock exchange.

del credere agency: an agency, factor, or broker who attempts to guarantee to his or her principal the payment of a buyer's debt.

delectus personae: "chosen or selected person" (*Latin*), as a designated partner.

delegated strategy: an approach that precludes participation by management. Through case discussion or sensitivity training, the employees determine an organizational development program. See *organic structure*. Cf. *autocratic*.

delegating: having trained people complete tasks for entrepreneurs to help them save time.

delegation: the process by which authority is distributed downward in the organization. See *chain of command*.

delinquency: failure to pay a debt when due.

delinquent tax: a tax that is unpaid after the date when the payment was expected.

delisting: the removal or cancellation, by the SEC, of rights previously given to a listed security. This usually occurs when a security fails to meet some of the requirements for the listing privilege.

delivered cost: the price at which goods are billed to a store, including transportation charges.

delivery:

(1) **general:** the transfer of possession of an item from one person to another.

(2) **securities:** the transmission of the certificate representing shares bought on a securities exchange; delivery is usually made to the purchaser's broker on the fourth business day after the transaction. See *good delivery; seller's seven sale; settlement day.*

delivery date:

(1) **retailing:** the date by which a vendor must ship purchases to a store in order to comply with the agreed-upon terms. Failure by the store to meet this deadline is considered reason for cancellation of the order.

(2) **securities:** formally, the first day of the month during which delivery is to be made under a futures contract. Since sales are made at the seller's option, however, the seller can make delivery on any day of the month, following proper notification to the buyer.

Delphi technique: a forecasting approach whereby, at intervals, the organization polls experts who predict long-range technological and market changes that eventually will affect the organization. Cf. *chartist*.

deluxe items: higher-priced, unique goods maintained for sale to wealthier customers.

demand:

(1) **business:** the willingness and capability to purchase goods or services. See *market demand*.

(2) **business law:** a claim or the assertion of a legal right.

(3) **finance:** a request to call for payment or for the carrying out of an obligation. See *sight draft*.

demand deposit: a deposit on account in a commercial bank on which checks can be drawn and funds taken out without any advance notification. Demand deposits are the greatest part of our money supply.

demand loan: a loan that has no fixed maturity date but is payable on demand on the bank making the loan. *Demand loans* can be called by a bank at any time payment is desired.

demand note: a note or mortgage that can be demanded at any time for payment by the holder. See *scrip*.

demand price: the maximum price a purchaser is willing to pay for a stated quantity of a commodity or service.

demand-pull inflation: an increase in the price level created by an abundance of money for too few commodities. The demand for items is greater than the capability to produce or supply them.

demand schedule: a table illustrating the number of units of an item that purchasers would be able and willing to buy at differing prices at a specified time period, all other variables remaining constant.

demarketing: term coined by Philip Kotler and Sidney J. Levy for the concept that part of marketing attempts to discourage customers, either individually or collectively, from desiring a good or service.

democratic leadership: a participative or group-centered leadership in which the leader in charge attempts to encourage and aid workers in achieving goals by (1) requesting maximum initiative from and participation by members in deciding on and carrying out certain policies; (2) distributing or decreasing his leadership or authority roles and establishing close relationships with members; and (3) motivating and developing, rather than ordering or criticizing. See *distributive leadership; permissive leadership*.

demographics: the statistics of an area's population, or a market, with distinguishing characteristics such as age, sex, income, education, marital status, etc. Includes all vital statistics.

demolition clause: coverage provided by an endorsement because standard fire policies exclude liability for any loss caused by the demolition of an undamaged portion of the building due to the enforcement of "ordinance or law regulating construction or repair."

demonetization:

(1) **finance:** the withdrawal of specified currency from circulation.

(2) **banking:** the reduction in the number of government bonds and securities by a commercial bank, resulting in an increase in the value of deposit and paper currency, including Federal Reserve notes.

demotion: change of a worker's status to a lower classification, salary, or title.

demurrage: detention of a freight car or ship beyond the time permitted for loading or unloading, with additional charges for detention. See *average demurrage agreement.*

demurrer: a method of procedure in a lawsuit whereby the defendant admits the validity of all the plaintiff's complaints but denies that the facts warrant a cause of action.

denomination value: the face value of currencies, coins, and securities.

department: a major executive or administrative unit within an organization.

departmentalization: the manner in which an organization is structurally divided; for example, by function, territory, product, customer, or task.

departmentation: the organizing process of establishing subunits based on some common characteristic. Jobs are thus grouped by common functions, products, territories, customers, or processes.

department manager: an executive charged with the operation of a selling department of a store. Often this individual is the buyer, but he or she may also be involved with stock and sales.

Department of Agriculture, U.S.: created on May15, 1862; works to improve and maintain farm income and to develop and expand markets abroad for agricultural products.

Department of Commerce, U.S.: the federal department established on March 4, 1913; promotes the Nation's international trade, economic growth, and technological advancement.

Department of Defense, U.S.: redesignated in 1949; responsible for providing the military forces needed to deter war and protect the security of the nation.

Department of Education, U.S.: establishes policy for, administers, and coordinates most Federal assistance to education. Its mission is to ensure equal access to education and to promote educational excellence throughout the Nation.

Department of Energy, U.S.: the federal department established on October 1, 1977, to control oil prices and allocations, to coordinate energy research and development efforts, to set rates for oil and oil-product appliances, and to establish energy conservation standards.

Department of Health and Human Services, U.S.: redesignated on April 11, 1953; involved with the Nation's human concerns.

Department of Homeland Security, U.S.: a new federal department established in 2002 following terrorist attacks on the U.S. By absorbing 20 U.S. existing agencies, its primary task is to secure the country.

Department of Housing and Urban Development, U.S.: established in 1965; responsible for programs concerned with the nation's housing needs, fair housing opportunities, and improvement and development of the nation's communities.

Department of the Interior, U.S.: created by act of March 3, 1849; mission is to protect and provide access to the nation's natural and cultural heritage and honor its trust responsibilities to tribes and other commitments to island communities; manages public lands and minerals, national parks, national wildlife refuges, and much more.

Department of Justice, U.S.: the federal agency created on June 22, 1870, with supervisory powers over federal prosecuting agencies, representing the federal government to the courts. The department has jurisdiction over issues of antitrust and civil rights and supervises the government's activities relating to immigration.

Department of Labor, U.S.: the federal agency created on March 4, 1913, to advance workers' welfare, working conditions, and employment opportunities in general.

Department of State, U.S.: established on July 27, 1789; advises the President in the formulation and execution of foreign policy and promotes the long-range security and well-being of the country.

Department of Transportation, U.S.: established on October 15, 1966; sets the nation's overall transportation policy; supervises 11 agencies.

Department of the Treasury, U.S.: the federal agency created on September 2, 1789, to impose and collect taxes and customs duties, to enforce revenue and fiscal laws, to disburse federal funds, to manage the public debt, and to coin and print money.

Department of Veterans Affairs, U.S.: the federal agency established on March 15, 1989 (succeeding the Veterans Administration). It operates programs to benefit veterans and members of their families.

department store: a retail organization that employs 25 or more people and sells merchandise in the following categories: home furnishings; apparel for men, women, and children; and home linens and dry goods.

department store banking: synonymous with *multiple banking.*

departure point: the time when dissatisfaction and frustration with his or her present job causes an entrepreneur to consider leaving to form a new venture.

dependency ratio: the ratio between the number of workers in a society and the number of people who are retired.

dependent: an individual who requires support from another, as distinguished from one who merely derives a benefit from the earnings of another.

dependent covenants: two or more related agreements by which the performance of one promise must take place before the performance of other promises (e.g., a buyer must pay for goods before the purchased items will be delivered).

dependent nations: nations that rely heavily on other nations for imports of essential goods.

depletion: an accounting practice consisting of charges against earnings based on the amount of an asset taken out of the total reserves in the period for which accounting is made. A bookkeeping entry, depletion does not represent any cash outlay, nor are any funds earmarked for the purpose.

depletion allowance: as permitted by the Internal Revenue Code, a deduction from taxable income derived from a wasting asset. The basis of the allowance is either a percentage of the gross income from specified property or a per-unit-of-product condition.

deposit: an amount of funds consisting of cash and/or checks, drafts, coupons, and other credit items that may be converted into cash upon collection. The deposit is given to a bank for the purpose of establishing and maintaining a credit balance.

depositary: an individual or institution identified as one to be entrusted with something of value for safekeeping (e.g., a bank or trust company).

depositary receipt: a mechanism to allow for the trading of foreign stocks on U.S. stock exchanges when the overseas nation involved will not allow foreign ownership of the stock of domestic firms. The shares are therefore deposited with a bank in the country of corporation and an affiliated or correspondent bank in the United States issues depositary receipts for the securities. U.S. investors buy these receipts and can trade them on an appropriate American stock exchange in the same way as other stocks. The major purpose of the instrument is to officially identify ownership of the stock in the foreign country.

deposit contraction: an excess of loan repayments to commercial banks over new loans.

deposit creation multiplier: the dollars of lending generated by an independent increase of one dollar in bank deposits.

deposit currency: checks and other credit items deposited with a bank as the equivalent of cash.

deposit expansion: an excess of new commercial bank loans over loan repayments.

deposit funds: funds established to account for collection that either are held in suspense temporarily and later refunded or are paid into some other fund of the government or held by the government as banker or agent for others. Cf. *escrow.*

deposit insurance: insurance to protect the depositor against bankruptcy of a bank or a savings and loan institution. See *Federal Deposit Insurance Corporation.*

depositor: an individual, partnership, business proprietorship, corporation, organization, or association in whose name funds have been placed in a bank.

depository bond: see *bond, depository.*

Depository Institutions Deregulation Committee: committee created by Congress in the spring of 1980, charged with deregulation of the bank and savings industry. It has a panel of five voting members: the Federal Reserve Board chairman, the Treasury Secretary, and the chairmen of the Federal Home Loan Bank Board, the Federal Deposit Insurance Corporation, and the National Credit Union Administration.

deposit premium: the deposit on premiums required by the company on forms of insurance subject to periodic premium adjustment.

depot store: a store carrying popular items that customers purchase because of the store's convenient location. In most cases, the customer is charged higher prices for the items than in supermarkets, discount stores, and other non–depot outlets.

depreciated cost: cost less accumulated depreciation and less other valuation accounts, having the effect of reducing the original outlay to a recoverable cost; the book value of a fixed asset.

depreciation: normally, charges against earnings to write off the cost, less salvage value, of an asset over its estimated useful life. It is a bookkeeping entry and does not represent any cash outlay, nor are any funds earmarked for the purpose. Synonymous with *capital consumption allowance.* See *declining balance depreciation.*

depreciation base: the amount that the internal Revenue Service recognizes as depreciable on a property's improvements. For depreciation purposes, the value of the land and that of the improvements must be determined separately.

depreciation charges: charges made by private business and nonprofit institutions against receipts to account for the decrease in value of capital assets as a result of wear, accidental damage, and obsolescence, plus an estimate of corresponding depreciation in owner-occupied dwellings.

depressed area: a community that is not part of the nation's economic growth pattern and has a high level of unemployment; sometimes referred to as a "distressed area."

depression: an economic condition in which business activity is down over a long period, prices drop, purchasing power is greatly reduced, and unemployment is high. Cf. *prosperity.*

Depression of the 1930s: the Great Depression, a severe economic crisis that afflicted the United States and also affected worldwide business; thought to have begun with the collapse of the stock market in October 1929 and finally ended in the early 1940s, when defense spending for World War II strengthened the general economy.

depth interview: a method, based primarily on the use of open-ended questions, to elicit from the person interviewed natural and lengthy statements about a predetermined subject. Cf. *interest inventory; interview, unstructured.*

derivative departments: departments formed through the subdivision of major departments (e.g., derivative production departments could include manufacturing and purchasing).

derivative deposit: a deposit that is created when a person borrows money from a bank (e.g., deposit currency). A customer is loaned a sum, not in money but by credit to his account, against which he or she may draw checks as required.

derived demand: the demand for an item that grows out of the wish to fulfill the demand for another item (e.g., when a demand for community tennis courts is filled, it leads to increased sales of supplies for the courts and tennis equipment). Cf. *suggestive selling.*

descriptive billing: a billing system in which an account statement is not accompanied by copies of original invoices. Instead, the statement contains sufficient detail to nature, date, and amount of each transaction processed during the statement period. Cf. *country club billing.*

descriptive decision making: a viewpoint of decision making that emphasizes what is occurring or what has happened in reaching a decision. It describes the decision and its process.

descriptive research: research concerned with determining the nature of something (e.g., the morale of employees). Cf. *applied research.*

desired investment: investments in plant, equipment, buildings, and inventories that were deliberately undertaken, as compared with inventory changes forced on a company by a period of slow sales.

desk audit: a systematic process of interviewing and/or observing workers at their place of activity to measure and identify factors affecting the completion of stated objectives. Synonymous with *work audit.*

deskilled: describing simple tasks or jobs that, because of work simplification or other reasons, require little or no skill to perform; also said of workers who perform such tasks or jobs. See *work simplification.*

desk jockey: (slang) an office employee; a person who works at an office desk.

detention time: additional charges made by the carrier when there is a lack of equipment or space on a store's receiving docks to enable the carrier to unload merchandise.

determinant attributes: product characteristics that help consumers discriminate among products and that influence product preferences. See *brand awareness.*

devaluation: an action taken by the   government to reduce the value of the domestic currency in terms of gold or foreign monies.

development:

(1) **general:** a gradual unfolding by virtue of which something comes to be.

(2) **administration:** a criterion of effectiveness that refers to the ability of an organization to increase its capacity to react to existing or anticipated pressures.

development expense: the cost of developing products, processes, or other commercial activities to make them functional.

development loan: a short-term loan, generally up to three years, for the development of unimproved land by the installation of utilities, drainage, sewers, and roads.

deviation:

(1) **general:** a measure of dispersion, calculated to be the difference between the particular number or item and the average, which is usually the arithmetic mean, or a set of numbers or items.

(2) **insurance:** a rate or policy form differing from that published by a rating bureau.

devisee: any person receiving title to real property in accordance with the terms of a will.

dexterity test: a measure of speed and accuracy in performing simple manual activities.

diagnostic skills: used by managers to understand cause-and-effect relationships and to recognize the optimal solutions to problems.

diagnostic systems: expert systems that lead machine operators and mechanics through step-by-step analyses of equipment problems and provide repair instructions.

diagonal communication: communication that involves the flow of information across departments or people at different levels of the hierarchy. It allows for messages to be transmitted directly instead of emanating from the bottom up to the top and down again.

diagonal expansion: a process whereby a business grows by creating new items that can be produced with the equipment that is already in use, requiring few additional materials.

dialectic process of change: the concept that any change introduced by management will create a new situation out of which new problems will develop.

diamond-water paradox: an argument of Adam Smith's theory that asks why there is such a high demand for diamonds and a low demand for water when water is a necessity and diamonds are a luxury.

diary method: a technique used to determine brand purchase and frequency of buying. The user makes arrangements with households to keep a continuous log of brands purchased day by day over a specified period. See *Videodex*. Cf. *aided recall; coincidental telephone method.*

Dictionary of Occupational Titles (DOT): published by the U.S. Employment Service, a reference book that lists alphabetically and describes 20,000 jobs. It is the most complete source book of its kind. Cf. *Standard Industrial Classification System.*

Diemer plan: a wage incentive plan providing for the regular day rates to be paid plus an increase of 0.5 percent salary for each 1 percent production above the task, with a bonus of 10 percent.

dies non: a day on which no business can be transacted (*Latin*).

differential advantages: selling characteristics that provide an advantage over competitors. These include price, product features, location, method of delivery, advertising skills, packaging, and brand name.

differential costs: the difference in costs between an actual situation and a proposed one.

differential marginal productivity: condition that exists when the marginal product of a productive factor drops when more of the productive factor is added to the given quantities of other factors.

differential oligopoly: an industry composed of a small number of sellers manufacturing products that are only slightly different. Cf. *oligopoly.*

differential piece-rate system: an inventive wage system whereby a fixed rate is paid for all production up to standard but there is a higher rate for all pieces once the standard is crossed.

differentiated marketing: a form of market segmentation in which the marketer employs different products and/or different marketing programs to reach two or more market segments.

differentiation: the process by which subunits in an organization develop particular attributes in response to the requirements imposed by their subenvironments. The greater the differences among the subunits' attributes, the greater the differentiation. Cf. *subenvironment.*

diffusion theory: the theory that tax income is eventually distributed throughout the population by price alterations or other means whereby funds find their way to the government.

digested securities: securities owned by investors who are not expected to sell them soon. Cf. *stag.*

dilution:
(1) **general:** the watering down or weakening of something.
(2) **securities:** the effect of a drop in earnings per share or book value per share caused by the potential conversion of securities or by the potential exercise of warrants or options.

dimension of planning: the five factors involved in planning: organization, subject, elements, time, and characteristics.

diminishing marginal utility law: the concept that, in a specified period, the consumption of an item while tastes stay the same can lead to increasing marginal utilities per unit of the item consumed, but a point will be reached when additional units of consumption of the item will lead to decreasing marginal utilities per unit of the item consumed.

diminishing returns: a condition that exists when, in successively applying equal amounts of one or two factors of production (e.g., land and capital) to the remaining factor(s), an additional application produces a smaller increase in production than the preceding application. Cf. *indifference schedule; point of indifference.*

direct advertising: print advertising sent by mail to prospects, salesmen, and dealers, in contrast to advertising presented by other media.

direct control: the process of developing better managers to make more skillful use of concepts, principles, and techniques to reduce the amount and degree of undesirable results.

direct cost: the cost of any good or service that contributes to the production of an item or service (e.g., labor, material). Cf. *fixed costs; indirect costs.* See *running costs.* Synonymous with *direct expense.*

direct costing: a technique for implementing the economic theory of marginal analysis to assist a firm in making short-term business decisions.

direct deposit of payroll: a payroll system in which employee earnings are deposited directly to the employee's account at a depository institution. direct expenditures: payments to employees, suppliers, contractors, beneficiaries, and other final recipients of government payment (i.e., all expenditures other than intergovernmental expenditure).

direct expense: synonymous with *direct cost.*

direct financial compensation: the pay a person receives in the form of wages, salaries, bonuses, and commissions.

direct financing: raising capital without resorting to underwriting (e.g., by selling capital stock).

directing: the process through which employees are led and motivated to make effective and efficient contributions to the realization of organizational goals.

direct investments: investments in foreign corporations when the investors have a controlling interest in the overseas firm.

directive counseling: the process of listening to an employee's emotional problems, deciding with the worker what should be done, and then telling and motivating the employee to do it. See *cooperative counseling; nondirective counseling.*

direct labor: the cost of wages paid to workers.

direct liability: a debtor's obligation arising from money, goods, or services received by him or her from another.

direct-mail list: names and addresses of potential customers, purchased by or given without charge to an organization.

direct marketing:
(1) a marketing strategy where the advertising message may be delivered by a variety of media rather than through the mail or a subordinate section of a local advertisement.
(2) the activity of selling to consumers or industrial users without the use of middlemen.

direct material: all raw material that is an integral part of the finished good and can be conveniently assigned to specific physical units.

director: any person elected by shareholders to establish company policies. The directors appoint the president, vice presidents, and all other operating officers. Directors decide, among other matters, if and when dividends shall be paid.

directorate: a corporation's board of directors.

directory advertising: advertising that appears in printed directories (e.g., telephone books, city directories).

direct expenditures: payments to employees, suppliers, contractors, beneficiaries, and other financial recipients of government payment (i.e., all expenditures other than intergovernmental expenditure).

direct overhead: factory, selling, or other expenses related directly to a specific product and resulting in a direct cost. Cf. *overhead*.

direct selling: a manufacturer selling directly to the user, the retailer, or the final consumer without the intervention of a middleman.

direct write-off method: the recording of actual losses from uncollectible accounts as expenses during the period in which accounts receivable are determined to be uncollectible. Cf. *allowance method*.

dirty float: a situation in which exchange rates are allowed to fluctuate in the market but national monetary authorities intervene to control the extent of the fluctuation.

disability income: a benefit provided by a specific health insurance contract that indemnifies the insured for loss of time in the event of sickness or accident. Cf. *state disability plan*. See *temporary total disability benefits; workmen's compensation*.

disagio: the charge made for exchanging depreciated foreign monies. Cf. *agio*.

disbursement: an actual payment of funds toward the full or partial settlement of an obligation.

discharge:

(1) **personnel:** to fire. Synonymous with *dismiss.*

(2) **business law:** the release of one party from meeting his or her obligation under a contract because other parties to the contract have failed to meet their obligation(s).

discharge of contract: the fulfillment of a contract's obligations.

disciplinary layoff: suspension of an employee because of violation of company rules.

disciplinary review board: an internally created organizational committee to review a worker's performance; often results in a warning to an employee that he or she is breaking company rules.

discipline: the state of employee's self-control and orderly conduct present in an organization.

discipline without punishment: a process whereby a worker is given time off with pay when disciplinary action is suggested to determine if he or she really wants to follow the rules and continue working.

disclaimer: a document, or a clause in a document, that renounces or repudiates the liability of an otherwise responsible party in the event of (1) noncompliance by such other party to certain conditions described in the instrument, (2) named external conditions, or (3) losses incurred because of a discrepancy in the goods delivered and the weight or count made by the shipper.

disclosure: see *full disclosure.*

discontinuous market: as differentiated from continuously listed securities, the unlisted stocks and bonds that form a separate market.

discotetic: describing the chaos resulting from continuous shifts and changes within an organization that fail to yield constructive results in attaining a primary objective or goal.

discount:

(1) **finance:** the amount of money deducted from the face value of a note.

(2) **securities:** the amount by which a preferred stock or bond sells below its par value.

(3) **securities:** to take into account (e.g., the price of the stock has discounted the expected dividend cut).

(4) **foreign exchange:** the relationship of one currency to another. (e.g., Canadian currency may be at a discount to United States currency).

(5) **sales:** the selling of an item or service at a price below the normal list price. See *bulk discount*. Cf. *rebate*.

discounted cash flow methods: capital budgeting techniques that take into account the time value of money. See *internal rate of return; net present value.*

discounted present value: a technique of evaluating projects where the discounted future cash flows are compared to the outlay needed.

discounted rate of return: the rate of return that equates future cash proceeds and the initial cost of the investment.

discount factor: the reciprocal of one plus the discount rate.

discount house (store): a retail operation in which prices are lower than at other stores selling the same merchandise.

discounting: an institution lending money to a business with a customer's debt obligation to the firm as security on the loan.

discounting notes receivable: securing cash through selling a note(s) receivable to a bank or other agent for an amount less than the proceeds at maturity. When the note is transferred to the financial institution without qualification, the original holder remains liable if payment is not made.

discounting the news: the situation occurring when a stock's price or the level of a major market indicator climbs or falls in expectation of a good or bad occurrence, then barely moves when the actual development takes place and is announced.

discount loading: in retailing, an internal bookkeeping computation that places all inventory and purchase figures on a comparable basis by recalculating all invoice prices to reflect an assumed desirable cash discount percent.

discount on bonds payable: the difference between the par value of bonds payable and a lower initial sales price. At maturity there is no discount and the bonds are shown at their principal value.

discount order quantity: the order quantity calculated based on a discount that a vendor gives if a fairly large minimum quantity is ordered.

discount period: the time between the date a note is issued or sold to a financial institution and its maturity date.

discount points: the amount of money sometimes paid by a borrower to the lender to make up the difference between the current interest rate and that allowed by a government-insured loan. The discount points paid by the borrower increase the effective loan yield to the lender. Each point is equal to one percent of the loan amount.

discount rate: the interest rate charged by the Federal Reserve System to its members; an interest rate used in evaluating expenditures that measures the relative value of benefits or returns obtained now, as compared with later.

discovery period: under certain insurance policies, a provision to give the insured a period of time after the cancellation of a contract in which to discover whether he or she has sustained a loss that would have been recoverable if the contract had remained in force. The period may be determined by statute.

discretionary account: an account in which the customer gives the broker or someone else the authority, which may be complete or within specific limits, to purchase and sell securities or commodities, including selection, timing, amount, and price to be paid or received.

discretionary costs: fixed costs arising from periodic, usually yearly, appropriation decisions that directly reflect top-management policies.

discretionary policy: monetary policy, purporting to compensate for a business cycle, that leads to a decision by a person or government.

discretionary spending power: money available to consume after necessities have been purchased. Cf. *disposable income.*

discrimination: prejudice or differentiation in the screening, hiring, promoting, discharging, and so on, of individuals based on race, religion, place of birth, or other non-job-related reasons. See *Civil Rights Act of 1964; sex differential.*

discriminatory discharge: firing of an employee for union activity; an unfair labor practice under the Taft-Hartley Act.

diseconomies of scale: situations that occur when costs increase as a business grows in size. For all firms, there is a point at which, as the company becomes larger, costs also increase. See *agglomeration diseconomies; internal economies scale; law of increasing costs; point of indifference.*

disequilibrium: a condition in which incentives to change exist; usually used in reference to markets in which either purchasers or producers, or both, have not yet adjusted prices and quantities to their satisfaction.

disestablishment: a National Labor Relations Board procedure to divest an organization of its claim to represent the employees and its status as a labor organization.

dishonored: a negotiable instrument offered for acceptance of payment that is turned down or cannot be obtained. See *notice of dishonor.*

disinflation: the result of a strategy to reduce the general price level by increasing the purchasing power of money.

disintermediation: the taking of money out of interest-bearing time accounts (e.g., savings and commercial bank accounts) for reinvestment at higher rates for bonds and the like. See *intermediation*.

disinvestments: reduction of capital goods.

dismiss:
    (1) **personnel:** to release an employee.
    (2) **business law:** to dispose of a case without a trial.

dismissal pay: payment in addition to regular wages to an employee who has been dismissed. It is usually based on both wage rate and length of service. Frequently the payee has the option of taking a lump sum or deferred payments. Synonymous with *severance pay; termination pay*.

dispatcher: an agent responsible for efficiently routing and sending merchandise to its destined location.

dispatching: the control and flow of pickups and deliveries of freight and the intercity movement of cargo.

display advertisement: an advertisement that uses attention-attracting features, such as illustrations, white space, or colors. Cf. *classified advertising*.

disposable income: personal income minus income taxes and other taxes paid by an individual, the balance being available for consumption or savings. See *discretionary spending power; personal saving*.

disproduct: a damaging item, particularly one that results from negligence on the part of the manufacturer.

disqualification: the inability to work or to continue in employment for physical, mental, legal, or other reasons.

dissatisfiers: used by F. Herzberg to describe events that do not bring about continuous worker satisfaction. The concept suggests that the continued presence of such conditions (e.g., improved working conditions, increased salary) will not bring satisfaction but that their absence can create dissatisfaction. See *decision to participate; maintenance factors; motivator-hygiene theory; organizational climate*. Cf. *satisfiers*. Synonymous with *hygiene factors*.

dissaving: a lowering of net worth, caused by spending more than one's current income.

disseminator role: a supervisor's role involving passing along special or privileged information that subordinates would not otherwise be able to obtain.

dissolution (corporate): termination of a corporation at the expiration of its charter, by order of the attorney general of the state, by consolidation, or by action of the stockholders.

dissolution (partnership): termination of a partnership at a specified time by the wishes of the partners or by operation of law because of incapacity, death, or bankruptcy of any partner.

distant: designation of a month in the distant future, or not near in time, when a contract has recently commenced.

distressed area: see *depressed area*.

distress for rent: the taking of a tenant's personal property in payment of rent on real estate. See *general lien*.

distress merchandise: goods that must be sold at reduced prices.

distress selling: selling because of necessity; occurs when securities owned on margin are sold because lowered prices have hurt equities.

distribution:

(1) **marketing:** the separation of merchandise into different categories and group levels.

(2) **finance:** the division of something among several people or entities.

(3) **finance:** the division of aggregate income of a community among its members.

(4) **securities:** the selling, over a time period, of a large block of stock without unduly depressing the market price. Cf. *secondary distribution*.

(5) **accounting:** the process of allocating income and expenses to the appropriate subsidiary accounts.

distribution center: a warehouse in which the emphasis is on processing and moving goods rather than on simple storage.

distribution cost analysis: when marketing an item in a particular location, the breaking down of all direct and indirect costs.

distributive leadership: the process of delegating leadership roles and responsibilities to or sharing them with other group members. See *democratic leadership*.

distributor: synonymous with *wholesaler*.

diversification:

(1) **securities:** spreading investments among different companies in different fields. Another type of diversification is offered by the securities of many individual companies whose activities cover a wide range.

(2) **securities:** the purchase of varying assets in order to minimize the risk associated with a portfolio.

(3) **manufacturing:** the manufacture or sale of unrelated products.

divest: to remove a vested right.

divest-and-exit strategy: efforts designed to eliminate a product or service line by selling or discontinuing it.

dividend: a portion of a firm's net profits that has been officially declared by the board of directors for distribution to stockholders. A dividend is paid at a fixed amount for each share of stock held by the stockholders. Cf. *Irish dividend*.

dividend check: a negotiable instrument in the form of a check drawn on a depository bank of the corporation issuing the dividend. It is signed by the secretary of the corporation.

dividend payout ratio: the ratio of dividends per share of common stock to earnings per share of common stock.

dividend rate: the indicated annual rate of payment to a shareholder based on a company's latest quarterly dividend and recurring extra or special year-end dividends.

dividends in arrears: missed dividends for past years that preferred stockholders have a right to receive under their cumulative-dividend preference when dividends are declared.

dividends per share: the dollar amount of dividends paid to stockholders for each share owned of a corporation's common stock.

divisionalization: the creation of autonomous units in an organization. Responsibility for performance rests with a divisional or sectional manager, who is permitted to operate the division as if it were separate from the parent organization. See *decentralization*.

division of labor:

(1) **administration:** see *horizontal specialization; vertical specialization*.

(2) **personnel:** breaking a job down into the smallest number of operations without jeopardizing performance. See *functional foremanship*.

dock:

(1) **transportation:** a landing area used for receiving ships between voyages.

(2) **personnel:** to deduct a part of an employee's wages (e.g., an hourly worker may be docked for coming to work late). See *docking*.

dockage and moorage: synonymous with *wharfage*.

docking: pay deduction for breakages, poor work, absenteeism, lateness, and similar causes.

DOE: see *Department of Energy, U.S.*

d.o.f.: see *degree of freedom*.

dole: welfare payments.

dollar:

(1) **general:** the monetary unit of the United States. See *purchasing power of the dollar.*

(2) **finance:** the monetary unit of other nations, (e.g., Canada, Ethiopia, Malaya).

dollar cost averaging: a system of buying securities at regular intervals with a fixed dollar amount. The investor buys by the dollar's worth rather than by the number of shares. If each investment is of the same number of dollars, payments buy more shares when the price is low and fewer when it rises.

dollar drain (gap): the amount by which imports from the United States into a foreign country exceed the nation's exports to the United States.

dollar merchandise plan: an estimate of anticipated sales, frequently over a six-month period, integrated with inventory estimates and purchase in harmony with sales and profit goals.

dollar overhang: excess of actual over desired holdings of dollars by foreign central banks.

dollar shortage: a nation's lack of sufficient money to buy from the United States, caused by a steadily favorable balance of payments for the United States.

domestic corporation: a corporation doing business in the state in which it has been incorporated.

Domestic exchange ratio: the relative costs of producing two goods domestically. The exchange ratio is the opportunity cost of one good in terms of the other. See *opportunity cost.*

dominant coalition: the major top-level decision makers of an organization.

domination: achieving objectives by direct command; utilizing power or influence to impose one's will on others within the firm.

doomsday strike: a threatened strike that may occur immediately, before the beginning of contract negotiations, thus putting pressure on management.

door-to-door selling: selling of a product or service directly from the manufacturer by the manufacturer's employee to potential customers in their homes or offices. This process eliminates the middleman, with the expectation of cutting costs. See *house-to-house salesman.*

dormant account: an account that has had little or no activity for a period of time. Synonymous with *inactive account.*

dormant partner: a partner not known to the public at large who is entitled to participate in the profits and is subject to the losses. See *secret partner.*

DOT: see *Dictionary of Occupational Titles.*

double coincidence of wants: situation in a barter exchange when each party must possess precisely what the other wishes and must be able to trade at the exact amount and terms agreeable to both.

double counting (entry): in bookkeeping, since every transaction is entered two times, counting the same quantity twice when evolving a total; procedure used in determining the gross national product.

double-decker: two outdoor advertising panels built one above the other.

double employment: holding down two jobs at the same time. Synonymous with *moonlighting.*

double entry: a method of recording transactions that requires that an increase in one account reflect an increase or decrease in another account. The total debits of each entry must equal the total credits. See *journalize. Cf.* single entry.

double indemnity: a provision in a life insurance policy, subject to specified conditions and exclusions, whereby double the face amount of the policy is payable if the death of the insured is the result of an accident.

double insurance: insurance purchased to insure against the same risk twice. Usually, it is impossible to obtain more than the loss suffered. If a risk is insured against twice, one firm will claim contribution from the other. See *excess coverage clause; nonconcurrency.* Cf. *other-insurance clause; pro rata distribution clause.*

double-page spread: an advertisement appearing on two facing pages.

double taxation: short for double taxation of dividends. The federal government taxes corporate profits once as corporate income; the remaining profits, distributed as dividends to stockholders, are taxed again as income to the recipient stockholders.

double time: twice the regular rate of pay for overtime, Sunday work, or holiday work.

double truck: see *double-page spread.*

douceur: a bribe or gratuity (French); term dating from the eighteenth century.

Dow-Jones averages: the averages of closing prices of 30 representative industrial stocks, 15 public utility stocks, 20 transportation stocks, and an average of the 65 stocks computed at the end of a trading day on the New York Stock Exchange. Cf. *NYSE Common Stock Index; Standard & Poor's 500 Stock Average.*

downer: a brief work stoppage to draw attention to a particular grievance. Cf. *strike.*

downgrading: a form of demotion created by a reduction in corporate functions.

down payment: a partial payment, made at the time of purchase, to permit the buyer to take the merchandise.

down periods: the shutdown of plant operations to permit cleaning, repair, and maintenance of equipment.

downsizing: the reduction of a firm's workforce, by attrition, layoff, or other means.

downstairs merger: a merger of a parent corporation into a subsidiary.

downstream: describing movement of a business activity from a higher to a lower level (e.g., a loan from a parent company to one of its subsidiaries).

downtime:

(1) **administration:** a period during which a worker is idled because a machine breaks down or the flow of materials is interrupted. Cf. *dead time.*

(2) **manufacturing:** the time interval during which a device is malfunctioning.

downward channel: the path used by management for sending orders, directives, goals, policies, memoranda, and so on, to employees at lower levels in the organization.

downward communication: the flow of information from higher levels of an organization to lower levels. Cf. *upward communication.*

Dow theory: a theory of market analysis based on the performance of the Dow-Jones industrial and transportation stock price averages. The market is said to be in a basic upward trend if one of these averages advances above a previous important high, accompanied or followed by a similar advance in the other. When both averages dip below previous important lows, this is regarded as confirmation of a basic downward trend. The theory does not attempt to predict how long either trend will continue, although it is widely misinterpreted as a method of forecasting future action. See *Dow-Jones averages.* Cf. *chartist.*

draw: the amount of money allowed a salesperson each week to pay his or her expenses until the results of the salesperson's efforts are known and total compensation is computed, usually based on commissions.

drawback: repayment of an important duty, in part or in full, made when imported items are re-exported instead of being retained for domestic consumption.

drawee: any party expected to pay the sum listed on a check, draft, or bill of exchange.

drawer: any party who draws a check, draft, or bill of exchange for the payment of funds.

drawing account: a regular allowance made available to salespeople employed on a straight commission basis. The commission earned is balanced against the drawing account at various intervals.

drawings: a temporary account for recording withdrawals of cash or other assets from a partnership or proprietorship by the owner(s).

drawn bond: see *bond, drawn.*

drop dead list: (slang) employees selected to be fired from their job.

drop shipment: merchandise shipped directly from the manufacturer to retailer. The wholesaler receives only the invoice and then bills the retailer.

drop shipper: a wholesaler who performs most wholesaling activities except storage and handling. He sends requests to the manufacturer, who ships directly to the customer. The customer pays the drop shipper, who has already paid his bill to the manufacturer. See *jobber.*

drummer: a traditional American style of salesman who calls on retailers of soft goods or meets them at buying centers.

dual banking: since some banks are chartered by the state in which they operate and others by the federal government, a system whereby each independent component cooperates with the other to offer its clientele complete banking services.

dual billing and posting: posting a customer's purchases to ledger independently from the preparation of a bill for the customer.

dual distribution: sales of a product through more than one distributive system.

dual labor market: a labor market consisting of a primary labor market, in which jobs are high paying and possess adequate working conditions and job security, and a second labor market, in which jobs are scarce, pay lower wages, have poor working conditions, and claim a high turnover of employees.

dual mutual funds: funds that divide their portfolios between capital growth investments and income investments.

dual-purpose fund: synonymous with *split investment company.*

dual savings plan: a plan whereby two separate operations are required to post a savings deposit or a withdrawal to an account.

dual-structure theory: identifies motivation factors, which affect satisfaction, as well as hygiene factors, which affect dissatisfaction.

dual supervision: a form of control whereby supervisory authority and responsibility for discharging the policies of the firm are divided between a line officer and a staff officer of similar rank, each of whom is answerable to the same manager. See *line-and-staff authority*.

due care: the standard of conduct displayed by an ordinary, reasonable, prudent individual. See *prudent man rule*.

due date: the date on which an instrument of debt becomes payable; the maturity date.

due process of law: all actions of a court taken to ensure the rights of private individuals before the law; all legal steps to protect these rights; a court order to compel compliance with its wishes (e.g., a summons issued to compel attendance in court).

dues: monthly sums paid by union members to the local. The amount of the dues is sometimes set by the international union but more often by the local.

dummy invoice: a statement prepared by a retailer as a temporary replacement for a vendor's invoice if the latter is not available when the goods are to be received, marked, and put in inventory.

dump: to offer large blocks of stock for purposes of disposal, with little concern for price or the effect on the market. See *profit taking*.

dumping:
(1) selling items to other countries at below cost to eliminate surplus or to hurt foreign competition.
(2) in the United States, selling imported items at prices less than the cost of manufacture. See *boomerang*.

dun: to press for payment of a debt; to demand repeatedly what one is owed.

Dun and Bradstreet (D&B): the oldest and largest mercantile agency in the United States, offering credit data and ratings on business concerns.

Dun's Market Identifiers: a published system that identifies firms with an absolute identification number and provides regularly updated economic information on each company (e.g., address code; number of workers; and corporate affiliation).

duopoly: an industry containing two businesses that sell the identical items. In a duopoly, both firms exercise control.

duopsony: a market situation in which only two buyers are seeking an item. Cf. *monopsony; oligopsony.*

duplication: in advertising, reaching the same person or household by two or more media.

durability:
(1) **general:** the lasting quality of an item.
(2) **finance:** money that can be used over an extended period or that can be replaced at minimal cost.

durable merchandise: goods that have a relatively lengthy life (television sets, radio, etc.).

duress (property): forced seizure or withholding of goods by an individual who is not entitled to possess them, and the demands made by such a person as a condition for the release of the goods.

Dutch auction: an auction sale in which the prices on items are continuously lowered until a bidder responds favorably and buys.

duty:
(1) **economics:** an actual tax collected.
(2) **business law:** a legal requirement established by law or voluntarily imposed by the creation of a binding promise. A legal right accompanies every legal duty.
(3) **customs:** a tax imposed on the importation, exportation, or consumption of goods. Cf. *customs.*

duty drawback: a tariff concession allowing a rebate of all or part of the duty on goods imported for processing before being re-exported. See *production sharing.*

duty free: describing items that are not affected by any customs duty. See *free list.*

duty to bargain: the obligation, under the Taft–Hartley Act, of employers and employees to bargain in good faith.

dynamic economy: an economy of growth and change.

dynamiter: (slang) a securities broker who attempts to sell fraudulent or unregistered stocks and bonds over the telephone. Cf. *boiler room tactic.*

dysfunction: synonymous with *malfunction.*

dysfunctional behavior: actions that are in conflict with top-management goal.

dysfunctional conflict: any conflict that results in decreased efficiency and greater factionalism within the organization.

E

each way: trading on both the buying and selling sides of a transaction. The broker earns a commission of 3 percent each way (i.e., 3 percent for selling and another 3 percent for executing the purchase order).

eager beaver: (slang) an employee who appears overly diligent to his coworkers, especially one who attempts to impress his superiors with his desire to work hard.

EAI: see *Enterprise for the Americas Initiative.*

early retirement benefits: the reduced pension received by some employees when they voluntarily leave their company prior to the mandatory retirement age.

earned income: income derived from goods and services rendered as well as pension and annuity income. See *Tax Reform Act of 1976.* Cf. *unearned income.*

earned income credit: under the Economic Growth and Tax Relief Reconciliation Act of 2001, the phaseout amount for the earned income credit was increased for joint returns by $1,000 for taxable years beginning in 2002–4; $2,000 in 2005–7; $3,000 after 2007. See *Economic Growth and Tax Relief Reconciliation Act of 2001.*

earned rate: the amount an advertiser pays for media space or time actually used.

earnest money: money given by a contracting party to another at the time of the signing of a contract to bind the bargain. This sum is forfeited by the donor if he or she fails to carry out the contract.

earning power: an employee's potential capacity on his or her job to earn wages over a period of time usually the normal span of years during which the worker is productive.

earnings: the total remuneration received by a worker for a given period as compensation for services rendered, for work performed, as a commission, as overtime, and so on. Cf. *payroll deductions; wage.* Synonymous with *net income.*

earnings per share: the portion of a corporation's net income that relates to each share of the corporation's common stock that has been issued and is outstanding.

earnings potential: the ability of a firm to generate positive future net cash flows from operations.

earnings report: a statement issued by a company showing its earnings or losses over a given period. The earnings report lists the income earned, the expenses, and the net result.

earn-out: an agreement between two merging firms where the amount of payment by the acquiring unit to the acquired firm's shareholders depends on the future earnings of the consolidated entity.

easy money: money that can be obtained at low interest rates and with relative ease as the result of sufficient supply of a bank's excess reserves.

E.C.: see *European Community.*

echelon: the level of activity within a firm characterized by the degree of decision-making assigned.

ECOA: see *Equal Credit Opportunity Act.*

e-commerce: see *electronic commerce.*

econometrics: the discipline of economics that measures economic data for the purpose of increasing knowledge and forecasting ability in that field.

economic: any action having to do with the evolution of goods and services that are purported to satisfy a human condition.

economic climate: the degree of market and financial risks associated with investments.

economic costs: payments to the owners of the requirements for manufacturing to convince them to supply their resources in a specified activity.

economic efficiency: synonymous with *Pareto optimality.*

economic element: the part of the mega-environment that encompasses the systems of producing, distributing, and consuming wealth.

economic goods: items produced from scarce resources.

Economic Growth and Tax Relief Reconciliation Act of 2001: attempting to jump-start the economy; signed into law by President George W. Bush on June 7, 2001, the Act will reduce individual income tax rates by: (a) creating a new 10% rate bracket and a rate-reduction credit in lieu of the 10% rate for 2001. There is no 10% bracket for estates and trusts. The new 10% bracket is estimated to cost $421 billion. (b) expanding the 15% bracket for joint return filers to twice the amount of the 15% bracket for singles, phasing in over five years beginning in 2005. (c) phasing in a decrease in each individual tax rate bracket above 15% on July 1, 2001. The 28%, 31%, 36%, and 39.6% brackets in existing law will be cut to 25%, 28%, 33%, and 35% respectively, over six years. (d) the Act gradually repealed the overall limitation on itemized deductions for all taxpayers. The repeal is phased in over five years. The amount by which itemized deductions otherwise would be reduced under the pre-Act law phaseout rules will be reduced by one-third in 2006 and 2007 and by two-thirds in 2008 and 2009. The overall limitation will be repealed for tax years beginning in 2009. (e) the Act will reduce the personal exemption phaseout beginning in 2006, and repeal it after 2009. Under the five-years phase-in, the otherwise applicable personal exemption phaseout will be reduced by one-third in 2006 and 2007 and by two-thirds in 2008 and 2009. The repeal will be fully effective for tax years beginning after 2009. The Act called for a $1.35 trillion in tax cuts over 11 years. See *earned income credit*.

economic growth rate: the percentage rate at which total annual output grows; an increase in real per capita income.

economic imperialism: efforts toward domination of the economies of developing nations by foreign business firms, which seek profits by controlling raw materials, labor, and markets in those nations.

economic indicators: classification of economic information to be used in business cycle analysis and forecasting.

economic integration: attempts by two or more nations to obtain the advantages of free trade by minimizing trade restrictions.

economic lot technique: an approach that purports to describe the amount of an item that should be made or sold at one time to reduce the total costs involved.

economic profit: the residual profit after explicit and implicit costs have been paid. Synonymous with *pure profit*.

Economic Recovery Tax Act of 1981: federal legislation signed by President Reagan in August 1981, providing reductions and revisions of tax liability in various areas (e.g., estate and gift taxes, pensions, stock options, depreciation and investment tax credit). See *individual retirement accounts; Keogh plan*.

economics:
(1) the branch of the social sciences concerned with the production, distribution, and consumption of goods and services.
(2) a description of events dealing with the consumption, distribution, exchange, and production of goods and services. See *behavioral economics; labor economics; normative economics; positive economics*.

economic standard order quantity: see *EOQ model*.

economic strike: a work stoppage because of money issues and working conditions rather than unfair labor practices. It is not protected under law, and employers may hire and retain replacements unless this is interdicted by a strike settlement. See *strike*.

economic system: the system concerned with the allocation of scarce resources.

economic value: the value given to an item as a function of its usefulness and its scarcity.

economies of scale: the result of production functions showing that an equal percentage increase in all inputs leads output to increase by a large percentage. See *agglomeration economies; natural monopoly*.

economizing: choosing among alternative uses of a scarce resource, such as a factor of production, money income, or time.

ECU: see *European Currency Unit*.

edge corporation: a foreign banking organization structured in compliance with the Federal Reserve Act.

editorial credit: identification of a specific retail operation as a source for a fashion item featured editorially (i.e., not in an advertisement) in a consumer magazine or newspaper.

Education, Department of (U.S.): see *Department of Education (U.S.)*.

E.E.C.: see *European Economic Community*.

EEOC: Equal Employment Opportunity Commission. See *Civil Rights Act of 1964*.

effective assortment: all available products that are natural substitutes and are well known enough to users to be judged in terms of all important determinant attributes (after reasonable information collection efforts).

effective communication: when the intended meaning of the source and the perceived meaning of the receiver are one and the same.

effective date:

(1) **general:** the date on which an agreement or contract goes into effect; the starting date.

(2) **insurance:** the date on which an insurance binder or policy goes into effect and from which time protection is provided.

effective debt: the total debt of a firm, including the major value of annual leases or other payments that are equivalent to interest charges.

effective delegation: assignment of specific duties, granting authority to carry out these duties, and creating the obligation of responsibility for necessary action.

effective gross income: the total possible income generated by a project, less an allowance and bad debts.

effective-interest amortization: a method of systematically writing off a bond premium or discount that takes into consideration the time value of money. This results in an equal rate of amortization for each period. Cf. *straight-line interest amortization.*

effective interest rate: the actual rate of return earned or paid.

effectiveness: the achievement of goals.

effective par: for preferred stocks, the par value that would ordinarily correspond to a given dividend rate.

efficiency: the measure of production relative to input of human and other resources. See *Taylorism.* Cf. *productive efficiency.*

efficiency expert: a specialist who analyzes and reports on the correct thing being done at the proper time, in the right place, by the appropriate person. Sometimes incorrectly called a time and motion study expert and/or an industrial engineer, an efficiency expert has narrower functions. See *work simplification.* Cf. *methods-time measurement; motion study.*

efficiency perspective: an approach to work design that focuses on the creation of jobs that economize on time, human energy, raw materials, and other productive resources.

efficient market hypothesis: the supposition in finance that securities' prices reflect all available information and react nearly instantaneously and in an unbiased way to new information.

effort bargain: a collective-bargaining agreement that identifies the quantity of work to be completed for a stated wage payment, not merely the number of working hours.

effort scale: a system for charting the amount of effort a buyer will expend to purchase a specified item.

effort-to-performance strategy: a person's perception of the probability that effort will lead to performance.

EFTA: see *European Free Trade Association.*

EFTS: see *electronic funds–transfer system.*

EIB: see *European Investment Bank.*

Eiffel Tower culture: a culture that is characterized by a strong emphasis on hierarchy and orientation to the task.

8-K: a report filed with the SEC by corporations whose stock are traded on a national exchange or in the over-the-counter market, stating the details of any material event. This form must be filed within 10 days of the close of the month in which the event occurred.

eighty-twenty principle: the concept that a business gets 80 percent of its activity from 20 percent of its product line, while spending 80 percent of its energy to get the remaining 20 percent of volume. This indicates a misdirected marketing effort.

elastic demand: demand that changes in relatively large volume as prices increase or decrease. When a small change in price results in a greater change in the quantity people buy, the demand for the item is said to be elastic. The demand for jewelry, furs, and second homes is considered to be elastic. See *cross-elasticity.*

elasticity:

(1) **banking:** the ability of a bank to meet credit and currency demands during times of expansion and to reduce the availability of credit and currency during periods of overexpansion. See *Federal Reserve notes.*

(2) **merchandising:** the impact on the demand for an item created by changes in price, promotion, or other factors affecting demand. See *coefficient of cross-elasticity.*

elasticity of power: the relative responsiveness of power to changes in available alternatives.

elastic supply: supply that changes in relatively large volume with a minor change in price.

eLearning: any instructional activity that takes place over the internet including courses, online conferencing, videoconferencing, etc.

electronic bulletin board: an example of e-mail-based communications that allows one or more group members to file messages on various topics to be picked up by other group members via television links.

electronic commerce (e-commerce):

(1) the buying and selling, and marketing and servicing of products, services, and information over a variety of computer networks.

(2) encompasses the entire online process of developing, marketing, selling, delivering, servicing, and paying for products and services purchased by Internet-worked, global virtual communities of customers, with the support of a worldwide network of business partners. Relies on the resources of the Internet, and other computer networks.

electronic funds–transfer system(s) (EFTS): a loose description of computerized systems that process financial transactions, process information about financial transactions, or effect an exchange of value between two parties. See *Bank Wire System; Fed Wire; paperless item processing system; preauthorized payment; prestige card; service counter terminal.*

electronic mail: see *e-mail.*

eleemosynary: the classification of quasi–public corporations and organizations engaged in charitable work. Cf. *not-for-profit.*

eligibility date: the date set by the National Labor Relations Board for eligibility to vote in a union representation election. Usually the eligibility date is determined by the last payroll period.

eligible investment: any income-producing investment that is considered to be a sound repository for the funds of savings banks and similar institutions.

e-mail: data and text circulated through interlinked computers; widely used to send and receive text messages between networked computers over telecommunication networks. Synonymous with *electronic mail*.

embargo: a condition resulting in the failure to accept freight at a specified location because of some crisis at the point of destination; the prohibition against handling certain goods.

embezzlement: the fraudulent appropriation to a person's own use of the money or property entrusted to his or her care. See *defalcation*.

emergency dispute: a strike or the threat of a strike that would affect the national welfare and/or safety. Under the Taft-Hartley Act, the president is authorized to determine whether a dispute imperils the nation's well-being and, if it does, to take appropriate action, which usually involves creating a fact-finding board.

emergent clusters: informal, unofficial groups.

emergent task elements: components of work roles that are not formally recognized by the organization but arise out of expectations held by others for the role incumbent.

emerging talent: those people within five to ten years of college who have shown extraordinary vision and leadership ability. They are often supported, coached, and tracked until they reach the high potential pool of talent. See *high potentials*.

empire building: enlarging one's status and power by increasing the number of subordinates, the amount of space and physical facilities, and the number of make-work projects.

employ: to hire or engage the services of an individual or his or her equipment.

employable: describing people in the population who are able to work and who fall within certain age limits. Cf. *hard-core unemployed*.

employee: anyone who works for a wage or salary and performs services for an employer.

employee assistance programs: programs designed to help employees deal with social problems, such as alcoholism, drug addiction, and excessive stress.

employee association: a group of workers organized to accomplish specific common interests and goals.

employee benefits: any supplements to wages or pay that employees get based on their working for the organization.

employee-centered leadership behavior: involves attempting to build effective work groups with high performance goals.

employee compensation: all forms of pay or rewards that go to employees and arise from their employment.

employee empowerment: granting employees power to initiate change, thereby encouraging them to take charge of what they do.

employee involvement: a participative process that uses the entire capacity of employees and is designed to encourage increased commitment to the organization's success.

employee leasing: process of dismissing employees who are then hired by a leasing company and then contracting with that firm to lease back the employees.

employee orientation: a formal process of helping new employees adjust to the organization, job, and work group.

employee-oriented behavior: leadership behavior designed to meet the social and emotional needs of group members.

employee-oriented leader: a person in authority who emphasizes interpersonal relations.

employee replacement chart: a chart that shows which personnel are performing extremely well, which are satisfactory, and which need to improve their performance, as well as the promotion potential of each person.

Employee Retirement Income Security Act of 1974 (ERISA): legislation signed by President Ford on Labor Day, 1974, to protect the interests of workers who participate in private pension and welfare plans and their beneficiaries. The law also allows an employee not covered by a pension plan other than Social Security to put aside, on a tax-deferred basis, a certain amount of money for retirement. See *individual retirement account; Keogh plan.*

employee rights: guarantees of fair treatment from employers, particularly regarding an employee's right to privacy.

employee right-to-know laws: laws that require employers to advise employees of job hazards.

employee stock ownership plans (ESOPs): programs created to give workers a feeling of participation in the management and direction of a company. Workers are encouraged to purchase stock of the company. See *compensation; retirement; self-employed.*

employer: a person, organization, or corporation that has workers in its employ.

employer interference: unfair labor practices, including the following: barring distribution of union literature or solicitation during non-working time; speeches to employees on company time and property before a representation election, unless the union has equal opportunity to reply; questioning of employees about union activity; closing or moving the plant, or threatening to do so; circulating an antiunion petition and inducing employees to sign under duress; across-the-board increases in wages; removal of privileges; spying; encouraging or discouraging union membership; and firing for union activity. See *Taft-Hartley Act.*

employer petition: a formal request by an employer to the National Labor Relations Board for holding an election to determine the representative for collective bargaining. See *representation election.*

employer rights: synonymous with *management prerogatives.*

employer's final offer: the last terms offered by an employer in an attempt to settle a contract dispute. For national emergency disputes, the National Labor Relations Board conducts a secret-ballot vote on this offer among the employees.

employment: the state of being employed or having work that renders payment.

employment agency: an organization that assists firms in recruiting employees and aids individuals in their attempts to locate jobs.

employment at will: the legal principle that holds that either employee or employer can terminate employment at any time for any reason.

employment contract: mutually written with implied expectations between employer and employee.

employment function: the aspect of personnel work that is responsible for recruiting, selecting, and hiring new workers. It usually is found in the employment section of large personnel departments.

employment requisition: a form issued to activate the recruitment process, typically including such information as the job title, starting date, and pay scale, and a brief summary of principal duties.

employment test: a selection method involving the assessment of a job applicant's characteristics through paper-and-pencil responses or simulated exercises.

emporium: a place of trade, usually a major center.

empowering employees: authorizing and enabling employees to do their jobs with greater autonomy.

empowerment perspective: an approach to work design that suggests that fitting the characteristics of jobs to the people who perform them increases personal growth and satisfaction at work.

EMS: see *European Monetary System.*

emulative product: a new offering by a competitor of the same general type of item.

encounter group: the participants in a sensitivity training program. See *sensitivity training.*

encounter stage: the stage in the socialization process in which a new employee sees what the organization is really like and confronts the possibility that expectations and reality may diverge.

encroachment: infringement on another's property without the owner's consent.

encumbrance (incumbrance):
(1) **general:** that which holds back or weighs down.
(2) **finance:** the amount expected to be paid for items ordered before they are received.

end money: a special fund created in the event that the costs of a project exceed original estimates.

endorsed bond: see *bond, endorsed.*

endorsee (indorsee): the person to whom a negotiable item payable or endorsed to order is negotiated by endorsement and delivery.

endorsement (indorsement):
(1) **general:** a show of support; a verification.
(2) **banking:** a signature written on the back of an instrument. An endorsement is required on a negotiable instrument in order to transfer and pass title to another party, who becomes a holder in due course. The endorser, in signing the endorsement, guarantees that he or she is the lawful owner of the instrument, knows of no infirmity in the instrument, accepted it in good faith for value received, and is a holder in due course and has the legal capacity to transfer title to another party in the normal course of business.
(3) **insurance:** when circumstances require that a policy be changed (e.g., change of name; addition of property; change in coverage), a form bearing the language necessary to record the change. Cf. *scratch endorsement.*

endorser (indorser): one who endorses; the person who transfers his title to an instrument to another by endorsement.

endowment:

(1) **insurance:** a life term contract providing for the payment of the face amount of the policy at a specified age, at the end of a specified period, or upon the death of the insured.

(2) **economics:** a gift to an institution, usually for a specific purpose. In most cases, the gift permits the giver to declare a deduction on his taxes.

endowment insurance: life insurance on which premiums are paid for at a given period, during which the insured is covered. If the person survives beyond the end of the premium period, he or she collects the face value.

Energy, Department of (U.S.): see *Department of Energy (U.S.)*.

engage:

(1) **general:** to employ or to arrange for services.

(2) **business law:** to commit by word or contact.

Engels' law: an economic theory claiming that the lower a person's income is, the greater the percentage of it that is spent for food. Frederick Engels was a nineteenth-century German collaborator of Karl Marx.

engross: to purchase a sufficient quantity of a commodity to secure a monopoly for purposes of reselling at a higher price.

enjoin:

(1) **general:** to command or direct.

(2) **labor relations:** a court action to prevent a union from engaging in an illegal stoppage or strike action. An employer or corporation may also be enjoined during a labor dispute. See *injunction*.

(3) **business law:** to stop; to forbid.

enlargement: see *European Union*.

Enron: a U.S. major corporation whose December 2001 bankruptcy became the symbol of corporate scandals. See *cook the books; Corporate Accountability Act of 2002; Sarbanes-Oxley Act*.

enterprise union: a union comprised of employees at a single company; typically found in Japan.

Enterprise for the Americas Initiative (EAI): announced by President Bush on June 27, 1990 to harness the hemispheric policy reforms taking place in the region to form a partnership of economic liberalization and growth. EAI's objectives include increased trade, investment, and debt reduction obligation to the U.S. government. Cf. *New*

American Community. See *North American Free Trade Agreement.*

entitlement: a special tax device for restoring equity under the existing marketing arrangements governing oil. The tax is paid by the large oil companies for excess new oil, and the government transfers the receipts to the smaller companies to offset their high payments for foreign oil.

entity: see *corporation.*

entity attraction: satisfaction with other persons in the workplace that comes about because these people share one's fundamental values, attitudes, or philosophy.

entrepot trade: reexport of imports from a warehouse. When the items are not sold from bonded warehouses, and duty has been paid, the reexporter may be entitled to a refund of the duty.

entrepreneur: one who assumes the financial risk of the initiation, operation, and management of a given business or undertaking. See *threshold companies.*

entrepreneur decision process: the decision to leave a present career or lifestyle because the entrepreneurial venture being considered is desirable, and external and internal factors make the venture possible.

entrepreneurial career: dynamic stages in the life of an entrepreneur, with each stage reflecting and interacting with other stages and events in the individual's life.

entrepreneurial culture: a culture typified by the presence of characteristics such as a flat management structure with multiple informal networks, a long-run time perspective, and a strategic orientation driven by perception of opportunity.

entrepreneurial judo: strategy that capitalizes on the weakness of an organization that holds a leadership position.

entrepreneurial process: the four distinct phases of creating a new venture: identifying and evaluating the opportunity; developing the business plan; determining the resources required; and managing the resulting entity.

entrepreneurial stress: a function of discrepancies between one's expectations and one's ability to meet those demands.

entrepreneurial trait school of thought: a school of entrepreneurial thought that focuses on identifying those traits that appear common to successful entrepreneurs.

entrepreneuring: (slang) the taking of risk in the running of an organization, usually a small business enterprise.

entry: a recording of data in an account or account book.

entry-level assignments: the lowest position within a job category; usually the lowest job from which one can be promoted.

entry strategies: ways of entering multinational business operations. They include exporting, licensing, franchising, foreign branch operations, joint ventures, and wholly owned subsidiaries.

environment: those institutions or forces outside the organization that potentially affect the organization's performance.

Environmental Protection Agency (EPA): federal agency founded on December 2, 1970, to develop and enforce standards for clean air and water; to establish standards to control pollution from pesticides, toxic substances, and noise; and to approve state pollution abatement plans. See *Toxic Substances Control Act of 1976.*

environmental selling: displaying items for sale in a setting that simulates a buyer's home.

environmental uncertainty: the state of the external environment of an organization as defined by the degree of complexity and the degree of change.

EOM (end-of-month) dating: a policy of commencing credit terms as of the month's end. For example, "7/20 EOM" means that a 7 percent cash discount is taken if the invoice is paid by the 20th of the month following the invoice date. Invoices dated after the 25th of the month are considered to be dated in the following month.

EOQ (economic order quantity) model: an inventory decision–making approach used to create a formula for determining when to order supplies and in what quantity.

ephemeralization: Buckminister Fuller's concept for increasing the rate of obsolescence of products in order to increase the rate of recycling of their elements.

equal coverage: a corporation indenture protective clause providing that, in the case of an additional issue of bonds, the subject bonds shall be entitled to the same security as that of the earlier issue.

Equal Credit Opportunity Act (ECOA): federal legislation prohibiting creditors from discriminating against credit applicants on the basis of sex or marital status. After March 1977, discrimination in credit on the basis of race, color, religion, national origin, age, and receipt of public assistance was prohibited. Compliance with the law comes under the jurisdiction of the Federal Trade Commission.

equal employment opportunity: giving people a fair chance to succeed without discrimination on factors unrelated to job performance, such as age, sex, race, religion, or national origin. See *Civil Rights Act of 1964, Title VII; Equal Employment Opportunity Act of 1972.*

Equal Employment Opportunity Act of 1972: became operational on July 2, 1965; an act strengthening the role of the Equal Employment Opportunity Commission by amending the Civil Rights Act of 1964. The law empowered the EEOC to initiate court action against noncomplying organizations. See *Civil Rights Act of 1964, Title VII.*

Equal Employment Opportunity Commission (EEOC): see *Civil Rights Act of 1964, Title VII.*

equalizers: people whose primary concern in negotiating or managing conflicts is to equalize outcomes for everyone involved in a situation.

Equal Pay Act of 1963: a federal law requiring that men and women performing equal work be paid equal wages, applicable to employers and workers covered by the Fair Labor Standards Act. The act prohibits lowering pay for men to equalize rates.

equal pay for equal work: the concept, frequently written into contract language, that like work shall command like pay, regardless of sex, race, or other individual characteristics of the employees.

equation price: a price attained by the adjusting action of competition in any market at any time, or in a unit of time, such that the demand and supply become equal at that price.

equilibrium price:
(1) **general:** the price that maximizes a firm's profitability.
(2) **manufacturing:** the price of goods determined in the market by the intersection of a supply and demand curve.

equilibrium quantity:
(1) **general:** the quantity that maximizes a firm's profitability.
(2) **manufacturing:** the quantity of goods determined in the market by the intersection of a supply-and-demand curve.

equipment leasing: the rental of expensive equipment to save a substantial and immediate cash outlay. In most cases the leasing agreement includes a maintenance arrangement with the lessor on the leased items.

equipment trust certificate: a type of security, generally issued by a railroad, to pay for new equipment (e.g., locomotives). Title to the equipment is held by a trustee until the notes are paid off. An equipment trust certificate is usually secured by a first claim on the equipment.

equitable conversion: permitting real property to be converted into personal property. Real property owned by a partnership is, for the purpose of the partnership, personal property, because the real property must be reduced to cash to determine a partner's interest.

equitable title: the right that exists in equity to secure total ownership to property when its title is in someone else's name.

equity:

(1) **business law:** the law of trusts, divorces, injunctions, and other rules of performance, enforced in courts of equity to determine fairness, right, and justice.

(2) **economics:** the value placed on the distribution of income.

(3) **securities:** the ownership interest of common and preferred stockholders in a company.

(4) **securities:** the excess of value of securities over the debit balance in a margin account. See *margin call.*

equity capital: stockholders' or owners' investments made in an organization.

equity financing: the selling of capital stock by a corporation. Cf. *debt financing.*

equity participation: having an ownership position in an organization as a result of contributing some resource, usually money.

equity securities: any stock issue, common or preferred.

equity transaction: a transaction resulting in an increase or decrease of net worth or involving the transfer between accounts that make up the net worth.

equity turnover: the ratio that measures the relationship between sales and the common stockholders' equity. It is used to compute the rate of return on common equity.

ergonomics: matching of machines and people to increase efficiency by expanding production, raising output quality or quantity, minimizing training, improving working conditions, and setting a better union-management atmosphere. See *human engineering.* Cf. *methods-time measurement; motion study.*

ERISA: see *Employee Retirement Income Security Act of 1974.*

errors and omissions: insurance coverage for liability arising out of errors or omissions in the performance of professional services other than in the medical profession; applicable to such services as engineering, banking, accounting, insurance, and real estate. See *retroactive extension.* Cf. *malpractice insurance.*

escalator clause:

(1) **labor relations:** a contract clause that provides for an adjustment of wages in accordance with such factors as cost of living, productiv-

ity, or material costs. Escalator clauses are designed to keep real wages reasonably stable during the term of a contract.

(2) **purchasing:** a clause permitting adjustments of price or profit in a purchase contract under specified conditions.

escape clause:

(1) **labor relations:** in a maintenance-of-membership agreement, a provision setting a period during which union members may withdraw from membership without affecting their employment.

(2) **business law:** a contractual provision outlining the circumstances under which either party may be relieved of any obligation previously incurred or agreed to.

escrow: a written agreement or instrument setting up for allocation funds or securities deposited by the giver or grantor to a third party (the escrow agent) for the eventual benefit of the second party (the grantee). The escrow agent holds the deposit until certain conditions have been met. The grantor can get the deposit back only if the grantee fails to comply with the terms of the contract, and the grantee cannot receive the deposit until the conditions have been met. See *billed escrow.* Cf. *deposit funds.*

escrow agreement: an arrangement whereby two parties agree to place a sum of money in the hands of a third party for conditional delivery under specified circumstances.

escrow bond: see *bond, escrow.*

ESOPs: see *employee stock ownership plans.*

ESP: see *Exchange Stock Portfolio.*

essay method: an approach to performance appraisal that requires the rater to compose a statement describing employee performance.

establishment: a factory, or several, under the ownership of one management, located in one geographic area, and producing related goods; more recently, those in power, and the system under which such power is exercised, maintained, and extended.

establishment of equilibrium: a career phase during which individuals reevaluate their progress, find that things are going along pretty well, and feel a large degree of contentment, optimism, and stability.

establish the differential: all of the sales promotion and publicity activities a company musters within its budgetary constraints to take advantage of a possible differential advantage.

estate:

(1) **general:** any right, title, or other interest in real or personal property.

(2) **business law:** all assets owned by an individual at the time of his or her death. The estate includes all funds, personal effects, interests in business enterprises, titles to property (real estate and chattels), and evidence of ownership, such as stocks, bonds, and mortgages owned, and notes receivable.

estate tax bond: see *bond, estate tax*.

esteem needs: Maslow's fourth set of human needs, including the human desire for self-respect and respect from others.

estimate: an informed guess about the future effect on an organization of specific current conditions.

estimated cost: the expected cost of a product to be manufactured. It includes standard costs projected to future operations.

estimated revenues: the account title used in governmental accounting to set up the budgeted revenues for a period. The estimated revenues are compared against the actual revenues at the end of the period.

ETC: see *export trading company*.

ethical advocate: ethics specialist who plays a role in top-management decision making.

ethics: personal beliefs about what is right and wrong or good and bad. See *Enron*.

ethics audit: systematic efforts to assess conformance to organizational ethical policies, aid understanding of those policies, and identify serious breaches requiring remedial action.

ethics hot line: a special telephone line established to enable employers to bypass the normal chain of command in reporting grievances and serious ethical problems.

ethod: the moral value of an organization to society—its universal appeal as a contributor to the wellbeing of mankind.

Euro: the present currency of exchange and trade in the European Union; most of its 15 nations began using the Euro on January 1, 2002.

Eurobond: a bond released by a U.S. or other non-European company for sale in Europe.

Eurocard: a European credit card developed by the West German banking system that is accepted in most Western European countries.

Eurocheque: a credit card for purchasing goods in several Western European countries.

Eurocurrency: monies of various nations deposited in European banks that are used in the European financial market. Synonymous with *Euromoney.*

Eurodollars: European claims for U.S. dollars. These claims arise when, through the purchase of a bill of exchange or other financial transaction, a foreign bank debits the account of a U.S. bank and credits a dollar deposit account.

Euromarket (Euromart): synonymous with *European Economic Community.*

Euromoney: synonymous with *Eurocurrency.*

European Coal and Steel Community (ECSC): proposed in 1950 by Jean Monnet, a leader in European confederation, the pooling of resources and duty restrictions on coal, iron, and steel between France, West Germany, Italy, Belgium, the Netherlands, and Luxembourg, known as the Schuman Plan. See *European Economic Community.*

European Common Market: synonymous with *European Economic Community.*

European Community (E.C.): the three European communities created by the Treaty of Paris and the Treaty of Rome, the European Coal and Steel Community, the European Atomic Energy Community, and the European Economic Community, merged in 1965 to form the E.C. In 1973, the six founder members (Belgium, France, Italy, Luxembourg, Germany, and the Netherlands) were joined by Denmark, the Irish Republic, and the United Kingdom. Greece became a full member on January 1, 1981, with Portugal and Spain joining in 1986. Aims to break down trade barriers within a common market and create a political union among the peoples of Europe; has its own budget raised from its own resources, e.g., customs duties, agricultural levies, a proportion of value-added tax; offers loans, subsidies, or grants through a variety of financial instruments. Sometimes called the *Common Market.* By 2004, a total of 25 European nations will be members. Presently called the *European Union.* See *Euro; European Economic Community; internal market.*

European Currency Unit (ECU): The Community's new basket-type unit of account was christened the European unit of account (EUA). With its introduction in 1975, the foundation was set for the ECU. When the European Monetary System (EMS) was launched on March 13, 1979, the EUA formula was retained unchanged, but a review clause was incorporated and the EUA was renamed the ECU and is now the European Community's sole unit of account; a central element of the European Monetary System, a composite monetary unit consisting of a basket of Community currencies and equivalent to the European Unit of account; subject to review every five years, or upon request, should the weight of any currency change by 25 or more percent. See *Euro*.

European Currency Unit bonds: the major ECU bonds are:

(1) Fixed rate bonds, with average maturities between three and 15 years and comparable interest rates. They account for about 88 percent of the total market.

(2) Adjustable rate bonds, with interest adjustments every three to six years at the investor's or issuer's option or according to bilateral agreement.

(3) Zero coupon bonds, with fixed interest payments at maturity.

(4) Floating rate notes, issued mainly by state-guaranteed banks and sovereign states, with interest-rate adjustments every three to six months to reflect market movements.

(5) Convertible bonds that permit conversion into bonds or shares. These are well suited to counterbalance exchange-rate risks.

(6) Cum warrant issues that entitle the holder to purchase additional bonds or the issuer's shares. See *European Currency Unit; European Currency Unit futures and options.*

European Currency Unit futures and options: under an ECU futures contract, the buyer (or seller) has the right and not the obligation to buy (or sell) at a specified future date a fixed amount of ECUs at a price agreed when the contract was concluded. Under an ECU options contract, the buyer has the right, but not the obligation, to buy (call) or sell (put) a fixed amount of ECUs at a specified future date. ECU options have been traded on the Philadelphia Stock Exchange since February 1986, while ECU futures have been traded on the Financial Instrument Exchange forming part of the New York Cotton Exchange and on the Chicago Mercantile Exchange since January 1986. The Chicago Mercantile Exchange introduced a special incentive system in May 1986, resulting in a surge in the number of futures contracts traded in Chicago. See *European Currency Unit.*

European Economic Community (EEC): an agreement made in 1957 among France, Italy, West Germany, Belgium, The Netherlands, and Luxembourg (the original Inner Six nations) for the purposes of establishing common import duties and abolishing tariff barriers between borders. Denmark, Ireland, and England joined the EEC in 1973. Synonymous with *Common Market; European Common Market; European Community; Euromarket (Euromart)*. See *European Free Trade Association*.

European Free Trade Association (EFTA): formed in 1959 by Austria, Denmark, Norway, Portugal, Sweden, Switzerland, and the United Kingdom (the original Outer Seven) to establish common regulations for tariffs and trade. Later, Iceland became a member and Finland an associate member. See *European Economic Community*.

European Investment Bank (EIB): established by the Treaty of Rome in 1958 to help implement specific economic policy objectives of the European Economic Community; committed to serving the E.C.'s mission as a market partner; an independent body with capital contributed by Community nations; goal is to contribute via investment loans in projects to "the balanced and steady development of the common market in the interest of the Community."

European Monetary System (EMS): officially introduced on March 13, 1979; any European nation with particularly close economic and financial ties with the European Community can take part in the exchange rate and intervention mechanisms; goal is to create a zone of monetary stability in Europe, through the implementation of certain exchange rate, credit, and resource transfer policies to ensure that monetary instability did not interfere with the process of genuine integration within the Community. The United Kingdom entered EMS in October 1990.

European Union: most recent name for the combined 15 nations of the European Community; by 2004 enlarged to 25 nations. See *European Community*.

Euro-sterling: sterling deposits accepted and employed by banks outside the United Kingdom; market in such sterling in centered in Paris, and is smaller than the Eurodollar.

Euro-zone: the common currency, the Euro, used in 2003 by 12 of the present 15 nations of the European Union.

evaluation:

(1) **human resources:** the judgment of a person's fitness for a job, a training project, or other new or existing programs.

(2) **marketing:** a step in the adoption process; a consumer's estimate of the value, quality, and reaction to a product or service. See *adoption process*.

even lots: lots or amounts of stock shares sold in units of 100 or multiples thereof. See *board lot*.

evidence of insurability: any statement or proof of a person's physical condition and/or other factual information affecting his acceptability for insurance. Cf. *declaration*.

ex-ante quantities: planned or intended consumption, investment, and so on, at the beginning of a time period.

exception principle: the concept that managers should permit their subordinates to make routine, recurring decisions and that only unusual or highly important problems should be referred to higher levels in the organization.

excess capacity: surplus ability to produce, especially unused factory space or staff.

excess coverage clause: a clause claiming that, in the event of a loss, a specific insurance will be considered in excess of any other insurance held against the identical risk. See *double insurance.*

excess insurance: a policy or bond covering the insured against certain hazards and applying only to loss or damage in excess of a stated amount. The risk of initial loss or damage (excluded from the excess policy or bond) may be carried by the insured himself or may be insured by another policy or bond, providing what is known as primary insurance. Cf. *service excess.*

excess loan: a bank loan made to one customer that is in excess of the maximum stated by law. Directors of banks approving such loans have been held by court decisions to be personally liable for the bank's losses.

excess materials requisitions: forms to be filled out by the production staff to secure any materials needed in excess of the standard amount allotted for output.

excess of loss reinsurance: reinsurance that indemnifies the ceding company for the excess of a stipulated sum or primary retention in the event of loss.

excess profits tax: a tax added to the normal tax placed on a business. It is usually levied during periods of wartime on profits above what the law declares as normal.

excess reserves: designating the amount of funds held in reserve in excess of the legal minimum requirements, whether the funds are on deposit in a Federal Reserve bank, in a bank approved as a depository, or in the cash reserve carried in a bank's own vaults.

exchange:
> (1) **business:** an organization or place for carrying out business or settling accounts.
> (2) **securities:** a place for trading in securities or commodities. See *clearinghouse; foreign exchange; stock exchanges.*
> (3) **finance:** the volume of monies available for use.
> (4) **retailing:** to return an item to a store to substitute another item.

exchange acquisition: a method of filling an order to purchase a block of stock on the floor of an exchange. Under certain circumstances, a member broker can facilitate the purchase of a block by soliciting sell orders. All orders to sell the security are lumped together and crossed with the buy order in the regular auction market. The buyer's price may be on a net basis or on a commission basis.

exchange current: the current rate of exchange.

exchange distribution: a method of disposing of large blocks of stock on the floor of an exchange. Under certain circumstances a member broker can facilitate the sale of a block of stock by soliciting and inducing other member brokers to solicit orders to buy. Individual buy orders are lumped together with the sell order in the regular auction market. A special commission is usually paid by the seller; ordinarily the buyer pays no commission.

exchange rate: the price of one currency in relation to that of another.

Exchange Stock Portfolio (ESP): the New York Stock Exchange basket product, the first program trading vehicle (October 1989) carrying the exchange's seal of approval. ESPs will allow institutional investors to buy or sell all 500 stocks in Standard & Poor's index in a single trade of a minimum of $5 million. Customized baskets of fewer stocks will also be available.

excise taxes: taxes levied by federal and state governments on the manufacture, sale, or consumption of commodities, or taxes levied on the right, privilege, or permission to engage in a certain business, trade, occupation, or sport.

exclusion:
> (1) **general:** any restriction or limitation.
> (2) **insurance:** a provision of an insurance policy or bond referring to hazards, circumstances, or property not covered by the policy.

exclusion allowance: the portion of an annuity payment that can be excluded from taxable income each year. This amount is determined by dividing the annuitant's investment in the contract by his life expectancy. In a tax–deferred annuity (TDA) program, the amount of annual contribution that may be excluded from taxable income by a participant is specified by law.

exclusive:
(1) goods obtainable from a limited number of stores or dealers.
(2) sales of merchandise limited to a single retailer in a given location. See *exclusive outlet selling.*

exclusive dealing contract: an agreement that a buyer will make all purchases of a specific item from only one seller and will refrain from carrying competing goods.

exclusive distribution: a manufacturer's protection of a dealer against the location of other dealers in the same area, often giving the right to sell an item to the exclusion of other sellers.

exclusive listing: an arrangement whereby a broker becomes the sole agent of the owner of a property, assuming the sole right to sell or rent the property within a specified time period.

exclusive outlet selling: one retailer or wholesaler in a location having exclusive control over the sale of an article or service, usually determined by contract.

exclusivity: the right acquired by an employee organization to be the sole representative of the bargaining unit.

ex-dividend (ex div, XD): identifying the period during which the quoted price of a security excludes the payment of any declared dividend to the buyer, and the dividend reverts to the seller. Synonymous with *without dividend.* Cf. *ex-stock dividend; record date.*

ex dock: from the (shipping) dock.

exec: (slang) an executive.

execute: to complete or make valid, as by signing, sealing, and delivering.

executed: signed, sealed, and delivered, as of contracts or other written agreements.

executive: an individual whose position calls for decision making and the use of power over employees in the daily activities of a firm.

executive coach: someone hired by the firm to help a specific executive work through or develop a particular skill. The coach works with an executive over a specified time frame to accomplish specific objectives.

executive committee: a formal group responsible for the direct operation and management of an organization.

executive compensation: the total monies paid to an executive, including regular salary plus additional payments (e.g., bonuses or director's fees). It does not include warrants or options to purchase stock. See *compensation*.

executive fallout: (slang) fired managers.

executive reality check: top managers periodically working at lower-level jobs to become more aware of operations.

executive recruiters: agencies retained by employers to seek out top management talent.

executive search firms: private organizations that seek new managers for a company, usually accomplished by approaching managers in their existing jobs and asking them if they want to work for a different company. Synonymous with *headhunting*.

executive trainee: a (usually) young person who works in various units of business to receive on-the-job training and to acquire familiarity with the entire operation. Cf. *apprentice*.

executory: until all parts of a contract are performed, the state of the part not performed.

exemplary damages: monies or fines imposed by a court (1) in punishment of the defendant, (2) to make an example of the wrongdoers, and (3) to deter others from doing the same thing.

exempt commodity: merchandise shipped in interstate commerce to which published rates do not apply.

exempt employees:
(1) **personnel:** employees who are not subject to the rulings of seniority
(2) **labor relations:** employees who are not subject to wage and overtime provisions of the Fair Labor Standards Act. Such employees may or may not be covered by a union contract.

exercise notice: a notice issued by a clearinghouse that was formed to insure stock deliveries, obligating a customer to send the securities covered by an option against payment of the exercise price.

exercise price: the fixed price at which a stock can be purchased in a call contract or sold in a put contract. See *puts and calls*. Synonymous with *striking price*.

ex gratia payment: a payment made by an insurance company, for which it is not liable under the terms of the insurance policy.

exhaust price: the price at which a broker is forced to sell a security that was margined and subsequently dropped in price.

exhibit:
(1) **general:** a display or public show.

(2) **administration:** materials presented in a report.

Eximbank (Ex-Im Bank): see *Export-Import Bank of the United States.*

exit interview: see *interview, exit.*

ex officio: by right or virtue of the office held (*Latin*).

exogenous demand: a demand for goods determined by factors outside the present economy and including exports and government expenditures.

expanding-pie assumption: the assumption that the amount of power or any resource held by people is not fixed but rather is expanding, and that all resources can gain. Cf. *fixed-pie assumption.*

expansion:

(1) **business:** extending or broadening the operation or area of a business. See *horizontal expansion.*

(2) **economics:** a business cycle fluctuation characterized by an increase in industrial activity. The opposite of *contraction.* Synonymous with *recovery (securities).*

expectancy theory of motivation: based on Vroom's theory that a person's motivational level depends on his or her objectives, perceived relationship between job performance and achievement of individual objectives, and perceived ability to influence his or her performance level.

expected exit value: the nondiscounted amount of cash a company expects to realize from holding a particular asset. Cf. *present value of expected cash flow.*

expected idle capacity variance: the excess of practical capacity over the master budget sales forecast capacity, expressed in physical or dollar terms.

expected return: the profit that is anticipated from a business venture.

expected yield: the ratio of expected return over the investment total, usually expressed annually as a percentage.

expedited arbitration: a faster, less expensive, and less legalistic way to resolve grievances regarding discipline cases, routine work issues, and cases of insignificant monetary cost to the disputing parties.

expendable fund: a fund whose assets may be applied by administrative action to general or specific purposes.

expenditure: an actual payment, or the creation of an obligation to make a future payment, for some benefit, item, or service received. If the expenditure is to acquire or improve a relatively permanent asset, it is a capital expenditure. If the amount involved is charged to an operating account, it is a revenue expenditure.

expenditure multiplier: the amount resulting from an increase in sales because of the induced spending created thereby.

expense: the cost of resources used to create revenue. Expense is the amount shown on the income statement as a deduction from revenue. Expense should not be confused with cost; all expenses are costs, but not all costs are expenses.

expense account:

(1) **accounting:** an account carried in the general ledger in which all operating expenses are recorded. Expenses are deducted from gross profits, or from the total of all income accounts, to compute the net profit of the business for the period.

(2) **administration:** money advanced to an employee, usually an executive, for travel, daily costs, and other items that are accepted by the organization as justified; monies paid by an employee that are reimbursed by the employer after the expenditures have been accepted.

expense approach: a method of accounting for prepaid expenses whereby these expenses are initially debited to an expense account, even though future benefits exist. A year-end adjustment is required to record the actual expense incurred during the period and to establish a companion asset account equal to remaining future benefits. Cf. *asset approach.*

expense budget: the planned cost of the expected volume of an activity to be undertaken.

expense constant: a flat amount included in some premiums, to cover the minimum expense of an insurance transaction.

expense ratio: the percentage of a premium used to pay all operating costs.

experience:

(1) **general:** events during a person's lifetime, usually pertaining to required knowledge or skill.

(2) **insurance:** the premium and loss record of an insured or of a class of coverage.

experience curves: a phenomenon in which costs of production decrease arithmetically as experience increases geometrically.

experienced meaningfulness: feeling that one's job is important and worthwhile.

experience rating:

(1) **personnel:** the basis for an adjustment, according to an employer's

unemployment or accident record, of the rate the employer pays for unemployment insurance or worker's compensation insurance.

(2) **insurance:** a type of individual risk rating that, based on insured experience on the risk, measures the extent to which a particular risk deviates from the average of its class and reflects this deviation in the rate for the risk. See *basic rate; line sheet; rating bureaus.* Cf. *judgment rates.* Synonymous with *merit rating.*

expert-estimate techniques: a method of forecasting employment needs in which a knowledgeable executive or committee decides how many people will be needed over the next six to twelve months.

expert power: the capacity to influence based on some expertise or knowledge. It is a function of the judgment of those less powerful that the expert has ability exceeding their own.

expiration:

(1) **general:** termination, cessation.

(2) **insurance:** the date on which a policy will cease to be in effect, unless previously canceled.

expire: to arrive at the termination period of an agreement, contract, or other instrument.

explicit costs: costs of a company that involves cash outlays to individuals, other businesses, or the government; include the purchase of resources, land, labor, and capital needed in a firm's production process, and indirect business taxes.

explicit interest: the amount of money or goods paid on a loan.

exploitative-authoritative leadership style: a basic leadership style in which management exhibits little confidence in its subordinates. Decision making tends to be highly centralized.

export: to ship an item away from a country for sale to another country.

Export-Import Bank of the United States (Eximbank; Ex-Im Bank): an independent federal banking corporation established in 1934 to facilitate and aid in financing exports and imports and the exchange of commodities between the United States and foreign nations. It offers direct credit to borrowers outside the United States as well as export guarantees, export credit insurance, and discount loans.

export promotion: a strategy for economic development that focuses on increasing a country's exports to generate foreign exchange and stimulate domestic production.

exports: items produced in one country and sold to another.

export subsidies: payments made by a government to companies that export specific goods in order to encourage them to compete in foreign markets.

export trading company (ETC): any of the companies or firms engaged in international trade as established or invested, especially by banks on special permission in the Export Trading Company Act of 1982.

exposure: the condition of being open to loss from a specific hazard, event, or contingency; also, funds, or the insurable values, that are so exposed to loss.

express warranty: a seller's position statement concerning the quality, benefit, or value to a consumer of his or her goods, intended to convince an individual to make a purchase. The consumer has the right to expect the seller to back up these statements based on the seller's express warranty.

ex-rights: without rights. A stock trades ex-right when the sellers, rather than the purchasers, are entitled to receive rights that have been declared but not paid.

ex-stock dividend: without any stock dividend (e.g., when the stock dividend is held as the property of the seller). Cf. *ex-dividend*.

extend:
(1) **accounting:** to multiply the unit price by the quantity of units to ascertain the total cost on an invoice.
(2) **business:** to allow a period of time for the payment of a debt beyond the date originally set.

extended:
(1) **business:** a situation in which liabilities have increased far in excess of existing assets.
(2) **business law:** a contractual obligation that has been prolonged beyond the originally stated date of maturity or termination.

extended bond: see *bond, extended*.

extended coverage endorsement: an endorsement extending a fire insurance policy, usually to cover loss caused by windstorm, hail, explosion (except of steam boilers), riot, civil commotion, aircraft, vehicles, and smoke.

extended term insurance: permanent plans of life insurance that provide term coverage for the face amount of the policy, in lieu of cash settlement, when premiums are discontinued for a fixed period.

extended terms: when a customer is given an additional period in which to pay.

extension:

(1) **banking:** moving the maturity date to a later time, resulting in a prolongation of the terms of a loan. See *lockup.*

(2) **finance:** the granting of borrowing rights or the permission to buy without immediate payment.

(3) **business law:** a postponement, by agreement of the parties, of the time set for any legal procedure.

(4) **marketing:** a basic type of innovation that involves extending the life of a product, service, or process that is already in existence.

external audit: an audit conducted by an outside accounting firm.

external bond: see *bond, external.*

externalities: external benefits or costs of activities for which no compensation is offered. Synonymous with *spillovers.*

external recruiting: human resource managers' attempting to find a qualified pool of candidates from outside of an organization.

external resources: resources outside the venture.

external users: investors, creditors, analysts, and other groups interested in the financial affairs of a company but not involved in managing its day-to-day activities.

extinguish: to wipe out, settle, or conclude, as a debt or obligation.

extra: short form of *extra dividend*, a dividend in the form of stock or cash in addition to a company's regular or usual dividend (not to be confused with *ex-dividend*).

extractive industry: a business that takes products directly from nature, especially from land or water (e.g., lumber, coal, or oil).

extra dating: adding days beyond the regular date for invoice payment. Extensions are usually for 30- or 60-day periods.

extra dividend: see *extra.*

extra expense insurance: designed for the business firm (e.g., a bank) that must continue to operate following a loss, usually at great additional expense. It should not be confused with business interruption insurance because it does not protect against interruption of business. Cf. *business interruption insurance.*

extranet: the use of the Internet to link a company with outsiders.

extraordinary gain or loss: income or loss to an entity caused by an unusual and infrequent event that is unrelated to the ordinary activities of the entity. Cf. *above-normal loss.*

extraordinary items: special nonoperating gains and losses that are unusual in nature, infrequent in occurrence, and material in amount.

extreme job specialization: subdivision of work to the point that it results in routine, monotonous jobs. See *specialization*.

extrinsic motivators: motivators within an organizational behavior modification program that are based on rewards provided by someone other than the person being motivated.

extrinsic rewards: rewards received from the environment surrounding the context of the work.

eyeball control: visual examination of inventory to determine whether there is sufficient stock on hand until requested by the wholesaler, retailer, or consumer. Cf. *inventory control*.

F

fabrication: the process of converting materials into unit, parts, or items. Cf. *assembling.*

face amount: the principal sum involved in a contract. The actual amount payable may be decreased by loans or increased by additional benefits payable under specified conditions or stated in a rider.

face value: the principal value of an instrument, on which interest is computed for interest-bearing obligations such as notes and bonds. The legal entity issuing a note, bond, or other obligation contracts to repay the face value of the obligation at maturity. Synonymous with *par value.*

facilitating agency:

(1) **general:** an organization that services other institutions but does not take title to goods (e.g., a stock exchange).

(2) **marketing:** an agency that aids in the performance of some marketing functions but does not own the items and is not involved in buying or selling.

facility: the aggregate amount of credit that a bank or other institutional lender grants to a borrower. It represents the combination of any loans outstanding plus the additional amount the bank is proposing to lend.

fact finding:

(1) **general:** investigating, collecting, and making known to a specified organization the facts regarding a specific situation.

(2) **labor relations:** investigation of a labor-management dispute by a board, usually named by a government official, that issues a report describing the points at issue and sometimes makes recommendations for a solution. Under the Taft-Hartley Act, the president must name a board of inquiry to investigate a fact-finding dispute that threatens the nation's welfare or safety. See *observer; public member.*

factor:

(1) **general:** an individual who carries on business transactions for another. See *factors.*

(2) **sales:** an agent for the sale of goods who is authorized to sell and receive payment for the merchandise.

factorage: the commission collected by a factor.

factor comparison method: a form of job evaluation that allocates a part of each job's wage to the key factors of the job, resulting in a relative evaluation of the job. See *job evaluation.*

factor hours: the sum of all hours worked by one employee who is operating two or more pieces of equipment simultaneously.

factoring banking: a method commonly employed by an installment loan department of a bank for

(1) computing the amount of interest to be refunded or credit when a 12-month loan is being liquidated before maturity. It is also a method for accruing earned discount.

(2) **finance:** selling accounts before their due date, usually at a discount.

factor price equalization theorem: the tendency, under simplified conditions, of trade between two countries that have different factor endowments to equalize factor price ratios in the two countries.

factors:

(1) **manufacturing:** ingredients needed for the production of any good or service. The primary factors are land, labor, capital, and enterprise.

(2) **finance:** limited agents who buy accounts receivable from small firms at discount. Funds are advanced upon the delivery of duplicate invoices as evidence of sale and delivery of the goods. Factors frequently perform all accounting functions in connection with the accounts receivable, in which case purchasers are notified to remit directly to factor. See *factor.*

factor's lien: a factor's right to retain the merchandise consigned to him or her as reimbursement for all advances previously made to the consignor. Cf. *particular lien.*

factory: a production facility in which assembled workers are organized for a common business activity.

factory expense: manufacturing overhead.

factory overhead: manufacturing costs excluding direct material and direct labor. Cf. *overhead.*

factory overhead incurred: manufacturing costs accumulated during a given accounting period.

factory pack: the direct premium that is attached to the product.

factory price: the selling price quoted for manufactured goods for pickup at the gate of a factory, usually including minimum packaging.

facultative: a specific transaction, one risk at a time, with the ceding and acceptance being optional on the part of the ceding company and the reinsurer (i.e., the reinsuring company may exercise its faculty to accept or reject the risk offered).

Fair Credit Billing Act: protects charge account customers against billing errors by permitting credit card customers to use the same legal defenses against banks or other third-party credit card companies that they previously could use against merchants.

Fair Credit Reporting Act of 1971: federal legislation giving the user of credit, the buyer of insurance, or the job applicant the right to learn the contents of his or her file at any credit bureau. See *Hatch Act.*

fair employment practices (FEPs): state and local laws governing equal employment opportunity that are often more comprehensive than federal laws.

fair market value: a value arrived at by bargaining between informed buyers and sellers.

fair plan: a facility operating under a government-insurance industry cooperative program to make fire insurance and other forms of property insurance readily available to persons who have difficulty obtaining such coverage. Cf. *assigned risk.*

fair price: the price that results in a fair return on funds invested or has a sufficient markup on goods or services sold to claim a reasonable profit.

fair rate of return: the profit that a public utility can earn to pay interest and dividends and expand facilities, as determined by federal and state law. See *rate regulation.*

fair representation doctrine: where unions have a legal obligation to provide assistance to both members and nonmembers in labor relations matters.

fair trade acts: laws passed by various states by which retailers are obliged to maintain specified prices on selected goods. In recent years fair trade pricing has been withdrawn by a great number of retailers and manufacturers.

fair trade price: the retail price fixed by the manufacturer of a branded item below which the retailer is prohibited by law from making sales. Increasingly, states are removing this form of pricing. See *price control; resale price maintenance.* Cf. *list price.*

fairy money: (slang) in advertising, coupons used by a consumer, thereby reducing the cost of the item for the consumer, with the difference paid by the manufacturer.

fallback pay: a guaranteed minimum pay level.

fall out of bed: (slang) a crash in stock prices; a sharp drop in the market.

false advertising: advertising that is misleading in a material respect, including not only false representation of the benefits or results of using the advertised commodity or its contents but also failure to reveal any potentially damaging consequences that are likely to follow from its use.

family brands: brands that appear on two or more products of a company (e.g., Hershey Company using the Hershey name for both candy bars and cocoa; Lipton Corporation using its name for both soups and tea). See *brand awareness.*

family-friendly organizations: companies that offer an umbrella of work/family programs such as on-site daycare, childcare and eldercare referrals, flexible hours, compressed workweeks, job sharing, telecommuting, temporary part-time employment, and relocation assistance for employees' family members.

family income rider: a special life term policy provision added to the basic policy, stating that a specified monthly income is to be paid to the beneficiary for the remainder of the income period if the insured dies before the expiration of the term.

family life cycle: the identified consumer marketing stages: single person; young married couple with no children; young married couple with children; older married couples with older, dependent children; older married couple with no children at home; and solitary survivor.

Farm Credit Administration: independent financial regulatory agency established on March 27, 1933; responsible for ensuring the safe and sound operation of the banks, associations, affiliated service organizations, and other entities that collectively comprise the Farm Credit System.

Farm Credit System: See *Farm Credit Administration.*

farm out: to subcontract.

FAS: see *free alongside ship.*

FASB: see *Financial Accounting Standards Board.*

fast-tracking: choosing of certain workers for rapid advancement while the remaining members of the work force are essentially bypassed. See *fast track-program.*

fast-track program: program that encourages young managers with high potential to remain with an organization by enabling them to advance more rapidly than those with less potential. See *fast-tracking.*

fat budget items: merchandise approved by buyers in the hope that the goods will substantially increase sales potential.

fatigue: diminished ability to do work, either mental or physical, as a consequence of previous exertion.

favorable trade balance: the situation that exists when a nation's total value of exports is in excess of its total value of imports.

favoritism: a superior's attitude and behavior toward a particular worker, group, or ideas, based on considerations other than objectivity, professional judgment, impartiality, fairness, or equity, when making a decision among alternatives in employee relations. See *nepotism*.

FCPA: see *Foreign Corrupt Practices Act of 1977*.

FDIC: see *Federal Deposit Insurance Corporation*.

fear of failure: the fear of not reaching organizational or personal goals and of potential public embarrassment if such failures are recognized.

fear of success: the fear of the burden and stress that may accompany success and the envy and dislike it may generate in others.

feasibility study: an inquiry to determine what can be achieved given certain specified resources and constraints.

featherbedding: securing pay for work not done or for unnecessary work. See *full-crew rule*. Cf. *overmanning*.

feature:

(1) **salesmanship:** the components of an item or service that yield a benefit.

(2) **securities:** the more active stocks in the general list.

Fed: (slang) the Federal Reserve System.

Federal Advisory Council: a committee of the Federal Reserve System that advises the Board of Governors on major developments and activities.

federal bond: see *bond, federal*.

federal budget expenditures: in the unified budget concept, expenditures of all federal agencies and trust funds. Expenditures are distinguished from net lending, and total budget outlays are the sum of expenditures and net lending. Expenditures of public enterprise funds and trust revolving funds are shown net of the receipts of such funds. See *social infrastructure expenditures*.

federal budget receipts: in the unified budget concept, receipts, net of refunds, of all federal agencies and trust funds. Interfund and intragovernmental transactions are excluded. Proceeds of borrowing or receipts of public enterprise and revolving funds are not included.

Federal Communications Commission: established in 1934; regulates interstate and foreign communications by radio, television, wire, satellite, and cable.

Federal Contract Compliance Office (OFCC): a unit of the U.S. Labor Department, created in 1962, that is responsible for drawing up uniform sets of rules to guide the government agencies that enforce affirmative action programs. It prohibits discrimination on the basis of race or sex by employers that hold federal contracts. See *affirmative action.*

Federal Corrupt Practices Act: synonymous with *Hatch Act.*

Federal Credit Union: a cooperative association organized under the Federal Credit Union Act for the purpose of accepting savings from people, making loans to them at low interest rates, and rendering other financial services to members.

Federal debt limit: a limit imposed by law on the aggregate face amount of outstanding obligations issued, or guaranteed as to principal and interest, by the United States. Guaranteed obligations held by the Secretary of the Treasury are exempted.

Federal Deposit Insurance Corporation (FDIC): government corporation that insures the deposits of all banks that are entitled to the benefits of insurance under the Federal Reserve Act. The FDIC was created through the Banking Act of 1933 and was affected by amendments of 1935. All national banks and state banks that are members of the Federal Reserve System are required by law to be members of the FDIC. In 1989, dissolved and replaced by the Bank Insurance Fund. See *BIF; Federal Home Loan Bank Agency; Savings Industry Bill.*

Federal Emergency Management Agency: established on March 31, 1979; central agency within the Federal Government for emergency planning, preparedness, mitigation, response, and recovery. Effective 2003, part of Department of Homeland Security.

Federal Equal Credit Opportunity Act of 1977: legislation prohibiting discrimination, when responding to credit requests, on the basis of race, color, religion, national origin, sex, marital status, or age; because all or part of a person's income derives from any public assistance program; or because a person has exercised in good faith any right under the Truth in Lending Law. It gives married persons the right to have credit information included in credit reports in the name of both the wife and the husband if both use or are responsible for the account. This right was created, in part, to ensure that credit histories will be available to women who are later divorced or widowed.

federal expenditures: federal purchases of goods and services, transfer payments, grants-in-aid to state and local governments, net interest paid, and subsidies, less current surplus of government enterprises.

federal funds market: a market in which a bank needing additional reserves can borrow deposits in the Federal Reserve System from a bank with excess reserves.

federal funds rate: the interest rate on loans in the federal funds market.

Federal Hazardous Substances Labeling Act of 1960: law establishing a list of hazardous household substances subject to stringent labeling standards. As a result, the words "danger," "warning," and "caution" now appear more often in labeling.

Federal Home Bank: one of 11 regional banks established in 1932 to encourage local thrift and home financing during the depression. The banks are owned jointly by various savings and loan associations. The Federal Home Loan Bank Board serves as a management body. See *Federal Home Loan Bank Agency.*

Federal Home Loan Bank Agency (FHLBA): the 12 regional Federal Home Loan Banks under President Bush's 1989 rescue plan for the savings and loan industry.

Federal Housing Finance Board: established in 1989; responsible for the administration and enforcement of the Federal Home Loan Bank Act, as amended.

Federal Insurance Contributions Act (FICA): federal legislation that defines Social Security taxes and benefits. FICA deductions are made from paychecks to support this program. See *payroll tax.*

federal Internal Revenue collections: total federal taxes collected through the Internal Revenue Service. These monies make up 99 percent of all federal taxes (customs and a few miscellaneous taxes are excluded).

Federal Labor Relations Authority: created on January 1, 1979; oversees the Federal service labor-management relations program; protects the rights of employees of the Federal Government.

Federal Loan Bank: one of 12 district banks originally established in 1916 to make available long-term mortgage loans, at equitable terms, to farmers to enable them to own their own farms. The Federal Loan Bank System is the largest holder of farm mortgages in the world.

Federal Maritime Commission: established on August 12, 1961; regulates the waterborne foreign commerce of the United States; ensures that the U.S. international trade is open to all nations on fair and equitable terms.

Federal Mediation and Conciliation Service (FMCS): an independent agency created in 1947 as the successor to the U.S. Conciliation

Service. Its functions include providing mediators for labor management disputes in which interstate commerce is involved. See *Maritime Labor Board; National Mediation Board*.

Federal Mine Safety and Health Review Commission: established in 1977; ensures compliance with occupational and health standards in the nation's surface and underground coal, metal, and nonmetal mines.

Federal Occupational Safety Act: federal legislation of 1970 requiring employers to provide their workers with safe and healthful working conditions.

Federal Open Market Committee (FOMC): the Federal Reserve System's most important policymaking group, with responsibility for creating policy for the system's purchase and sale of government and other securities in the open market.

Federal Reserve Bank: one of 12 banks created by and operating under the Federal Reserve System. Each Federal Reserve Bank has nine directors.

Federal Reserve Board: the seven-member governing body of the Federal Reserve System. The governors are appointed by the president, subject to Senate confirmation, for 14-year terms. Created in 1913 to regulate state-chartered banks that are members of the Federal Reserve System, the board has jurisdiction over bank holding companies and also sets national money and credit policy. Synonymous with *supreme court of finance*.

Federal Reserve notes: notes issued by the Federal Reserve banks under the Federal Reserve Act when certain areas require large volumes of currency, or in seasons of the year when the public demand for currency is very heavy. When the need for currency relaxes, Federal Reserve banks retire these notes. Federal Reserve notes are issued to member banks through their respective Federal Reserve banks in denominations of $1, $5, $10, $20, $50, $100, $500, $1,000, $5,000, and $10,000. They answer the need for an elastic currency with full legal tender status.

Federal Reserve System: the title given to the central banking system of the United States as established by the Federal Reserve Act on December 23, 1913. The system regulates money supply; determines the legal reserve of member banks; oversees the mint; effects transfers of funds; promotes and facilitates the clearance and collection of checks; examines member banks; and discharges other functions. See *Federal Reserve Board*.

Federals: name given to items drawn on banks in a large city in which a Federal Reserve bank is located, although the banks do not belong to the city's clearinghouse association.

Federal Savings and Loan Association: see *Savings Association Insurance Fund; Savings Industry Bill.*

Federal Trade Commission (FTC): an agency established in 1914 to enforce antitrust laws by seeking voluntary compliance or civil remedies. The enabling legislation, which also declared unfair methods of competition illegal, was amended by the Wheeler Lea Act of 1930. See *Equal Credit Opportunity Act.*

Fed Wire: a communications network linking Federal Reserve banks, branches, and member banks; used both to transfer funds and to transmit information. Cf. *Bank Wire System.*

federated associated: a cooperative organization that is an association of associations.

fee basis: an arrangement with an advertising firm whereby the agency agrees to accept a fixed fee for stated services to be rendered.

feedback:

(1) **manufacturing:** the return of part of the output of a machine, process, or system to another machine, process, or system (e.g., to the computer) as input for another phase, especially for self-correcting or control purposes.

(2) **salesmanship:** market data collected in the field from surveys, polls, and/or interviews.

(3) **administration:** a means for measuring how an organization learns by reinserting into its system information derived from its own activity, thus enabling the organization to modify its system.

(4) **human resources:** the degree to which carrying out the work activities required by a job results in the individual obtaining direct and clear information about the effectiveness of his or her performance.

fees: payments for the performance of certain activities.

feminine organization: an organization characterized by humanistic treatment of individuals, nonopportunism, careers defined through service to others, commitment to employee growth, creation of a caring community, and power sharing.

FEPs: see *fair employment practices.*

fiat money: money circulated by government decree that has no precious metal backing. See *gold exchange standard.* Cf. *full-bodied money; paper money; real money.*

FICA: see *Federal Insurance Contributions Act.*

fidelity bond: see *bond, fidelity.*

fidelity insurance: coverage against loss from embezzlement or theft by employees.

fiduciary: an individual, corporation, or association, such as a bank, to which certain property is given to be held in trust, according to an applicable trust agreement. The property is to be utilized or invested for the benefit of the property owner to the best ability of the fiduciary. Administrators and executors of estates and trustees of organizations are common examples of fiduciaries. Investments of trust funds, unless specified in the trust indenture, are usually restricted by law.

fiduciary accounting: maintaining property accounts in the hands of a trustee, executor, or administrator.

fiduciary bond: see *bond, fiduciary.*

Fiedler's model: a model of leadership that specifies that a group's performance is contingent on the motivation system of the leader and the degree to which the leader has control and influence in a particular situation.

field examiner: an employee of the National Labor Relations Board whose primary duties are to pass on union petitions for an election, to conduct certification elections, and to investigate unfair labor practice charges.

field man: a company employee who travels in a certain territory, developing new agencies and servicing agencies that already represent the company.

field theory: see *Lewin model of behavior.*

field warehousing: a method for receiving collateral pledged in business loans. The warehouseman usually leases part of the borrower's facility and appoints a custodian to care for the items.

fieri facias: that you cause it to be made (*Latin*); a court order directing the sheriff to impose a tax on goods or personal property of the defendant to satisfy the judgment of a plaintiff.

FIFO (first in–first out):

(1) **manufacturing**: relating to inventory valuations (and the balance sheet figures for inventory should be qualified accordingly). That means that the cost shown for the first shipment of an item is used for valuations. This could inflate or deflate profits.

(2) **finance**: a method of computing dividends or interest and the effect withdrawals have on earnings for the period. The FIFO method

is considered to be using the oldest money on deposit for withdrawals during the interest period. It was originally designed to discourage withdrawals by exacting the maximum penalty. Cf. *LIFO*.

fifteen and two: the usual discount to advertising agencies permitted by most media, whereby 15 percent of the gross bill is the commission retained by the agency and 2 percent of the net bill is a cash discount given to the advertiser.

fifty-six: (slang) the days that replace Saturdays and Sundays for workers who are on the job on those days.

figurehead role: managerial duties that are symbolic in nature. As head of the organization or of a subunit, the manager represents the unit in formal matters, including ceremonies.

file:

(1) **general:** any collection of informational items that are similar to one another in purpose.

(2) **human resources and administration**: a collection of related records treated as a unit.

(3) **business law:** to place a legal document on public record.

file maintenance:

(1) the activity of keeping a file up to date by adding, changing, or deleting data.

(2) the processing of a master file required to handle nonperiodic changes in it.

filtering: alteration of information by the sender to create an inaccurate impression.

final expense fund: synonymous with *clean-up fund*.

final-offer arbitration: method of resolving collective bargaining deadlocks whereby the arbitrator has no power to compromise but must select one or another of the final offers submitted by the two parties.

final sales: the total of net sales to consumers, governments, and foreigners. Final sales exclude sales made to producers, except sales of durable plant and machinery.

finance:

(1) **general:** to raise money by sale of stock, bonds, or notes.

(2) **economics:** the theory and practice of monetary credit, banking, and comprehensive promotion methods. This theory covers investment, speculation, credits, and securities.

finance company: any institution other than a bank that makes loans to businesses or individuals. See *sales finance company*

financial accounting: the area of accounting concerned with periodically measuring and reporting on the financial status and operating results of organizations to interested external parties. Cf. *managerial accounting.*

Financial Accounting Standards Board (FASB): an independent accounting organization, formed in 1973, that is responsible for creating generally accepted accounting principles. FASB is a self-regulatory organization affecting accounting firms and practitioners.

financial analysis: the use of specific techniques to study a firm's financial documents and to control the flow of funds, products, and services, both inside and outside the firm.

financial controls: the vital factors in control process: budgets, financial analysis, and breakeven analysis.

financial expense: interest expense on long-term debts.

financial forecasts: the presentation of futuristic data, especially the financial statements.

Financial Institutions Reform, Regulation and Enforcement Act (FIRREA): 1989 federal legislation for bailing out the savings and loan industry. See *Savings Industry Bill.*

financial intermediaries: organizations that operate in money markets to permit buyers and sellers, borrowers, and lenders to meet easily. See *financier.*

financial leverage: the extent to which a company utilizes stock with a fixed return to finance assets. Increased financial leverage results in dramatizing changes in operating income upon earnings per share.

financial markets: the money and capital markets of the economy. The money markets buy and sell short-term credit instruments. The capital markets buy and sell long-term credit and equity instruments.

financial position: the status of a company, indicated by combining the assets and liabilities as listed on a balance sheet.

financial ratios: the relationship that exist between various items appearing in balance sheets, income accounts, and occasionally other items. These ratios are used to measure and evaluate the economic condition and operating effectiveness of a firm.

financial reporting: periodic reporting on the financial position of an organization or part of one in terms of operating results, activities, and financial transactions.

financial responsibility law: a law under which a person who is a responsible party involved in an automobile accident may be required to furnish security up to certain minimum dollar limits. Each state has some form of financial responsibility law.

financial solvency: the normal business condition in which current assets are above current liabilities. Cf. *insolvency.*

financial statement: any statement made by an individual, a proprietorship, a partnership, a corporation, an organization, or an association regarding the financial status of the legal entity.

financier: an individual who earns his or her living by supplying money for other people's businesses. In most cases the financier receives a cash profit or retains a percentage of the business. See *financial intermediaries.*

financing transactions: movements of currency, gold, and gold equivalents used to settle a balance-of-payments deficit. See *balance-of-payments deficit.*

finder's fee: a payment to an individual for bringing together a buyer and seller.

fine-tuning: an effort to steer aggregate demand toward a target level through monetary and fiscal instruments.

finished-goods inventory: all items a manufacturer has made for sale to customers. Cf. *work-in-process inventory.*

fire fighting: (slang) a management approach to responding to problems by making small changes as needed rather than by developing a program of planned change.

fire insurance: coverage for losses caused by fire and lightning, plus resultant damage caused by smoke and water. See *casualty insurance; smoke damage insurance.*

fire sale: goods sold at reduced prices because they have been damaged or water-soiled in a fire.

firing: see *layoff.*

firm:
(1) **general:** describing full acceptance of an obligation to perform, deliver, or accept (e.g., a firm bid, a firm offer).
(2) **business:** any business, corporation, proprietorship, or partnership.
(3) **business law:** an unincorporated business or a partnership. Unlike a corporation, a firm is not recognized as a separate person apart from those managing it (i.e., it is not an entity). Cf. *corporation.*

firm growth pattern: where each industry has established track records by which a firm grows.

firm order: a definite order that cannot be canceled. It may be written or oral.

FIRREA: *Financial Institutions Reform, Regulation and Enforcement Act*

first-dollar coverage: insurance that provides payment for the full value of each loss up to the insured amount with no deductibles.

first in–first out: see *FIFO.*

first level: the beginning-level position in an organization.

first-level outcome: a factor that brings about a second-level outcome. For example, productivity (first-level outcome) leads to promotion (second-level outcome) in many companies.

first-line management: the management level just above the workers, as represented, for example, by a plant foreman.

first-party insurance: insurance indemnifying the policyholder against loss or damage to his own property (e.g., fire insurance).

firsts: the top grade of any item. Cf. *seconds.*

first-tier forces: external environmental forces that affect virtually all organizations. They include the economy, suppliers, customers, and competitors.

fiscal: relating to financial matters.

fiscal charges: expenses or charges that are normal for a given type of business and must be incurred in order to engage in that type of business.

fiscal drag: the tendency of a high-employment economy to be restrained from its full growth potential because it is incurring budgetary surpluses.

fiscal period: a 12-month accounting period for which business activities are reported.

fiscal policy: a planned course of action on budgetary issues. Cf. *monetary policy.*

fiscal year (FY): a corporation's accounting year. It can be any 12 consecutive months (e.g., February 1 of one year through January 31 of the next). Most companies operate on a calendar-year basis.

five competitive forces model: a model, developed by Michael Porter and used in the examination of an organization's task environment, that offers an approach to analyzing the nature and intensity of competition in a given industry.

fixed annuity: an annuity contract providing payments that remain constant throughout the annuity period. These payments do not vary with investment experience.

fixed assets: permanent assets required for the normal conduct of a business, which normally are not converted into cash during the period after they were declared fixed (e.g., furniture, land, buildings). See *illiquid*.

fixed budget: a budget that remains the same after it is established, regardless of whether the activity level of the organization or program is higher or lower than projected.

fixed capital: capital invested, usually by stock- and bond-holders, as distinguished from current assets, which are partly supplied by banks.

fixed charges: business expenses that are not related to the level of operations.

fixed cost (expense): a cost (or expense) for a fixed period and range of activity that does not change in total but becomes progressively smaller per unit as the volume increases. Synonymous with *period cost*. See *capacity costs*. Cf. *direct cost*.

fixed factors of production: those productive resources that a company cannot alter in the short run (e.g., basic plant facilities).

fixed income: income that does not fluctuate with the general price level. People on fixed incomes have the most difficulty when prices are rising (e.g., retired pensioners in a period of inflation).

fixed liabilities: all liabilities that will not mature within the ensuing fiscal period (e.g., mortgages due 20 years hence; bonds outstanding).

fixed-pie assumption: the assumption that the amount of power or any resource held by people is fixed and that one resource gains only at the expense of another. Cf. *expanding-pie assumption*.

fixed routing: calling on customers on a regular basis. Cf. *irregular routing*.

fixed salary: compensation based on an agreed rate for a set period of time.

fixing the price:

(1) **finance:** establishing a price on something arbitrarily rather than through the free enterprise system.

(2) **securities:** computing the price at which a commodity will be billed for rapid delivery. See *spot   market*.

fixture:

(1) **leasing:** any equipment or furnishing (e.g., lamps, shelves) added to rented space to aid in business activity.

(2) **business law:** any chattel or personal property that is attached to real property permanently.

flagging an account: temporarily suspending activity on an account until it is brought up to date or for other relevant reasons. See *rubricated account*.

flag of convenience: the national flag flown by a ship that is registered in a country other than that of its owners (e.g., to avoid taxes or high domestic wages).

flagship store: a downtown or home office store where executive, merchandising, and sales personnel are located.

flash sales report: an unaudited report of a previous week's or day's sales.

flat:

(1) the price at which a bond is traded, including consideration for all unpaid accruals of interest. Bonds that are in default of interest or principal are traded flat.

(2) income bonds, which pay interest only to the extent earned, are usually traded flat. Cf. *loaned flat.*

(3) with no interest.

flat cancellation: the cancellation of a policy as to what would have been its effective date, before the company has assumed liability. This requires the return in full of any paid premiums. Cf. *pro rata cancellation.*

flation: neither inflation or deflation; a period of economic stability. Cf. *creeping inflation; inflation.*

flat organization: an organizational hierarchy characterized by a wide span of control between the top executive and the first-level supervisors. It usually requires better than ordinary communications, independence, availability of sound control, and ability to delegate. Cf. *tall organization structure.*

flat pyramid structure: an organization type that reduces the layers of management, widens the span of control of managers at various levels, and is often more decentralized with regard to decision-making autonomy.

flat rate:

(1) **advertising**: a standard rate for advertising space or time, with no discounts given for volume or repeat times.

(2) **finance:** a uniformly charged rate for each unit of goods and services, irrespective of quantity, frequency of purchases, and so on.

(3) **fire insurance**: the rate used when no coinsurance clause is attached to the policy (i.e., the rate from which the credit for coinsurance has not been deducted). In some states this is called the gross rate.

fleet policy: an insurance contract covering a number of automobiles. The automobiles may be specifically designated, or provision may be made for automatic coverage on a reporting basis of all automobiles owned by the insured (e.g., a taxi company). To be eligible for such coverage, all automobiles must be owned by a single insured. Cf. *open policy.*

flexible account: see *charge account.*

flexible budget: a budget, usually referring to overhead costs, that is established for a range rather than for a single level of activity. Direct materials and labor are sometimes included in the flexible budget.

flexible freeze: when George Bush was inaugurated as the 41st President of the United States on January 20, 1989, he announced this plan that would hold overall spending to the rate of inflation so that the presumably faster growth of revenues could close the budget gap within four or five years.

flexible hours: where work is carried out during period other than the traditional 9 A.M. to 5 P.M. periods.

flexible multi-item factory: a factory that is usually labor intensive and thus capable of producing several different products without large capital costs.

flexible reward system: allows employees to choose the combination of benefits that best suit their needs.

flexitime: a system that allows employees to choose their own starting and finishing times within a broad range of available hours. Workers still have to work their regular number of hours.

flextime: see *flexitime.*

flexyear: an employee scheduling concept that permits workers to be off the job part of the year. Employees usually work a normal work year in less than twelve months.

flier:

(1) **advertising:** a handout used to promote an idea, product, or person (e.g., a political candidate).

(2) **securities:** a speculative purchase or investment, usually made by an individual who does not normally speculate or trade actively in the market.

flight of capital: the movement of capital, which usually has been converted into a liquid asset, from one place to another to avoid loss or to increase gain.

flight saturation: maximum concentration of spot advertising in a relatively short period.

float:

(1) **banking:** the amount of funds in the process of collection, represented by checks in the possession of one bank but drawn on other banks, either local or out of town. See *uncollected funds.*

(2) **securities:** the portion of a new security that has not yet been bought by the public. Cf. *undigested securities.*

floatation (flotation):

(1) **securities:** launching an issue of securities. See *float.*

(2) **finance:** the process of financing a business activity.

floater policy: a policy under whose terms protection follows movable property (e.g., jewelry, furs), covering it wherever it may be. See *blanket policy.* Synonymous with *all-risks insurance.*

floating assets: synonymous with *current assets.*

floating charge: a business loan that is secured on assets rather than on a particular item. The lender has priority of repayment from the fund of assets that exist when a receiving order is made against the firm.

floating debt: any short-term obligation; usually, the portion of the public debt held in Treasury bills or other short-term obligations.

floating rates: the automatic determination of appropriate exchange rates by market forces, not by a nation's reserve holdings. Nations that do not follow these rates are pressured into line; otherwise they would see the value of their currency driven to unacceptably low levels or driven up to the point where no other nation would be able to purchase its goods.

flood insurance: coverage against loss resulting from the flood peril, widely available at low cost under a program developed jointly in 1968 by the private insurance industry and the federal government.

floor: the huge trading area where stocks and bonds are bought and sold on an exchange. See *pit.*

floor broker: a member of a stock exchange who executes orders on the floor of the exchange to buy or sell listed securities.

floor limit: the largest amount for which a merchant may accept noncash payment (check or credit card) without obtaining an authorization. A zero floor limit calls for authorization for every transaction, and this is becoming more feasible as the time and cost of obtaining authorization decline.

floorwalker: a person who moves about a store through various selling departments and assists customers in ways not handled by sales personnel.

flow chart:

(1) **administration:** a graphical representation for the definition, analysis, or solution of a problem, in which symbols are used to represent operations, data, flow, equipment, and other variables.

(2) **operations research**: a system analysis tool that displays a graphi-

cal picture of a procedure. May be general or detailed. See *methods study*.

flower bond: see *bond, flower*.

flow of work: the way in which organizational activities or processes are completed.

flow process chart: a graphic approach used for the classification and analysis of organizational activities in terms of the various individual operations, transfers, inspection points, and storages, so as to make these activities as feasible, economical, and efficient as possible.

flow-through: synonymous with *pass-through*.

fluctuating unemployment: unemployment caused by temporary, often voluntary economic adjustments (e.g., when people voluntarily shift jobs, or when people are laid off during certain months of the year in seasonal industries).

fluctuation: the ups and downs of prices. See *hedging; seasonal fluctuations; yo-yo stocks*.

fluid savings: savings that have been neither spent nor invested.

flying squadron: supervisors who rotate assignments among several departments to increase their overall understanding and skills. Synonymous with *job rotation*.

FMCS: see *Federal Mediation and Conciliation Service*.

FOB: freight (free) on board. Identifying the point from which a store is to pay transportation on incoming shipments. When the terms are FOB shipping point, the store must pay all charges from the vendor's shipping point. When the terms are FOB store, the vendor must pay all charges up to the store's receiving dock. Cf. *free alongside ship*.

focused market unit: a market oriented division that services potential customers regardless of their location.

fog of war: a military concept that has found its way into management: a confusion that attends the smoke of battle; a rationalization for distorting the truth.

follow-up control: a management approach of checking whether assigned work has been completed in accordance with instructions or training given previously to an employee or a group of workers.

FOMC: see *Federal Open Market Committee*.

football-bell structure: a theory proposed by Professors Leavitt and Whisler that by 1980 organizations would be characterized by a small group of middle managers, more innovators in the top ranks, and fewer lower-level managers. Cf. *line organization*.

footing: adding a column of figures. Synonymous with *casting up*.

forced billing: a means used to secure payments for freight delivery when no bill can be found.

forced-choice method: an approach to performance appraisal that requires the rater to choose from statements designed to distinguish between successful and unsuccessful performance.

forced sale: the sale or loss of property when one does not wish to dispose of it, as in bankruptcy. Synonymous with *judicial sale.*

forced saving: the situation that occurs when consumers are prevented from spending a portion of their income on consumption.

Foreign Corrupt Practices Act (FCPA) of 1977: legislation that requires all companies registered with the Securities and Exchange Commission to keep accurate accounting records and to maintain an adequate system of internal control. See *Trade Bill of 1988.*

foreign exchange (F/X): instruments used for international payments (i.e., currency, checks, drafts, and bills of exchange).

foreign exchange rate: the price of one currency in terms of another.

foreign income: income earned by Americans from work performed in another country.

foreign investment: the purchase of assets from abroad.

foreign trade multiplier: the concept that fluctuations in exports and/or imports may lead to significant variations in national income.

foreman: a member of the management team responsible for implementing the policies and procedures in his or her department, directing the workers assigned to the department. See *functional foremanship.* Synonymous with *gang boss; straw boss.*

forfaiting: the purchase, without recourse, of receivables from the export sales of items.

forgery: false writing or alteration of an instrument to injure another person or with fraudulent intent to deceive (e.g., signing another person's name on a check to obtain money from a bank).

forgery bond: see *bond, forgery.*

formal appraisal: a formalized appraisal process for rating current subordinate performance, identifying subordinates deserving raises or promotions, and identifying subordinates in need of further training.

formal authority: power rooted in the general understanding that specific individuals or groups have the right to exert influence within certain limits by virtue of their position within the organization.

formal communication: any communication that follows an organization's prescribed lines of authority.

formal group: a designated work group defined by the organization's structure.

formalization: attainment of a firm's objectives through uniform procedures that are established and legitimated by top management.

formal leadership: the process of influencing others to pursue official objectives.

formal networks: task-related communications that follow the authority chain.

formal organization: the established organizational structure used to achieve goals and objectives. Cf. *informal organization.*

formal rewards: rewards, such as increases in pay or receipt of a promotion, that are stipulated by an organization to help its managers develop power.

form analysis: the method and practice of examining and analyzing organizational forms, charts,

documents, and other records to discover the most appropriate way of facilitating procedures.

formula investing: an investment technique. One formula calls for shifting funds from common shares to preferred shares or bonds as the market average rises above a certain predetermined point and returning funds to common share investments as the market average declines.

forward exchange: a foreign bill of exchange purchased or sold at a stated price that is payable on a given date.

forwarding: carrying information from one page to another in an account or journal.

forward integration: see *integration, forward.*

forward market: the claim to sell or purchase securities, foreign currencies, and so on, at a fixed price at a given future date. This market deals in futures.

forward prices: a proposal for minimizing price uncertainty and encouraging greater stability in farming by utilizing the price system as an adjustment mechanism.

forward stock: stock that is brought into the selling department. See *inventory.* Cf. *reserve requisition control.*

foul bill of lading: a bill of lading identifying shortage or damage that existed at the time of shipment.

401 (k) plan: a company sponsored current pay reduction program, whereby the amount withheld, often matched by the employer, is not taxed until it is withdrawn from the plan.

fourth-class mail: merchandise, printed matter, mailable live animals, and all other matter not included in first-, second-, or third-class mail.

fourth market: the buying and selling of unlisted securities directly between investors.

fractional currency: any currency that is smaller than a standard money unit (e.g., any U.S. coin worth less than $1).

fragmented (fractional) bargaining: part of the collective-bargaining negotiation dealing with a set of grievances of a particular group that is looked on as a smaller but critical aspect of the total bargaining activity.

franchise:

(1) **manufacturing:** a privilege granted to a dealer for distribution of a manufacturer's product. Cf. *refusal to sell.*

(2) **business law:** a certificate of incorporation.

franchise clause: a provision that payment shall not be made unless the loss or damage equals or exceeds a specified amount, known as the franchise. Cf. *deductible clause.*

franchised dealer: a retail dealer who, under terms of a franchise agreement, carries a supplier's products.

franchisee: the person or entrepreneur who purchases the right to use, manufacture, or sell any trademark, copyright, or patent.

franchiser: an individual or company that licenses others to sell its products or services.

franchise store: an independently owned store that sells branded items produced by a franchise holder. The store pays the franchiser a percentage of sales for the use of the name.

franchise tax: the tax levied on a corporation for conducting business under its corporate name.

franco delivery: the full delivery of items to a consignee with all charges paid (e.g., a prepaid delivery). Cf. *cash on delivery.*

Frankenstein foods: food, primarily exported from the U.S., that is genetically modified. The European Union has refused to approve these imports since 1998.

fraud: intentional misrepresentation of the truth in order to deceive another person. Aspects of fraud include the false representation of fact intentionally made, with the intent that the deceived person act thereon; knowledge that the statement would deceive; and knowledge that the person deceived acted, leading to his injury. See *bad faith; lapping; voidable contract.*

fraudulent conveyance: conveyance of property entered into by a debtor with the objective of defrauding creditors.

free alongside ship (FAS): shipping terms whereby an exporter pays all charges involved up to the moment of delivery. Cf. *FOB; free overside.*

free and open market: a market in which supply and demand are freely expressed in terms of price as contrasted to a controlled market, in which supply, demand, and price may all be regulated.

free astray: freight that is miscarried or delivered to the wrong location, then is billed and forwarded to the correct location without additional charge.

free bond: see *bond, free.*

freedom of contract: the right of persons engaged in producing goods and services to enter into agreements resulting in production. These agreements must be within the law and cannot be planned to damage individuals or society. Article I, Section 10, of the U.S. Constitution forbids the states to pass any law impairing the obligation of contracts. See *contract clause.*

free economies: economies that operate on the basis of supply and demand, with price acting as the control mechanism. There is no central authority to allocate resources, as in a planned economy.

free enterprise: the condition under which a firm or individual is able to function competitively without excessive government restrictions.

free goods: items that are so abundant that it is not profitable to attempt to charge for them (e.g., sunlight).

free goods offer: merchandise received by a buyer at no cost for having purchased some unit of goods. Cf. *giveaway.*

free list: a statement prepared by a customs department of items that are not liable to the payment of duties.

free market: describes the unrestricted movement of items in and out of the market, unhampered by tariffs or other trade barriers.

free overside: in export price quotations, the seller paying all costs and accepting full responsibility for the goods until they have been safely unloaded at the place of importation in a foreign country. Thereafter, the buyer will pay all costs such as customs duty. Cf. *free alongside ship.*

free port: a port where no duties are paid on either imports or exports.

free reserves: a Federal Reserve Bank term describing the margin by which excess reserves exceed the bank's borrowings.

free ride: a situation in which an investor buys and sells in a short period, usually less than five days. The purchaser does not put up any money but still takes a profit.

free rider: a union term for an employee who fails to join the union that has negotiated a contract governing his wages and working conditions and is legally bound to protect his interests in the workplace. Cf. *Rand formula.*

free trade: trade among countries in the absence of policy restrictions that may interfere with its flow.

free trade agreement: a comprehensive agreement designed to remove barriers to substantially expand all trade through elimination tariffs and quotas enhancing market access and restraining certain government actions, such as subsidies. Cf. *reciprocal trade agreement.*

Free Trade Area of the Americas (FTAA): proposed free trade zone of 34 nations from North, Central, and South America, plus nations of the Caribbean, to lower tariffs and increase free trade by the year 2005.

freeze:

(1) **general:** to fix prices at present levels, as with a price freeze. A freeze rarely takes place except during national crises or wartime.

(2) **government:** government seizure or impounding of property, goods, and so on. This action demands an executive order or the passage of a law, usually during emergencies.

freight: all merchandise, goods, products, or commodities shipped by rail, air, road, or water, other than baggage, express mail, or regular mail.

freight absorption: a seller not charging a customer for freight out.

freight allowed: an agreement whereby a store pays the transportation charges on incoming goods but is permitted to charge back all or part of that cost to the vendor.

freight forwarder: an organization that consolidates the less-than carload or less-than-truckload shipments of manufacturers into carload or truckload shipments.

freight (free) on board: see *FOB.*

freight inward: freight paid on shipments received.

freight outward: freight paid by a seller on outgoing customer shipments.

frictional unemployment: time lost in changing jobs, rather than as a result of lack of job opportunities. Cf. *cyclical unemployment.*

Friedmanite: an individual who upholds the monetary theories of Milton Friedman, who advocated direct control of money supply by governments in lieu of tax manipulations, government projects, and so on. Cf. *Keynesian economics; neo-Keynesian.*

fringe benefits: nonwage benefits (paid vacations, pensions, health and welfare provisions, life insurance, etc.) whose cost is borne in whole or in part by the employer.

fringes: *(slang)* fringe benefits.

front money: a sum that includes funds needed to pay for land; permanent financing; legal engineering, and architectural fees; title insurance; and other closing costs not included in a construction loan.

front office: popular description for the offices of the major executives within a company.

frozen:

(1) **general:** not easily available.

(2) **finance:** incapable of conversion to cash. Cf. *liquid.*

frozen account: an account on which payments have been suspended until a court order or legal process makes the account again available for withdrawal. The account of a deceased person is frozen pending the distribution by a court order grant to the new lawful owners of the account. Where a dispute has arisen regarding the true ownership of an account, it is frozen to preserve the existing assets until legal action can determine the lawful owners of the asset. See *attached account; deceased account; sequestered account.* Cf. *blocked accounts.*

frozen asset: any asset that cannot be used by its owner because of pending or ongoing legal action. The owner cannot use the asset or dispose of it until the process of the law has been completed and a decision has been passed down from the courts.

frozen pension: a pension that is paid up in full; the pension given when an employee leaves a company. See *annuity.*

FTC: see *Federal Trade Commission.*

full-bodied money: gold; currency that is worth its face value as a commodity. Cf. *fiat money*

full-cost pricing: the practice that includes all appropriate manufacturing costs in determining inventory.

full coverage: any form of insurance coverage that provides for payments of losses in full, subject to the limit of the policy, without application of a deductible. Cf. *deductible insurance; ordinary life.*

full-crew rule: a regulation stating the minimum number of workers required for a given operation. It was originally designed as a safety precaution for both workers and the public. See *featherbedding.*

full disclosure: found in the Securities Exchange Act of 1934; the requirements that every company that has securities listed on an exchange must register with the SEC and file annual and other reports disclosing financial and other data for the information of the investing public. Management must also disclose basic financial information used in stockholders' meetings.

full employment: the condition existing when all people capable of working are working to the limit of their capability, when there are more jobs to be filled than there are people looking for jobs, and when employers can obtain additional labor only by raising real wage rates.

full liability: liability that is not shared with others.

full lot: usually, 100 shares of stock traded on the New York Stock Exchange. Synonymous with *board lot; round lot*. Cf. *odd-lot orders.*

full mark: in retailing, a 100 percent markup.

full service agency: an advertising firm that handles the planning, developing, production, and placement of advertising for its clients.

full-service bank: a commercial bank that is capable of meeting the total financial needs of the banking public. Because the charters of some financial institutions limit their activities, this term draws attention to the advantages enjoyed by customers of a commercial bank. Cf. *multiple banking; one-stop banking.*

full-service wholesaler: a wholesaler who provides the full line of services, including taking the merchandise title, retaining a sales force, and making credit available to consumers.

full showing:

(1) **transportation:** the advertising message used on public transportation carriers.

(2) **advertising:** a full or 100 percent display of outdoor advertising.

fully allocated costs: the accountant's definition of production costs, including a proportional share of overhead, depreciation, insurance, and so on, usually for a multiproduct firm whose distribution of these costs is somewhat arbitrary.

fully vested: an employee covered by a pension plan who has rights to all the benefits bought with the employer's contributions to the plan, even when the worker is not employed by that employer at retirement.

function: a type of work activity that can be identified and distinguished from other work.

functional attraction: satisfaction with other persons in the workplace that comes about because these other people help one attain valued work outcomes.

functional audit: a technique for evaluating organizational internal strengths and weaknesses that involves an exhaustive appraisal of the important positive and negative attributes of each major functional area.

functional authority: a management style that permits staff experts to make decisions and take actions that are normally reserved for line managers.

functional conflict: conflict that supports the goals of the group and improves its performance.

functional costing: classifying costs by allocating them to the various functions performed (warehousing, delivery, billing, etc.).

functional departmentation: grouping jobs into subunits based on the primary functions of the organization, such as engineering, production, and marketing. Cf. *geographical departmentation; matrix departmentation; process departmentation; product departmentation.*

functional discount: a deduction taken to effect different prices for different customers (e.g., retailers get 40 percent off the list price, wholesalers 40 to 50 percent off). Cf. *price discrimination.*

functional distribution: the payment of wages, rent, interest, and profit to the factors of production according to their respective contributions.

functional foremanship: the application of division of labor at the foreman level. It involves splitting the task of the foreman into an arbitrary number of subtasks (usually eight) and assigning each subtask to an employee.

functional income distribution: payment of wages, rents, interests, and profits to manufacturers in return   for supplying their labor, land, capital, and management talents.

functionalism: the ability to perform a task; the division of work to ensure that tasks are performed (production, marketing, etc.) See *division of labor.*

functional manager: a manager who is responsible for a specialized area of operations, such as accounting, personnel, finance, marketing, or production.

functional obsolescence: obsolescence created by structural defects that reduce a property's value and/or market ability. See *weakest link theory.* Cf. *planned obsolescence; product development.*

functional organization: originated by F. W. Taylor; currently refers to a type of organization in which the direction and management of work is divided according to specialized functions or duties, rather than pure line or staff areas of specialization.

functional plan: a tactical short-term plan showing how each department of a business will contribute to top management's plans.

functional status: status derived from one's profession or type of work.

functional strategy: the overall course of action and basic policies that each department is to follow in helping the business accomplish its strategic goals.

functional superstructure: superstructure in which upper-level managers are organized around the basic organizational functions similar to the departmentalization-by-function approach adopted at lower levels.

fund:
(1) **business:** an asset of an organization that is set aside for a particular purpose; not to be confused with *general fund*. See *sinking fund*.
(2) **finance:** cash, securities, or other assets placed in the hands of a trustee or administrator to be expanded as defined by a formal agreement.
(3) **accounting:** current assets less current liabilities.

fundamental disequilibrium: a situation of chronic balance-of- payment problems brought on by an unrealistic, protected foreign exchange rate.

funded debt:
(1) **general:** the condition that exists when the method of paying off a debt and its interest is determined for specific periods.
(2) **finance:** usually, interest-bearing bonds or debentures of a company; may include long-term bank loans, but does not include short loans or preferred or common stock.

funded retirement plan: a plan whereby the employer sets aside sufficient monies to meet the future payout requirements of the firm's retirement plan.

funding: the gathering together of outstanding debts of a business, leading to a reissuing of new bonds or obligations for the purpose of paying off debts.

funding bond: see *bond, funding*.

funding gap: a barrier women entrepreneurs experience when they begin a venture and are frustrated in an attempt to secure initial financing. See *glass ceiling*.

fungible: goods or securities for which any unit is the equal of any other like unit (e.g., wheat, corn).

funny money: convertible preferred stocks, convertible bonds, options, and warrants that appear to have characteristics of common stock equity but which did not reduce reported earnings per share before 1969.

fusion process: a type of socialization process whereby the goals and interests of an employee become somewhat similar to those of the organization in which he or she works.

futures:

(1) **finance:** foreign currencies bought or sold based on a rate that is quoted as of some future date.

(2) **securities:** contracts for the sale and delivery of commodities at some future time, made with the expectation that no commodity will be received immediately. See *gray market; hedging; Tax Reform Act of 1976*.

futures contract: a contract under which the seller promises to sell the purchaser a given amount of foreign currency at a stated price at some time in the future, regardless of the actual market price of the currency at that future data. A futures contract thereby protects a businessperson against an increase in the price of foreign currency between the time he or she places an order for a shipment of foreign goods and the future delivery date.

future sum: the money that a borrower agrees to repay for an obligation. It is the interest or discount plus service or other charges, added to the total amount borrowed.

future worth: equivalent value at a future date of the time value of money.

futuriasis: a manager's preoccupation with the future, with little regard to common sense or the reality of daily living.

futurists: individuals useful in social forecasting who track significant trends in the environment and attempt to predict their impact on an organization.

F/X: see *foreign exchange*.

FY: see *fiscal year*.

G

GAAP: generally accepted accounting principles. See *Financial Accounting Standards Board*.

gain on disposal: sale of a noncurrent asset for more than book value.

gain sharing: an incentive system whereby wage increments given to employees for increased output become progressively smaller as output increases.

galloping inflation: the rapid and unlimited rise of prices; swiftly increasing inflation that, if not controlled and minimized, could lead to a major crisis in the economy. Synonymous with *hyperinflation; runaway inflation*. Cf. *inflation*.

gamemanship: management actions that try to improve the manager's apparent performance in terms of the control system without producing any economic benefits for the firm.

gang boss: synonymous with *foreman*.

gangplank principle: developed by Henri Fayol; a principle holding that individuals at the same hierarchical level should be allowed to communicate directly, provided that they have permission from their supervisors to do so and that they tell their supervisors afterward what they have agreed to. The purpose of the principle is to cut red tape while maintaining hierarchical integrity.

Gantt chart: a means designed by H. L. Gantt to measure graphically the relationship between actual and anticipated production records. Cf. *milestone scheduling*.

gap analysis:
(1) **human resources:** approach to strategy formulation that involves comparing current and desired performance to determine a plan of action.
(2) **international business:** a tool used to discover why a company's sales of a given product are less than the market potential in a country; the reason may be a usage, competitive, product line, or distribution gap.

garbage-can model: a nonrational model of management decision-making stating that managers behave in virtually a random pattern in making non-programmed decisions.

garnishee: a debtor of a defendant who possesses money or property that a third party (a plaintiff) wishes to acquire to satisfy a debt due him or her by the defendant; an individual upon whom a garnishment is served.

garnishment: a writ from a court directing an employer to withhold all or part of the money due an employee in wages and to pay such funds to the court or to the plaintiff in the action (the person to whom the employee is indebted) until a given debt is liquidated. Cf. *offset*.

GATT: see *General Agreement on Tariffs and Trade*.

GAW: see *Guaranteed Annual Wage*.

gazumping: (slang) an unethical practice whereby a salesman raises his price just before the deal is about to be completed, often using inflation as the reason.

gender-role stereotypes: the association of women with certain behaviors, and possibly, often lower-level jobs. See *glass ceiling*.

general accounting executive: the executive primarily responsible for the organization's general accounting functions and for the preparation of reports and statistics reflecting earnings, profits, cash balances, and other financial results. Duties involve supervision of general ledger maintenance, and may include responsibility for accounts payable and other subsidiary ledgers.

general advertising: national or nonlocal newspaper advertising.

General Agreement on Tariffs and Trade (GATT): on January 1, 1948, a multilateral trade treaty was signed embodying reciprocal commercial rights and obligations as a means of expanding and liberalizing world trade; it set out common regulations and obligations concerning international trading arrangements and a framework for the negotiation of agreements to liberalize world trade by withdrawing barriers and problems that hinder such trade; accepted by over 100 fully participating nations, and nearly 30 participating under special arrangements, accounting for almost 80 percent of world trade. Replaced by the World Trade Organization (WTO) in 1995. See *Kennedy Round; Montreal Round; most favored nation status; Multifibre Arrangements; Tokyo Round; World Trade Organization*.

general average: a contribution by all the parties in a sea adventure to make good a loss sustained by one of their number because of voluntary sacrifices of part of the ship or cargo to save the remaining part and the lives of those on board from an impending peril.

general control expenditures: expenditures (for personnel administration and other general administration) of the legislative and judicial branches of the government, the office of the chief executive, auxiliary agencies, and staff services.

general equilibrium analysis: an economic inquiry in which the interaction of all markets is considered.

general equilibrium system: a model that attempts to define all relevant market interactions.

general expenditures: total expenditures less utility, sales of alcoholic beverages, and insurance trust expenditures when used in reference to state or local governments separately. When combined for state local totals, these items become direct general expenditures, to avoid duplicating intergovernmental payments. Cf. *general revenue.*

general fund: money that can be utilized (i.e., money that has not already been authorized for a particular project).

general journal: an accounting record into which journal entries are made.

general leader: a leader who takes a middle-ground approach between close supervision and laissez-faire leadership.

general ledger: the most important bank record, reflecting every transaction that takes place in the bank during the business day, posted from various departmental subsidiary records.

general lien: a lien against an individual but not his real property. It gives the right to seize personal property until a debt has been paid. The asset involved does not have to be that which created the debt. See *distress for rent; seller's lien; vendor's lien.* Cf. *particular lien.*

general macroeconomic equilibrium: a condition in which aggregate demand equals aggregate supply and the demand for money equals its supply.

general manager: a manager who is responsible for more than one specialized area, such as a company or plant. People from various functions report to this type of manager.

general partner: partner who, along with others, is liable for the partnership debts.

general revenue: total revenue less utility, sales of alcoholic beverages, and insurance trust revenue when used in reference to state or local governments separately. When combined for state-local totals, it refers only to taxes and charges and miscellaneous revenue, to avoid duplicating intergovernmental revenue. Cf. *general expenditures.*

general sales tax: a tax on most items, collected at the time of purchase. In many states purchases of food and medicine are excluded from this tax.

General Services Administration: established in 1933; sets policy for and provides economical and efficient management of Government property and records.

genetically modified foods: see *Frankenstein foods.*

geographical departmentation: grouping jobs into subunits based on geographical areas or territories. Cf. *functional departmentation; matrix departmentation; process departmentation; product departmentation.*

geographical differential: the variation in wage rates for identical work between areas or regions of the country.

Giffen good: see *inferior goods.*

gift certificate: a certificate that has an identified cash value, to be used in purchasing goods or services from the issuing store or business.

gilt-edged bond: see *bond, gilt-edged.*

gin out: (slang) to produce, implement, or execute a strategy.

giro: developed in the banking system of Germany, a payment system in which a bank depositor instructs his bank to transfer funds from his account directly to creditor accounts and to advise the creditors of the transfer.

giveaway:

(1) **finance:** a premium available without charge. Cf. *free goods offer.*

(2) **media:** the award of prizes to studio contestants, radio listeners, or television viewers.

give-up: a member of a stock exchange on the floor acting for a second member by executing an order for him with a third member. See *two-dollar brokers.*

glass ceiling:

(1) an invisible barrier to women and minorities in corporations; often used to keep salaries lower than for men doing equal work. The top corporate positions continue to be monopolized by white males, according to recent U.S. Labor Department studies. See *funding gap; gender-role stereotypes.*

(2) the transparent but strong barrier keeping women and minorities from moving up the management ladder.

global corporation: sells essentially a standardized product throughout the world, components of which may be made in or designed in different countries.

globalization:

(1) the extension of a firm's sales or manufacturing to new markets abroad.

(2) developing relatively standardized products with global appeal, as well as rationalizing operations throughout the world. See *responsible global capitalism.*

glut: to oversupply.

gnome: a banker or money expert who conducts business in the international finance market.

GNP: see *gross national product*.

goal: an objective or something specific to be achieved.

goal incongruence: a condition in which there are major incompatibilities between the goals of an organization member and those of the organization, the effects of which can be reduced by the establishment of standards.

goal setting: establishing steps to meet the objectives of an individual or firm.

godown: in the Far East, a commercial storage warehouse.

go-go fund: (slang) an investment purporting to yield sizable earnings in a short time period, resulting in risky, speculative market activity.

going ahead: a broker deciding to make a trade for his own account rather than filling all his customer's orders first. A dishonest broker might go ahead (i.e., transact his own business first).

going-concern assumption: the idea that an accounting entity will have a continuing existence for the foreseeable future.

going down the tube: (slang) the failure of a new venture.

going public: a firm's shares becoming available on a major exchange, as distinguished from being held by a few shareholders.

goldbricking: (slang) giving the appearance of working; also applied to actions of workers or unions (e.g., limiting output, loafing on the job).

gold bullion standard: a monetary standard according to which
(1) the national unit of currency is defined in terms of a stated gold weight,
(2) gold is retained by the government in bars rather than coin,
(3) there is no circulation of gold within the economy, and
(4) gold is made available for purposes of industry and for international transactions of banks and treasuries.

gold certificates: receipts that the Treasury gives to the Fed, verifying the gold deposits that the Fed makes at Fort Knox, Tennessee.

golden circle: in marketing, a group of brands in a particular product field, all of which are equally acceptable to consumers.

gold exchange standard: an international monetary agreement according to which money consists of fiat national currencies that can be converted into gold at fixed price ratios.

gold points: the range within which the foreign exchange rates of gold standard countries will differ. Gold points are equal to the par rate of exchange plus and minus the cost of transporting gold. The cost of insurance is included.

gold standard: a monetary agreement according to which all national currencies are backed 100 percent by gold and the gold is utilized for payments of foreign activity. Cf. *limping standard*.

good delivery: basic qualifications that must be met before a security sold on an exchange may be delivered. The security must be in proper form to comply with the contract of sale and to transfer title to the purchaser.

good-faith bargaining: the requirement that both parties to a labor dispute meet and confer at reasonable times, with their minds open to persuasion and with a view to reaching agreement on new contractual terms. A requirement to reach agreement on any specific proposal is not implied. See *arm's length bargaining; duty to bargain*.

good money: if two kinds of money of equal nominal value are in circulation, the one preferred by the general public because of metal content. People will tend to hoard the good money and spend the bad money, driving the good money out of circulation. See *Gresham's law*.

goods and services:

(1) **economics:** the result of industrial work, equaling the gross national product for one year.

(2) **business law:** any movable personal property, excluding livestock and excluding intangible property such as leases.

goods on approval: items obtained when a potential buyer requests and receives from a seller the right to examine them for a stated time period before deciding whether to purchase them.

good 'til canceled order (GIC): an order to buy or sell that remains in effect until it is either executed or canceled. Cf. *orders good until a specified time; resting order*. Synonymous with *open order*.

goodwill: the intangible possession that enables a business to continue to earn a profit in excess of the normal or basic rate of profit earned by other businesses of similar type.

goon: (slang) a person hired to create a disturbance during a labor dispute or to induce nonstrikers to join the job action.

go-stop: synonymous with *stopgo*.

gouge: (slang) to acquire an excessive profit by either overcharging or defrauding.

government bond: see *bond, government.*

government deposits: funds of the U.S. government and its agencies, which are required to be placed in depositories designated by the Secretary of the Treasury.

government expenditures: gross expenditure amounts without deduction of any related receipts.

government insurance: protection up to $10,000 provided by the U.S. government to individuals who have served or are serving in the armed forces, to cover additional war hazards.

government markets: federal, state, and local government groups and agencies that are the target of marketing activity.

government monopoly: a monopoly owned and controlled by either a local, state, or federal government (e.g., the U.S. Postal System; water supply systems).

government revenue: all money received by a government other than from issue of debt, liquidation of investments, and agency and private trust transactions. It includes tax collections, charges and miscellaneous revenue, intergovernmental revenue, utility, sales of alcoholic beverages, and insurance trust revenue for all funds and agencies of a government. Revenue is net of refunds and other correcting acts.

government saving: tax receipts less government expenditures.

graceful degradation: (slang) in computer industries, the attainment of acceptable levels of reduced service.

grace period: in most contracts, a provision that the policy will remain in force if premiums are paid at any time within a period (the grace period) varying from 28 to 31 days following the premium due date.

grade labeling: as authorized by government agencies, the labeling of certain consumer items as specified by standards (e.g., the grading of meat). See *Federal Trade Commission.*

grades (grading): the classification of major commodities into well-defined grades; the standardization of quality differences of staple commodities for purposes of identification during trading periods.

graduated securities: stocks that have moved from one exchange to another (e.g., from the American Stock Exchange to the New York Stock Exchange).

graduated tax: a progressive tax whereby the rate of tax per unit of the tax base increases as the number of units increases.

graduated wage: wages that are adjusted on the basis of length of service with the organization or are coupled with performance standards.

grandfather clause: any condition that ties existing rights or privileges to previous or remote conditions or acts; more popularly used, when a new regulation goes into effect, to exempt people who are already engaged in the activity being regulated.

grants-in-aid: payments made by one government unit to another for specified purposes. They represent federal support for a state or locally administered program or state support for a local program. Cf. *revenue sharing.*

grand strategy: a master strategy that provides the basic strategic direction at the corporate level.

grapevine: an informal communication network in an organization that bypasses the formal channels of communication.

grass-roots method: a sales forecasting method that relies on input from salespeople in the field.

gray knight: an opportunistic second bidder in a company takeover that is not sought by the target who attempts to take advantage of the problems between the target and the initial bidder. Cf. *white knight.*

gray market:
(1) sources of supply from which scarce items are bought for quick delivery at a premium well above the usual market price. Individuals engaged in this legal activity speculate on future demands. Cf. *black market.*

(2) the market for goods and services among older consumers.

great person approach: leadership approach that states that some people are born with the necessary attributes to be great leaders.

green hands: workers who are new to a job and inexperienced in performing their tasks.

green power: the power of money.

Gresham's law: the concept that bad money drives away good money. This refers to the way in which people protect themselves from loss by spending money of questionable value and holding onto money of known better value. Cf. *quantity theory.* See *good money.*

grid technique: see *managerial grid; repertory grid.*

grievance: a complaint handled formally through contractually fixed procedures. If unsettled, a grievance may lead to the arbitration process. Synonymous with *gripe.*

grievance machinery: procedures identified in a collective-bargaining agreement to resolve problems that develop in interpretation and/or application of the contract.

grievance mediation: a process where a neutral party assists in the resolution of an employee
grievance.

grievance procedure:

(1) a systematic process through which employees complain about matters affecting them.

(2) a means that an employee uses to lodge a complaint against an employer, usually one regarding wages, hours, or some condition of employment, such as unfair supervisory behavior.

gripe: synonymous with *grievance*.

gross:

(1) **general:** coarse; common.

(2) **merchandising:** twelve dozen.

(3) **finance:** a total amount before any deductions have been made.

gross debt: all long-term credit obligations incurred and outstanding, whether backed by a government's full faith and credit or nonguaranteed, and all interest-bearing short-term credit obligations.

gross earnings: the total income of a business, usually segregated according to types in financial income statements.

gross income: revenues before any expenses have been deducted.

gross investment: the total value of real productive assets produced in one year.

gross line: the amount of insurance a company has on a risk, including the amount it has reinsured. Net lines plus reinsurance equals gross line.

gross margin:

(1) **sales:** the amount, determined by subtracting cost of goods sold from net sales, that covers operating and financial expenses and provides net income. Synonymous with *gross profit*.

(2) **retailing:** the dollar difference between net sales and the net cost of goods sold during a stated time frame. Gross margin percentage is calculated by dividing net sales into this figure.

gross national debt: the total indebtedness of the federal government, including debts owed by one agency to another.

gross national disproduct: the total of all social costs or reductions in benefits to the community that result from producing the gross national product (e.g., pollution of rivers is part of the gross national disproduct).

gross national expenditure: the full amount spent by the four sectors of the economy (household, government, business, and foreign) on the nation's output of goods and services. It is equal to the gross national product.

gross national income: synonymous with *gross national product*.

gross national product (GNP): the total retail market value of all items and services produced in a country during a specified period, usually one year. Distribution is presented in terms of consumer and government purchases, gross private national and foreign investments, and exports. Synonymous with *gross national income*.

gross price method (of recording purchase or sales discounts): the purchase (or sale) recorded as its invoice price, not deducting the amounts of discounts available. Discounts taken are recorded in a contra account to purchases (or sales).

gross private domestic investment: purchases of newly produced capital goods plus the value of the change in the volume of inventories held by business. Purchases include all new private dwellings, whether leased to tenants or owner occupied.

gross profit: synonymous with *gross margin*.

gross profit method: a way of determining ending inventory. The estimated gross profit ratio x net sales = gross profit, which is then subtracted from net sales to obtain cost of goods sold. Then, cost of goods sold is subtracted from the total of the beginning inventory plus net purchases to obtain an estimate of ending inventory.

gross profit ratio: that portion of sales remaining after a company has paid for the cost of producing the goods.

gross rate: see *flat rate*.

gross rating point buy:

(1) **advertising:** the number of advertisements needed in a medium to achieve the desired percent of exposures of the message to the population of a market.

(2) **outdoor advertising:** the number of panels required to deliver in one day the desired percent of exposure opportunities. 100-buy is considered that number which would reach the entire population.

gross revenue: total revenues received from selling goods or performing services; a revenue before any deductions have been made for returns, allowances, or discounts. Synonymous with *gross sales*. Cf. *revenue*.

gross sales: total sales over a specified period, before customer returns and allowances have been deducted. Synonymous with *gross revenue*.

gross savings: the sum of capital consumption (depreciation) and personal and corporate savings.

group banking: a form of banking enterprise whereby several existing banks form a holding company. The holding company supervises and coordinates the operations of all banks in the group. A majority of the capital stock of each bank in the group is owned by the holding company.

group bonus: a method of wage payment based on the performance of a team on the job. The bonus is an incentive for work completed beyond the average.

group depreciation: a means of calculating depreciation charges where similar assets are combined, rather than depreciated separately. Gain or loss is not recognized on retirement or items from the group until the last item in the group is sold or retired.

group discount:

(1) **broadcasting:** a special discount for the use of a group of broadcasting stations simultaneously.

(2) **merchandising:** a special discount for the purchase of large quantities of an item or service (e.g., group discounts on air fares).

group dynamics: the study of techniques and procedures for altering the structure and/or behavior of a social group. It emphasizes eliciting from members some behavior that will bring about a desired change in group structure or behavior without attempting to modify the behavior of individuals. See *structural intervention*.

group enrollment card: a document signed by an individual who is eligible for group insurance as notice of his wish to participate in the group plan. In contributory insurance, this card also provides an employer with authorization to deduct contributions from an employee's pay.

group formation: the process of grouping the members of an organization into work groups or units.

group health insurance: a means for insuring a group of people (e.g., the employees of a firm) against the costs of ill health under one policy.

group incentive plan: a plan under which pay is based on total or group output. Added compensation is given to individual employees when the team to which the individual belongs produces in excess of preestablished levels or standards.

group insurance: any insurance plan incentive for work completed beyond the average under which a number of employees and their dependents are covered by a single policy, issued to the employer or to an association with which the employees are affiliated, with individual certificates given to each insured person. See *noncontributory*.

group life: a form of life insurance available to members of a group of people, typically members of a company, under a master policy.

Group of Ten: under arrangement to borrow, 10 of the principal industrial nations (United States, the Netherlands, United Kingdom, Sweden, France, Japan, Germany, Italy, Belgium, and Canada). With Switzerland (an unofficial member), the 1962 General Agreement to Borrow makes their currencies available to the International Monetary Fund to lend up to specified amounts when supplementary funds are needed by the IMF. Synonymous with *Paris Club*.

group order ranking: an evaluation method that places employees into a particular classification.

group selling: the presentation for sale of goods or services to two or more people simultaneously; designed to increase the size and sales of a firm.

groupshift: a change in decision risk between the group's decision and the individual decision that members within the group would make; can be toward either conservatism or greater risk.

groupthink: phenomenon in which the norm for consensus overrides the realistic appraisal of alternative courses of action.

grow-and-penetrate strategy: active investment and marketing efforts designed to increase the size and sales of a firm.

growth-need strategy: the degree to which an individual needs personal growth and development on the job.

growth-share matrix: a display matrix showing market growth on the vertical axis and relative market share on the horizontal axis, used in analyzing the cash flow and investment requirements of a firm's products.

growth stage: the second phase in a product's lifecycle, characterized by arise in sales and profits and the appearance of competitors in the market.

growth stock: stock of a corporation whose existing and projected earnings are sufficiently positive to indicate an appreciable and constant increase in the stock's market value over an extended time period, the rate of increase being larger than those of most corporate stocks.

guarantee: a written statement assuring that something is of stated quantity, quality, content, or benefit, or that it will perform as advertised for a stated period. In some cases all or part of the purchaser's money will be refunded if the item fails to meet the terms of a guarantee. See *guaranty*.

Guaranteed Annual Wage (GAW): a plan whereby an employer agrees to provide his employees a specified minimum of employment or income for a year. Unions argue that GAW plans add to income and employment stability. Management argues that GAW does not take into account the fluctuations in demand for goods and thus is a poor business practice. See *makeup pay*. Cf. *Halsey premium plan*.

guaranteed bond: see *bond, guaranteed*.

guaranteed debt: obligations of certain semipublic and public corporations that are guaranteed by the federal government as contingent liabilities.

guaranteed income: proposals that the government ensure, as a matter of right, that everyone has a minimal income, even those who are unable or unwilling to work.

guaranteed letters of credit: traveler's letters of credit or commercial letters of credit, whereby the party requesting the credit issuance does not pay the bank in cash for the equivalent amount of the credit upon its issuance. The bank substitutes its own credit for people or firms, to encourage more domestic and foreign trade.

guaranteed rate: a minimum wage rate guaranteed to an employee who receives incentive pay.

guaranteed stock: usually, preferred stock on which dividends are guaranteed by another company under much the same circumstances as a bond is guaranteed.

guaranteed working week: the result of a labor-management agreement whereby workers will be paid for a full working week even when there is insufficient work for the employees during the week.

guarantor: one who makes a guaranty; an individual who, by contract, is prepared to answer for the debt, default, and miscarriage of another. See *guaranty*.

guaranty: a contract, agreement, or undertaking involving three parties. The first party (the guarantor) agrees to see that the performance of a second party (the guarantee) is fulfilled according to the terms of the contract, agreement, or undertaking. The third party is the creditor, or the party to benefit by the performance.

guest worker: a foreign work who is allowed to enter a country for purposes of employment but cannot bring his or her family.

guided missile culture: a culture that is characterized by a strong emphasis on equality in the workplace and orientation to the task.

guiding principles: principles drawn up by various underwriting organizations to deal with situations in which the coverage provided by one type of insurance policy overlaps that provided by another, resulting in disputes between companies as to how a loss should be apportioned. Use of these principles minimizes the disputes, thus securing payments to the insured.

gunslinger: (slang) a high-performance, high-risk fund that takes a capital role, or the manager of such a fund.

H

Hackman-Oldham job enrichment model: a model that focuses on certain job characteristics that lead to critical psychological states for the worker. These states affect personal and work outcomes, which are moderated by employee growth-need strengths.

haggling: synonymous with *higgling*.

half-stock: common or preferred stock that has a par value of $50.

halo effect: drawing a general impression about an individual based on a single characteristic.

Halsey premium plan: an incentive wage plan that provides for a guaranteed wage in addition to an extra bonus for performance in excess of the norm. Cf. *Guaranteed Annual Wage*.

hammering the market: the persistent selling of securities by speculators operating on the short side who believe that prices are inflated and that liquidation is imminent. When the market is primarily affected by the bears, these individuals are said to be hammering the market.

handbill:

(1) **advertising:** a form of direct advertising, usually a single sheet or a small pamphlet, distributed by hand.

(2) **finance:** paper currency.

handling cost: the cost involved in handling inventory. In some situations, the handling cost incurred may depend on the size of the inventory.

hand of government: a view of corporate social responsibility which argues that the interests of society are best served by having the regulatory hands of the law and the political process, rather than the invisible hand, guide the results of the corporation's endeavors. Cf. *hand of management*.

hand of management: a view of corporate social responsibility which states that corporations and their managers are expected to act in ways that protect and improve the welfare of society as a whole as well as advance corporate economic interests. Cf. *hand of government*.

hard cash: metallic currency, as distinguished from paper money.

hard-core unemployed: a group within the labor-age population that is able and willing to work but remains unemployed. Cf. *cyclical unemployment; employable; unemployable*.

hard goods: major appliances, including refrigerators, dryers, washing machines, and air conditioners.

hard loan: a foreign loan that must be paid in hard money.

hard money (currency):

(1) currency of a nation that has stability in that country and abroad.

(2) coins, in contrast to paper currency or soft money.

(3) a situation in which interest rates are high and loans are difficult to arrange. Synonymous with *dear money.*

hard sell: a dynamic, determined, and insistent approach to sales. Cf. *soft sell.*

hardship index: a measure of a person's income that is too small to satisfy the economic necessities of himself or herself, of his or her dependents, based on factors of unemployment, low income, etc.

hardship point: in a sales territory, a customer or prospect situated at a geographically isolated spot.

harvest strategy: investment and marketing efforts designed to draw excess cash and profits generated by a particular product or service line for use elsewhere.

hash total: a summation of fields that is used for checking purposes and has no other useful meaning.

Hatch Act: the Federal Corrupt Practices Act. Section 313 of this law was amended by Section 304 of the Taft-Hartley Act to make it unlawful (1) for banks and corporations authorized by Congress to make a contribution or expenditure in connection with election to any political office or activity; and (2) for any corporation or labor organization to make a contribution or expenditure in connection with any election or political activity. Synonymous with *Federal Corrupt Practices Act.*

Hawthorne effect: tendency of people who are being observed to react differently than they would otherwise. See *Hawthorne studies.*

Hawthorne studies: a series of performance studies undertaken at the Chicago Hawthorne Plant of Western Electric between 1924 and 1933. These investigations showed the importance of the social system of an organization and became the foundation of human relations theory. See *Hawthorne effect; human relations movement.*

Hazardous Substances Labeling Act of 1960: see *Federal Hazardous Substances Labeling Act of 1960.*

headhunter: (slang) an individual or agency involved in finding managers and executives for a client organization. A flat fee or commission is paid to the headhunter.

headhunting: synonymous with *executive search.*

head-on position: an outdoor advertising location that faces the flow of traffic, rather than being placed on an angle or parallel to the traffic.

Health and Human Services, Department of (U.S.): see *Department of Health and Human Services.*

health insurance: insurance that provides indemnity for loss of time and for medical expenses due to sickness. Cf. *accident insurance; hospitalization insurance.*

health maintenance organizations (HMOs):
(1) organizations of physicians and health care professionals that provide a wide range of services to subscribers and dependents on a prepaid basis.
(2) professional comprehensive health care for a fixed, prepaid fee.

hearing: a process whereby an accused employee formally presents evidence and testimony before an examiner or an official representing a board, in response to charges that have been preferred against him or her.

hearing office: a person who holds a full-time position with an organization but assumes a neutral role when deciding cases between the aggrieved employees and management.

heavy industry: the industries engaged in producing basic products, such as metals, or in manufacturing machinery and other equipment.

heavy market: a declining securities and commodities market created when the supply of bids for buying shares exceeds the demand for them, resulting in a price drop.

hedge fund: a partnership of people who pool their resources for purposes of investment. Cf. *investment company.*

hedging: a type of economic insurance used by dealers in commodities and securities, manufacturers, and other producers to prevent loss due to price fluctuations; consists of counterbalancing a present sale or purchase with a purchase or sale of a similar or different commodity, usually for delivery at some future date. The desired result is that the profit or loss on a current sale or purchase is offset by the loss or profit on the future purchase or sale.

hedging clause: a caution to customers attached to circulars, brochures, advertisements, and so on; a protective statement of warning for securities customers that customarily reads: "The information furnished herein has been obtained from sources believed to be reliable, but its accuracy is not guaranteed."

Hersey and Blanchard model: leadership model; identifies different combinations of leadership presumed to work best with different levels of organizational maturity on the part of followers.

hesiflation: suggested by former Secretary of the Treasury Henry H. Fowler for a reduced growth pattern in the economy combined with strong inflationary pressures. Cf. *inflation; stagflation.*

hetarchy: organizational structure in which management of an alliance of companies is shared by so-called equals rather than being set up in a superior-subordinate relationship.

heuristic:

(1) **general:** describing any method used to assist a person in discovering or learning something for himself or herself.

(2) **human resources:** describing a procedure or methodology designed to outline a program that will obtain desired results as an improvement over current procedures and is satisfactory in relation to the limits of time, cost, manpower, and the limited use of the result.

hidden assets: assets of a firm that are not easily identifiable by examining the balance sheet.

hidden clause: in a contract, any obscure provision that stipulates requirements that may be against the buyer's interests.

hidden offer: a special offer buried in the copy of an advertisement as a test of readership.

hidden persuader: popularized by Vance Packard in 1957 in connection with the motivational and manipulative techniques used by ad agencies in their campaign programs. See *motivational research.*

hidden tax: a tax included in the price of goods and services that is not easily identifiable by the payer of the tax.

hierarchical communication: exchange of information between managers and employees.

hierarchy: positions ranked in relative importance within a firm by degree of authority. See *chain of command; vertical strain.*

hierarchy gap: the difference in perceived satisfaction between employees at the upper levels of the organization and those at the other levels.

hierarchy of effects models: models of advertising communications that conceptualize communications as proceeding through a succession of stages from awareness to purchase.

hierarchy of needs: the theoretical model developed by Abraham Maslow, detailing the sequence of accomplishment necessary for personal fulfillment. When physiological needs have been satisfied, the individual directs his attention in turn to needs for security, belonging, esteem, and self-actualization.

hierarchy of objectives: the interrelationship of objectives within an organization. Short-term objectives are related to intermediate range objectives, which are in turn related to long-range objectives.

higgling: the procedure whereby, when the buyer offers a low price and the seller asks a high price, a third price is arrived at through bargaining to satisfy both parties. Synonymous with *haggling.*

high finance:

(1) **general:** utilizing another's funds in a speculative fashion, which may result in a loss to the funds' owner.

(2) **finance:** borrowing to the maximum of one's credit.

(3) **finance:** extremely complicated transactions.

high grade: an item of superior quality (e.g., high-grade stock or steak).

high potentials (hi-po's): executives with the greatest potential for filling the top slots for a given company. These are not necessarily a company's highest performers, but those with both the management skills, business acumen, and vision to lead the firm. See *emerging talent.*

hightime: extra pay for a worker who is employed in places high above ground or deep below ground.

high-value individual: one who will work very hard to achieve materials or career success, sometimes to the detriment of social relationships or spiritual achievements.

high-yield bond: see *bond, junk.*

hi-po's: see *high potentials.*

hir: a new pronoun recently coined by the American Management Associations to indicate the third person singular of either sex. National acceptance is urged for "he," "she," "him," and "her" to yield to the sexless "hir."

hiring hall: a union-operated place where out-of-work members apply for jobs (in an industry for which the hiring is done through the union). There are legal restrictions on how such hiring is conducted. In many hiring halls the workers are assigned in strict order of their registration for jobs. Cf. *oligopsony; shapeup.*

hiring specification: a written description of the education, experience, and skills needed to perform a job or position effectively.

historical cost: the principle requiring that all information on financial statements be presented in terms of the item's original cost to the entity. The dollar is assumed to be stable from one time period to another.

hi-tech: contraction of high technology.

hit the bricks: (slang) to go on strike.

HMOs: see *Health Maintenance Organizations.*

hoarding: collecting for the sake of cumulating; a planned effort by persons to accumulate items beyond normal need (e.g., purchasing dozens of cartons of cigarettes in anticipation of a price hike). Cf. *stockpiling.*

holdback: the portion of a loan commitment that is not funded until some additional requirement is met.

holdback pay: monies due an employee for services rendered but not yet paid to him or her.

holder in due course: a person who has taken an instrument under the following conditions: (1) that it is complete and regular upon its face; (2) that he or she became a holder of it before it was overdue and without notice that it had been previously dishonored, if such was the fact; (3) that the holder took it in good faith and for value; and (4) that, at the time it was negotiated to him, the holder had no notice of any infirmity in the instrument or defect in the title of the person negotiating it. See *endorsement (banking).*

holder of record: stockholders who own shares as of a specific date, to whom dividends are declared payable.

holding company: a corporation that owns the securities of another, in most cases with voting control. See *group banking.* Synonymous with *parent company; proprietary company.*

holding power: the ability of a product, program, or entity to retain an audience over time.

hold order: a written order directing that specific operations or work be interrupted or terminated, pending a change in design or other disposition of the material.

hold out: (slang) to refuse to work unless one is treated better or receives an increase in wages.

hold points: stock points for semi-finished inventory.

holiday pay: wages for holidays not worked; the premium rate established for work performed on holidays. Most union contracts specify holidays and establish premium rates.

hollow corporations: manufacturers that do little or no manufacturing and are increasingly becoming service-oriented, performing profit-making functions from design to distribution but lacking their own production base.

Homeland Security, Department of (U.S.): see *Department of Homeland Security (U.S.).*

honcho: (slang) a boss, senior executive, or headman.

honor: to pay or to accept a draft that complies with the terms of credit.

honor bond: see *bond, honor.*

hooking: the process of trapping a worker in order to have him spy on the union or his fellow workers. Synonymous with *roping.*

Hooperating: the percentage of individuals who are listening to radio stations, ascertained by using the telephone coincidental method of data gathering. These data are supplied by C. E. Hooper, Inc. See coincidental telephone method; *share of audience.* Cf. *Nielsen rating.*

horizontal channel: the flow of information across lines of communication. It can be classified as either a formal or an informal channel.

horizontal coordination: an aspect of organization structure involving the linking of activities across departments at similar levels.

horizontal corporation: a structure that is organized around customer-oriented processes performed by multidisciplinary cross-functional teams rather than formal functional departments.

horizontal expansion: expansion of a business by absorbing facilities or buildings to handle an increased volume of business in which the firm is already engaged.

horizontal integration: see *integration, horizontal.*

horizontal job enlargement: a type of work design based on the idea that increasing the number of tasks a jobholder performs will reduce the repetitive nature of the job and thus eliminate worker boredom.

horizontal loading: increasing the number of tasks or activities that a worker is doing by giving him or her more of the same to do.

horizontal merger: a combination formed when two or more businesses producing the same goods or services merge.

horizontal mobility: see *labor mobility.*

horizontal price fixing: an agreement on prices among competitors at similar levels of distribution.

horizontal promotion: a form of advancement of an employee whereby there is no change in the worker's job classification (e.g., promotion from junior to senior clerk, since the change involves no departure from the clerical classification). In horizontal promotion, pay may or may not be affected.

horizontal publication: a business publication edited for employees in similar job classifications in different industries (e.g., JOURNAL OF

MARKETING, NEW ENGINEER*).*

horizontal restructuring:
(1) acquiring ownership or control of competitors who are competing in the same or similar markets with the same or similar products or services.
(2) altering the lines of authority, means of conducting business, identifying savings via firings, etc.

horizontal specialization: factors in the division of labor that involve specialties (e.g., marketing, production). Cf. *vertical specialization.*

hornblowing: (slang) bragging about one's talents; advertising that is presented in an aggressive fashion.

horse trading: (slang) a form of bargaining designed to gain a one-sided advantage only, whether price or other benefits are involved. Trickery, deception, and/or other unethical methods are employed.

hospitalization insurance: insurance that provides indemnity for hospital, nursing, surgical, and miscellaneous medical expenses resulting from bodily injury or illness. Cf. *accident and health insurance; health insurance.* See *major medical expense insurance; medical expense insurance.*

hostile: offering resistance or opposition to being acquired by another corporation.

hostile environment: an unfriendly, often antagonistic situation as found in an office, or in dealings between employer and employee or representative, such as a union.

hot cargo: goods made or shipped by nonunion labor. Many unions refuse to handle such products, especially when they are produced or shipped by a struck company. See *unfair goods.*

hot cargo provisions: contract provisions that allow workers to refuse to work with or handle unfair goods. The Landrum-Griffin Act of 1959 outlawed such provisions, except for those affecting suppliers or subcontractors in construction work and jobbers in the garment industry. See *unfair goods.*

hot group: an energetic, high-achieving work group, usually small, whose members are excited by or obsessed with completing a challenging task.

hot: (slang) a security that is drawing considerable public interest and for which demand causes the issue to jump to an immediate premium, usually several points.

hot items: (slang) any goods that show quick salability.

hot money: (slang) money that is received through means that are either illegal or of questionable legality.

hot-stove rule: the concept that disciplinary action should have the same characteristics as the penalty a person receives from touching a hot stove; that is, the discipline should be given with warning and should be immediate, consistent, and impersonal.

hourly rated workers: employees whose pay is figured on hours actually worked during a week. Cf. *Guaranteed Annual Wage; guaranteed rate.*

house agency: an advertising agency that has only one client.

household saving: household disposable income less existing household consumption.

housekeeping: the general care, cleanliness, and maintenance of an insured property. The standard of housekeeping is a primary consideration of underwriters and inspectors, since poor housekeeping is a major cause of fires and accidents.

house of issue: an investment banking firm engaged in underwriting and distribution of security issues.

House of Labor: popular name for the American Federation of Labor–Congress of Industrial Organizations.

house organ: a publication (newspaper, magazine) issued periodically by a company to its employees to keep them informed about the company, its personnel, and pertinent activities.

house-to-house salesman: a sales representative who visits homes in an attempt to make direct sales. See *door-to-door selling.*

Housing and Urban Development, Department of (U.S.): see *Department of Housing and Urban Development (U.S.).*

HRIS: see *human resource information system.*

HRM: see *human resource management.*

HR 10: see *Keogh plan.*

huckster: a peddler or petty retailer who will attempt to sell anything profit-making.

human capital stock: the value of future labor earnings.

human engineering: an applied science of psychology and engineering concerned with the design of equipment and the arrangement of the physical conditions of work in relation to human sensory capacities, psychomotor abilities, learning, body functions, safety, and satisfactions. See *ergonomics.* Cf. *industrial psychology.*

human factors engineering: a process that applies information about human characteristics and behavior to the design of things that people use, to the way they are used, and to the environment in which people live and work. See *human engineering*.

human process interventions: organizational change techniques aimed at enabling employees to develop a better understanding of their own and others' behaviors for the purpose of improving the behavior in such a way that the organization benefits.

human relations movement: emerged following the Hawthorne studies, where human relationists believed that employee satisfaction is a key determinant of performance. See *Hawthorne studies*.

human relations theory: a theory that stresses the importance of individuals in determining the future of an organization. It is a systematic, developing body of knowledge that is devoted to explaining the behavior of industrial man. See *Hawthorne studies; multiple management; organic structure*. Cf. *classical design theory; unilateral strategy*.

human relations view of conflict: the belief that conflict is a natural and inevitable outcome in any group.

human resource accounting: the reporting of and emphasis on the relevance of skilled and loyal employees in a firm's earning picture.

human resource forecasting: the attempt, using specific techniques, to predict and project future personnel needs.

human resource information system (HRIS): a system, frequently computerized, for collecting, storing, maintaining, retrieving, and validating data concerning an organization's personnel.

human resource management (HRM): the management function that deals with recruitment, placement, training, and development of organization members.

human resource planning: estimating the size and makeup of the future work force.

human resources: synonymous with *personnel*.

human skills: the ability to work with, understand, and motivate other people, both individually and in groups.

Hume's species flow mechanism: the process whereby economies operating on the gold standard suffer inflation if exports exceed imports (and deflation if imports exceed exports). The economy's competitiveness in international trade is altered as a result, and exports and imports ultimately are forced into balance.

hurdle rate: the minimum rate of return that an investment must provide in order to be respectable.

hybrid structure: a type of departmentalization that adopts part of both functional and divisional structures at the same level of management.

hygiene factors: synonymous with *dissatisfiers; maintenance factors.*

hype: (slang) an activity that attempts to encourage consumer interest and sales (e.g., advertising).

hyperinflation: synonymous with *galloping inflation.*

hypothecated account: an account that is pledged or assigned as collateral for a loan. Savings accounts and trust accounts are usually selected for purposes of hypothecation.

hypothecation:

(1) **banking:** an agreement or contract that permits a bank or a creditor to utilize the collateral

pledged to secure a loan in case the loan is unpaid at maturity. See *respondentia.*

(2) **securities:** the pledging of securities as collateral (e.g., to secure the debit balance in a

margin account). Cf. *pledging.*

hypothesis: a specific, testable prediction, typically derived from a theory about the relationship between two variables.

I

IBRD: see *International Bank for Reconstruction and Development.*

ICC: see *Interstate Commerce Commission.*

iceberg company: a firm two-thirds of which is below the break-even point. See *break-even point.*

ICFTU: see *International Confederation of Free Trade Unions.*

ideal bureaucracy: a hierarchy of authority and a system of rules and procedures designed to create an optimally effective system for large organizations.

ideal capacity: the absolute maximum number of units that could be produced in a given operating situation, with no allowance for work stoppages or repairs. Cf. *peak capacity.*

idem sonans: a legal document in which absolute accuracy in the spelling of names is not demanded (e.g., "Eliot" or "Elliot" would be acceptable as designation of a person named Elliott.)

identity of task: the degree to which a job allows for completion of a whole or identifiable piece of work.

idle money:
(1) **finance:** uninvested available funds.
(2) **banking:** inactive bank deposits. See *unclaimed balances.* Cf. *inactive account.*

idle time: time when an employee is unable to work because of machine malfunction or other factors not within the control of the worker. Usually the worker receives compensation during idle time.

ignorantia juris neminem excusat: "ignorance of the law is no excuse" (*Latin*); the principle according to which a person can be cited for parking illegally even if he says he did not see the "No Parking" sign.

illegal strike: a strike in violation of a contract, one that is not properly voted by the union membership or not authorized by established union or legal procedures, or one in violation of a court injunction. See *snap strike; strike.*

illiquid:
(1) **finance:** not easily convertible into cash; the opposite of liquid. Illiquid assets can be converted into cash, but usually at a major loss in value. Fixed assets are illiquid assets.
(2) **business law:** not established by any documentary evidence.

illth: consumer items that are harmful to people who consume them and to the general welfare.

ILO: see *International Labor Organization.*

image:

(1) **marketing:** a buyer's mental picture of himself or herself; how an individual sees a product.

(2) **merchandising:** the feelings of customers toward a store.

image building: a public relations approach to advancing, upgrading, or generally improving the customer's attitude toward an item, service, organization, or person.

IMF: see *International Monetary Fund.*

immediate objectives: objectives that the organization can accomplish now without obtaining more resources or doing additional research.

immediate supervisor: a member of management who is placed directly over and is responsible for the activities of a worker, position, area, or function. See *foreman; supervisor.*

immoral management: management decisions that imply a positive and active opposition to what is ethical.

immunity: that which confers the ability to escape from the legal duties or penalties imposed on others. See *indemnity.*

impact: the way in which an advertisement or a medium affects the audience receiving it. See *motivational research.*

impact of a tax: the placement of legal responsibility for paying a tax (in contrast to the incidence of a tax) which is concerned with the extent to which the tax is passed on to others through price changes.

impairment:

(1) **finance:** the amount by which stated capital is reduced by dividends and other distributions and by losses.

(2) **accounting:** the total, where liabilities exceed assets by reason of losses.

impartial chairman: an arbitrator jointly employed by union and management to decide (i.e., settle) or arbitrate disputes arising out of interpretation of a contract; chairman of a fact-finding board. See *fact finding.*

impasse: the point in negotiations at which any party has determined that no further progress in reaching agreement can be made. In public negotiations, impasses often require a third party, such as a mediator.

imperfect competition: circumstances under which prices are usually altered by one or more competitors. This occurs because of unusual conditions in the market or advantages secured by some buyers or sellers. Cf. *competition (business).*

impersonal, aggressive management: management that strives forcefully to achieve various goals but treats its employees in a rather cold or distant fashion. Cf. *paternal, aggressive company; paternal; passive company.*

impersonal, passive management: management that rather apathetically pursues various tasks and treats its employees in a rather cold or distant fashion. Cf. *paternal, passive company.*

impersonality: the idea that all employees are subject to the same rules and regulations and are thus saved from the personal whims of the manager.

implementation: planning and/or putting an idea, schedule, method, or proposal into actual practice.

implemented improvement system: a Japanese-style suggestion system that is often used by total quality management firms.

implicit costs: costs originating within the business that are the responsibility of the owner (e.g., time, money).

import: to receive goods and services from abroad; an imported item.

import duty: any tax on imported items.

import quota: a protective ruling establishing limits on the quantity of a particular product that can be imported.

import substitution: reducing imports through local manufacture of the item. Import substitution is a common policy in developing nations, where foreign exchange is very scarce and where importers have developed the local market.

imposition: a demand or tax (e.g., bridge tolls, tariffs) on items, property, and so on, made by a taxing authority.

impost: a tax, usually an import duty.

imprest (petty cash) fund: a fund of a designated amount out of which payments for expenses of small amounts are made. This system is commonly employed in businesses.

imprint: the identification printed on a container during the process of manufacture. It may give the brand, container capacity, material quality, freight classification, and similar data.

improshare: a program under which bonuses are based upon the overall productivity of the work team.

improved value: the market value of a property after appreciation.

improvement mortgage bond: see *bond, improvement mortgage.*

impulse merchandise: items susceptible to spontaneous rather than purposeful purchasing. These goods benefit from display in store locations that have a considerable flow of customers.

impulse purchase: unpremeditated buying of merchandise.

imputed: a value that is estimated when no cash payment is made to establish that value.

imputed cost: a cost that is not specified but is implied to exist by the policies of the organization (e.g., interest that would have been earned on cash spent to purchase inventories).

inactive account: an account that has little or no movement. The balance may be stationary, neither deposits nor withdrawals having been posted to the account for a period of time. Cf. *idle money.* Synonymous with *dormant account.*

inactive stock (bond): an issue traded on an exchange or in the over-the-counter market for which there is a relatively low volume of transactions. Volume may be a few hundred shares a week or even less. See *cabinet crowd.*

inalienable: not able to be sold or transferred. Synonymous with *nonassignable.*

in-and-out: purchase and sale of the same security within a short period—a day, a week, or a month. An in-and-out trader is generally more interested in day-to-day price fluctuations than in dividends or long-term growth.

in-basket training: a training method in which the participant is given a number of business papers that would typically come across a manager's desk. The participant is required to establish priorities and act on the information contained in these papers.

in bond: items shipped by a producer several months before a store's usual selling season. The items are held in bond in the store's warehouse until the selling season.

Inc.: abbreviation for *incorporated.*

incentive pay: a wage system based on the productivity of a worker above a specified level. It may take the form of a piece rate, a rate for performance above a fixed standard, or a rate arrived at by some other agreed-upon method. See *accelerating premium pay; annual improvement factor; Atkinson system; base rate; basic piece rate; Diemer plan; differential piece-rate system; gain sharing; group bonus; group incentive plan; Halsey premium plan; Lincoln incentive management plan; piece rate (wage); push money; Rucker plan; Scanlon plan; task and bonus system; zero defects.* Cf. *automatic progression; Guaranteed Annual Wage; merit increase; speed-up; step-up.*

incentive plan: a reward scheme that attempts to tie pay directly to job performance (e.g., a piece rate, a sales commission).

incentive raise: a salary increment given after the completion of a specified, usually probationary, period.

incestuous share dealing: companies' buying and selling of one another's company securities for purposes of creating a tax or other financial advantage.

income: money or its equivalent that is earned or accrued, arising from the sale of goods or services. See *gross income; net income; profit; revenue.*

income account: an account in the general ledger of a bank. Expenses are listed under the assets, and the total expenses are usually deducted from the income accounts total to show the net profit to date as a portion of the undivided profits accounts.

income and expense statement: a summary of incomes and costs of operation over a specified time period. Synonymous with *profit and loss statement.*

income averaging: see *averaging.*

income bond: see *bond, income.*

income distribution: the way in which personal income is dispensed throughout the various socioeconomic levels in a nation.

income effect: the change in the quantity of an item demanded because a person's purchasing power has been altered.

income of unincorporated enterprises: income of businesses not organized as corporations; a mixture of return to labor or capital.

income segmentation: dividing markets or customers on the basis of their earnings.

income statement:

(1) **general:** the profit and loss statement of a given concern for a particular period of time.

(2) **accounting:** a copy of the income cash ledger for a particular trust account.

income summary: a clearing account used to close all revenues and expenses at the end of the accounting period. The balance of the income summary account before it is closed represents the operating results (income or loss) of a given accounting period.

income tax: a tax on annual earnings and profits of a person, corporation, or other organization. Traditionally, there are federal, state, and city taxes, although not all states and not all cities tax income.

Income Velocity of Money: the average number of times each year that a dollar is spent on purchasing the economy's annual flow of final goods and/or services—its gross national product.

incontestable clause: a clause stating that after a certain period, an insurance policy may not be disputed except for nonpayment of the premiums.

inconvertible money: irredeemable funds; circulating money that cannot be converted into the standard. United States money has been inconvertible since 1933 because it is not redeemable in gold. See *fiat money.* Synonymous with *irredeemable money.*

incorporated: the liability of the company's owners is limited to the extent of their investments if the company fails or encounters financial or legal difficulties.

incorporation: the procedure for obtaining a state charter to form a corporation. See *incorporated.*

increasing-cost industry: an industry that experiences increases in resource prices or in manufacturing costs as it expands when new firms enter it.

increment: a salary increase within a pay grade. It is usually based on seniority and performance.

incremental: additional investment required for a project or additional cash flows resulting from a project.

incremental adjustment: method of managerial problem solving in which each successive action represents only a small change from existing activities.

incremental influence: the influence of a leader over and above the influence base bestowed on him or her because of position in the organization.

incrementalism: a decision-making approach whereby executives begin with a current situation, consider a limited number of changes in that situation based on a small number of alternatives, and test those changes by instituting them one at a time.

increment tax: a tax on the increased value of a property, levied or assessed on the basis of its appreciation.

incumbent: a worker who is legally authorized and is now occupying an office or position.

incumbrance: see *encumbrance.*

incurably depreciated: damaged property that is beyond rehabilitation or property that is uneconomical to repair. Cf. *constructive total loss; particular average.*

incurred losses: loss transactions occurring within a fixed period, usually a year. For example, calendar-year incurred losses are customarily computed in accordance with the following formula: losses paid during the period, plus outstanding losses at the end of the period, less outstanding losses at the beginning of the period.

indebtedness: a debt that is owed; any form of liability.

indefinite tenure: an unspecified period of time a worker may, upon satisfactory performance, expect to serve under his or her current employers without fear of arbitrary dismissal.

indemnify: to compensate for actual loss sustained. Many insurance policies and all bonds promise to indemnify the insureds. Under such a contract, there can be no recovery until the insured has actually suffered a loss, at which time he or she is entitled to be compensated for the damage that has occurred (i.e., to be restored to the same financial position enjoyed before the loss).

indemnity:

(1) **securities:** an option to buy or sell a specific quantity of a stock at a stated price within a given time period.

(2) **finance:** a guarantee against losses.

(3) **finance:** payment for damage.

(4) **business law:** an act of legislation that grants exemption from prosecution to certain people.

(5) **insurance:** a bond that protects the insured against losses from others failing to fulfill their obligations. See *bond, indemnity.*

indemnity bond: see *bond, indemnity.*

indent: the request from a purchaser to an importer to import specific items at a stated price. The importer has a given time period in which to accept or refuse the offer.

indenture:

(1) **finance:** a written agreement under which debentures are issued, setting forth maturity date, interest rate, and other terms.

(2) **business law:** an agreement binding one person to work with or without pay for another for a stated period (e.g., apprenticeship). Such agreements are obsolete.

(3) **business law:** see *trust indenture.*

indenture bond: see *bond, indenture.*

independent:

(1) **human resources:** an individual whose behavior is self-determined.

(2) **administration:** an organization that does not belong to an association of companies or chains.

independent audit: an audit performed by an auditor who is independent of the organization whose accounts are being audited. See *audit*.

independent bank: a bank that operates in one locality. The directors and officers are generally local to the community.

independent integrator: an individual or group that coordinates the activities of several independent departments but is independent of them.

independent store: a retail operation that is controlled by individual ownership or management, not by outside management.

independent union: a union that is not affiliated with the AFL-CIO.

index:

(1) **general:** an ordered reference list of the contents of a file or document, together with keys or reference notations for identification or location of those contents.

(2) **economics:** a statistical yardstick expressed in terms of percentages of a base year or years. For example, the Federal Reserve Board's index of industrial production is based on 1967 as 100. In April 1973 the index stood at 121.7, which meant that industrial production during that month was about 22 percent higher than it had been in the base period.

index frontrunning: where the aim is to make money in futures by manipulating the stock indexes. This is done by trading in stocks that make up indexes, either by acting for large institutional clients or for the firm's own account (self-front running).

indexing:

(1) **economics:** the automatic adjustment of wages, taxes, pension benefits, interest rates, or any other payments of charges according to changes in the cost-of-living or other economic indicator, especially to compensate for or keep pace with inflation.

(2) **investment:** an investment strategy of purchasing and holding a mix of stocks to match the performance of a broad stock-market barometer such as the S&P 500. Many institutional index funds are active program traders, swapping their stocks for futures when profitable to do so.

index number: a measurement of relative change arrived at by employing statistical procedures. See *base period*.

Index of National Enervation and Related Trends (INERT): a U.S. Department of Commerce measure of the rate of increase of the figure for the gross national product.

indifference schedule: a table illustrating all combinations of two commodities that are equally satisfactory or that yield the same total utility to a recipient at a specified time. Cf. *diminishing returns.*

indirect-action environment: those elements of the external environment that affect the climate in which operations of the organization take place, including the economy and the political situation, but which do not affect the organization directly.

indirect business tax and nontax liability: all tax liabilities incurred by business, except for corporate income and social insurance taxes, plus general government nontax revenues from business. Nontax liabilities consist mainly of certain charges for government products and services, fines and penalties, donations, and special assessments by state and local governments.

indirect control: a management technique that traces the cause of an unsatisfactory result to the responsible person so that incorrect activities or practices can be corrected.

indirect costs: costs not usually identifiable with or incurred as the result of the manufacture of goods or services but applicable to a productive activity generally. Included are costs from manufacturing operations (wages, maintenance, overhead, etc.). See *reapportionment; running costs.* Cf. *direct cost.*

indirect damage: a consequential loss.

indirect financial compensation: all financial rewards, such as insurance plans, that are not included as direct pay.

indirect labor costs: wages of nonproduction employees, such as maintenance crews, inspectors, timekeepers, tool crib attendants, and sweepers. See *tandem increase.* Cf. *production workers.*

indirect liability: the liability of a party who endorses the note of a maker for a bank or guarantees a note as guarantor for a maker.

indirect material costs: the costs of materials that are included as manufacturing overhead and assigned to products on some reasonable allocation basis.

indirect production: producing an item needed for the manufacture of major goods or services (e.g., producing a machine designed specifically to produce a given consumer product).

indirect taxes: taxes applied to goods, which can be readily shifted to other individuals.

individual brand: a name applied to one product only (e.g., Crest, Tide).

individual characteristics: the interests, values, attitudes, and needs that workers bring to the job.

individualism:

(1) **general:** conducting one's affairs in one's own way.

(2) **economics:** the principle behind laissez-faire doctrine; the concept that individual economic freedom should not be restricted by governmental regulation.

individualized consideration: leadership factor that involves delegating projects to help develop each follower's capabilities, paying personal attention to each follower's needs, and treating each follower as an individual worthy of respect.

individual pay: amount a manager decides to pay an individual within an established pay range.

individual proprietorship: Synonymous with *proprietorship.*

individual ranking: an evaluation method that rank-orders employees from best to worst.

individual retirement accounts (IRAs): originally, individual pension accounts available to anyone who was not covered at work by a qualified pension plan. Effective January 1, 1982, all wage earners, including those who are already in company pension plans, are able to make tax-deductible contributions to IRAs. See *Economic Recovery Tax Act of 1981; Employee Retirement Income Security Act of 1974; Keogh plan.*

individual-role conflict: conflict between individual capacity or interest and job requirements.

indivisibility: the claim that certain production factors cannot be divided into smaller components (e.g., unlike a pulley system, which can function at reduced efficiency if one or more wheel-chain elements are omitted, an automobile that is divided into a set of wheels, an engine, and so on, cannot perform a function of lesser efficiency).

indorsee: see *endorsee.*

indorsement: see *endorsement.*

indorser: see *endorser.*

induced consumption: additional consumer buying caused by new capital formation.

induced investment: new capital formation caused by an upturn in consumer buying.

induction and orientation: activities intended to ease an individual's entrance into an organization through inducing the individual to the organization.

inductive method: a form of reasoning that approaches a problem from the particular and arrives at a generalization, emphasizing data gathered by observing the empirical world. Cf. *deductive method*.

industrial advertising: advertising goods or services for use in the manufacture or distribution of other goods and services.

industrial bank: a financial institution originally organized to extend loans to employees. The bank derives its funds through a form of worker savings. Most industrial banks have now been merged into commercial banks. Cf. *labor banks*.

industrial classification: analysis and synthesis of the factors pertinent to a business into a logical and systematic hierarchy, in which like things are combined in terms of their similarity, then categorized according to their essential differences.

industrial concentration: a factor reflecting the extent to which a large proportion of an industry's sales are produced by a few companies.

industrial democracy: an industrial organization that is required by law to permit its members to govern themselves.

industrial distributor: a full-service wholesaler representing industrial manufacturers and selling to industrial buyers.

industrial dynamics: a concept developed by Jay Forrester of MIT in 1957, to be used in investigating the behavior of industrial systems to demonstrate how policies, decisions, structure, and delays are interrelated to influence growth and stability.

industrial engineering: the applications within engineering dealing with the design, improvement, and installation of integrated systems of workers, materials, and equipment. It draws on specialized knowledge and skill in the mathematical, physical, and social sciences, together with the principles and methods of engineering.

industrial espionage: the effort by an outsider to illegally obtain protected technology from its originator.

industrial insurance: life insurance on an individual in an amount under $1,000, with premiums payable weekly to an agent who calls at the insured's home to collect. See *debit*.

industrialist: an individual who owns, controls, or plays a crucial role in the operation of an industrial organization.

industrial psychology: the branch of applied psychology concerned with the behavior and motivation of individual workers. Activities include testing, selection, training, and other aspects of individual and/or group interactions on the job. Cf. *human engineering*.

industrial relations: any activity, event, or interaction between employer and employee. It commences with the job interview and lasts throughout the working lifetime of an employee. The most popular usage of the term limits it to union-management relations.

industrial standardization: the orderly and systematic formulation, acception, usage, and revision of the given requirements to be achieved in order to attain a goal.

industrial union: a union whose members are employed in a particular industry, embracing various skilled and unskilled occupations. The union relies for its bargaining strength on the breadth of its membership rather than on the prestige associated with particular skills that they possess. Synonymous with *vertical union*.

industry-wide agreement: synonymous with *joint agreement*.

inelastic demand (inelasticity): the condition that exists when a price increase leads to a higher total sales revenue, or a price decrease leads to a lower sales revenue. A perfectly inelastic demand occurs when the demand for an item does not change with changes in price. Cf. *price out of the market*.

inelastic supply: a condition in which the quantity of an item produced does not alter, or changes minimally, with a price change.

inequities: rates or conditions substantially out of line with those paid or existing for comparable work in a plant, locality, or industry.

INERT: see *Index of National Enervation and Related Trends*.

infant industry argument: a dispute in support of import restrictions, claiming that specific new domestic firms have not reached their ultimate level of technical superiority and consequently require temporary protection from products from abroad.

inferior goods: any items for which demand decreases as income increases.

inflation: an increase in the price level, creating a decrease in the purchasing power of the monetary unit. Cf. *deflation; flation; galloping inflation; hesiflation; overheating; prime interest (rate); simultaneous inflation and unemployment; speculation; stagflation*.

inflation, runaway: synonymous with *galloping inflation*.

inflation accounting: the bookkeeping practice that shows the impact of inflation on corporate assets and profits.

inflationary bias: the tendency toward a persistent upward trend in the price level.

inflationary gap: the amount by which government and private spending exceeds the amount needed to maintain a stable price level and full employment.

inflationary spiral: the situation in a time of rising prices when employees demand higher wages, which in turn increases costs, leading sellers and producers then to demand still higher prices. See *stabilization policy; wage stabilization.* Cf. *Pigou effect concept.*

inflation guard endorsement: an endorsement that, when added to a policy providing coverage against direct physical loss to buildings, automatically increases the amount of insurance applicable to building items at the end of each period of three months after the policy inception date.

influencer: any person who, though not directly involved in a purchase, affects the buying decision of another person.

inflump: see *simultaneous inflation and unemployment.*

informal groups: natural (i.e., unorganized) groups of employees in the work situation.

informal leader: a leader whose power and authority over a group is derived from his acceptance by the group, rather than from his office, position, status, or rank in the formal chain of command in the formal organization.

informal organization: a rather complicated and nebulous network of communication and interaction patterns of workers, supervisors, groups, or cliques within the formal organizational structure. Such a phenomenon usually arises spontaneously in order

(1) to augment, interpret, speed up, or change the formal communication system (or the lack of it);

(2) to regulate the flow, extent, manner, and enforcement of formal authority;

(3) to humanize the formal organization by trying to maintain a feeling of individuality among the members, while providing some security, unity, integrity, and feelings of belonging; and

(4) to meet related psychological and social needs to such an extent as to give the impression of being the organization. Cf. *formal organization.*

informal performance appraisal: the process of continually feeding back to subordinates information regarding their work performance.

informational roles: the roles of monitor, disseminator, and company spokesperson.

information superhighway: high-speed digital communication network that may combine telephone lines, cable lines, microwave transmissions, and fiber optics to let anyone anywhere use interactive television, telephones, PCs or other devices to interact with databases around the world.

infrastructure: the basic structure of a nation's economy, including transportation, communications, and other public services on which the economic activity relies.

infringement:

(1) **manufacturing:** production of a machine that yields the same results by the same action as a patented machine. This is a patent infringement.

(2) **merchandising:** reproduction of a registered trademark and its use on merchandise to mislead the public into believing that the items bearing the reproduced trademark are the product of the true owner of the trademark. This is a trademark infringement.

in-house advertising agencies: advertising agencies that are owned and controlled by client organizations.

initial mark-on: the difference between the retail value of goods and the delivered cost when they are first priced and placed on display.

initiating structures: a leader's behavior in delineating the relationship between leader and work group and the leader's work toward establishing well-defined patterns of organization, channels of communication, and procedural methods.

injunction: a court order advising that if a party does commit the enjoined-against act, there will be a penalty. A temporary restraining order is issued for a limited time. A permanent injunction is issued after a full hearing. In 1932, the Norris-LaGuardia (Anti-Injunction) Act forbade the federal courts to issue injunctions unless certain conditions were fulfilled first. See *blanket injunction*.

in kind: the replacement of lost or damaged property with material or property of a similar description and quality. Cf. *kind*.

inland marine insurance: insurance developed originally by marine underwriters to cover goods while in transit by other than ocean vessels. It now covers any goods in transit (except transoceanic) and also includes numerous floater policies. Cf. *ocean marine insurance*.

innocent purchaser: an individual who, in good faith, does not expect any hidden property defects to appear when he has gained title to real property.

innovation: a process by which entrepreneurs and others convert opportunities into marketable ideas.

innovation-dominated strategy: a focus of key managers on the creation and/or implementation of new technologies, products, or services.

innovative diffusion: a process where anything in the market perceived as new by some group becomes adopted for regular usage.

innovative efficiency: as part of the concept of marketing efficiency, the offering of items and services demanded by and supplied to the market by activities which, together with the offerings, are the most appropriate that can be brought into being under the present knowledge of markets and technology.

in-pack: a direct premium found in a product package.

in personam: a legal judgment that binds the defendant to a personal liability. Cf. *in rem*.

in play: (slang) Wall Street jargon for a company being sought in a takeover attempt.

in-progress inventory: goods that are partially completed but will require additional labor and materials to become finished goods.

inquiry test: a technique for testing advertisements by noting the number of inquiries from listeners, viewers, or publication readers.

in rem: a legal judgment that binds, affects, or determines the status of property. Cf. *in personam*.

insertion order: written instructions for an advertisement to be placed in a particular issue of a publication at a stated rate.

inside-outside approach: a strategy approach whereby managers look first at the organization and then at the environment. Cf. *outside-inside approach*.

insider: an individual who, because of his or her employment position, has special information dealing with the financial status of a firm before that information is released to the public or to stockholders. See *smart money*.

insider trading: the practice of participating in transactions based on privileged information gained by one's position and not available to the public. When such transactions affect the price, giving an unfair advantage to a trader, it is illegal.

inside salesperson: in industrial and wholesale companies, a salesperson who remains in a central office to take calls from customers.

inside union: synonymous with *company union*.

insolvency: the inability to pay one's debts as they mature. Even though the total assets of a business might exceed its total liabilities by a wide margin, the business is said to be insolvent if the assets are such that they cannot be readily converted into cash to meet the current obligations of the business as they mature. Cf. *financial solvency*.

insolvent: an individual who has ceased to pay his or her debts or is unable to pay such debts as demanded by creditors. See *bankrupt; bankruptcy*.

inspection: the process of examining units or goods to determine acceptability against a standard and to accumulate information about product quality.

inspection order: an authorization to perform an inspection operation.

installment account: see *charge account*.

installment bond: see *bond, installment*.

installment buying: acquiring goods or services with no down payment or a small down payment, to be followed by payments at regular intervals.

installment credit: a form of consumer credit involving regular payments, permitting the seller to reacquire the purchased item if the buyer fails to meet the payment schedule.

installment loan: synonymous with *personal loan*.

instant (inst.): the present month (e.g., on the 10th inst.). Cf. *proximo*.

instant vesting: the right of employees to change employers within a given industry or area without losing pension rights. See *multiemployer pension plans*.

institution: an organization (e.g., bank, insurance company, investment company pension fund) that holds substantial investment assets, often for others.

institutional advertising: an attempt to sell the image of a firm—its quality, services, role in community services, merchandise, and so on—rather than specific items. Goodwill and position are foremost in the development of institutional advertising.

institutional decisions: decisions that involve long-term planning and policy formulation aimed at assuring the organization's survival as a productive part of the economy and the society.

institutional investor: a company that has substantial funds invested in securities (e.g., a bank, a labor union, a college).

institutional level: the upper level of an organization, concerned with relating the overall organization to its environment.

institutional managers: top-level managers whose concern is surveying the environment and developing cooperative and competitive strategies that will ensure the organization's survival. Such managers tend to adopt philosophical viewpoints.

institutional operation: a factory or group of plants under one management that performs all processes of production, including preparation for sale.

institutional power: a need for power in which individuals focus on working with others to solve problems and to further organizational goals.

institutional zone: zone of responsibility in which managers are primarily responsible for two aspects of an organization's external environment.

in stock: merchandise on hand, available for shipment or sale.

instrument: any written document that gives formal expression to a legal agreement or act.

instrumentality: the relationship between first- and second-level outcomes.

instrumental leadership: a style characterized by managers who plan, organize, control, and coordinate the activities of subordinates to reach departmental or group goals.

instrumental performance: the performance of the physical product per se.

insubordination:
(1) not submitting to authority; being disobedient.
(2) a worker perceived by the employer to disobey rules and regulations, usually following repeated warnings.

insufficient funds: when a depositor's balance is inadequate for the bank to pay a check that has been presented. A service charge is often placed on the customer when the balance is not sufficient to pay the check.

insufficient-reason criterion: the assumption, when a manager is operating under conditions of uncertainty, that there is an equal probability that each of the possible states of nature or competitive actions might occur.

insular bond: see *bond, insular.*

insurable interest (life version): the monetary interest of the beneficiary of a life insurance contract in the continued life of the person insured. Insurable interest exists only to the extent that the beneficiary will suffer financial loss as the result of the death of an insured.

insurable interest (property and liability version): any interest in or relation to property of such nature that the occurrence of an event insured against would cause financial loss to the insured.

insurable title: a form of title that may have objections but on which a title-insuring company is willing to issue its policy of title insurance.

insurance:

(1) **general:** a method whereby those concerned about some form of hazard contribute to a common fund, usually in an insurance company, out of which losses sustained by the contributors are paid. See *self-insurance.*

(2) **business law:** a contractual relationship that exists when one party (the insurer), for a consideration (the premium), agrees to reimburse another party (the insured) for loss to a specified subject (the risk) caused by designated contingencies (hazards or perils), or to pay on behalf of the insured all reasonable sums for which he may be liable to a third party (the claimant).

insurance company: an organization chartered under state or provincial laws to act as an insurer. In the United States, insurance companies are usually classified as fire and marine, life, casualty, and surety companies and may write only the kinds of insurance for which they are specifically authorized by their charters.

insurance coverage: the total amount of insurance that is carried.

insurance management:

(1) **general:** in relation to the exposure of assets to risks, the function that examines the impact of the transferral of risk, or self-insurance of the risk, and the resulting effects of that transfer or self-insurance.

(2) **insurance:** the liaison between buyers of insurance for business needs and the sellers of this coverage.

insurance of title: insurance showing who owns a specific interest in a designated property and showing as exceptions to the insured interest the defects, liens, and encumbrances that exist against that insured interest.

insurance policy: broadly, the entire written contract of insurance. More specifically, it is the basic written or printed document, as well as the coverage forms and endorsement added to it.

insurance premium: see *premium (insurance).*

insurance trust: an instrument composed wholly or partially of life insurance policy contracts.

insurance trust expenditures: cash payments to beneficiaries of contributory social insurance programs (employee retirement funds, unemployment compensation, sickness insurance, etc.), excluding cost of administration, intergovernmental expenditures for social insurance, and noncontributory payments to former employees.

insurance trust revenue: revenue from contributions required of employers and employees for financial social insurance programs operated by state and local governments, plus earnings on assets held for such systems.

insured: the person(s) protected under an insurance contract.

insured bank: a bank that is a member of the Federal Deposit Insurance Corporation.

insured warranty: an express warranty additionally covered by an insurance policy that protects a buyer, especially of a new house, in case the builder refuses to pay for any repair cost within a stated period of time.

insurer: the party to the insurance contract who promises to indemnify losses or provide service.

insuring clause: part of an insurance policy or bond that recites the agreement of the insurer to protect the insured against some form of loss or damage. This is the core of the contract of insurance.

intangible asset: an asset that has no substance or physical body. It is incorporeal. The most widely known types of intangible assets are goodwill and patent rights. These assets are purchased, sometimes for very substantial outlays of capital. Their value to the purchaser lies in the use he or she can make of them, although they cannot be seen.

intangible rewards: feelings that derive from recognition, applause, and so on, and have no monetary value. Synonymous with *psychic income.*

intangible tax: a state tax levied on all deposits in a bank (stocks, bonds, notes, etc.), excluding certain exempted items. The tax is against the individual accounts.

integrated commercial: a broadcast commercial that appears or is heard as part of the program's entertainment.

integrated strategic management: an organizational development program to create or change a company's strategy by analyzing the current strategy, choosing a desired strategy, designing a strategic change plan, and implementing the new plan.

integration: centralization of authority in the hands of a top administrator or executive.

integration, forward: the expansion of the area of operation of a business to include activity near the ultimate user (e.g., a manufacturer building a retail outlet).

integration, horizontal: the absorption by one firm of other firms functioning on the same level of production; the attempt to dominate a market at a specific production stage by monopolizing resources at that stage.

integration, vertical: the absorption by one firm of other firms involved in all stages of manufacture, from raw materials to sales of the finished goods.

integrative growth: expansion of a firm's operation by acquiring the assets of suppliers, customers, or competitors.

integrator: a worker who is neither line nor staff but has informal power to bring together the efforts of overlapping working units.

intellectual property: a wide range of goods and services, including branded merchandise, patented products, and creative work, such as books and movies.

intensive distribution: placement of an item in all available outlets.

interaction analysis: a technique developed by R. R Bales whereby, through observations of groups working on solving a problem, a profile of human relationship develops that is measurable. See *managerial grid*.

inter alia: "among other things" (*Latin*).

interactive control systems: control methods that involve direct, face-to-face interaction with employees so as to monitor rapidly changing information and respond proactively to changing conditions.

Inter-American Development Bank: a bank established in 1959 to encourage economic development of the 21 member nations in Latin America. Twenty representatives from Latin American countries and the United States initiated this effort.

interchangeable bond: see *bond, interchangeable*.

interchangeable parts: the basis of the entire concept of mass production: the ability to interchange any part of a machine with an identical part in any similar piece of equipment. See *assembly-line production*.

intercorporate stockholding: an unlawful condition whereby a corporation holds stock in other corporations, thus interfering with competition (e.g., restraint of trade).

interdepartmental conflict: a form of conflict that arises between two or more departments because of conflicting interests, limited resources, communication problems, and/or differing perceptions.

interest:

(1) **finance:** the price paid for the borrowed use of a commodity, usually money. See *money rates*. Cf. *pure interest*.

(2) **marketing:** following the awareness stage in the adoption process, the consumer's curiosity in pursuing the value of a product or service.

interest group: those working together to attain a specific objective with which each is concerned.

interest coverage: the frequency with which interest charges are earned, found by dividing the sum of the fixed charges into the earnings available for such charges, either before or after deducting income taxes.

interest inventory: a questionnaire concerning the activities a person likes or in which he or she has an interest. *Cf. depth interview; interview, structured.*

interest rate: the ratio of the payment for the use of financial capital to the amount borrowed.

intergovernmental expenditures: payment to other governments as fiscal aid or as reimbursements for the performance of services for the paying government. Synonymous with *revenue sharing. Cf. direct expenditures.*

intergovernmental revenue: revenue received from other governments as fiscal aid, shared taxes, and reimbursements for services performed. Synonymous with *shared revenue.*

interim bond: see *bond, interim.*

interindustry competition: the competition that develops between companies in different industries.

Interior, Department of the (U.S.): see *Department of the Interior.*

interlocking directorate: the condition in which one or more members of the board of directors of one business are also members of the board of directors of other corporations.

Intermarket Trading System (ITS): an electronic network designed to link the nation's six major securities exchanges (New York, Midwest, Philadelphia, Boston, Pacific, and American). This national system began operations on April 17, 1978.

intermediate bond: see *bond, intermediate.*

intermediate goods: items transformed by production into other items.

intermediate-range planning: planning that covers a time period of one to five years.

intermediate report: a report by the National Labor Relations Board trial examiner, after a hearing on charges of unfair labor practices, on the examiner's findings and recommendations. If either party objects to the report, the entire matter goes to the NLRB for a decision, which may be appealed in the courts.

intermediate-term credit: credit that is extended for a period of from three to 10 years.

intermediation: the process by which savers place funds in a financial institution, enabling the institution, acting as an intermediary, to place those funds in housing loans and other investments. See *disintermediation*.

intermittent process: any process designed to produce a variety of items (e.g., a job-order machine shop).

internal audit: a business audit carried out by the firm itself on a continuous basis. Cf. *look back*.

internal bond: see *bond, internal*.

internal check: coordinated methods and measures adopted by an organization to check the accuracy and validity of data and to safeguard assets.

internal controls: methods and measures employed to promote efficiency, to encourage acceptance of managerial procedures and policies, to check the validity of management data, and to protect assets.

internal customer: anyone in the organization who cannot do a good job unless others do a good job.

internal economies scale: factors that bring about increases or decreases to an organization's long-run average costs or scale of operations resulting from size adjustments with the company as a product unit. They occur primarily because of physical economies or diseconomies. See *diseconomies of scale*.

internal financing: raising money within a firm through normal operations.

internal forecast: a forecast relating to a firm's output and its internal operations.

internalize: of a business firm, to bear or derive costs or benefits directly by itself or by utilizing in-house resources, as without the aid of a government agency or without the use of middle people.

internal locus of control: viewpoint in which the potential entrepreneur has the ability or control to direct or adjust the outcome of each major influence.

internal market: activities within the European Union member states. The Commission's 1985 White Paper urged the completion of the internal market as a prerequisite for an efficient, modern Europe that can provide industry and commerce with a structural framework in which they can be fully competitive. Directives, decisions, and recommendations are required for dealing with three primary barriers, which are: physical barriers; technical barriers on public contracts, the free movement of workers and members of their professions, capital movements and the services market, the creation of an environment favorable to industrial cooperation; and tax barriers. See *European Union; Single European Act; White Paper.*

internal rate of return: an interest rate that, if paid on the costs of a project, would ensure that costs were equal to benefits. Synonymous with *ROI.*

internal recruiting: finding employees already inside an organization who are qualified for job openings.

Internal Revenue Service (IRS): the federal agency empowered by Congress to administer the rules and regulations of the Department of the Treasury, which includes the collection of federal income and other taxes. It is divided into nine regions, with 64 districts, and is also responsible for the investigation and prevention of tax frauds.

internal users: the managers of a company who are responsible for making the day-to-day decisions that lead the organization to its profit and service goals.

International Bank for Reconstruction and Development (IBRD): the World Bank, proposed at Bretton Woods, New Hampshire, in July 1944, and commencing operation in June 1946. After phasing out activities of reconstruction, its primary efforts are to provide loans for economic development. See *International Monetary Fund.*

International Bureau for the Protection of Industrial Property Rights: multilateral agreement to protect patents, trademarks, and other property rights.

international business:

(1) any firm that engages in international trade or investment. Cf. *international management.*

(2) those business activities that involve the movement of resources, goods, services, and skills across national boundaries.

International Confederation of Free Trade Unions (ICFTU): a federation of labor groups in the free nations of the world. ICFTU was formed in 1949 after its predecessor, the World Federation of Trade Unions, fell under unbreakable Communist control. It comprises unions in more than 100 countries, and its headquarters is in Brussels. The United States affiliates of ICFTU are the AFL-CIO and the United Mine Workers of America.

international corporation: a corporation with business interests in different countries. It often focuses on the import or export of goods and services.

International Labor Organization (ILO): a tripartite body of representatives from labor, management, and government, initially organized as an agency of the League of Nations in 1919, now continued under United Nations auspices. The ILO disseminates labor information and sets minimum international labor standards, called conventions, which are offered to member nations for adoption.

International Labor Review: the official monthly magazine of the ILO, describing working conditions and presenting statistical data of member countries.

international management: process of applying management concepts and techniques in a multinational, multicultural environment. Cf. *international business.*

International Monetary Fund (IMF): an organization established to restore orderly exchange practices following World War II. IMF was formed and became operational on March 1, 1947. Member nations can borrow foreign currencies from the fund under specified conditions. Membership in the IMF is a prerequisite to membership in the International Bank for Reconstruction and Development. See *special drawing rights.*

international payments mechanism: the organization of markets whereby the monies of different nations are exchanged. See *swap.*

international representative: an agent of a national or international union, who may be primarily an organizer, an administrator, or an all-around troubleshooter.

international reserves: a means of payment generally acceptable in settlement of balances among countries (e.g., gold, dollars, pounds SDRs).

Internet: global network of servers connecting millions of computers with personal, industrial, and organizational users. Cf. *Intranet*

internship: an extensive period of training during which selected employees are given a complete introduction to their jobs and an opportunity to apply the theories and methods they learned earlier at school.

interpersonal orientation: a focus that allows an observer to determine whether a person is more concerned with achieving good social relations or with accomplishing a task. There are various techniques (e.g., the managerial grid) for measuring whether the employee is more oriented toward people or toward tasks. See *managerial grid*.

interselling: assigning sales personnel so that each is able to work in two or more related departments rather than being limited to one.

interstate carrier: a common carrier whose business extends beyond the boundaries of one state.

interstate commerce: commerce that involves more than one state, including transportation of goods and services across the boundaries.

Interstate Commerce Commission (ICC): a federal agency established to enforce the Interstate Commerce Act and other related acts affecting common carriers engaged in interstate commerce.

interstore transfer forms: forms containing data from a list of items to be shipped from the central warehouse to a branch store, or from one branch store to another.

interval reinforcement: a schedule of rewards that ties reinforcements to time. Such a schedule can be fixed or variable.

intervention:

(1) **labor relations:** entry by a union or unions in a representation election ordered by the National Labor Relations Board, in competition with the union or unions that originally had sought the election.

(2) **administration:** the process by which either outsiders or insiders assume the role of altering a program within an organization.

interview: a conversation designed to yield information for purposes of research or assistance in guidance, counseling, or treatment. See *interview, structured; interview, unstructured*.

interview, exit: a conference with an employee before termination of his or her relationship with the organization to determine reasons for leaving, future plans, and general attitudes toward the job and the company.

interview, structured: an interview in which the asking of definite questions closely controls the subjects discussed. Cf. *interest inventory*.

interview, unstructured: an interview in which the interviewer does not determine the format or subject to be discussed, thus leaving the interviewee in major control of the conversation. Cf. *depth interview*.

in the black: (slang) a business that is functioning with a profit.

in-the-money: (slang) a call option in which the striking price is below the market price of the underlying stock.

in the red: (slang) a business that is functioning with a loss.

in toto: "in the entire amount" (*Latin*).

Intranet: an organization's private Internet; links together the different divisions and functions inside a company. Cf. *Internet*.

in transit: describing items that have left the consignor's location and are en route to the destination.

intrapreneur: an employee who remains in the organization but is given freedom to create new products, services, and/or production methods.

intrapreneurial culture: instilling the entrepreneurial spirit in an existing organization in order to innovate and grow.

intrapreneurship: entrepreneurial activities that receive organizational sanction and resource commitments for the purpose of innovative results.

intrasender role conflict: inconsistency between one person's various expectations regarding another's behavior. A manager, for example, may expect both rapid work and a high quality level that is impossible at a rapid pace.

intrastate carrier: a common carrier whose business is conducted entirely within the boundaries of a state.

intrastate commerce: commerce conducted solely within a state's geographic borders.

intrastate traffic: cargo that is shipped only within one state.

intrastore transfer: the purchase of goods from one selling department for use by another selling department.

intrinsic rewards: rewards associated with the job itself, such as the opportunity to perform meaningful work, to complete cycles of work, to see finished products, to experience variety, to carry out highly visible cycles of activity, and to receive feedback on work results.

intrinsic value: the market value of the material in something (e.g., the value of the metal in a gold tooth filling).

intuitive pricing: the practice of establishing price based on the intuition of the responsible party.

inventory: the name given to an asset of a business. Inventories are of two general types, direct and indirect. *(a)* Direct inventory in an industrial concern consists of raw materials, work in process, and finished goods. Direct inventories represent various stages of fabrication; in commercial and retail businesses, they are inventories purchased for resale. *(b)* Indirect inventories, in general, are all supplies used to carry on the business and not purchased for resale. Indirect inventories are usually considered deferred assets. Cf. *book inventory; perpetual inventory; work-in-process inventory.*

inventory, composite: see *book inventory; composite inventory.*

inventory change: the amount of increase or decrease in business inventories during a specified period.

inventory control:
(1) the control of merchandise on hand by accounting and physical methods. See *EOQ model.* Cf. *eyeball control.*
(2) an approach used in emergencies to regulate inventories for the purpose of increasing utilization of items and preventing hoarding.

inventory cutoff: the determination of which inventory items are to be included in the year-end inventory balance.

inventory model: a type of production control model that answers two questions relating to inventory management: "How much?" and "When?" An inventory model tells the manager when goods should be reordered and what quantity should be purchased.

inventory shortage (shrinkage): inventory reduced by theft, internal or external fraud, waste, sabotage, or careless operation.

inventory turnover: the number of times, on the average, that inventory is replaced during a period. It is calculated by dividing cost of goods sold by average inventory.

inventory valuation adjustment: in contrast to corporate profits and income of unincorporated enterprises, which include inventory profit or loss in customary business accounting, the accounting for current output in the national income accounts, which includes only the value of the change in volume in inventories.

inverse demand pattern: the situation that exists when price and volume vary at the same time and more is sold at a high price than at a lower one.

invested capital: the amount of capital contributed to a company by its owners.

investment: the use of money for the purpose of making more money, to gain income or to increase capital, or both.

investment banker: the middleman between the corporation that is issuing new securities and the public. The usual practice is for one or more investment bankers to buy a new issue of stock or bonds outright from a corporation. The group forms a syndicate to sell the securities to individuals and institutions. The investment banker is the underwriter of the issue.

investment banking: the financing of the capital requirements of an enterprise, rather than the current working capital requirements of a business.

investment center: an organizational unit in which a manager has responsibility for costs, revenues, and investments. Cf. *profit center.*

investment club: a voluntary grouping of people who pool their monies to build up an investment portfolio, which members hope will give them a better return per individual than each could have expected separately.

investment company: a company or trust that uses its capital to invest in other companies. There are two principal types: the closed-end type and the open-end or mutual fund. Shares in closed-end investment companies are readily transferable in the open market and are bought and sold like other shares. Capitalization of these companies remains the same unless action is taken to change, which is seldom. Open-end funds sell their own new shares to investors, stand ready to buy back their old shares, and are not listed. Open-end funds are so called because their capitalization is not fixed; more shares are issued as people want them. See *reinvestment privilege.* Cf. *hedge fund; monthly investment plan; no-load funds; regulated investment company; split investment company.* Synonymous with *securities firm.*

Investment Company Act of 1940: federal legislation requiring the registration and regulation of investment companies with the SEC.

investment counsel: a person whose principal business consists of acting as investment adviser. A substantial part of the person's business consists of rendering investment services.

investment decisions: decisions that commit present funds in exchange for potential future funds. These decisions are controlled through a capital budget.

investment portfolio: the list of securities owned by a bank, an individual, or a business enterprise.

investment schedule: a table of the amount of gross investment that would be undertaken at alternative rates of GNP.

investor: an individual whose principal concerns in the purchase of a security are regular dividend income, safety of the original investment, and, if possible, capital appreciation. See *long position.* Cf. *speculator.*

invisible hand: first used by Adam Smith to describe the ability of the perfectly competitive market to bring about the greatest benefit for all, even when all merchants selfishly maximize their own profits.

invoice: an instrument prepared by a seller of goods or services and rendered to the buyer. The instrument usually lists all items making up the bill for the convenience of the buyer; to prevent disagreements, the amount is stated on the instrument.

involuntary bankruptcy: see *bankruptcy.*

involuntary conversion: a transaction in which an asset is destroyed or is taken by a government agency through condemnation proceedings.

involuntary investment: the involuntary increase or decrease in business inventory as a result of either an excess of household saving over intended investment or an excess of intended investment over savings.

involuntary lien: a lien on property that is demanded without the consent of the owner (e.g., construction of sewers and sidewalks near an owner's property; property tax increases). Synonymous with *lien in invitum.*

involuntary transfer: where an employer shifts an existing worker into another position within the company, often done without the employee's wish or will.

involuntary unemployment: the situation that exists when people who wish to work are unable to locate opportunities at going wage rates for the related skills and experiences they have to offer.

iota: a minute amount of any item.

IOU: an informal written agreement acknowledging a cash debt ("I owe you").

IRA: see *individual retirement accounts.*

Irish dividend: an assessment imposed on a security, rather than a dividend. Cf. *dividend.*

iron law of wages: the concept that wages tend to equal what the employee needs to maintain a subsistence level of living. Synonymous with *brazen law of wages; subsistence law of wages.*

irredeemable bond: see *bond, irredeemable.*

irredeemable money: synonymous with *inconvertible money.*

irregular routing: a sales-call pattern in which the sales representative determines the frequency of calls to be made. Cf. *fixed routing.*

irregulars: items having defects that may affect appearance but not wear.

irreparable harm: injury or damage that is so constant and universal that no fair or reasonable redress can be achieved in court. Therefore, the plaintiff seeks resolution by injunction.

I-S curve: a graphical presentation of combinations of interest rates and levels of national income for which aggregate supply and aggregate demand are equal; named for the notion that investment, I, should absorb savings, S.

island display: merchandise shown in a store's aisle or open space.

island position: the placement of newspaper advertising copy that is surrounded by editorial matter or page margin.

issue: any of a company's securities, or the act of distributing such securities.

issued stock: authorized stock originally issued to stockholders, which may or may not still be outstanding.

issues management: process by which managers keep abreast of current issues and bring organizational policies in line with prevailing public opinion.

item:

(1) **general:** one member of a group.

(2) **human resources:** the smallest unit of test material to be addressed by the person being tested.

itemized appropriation: a restriction of an appropriation to be made only for and in the amounts listed; a step-by-step listing of all pertinent funds set aside to pay a specific cost.

itemized deductions: a listing of allowed expenses that are subtracted in arriving at taxable income. See *Tax Reform Act of 1976; Tax Reform Act of 1986.*

item merchandising: the special planning and control effort to discover and take advantage of the sales opportunities presented by those items that are in greatest customer demand.

itinerant worker: a worker who is not a permanent member of a community and finds work by moving from opportunity to opportunity.

J

January effect: where stocks of companies with lower-than-average market capitalizations outperform the stocks of larger companies in the month of January.

jawboning: (slang) pressured urging by an influential individual to submit to specific rules and regulations. Cf. *moral suasion*.

J-curve effect: the theoretical initial impact of a currency devaluation on the trade balance, which actually continues to deteriorate for a while, because it takes time for the volume of higher-cost imports to decrease and that of lower-cost exports to increase. The name comes from the upsweep of the hook like letter J at the foot.

jebble: (slang) synonymous with *bluefingers*.

jerry-built: constructed cheaply, flimsily, and often temporarily.

JIT: see *job instruction training*.

JMT: see *job methods training*.

job:

   (1) **general:** a specific group of tasks prescribed as a unit of work.

   (2) **merchandising:** to purchase or sell merchandise in quantity, not in selected categories.

job action: an employee protest that falls short of a strike (e.g., a slowdown).

job analysis: a systematic study of the specific tasks, conditions, rate of pay, and so on, required for a particular job; usually includes a statement of the personal qualities needed to perform a given job. Cf. *time and motion study*.

jobber: a middleman who handles merchandise in odd or job lots. Some jobbers take possession of the title to the goods, which they resell to another jobber, to a retailer, or directly to the consumer. Others have a buying agreement with the manufacturer to dropship the merchandise on orders obtained by the jobber. See *rack jobber*.

job bidding: see *bidding*.

job-center behaviors: leader behaviors devoted to supervisory functions, such as planning, scheduling, coordinating work activities, and providing the resources needed to task performance.

job characteristics model: a model that helps explain how jobs can be redesigned so that they become more motivational.

job classification: evaluation of job content and required skills, for the purpose of setting up wage brackets for each classification.

Synonymous with *job grading*.

job cluster: a group of similar jobs in a company.

job content: the duties, functions, and responsibilities for a given job classification.

job cycle: the time it takes an employee to complete every task in his or her job before repeating the cycle.

job definition: the statement of the task requirements of a job. There is a job definition for each job in a company.

job depth: the amount of control an employee can exert to alter or influence his or her job and the surrounding environment.

job description: a statement, usually in writing, of the responsibilities, approaches, conditions, and other relevant factors built into a job.

job design: the process of task delineation necessary to meet various personal, work, organizational, and environmental parameters.

job dilution: the division of the tasks of a job into levels of skill. The tasks needing greater skill are performed by skilled employees, and the remaining tasks are carried out by relatively unskilled employees who have a lower level of training.

job dynamics: the situational factors surrounding the tasks in a job that must be considered to define the job adequately.

job enlargement: a procedure for increasing the scope and responsibilities of a job to increase employee satisfaction. Cf. *loose jobs (rate)*.

job enrichment: an approach of F. Herzberg that attempts to improve task efficiency and satisfaction by means of building into people's jobs greater scope for personal achievement and recognition, more challenging and responsible work, and greater opportunity for advancement and growth. See *dissatisfiers; O-E-C syndrome; organic structure; satisfiers*.

job environment: all the physical, psychological, and social factors, situations, events, or relationships that surround and affect a firm and its workers.

job evaluation: a systematic rating of job content on such factors as skill, responsibility, and experience. The evaluation is primarily used to minimize wage inequities.

job factors: categories of common job characteristics used in job evaluation.

job families: groups of different jobs that require similar skills.

job grading: a form of job evaluation that assigns jobs to predetermined job classifications according to the job's relative worth to the organization. Synonymous with *job classification*.

jobholder reports: reports given to workers about a company's economic performance.

job identification section: the section of a job description that contains the job title and a job number or code. See *job description*.

job instruction training (JIT): a program of training workers within industry based on a specific outline of procedures, including rules for getting ready to instruct and rules on how to train.

job involvement: degree to which a person identifies with his or her performance's importance.

job lot:

(1) **merchandising:** a miscellaneous grouping of items of various styles, sizes, colors, and so on, bought at a reduced by a store or an individual middleman.

(2) **business:** a contract that has a smaller unit of trading than is featured in the regular contract.

job management: collectively describes the functions of job scheduling and computer command processing.

job methods training (JMT): a training approach designed to teach management the techniques of methods improvement through the recommended steps of (1) breaking down the job, (2) questioning every detail, (3) developing and improving the methods, and (4) applying the improved methods.

job order: an order authorizing the production of a specified quantity of goods or specifying services to be rendered, and dispatching personnel to perform them.

job-order costing: a method of product costing whereby each job, product, or batch of products is costed separately. Cf. *process costing.*

job-oriented behavior: leadership behavior that focuses on careful supervision of employees' work methods and performance level.

job performance standards: work requirements that are expected from an employee on a particular job.

job placement: assignment of a person to a job.

job posting: see *posting.*

job price protection: the guarantee of quoted prices on adequate material to complete a specific project in which a buyer is involved.

job pricing: the placement of a dollar value on the worth of a job.

job processing: reading job control statements and data from an input stream, initiating job steps defined in the statements, and writing system output messages.

job progression ladder: a particular career path in which some jobs have prerequisites.

job range: the number of operations a job occupant performs to complete his or her work.

job ranking: job evaluation that subjectively ranks jobs according to their overall worth to the company. See *job evaluation*.

job rate: the lowest or minimum rate paid to a qualified or experienced employee for a specific task or job.

job relationships: the interpersonal relationships required of or made possible by a job.

job relations training (JRT): a type of human relations training program designed to teach management (1) some of the general knowledge that is required to deal with workers as individuals and (2) some basic techniques for dealing with individual problems through the recommended steps of getting the facts, evaluating and making decisions, taking the necessary steps toward solution of the problem, and checking the results.

job requirements: duties, tasks, and responsibilities that make up a job.

job rotation: a personnel practice that involves moving an employee from one work station to another to increase overall performance by promoting a greater understanding of multiple tasks in the organization. Synonymous with *flying squadron*.

Jobs and Growth Tax Relief Reconciliation Act of 2003: Synonymous with *Tax Act of 2003*.

job satisfaction: the positive or negative aspects of an employee's attitude toward his or her job or some part of it.

job scope: the relative complexity of an assigned task as reflected by its cycle time.

job security: a means of protecting a worker's job, usually described in a union contract, and often invoked when new methods or machines are introduced.

job sharing: a scheduling innovation that permits two or more employees to do the same job by working different hours, days, or even weeks. The total hours worked by job sharers are usually equivalent to the hours worked by one full-time worker.

job shop: type of operation in which work centers are arranged around particular types of equipment or functions.

job simplification: job design approach whereby jobs are configured so that jobholders have only a small number of narrow activities to perform.

job specialization: division of work into standardized, relatively simple tasks.

job specification (specs): a carefully written description of a specific job, with duties and opportunities described. It identifies the requirements of the job and the desired qualifications needed for a worker to perform effectively. Cf. *job standardization.*

job stabilization: a process of creating and/or maintaining continuous job opportunities.

job standardization: the use of clearly defined work procedures and requirements to be met to reduce individual variations in a specific work task. Cf. *job classification.*

job step: a unit of work associated with one processing program or one catalogued procedure and related data. A job consists of one or more job steps.

job stress: an individual's internal frustration and anxiety regarding certain job- or organization-related situations.

jockey: (slang) an investor who has sufficient equity and gains financial control over the major decisions needed to conduct day-to-day business.

Johari window: a model illustrating the communication between any two people ("Joe and Harry").

joint account: an account owned by two or more people, subject to deposit or withdrawal by the signatures of any of the joint owners. In banks, any account owned by two or more parties is referred to as a joint account, regardless of whether all parties or any one of the parties may sign checks.

joint adventure: two persons entering into a single business for their mutual benefit (e.g., a partnership). See *joint venture.*

joint agreement: a statement covering salary and working conditions, agreed to and signed by employers and union representatives within an industry. Synonymous with *industry-wide agreement.*

joint and several account: an account in which, when two or more persons desire to deposit in a jointly owned account, and the account is drawn against by either check or withdrawal order, the signature of any one of the owners will be honored.

joint and several bond: see *bond, joint and several.*

joint contract: a contract whereby two or more people who make a promise to another person are joint obligors to the contract and to the other party identified.

joint control bond: see *bond, joint control.*

joint cost:

(1) **accounting:** a cost that is common to all the segments in question and that can be assigned to the segments only by arbitrary allocation.

(2) **production:** the costs of two or more items that must be manufactured together.

joint demand: demand for two or more items that are usually used together because of necessity or consumer preference.

joint life insurance: insurance on two or more persons, the benefits of which are payable on the first death.

jointly and severally: encountered in loan transactions, when several persons sign a note for a loan. When used, each person is legally obligated to become individually liable for the payment of the note; the group involved also must become liable.

joint production costs: the costs of two or more produced goods that are made by a single process and are not identifiable as individual products up to a certain stage of production, known as the split-off point.

joint profit maximization: collusion by firms in an oligopolistic industry, which enables them to obtain the maximum (monopoly) profit.

joint stock company: an association that is neither a partnership nor a corporation but has some of the characteristics of each.

joint study committee: a committee that includes representatives from management and unions who meet away from the bargaining table to study some topic of mutual interest in hopes of finding a solution that is mutually satisfactory.

joint tenancy: two or more people holding equal ownership of property. Upon the death of one of the parties, the decedent's interest automatically passes on to the surviving owner(s).

joint venture: a commercial undertaking by two or more people, differing from a partnership in that it relates to the disposition of a single lot of goods or the termination of a specific project. Cf. *partnership; syndicate.*

journal: a record of original entry. This record may be written in ink at the time a transaction is made or may be created in original printing or carbonized as the posting of the entry is made by machine. Cf. *ledger.*

journal entry: a method of directly recording on a profit and loss statement a transaction that did not necessarily have the direct approval of management, such as rent, monthly assessments, leases, or taxes, and/or reclassifying charges from one account or location to another.

journalize: to record a transaction in an entity's records using the double-entry system. Debits, credits, and any necessary explanations are recorded in the journal.

journeyman: a craftsman who has completed an apprenticeship and is entitled to the highest minimum rate established for the job classification.

JRT: see *job relations training.*

judgment: a debt or other obligation, as determined by the decision or decree of a court.

judgment bond: see *bond, judgment.*

judgment in rem: a judgment against a thing (e.g., a bank account, personal property), as contrasted a judgment against an individual. See *lien.*

judgment note: a note authorizing a creditor to enter a judgment against a debtor in case of nonpayment, without the need for court action.

judgment rates: rates established by the judgment of an underwriter, utilizing his or her professional skills and experience, without the application of a formal set of rules or a schedule. Cf. *experience rating.*

judgment strategy: the use of personal beliefs and experiences for choosing among alternatives and deciding how the selected alternative should be implemented.

judicial review:

(1) **labor relations:** an action brought before a court to determine the legality of decisions issued by a labor relations board. The review is concerned only with whether the decision is in violation of a statute; the merits of the case are not at issue.

(2) **business law:** a legal examination of a situation that is ordered, sanctioned, prescribed, or enforced by a judge or court (e.g., a judicial proceeding).

judicial sale: a sale of real or personal property ordered by a legal body or court. Synonymous with *forced sale.*

juice man: (slang) a loaner of money at exorbitant interest rates. Synonymous with *loan shark.*

junior board: a group of lower-level managers who meet periodically to discuss various issues and to provide ideas and suggestions that may be valuable to upper-level management in identifying and solving problems.

junior bond: see *bond, junior.*

junior issue: an issue whose claim for dividends or interest, or for principal value, comes following that of another issue, called a *senior issue.*

junk bond: see *bond, junk.*

jurisdictional dispute: a conflict between rival unions over which should maintain control over a given job or activity and be recognized as the collective-bargaining agent. See *intervention (labor relations).*

jurisdictional strike: a walkout by one union because of a dispute with another union over representation rights or performance of certain jobs. Jurisdictional strikes are unfair labor practices according to the Taft-Hartley Act.

jury of executive opinion: a forecasting approach utilizing the opinions of senior executives.

Justice, Department of (U.S.): see *Department of Justice, U.S.*

justified price: a fair market price that an informed buyer will give for property.

K

kaisen: Japanese for "continuous improvement."

Kameralism: a concept of mercantilism concerned with the production of wealth by the state and how the wealth is used; sometimes spelled *cameralism*.

karoshi: in Japanese, being overworked or having job burnout.

KD: see *knocked down*.

keiretsu: groups of linked Japanese companies that are considered to be Japan's most important contribution to modern capitalism. In the marketplace, the members of one keiretsu battle their rivals in other groups. Such companies enjoy a safety net that encourages long-term investments and high-tech risk-taking.

Kennedy Round: made possible by the U.S. Trade Expansion Act of 1962, which achieved substantial cuts in industrial but not in agricultural tariffs; covered three elements in the trade negotiations which the ministerial meeting in the GATT in May 1963 agreed to launch on May 4, 1964, and which were completed June 30, 1967. These were: (1) a substantial reduction in tariffs and other barriers to trade by an average of 35 to 40 percent; (2) measures to improve access to world markets for agricultural products; and (3) expansion of outlets for the exports of less developed nations; sometimes used to cover only the tariff element in these negotiations. See *General Agreement on Tariffs and Trade*. Cf. *Tokyo Round; Uruguay Round*.

Keogh plan (HR 10): a form of tax-qualified retirement plan established by a nonincorporated business or self-employed individual. Investment contributions and appreciation are generally tax deferred until actually received in the form of benefits. See *Economic Recovery Tax Act of 1981; individual retirement accounts*.

key:

(1) **general:** crucial, essential (e.g., a key decision).

(2) **administration:** a crucial, important member of an organization.

keyed advertising: see *keying an advertisement*.

key industry: an industry that, because of a unique characteristic, holds major importance in the country's economy (e.g., steel; automobiles).

keying an advertisement: placing a code or letter in a coupon or in the advertiser's address so that the specific advertisement producing an inquiry can be noted.

key jobs: positions that are common in a firm and its labor market.

Keynesian economics: developed by the British economist John Maynard Keynes, a system showing that national income and employment are dependent on real investments and consumer spending. See *liquidity preference; liquidity trap; New Economics; paradox of thrift; savings and investment theory.* Cf. *Friedmanite; quantity theory.*

key performance: aspects of a unit or organization that must function effectively if the entire unit or organization is to succeed. Synonymous with *key result.*

key question: a question of major importance asked of an interviewee by an interviewer or of a respondent by a written questionnaire, to be used in making a determination or evaluation.

key result: synonymous with *key performance.*

key result area: an aspect of a company's operations that has direct bearing on profitability.

key subordinates: workers who are crucial to a manager's success in a particular job.

kickback:
(1) **labor relations:** the racketeering practice of forcing employees, as a condition of employment, to return a part of the wages established by law or by union contract to the employer. This practice is outlawed in federally financed employment.
(2) **general:** an illegal rebate given secretly by a seller for granting an order or contract (e.g., payoff).

kicked upstairs: (slang) removal of an individual from a lower position, where his or her performance is not considered acceptable, by promotion to a higher position. See *Peter Principle.*

killing: (slang) an unusually profitable trade.

Kimball tags: prepunched tags affixed to goods, containing size and style data that are utilized in speeding inventory control.

kind: when used in "distribution in kind," the distribution of the property itself, not its cash value. Cf. *in kind.*

kite (kiting):
(1) **banking:** writing a check in an amount sufficient to overdraw the account, but making up this deficiency by depositing another check, also in excess of deposits, but issued on some other bank. This unorthodox procedure is considered to be evidence of fraudulent intent (e.g., mailing the rent check when your account has insufficient funds, but counting on receiving and depositing some money before the landlord has a chance to present the check for collection). See *forgery.*

(2) **finance:** used for an accommodation bill.

kiting stocks: manipulation of stock prices to unprecedented high levels.

km: see *knowledge management*.

knocked down: applied to sales or shipments of equipment that are to be assembled by the receiver.

knocked-down price:

(1) **general:** a lowered or reduced price.

(2) **retailing:** a seller's asking price that has been lowered for purposes of making the sale. Cf. *upset price*.

knocker: (slang) a door-to-door salesman.

knowledge management (km): the application of people, processes, or technology that optimizes knowledge sharing and retention for an organization.

knowledge workers: employees whose responsibilities include a rich array of activities such as planning, decision making, and problem solving.

L

L: a measure of money supply that consists of M3 plus Eurodollars owned by American residents, banker's acceptances, commercial paper, and certain Treasury obligations. Cf. *M1; M1-A; M1+; M1-B; M2; M3.*

labeling acts: see *Federal Hazardous Substances Labeling Act of 1960.*

labor:

(1) **general:** the human effort expended for the purpose of acquiring money or other compensation.

(2) **economics:** the effort of people applied to the production and marketing of goods and services toward an economic goal, resulting in the payment of money or another form of compensation.

labor agreement: an accord reached after collective bargaining.

laboratory training: see *sensitivity training.*

labor-augmenting technical change: a technical change that has the same effect on output as if the number of laborers had been increased. Cf. *labor-saving equipment; resource-augmenting technical change.*

labor banks: banks whose stock is owned by labor unions and their membership. Cf. *industrial bank.*

labor claim: a plant employee's regular report indicating the job worked on, the number of pieces, numbers of hours, etc., and often the amount of money claimed. A labor claim is usually made on a labor chit or time ticket.

Labor, Department of (U.S.): see *Department of Labor, U.S.*

labor dispute: as defined by the National Labor Relations Act, any controversy concerning terms, tenure, or conditions of employment, or concerning the association or representation of persons in negotiating, fixing, maintaining, changing, or seeking to arrange conditions of employment, regardless of whether the disputants stand in the relations of employer or employees. See *emergency dispute.*

labor economics: a specialty in the field of economics concerned primarily with the relationship between the worker and his or her job. Areas covered include supply of labor; hours and wages; conditions of work; and other forces relating to the general economic welfare of the worker.

labor flux: see *turnover (human resources).*

labor force: as defined by the U.S. Bureau of the Census, people over 14 years of age who are gainfully employed, looking for work, or absent from work (e.g., because of illness or vacation).

labor grade: a job or job group in a rate structure, usually set through job classifications and evaluations or by agreement with a union.

labor intensive: the use of additional manpower to increase output or earnings. See *labor pool.*

Labor-Management Relations Act of 1947: see *Taft-Hartley Act.*

labor market:

(1) the number and types of people in the workforce.

(2) the area from which applicants are to be recruited.

labor market analysis: the study of an employer's labor market to evaluate the present or future availability of workers.

labor mobility: the ease with which workers change positions and jobs. Horizontal mobility pertains to the way workers move from job to job at a similar skill level. Vertical mobility pertains to the way workers change jobs by moving up and sometimes down the occupational ladder.

labor monopoly: the claim that some unions—by dominance in an industry or through control of hiring procedures, control of apprenticeship rules, or other practices—have monopoly power over the supply of labor.

labor pool: the established source of trained people from which prospective workers are recruited. See *labor intensive.*

labor relations: a general term to identify all matters arising from the employer–employee relationship. See *industrial relations.*

labor-saving equipment: any machine or mechanized equipment that reduces the need for labor by a reduction of workers or by curtailing the number of hours of potential employees. In the 1960s automation was considered to be a technological breakthrough that would result in displacement of workers. Cf. *automation; labor-augmenting technical change; redeployment; technological unemployment*

labor skate: semihumorous name for a full-time union employee. Synonymous with *pie-card.*

lag indicators: a series of economic indicators that often follow changes in the economic cycle.

laissez-faire:

(1) **management:** a leadership style of minimal involvement. Synonymous with *loose-rein supervision.*

(2) **economics:** a policy of the classic capitalistic model, suggesting that government should not interfere with the economy. See *individualism.* Cf. *controlled economy; statism.*

lame duck:
   (1) **securities:** a speculator whose venture has failed.
   (2) **securities:** a member of a stock exchange who is unable to meet his or her debts.
   (3) **human resources:** an individual who is going out of office shortly and is thus thought to be ineffectual or helpless.
land revenue: any form of payment derived from ownership of land. It may take various forms (e.g., farm produce, forest rights, mineral deposits.).
land value tax: a governmental levy on the value of land only (i.e., not including structures or agricultural produce on it).
Lanham Act of 1947: federal legislation governing trademarks and other symbols for identifying goods sold in interstate commerce. As amended, it allows a manufacturer to protect his brand or trademark in the United States by having it recorded on a government register in the U.S. Patent Office, and provides for the legal right to register any distinctive mark. See *trademark.*
Laplace criterion: a basis for decision making whereby a manager applies equal probabilities to all states of nature. Synonymous with *Bayes criterion.*
lapping: theft from a customer that is covered by theft from another customer by placing false entries in account books. See *fraud.*
lapse:
   (1) **insurance:** the failure of the insured to pay the cost of the premium when due or within the grace period allowed.
   (2) **business law:** the termination of a right through disuse or failure to meet standard obligations over a fixed time period.
lapsing schedule: a form on which are recorded the costs of fixed assets or the total yearly additions to a group of fixed assets, together with the details of the distribution of their costs over the accounting periods succeeding their purchase.
last in–first out: see *LIFO.*
latent defect: a defect in goods that is not visible to the naked eye.
lateral communication: communication that takes place among departments or people on the same hierarchical level.
lateral relationships: horizontal relationships among organizational components (i.e., direct relationships among units at the same organizational level).
late tape: the situation that occurs when the ticker tape in an exchange

or securities office is unable to print fast enough to keep up with the heavy trading on the trading floor.

lawful money: all forms of money that are endowed by federal law with legal tender status for the payment of all debts, both public and private.

law of increasing costs: the concept that the average total unit cost in a production process increases as the volume of a firm increases. See *diseconomies of scale; marginal cost.* Cf. *proportional law.*

law of triviality: as formulated by C. Northcote Parkinson, a law stating that the time spent on any agenda item will be in inverse proportion to the monetary sum involved. See *Parkinson's laws.*

lawyer: (slang) a friend who advises another in a store regarding whether or not to purchase an item, frequently resulting in the customer's not buying the item.

layaway plan: a method of deferring payments whereby goods are retained by the store until the customer has completed payments for them.

layoff: a temporary and indefinite separation from work, caused by a slack season, shortage of materials, market declines, or other factors outside the control of the worker. Layoff is to be distinguished from *discharge* or *firing.* See *share-the-work.*

L/C: see *letter of credit.*

LCL: see *less than carload lot.*

LDC: see *less-developed country.*

lead:

　(1) **general:** to direct and govern.

　(2) **salesmanship:** the name and address of a potential customer. See *referral leads.*

leader: a person who, at a given time and place, by his or her actions modifies, directs, or controls the attitudes or behavior of others, often referred to as followers.

leader, autocratic: an individual who controls employees through domination and the power of his or her title. See *Caesar management; Theory X and Theory Y.* Cf. *leader, autocratic.*

leader, democratic: an individual who controls employees through personal talents and who is open, flexible, and sensitive to the needs and feelings of all those under his or her jurisdiction. See *organic structure; Theory X and Theory Y.* Cf. *leader, participative.*

leader, merchandising: a store that promotes several items at attractive prices for the purpose of inducing customers into the store. See *loss leader.*

leader, participative: a leader who uses various styles of leadership and who tries to get people actively involved in making decisions that will affect them. Cf. *Caesar management; leader, autocratic; leader, democratic.*

leader-member relations: a leader's feeling of being accepted by the group. It is the most important influence on a leader's effectiveness.

leader-participation model: a leadership theory that provides a set of rules to determine the form and amount of participative decision-making in different situations.

leader power position: the extent to which a leader has legitimate, coercive, and reward power to influence subordinates.

leadership: in a group or organization, the exercise of command and direction in a skillful and responsible fashion. See *trait theory of leadership.*

leadership continuum: a sliding scale of leadership styles from auto-cratic to highly participative. A leader chooses the proper style of leadership based on forces in the leader, in the subordinates, and in the situation.

leadership style: the way a manager behaves in his or her role as leader. The two most widely discussed leadership styles are task–oriented and relationship–oriented behavior. See *Theory X and Theory Y.*

leadership substitutes: variables that reduce a leader's power to improve or retard the performance or satisfaction of subordinates.

leadership training: workshops, conferences, seminars, and other pro-grams designed to upgrade skills and to offer information of use to those in leadership positions.

lead-in: part of the interaction that permits a sales representative to move toward a summing up or to close with a customer.

lead indicators: a series of economic indicators that often precede changes in the economic style.

leading from strength: a rule of strategy holding that an organization should draw on its strong points in fashioning its strategy.

leadman: an employee whose job involves some supervision, planning, and organization of tasks and materials performed by a group. A lead-man usually receives additional pay.

lead time: the elapsed time between the beginning of an economic or manufacturing function and the completion of that function.

leakage: any factor or pressure that prevents new capital formation from exerting its full effect on the national income.

lean manufacturing: a management philosophy that assumes that any manufacturing process that does not add value to the product for the customer is wasteful.

learning curve: a graphic representation of the measured changes at successive units of practice.

leased department: a department that is managed by a host store but is actually operated for the store by an outside organization, which pays the store a percentage of sales as rental.

leased employees: individuals provided by an outside firm at a fixed hourly rate, similar to a rental fee, often for extended periods.

least-cost decision: a decision to undertake an investment with the smallest negative net present value.

least-preferred coworker (LPC): the motivational system or behavioral preferences of a leader. High-LPC leaders are relations-oriented; low-LPC leaders are task-oriented.

leave of absence: time off from work, usually without loss of seniority, granted with the assumption that the employee will be reinstated. Usually, long leaves of absence are without compensation.

leave year: the period from the beginning of the first complete pay period in the calendar year to the beginning of the first complete pay period in the following calendar year.

ledger: a record of final entry in bookkeeping. An account is established for every type of transaction, and a ledger account is posted with every transaction affecting that account. Cf. *journal.*

legal asset: any property that can be used for payment of a debt.

legal bond: see *bond, legal.*

legal capital: the amount of contributed capital not available for dividends, as restricted by state law for the protection of creditors; usually equal to the par or stated value or the contributed amount of issued capital stock.

legal entity: any individual, proprietorship, partnership, corporation, association, or other organization that, in the eyes of the law, has the capacity to make a contract or an agreement and the abilities to assume an obligation and to discharge an indebtedness. A legal entity is a responsible being in the eyes of the law and can be sued for damages if the performance of a contract or agreement is not met.

legal interest: the maximum rate of interest permitted by state law. This rate is used in contracts in which no rate has been stated. Cf. *loan rate; usury.*

legal list: a list of investments selected by various states in which certain institutions and fiduciaries, such as insurance companies and banks, may invest. Legal lists are often restricted to high-quality securities that meet certain specifications. See *prudent man rule.*

legal monopoly: a privately owned organization that is granted an exclusive right by the government to function in a specified market under strict control and pricing by the government (e.g., public utilities). Cf. *legal monopoly.*

legal reserve:

(1) **insurance:** policy reserves maintained by an insurance company to meet future claims and obligations, according to the standards established by the insurance laws of the various states. Cf. *reserve.*

(2) **banking:** part of a bank's cash assets that must be retained as protection for depositors according to a ruling from the Federal Deposit Insurance Act.

legal security: a stock or bond that can be bought by a fiduciary and retained for beneficiaries.

legal tender: any money that is recognized as being lawful for use by a debtor to pay a creditor, who must accept same in the discharge of a debt unless the contract between the parties specifically states that another type of money is to be used.

legitimate power: the power a leader has in the managerial hierarchy because of rank. For example, a department manager who is ranked higher than the foreman in the managerial hierarchy possesses more legitimate power.

leisure ethic: to regard work as totally undesirable and to work only to survive.

lend: to give up something of per sonal value for a definite or indefinite period of time, without relinquishing ownership. See *loan.*

lender: an individual or financial institution that makes a trade of placing an interest on the use of money, with the expectation that the money (or other item) will be returned with the interest. See *note.* Synonymous with *creditor.*

lender of last resort: a central bank that will lend to individual banks whenever they experience large withdrawals.

lending institution: a finance company, bank, loan organization, or the like, that lends money and makes money by advancing funds to others. See *personal finance company.*

length of service: the period of a worker's continuous service with a particular firm. It is calculated from the date the worker is placed on the payroll to the time the length of service is computed.

leniency bias: a tendency to rate employees higher than their performance justifies.

less-developed country (LDC): a country showing

(1) a poverty level of income,

(2) a high rate of population increases,

(3) a substantial portion of its workers employed in agriculture,

(4) a low proportion of adult literacy,

(5) high unemployment, and

(6) a significant reliance on a few items for export.

See *underdeveloped country.*

less than carload lot (LCL): goods requiring less space when shipped than that available in a single freight car; the rate applied to such a shipment.

let: to award or assign work to be done by or equipment to be rented from a supplier.

let out: (slang) to dismiss from employment; to fire.

letter of credit (L/C): an instrument or document issued on behalf of a buyer by a bank on another bank or banks or on itself. It gives the buyer the prestige and the financial backing of the issuing bank. The acceptance by the bank of drafts drawn under the letter of credit satisfies the seller and the seller's bank in the handling of the transaction. The buyer and the accepting bank also have an agreement as to payment for the drafts as they are presented. See *authority to purchase; guaranteed letters of credit; revolving letter of credit.* Cf. *traveler's letter of credit.*

letter of indication: a bank's letter of identification given to a traveler who has bought a letter of credit.

letter stock: an unregistered stock, usually issued by a new, small firm to avoid the expense of formal underwriting. These securities are sold at a discount to mutual funds and to investors who specialize in speculative purchases.

level: denotes the structure of a product.

level-by-level planning: in materials planning, a method involving the determination of gross requirements at the highest level; comparison of this gross requirement with available inventory determines the net requirements at that level. The net requirements at that level are the gross requirements for the next level of inventory down.

leveling: a procedure in time and motion study used to measure and evaluate an employee's output. The output is expected to be that of an average trained worker. A stopwatch is used to measure the time needed to complete a task. See *time and motion study*. Cf. *performance appraisal*.

level of abstraction: in performance appraisal, refers to the problem of specifying a level of analysis in forming performance standards.

level of aspiration: a degree or quality of achievement or failure by which an individual or group perceives or measures its own performance.

level(s) of authority: points or layers in the organizational hierarchy.

level premium insurance: insurance in which the annual premium remains the same throughout the period over which premiums are paid.

leverage: the effect on the per-share earnings of the common stock of a company when large sums must be paid for bond interest, preferred stock dividends, or both, before the common stock is entitled to share in earnings. Leverage may be advantageous for the common stock when earnings are good but may work against the common stock when earnings decline.

leveraged buyout: where loans are used to finance most of the purchase price. A company is considered highly leveraged when debt far outweighs equity as a percentage of its total capitalization, and most of its cash flow is used to cover debt service. Synonymous with *leveraged takeover*.

leveraged marketing: where industrial item companies diversify into high-profit consumer items by taking basic industrial products or processes and applying them to consumer uses.

leveraged recap: allows a firm under attack to act as its own white knight. Recapitalizing a company involves substituting most of the equity on a firm's books for debt. The assumption of debt discourages a corporate raider, who can no longer borrow against those assets to finance the acquisition. The company creates the debt by borrowing funds so it can pay shareholders a huge dividend for the bulk of their holdings. See *white knight*.

leveraged takeover: synonymous with *leveraged buyout*.

leverage ratios: ratios used during ratio analysis that indicate the relationship between organizational funds supplied by the owners of an organization and organizational funds supplied by creditors.

leveraging: the advantage of (or disadvantage) obtained from using borrowed money to finance a business when the net interest rate of the borrowed funds is less (more) than the company's earnings rate.

levy:

(1) **general:** a tax assessment.

(2) **finance:** a demand made on the members of a company to contribute added working capital or to make good on a loss.

(3) **finance:** to assess, declare, and receive a sum of money against a person or property for public objectives.

Lewin model of behavior: developed by Kurt Lewin, whose field theory shows the relationships between the person and his or her environment, a model that suggests that behavior (B) is a function (f) of the personality (P) of the individual and the climate in which the person lives (E). In equation form, it is stated: $B=f$ (P,E).

liabilities:

(1) **finance:** all the claims against a corporation. See *indirect business tax and nontax liability.*

(2) **banking:** the funds a bank owes. The largest liability for a bank is deposits. See *accrued liabilities; capital liability; continent liabilities; current liabilities; fixed liabilities; floating debt; long-term liabilities; secured debt.*

liability:

(1) **insurance:** a form of coverage that pertains, for the most part, to claims arising out of the insured's claim for injuries or damage caused by ownership of property, manufacturing operations, contracting operations, sale or distribution of products, and operation of elevators and the like, as well as professional services. See *third-party insurance.*

(2) **business law:** any obligation an individual has by virtue of law (e.g., a debt; a responsibility). See *liabilities; vicarious liability*

liability insurance: any form of coverage whereby the insured is protected against claims of other parties. Most liability insurance is written by casualty companies, but some forms (especially those referring to property in the care of the insured) are underwritten in connection with fire or marine business. The insured's liability for damages usually results from negligence.

liability ledger: the record of all outstanding loans made by a bank to every borrower.

liability limits: the sum or sums up to which an insurance company protects the insured on a particular policy. Bodily injury and property damage liability covered by general liability policies is subject to a limit for each occurrence. In certain forms, however, such as malpractice, product, and manufacturers' and contractors' liability, there is also an aggregate limit of liability for the total amount of all claims during the policy period. Automobile policies covering liability for bodily injury have two limits: (1) a limit of liability to any one person, and (2) subject to this personal limit, another (usually higher) limit for any single accident involving more than one person. Automobile coverage for property damage liability is written with a limit per accident. Basic limits of liability are the lowest limits that are ordinarily written and are also the limits for which the cost of units of protection and minimum premiums are computed. Cf. *umbrella liability.*

liaison role: the role of a manager in making contacts outside the vertical chain of command in an effort to bring information into the unit and gain favors from others. This role includes interacting in a network of contacts with peers and others in order to get that information.

liaison unit: an organizational unit that has responsibility for coordinating the activities of two or more components of an organization.

liberal return policy: the practice of a store to accept goods returned for refund or exchange with a minimum of difficulty to the customer.

licensed lender: a lending group of people or organization(s) authorized by license to conduct business in the state in which residence is shown.

licensing: a business arrangement in which the manufacturer of a product (or a firm with proprietary rights over technology or trademarks) grants permission to a group or an individual to manufacture that product in return for specified royalties or other payments.

lie-detector: see *polygraph.*

lien: a claim on another's property as security against payment of a debt. See *bond, indemnity; quantum meruit.*

lien in invitum: a lien placed on property without the owner's approval. Synonymous with *involuntary lien.*

lienor: the holder of a *lien.*

life annuity: an insurance policy that provides an annual income for the insured, beginning at retirement and continuing for the duration of the individual's life. See *annuity.*

lifecycle hypothesis: a theory of the saving decision stating that consumers save to be able to maintain a stable level of consumption in the future. See *marginal propensity to consume; marginal propensity to invest; marginal propensity to save.*

lifecycle theory: a leadership theory, developed by Paul Hersey and Kenneth Blanchard, that contends that appropriate leadership behavior requires varying degrees of task and relationship orientation as the maturity of the followers increases.

LIFO (last in–first out):

(1) **accounting:** in valuation of inventories, the system whereby the price shown on the last incoming shipment of a particular item is the one used for current valuations and cost.

(2) **banking:** a method of determining the effect of withdrawals on savings account dividends or interest computations. With LIFO, withdrawals are made from money that was deposited last. The withdrawal penalty under this plan is loss of interest on the last money deposited. Cf. *FIFO.*

light gold: gold coins that have been reduced in weight, either by error of the mint or as the result of usage.

limitations of actions (statutes of): the laws for each state that identify the definite time limit within which a lawsuit can be brought under law. The terms within the statutes vary by state, but the time within which a commercial case action should be brought is usually 6 years.

limited: see *limited company.*

limited coinage system: the U.S. Mint's program under which the right of the individual to bring bullion for purposes of being coined is limited.

limited collision coverage: a form of collision coverage that is applicable only when the insured is not at fault in an accident. Cf. *no-fault automobile insurance.*

limited company: a British business corporation. Use of the abbreviation "Ltd." indicates registration under the Companies Act and formally establishes the limited liability of stockholders.

limited distribution: the number of dealers in an area that a company considers will produce maximum profitability.

limited function wholesaler: a wholesaler middleman who does not perform all the marketing functions.

limited liability: legal exemption of stockholders from financial liability for the debts of the firm beyond the amount they have individually invested. See *partnership.* Cf. *nonassessable stock.*

limited life: a characteristic of a single proprietorship or partnership whereby the business ceases to exist on the death of the owners.

limited line stores: smaller retail operations that carry most goods in a narrow line of items (e.g., a women's apparel shop that carries casual and formal ladies' garments, sportswear, and lingerie, but not baby clothes).

limited-line strategy: a company's decision to concentrate on only a small number of variations of a product.

limited order: an order in which the customer has set restrictions with respect to price. See *composite limit order book; market order; no-limit order; percentage order; stop limit order.*

limited partner: a member of a partnership who is not personally liable for incurred debts of the partnership. By law, at least one partner must be fully liable.

limited payment life: a policy providing permanent protection, but with premiums payable only for a specified, limited number of years.

limited policy: a policy providing insurance against accidents of specified types, or one that is restricted in indemnity payments, in contrast to a full-coverage policy.

limited price order: an order to buy or sell a stated amount of a security at a specified price or at a better price, according to the directions within the order. Cf. *limited order.*

limited tax bond: see *bond, limited tax.*

limiting factor: anything that restricts or constrains the production or sale of a product or service.

limping standard: a modification of the gold monetary standard leading to the acceptance of certain silver coins as standard money to the extent that they are made unlimited legal tender and are not required to be redeemed in gold. Cf. *gold standard.*

Lincoln incentive management plan: a combination profit-sharing and incentive plan, developed by J. F. Lincoln in 1934, leading to better worker performance and sizable extra payments for the employee.

line:

(1) **merchandising:** the silhouette and description of any apparel style.

(2) **retailing:** items carried by a merchant. Cf. *product line.*

(3) **insurance:** a type or class of insurance or of insurance risks. See *accommodation line; gross line.* Cf. *multiple-line underwriting.*

(4) **transportation:** a system or carrier.

(5) **human resources:** the chain of command and business responsibility.

(6) **labor relations:** see *assembly-line production*.

line and staff authority: a part of the organization identified as those having the right to decide and to order others to perform activities (line) and those having the right to plan, recommend, advise, or assist, but not to order others to perform activities (staff).

line-and-staff organization: an organization that, because of its size or the complexity of its functions or goals, has an advisory support staff in addition to the line staff.

line authority: authority that is exerted downward (i.e., over subordinates) in an organization.

line departments: departments directly involved in accomplishing the primary purpose of the organization.

line item: an income or expense account on a profit and loss statement.

line manager: a high-level officer who has direct responsibility for carrying out a superior's requests and is authorized to pass along his or her own orders to subordinates. See *line organization; middle management*.

line of credit: an agreement between a bank and a customer whereby the bank agrees to lend the customer funds over a future period, up to an agreed maximum amount. The bank has the option to withdraw from the agreement if the financial status of the borrower changes or if the borrower fails to use the line of credit for its intended use as set forth in the agreement. The customer may borrow as much of the line as is required and pay interest on borrowed portions only. Lines of credit are widely used by large organizations to finance future commitments and for purchasing inventory.

line of discount: the maximum credit that a bank will extend to a retailer on the basis of his or her accounts payable, which the merchant discounts with the bank.

line organization: the oldest and least complex company structure, in which top officials have total and direct authority and subordinates report to only one supervisor. Cf. *football-bell structure*.

line-out: a group of workers who carry out a complete production operation as a team.

line position: position that has authority and responsibility for achieving the major goals of the organization.

line pricing: a pricing strategy in which all products in a multiple product line are priced at the same level.

line sheet: a guide prepared by an insurance company for its underwriters, setting forth the amount of liability the company is willing to assume on various classes of risks. See *experience rating*.

line-staff conflict: disagreements between a line manager and the staff manager who is giving him or her advice.

linkage: the pressures an industry can exert on the rest of the economy.

linking pin: a term coined by Rensis Likert for a worker who belongs to two groups whose tasks overlap. This person is given responsibility for coordinating the activities of both groups.

liquid: capable of being readily converted to cash. Usually the assets of an entity are considered to be most liquid when they are in cash or marketable securities. Synonymous with *collectible*. Cf. *frozen*.

liquid assets: assets that are easily converted into cash (e.g., government bonds). See *flight of capital*.

liquidate:
   (1) **general:** to convert assets into cash.
   (2) **accounting:** to discharge or pay off an indebtedness.
   (3) **finance:** to settle accounts by apportioning assets and debts.

liquidated damages: the payment by all parties of an agreed-upon sum of money as damages for breaching their contract. The courts can declare the damages to be a penalty and therefore unenforceable if the amount is excessive.

liquidating dividend: the dividend declared in the closing of a firm to distribute the assets of the organization to properly qualified stockholders.

liquidation: winding up the affairs of a business by converting all assets into cash, paying off all outside creditors in the order of their preference, and distributing the remainder, if any, to the owners in proportion and in the order of preference, if any, of ownership.

liquidator: a person who liquidates; a person who is legally in charge of liquidating a business.

liquidity:
   (1) **finance:** the solvency of a business, with special reference to the speed with which assets can be converted into cash without loss. Cf. *marketablility*.
   (2) **securities:** the ability of the market in a particular security to absorb a reasonable amount of buying or selling at reasonable price changes.

liquidity preference: the part of Keynesian theory that deals with the preference of people to hold their assets in cash rather than in a less liquid form, such as an investment. See *Keynesian economics*. Cf. *marginal propensity to invest*.

liquidity ratios: ratios used during ratio analysis that indicate an organization's ability to meet upcoming financial obligations.

liquidity trap: in the liquidity preference theory of John Maynard Keynes, the concept that, at some low interest rate, the speculative desire for cash becomes infinitely elastic. Cf. *quantity theory.*

liquid ratio: the ratio of readily available current assets to current liabilities.

list broker: a commission agent who rents direct-mail lists to advertisers.

listed securities (stocks): any bonds or stocks that have been admitted for trading on a stock exchange and whose issues have complied in every way with the listing requirements of the exchange.

list price:

(1) **general:** the price of an item, subject to sale and cash discounts; any quoted price in excess of that obtained in an actual sale.

(2) **retailing:** the retail price suggested or fixed by the manufacturer rather than the retailer. Cf. *fair trade price.*

Little Board: the American Stock Exchange. See *American Stock Exchange.* Cf. *Big Board.*

Little Wagner Acts: see *Baby Wagner Acts.*

living document doctrine: part of a contract stipulating that a union may reopen wage negotiations at any time. Cf. *contract bar.*

Lloyds: an association of English insurance underwriters, the oldest of its kind in the world. The Corporation of Lloyds also provides a daily newspaper (LLOYDS LIST AND SHIPPING GAZETTE), a classification of ships (LLOYDS REGISTER OF SHIPPING), and other publications.

L-M curve: a graphical presentation of combinations of interest rates and incomes for which the demand for money equals its supply.

load:

(1) **shipping:** a package or group of packages included in a shipping unit (a carload, an airplane load, etc.).

(2) **shipping:** an item or group of items included in a single outer shipping container.

(3) **securities:** the portion of the offering price of shares of open-end investment companies that covers sales commissions and all other costs of distribution. The load is usually incurred only on purchase; there is seldom any charge when the shares are sold. Cf. *no-load funds.*

load-factor pricing: changing the price of a product at various periods to maximize the utilization of manufacturing facilities in order to minimize seasonal or time-of-day decline in demand, or to attract lower-income groups of purchasers.

load funds: mutual funds sold by sales representatives. For the shares they sell, there is a sales charge or load. Cf. *no-load funds.*

loading:

(1) **finance:** the amount added to an installment agreement to cover selling and administrative overhead, interest, risk, and so on.

(2) **securities:** the amount added to the prorated market price of underlying securities to represent fees and overhead.

(3) **business:** the addition of overhead to prime cost.

(4) **insurance:** the amount added to net premiums to cover a company's operating expenses and contingencies, including the cost of securing new business, collection expenses, and general management expenses; precisely, the excess of gross premiums over net premiums.

loading charge: a premium, usually from 6 to 8 percent, charged by open-end investment funds on selling new securities, to cover selling costs.

loading of cash discounts: building up gross invoice price of goods and crediting cash discounts with the amount of the load. This is accomplished by adjusting the invoice or by altering the store's book-keeping entry.

load up: to buy a security or commodity to one's financial limit for purposes of speculation.

loan: a business transaction between two legal entities whereby one party (the lender) agrees to lend funds to a second party (the borrower). The funds may be lent with or without a fee, which is called interest or discount. Loans may be demand or time loans, depending on the agreement as to maturity, and they may be for short or long terms. See *lend; lender; lending institution.*

loanable funds theory of interest: a concept that the interest rate is determined by the demand for and supply of loanable funds only, as distinguished from all money.

loan-closing payments: expenses incurred when a mortgage loan is terminated (mortgage costs; legal fees for preparing the papers; appraisal and recording fees, etc.).

loan crowd: stock exchange members who will borrow or lend securities to investors who have sold short. These individuals usually meet at a designated place in the exchange. See *short sale.*

loaned flat: stock that is borrowed without an interest payment.

Sometimes securities are sold short, requiring the seller to borrow them if this becomes necessary to make delivery. When he or she is able to borrow without making an interest payment for the shares, the seller is dealing in a stock that is loaned flat. See *loan stock.* Cf. *flat.*

loan fee: any charge made to the borrower in connection with a loan. Synonymous with *loan origination fee; premium servicing fee.*

loan interest: the amount of money paid for the use of capital or borrowed funds.

loan origination fee: synonymous with *loan fee.*

loan rate: the rate charged for borrowing money at a specific date for a stated period. Cf. *legal interest.*

loan shark: an unauthorized moneylender who charges excessive interest for instant cash, accepting poor credit risks, and so on; a racketeer who threatens punishment if the repayment is not on schedule. See *usury.* Synonymous with *juice man.*

loan stock: securities that have been loaned to a broker or short seller to fulfill the terms of a short-selling contrast by delivering shares.

loan value: the amount of money that can be borrowed on a life insurance policy.

lobbyist: a person or group of persons trying to affect and influence (through personal intervention) the proceedings of government agencies.

lobster shift: synonymous with *midnight shift.*

locals: managers and professionals who have an inside-the-organization orientation. They tend to be loyal to the organization's norms and values.

local union: the organization of members of an international union in a particular plant, region, or locality.

lock-away: a British term for a long-term security.

locked in: an investor who does not sell a security because its profit would immediately become subject to the capital gains tax. See *Tax Reform Act of 1976.*

locker stocks: a manufacturer's or wholesaler's shipment of additional inventory that is retained unopened in the store's central warehouse. When the buyer requires an item held in locker stock, payment is made to the vendor for the entire shipment.

Lockheed model: a model that identifies relevant variables for establishing spans of control, including the complexity of functions, the coordination of subordinates required, and the direction and control required by subordinates.

lockout: the phase of a labor dispute in which management refuses work to employees or closes its plant to force a settlement. The antithesis of a strike, the lockout is used to avert a threatened strike.

lockup:

(1) **securities:** securities that have been withdrawn from circulation and placed in a safe deposit box as a long-term investment.

(2) **banking:** a note or obligation that has been renewed, the time of repayment having been extended beyond the original due date.

locus of authority: where the power to make various decisions resides within the organization. Cf. *locus of control.*

locus of control: degree to which people believe they are master of their own fate. Cf. *locus of authority.*

logo (type): two or more letters, often making a short word, that represent the name or signature of an advertiser (e.g., NBC).

lonely pay: (slang) increased wages demanded by unions to offset reduced working hours resulting from technological advances.

long: signifying ownership of stocks ("I am long 100 U.S. Steel" means that the speaker owns 100 shares); holding a sizable amount of security or commodity in anticipation of a scarcity and price rise. See *carry.*

longevity pay (wage): salary adjustments based on seniority or length of service.

long-lived assets: resources that are held for an extended time, such as land, buildings, equipment, natural resources, and patents.

long of exchange: a trader in foreign currency who has bought and holds foreign bills in an amount exceeding the bills of his or her own that have been sold and remain outstanding.

long position: the status of a holder of securities who expects an increase in the price of his or her shares or who holds these securities for income.

long-range planning: a systematic procedure for directing and controlling future activities of a firm for periods longer than a year. It predicts the future and establishes a strategy of action and expected results.

long rate: the reduced premium rate when a policy runs longer than one year.

long run: an extensive time period that permits a firm to develop its capability to manufacture.

long-run planning capacity: the rate of activity needed to meet average sales demand over a period long enough to include seasonal and cyclical fluctuations.

long-term capital gain: the gain realized when capital assets that have been held for longer than 12 months are sold at a profit. See *Tax Reform Act of 1976.*

long-term capital loss: the loss realized when capital assets that have been held for longer than 12 months are sold at a loss. See *Tax Reform Act of 1976.*

long-term contract: a collective bargaining agreement negotiated for a period longer than one year.

long-term corporate bond: see *bond, long-term corporate.*

long-term debt: liabilities that become due more than one year after the signing of the agreement. Usually, these are formal legal agreements demanding periodic payments of interest until the maturity date, at which time the principal amount is repaid.

long-term disability policies: insurance policies that pay covered workers a proportion of their wage or salary when they are disabled. Usually these policies require a six-month waiting period before they begin to pay.

long-term liabilities: debts or other obligations that will not be paid for or otherwise discharged within one year or within the normal operating cycle.

long-term operational assets: long-lived assets acquired for use in the business rather than for resale, including property, plant, and equipment; natural resources; and intangible assets.

long ton: 2,240 pounds. Cf. *short ton.*

look back: the auditing of past records to locate errors that have come to the attention of a bank's auditing department. Cf. *internal audit.*

loose jobs (rate): the situation that exists when the earnings for a worker are not in line with pay for similar positions requiring similar skills. See *incentive pay; piece rate (wage).* Cf. *job enlargement.*

loose-rein supervision: a leadership style based on the philosophy that the less supervision is exerted, the better it will be for the firm. Synonymous with *laissez-faire.* See *open system.*

Lorenz curve: a graphic device for plotting the degree of inequality in the distribution of income.

loss:

(1) **insurance:** any decrease in quantity, quality, or value of property. With reference to policies of indemnity, this term is often used as an

expression of the amount of damage that might or might not be covered in whole or in part, depending on the cause of the loss and the coverage afforded. In its application to liability policies, loss refers to payments made on behalf of the insured.

(2) **accounting:** any item that can be listed as an expense.

(3) **finance:** the excess of the cost of depreciated cost of an asset over its price of sale.

loss constant: a flat amount included in some insurance premiums that measures the average provision for losses.

loss expectancy: an underwriter's estimate of damage that would result from the peril insured against. An underwriter must consider (1) "probable maximum loss expectancy," which is an estimate of damage under conditions of normally expected control and protection against the peril, and (2) "above-normal loss (ANL) expectancy," the estimate of damage that would occur if the peril were not controlled by the protection to be reasonably expected. See *maximum foreseeable loss.*

loss information service: a listing service provided to an insurance company by the National Board of Fire Underwriters, giving the names of individuals involved in arson or fires of suspicious origin.

loss leader: a retail merchandising strategy of advertising an item at a price below cost, to attract customers to the store in the expectation that they will purchase other items at full profit margins. See *leader, merchandising; price lining.*

loss on disposal: the result of a sale of noncurrent asset for less than the book value of unrecovered cost.

loss-prevention service: loss-control and inspection work done by insurance companies or independent organizations for the purpose of recommending the change or removal of conditions that are likely to cause loss.

loss ratio: a percentage arrived at by dividing the amount of the losses by the amount of the insurance premium. Various loss ratios are computed (e.g., earned premium to incurred losses; written premium to paid losses).

loss reserve: a part of an insurance firm's assets retained in available form to meet expected claims.

lost policy release: a statement signed by the insured releasing the insurance company from all liability resulting from a lost or mislaid contract of insurance.

lot:

(1) **accounting:** any group of goods or services making up a single transaction.

(2) **securities:** a quantity of shares, usually 100. Cf. *block; odd-lot orders.*

low: the lowest price paid for a purchase of securities in a specific time period.

low-bailer: (slang) an executive who underestimates his expected financial situation.

low-cost unit factory: production location with lower costs, because of either low wages or large capital investment.

lower-order needs: needs that are not satisfied externally; physiological and safety needs.

lower turning point: a short period during which a downswing ends and an upswing begins. Cf. *upper turning point.*

low grade: of inferior quality, applied to merchandise, stock, and so on.

low-margin retailing: discount selling or mass merchandising.

loyal worker:

(1) **general:** an employee who is faithful to his or her employer.

(2) **labor relations:** used by an employer to describe a worker who refuses to join fellow employees in an organizing drive, who votes against the union in a representation election, or refuses to take part in a strike. Cf. *blackleg.*

Ltd.: see *limited company.*

Lud: see *Luddites.*

Luddites: nineteenth-century English workers who resisted the introduction of labor-saving equipment in the factories that employed them. A workingman named Lud is credited with destroying stocking frames in 1779. Now used for any who fear or resist technological progress. See *sabotage, industrial.*

lump-sum merit program: program under which employees receive a year-end merit payment, which is not added to their base pay.

lump-sum purchase: a group of assets obtained for an indicated figure, without breakdown by individual assets or classes of asset.

luxuries: comforts and beauties of life that are excess of what is needed for normal or standard living. See *optional consumption.*

luxury tax: a tax imposed on items that are not considered essential for daily living. In most cases, goods so taxed are expensive.

M

MI: a measure of money supply that consists of cash held by the public and private demand deposits, such as checking accounts at commercial banks. Cf. *L, M1-A, M1-B, M2, M3.*

MI-A: a measure of money supply that consists of cash held by public and private demand deposits, such as checking accounts at commercial banks, but excludes demand deposits held by foreign-owned banks and nonbank depository institutions. Cf. *L, M1, M1-B, M2, M3.*

MI+: the Federal Reserve Board's basic and most closely watched measure of the nation's money supply M1. Cf. *L; M1; M1-A; M1-B; M2; M3.*

MI-B: a measure of money supply that consists of M1-A plus other checkable deposits at all depository institutions, such as NOW and ATS accounts, and credit-union share drafts. Cf. *L, M1, M2, M3.*

M2: a measure of money supply that consists of M1-B plus savings and time deposits under $100,000 at all depository institutions, overnight repurchase agreements and Eurodollars, and shares in individual money-market funds. Cf. *L; M1; M1-A; M3.*

M3: a measure of money supply that consists of M2 plus savings and time deposits over $100,000 at all depository institutions, term repurchase agreements, and shares in institutional money-market funds. Cf. *L; M1; M1-A; M1-B.*

Machiavellian manager: a person of low moral and ethical values who operates with the philosophy that the end justifies the means, regardless of who gets hurt along the way.

macroeconomics: the study of statistics (e.g., total consumption, total employment) of the economy as a whole, rather than as single economic units. Synonymous with *aggregate economics.*

macrolevel approach: a means of change that affects the entire organization. Cf. *microlevel approach.*

macromarketing: a study of the economic exchange process of a total economy. Cf. *micromarketing*

macro-organizational behavior: subfield of organizational behavior that focuses on understanding the structure and processes of entire organizations. Cf. *micro-organizational behavior.*

made work: employment created or work activities spread out by assigning employees activities that fulfill no productive requirement.

Madison Avenue: (slang) communications and advertising enterprises once typically found along Madison Avenue in New York City.

Madrid Convention: resulted in 22 member nations agreeing to automatic trademark protection for all members. The United States is a participant only to the extent that a subsidiary of a U.S. company located in one of the member nations can effect protection for its firm in all member nations.

Magnuson-Moss Warranty Act: federal legislation of 1975 requiring that all consumer items distributed interstate and sold with a written warranty must have the warranty designated at "full"(the firm promises to remedy any defect of malfunction) or "limited."

maintained mark-on: the difference between the cost for delivering goods and the price at which they are sold.

maintenance:

(1) **general:** the upkeep of any form of property (land, machinery, tools, etc.).

(2) **accounting:** all expenditures made to preserve an asset's value.

(3) **business law:** support or sustenance that a person is legally bound to give to another.

(4) **business law:** interfering unlawfully in a suit between others by assisting either party (e.g., giving one party money).

maintenance bond: see *bond, maintenance.*

maintenance factors: elements of the work setting that lead to employee dissatisfaction when they are not provided adequately. Synonymous with *dissatisfiers; hygiene factors.*

maintenance mechanism: a mechanism that attempts to stop a system from changing so rapidly that it is thrown out of balance.

maintenance-of-membership: a contract provision requiring union members to retain good-standing membership during the life of the contract as a condition of employment. See *escape clause.*

major duty: any activity or group of closely related activities of a job that is a determinant of a required qualification for employment in that position or that occupies a significant amount of the worker's time.

majority stockholders: those who own more than 50 percent of the voting stock of a corporation, thus having controlling interest. See *working control.*

major medical expense insurance: insurance that offers protection against huge expenses resulting from a major injury or serious illness. The form of insurance usually pays from 75 to 80 percent of doctor and hospital bills after a deductible has been paid by the policy holder. See *catastrophic insurance.*

make good:
   (1) **general:** to discharge an obligation or debt.
   (2) **advertising:** to repeat a message without additional charge or to refund space or time charges as compensation for an error in or omission of an advertisement.

make-or-buy decision: a firm's decision of whether to produce an item itself or purchase it elsewhere.

maker:
   (1) **general:** a manufacturer, processor, or producer of merchandise or products.
   (2) **business law:** an individual, firm, or other legal entity that signs a note, check, or other negotiable form as a responsible party.

makers and shakers: (slang) those who are in power.

make the cash: to decide whether the funds on hand, following receipts and payments, balance with the record of sales and payments of obligations.

makeup pay (wages): the difference between the amount a pieceworker has actually earned and the earnings to which the worker is entitled under contract or according to a minimum.

makeup time: the part of available time used for reruns due to malfunctions or mistakes during a previous operating time.

make whole: an order to an employer to pay a worker all wages lost from the date of firing, minus what he or she may have earned elsewhere meanwhile. Used in an arbitration award or government agency ruling, the order reinstates a discharged employee.

make-work fallacy: the fallacious belief that the destruction of wealth or the uneconomic utilization of manpower is good for the general economy because it stimulates employment.

mala fides: see *bad faith.*

malfeasance: a wrongdoing; a criminal act (e.g., a public official taking graft).

malfunction: usually, the failure of equipment to operate as designed. Synonymous with *dysfunction.*

Maloney Act: see *National Association of Securities Dealers.*

malpractice insurance: coverage afforded to a professional, such as a doctor or a lawyer, against liability claims for damages resulting from alleged improper performance of the insured's services. Cf. *errors and omissions.*

managed exchange rates: aggressive efforts by a government to dictate the rate of exchange through economic policies rather than permitting market forces to determine the value of the nation's currency.

management:

(1) **general:** the individual or group of individuals responsible for studying, analyzing, formulating decisions, and initiating appropriate actions for the benefit of an organization.

(2) **administration:** the functions of planning, coordinating, and directing the activities of an organization.

management access time: the time between a manager's request for certain information and the receipt of the information.

management accounting: a resource of management that supplies financial information at all levels to be used in planning and administering the business.

management assessment center: development and/or selection device wherein management candidates spend two or three days performing realistic management tasks under the observation of appraisers.

management audit: a system for examining, analyzing, and appraising a management's overall performance. Ten categories of the audit are: economic function; corporate structure; health of earnings; service to stockholders; research and development; directorate analysis; fiscal policies; production efficiency; sales vigor; and evaluation of executive performance. Cf. *market audit.*

management by crisis: a leadership style that attempts to deal with shortcomings and failures by waiting until things get so bad that people will accept drastic measures. It is usually destructive and fails to attain stated organizational goals.

management by exception: the practice by an executive of focusing attention primarily on significant deviations from expected results. See *variance.*

management by objectives: see *MBO.*

management by walking around (MBWA): a management approach to communicating with personnel and getting feedback from them. It consists of the entrepreneur walking around the company, talking to personnel, asking questions, and learning about operations on a first-hand basis.

management company: a firm that manages and sells the shares of open-end investment companies and claims a fee or commission.

management consulting: the service performed, for a fee, by independent and objective professionals, or by an organization, to assist managers in analyzing management problems, to recommend practical solutions, and, at times, to help in the implementation of the recommendations.

management development: leadership training for middle- or top-level personnel to upgrade their skills.

management forecasts: opinions of supervisors, department managers, or others knowledgeable about the organization's future employment needs.

management functions: the basic activities required of managers in the performance of their jobs. The major management functions are planning and decision making, organizing for effective performance, leading and motivating, and controlling performance.

management game: a dynamic training approach utilizing a model of the business world. In most cases, this problem-solving technique attempts to examine broad business issues in a classroom setting, free of real-world consequences.

management information system (MIS): a specific data-processing system that is designed to furnish management and supervisory personnel with current information in real time. In the communication process, data are recorded and processed for operational purposes. The problems are isolated for referral to upper management for higher-level decision making, and information is fed back to top management to reflect the progress in achieving major objectives.

management inventories: summaries of the skills and abilities of management personnel, as distinguished from skills inventories, which are used for nonmanagement employees. See *skills inventories.*

management prerogatives: the rights believed by management to be exclusively theirs and not subject to collective bargaining. There is no accepted definition, however, of which rights should be nonbargainable. Synonymous with *employer rights.*

management process: the activities that take place in the managerial subsystem.

management process school: a modern school of management thought whose adherents believe that the way to study management is through a systematic analysis of the managerial function (i.e., planning, organizing, and controlling).

management systems: four basic leadership styles identified by Rensis Likert: exploitive-authoritative; benevolent-authoritative; consultative-democratic; and participative-democratic.

manager: an individual responsible for the control or direction of people, a department, or an organization.

managerial accounting: the area of accounting concerned with assisting managers in decision making, specifically for planning, budgeting, and controlling costs and revenues. Cf. *financial accounting*.

managerial control: the monitoring and modification of organizational activity and resource to ensure that predetermined standards are met and that plans are carried out.

managerial diversity: planning and implementing organizational systems and practices to manage people in a way that maximizes the potential advantages of diversity while minimizing its potential disadvantages.

managerial domain: pressures on a business to manage in a more hierarchical fashion caused by such factors as power, status, financial rewards, performance, etc.

managerial grid: a means of measuring a manager's leadership style in terms of concern for production and concern for task. The grid technique was developed by Robert Blake and Jane Mouton of the University of Texas.

managerial performance: the extent to which a manager achieves coordinated work through the efforts of subordinates. Coordinated work results from appropriate use of relevant planning, organizing, and controlling techniques and methods.

managerial roles: the organized set of behavior that belongs to the manager's job. The three main types of managerial roles are interpersonal, informational, and decision roles.

managerial zone: area of responsibility in which managers create and manage systems to coordinate and integrate various parts of the technical core.

managers: individuals who achieve goals through other people.

managing diversity: process of helping all employee, including women and minorities, reach their full potential.

man-catcher: (slang) an employment agency.

mandate of protest: synonymous with *notice of dishonor.*

mandatory retirement: often fixed at age 65, when a worker traditionally retired from his organization. Recent court rulings have challenged this regulation. Today, with exceptions controlled by positions that require dexterity skills, such as airline pilots, a firm cannot enforce a mandatory retirement age.

manifest: a statement itemizing the contents, value, point of origin, destination, and so on, of cargo that is shipped.

manipulation:

(1) **general:** an artful approach, often in an unfair or fraudulent fashion.

(2) **securities:** an illegal operation that involves buying or selling a security in order to create a false or misleading appearance of active trading or to raise or depress the price to induce purchase or sale by others. See *rigged market; SEC; stock jobbing.*

manit: one man-minute of production.

manning table: a listing of the number of employees or the positions to be used in a machine's operation, a described task, or a unit within a firm.

manpower: all employees in an organization, from chief executive officer down.

manpower planning: a forecast of the future manpower requirements of an organization and establishment of a plan to meet these needs.

man-to-man rating: an employee evaluation technique whereby supervisors or other raters compare employees, usually two at a time, in terms of their work effectiveness; behavior and attitude on the job; potential for further development; need for additional training, guidance, or incentives; and other related factors.

manual:

(1) **general:** operated by hand, without the use of tools or machinery.

(2) **communications:** a listing of information, instructions, prices, and so on, that is a handy reference book; a handbook.

manual rating: synonymous with *experience rating.*

manual skill: the ability to use one's hands efficiently in the operation of tools and machinery.

manufacture: to produce, make, or fabricate something, by hand or using equipment.

manufacturer's agent: an agent (wholesale or middleman) who takes neither title to nor possession of the merchandise he or she sells. The agent represents several noncompeting producers of goods that are purchased by one type of trade (e.g., a manufacturer's agent in women's apparel might sell dresses, blouses, belts, coats, stockings, and so on, for different manufactures). Synonymous with *manufacturer's representative.*

manufacturer's representative (MR): an independent sales agent for a group of manufacturers (principals) in a described sales territory. Synonymous with *manufacturer's agent*.

manufacturing: converting raw materials into a completed product by a mechanical, electrical, or chemical (i.e., not manual) process.

manufacturing costs: costs incurred in the manufacturing process to bring a product to completion, including direct materials, direct labor, and manufacturing overhead costs.

manufacturing inventory: covering all items of inventory for a manufacturing entity. Items included are usually raw materials, work in process, and completed goods.

manufacturing management: the responsibility within management for the planning, direction, and control of production and allied services performed in a manufacturing industry.

manufacturing order: instructions for directing production.

manufacturing overhead: all expenses arising from manufacturing activities except those of labor and materials.

maquiladadora: a Mexican assembly plant, usually near the U.S. border, that imports U.S.-made parts, assembles them, and returns the completed items to the United States, without being required to pay the usual duty on the imported parts and with a duty paid only on the value added when the completed items are returned to the United States.

margin:

(1) **finance:** the difference between the market value of collateral pledged to secure a loan and the face value of the loan itself. See *remargining*.

(2) **securities:** the amount paid by the customer when he or she uses a broker's credit to buy a security. Under Federal Reserve regulations, the initial margin required in recent decades has ranged from 50 to 100 percent of the purchase price. See *Regulation T*.

(3) **accounting:** the difference between the cost of sold items and the total net sales income. See *contribution margin; profit*.

marginal: an existing situation characterized by the occurrence of the smallest possible increment or decrement in certain variables.

marginal analysis: analysis of economic information by examining the results of the value added when one variable is increased by a single unit of another variable. See *direct costing*.

marginal borrower: a borrower who will reject an opportunity to borrow if the interest charge is increased.

marginal business saving rate: the proportion of an additional dollar of GNP income that goes into gross business saving.

marginal buyer: a buyer who will refuse to buy if the price is increased.

marginal cost: the increase in the total cost of production that results from manufacturing one more unit of output. See *law of increasing costs.*

marginal-cost pricing (MCP): a concept or system of charging consumers for goods or services at prices that are equal to the level of actual marginal costs, often recommended for regulated industries, such as public utilities.

marginal customer: a purchaser judged by a seller to be at the border of providing enough profit to be continued.

marginal efficiency of investment: a schedule showing the expected rate of return on the last or least profitable unit of investment for an alternative amount of potential investment in a given time period.

marginal lender: a lender or investor who will refuse to lend or invest if the rate of interest is lowered.

marginal producer: a producer who is just able to meet his costs of production, with little actual profit.

marginal product: the additional product derived by increasing a given factor of production by one further unit. See *differential marginal productivity.*

marginal productivity wage theory: the theory that, under competitive conditions, the wages of all employees will be established by the productivity, measured in money, of the last worker to be employed.

marginal profits: the increase in total profits that is obtained by producing an additional unit of output.

marginal propensity to consume (MPC): the percentage of increases in income that is spent for consumption purposes.

marginal propensity to invest (MPI): the percentage of increases in sales that is spent on investment items. Cf. *liquidity preference; oversaving; quantity theory.* Synonymous with *accelerator.*

marginal propensity to save (MPS): the percentage of increases in income that individuals save. Cf. *life cycle hypothesis; multiplier principle; oversaving; quantity theory.*

marginal revenue: the added revenue a business receives from the sale of one additional unit. In the short run, under conditions of competition, this is the same as the market price.

marginal revenue product: the added revenue a business receives by the addition of one more unit of a production factor (e.g., another employee; another piece of equipment).

marginal seller: a seller who refuses to sell if the price is lowered. See *upset price.*

marginal trading: the purchase of a security or commodity by one who borrows funds for part of the purchase price rather than paying for the entire transaction with his or her own money.

marginal utility: the increase in satisfaction one receives from adding or consuming one more unit of an item; the value of a commodity.

marginal worker: a worker the value of whose production equals his actual wage.

margin call:

(1) **general**: a demand upon a customer to put up money or securities with a broker. The call is made when a purchase is made or when a customer's equity in a margin account declines below a minimum standard set by the exchange or firm.

(2) **securities:** a bank's request for more margin from a borrower when the borrower has securities pledged as collateral for a loan, and a declining market for the securities forces the value of the securities downward. The bank is responsible for seeing that the margin meet the established margin requirements.

margin of profit: operating income divided by sales. Income taxes are usually excluded and depreciation is usually included in the operating expenses.

margin of safety:

(1) **general:** the balance of income left after payment of fixed charges.
(2) **sales:** the amount by which sales exceeds the break-even point, thus providing a cushion against a drop in sales or other unforeseeable forces.

(3) **securities:** the difference between the total price of a bond issue and the true value of the property for which it is issued.

margin requirement: the portion of a total purchase price of securities that must be put up in cash.

marine protection and indemnity insurance: insurance against legal liability of the insured for loss, damage, or expense arising out of or incident to the ownership, operation, chartering, maintenance, use, repair, or construction of any vessel, craft, or instrumentality in use in ocean or inland waterways, including liability of the insured for personal injury or death and for loss of or damage to the property of another person. See *assailing thieves; barratry; certificate of insurance; constructive total loss; general average; inland marine insurance; liability insurance; loss; ocean marine insurance; particular average.*

Maritime Labor Board: formed by Congress in 1938, the agency responsible for mediating labor disputes between companies and organized seamen and longshoremen and for developing a general maritime labor policy. See *Federal Mediation and Conciliation Service.*

markdown:

(1) **retailing:** a reduction of an originally established selling price.

(2) **securities:** a revaluation of stocks based on a decline in their market quotations.

markdown cancellation: the increase in the retail price of an item that has been reduced. The increase can be up to the retail price at which the item was originally placed for sale, but not higher.

market:

(1) **general:** people who possess the ability and desire to purchase, or prospects for a product or service.

(2) **business:** geographical area that includes a significant number of potential customers.

(3) **economics:** an estimated or realized demand for an item or service.

marketability: the rapidity and ease with which a given asset can be converted into cash. Cf. *liquid.*

marketable: that which can be sold.

marketable securities: short-term investments that can be sold readily in established markets.

market analysis: an aspect of market research involving measurement of the extent of a market and determination of its characteristics. See *chartist; Delphi technique; Dow theory.*

market audit: a method for studying the marketing activities and structure of a business. It is designed primarily to identify areas in which improvements are necessary to boost profits. Cf. *management audit.*

market channel: the path of the direct or indirect transfer of ownership to a product as it goes from a manufacturer to industrial or retail customers.

market demand: the total amount of an item that is wanted at a specified price at a specific time. Cf. *overall market capability; potential demand.*

market equilibrium: the balance that occurs when buyers and sellers decide to stop trading at the prevailing prices.

market failure: a condition under which markets do not allocate resources efficiently, usually because of ignorance or externalities. See *externalities.*

market fit: the likelihood that a new item will be purchased by the same people who buy a firm's other goods. Cf. *test marketing.*

marketing: activities that accelerate the movement of goods or services from the manufacturer to the consumer, including everything connected with advertising, distribution, merchandising, product planning, promotion, publicity, research and development, sales, transportation, and warehousing of goods or services. Cf. *merchandising.*

marketing boards: agencies established to monopolize the sale of specified products, especially agricultural commodities. Marketing boards are similar to labor unions in that they organize large numbers of small producers to negotiate with a small number of purchasers.

marketing concept: a business philosophy consisting of the notions that marketing strategy should be developed based on customer needs and desires and that all marketing functions should be structured within the firm, with one person having overall responsibility. See *consumer behavior research; marketing management; market research.*

marketing cost analysis: examination of the costs incurred from the time items are produced to final delivery and payment, with a view toward providing useful quantitative financial data for the marketing firm.

marketing-dominated strategy: a focus of key managers on managing the consumer.

marketing functions: buying, selling, shipping, warehousing, grading and standardization, financing, assuming responsibility for taking the risk, and data accumulation.

marketing information system: the entire system employed by a firm to gather, analyze, store, and disseminate relevant marketing information to those who require these data.

marketing intelligence: the part of the marketing information system that includes the procedures a company routinely uses to keep abreast of developments in the external environment.

marketing management: the planning, directing, and controlling of the total marketing operation, including formulation of marketing goals, policies, programs, and strategy, and often embracing product development, organizing and staffing to discharge plans, supervising marketing operations, and monitoring performance. See *product manager.*

marketingmanship: the measure of skill in marketing a product or service.

marketing mix: the concept of Neil Borden that market strategy is based on the product, price, promotion, and channels in an integrated marketing program.

marketing research: the process of gathering, recording, and analyzing information pertaining to the marketing of goods and services. See *market research*.

market off: an expression indicating that prices on the various stock exchanges were down for the day.

market order: an order to buy or sell stocks or bonds at the price prevailing when the order reaches the market. See *limited order; no limit order; percentage order; stop order.*

market-oriented production: production of a product or products in a foreign country that uses that product.

market out clause: a clause in underwriting statements of securities, whereby the underwriter reserves the privilege of terminating an agreement to sell securities at a stated price if unfavorable market conditions occur, rendering sale at this price unprofitable.

market outline: a summary of the relative place of a type of brand or item in the total market. See *positioning*. Cf. *market structure analysis.*

market penetration: the degree to which a product captures a percentage of the total market for that item. This includes the absence of competition for the item.

marketplace: a general statement identifying business and trade activities.

market potential: maximum sales potential for all sellers of a product or service over a fixed period.

market power: the ability of a purchaser or seller to control price and quantity of an item.

market presence: in advertising, being present in the marketplace, having a reputation or identity with competitors or consumers.

market price:

(1) **finance:** the price established in the market where buyers and sellers meet to buy and sell similar products.

(2) **finance:** a price determined by factors of supply and demand rather than by management decisions.

(3) **securities:** the last reported price at which a stock or bond sold.

market profile: data about potential customer or an analysis by individual background (sex, age, etc.) of people who make up the market for a particular item or service. See *market segmentation; market target.* Cf. *market structure analysis.*

market rate: the interest rate charged a firm in order to borrow funds.

market representative: the executive of a firm's buying office who gives his or her time and effort to a particular grouping of goods and makes data about it available to buyers of owned or operated stores.

market research: the part of marketing research that deals with the pattern of a market, measuring the extent and nature of the market, and identifying its characteristics. Market research precedes marketing research. See *marketing research; product planning.* Cf. *concept testing.*

market segmentation: separating the market for an item into categories of location, personality, or other characteristics for each division. See *market profile; zoning price.*

market share: a firm's percentage of its industry's total sales.

market skimming: an introductory pricing strategy of charging a high price in order to recover investment quickly.

market strategy: a marketing approach designed to enable a product to fulfill the objectives set for it by management.

market structure analysis: the study of competitive product offerings and buyer product preferences that account for the design features of items and the item preference characteristics of purchaser/consumer segments. Cf. *market outline; market profile.*

market target: the people or groups for whom an item and its program or marketing are intended. A strategy and a meaningful approach to fulfilling a stated goal must be established with respect to a market target. See *market profile; positioning.* Cf. *target customer.*

market value:

(1) **general:** the price that property will command on the open market; the price for which an owner is prepared to sell property and the amount a purchaser is willing to pay.

(2) **securities:** the price of a security or commodity on the daily quotation, indicating the amount required for buying or selling.

market value clause: a provision that sometimes appears in property damage insurance forms covering certain risks. It obligates the insurance company, in the event of a loss, to recognize the established market value of the destroyed and damaged property as its actual cash value as of the date of the loss and to adjust the loss accordingly.

marking: placing the correct tag on new goods, usually containing price, size, and style data. See *Kimball tags.*

mark-on: the difference between the billed-cost price and the original retail price of an item. See *initial mark-on.*

markup:
(1) **sales:** increase, in dollars or percentage, between cost and selling price.
(2) **finance:** increasing the value of assets (i.e., securities) to show an improvement in their market value.

Massachusetts trust: see *business trust.*

mass communication: the delivery of quantities of identical messages at the same time by communication firms or media.

mass marketing: the approach used to sell large volumes of items to everyone. This usually requires distribution in discount stores and supermarkets.

mass production: the utilization of mechanization to produce a large quantity of standardized items.

master:
(1) **general:** a skilled tradesman who is certified, usually by passing an examination, to train beginners and to operate his/her own business.
(2) **administration:** someone who has control or dominance over others.

master agreement: a contract covering a number of companies and one or more unions, or an agreement covering several plants of a single employer. This is supplemented by local contracts covering conditions that vary among individual plants or companies.

master budget: a budget comprising all the departmental budgets.

master policy: a policy issued to an insured to cover property at more than one location. If locations are in more than one state, it is customary to issue underlying policies in the respective states to meet legal requirements.

master schedule: a schedule in production control that applies only to a completed product and its major elements.

master tariff: a tariff that controls the use of other tariffs.

matched and lost: when two bids to buy the same stock are made on the trading floors simultaneously (i.e., matched), and each bid is equal to or larger than the amount of stock offered. The bids are considered to be on an equal basis, and the two bidders then flip a coin to decide who buys the stock. This also applies to offers to sell.

material budget: a forecast of how much material will be necessary to achieve a result.

material control: the attempt to supply commodities needed in manufacturing at the lowest cost per unit consistent with required quality and with the lowest inventory investment. Cf. *quality control.*

material cost: the cost of an item that is a direct result of the cost of raw material and does not include indirect expenses such as wages and overhead.

materiality: the concept that accounting should disclose only those events important enough to have an influence on the decision maker.

material management: the material handling functions as they relate to the physical distribution chain.

materials handling: the physical movement of materials and products within a work facility.

materials requisition form: a document used to request raw materials from the storeroom.

matrix departmentation: using two forms of departmentation to group jobs into subunits. Functional departmentation occurs vertically and product or program departmentation horizontally. The resulting organization chart is a matrix. Cf. *functional departmentation; geographical departmentation; process departmentation; product departmentation.*

matrix organization: an organizational structure in which organization members have a dual allegiance, to a particular assignment or task and to their department.

mature economy: the condition of a nation's economy with a declining rate of population growth and a decrease in the proportion of national income utilized for new capital investment, accompanied by a relative increase of national income used in purchasing consumer goods. Cf. *underdeveloped country.*

maturity:

(1) **finance:** the date on which a note, time draft, bill of exchange, bond, or other negotiable instrument becomes due and payable. The maturity date of a note, time draft, or bill of exchange drawn for a future date is set to run a specified number of days from the date of the loan or acceptance of maturity. Presentation and request for payment of the instrument are made on the maturity date.

(2) **business law:** the completion of a contract (e.g., an insurance policy).

maturity date: the date on which a financial obligation becomes due for payment and/or the date an obligation or contract expires.

maturity stage: the beginning of the demise of a product. The product's lifecycle conclusion is measured by the leveling off of demand, a decline in profit, and increasing competition. Small and financially insecure institutions tend to drop out of the market in the maturity stage.

maturity value: the money that is to be paid when a financial obligation or other contract becomes due.

maxim: a proposition of law needing no proof or argument because of its general acceptance. The mere announcement of a maxim invokes the authority understood to exist for its enforcement.

maximax criterion: a basis for decision making whereby a manager determines the greatest payoff for each possible strategy and then chooses the one that is most favorable, thus maximizing the maximum gain. Cf. *maximin criterion.*

maximin criterion: a basis for decision making whereby a manager determines the most negative payoff for each possible strategy and then chooses the one and that is most favorable, thus maximizing the minimum gain. Cf. *maximax criterion.*

maximizing: decision-making behavior in which a manager selects the best alternative from all possible alternatives.

maximum foreseeable loss: the estimate of the damage that would result if the occurrence insured against were not controlled by the protection that might reasonably be expected. See *loss expectancy.* Cf. *normal foreseeable loss; probable maximum loss.*

maximum loan-to-value ratio: the highest loan-to-value ratio (loan amount as a percentage of assessed valuation) that a lender is willing to undertake.

MBO (management by objectives): a process whereby superiors and those who report to them jointly establish objectives over a specified time frame, meeting periodically to evaluate their progress in meeting these goals.

means-end chain: a hierarchy of objectives for an organization in which objectives (ends) of component units becomes the means by which the broader objective is achieved.

means-goal staircase: systematic linkage of the goals of lower-level units or individuals with those of higher-level units or individuals.

measure of value: a function of money that gives the standard for identifying the results of production, using the monetary unit as the common denominator.

mechanic's lien: the legal, enforceable claim of a person who has performed work on or provided materials for a given property. Such claims are permitted by law in certain states as a claim against the title to the property. A mechanic's lien may also grant the claimant a degree of preference in case of liquidation of an estate or business. Cf. *artisan's lien ; particular lien*.

mechanistic structure: an organization in which all activities are specified and regulated so that the organization functions like a machine. See *bureaucracy*.

mechanization: the use of machines to replace human effort. Cf. *automation*.

media: the means used by transmitters of messages to deliver them to the intended receivers in a communication system. In advertising, the term refers to newspapers, radio, television, magazines, billboards, direct mail, and other such institutions that are used to carry advertisements.

media analysis: the study and evaluation of various media approaches for promoting items and services to a wide or specific audience. See *zero-base media planning*. Cf. *audience study*.

media director: an advertising agency executive who is responsible for choosing the media to be employed and scheduling the appearance of promotional material in such media.

mediation: an attempt by a third party, usually a government official, to bring together the parties to an industrial dispute. The mediator has no power to force a settlement. Mediation is different from conciliation, which also brings the two groups together, in that mediation includes suggestions for a compromise solution by a third party. See *Federal Mediation and Conciliation Service; Maritime Labor Board*. Cf. *arbitration; conciliation*.

mediator: a person, acting as a third party, who attempts to resolve a labor dispute. Cf. *arbitrator*.

medical expense insurance: coverage available in various forms against expenses incurred for medical treatment and care as a result of bodily injury or illness (e.g., major medical expense, surgical expense, or hospitalization insurance).

medical payments insurance: coverage available in various liability insurance policies in which the insurer agrees to reimburse the insured and others, without regard for the insured's liability, for medical or funeral expenses incurred as the result of bodily injury or death by accident under the conditions specified in the policy.

medium (plural: media): any means for transmitting a message to an intended recipient in a communication network. Examples include newspapers, radio, television, magazines, billboards, and direct mail. See *SRDS.*

medium-range planning: development of major plans that extend beyond the traditional operating period of one year. An average medium-range planning period is five years.

megabuck: (slang) a million dollars.

megacompany: synonymous with *megacorporation.*

megacorporation: a company formed from two or more companies or a number of companies of various sizes. Synonymous with *megacompany.*

megamerger: a gigantic-scale merger of two or more large companies involving billions of dollars.

megaselling: any selling involving orders of significant amounts of funds.

megatrend: a long-range trend extending to a decade, especially one involving predictions about the United States in the next 10 years.

melon: (slang) unusually large profits that have not been dispersed to eligible persons. See *cutting a melon.*

meltup: where stock prices explode upward, propelled by program trading and huge amounts of idle cash.

member bank: all national banks and any state bank that has applied successfully for membership in the Federal Reserve System.

member-bank reserves: funds that commercial banks are required to keep on deposit at regional Federal Reserve Banks. See *reserve.*

member corporation: a securities brokerage firm, organized as a corporation, that has at least one person who is a member of a stock exchange as a director and a holder of voting stock in the corporation.

member firm: a securities brokerage firm organized as a partnership and having at least one general partner who is a member of a stock exchange.

mentor: an experienced member of an organization who coaches, guides, and counsels newer members.

mercantile agency: an organization that supplies its subscribers with credit data on individuals and firms. In addition, some mercantile agencies gather statistical information and serve as collection depositories of past-due accounts. See *Dun and Bradstreet.*

mercantile rate of return: the ratio, expressed in percentages, between the figure showing on the contemporary income statement and the figure appearing on the contemporary balance sheet.

mercantilism: the economic policy under which nations measure their power by the amount of precious metal they have acquired. See *Kameralism*.

merchandise:

(1) **general:** purchased articles of business held for sale.

(2) **sales:** to plan or promote the sale of goods.

merchandise charge: extraneous costs (including shipping, insurance, demurrage, etc.) added to the cost of goods prior to mark-on.

merchandise control: collection and analysis of data on purchases and sales items, either by unit or by dollars.

merchandise inventory: products held by an entity for resale to customers.

merchandise manager: an executive who is responsible for supervising the purchasing, selling, and inventory control activities in a store.

merchandise mart: a building, usually large, that contains manufacturers' showrooms where retailers can examine the goods and place orders. Cf. *resident buyer; sales office.*

merchandise transfer: the transfer of goods from one accounting unit of a store to another. Merchandise can be transferred from department to department, from one branch store to another branch, or from home office to branch store.

merchandising:

(1) **retailing:** all activities connected with the buying and selling of merchandise, including displays, promotions, pricing, and buying.

(2) **manufacturing:** the activities required in the attempt to make a product interesting to buyers, (packaging, promotion, pricing arrangements, etc.). Cf. *marketing.*

merchandising the advertising: selling the advertising and sales promotion program to channel intermediaries in order to generate their enthusiasm and gain their support.

merchant: an individual who takes title to goods by buying them for the purpose of resale.

merchant wholesaler: a middleman who receives title to merchandise purchases for resale to firms that plan to resell the goods or process them in some fashion for resale. Cf. *wholesaler.*

merger:

(1) **general:** the combining of two or more entities through the direct

acquisition by one of the net assets of the other. A merger differs from a consolidation in that no new entity is created by a merger, whereas in consolidation a new organization comes into being and acquires the net assets of all of the combining units. See *conglomerate.* Cf. *takeover.*

(2) **economics:** any business combination. See, for example, *downstairs merger; horizontal merger.*

merit guidelines: guidelines for awarding merit raises that are tied to performance objectives.

merit increase (pay): an individual wage increase in recognition of superior performance or service, commonly specified as negotiable in a contract between union and management. Cf. *incentive pay.*

merit rating:

(1) **insurance:** a system of evaluation in which the past experience of the individual risk is a factor in determining the rate. Synonymous with *experience rating.*

(2) **human resources:** periodic evaluation of workers' efficiency as a basis for pay increases and/or promotion.

metapolicymaking: a strategy for making policy on how to make organizational policy.

methods analysis: synonymous with *time and motion study.*

methods study: analysis of the flow of work, particularly the utilization of materials, to permit more efficient use of manpower.

methods-time measurement (MTM): the listing of basic human movements and the assignment of time values to each. MTM is used in establishing time standards for varying tasks. Cf. *efficiency expert; ergonomics.*

metrocorporation: the corporation seen as having unlimited social responsibilities, with its managers holding themselves accountable to several groups in society. This view of the corporation is the opposite of the traditional one, in which managers are mainly accountable to the stockholders. Cf. *traditional corporation; well-tempered corporation.*

MFA: see *Multifibre Arrangements.*

MFN: see *most-favored nation status.*

Michels' Iron Law: Michels' statement that whoever says organization, says oligarchy, or rule by the few.

microbridge: a shortened version of *minibridge,* involving import-export shipments that originate or terminate at specified inland U.S. points. See *minibridge.*

microeconomics: the examination of the economic behavior of individual units in the economy, such as households or corporations.

microlevel approach: a method used to respond to changes of small magnitude, such as for individuals or groups. Cf. *macrolevel approach.*

micromarketing: a study of the economic exchange process of individual firms. Cf. *macromarketing.*

micromotion study: a time or motion study in which photographs or motion pictures are taken as part of an investigation of the details of body movements needed to complete a task. Cf. *time and motion study.*

micro-organizational behavior: subfield of organizational behavior concerned with understanding the behaviors of individuals working alone. Cf. *macro-organizational behavior.*

microstudy (of the organization): the analysis of job tasks and design.

midcareer plateau: the stage of a career at which the individual has no opportunity for further advancement.

middleman: an individual who buys merchandise with the expectation of reselling it for profit. At times a middleman may arrange for such transactions without actually having possession of the goods.

middle management:
(1) **general:** management personnel who report directly to top management.
(2) **administration:** the level of management responsible for carrying out the directives of top management.

mid-life crisis: career phase during which individuals evaluate their work progress, determine that things are not going well for them, and encounter strong psychological stress which can result in their doing foolish or bizarre things.

midnight shift: in an operation running on a 24-hour day, the work shift commencing at midnight and usually terminated at 8 A.M. Synonymous with *lobster shift; third shift.*

migrant worker: an individual without a permanent home who shifts from one region of the country to another, taking advantage of seasonal demand for his or her services during the harvesting seasons of various types of produce.

milestone scheduling: a scheduling and controlling procedure that employs bar charts to monitor progress. In essence, it is very similar to a Gantt chart, but its use is not restricted to production activities. Cf. *Gantt chart.*

military-industrial complex: the community of interests created between armed services officials and manufacturers of weapons and defense material.

milking: (slang) management's attempt to squeeze the last remaining profits from the firm without leaving sufficient reserves for improvements or for a downturn period.

mill supply house: the industrial equivalent of a general line, full-service merchant wholesaler, often focusing on supplying one industry.

minibridge: see *microbridge*.

minimum premium: the smallest premium an insurance company may charge under the manual rules for writing a particular policy or bond for a designated period. It is calculated to allow defraying of the necessary expenses of the insurance transaction and to leave an adequate amount to contribute to the payment of losses.

minimum (charge) rate: the lowest rate a public utility company charges for a commodity or service, even though on a per unit, per hour basis the amount of the charge would be less (e.g., the minimum monthly charge for your telephone, regardless of the frequency of telephone calls made).

minimum subscription: the figure given in a firm's prospectus identifying the minimum that must be raised for the organization to become operational.

minimum wage: the lowest allowable rate, by union contract, or by federal or state law, for a given job; most widely used in reference to the federal wage-hour law (Fair Labor Standards Act), which sets a minimum hourly rate for all workers to which it applies, and to supplementary state and municipal statutes. See *union rate; wage floor.* Cf. *substandard rate.*

minority interest: the part of the net worth of a subsidiary that relates to shares not owned by the controlling company or by other members of the combined group. Cf. *controlling interest.*

minority investment: a holding of less than 50 percent of a corporation's voting stock.

minority union: a union that does not enjoy exclusive bargaining or majority status. Usually it is an organization that has been unable to obtain a majority of the workers in the appropriate unit for certification but still retains its identity as a group within the firm.

mint ratio: the ratio of the weight of one metal to another, and to their equivalent in terms of the national unit of currency, such as the dollar (e.g., x grains of silver = x grains of gold = \$1.00).

minute book: an official record of a corporation's scheduled meetings (stockholders' gathering, board of director's meeting, etc.).

MIP: see *monthly investment plan.*

mirror principle: a human relations approach suggesting that people will respond in the same fashion as they are treated. Cf. *antagonistic cooperation; Theory X and Theory Y.*

MIS: see *management information system.*

misrepresentation:

(1) **insurance:** willfully misleading an insurance company with regard to information affecting the acceptance of a risk, the issuance of a policy, or the settlement of a claim. See *declaration; warranty.*

(2) **business law:** giving a positive statement or claiming an alleged fact that is not true, thus leading to a false conclusion.

missent item: an item that has been sent in error to another bank.

mission: organization's purpose or fundamental reason for existence.

missionary sales: the activity of personnel from a manufacturer who work closely with various firms and middlemen to increase the product sales.

missionary worker: a worker who is hired to break a strike using non-violent techniques.

mission statement: broad declaration of the basic, unique purpose and scope of operations that distinguishes the organization from others of its type.

MITI: Japan's Ministry of International Trade and Industry.

mix: see *audience composition; product mix; promotional mix.*

mix control: the control of the individual products going through the factory.

mixed capitalism: an economic system in which the major portion of the tools of production is owned and operated by the private sector and the market process is the principal factor in determining the allocation of resources.

mixed car: commodities shipped in the same railway car to which otherwise a variety of rates would apply.

mixed conflict situation: a relationship that is both highly distributive and highly integrative.

mixed costs: costs which include both fixed and variable elements within a relevant range of activity. Synonymous with *semivariable costs.*

mixed economy (system): an economic system that combines characteristics of both capitalism and socialism. Resources are allocated partly through decentralized markets and partly by means of decisions of a centralized government.

mixed-enterprise corporation: in Canada, a business company that is owned or controlled jointly by private interests and a government agency, chiefly for the purpose of promoting national objectives.

MNC: see *multinational corporation.*

models of development: economic success stories, such as postwar Japan, that are examined for clues about how to accelerate the growth of countries.

model stock: the right goods at the right time in the right quantities at the right price.

modified half-year convention: under the class life system, the practice whereby assets put into service before midyear are eligible for a full year of depreciation, and assets put into service after midyear are not eligible for depreciation until the following year.

modified union shop: one in which nonunion workers already employed need not join the union, but all new employees must join and those who are already members must remain in the union. Cf. *closed shop; open shop; union shop.*

mom and pop outlets: small stores, generally operated by members of a family with limited capital.

monetarist: a believer in the concept that a balanced economy depends on the supply of money.

monetary aggregates: the money supply consisting of either M1 or M3, seasonably adjusted.

monetary assets: assets, such as cash, accounts receivable, and other items having a contractual claim to a fixed amount of cash.

monetary base: a monetary aggregate composed of funds retained by banks and by the public, and including member-bank deposits at the various Federal Reserve banks.

monetary items: assets or liabilities that are fixed, either by nature or by contract, as to the amount of future dollars they can command in the marketplace.

monetary liability: the promise to pay a claim against a specified quantity of money, the amount of which is unaffected by inflation or deflation.

monetary policy: a policy of the Federal Reserve System that attempts to affect the terms on which credit can be obtained in private markets. Its purpose is to regulate the nation's sales level, level of employment, and prices. See *discretionary policy.* Cf. *fiscal policy.*

monetary reserve: the amount of bullion held by the government or by banks as security for fiduciary or credit money in circulation. See *reserve*.

monetary rule: a proposal that the Federal Reserve System should increase the money supply at a constant percentage rate.

monetizing a loan: the process in granting a loan whereby a borrower's note is converted into money, usually in the form of a demand deposit. See *demand deposit*.

monetizing the debt: increasing government debt financed through purchases of government securities by commercial or Federal Reserve banks.

money: any denomination of coin or paper currency of legal tender that passes freely as a medium of exchange; anything that is accepted in exchange for other things (e.g., precious metals). Major characteristics of money include easy recognition, uniformity in quality, easy divisibility, and a relatively high value within a small area. Cf. *currency; purchasing power*.

money illusion: the perception that an increase in all prices and incomes by the same proportion produces an increase in consumption, although real incomes remain the same.

money income: the amount of money received for work performed.

money manager: a professional manager employed to systematically invest funds entrusted to grow in value, especially as in a pension fund or a mutual fund.

money market (brokers): all financial organizations that handle the purchase, sale, and transfer of short term credit instruments and notes.

money market fund: a mutual fund that specializes in high-yield short term instruments of credit, such as certificates of deposit, Treasury bills, commercial paper, and repurchase agreements.

money measurement concept: the idea that money, as the common medium of exchange, is the accounting unit of measurement, and that only economic activities measurable in monetary terms are included in the accounting model.

money of account: a monetary denomination used in reckoning value in transactions or accounts, especially one not used as a coin, such as the U.S. mill.

money order (postal, bank): an instrument commonly purchased for a fee by an individual who does not maintain a checking account but wishes to send money to others. The names of the purchaser and payee are shown on the face of the money order. An advantage of the money order over checks is that presentation for payment at the original place of purchase is not required. A disadvantage is that a bank or other financial institution may charge for the service of supplying a money order.

money price: the number of money units that must be sacrificed to purchase a particular commodity.

money rates: interest rates that lenders charge their borrowers.

money supply: the total sum of currency circulating in a country. See *price-specie flow theory*.

money wages: the number of dollars received by employees, as contrasted with what those dollars will purchase. See *purchasing power of the dollar; real wages*.

monger: a trader or seller, often used in a derogatory fashion.

monitor role: an informational role in which a manager continually scans the environment to collect information pertinent to the organization or unit he or she manages.

monometallism: a monetary system in which the monetary component is defined in terms of only one metal, which is accepted in unlimited quantities for producing coins. See *real money*. Cf. *bimetallism*.

monopolistic competition: a form of competition in which the product of each competitor in a particular field differs from other competitors' products in some way so that an exact duplicate cannot be obtained from another source. Most competition in the United States is monopolistic competition.

monopoly:
(1) **general:** ownership of the source of a commodity or domination of its distribution. See *competition; engross*.
(2) **economics:** exclusive dominance of the supply and price of a commodity that is acquired by a franchise or government patent. Cf. *bilateral monopoly; legal monopoly; natural monopoly; oligopoly; partial monopoly; perfect (pure) monopoly; strategic resource monopoly*.

monopsony: a market situation in which there is only one buyer for an item. Cf. *duopsony; oligopsony*.

monotony: a condition that results in a worker showing low interest and boredom. The reasons for monotony are job related, but other external and internal factors may play a major role in creating this condition.

monthly investment plan (MIP): a pay-as-you-go method of buying odd lots of exchange-listed shares on a regular payment plan for as little as $40 a month for every three months, and up to $1,000 per payment. Under MIP the investor buys a stock designated by a securities broker by the dollar's worth. If the price advances, he or she gets fewer shares; if it declines, more shares. The investor may discontinue purchases at any time without penalty. Cf. *investment company.*

Montreal Round (trade meeting): In December 1988, a 96-nation trade meeting was called to give political momentum to the four-year round of world trade talks (the Uruguay Round) that began in 1986. Resolved were: liberalizing trade in services; swifter settlement of trade disputes; freer trade in tropical products; reducing tariffs by 30 percent; easing nontariff barriers; easing some investment restrictions; and monitoring countries' trade policies. See *General Agreement on Tariffs and Ttrade.*

moonlighting: holding two jobs at one time, usually a full-time job and a part-time job. Synonymous with *double employment; secondary employment.*

morale: the extent to which an employee's needs are met and the extent to which the person perceives that satisfaction as stemming from his or her total job situation. See *dissatisfiers; organizational climate; satisfiers.* Synonymous with *satisfaction.*

moral hazard: the possibility of loss being caused or aggravated by dishonesty or carelessness of the insured or his or her agents or employees. It arises from the character and circumstances of the insured, as distinguished from the inherent nature of the property covered, or its location. See *physical hazard.*

moral suasion: in banking, Federal Reserve System pressure exerted on U.S. banking, unaccompanied by an effort to compel compliance with the suggested action. See *jawboning.*

moratorium: the legally invoked period of delay during which a debtor need not fulfill obligations when they fall due.

morning loan: banks loans made to stockholders on an unsecured basis, with the broker handling stock deliveries until reimbursement has been made.

morphological research: a form of marketing research that focuses on how decisions are made.

mortality:

(1) **general:** death on a large scale; the proportion of deaths to the

population of a region, city, or nation.

(2) **accounting:** the expectancy of an asset or class of assets to expire or depreciate through use or the passage of time.

mortality guarantee: a guarantee in a contract that contract owners will not be affected by losses arising if mortality experience is different from that assumed in the contract.

mortality table: an actuarial table based on a sample group of the population, giving the percentage of people who live to any given age.

mortgage:

(1) **general:** a written conveyance of title to property, but not possession, to obtain the payment of a debt or the performance of some obligation, under the condition that the conveyance is to be void upon final payment.

(2) **finance:** property pledged as security for payment of a debt.

mortgage banker:

(1) a banker who specializes in mortgage financing.

(2) an operator of a mortgage financing company. Mortgage financing companies are mortgages themselves, as well as being mortgage agents for other large mortgages.

mortgage bond: see *bond, mortgage.*

mortgage broker: an individual or corporation that rarely originates loans but brings together a lender and a borrower for a fee.

mortgage clause: a provision attached to a fire or other direct damage insurance policy, stating (1) that the loss shall be payable to the mortgagee according to the amount of his or her interest, (2) that the mortgagee's right of recovery shall not be defeated by any act or neglect of the insured, and (3) that the mortgagee has other rights and privileges.

mortgage finance company: see *mortgage banker.*

most-favored nation status: in international business treaties, a provision against tariff discrimination between two or more nations. It provides that each participant will automatically extend to other signatories all tariff reductions that are offered to nonmember nations. Cf. *open door policy; retaliatory duty.*

motion study: measurement and observation of the movements of equipment and materials as they relate to workers' motions. The objective is to increase performance, make correct performance easier, and reduce wasted time. Cf. *efficiency expert; ergonomics; therbligs; time and motion study.*

motivating potential score: predictive index suggesting the motivation potential in a job.

motivation: a stimulus that differentially energizes certain responses within a person.

motivation, unconscious: a motivation (e.g., to buy) inferred from a person's pattern of behavior but of which the individual is not aware. See *hidden persuader; self-concept theory.* Cf. *rational buying motives.*

motivational needs: psychological forces that affect thinking and behavior (e.g., needs for self-actualization, belonging, feelings of security). A theory developed by A. Maslow details an individuals motivational needs. See *hierarchy of needs.*

motivational research: a technique developed by E. Dichter, purporting to correlate behavior, needs, emotions, and desires with consumer activity. See *consumer behavior research; hidden persuader.*

motivator-hygiene theory: F. Herzberg's theory that identifies conditions of a job that operate primarily to dissatisfy employees when they are not present (i.e., hygiene factors, salary, job security, etc.) and job conditions that lead to high levels of satisfaction when present (e.g., achievement, growth). Failure to meet the latter conditions is not highly dissatisfying. See *dissatisfiers; two-factor theory.*

movement: an increase or decrease in the price of a specific stock.

moving average: a perpetual inventory cost-flow assumption whereby the cost of goods sold and the ending inventory are determined to be a weighted-average cost of all merchandise on hand after each purchase.

moving budgeting: a form of budgeting that involves periodic updating through time.

MPC: see *marginal propensity to consume.*

MPI: see *marginal propensity to invest.*

MPS: see *marginal propensity to save.*

MTM: see *methods-time measurement.*

MTN: see *multilateral trade negotiations.*

muckracker: an individual who seeks to uncover business corruption or other activities that are unethical or harmful to the well-being of society.

multiallegiant worker: an employee who possesses allegiance to a variety of institutions (e.g., company, church, family, professional society).

multicompany: diverse organizations or a variety of firms under a single management.

multicultural organization: an organization in which employees of mixed backgrounds, experiences, and cultures can contribute and achieve their full potential for the benefit of both themselves and the organization.

multidivisional firm: an organization that has expanded into different industries and diversified its products.

multiemployer bargaining: the result of a collective-bargaining agreement covering more than one company in a given industry. It may be industry-wide, regional, or limited to a city or a metropolitan area. A related process is pattern bargaining, in which key terms reached in one settlement are closely followed by other settlements in similar companies. Synonymous with *multiunit bargaining.*

multiemployer pension plans: plans in which several employers pool pension contributions in a single fund, which is administered by labor and management of all companies involved. Workers can transfer between the participating firms without any loss in pension rights. See *instant vesting; portability.*

Multifibre Arrangements (MFA): a system of limits, under GATT, on imports of textiles and clothing from less costly countries. See *General Agreement on Tariffs and Trade.*

multi-industry: the management of firms involved in different activities.

multilateralism: the practice or system of freedom of trade and convertibility of currencies among many nations. Cf. *bilateralism.*

multilateral trade negotiations (MTN): the negotiations, usually over multiple sessions, conducted among many nations with respect to the conditions and rules of international trade, e.g., the Kennedy Round and the Tokyo Round.

multinational corporation (MNC): a corporation that participates in international business activities; a firm that produces, markets, and finances its operations throughout various nations of the world. Cf. *production sharing.*

multiple banking: the offering of all types of banking services to a bank's customers, as distinguished from specialization in a few services, as in savings and loan associations and other banking institutions. Synonymous with *department store banking.* Cf. *full-service bank.*

multiple brands: several brand names used by a manufacturer on essentially the same product to open up new market segments.

multiple expansion of bank deposits: the situation that occurs when a loan made by one bank is used to finance business transactions and becomes a deposit in another bank. A portion of this loan can be used by the second bank as a required reserve, and the remainder can be loaned out for business use, so that it is eventually deposited in a third bank.

multiple-line underwriting: the issuance of fire and casualty insurance by a single company, by authority granted under multiple line underwriting laws. Cf. *line*.

multiple-line underwriting laws: statutes granting underwriting powers that enable a single company to write both fire and casualty insurance.

multiple-location risks insurance: insurance that provides protection of property owned or controlled by one person or corporation in a number of different locations. See *master policy*.

multiple management: worker participation in a firm's management by assisting in the development and execution of policy. See *human relations theory*. Cf. *Caesar management; unilateral strategy*.

multiple pricing: a price reduction offered if more than one unit is purchased.

multiple sales: the result of selection by customers of multiple rather than single items to purchase.

multiple scenarios: a set of different assumptions used in planning.

multiplier principle: the reciprocal of the marginal propensity to save. The multiplier is a figure that identifies the changes in investment and spending to alterations in aggregate income. See *Keynesian economics*. Cf. *marginal propensity to save*.

multiunit bargaining: synonymous with *multiemployer bargaining*.

municipal bond: see *bond, municipal*.

municipals: a popular term for the securities of a governmental unit.

munifunds: synonymous with *mutual funds*. See *investment company*.

muniment of title:

(1) **general:** anything that protects or enforces.

(2) **business law:** deeds and contracts that show conclusive proof of ownership.

Murphy's law: the theory that if something can go wrong, eventually it will.

mutual assent: agreement by all parties to a contract to the same thing. Each party must know what the other wishes.

mutual company: a corporation without capital stock (e.g., a mutual savings bank) in which the profits, after deductions, are distributed among the owner–customers in proportion to the business activity they carried out with the corporation.

mutual funds: see *investment company*

mutual goal setting: an employee evaluation system consisting of a series of discussions between a supervisor and a subordinate in which the goals of future performance are identified and/or reviewed.

mutual rating: a relatively infrequent employee evaluation system whereby a worker is formally evaluated and rated by all or most members of the unit in which he or she works.

mutual savings bank: a banking organization without capital stock, operating under law for the mutual benefit of the depositors. The depositors are encouraged to practice thrift, and the savings of these small depositors are invested in very high grade securities and some first-class mortgages. Dividends from these investments are mutually distributed after deduction of expenses of the association and reserves for a guaranty fund for depositors. The principal idea of a mutual savings bank is to perform a social service for small depositors who cannot invest their savings at high yield. See *mutual company.*

N

NAC: see *New American Community.*

NAFTA: see *North American Free Trade Agreement.*

named insured: person, firm, or corporation or any of its members, specifically designated by name as insured(s) in a policy, as distinguished from others who, although unnamed, are protected under some circumstances.

named-peril insurance: coverage that specifies the perils that are insured against. Cf. *all-risks insurance.*

narrow market: a condition that exists when the demand for a security is so limited that small alterations in supply or demand will create major fluctuations in the market price.

narrow span of control: span of control in which only a small number of people, usually from two to six, report to a superior.

NASD: see *National Association of Securities Dealers.*

NASDAQ: see *National Association of Securities Dealers Automated Quotations.*

National Alliance of Businessmen: a coalition of business firms founded in 1968 to combat structural unemployment among the nation's hard-to-employ by reducing the barriers to their employment.

National Association of Insurance Agents (NAIA): the countrywide organization of stock fire and casualty insurance company agents whose primary purpose is the protection and advancement of the American agency system. See *American agency system.*

National Association of Manufacturers (NAM): a major organization of employers, founded in 1895 and structured with departments of trade, law, industrial relations, and publicity.

National Association of Securities Dealers (NASD): an association established in accordance with the Maloney Act of 1938, which amended the Securities Exchange Act of 1934, providing for self-regulation of the over-the-counter securities market by associations registered with the SEC. The NASD is the only association so registered. Most companies that offer variable annuities are NASD members.

National Association of Securities Dealers Automated Quotations (NASDAQ): an automated information network that provides brokers and dealers with price quotations on securities traded over the counter.

national bank: a commercial bank organized with the consent and approval of the Comptroller of the Currency and operated under the supervision of the federal government. National banks are required to be members of the Federal Reserve System and must purchase stock in the Federal Reserve Bank in their district.

National Bankruptcy Act of 1898: a federal law stating the conditions under which an individual or business may declare bankruptcy and detailing the procedures for declaration. See *reorganization*.

national brand: a brand distributed widely, through numerous outlets, in contrast to a private brand or label owned by a distributor or retailer.

National Credit Union Administration: established on March 10, 1970, reorganized in 1978; responsible for chartering, insuring, supervising, and examining Federal credit unions and administering the National Credit Union Share Insurance Fund.

National Credit Union Share Insurance Fund: see *National Credit Union Administration*.

national income: the total of the incomes received by all the people in a country over a stated period. It is equal to the gross national product minus depreciation minus sales taxes and other small items.

National Industrial Conference Board: founded in 1916, an organization that serves as a clearinghouse for the dissemination of information, publications of statistical materials, and other industrial relations data.

National Institute of Occupational Safety and Health (NIOSH): an organization created by the Occupational Safety and Health Act to conduct research and to develop additional safety and health standards.

National Labor Relations Act of 1935: see *Wagner Act*.

National Labor Relations Board (NLRB): a five-member body created by the Wagner Act of 1935 and charged with the administration of the act. Its members and general counsel are named by the president. The board supervises representation elections to determine the choice of a bargaining agent and prepares cases arising from charges of unfair labor practices.

National Mediation Board: created on June 21, 1934, by an act amending the Railway Labor Act of 1926; attempts to settle disputes between rail and air carriers and between their employees. It also conducts representation elections. Its three members are appointed by the President with the Senate confirmation. See *Federal Mediation and Conciliation Service*.

national union: the parent organization that charters local unions.

national wealth: the combined monetary value of all the material economic products owned by all the people in a country. Cf. *wealth.*

nationwide marine definition: a statement of the types of insurance that may properly be written under marine or inland marine policies. Because the definition is filed as part of rating plans in many states, it has real legal significance.

natural business year: a 12-month period, usually selected to end when inventory or business activity is at a low point.

natural capital: land that is used as a factor of production.

natural monopoly:

(1) a monopoly that results from natural conditions (e.g., a crop that demands special climate is subject to monopolization by a grower in the area having that climate).

(2) among industries that experience economies of scale, the situation in which cost per unit is lowest when there is only one company in the industry.

natural resources: all materials furnished by nature (minerals, timber, water, etc.).

near money: highly liquid assets (e.g., government securities) other than official currency.

need for achievement: desire to accomplish a task or goal more effectively than in the past.

need for control: strong desire that entrepreneurs have to control both their venture and their destiny.

need hierarchy model: see *hierarchy of needs.*

needle trades: apparel-producing industries.

needs assessment: diagnosis of present problems and future challenges that can be dealt with through training or development.

negative elasticity: the concept that demands moves in the same direction as price.

negative file: an authorized system file containing a simple list of accounts for which credit, check cashing, and other privileges should be denied. Cf. *positive file.*

negative income tax: a proposed system to provide financial aid to individuals with incomes below a certain minimum. Rulings of the Internal Revenue Service would be followed, but the procedure would be to distribute rather than collect revenue.

negative reinforcement: a method of making a desired response more likely when a behavior causes something undesired to be taken away.

negative sum game: the concept that the amount losers lose will always exceed the amount winners win.

negative verification: if a bank does not hear otherwise from a depositor, the assumption that the depositor finds no discrepancies between the statement presented and his or her records. Many banks have a legend printed on the statement form going to the depositor to the effect that, if no difference is reported within 10 days, the account will be considered correct.

negligence:

(1) **business law:** failure to do that which an ordinary, reasonable, prudent person would do, or doing some act that an ordinary, prudent person would not do. Reference must be made to the situation, the circumstances, and the awareness of the parties involved. See *contributory negligence.*

(2) **insurance:** failure to use the degree of care that is considered to be a reasonable precaution under the given circumstances. Acts of omission or commission, or both, may constitute negligence.

negotiable:

(1) **general:** anything that can be sold or transferred to another for money or as payment of an obligation.

(2) **securities:** a security whose title is transferable by delivery.

negotiable instrument: as stated in the Uniform Negotiable Instruments Act: "An instrument, to be negotiable, must conform to the following requirements: (a) it must be in writing and signed by the maker or drawer; (b) it must contain an unconditional promise or order to pay a certain sum in money; (c) it must be payable on demand, or at a fixed or determinable future time; (d) it must be payable to order or to bearer; (e) where the instrument is addressed to a drawee, he must be named or otherwise indicated therein with reasonable certainty."

negotiable order of withdrawal: see *NOW account.*

negotiated price: the result obtained by a purchaser who desires something different from what is available or is powerful enough to force the seller to accept prices lower than those usually charged. See *upset price.*

negotiation:

(1) **finance:** the act by which a negotiable instrument is placed in circulation by being physically passed from the original holder to another person.

(2) **labor relations:** the deliberation or discussion by representatives of labor and management to set conditions of work (e.g., wages, hours, benefits, working conditions, a mechanism for handling grievances); the bargaining that goes on between these parties. See *collective bargaining.* Cf. *arbitration; mediation.*

negotiator role: the role of a manager in discussing and bargaining with other units to obtain advantages for his or her unit.

Nenko system: the general pattern of human resource management commonly used in large-scale Japanese organizations.

neoclassical economics: an economic approach, developed between 1870 and 1918, that uses mathematics in the analysis of data and models. Neoclassicists were primarily concerned with refining the concepts of price and allocation theory, marginalism, and the theory of capital.

neo–human relations movement: an integrative approach to management theory that combines a positive view of human nature with the scientific study of organizations to prescribe how effective managers should act in most circumstances.

neo-Keynesian: a follower of concepts dealing with tax adjustment and government spending as primary forces of economic expansion. See *Keynesian economics.* Cf. *Friedmanite.*

nepotism: the practice of placing relatives in organizational positions without regard to the claims by others that better-qualified people can be found (e.g., the president of the firm, without consideration of qualifications, hiring his nephew).

net: that which remains after certain designated deductions have been made from the gross amount.

net assets: the property of a business, corporation, organization, or estate that remains after all obligations have been met.

net asset value: the resulting per share value derived when investment companies compute assets daily, or even twice daily, by totaling the market value of all securities owned, then deduct all liabilities and dividing by the number of shares outstanding.

net avails: the funds given to a borrower in the discounting of a note. It is equal to the face value of the note minus the discount.

netback: selling an item less out-of-pocket costs to move it from the plant to the point of sale.

net business formation: the index for measuring the net number of new businesses established each month. It is compiled from data on companies receiving charters of incorporation. Used as a leading indicator of the nation's health.

net cash flow: the net cash consumed or produced in a period by an activity or product during a unit of time, including all revenue and expenses except noncash items such as depreciation. Cf. *cash flow*.

net change:
(1) **securities:** the change in the price of a security between the closing price on one day and the closing price on the following day on which the stock is traded. The net change is ordinarily the last figure on the stock price list. The notation "+ 1 1/4" means "up $1.250 a share from the last sale on the previous day the stock traded."
(2) **production:** a materials planning system where the materials plan is not recalculated periodically, but instead is updated as each requirement change occurs.

net cost:
(1) **accounting:** the true cost of an item. The net cost is determined by subtracting all income or financial gain from the gross cost.
(2) **insurance:** the total premiums paid on a policy less any dividends, and the surrender value as of the time the net cost is determined.

net credit period: the maximum time a company takes to pay a bill according to the terms of sale.

net current asset value (per share): working capital divided by the number of common shares outstanding.

net debt: the sum of fixed and existing liabilities less the sinking fund and other assets that are earmarked for payment of the liabilities.

net earnings: the figure that results when income taxes applicable to operating earnings are deducted from the excess of gross operating income over gross operating expenses (referred to as "operating earnings before taxes").

net export of goods and services: the excess of exports of goods and services (domestic output sold abroad and production abroad credited to U.S.-owned resources) over imports (U.S. purchases of foreign output, domestic production credit to foreign-owned resources, and net private cash remittances to creditors abroad).

net income: the remains from earnings and profits after all costs, expenses, and allowances for depreciation and probable loss have been deducted. Synonymous with *earnings*.

net interest: synonymous with *pure interest*.

net investment: the actual change in value of productive assets in a given year, determined by subtracting from gross investment the value of depreciation or the value of all capital that has been consumed.

net long-term debt: total long-term debt, less cash and investment assets of sinking funds and other reserve funds specifically held for redemption of long-term debt.

net loss: the excess of expenses and losses during a specified period over revenues and gains in the same time frame.

net national product: gross national product minus capital consumption (depreciation); the market value of the net output of goods and services produced by the nation's economy.

net-net income: uses the repetition of the word "net" to emphasize the actual profit, resulting in usable cash, after all expenses have been paid.

net present value (NPV): the difference between the present values of an investment's expected cash inflows and outflows.

net price: the price after deductions, allowances, and discounts have been made.

net profit: the excess of all revenues over all costs and expenses incurred to obtain the income in a given enterprise during a given period of time. If the total expenses exceed the income, such amount is known as net loss. Synonymous with *net revenue*.

net rate: an advertising medium's published rate, less the agency commission. See *fifteen and two*.

net realizable value: the selling price of an item less reasonable selling costs.

net revenue: synonymous with *net profit*.

net sales: gross sales, minus returns and allowances, over a stated period. Synonymous with *sales (marketing)*.

net tax liability: the amount of tax computed by subtracting tax credits from the gross tax liability.

net working capital: the excess of existing assets over present liabilities.

network planning: a family of planning and control techniques whereby all of the planning steps are schematically tied together through a common network.

net worth:

(1) **general:** the owner's equity in a business, represented by the excess of the total assets over the total amounts owed to outside creditors at a given time.

(2) **accounting:** the figure determined by deducting the amount of all personal liabilities for the total value of personal assets.

net yield: the return from an investment following subtractions for costs and losses incurred in operating the investment.

neutral tax: a tax that does not affect the allocation of resources.

never-outs: items that should never run out of stock during a season because of continuous demand.

New American Community (NAC): first described by J. M. Rosenberg in January 1991 at the University of Yucatan in Merida, Mexico, (and in his 1992 book of the same title) to eventually include 700 million people from 33 nations of North, Central, and South America, in a treaty of benefits for free trade, social-educational-health welfare, research and development, etc. Cf. *Enterprise for the Americas Initiative.* See *North American Free Trade Agreement.*

new business venture group: a separate company unit with a mandate to develop one or more new businesses or items that fall outside the natural charter of the firm's existing activities.

New Economics: the economic theory, initially developed by John Maynard Keynes in the 1930s, that claims that an economy may be in equilibrium at any level of employment and that appropriate government fiscal and monetary policies are required to maintain full employment and keep economic growth with minimal inflation. See *Keynesian economics.*

new issue: a stock or bond sold by a corporation for the first time. Proceeds may be issued to retire outstanding securities of the company to finance new plant or equipment or to secure additional working capital.

new social contract: an assumption that employer-employee relationships will be shorter-term based on convenience and mutual benefit, rather than for life.

new-venture development: the first stage of a venture's lifecycle that involves activities such as creativity and venture assessment.

New York Coffee and Sugar Exchange: founded in 1882 and originally known as the New York Coffee Exchange, the principal U.S. exchange for the trading of coffee and sugar futures contracts.

New York Curb Exchange: former name for the *American Stock Exchange.*

New York Mercantile Exchange: an exchange founded in 1872 as a market for cheese, butter, and eggs. Its principal commodities now include potatoes, silver coins, and platinum. In January 1990, the New York Mercantile Exchange and the Commodity Exchange (Comex) agreed to merge.

New York Stock Exchange (NYSE): the largest, most prestigious security exchange in the world, reorganized under its existing name in 1863. The New York Stock and Exchange Board in 1817 moved indoors to a second floor room at 40 Wall Street in New York City. On January 2, 1863, its name was changed to the New York Stock Exchange; on the next day, the first subsidiary, the New York Stock Exchange Building Company, was created. See *American Stock Exchange; NYSE Common Stock Index*.

NICs: newly industrializing countries (i.e., Mexico, South Korea, Brazil, Taiwan).

Nielsen Drug (Food) Index: developed by A. C. Nielsen, statements on the market change of products, by type and brand, issued through panels of experts from drugstores and other stores.

Nielsen rating: the percentage of households tuned to a stated radio or television program, as reported by the A. C. Nielsen Company. A device called an Audimeter is installed out of sight in each sample household and is electronically connected to each television set in the home. The Audimeter produces a minute-by-minute photographic record identifying the times the sets are turned on and off and the stations tuned in. See *Audimeter*. Cf. *Hooperating*.

night differential: extra, nonovertime pay for time worked between 6 P.M. and 6 A.M.

NIOSH: see *National Institute of Occupational Safety and Health*.

NLRB: see *National Labor Relations Board*.

no-bill: (slang) an employee who is unwilling to join a union.

no-fault automobile insurance: personal injury protection in a form of state-mandated insurance under which a person's financial losses resulting from an automobile accident (e.g., medical and hospital expenses and loss of income) are automatically paid by his or her own insurance company without regard to the identity of the party at fault. One result of this form of insurance is that the responsible party cannot be sued, at least up to a certain limit. See *broadened collision coverage*. Cf. *limited collision coverage; nonownership automobile insurance*.

no-limit order: a request to buy or sell a security without any stipulation about price. See *limited order; market order*.

no-load funds: mutual funds that are not sold by a salesperson. They do not involve extensive marketing schemes and contain no sales charge or load. Cf. *investment company; load; load funds*.

no-lockout agreement: a collective bargaining clause stating that the employer will not withhold work from individuals or close down the plant to force acceptance of management's terms.

nominal: used as a modifier to indicate that values are expressed in current money prices.

nominal partner: an individual who lends his or her name to a business organization but is not a true partner because he or she may not have given sufficient financial backing or does not take a full share of the profit.

nominal price:

(1) **finance:** an amount of money so small in relation to the item purchased that it hardly justifies use of the word "price."

(2) **securities:** an estimated price for a security or commodity that is not traded often enough to warrant setting a definite market price.

nominal yield: the rate of return stated on a security, calculated on its par or face value.

nonaccrual asset: an asset, such as a loan, that has been questioned on bank examination and is known to be a slow or doubtful (of payment) loan. A reserve is set up or applied on this type of loan, and it is excluded from the earning or accrual assets.

nonassessable stock: most securities; stock whose owners cannot be assessed in the event of failure or insolvency. Cf. *limited liability*.

nonassignable: synonymous with *inalienable*.

noncallable bond: see *bond, noncallable*.

nonconcurrency: the situation that exists when two or more policies provide different coverages on the same risk. See *double insurance*.

noncontributory: a group insurance plan under which the policyholder (employer) pays the entire cost.

noncontributory retirement system: a system in which the employer bears the entire cost of deferred compensation for the worker.

noncontrollable costs: costs assigned to a responsible center whose amounts cannot be influenced by and are only indirectly the responsibility of the manager of that center.

noncrisis problem: type of problem in managerial decision-making involving an issue that requires resolution but does not simultaneously have the importance and immediacy characteristics of a crisis.

noncumulative: a preferred stock on which unpaid dividends do not accrue. As a rule, omitted dividends are gone forever.

noncumulative quantity discount: a price reduction that is given based on the size of the individual order placed.

noncurrent: that which is due more than one year after the date of issuance.

noncurrent accounts: all operational asset, long-term investment, long-term liability, and owner's equity accounts; all accounts except for working capital accounts.

noncurrent liabilities: claims against the assets of an entity that will become due a year or more in the future.

nondirective counseling: a client-centered process of skillfully listening and encouraging an employee to explain bothersome problems, understand them, and determine appropriate solutions. See *cooperative counseling; directive counseling.*

nondirective interview: an interview in which the applicant is allowed the maximum amount of freedom in determining the course of the discussion, while the interviewer carefully refrains from influencing the applicant's remarks.

nonexempt employees: employees covered by the overtime provisions of the Fair Labor Standards Act.

nondurable goods: items that have a relatively brief lifetime (e.g., food, clothing).

nonfinancial compensation: a form of compensation—other than pay and benefits—that includes the satisfaction a person receives by performing meaningful job-related tasks.

nonforfeiture options: privileges allowed under terms of a life insurance contract after cash values have been created. Four such privileges exist: (1) surrender for full cash value; (2) loans up to the full amount of the cash value; (3) paid-up policy for the amount of insurance that cash value, as a single premium, will buy at net rates; (4) term insurance for the full face amount of the original policy for as long as the cash value will last to pay necessary premiums.

noninstallment credit: credit granted with payment to be made in a lump sum at a future date.

non-interest-bearing note: a note whose maker does not have to pay any interest.

nonmanufacturing expenses: expenditures that are not closely associated with the manufacture of products, including selling and administrative expenses.

nonmarket production: production that occurs outside the market (e.g., production regulated by custom or law rather than by prices). This is a common phenomenon in less-developed nations.

nonmember bank: a U.S. bank that is not a member of the Federal Reserve System. Such institutions are either state or private banks.

nonmonetary items: assets or equities that are not fixed as to the amount of future dollars they can command and hence fluctuate in value according to their demand in the marketplace.

nonownership automobile insurance: insurance under which an accident victim is automatically compensated for medical expenses, income losses, and so on, without regard for who created the accident or owned the car. Cf. *no-fault automobile insurance.*

nonperformance: the failure of a contracting party to provide goods or services according to an agreement.

nonprice competition: markets in which a seller maneuvers for influence on the basis of special aspects of the items to be sold, promotion, or marketing strategy. Most larger organizations avoid price competition by emphasizing nonprice marketing forces. Cf. *competition (business); trading down; trading up.*

nonprofit corporation: see *not-for-profit.*

nonprofit marketing: the application of marketing concepts and activities to nonprofit organizations.

nonrecurring charge: any cost, expense, or involuntary loss that is thought not likely to occur again.

nonrenewable natural resources: natural resources that are used up in the process of production.

nontaxable income: income that is not liable to income tax.

nontraceable costs: costs that are not directly identified with the responsibility centers to which they are assigned.

nonverbal communications: messages conveyed through body movements, the intonations or emphasis we give to words, facial expressions, and the physical distance between the sender and receiver.

nonzero sum situation: a competitive situation in which not only the winning group benefits but the other group also wins or its position remains unchanged.

no par value stock: stock of a corporation that has designated par value.

no-passbook savings: the same as a regular passbook savings account, except that no passbook is used. Deposits and withdrawal slips are receipted by the teller, with a copy returned to the depositor for personal records. A periodic statement is rendered in place of a passbook. Withdrawals must be made by the depositor personally. Cf. *passbook.*

no protest: instructions given by one bank to another collecting bank not to object to items in case of nonpayment. The sending bank stamps on the face of the item the letters "N.P." If the item cannot be collected, the collecting bank returns the item without objecting.

no-raiding agreements (pacts): agreements between international unions not to persuade workers to leave one union and join another when the first union has established bargaining relationships. Once a union is organized, no other union will attempt to break a member away. Affiliates of the AFL-CIO have signed a general no-raiding pact. Several unions have bilateral agreements covering attempts to organize unorganized workers. See *rival unionism.*

normal foreseeable loss: the estimate of the damage that would result if the occurrence insured against received the normally expected protection and control. Cf. *maximum foreseeable loss.*

normal good: an item whose consumption changes directly with money income when prices remain constant (e.g., consumer goods). Cf. *superior goods.*

normal price: the price to which the market price tends to return following fluctuations up or down.

normal profit: the lowest price that an entrepreneur will accept as compensation for his or her activity. It is part of an organization's total economic costs, since it is a payment that must be received by the owner to keep him or her from withdrawing capital and effort that might have to be used in another way.

normal sale: a transaction that pleases both the seller and buyer of property and in which no unforeseen or abnormal situations surface.

normal time: the time needed by an average employee to complete some arbitrarily determined unit of work, performing at a normal pace under standard conditions and procedures but without allowances for work fatigue or interruptions. See *pacers.* Cf. *time standard.*

normal value: the price of a property commanded on the open market.

normative decision models: the various step-by-step procedures that prescribe how managers should make decisions to reach their goals.

normative economics: the study of economics that include the value judgments of the economist. See *overbought; oversold.* Cf. *positive economics.*

North American Free Trade Agreement (NAFTA): free-trade accords, first signed between the U.S. and Canada in 1989 and negotiated with

368 no sale final • notice of dishonor

Mexico in 1992. See *Enterprise for the Americas Initiative; New American Community.*

no sale final: an organizational policy that a sale is not final until the customer is totally pleased with the purchase made.

no-strike clause: a contract clause barring a strike during the life of an agreement. Cf. *contract bar.*

nostro account: an account maintained by a bank with a bank in a foreign country. Nostro accounts are kept in foreign currencies of the country in which the monies are held, with the equivalent dollar value listed in another column. Cf. *vostro account.*

nostro overdraft: part of a bank's statement indicating that it has sold more foreign bills of exchange than it has bought, resulting in the domestic bank's owing currencies to foreign banks in the amount of the nostro overdraft.

notarial protest certificate: synonymous with *notice of dishonor.*

notary public: a person commissioned by a state for a stipulated period (with the privilege of renewal) to administer certain oaths and to attest and certify documents, thus authorizing him or her to take affidavits and depositions. A notary is also authorized to protest negotiable instruments for nonpayment or nonacceptance. See *notice of dishonor.*

notation credit: a credit that specifies that any person purchasing or paying drafts drawn or demands for payment made under it must note the amount of the draft or demand on the letter or advice of credit.

note: an instrument, such as a promissory note, that is the recognized legal evidence of a debt. A note is signed by the maker (the borrower), promising to pay a certain sum of money on a specified date at a certain place of business, to a certain business, individual, or bank (the lender).

note of hand: any promissory note.

note payable: a liability, evidenced by a formal written promise to pay a specified sum at a fixed future date. Notes may be either short (one year or less) or long term.

note receivable: a promissory note collected by a business from a customer.

not-for-profit: the activities of an organization established with the sole goal of providing service for society rather than for the purpose of making a profit. See *eleemosynary.*

notice of dishonor: a document pre pared by a notary public when a maker or drawee has refused to pay for or accept an instrument. When a holder in due course presents an instrument for payment or acceptance by a drawee, and the maker or drawee fails to honor the instrument, the holder in due course gives it to a notary public. The notary public also presents the instrument to the maker or drawee as a legal formality. If the maker or drawee again dishonors the instrument by refusing to pay for or accept it, the notary public prepares the notice of dishonor. Synonymous with *mandate of protest; notarial protest certificate; protest jacket.*

novation:

(1) **general:** the replacement of a new debt or obligation for an older one. Cf. *renewal; standstill agreement.*

(2) **finance:** the replacement of a new creditor or debtor for a former creditor or debtor.

NOW (negotiable order of withdrawal) account: a checking account requiring no service charge or minimum balance. This is a growing trend among savings institutions.

NPV: see *net present value.*

n.s.f: not sufficient funds.

n.s.f. check: a check that is not honored by a bank because of insufficient cash in the customer's bank account. See *insufficient funds.*

nucleus group: full-fledged members of an informal organization.

nullification of agreement: setting aside the terms of an agreement. Cf. *repudiation.*

number of days sales in inventory (or receivables): days of average inventory on hand (or average collection period for receivables).

nursery finance: institutional loans to profitable organizations that plan to go public shortly. See *adventure; risk capital; venture capital.*

nut: a colloquialism for uneliminatable operating cost, essentially the same as *variable cost.*

NYSE Common Stock Index: a composite index covering price movements of all common stocks listed on the Big Board. It is based on the close of the market December 31, 1965, as 50.00 and is weighted according to the number of shares listed for each issue. The index is computed continuously and printed on the ticker tape each half-hour. Point changes in the index are converted to dollars and cents to provide a meaningful measure of changes in the average price of listed stocks. The composite index is supplemented by separate indices for four industry groups: industrials, transportation, utilities, and finances. Cf. *Dow-Jones averages.*

O

OA: see *operational analysis.*

O/A: open account.

OB: see *organizational behavior.*

OASI: see *old-age and survivors' insurance.*

objective rationality: a decision-making condition under which a manager identifies all possible alternatives, accurately predicts the consequences of each, and selects the one that will maximize returns to the firm.

objective value: the price an item can command in terms of other items in the market.

obligation: the legal responsibility and duty of a debtor (the obligor) to pay a debt when due, and the legal right of the creditor (the obligee) to enforce payment in the event of default.

obligation bond: see *bond, obligation.*

obligee: a creditor or promisee.

obligor: a debtor or promisor.

observer: an employee who attends a meeting of management and union negotiators but does not participate in the discussions or in the voting. Cf. *public member.*

obsolescence: the state of being out of date and therefore of little use to society. See *functional obsolescence; planned obsolescence; product obsolescence.*

occupation: a person's trade, business, or vocational choice.

occupational accident: an accident that occurs in the course of employment and is caused by inherent or related hazards.

occupational disease: a pathological condition caused by or resulting from employment (e.g., chemical or radium poisoning; pneumoconiosis; the bends in tunnel boring or diving).

occupational health: all activities related to protecting and maintaining the health and safety of working people.

occupational information: information resulting from analysis of questionnaires and other materials that describe the functions and characteristics of specific occupations. See, e.g., *Dictionary of Occupational Titles.*

occupational mobility: the extent to which individuals in a particular occupation move into work other than that for which they were specially trained.

Occupational Outlook Handbook: a publication of the U.S. Department of Labor that indicates future needs for various jobs. See *Dictionary of Occupational Titles.*

Occupational Safety and Health Act of 1970: federal legislation providing for health and safety standards for individuals in the performance of their labors. The act created the Occupational Safety and Health Administration (OSHA) in the U.S. Department of Labor to set the rules and enforce the laws. OSHA also administers training and educational programs on occupational safety and health standards for employers and workers, supervises regional inspections, and issues citations to employers who do not meet federal occupational safety and health standards.

Occupational Safety and Health Review Commission: see *Occupational Safety and Health Act of 1970.*

ocean marine insurance: coverage on vessels of all types, including liabilities connected with them, and on their cargoes. Cf. *inland marine insurance; marine protection and indemnity insurance.*

OD: see *organizational development.*

odd-lot dealer: a member firm of an exchange that buys and sells odd lots of stock, one to 9 shares in the case of stocks traded in 10-share units and one to 99 for 100-share units. The odd-lot dealer's customers are commission brokers acting on behalf of their customers.

odd-lot orders: purchases or sales of stock that are not in 100-share units. Cf. *full lot; lot; round lot.*

odd pricing: pricing at odd amounts (e.g., at 99 cents instead of at a dollar). Synonymous with *psychological pricing.*

OECD: see *Organization for Economic Cooperation and Development.*

O-E-C (organizing, evaluating, and coaching) syndrome: an approach to work improvement by studying jobs through analysis of work and tasks, minimizing the damaging impact of control by others, and emphasizing the dynamics of personal growth. See *job enrichment.*

OEEC: see *Organization for Economic Cooperation and Development.*

OEM: see *original-equipment manufacturer.*

OFCC: see *Federal Contract Compliance Office.*

off: a given day on which the prices of stocks and commodities drop.

off-balance-sheet financing: raising money in such a way that no further liabilities are clearly displayed on the balance sheet.

off-board: an over-the-counter transaction in unlisted securities or a transaction involving listed shares that was not executed on a national securities exchange. Cf. *over-the-counter securities.*

off-brand: a brand that is not considered acceptable to a consumer.
offer:
  (1) **general:** to present for acceptance or refusal.
  (2) **securities:** the price at which a person is ready to sell, as opposed to bid, the price at which a person is ready to buy.
offering: an issue of securities or bonds offered for sale to the public. See *secondary offering; special offering.*
Office of Federal Contract Compliance Programs: see *Federal Contract Compliance Office.*
Office of Personnel Management: established on December 28, 1978; administers a merit system to ensure compliance with personnel laws and regulations and assists agencies in recruiting, examining, and promoting people on the basis of their knowledge and skills.
Office of Savings Associations (OSA): the agency of the savings and loan industry replacing the Federal Home Loan Bank Board.
office of the president: exists when two or three co-equal chief executives in an organization divide the work and coordinate their respective efforts.
Office of Thrift Supervision: see *Savings Industry Bill.*
officer's check: synonymous with *cashier's check.*
official reserve transactions balance: the account on the balance- of-payments statement that records the total of the balance on the goods-and-services account, the balance on the unilateral-transfers account, and the balance on the capital account, plus the allocation of special drawing rights and net errors and omissions. See *special drawing rights.*
off-premises clause: a policy clause providing insurance protection on personal property while it is away from the premises named in the policy. See *floater policy.*
offset:
  (1) **accounting:** either of two equivalent entries on both sides of an account.
  (2) **banking:** the right accruing to a bank to take possession of any balances that a guarantor or debtor may have in the bank to cover a loan in default. A depositor who has both a deposit credit balance and a loan balance is denied the right of offset in case the bank becomes insolvent and closes. Cf. *garnishment.*
offsets to long-term debt: cash and investment assets of sinking funds, bond reserve, and other reserve funds held specifically for redemption of long-term debt, and assets of credit funds that are pledged to redeem debt incurred to finance loan activities of such funds.

off-shift differential: a premium payment for work hours other than those of a worker's regular shift. See *midnight shift.*

offshore banking: locations, often found on an island, where liberal banking laws seek funds in Eurocurrency.

offshore manufacturing: manufacturing outside the borders of a particular country.

off-the-books: transactions for which payments are not entered in account books and not reported to the tax-revenue authorities, chiefly in order to evade taxes.

off-the-job training: training that is accomplished in an area away from the actual work setting.

of record: stockholders as recorded on a firm's books on a specific date, entitling them to a particular dividend.

OJT: see *on-the-job training.*

Okie: (slang) a migratory worker.

Okun's law: a concept developed by Arthur Okun that relates declines in the idleness rate of workers to increases in the gross national product, using data that exclude the first two quarters of every economic recovery period.

old-age and survivors' insurance (OASI): the source of retirement income and other payments made to survivors of those eligible under Social Security legislation.

old boy network: (slang) an arrangement whereby jobs are offered to the relatives or friends of the hiring (or other) executive.

oligopoly: an industry in which a small number of producers sell identical products. See *cooperative equilibrium.* Cf. *differential oligopoly; monopoly; perfect (pure) monopoly.*

oligopoly price: a price that develops when there is a market of numerous buyers and few sellers, thus resulting in the sellers having the greatest power.

oligopsony:

(1) **finance:** control by a number of buyers who attempt to influence the demand for a specific commodity. Cf. *duopsony; monopsony.*

(2) **labor relations:** employers who have some control in obtaining labor in a particular labor market locality. Cf. *hiring hall.*

oligopsony price: a price that develops when there is a market of few buyers and numerous sellers, thus resulting in the buyers having the greatest power.

ombudsman: a person outside the normal chain of command who handles complaints and grievances of an individual or a small group of individuals.

on account:
   (1) a payment made toward the settlement of an account.
   (2) a purchase or sale made on open account.

on a scale: in buying or selling securities, the situation in which a customer purchases or sells equal amounts of a stock at prices that are spaced by a constant interval as the market price rises or drops.

on consignment: items turned over by an owner (the consignor) to someone else (the consignee) with the expectation that the items (the consignment) will be sold by the consignee. If all the items are not sold, the owner is entitled to the return of the items. Cf. *purchase allowance.*

on demand: a bill of exchange that is payable on presentation. See *demand note.*

one-bank holding company: a corporation that owns control of one commercial bank.

one-price policy: a situation in which the price for goods is firm and cannot be negotiated.

one-stop banking: the service provided by a bank whose clients can do all their banking business at that bank. Cf. *full-service bank.*

one-time rate: the advertiser's rate paid when there is not enough space or time purchased to earn volume discounts.

ongoing operations: perceived problem area among entrepreneurs involving lack of experience in financial planning, cash flow, and difficulty in attracting business.

on margin: securities purchased when the buyer has borrowed part of the purchase price from the broker.

on order: goods paid for but not yet received.

on-the-job training (OJT): use of the actual work site as the setting for instructing workers while at the same time engaging in productive work. Cf. *training, vestibule.*

OPEC: see *Organization of Petroleum Exporting Countries.*

open account: credit extended that is not supported by a note, mortgage, or other formal written evidence of indebtedness (e.g., shipments of merchandise for which a buyer is billed later).

open career: a career system that permits entrance to positions at any or all grade levels.

open credit: credit that is allowed without immediate proof of a customer's credit-worthiness.

open door policy: a policy whereby citizens and products of foreign countries receive the same treatment as domestic citizens and products. Cf. *most-favored nation status; peril point.*

open economy: an economy that is free of trade restrictions.

open-end agreement: a union contract that has no expiration date but includes a provision that either party can give notice of a desire to terminate the agreement.

open-end bond: see *bond, open-end.*

open-end contract: an agreement whereby a supplier contracts to meet the buyer's requirements for a specific item during a stated period, whatever those requirements may be. The agreement is open-end because all the terms are left indefinite.

open-ended: a process or system that can be cut back.

open-end funds: mutual funds in which new shares of the fund are sold whenever there is a request, with the expectation that the seller will eventually request to buy back the shares at no additional charge. See *investment company.*

open-end investment company: an investment firm that sells and reclaims its capital stock continuously, selling it at book value, adding a sales charge, and redeeming it at a slight discount or at book value.

opening:

(1) **merchandising:** the first showing of a new season's line of items by a manufacturer or an entire industry.

(2) **human resources:** an unfilled position in an organization.

opening purchase: a transaction in which an investor becomes the holder of a security.

open interest: the number of outstanding contracts in the exchange market or in a particular class or series.

open-market operations: operations carried out by the Federal Reserve System in which it buys or sells government bonds in the same market used by other institutional investors.

open order:

(1) **merchandising:** an order made without price or delivery stipulation, or an order shipped to a market representative without specifying the vendor.

(2) **securities:** an order to buy or sell securities that has not yet been executed. Such orders may be placed at market price or at a fixed price. Synonymous with *good 'til canceled order.*

open outcry: synonymous with *outcry market.*

open policy: in marine insurance, a continuous, open-term contract designed to insure automatically all cargo moving at the insured's risk. Cf. *fleet policy.*

open prospectus: a brochure that aims to obtain financial backing but does not clearly identify the use to be made of the investment. Cf. *prospectus.*

open rate: an advertising rate that is subject to discounts for volume or frequency.

open shop: an unorganized establishment or one in which union membership is not a condition of employment or continuing employment. Cf. *closed shop; modified union shop; union shop.* See *free rider.*

open stock: replacement items or additions of goods carried in quantity and retained in a warehouse for several years.

open system: an organizational department in which autonomy, interaction, and a relaxed atmosphere are encouraged. See *loose-rein supervision; organic structure.*

open the kimono: (slang) to reveal to prospective customers company plans regarding future products, to impress upon the buyer that the firm is ahead of its competitors in developing new or superior items.

open-to-buy (OTB): the quantity of goods that a store can receive in stock over a stated time without exceeding its planned inventory levels.

open trade: any transaction that has not yet been closed.

open union: a union that admits any qualified worker upon payment of an initiation fee.

operating budget: a quantitative expression of a plan of action that shows how a firm will acquire and use its resources over a specified period of time.

operating cycle: the general pattern of business activity whereby cash and other resources are converted to inventory and operational assets and eventually into a product or service that can be sold and for which cash and other resources are received.

operating earnings before taxes: see *net earnings.*

operating expense: any expense incurred in the normal operation of a business. This is to be distinguished from expenditures, which are disbursements that are capitalized and depreciated over a period of years. See *margin of profit.* Cf. *capital outlay.*

operating income: income to a business produced by its earning assets and by fees for services rendered.

operating losses: losses incurred in the normal operation of a business.

operating management: the process of managing the implementation of programs and projects in each area of performance, measuring and evaluating results, and comparing results with objectives.

operating profit ratio: the ratio of a firm's operating profit to its net sales. See *turnover ratio.*

operating statement: a statement for a store's management, providing net sales, costs, expenses, and the net operating profits or loss for a fixed period.

operation: any process or action that is part of a series in work.

operational analysis (OA): a form of industrial engineering that separates work into activities and designs the work flow to construct the most efficient scheduled sequence of output. Synonymous with *operations research.*

operational control: the influence of management on the inputs and activities in the daily performance of a firm.

operational plan: a short-range plan (less than one year) that relates to the scheduling of internal operations or processes.

operations: production activities of an organization.

operations budgeting: the setting of immediate goals for sales, production, expenses, costs, and the availability of cash.

operations management: an area that takes into account the design, operations, and control of organizational systems. It is heavily concerned with such functions as work flow, production planning, purchasing, materials requirements, inventory control, and quality control.

operations research (OR): the application of scientific methods, techniques, and tools to problems involving the operation of a system, to provide those in control of the system with optimum solutions to the problems. See *cost-benefit analysis.* Cf. *organizational analysis and planning.* Synonymous with *operations analysis.*

operative: a rank-and-file worker in an organization.

operative personnel: workers at the lower end of the organizational hierarchy who have no subordinates to supervise.

OPIC: see *Overseas Private Investment Corporation.*

opinion leader: a member of an organization who, because of ability, power, access to information, or prestige, can influence the attitudes, opinions, or behavior of those around him or her. See *informal leader.*

OPM:

   (1) **general:** operations per minute.

   (2) **finance:** other people's money.

opportunistic marketing: marketing stage in a growing venture in which the organization attempts to develop high sales volume through market penetration.

opportunity cost: a maximum alternative profit that could have been obtained if the productive good, service, or capacity had been applied to some other use.

opportunity cost of capital: the expected rate of return from employing funds effectively in the company.

opportunity orientation: pattern among successful growth-minded entrepreneurs to focus on opportunity rather than on resources, structure, or strategy.

optimization: combining elements in just the right balance, often to secure maximum profit.

optimum capacity: the quantity of output that permits the minimum cost per unit to be incurred.

option:

(1) **securities:** an agreement, often for a consideration, to buy or sell a security or commodity within a stipulated time in accordance with the agreement. See *puts and calls.* Cf. *covered option; straddle.*

(2) **insurance:** the right of an insured or a beneficiary to select the form of payment of the proceeds of an insurance contract.

optional bond: see *bond, callable.*

optional consumption: the buying of items and services that are not required for daily fulfillment and well-being. See *luxuries.* Cf. *consumption possibility frontier.*

optional dividend: a stockholder's right to choose either a stock dividend or a cash dividend.

optional valuation date: the date on which the size of an individual's estate is computed for purposes of tax payment. It can be set at the date of death or as of six months following death, provided that the assets are not disposed of in the interim.

optionee: the holder of an option.

option spreading: the simultaneous purchase and sale of options within the same class. The options may be either at the same striking prices with different expiration months, or at different striking prices with the same or different expiration months. The spread is the dollar difference between the buy and sell premiums.

OR: see *operations research.*

orchestrator: high-level manager who articulates the need for innovation, provides funding for innovating activities, creates incentives for middle managers to sponsor new ideas, and protects idea people.

order:

(1) **general:** a request to deliver, sell, receive, or purchase goods or services.

(2) **general:** a command or decree.

(3) **finance:** identifying the one to whom payment should be made (e.g., "made to the order of . . .").

(4) **securities:** request to buy or sell. See *buy; day order; limited order; negotiation; open order; stop order.*

order-filling cost: a marketing cost incurred in storing, packing, shipping, billing, credit and collection, and other similar aspects of selling merchandise.

order-getting cost: a marketing cost incurred in an effort to attain a desired sales volume and mix.

ordering cost: a major cost component that is considered in inventory control decisions. Each time the firm orders items for inventory, it must formally contact the supplier, which usually involves some clerical and administrative work. Labor is also used in placing the order and putting the items in inventory. The clerical, administrative, and labor costs make up the ordering cost element in inventory control models.

orders:

(1) **general:** requests made for the delivery of goods or services.

(2) **securities:** instructions to a broker to buy or sell shares.

orders good until a specified time: a market of limited price order that is to be represented in the trading crowd until a specified time, after which such order or the portion not executed is to be treated as canceled. Cf. *good 'til canceled order.*

ordinary annuity: a series of equal amounts to be received or paid at the end of equally spaced time intervals.

ordinary income: in income tax filing, reportable income that does not qualify as capital gains.

ordinary interest: interest that is calculated based on 360 days to the year.

ordinary life: a type of insurance policy that continues in force throughout the policyholder's lifetime and is payable on his death or when he attains a specified age. Synonymous with *whole life.* Cf. *full coverage.*

ordinary stock: common or equity stock.

organic structure: an organization design characterized by a decentralized hierarchy, flexible work procedures, and democratic leadership, with informal and open communications. See *human relations theory; job enrichment.* Cf. *classical design theory; organization, formal; Theory X and Theory Y.* Synonymous with *organization, informal.*

organization: any structured system of roles and functional relationships designed to carry out a firm's policies or, more precisely, the programs such policies inspire.

organization, formal: a highly structured organization with little flexibility in the delegation of authority and assignment of tasks and responsibilities. See *unilateral strategy; vertical strain.* Cf. *organic structure.*

organization, informal: a flexibly structured organization, free of rigid rules for activity and authority. Synonymous with *organic structure.*

organizational analysis and planning: the study of the objectives, the surroundings, and the human, physical, and financial assets of a business, to determine the most effective design for utilizing ideas and power generated by the firm's ultimate authority for accomplishment of its stated goals. Cf. *operations research; situational design theory; universal design theory.*

organizational behavior (OB): field of study that investigates the impact that individuals, groups, and structure have on behavior within organizations, for the purpose of applying such knowledge toward improving an organization's effectiveness.

organizational change: the intentional attempt by management to improve the overall performance of individuals, groups, and the organization by altering the organization's structure, behavior, and technology.

organizational chart: a graphic presentation of the relationships and interrelationships within an organization, identifying lines of authority and responsibility. See *span of control.*

organizational citizenship: extent to which an individual's behavior makes a positive overall contribution to the organization.

organizational climate: a set of properties of the work environment perceived by employees and assumed to be a major factor in influencing their behavior. Cf. *dissatisfiers; morale; satisfiers.*

organizational conflict: disagreement between individuals or groups within the organization stemming from the need to share scarce resources or engage in interdependent work activities, or from differing statuses, goals, or cultures.

organizational design: determination of the organizational structure that is most appropriate for the strategy, people, technology, and tasks of the organization.

organizational development (OD): a planned process of reeducation and training designed by administrative personnel to facilitate adaptation to demands placed on the environment of the company. See *multiple management; unilateral strategy.*

organizational downsizing: popular trend aimed at reducing the size of corporate staff and middle management to reduce costs.

organizational effectiveness: the degree to which an organization attains its objectives and goals.

organizational efficiency: a measure of the amount of resources used by an organization to produce a unit of output.

organizational goal: an end or a state of affairs that an organization seeks to reach.

organizational level: the middle level of a company, concerned with coordinating and integrating work performance at the technical level.

organizational managers: middle-level managers whose goal is to coordinate the technical and institutional levels of the firm in some harmonious fashion and who tend to assume a political or mediating viewpoint.

organizational mirror: an organization development technique in which each group takes its turn at being critiqued by other groups. The goal is to improve intergroup relations.

organizational moles: people who use the grapevine to enhance power and status.

organizational multiplier: the factor by which a primary change in a particular sector of an organization is multiplied to determine the total change in the whole organization.

organizational norm: an organization's expression of what it considers the proper way of behaving or the proper code of conduct.

organizational picketing: see *picketing.*

organizational politics: activities carried out by people to acquire, enhance, and use power and other resources to obtain their desired outcome.

organizational scan: step in strategic planning process that identifies an organization's present strengths and weaknesses by examining its internal resources.

organizational socialization: process by which employees learn about the firm's culture and pass their knowledge and understanding on to others.

organizational stakeholder: an individual or group whose interests are affected by organizational activities.

organizational strategists: people who spend a large portion of their time on matters of vital or far-ranging importance to the organization as a whole.

organizational structure: arrangement and interrelationship of the various component parts and positions of a company.

organizational system: a system composed of human beings, money, materials, equipment, that are related in the accomplishment of some goal or goals.

organization budget: a budget system based on establishing subsidiary budgets or cost limitations for each unit of the organization.

organization character: the product of all of an organization's features, such as its people, objectives, technology, size, age, unions, policies, successes, and failures.

organization expense: direct costs of forming a new corporation (incorporation fees, taxes, legal fees, etc.).

Organization for Economic Cooperation and Development (OECD): created in 1948, an organization of 17 European nations (including the German Federal Republic), known until 1960 as the Organization for European Economic Cooperation (OEEC). Initially, OEEC developed and implemented economic recovery programs following World War II. It was enlarged to 21 members, including the United States, Canada, and Japan, with the change of its name to OECD. Headquartered in Paris, it promotes the economic growth of member nations, the expansion of world investment and trade, and the economic development of emerging countries.

Organization for European Economic Cooperation (OEEC): see *Organization for Economic Cooperation and Development.*

Organization of Petroleum Exporting Countries (OPEC): founded in Iraq, a group comprising 13 members, concentrated in the Middle East but also including countries in Africa, South America, and the Far East. By virtue of their large exports, Saudi Arabia and Iran have been the most powerful influences. See *petrodollars.*

organization structure: the formally defined framework of an organization's task and authority relationships. The organization structure is analogous to the biological function of the skeleton.

organized labor: union labor, collectively or with respect to individual shops.

organizer: a union employee whose primary task is to recruit nonunion workers for membership in the union.

organizing function: the managerial activity involved with creating a formal structure of tasks and authority.

orientation programs: programs that familiarize new workers with their roles, the organization, its policies, and other employees.

original equipment (OE): items sold to manufacturers for use in equipping their units; for example, tires and batteries sold to automobile manufacturers.

original-equipment manufacturer (OEM): a manufacturing company that purchases computers, components, equipment, etc., from another company or companies and puts them together as its own product for resale to end users.

original issue discount: the excess of the face value of a bond over the selling price at the time of issue. The discount is amortized as an expense over the bond's life.

original retail: the sales price of items that is the total of cost plus the original markon.

OS: operating system.

OSA: see *Office of Savings Associations.*

OS&D: see *over, short, and damaged.*

OSHA: see *Occupational Safety and Health Act of 1970.*

ossification: condition that may occur in small-business growth that is characterized by lack of innovation and avoidance of risk.

ostensible partner: partner who is active in a business and known to be a partner.

OTC: see *over-the-counter securities.*

other-insurance clause: a provision in almost every insurance policy stating what is to be done at the time of loss in case any other contract of insurance protection includes the same property and perils. Cf. *double insurance.*

other-shoe syndrome: a fear that once management begins to dismiss personnel, morale and job satisfaction will decline in anticipation of a further decrease in manpower.

outbid: to offer a higher price for an item than that offered by other bidders.

outcome interdependence: degree to which the work of a group has consequences felt by all of its members.

outcry market: commodity tradings, by private contract, that must be shouted out, as on the floor of an exchange, for the agreement to be recorded. Synonymous with *open outcry*.

outgo: any expense or other cost in running a business.

outlaw strike: see *strike.*

outlay: any expenditure.

outlay costs: the actual cash outflows directly associated with the production and transfer of goods or services.

out-of-pocket expense: a cost incurred by an individual, often when on a business trip. The item or service is paid in cash or by check or charge account, and the employee expects reimbursement from the company.

out of stock: goods that are not in the store when requested by a customer.

out-of-the-money: a call option in which the striking place is above the market price of the underlying stock.

out-of-work benefits: payments by a union to unemployed members. Cf. *strike benefits; strike pay.*

outplace: to assist an employee who is about to be fired by sending him or her to an agency or organization that specializes in helping such people find new employment.

output:
(1) **manufacturing:** the quantity yielded in any operation.
(2) **economics:** the average dollar gross domestic product produced in a stated period.

outside-inside approach: a strategy approach whereby managers look first at the environment and then at the organization. Cf. *inside-outside approach.*

outside market: an over-the-counter market or a market in which unlisted securities are handled.

outsourcing: act of subcontracting operations to other employers.

outstanding:
(1) **business:** any unpaid or uncollected debt.
(2) **securities:** stock in the hands of stockholders, as distinguished from stock that has not yet been issued or, if issued, has not been released by the corporation. Cf. *absorbed.*

outtakes: known information that is deleted from a presentation to workers, the board of directors, or other groups.

overage:
(1) items additional to those shown on a bill of lading.
(2) the situation created by a spending program that exceeds a specified budget target during a specified time period. Cf. *shortfall.*

overall cost leadership strategy: business-level strategy that emphasizes low costs.

overall market capability: the quantity of an item or service that is absorbed in the general market without allowing for price or market considerations. For example, the overall market capability for television sets includes everyone who owns a television and everyone who would like to own a television but hasn't purchased one to date. Cf. *potential demand; potential market saturation.*

overall performance ratio: a measure of overall performance, including management of operations, use of assets, and management of debt and equity, computed by dividing net income by average stockholders' equity.

overapplied overhead: the excess of the amount of overhead cost applied to a product over the amount of overhead cost incurred.

overbought: reflecting an opinion about price levels of a security that has had a sharp rise or of the market as a whole after a period of vigorous buying, which some are arguing has left prices too high. See *normative economics.*

overcapitalize:

(1) **general:** to provide an excessive amount of capital to a business. See *capitalize; watered stock.*

(2) **finance:** to place too high a value on the nominal capital of a company.

overcontrol: limiting of individual job autonomy to such a point that it seriously inhibits effective job performance.

overdetermination: occurs because numerous organizational systems are in place to ensure that employees and systems behave as expected to maintain stability.

overdraft: a check drawn for more than the drawee's balance on deposit with a bank. The bank can return the check (the overdraft) either to the bank from which it came or to the person who presented it for payment, marked "insufficient funds." The bank can also elect to render the customer a service and pay the check.

overdraw: to write a bank check for an amount exceeding the deposit in the bank on which the check is drawn. See *cushion checkingl; kite (kiting).*

overextension:

(1) **finance:** credit received or extended beyond the debtor's ability to pay.

(2) **securities:** the condition of a dealer in securities who becomes obligated for an amount beyond his or her borrowing power or ability to pay.

(3) **administration:** the expansion by a business concern of buildings, equipment, and so on, in excess of the company's present or prospective future needs.

overfinancing: the result of an investment that does not produce a positive cash flow after amortization or that finances a property for more than its value.

overhead: costs of materials and services not directly adding to or readily identifiable with the product or service of the entity. See *conversion costs.* Cf. *direct overhead; factory overhead.*

overhead application rate: the rate at which estimated overhead costs are assigned to products throughout the year. It is calculated as total estimated overhead costs divided by a suitable allocation base, such as direct-labor hours, direct materials used, or direct-labor costs.

overheating: excessive price or money activity that some economists believe will lead to inflation. Cf. *inflation.*

overinsurance: insurance against property loss or damage that is in excess of the possible amount of damage or loss.

overinvestment theory: a business cycle concept stating that economic variations are a function of too much investment in the economy as businesspeople try to measure increasing demands during an upswing, and of major cutbacks in investment during a downswing when they realize that they expanded too much during the previous prosperity.

overissue: the release of stock in excess of the authorized or ordered amount. See *registrar; undigested securities.*

overline: an amount of liability larger than the amount an insurance company wishes to underwrite. See *referral risks.*

overlying bond: see *bond, overlying.*

overmanning: using more workers in an operation than are required for an efficient activity. Cf. *featherbedding.*

overnight multiple: the anticipated impact of a public offering on the holdings of insiders. It usually multiplies the value of the offering significantly.

over (or short): the difference between established sales statements and the actual audited figure. This discrepancy is often a result of errors in making change or missing sales checks.

overproduction: producing more than can be sold at any price or at a profitable price.

overqualification: having more skills or aptitude than are required to perform a task or hold a position.

override: a commission paid to managers that is added to their salary. Cf. *commission (general)*.

overrun: the number of pieces of printed advertising in excess of the specified quantity. A 10 percent overrun is usually acceptable at pro rata cost.

oversaving: the condition that exists when planned saving exceeds planned investment. The quantity of cash removed from income movement thus exceeds the amount returned to it, resulting in the decline of income. Cf. *marginal propensity to invest, marginal propensity to save; saving*.

Overseas Private Investment Corporation (OPIC): a federal agency that insures U.S. companies against seizure of their overseas property by foreign governments, damage to property from acts of war, or conditions under which they are unable to take their profits out of the foreign country.

over, short, and damaged (OS&D): the discrepancy between the amount and/or condition of cargo on hand and that shown on the bill. Cf. *clean bill of lading*.

oversold:

(1) **general:** the situation of a manufacturer who has become obligated to deliver more than he or she is able to supply within the stated period.

(2) **securities:** an opinion that a single security or a market is believed to have declined to an unreasonable level. See *normative economics*.

oversubscribed: a situation in which, for a given issue of shares, more orders have been received than can be filled. Cf. *undigested securities*.

over-the-counter (OTC) securities: securities that are not listed or traded on any of the regular exchanges. Such securities are traded through dealers in unlisted stocks. Sales or purchases are arranged by these dealers or through a chain of them until the desired securities and prices are obtained. Members of regular stock exchanges also handle trades in unlisted securities, but not through the exchange. See *National Association of Securities Dealers Automated Quotations; third market*. Cf. *off-board*. Synonymous with *unlisted securities*.

overtime: hours worked by an employee beyond the standard hours agreed to in the contract. Hours in excess are paid in penalty or at the overtime rate, which frequently is 1.5 times the normal rate.

overtrading: the activity of a firm that, even with high profitability, cannot pay its own way for lack of working capital and thus finds itself in a liquidity crisis.

own brand: an item bearing the name or brand of the store selling the item rather than the name of the producer.

owner-operator: a regular driver who owns equipment and is a subcontractor to a carrier on a long-term basis.

owners' equity: the ownership interest in the assets of an enterprise. It equals net assets. Synonymous with *stockholders' equity.*

ownership: possession of a legal title with the rights to enjoy the benefits derived from any assets accompanying or accruing from such title.

ownership advantages: resources owned by a firm that grant it a competitive advantage over its industrial rivals.

ownership norms: norms in a society's culture that support or reject the private ownership of organizations and property.

P

pacers: fast-working employees, identified by management, who are used to establish the pace of expected work for others. See *normal time; time standard*.

pace setter: a speedy, skilled employee whose output in a given period sets the basis on which piecework rates are determined for other workers doing similar work.

pack: to add to the total cost of merchandise charges for items not included or inflated charges; to give an undeserved discount without lowering the actual price.

package: the total gains, including fringe benefits, that result from collective bargaining.

package policies: combination insurance policies in which several coverages are included in one contract.

packaging: the preparation of merchandise for shipping and marketing.

paid-in capital: capital contributed by stockholders and assigned to accounts other than capital stock.

paid-in surplus: excesses of a business arising from sources other than profits; the surplus from the sale of capital stock at a premium.

paid-up insurance: a policy on which no further premium payments need to be made; the insurance company will be held liable for any benefits claimed under terms of the contract.

paid-up stock: capital stock on which the initial buyer has paid, in services, goods, or funds, an amount at least equal to the par value.

painting the bus: (slang) altering the appearance of a presentation, proposal, or idea without changing any of the basics. See *window dressing*.

paired comparison: an evaluation method that compares each employee with every other employee and assigns a summary ranking based on the number of superior scores that the employee achieves.

panic: a sudden, spreading fear of the collapse of business or the nation's economy, resulting in widespread withdrawal of bank deposits, stock sales, and similar transactions. A depression may but does not always follow a panic.

paper: a loan contract.

paperless item processing system (PIPS): an electronic funds-transit system that is capable of performing transit functions by establishing accounting transactions by which bank funds are shifted from one ledger or subledger to another.

paper local: a local union that has a charter but no members. It cooperates with an employer to freeze out legitimate efforts to organize the workers through coercion of employees, kickbacks of union dues to the employer, and other outlawed methods. Paper locals are denounced by the AFL–CIO in its Code of Ethical Practices.

paper money: currency on which a value is printed. Unlike coins, the bills have no value in themselves but usually represent bullion held in government vaults. Cf. *fiat money.*

paper profit: an unrealized profit on a security still held. A paper profit becomes a realized profit only when the security is sold. See *short sale.*

paper standard: a monetary system based on paper money that is not convertible into gold or any other item of intrinsic value.

papoose: (slang) a nonunion employee who works with union employees.

par: the exchangeable value of an instrument when it is equal to that expressed on the face of the instrument, without consideration of any premium or discount. See *face value.*

paradox of thrift: a concept of John Maynard Keynes that any effort by society to raise its savings rate can lead to a reduction in the amount it really can save.

parallel standard: a monetary standard whereby two or more metals are coined and authorized unconditionally as legal tender. Cf. *bimetallism.*

parent company: a controlling organization that owns or manages business properties. Synonymous with *holding company; proprietary company.*

parent ego state: an ego state consisting of the supervisory attitudes and behaviors that children perceive in their parents and later replicate in supervisory situations.

Pareto optimality: distribution of resources that will make at least one person better off and no one else worse off. Synonymous with *economic efficiency.*

Pareto's law: the theory of Vilfredo Pareto, Italian sociologist and economist, that income tends to become distributed in the same proportion among consumers throughout the world, regardless of differing forms of taxation.

par exchange rate: the free market price of one country's money in terms of another country's currency.

Paris Club: synonymous with *Group of Ten.*

par item: any item that can be collected at its par or face value upon presentation.

parity:

(1) **securities:** the state or quality of being equal or equivalent; equivalence of a commodity price expressed in one currency to its price expressed in another.

(2) **economics:** equality of purchasing power established by law between different kinds of money at a given ratio.

(3) **human resources:** the equivalence established between the wage schedules of some categories of employees. It is usually used in the public sector to describe the percentage ratio maintained between the salaries of police and firemen.

parity principle: the concept that the amount of authority that rests with an individual should be equal to the employee's responsibility.

parity value for currency: the official exchange rate of a currency. When exchange rates are fixed, monetary authorities are required to purchase and sell other currencies in money markets as necessary to preserve parity. See *parity.*

Parkinson's laws: as developed by C. Northcote Parkinson, laws stating that (1) work invariably expands to fill the time available for its completion, and (2) expenditures climb to reach income. See *law of triviality.*

par list: a Federal Reserve System list of banks that will remit in full for items that are payable to the system.

par of exchange: the market price of money in one national currency that is exchanged at the official rate for a specific amount in another national currency or for another commodity of value (gold, silver, etc.).

partial equilibrium analysis: an inquiry that looks at only one market of an economy under the assumption that solutions in other markets will not be altered by a change in the market examined.

partial-factor productivity: productivity approach that measures organizational productivity by considering the total output relative to a specific input, such as labor.

partial loss: a loss that does not completely destroy or render useless the insured property nor exhaust the insurance applied to it.

partial monopoly: a situation that exists when there are so few sellers of an item or service that each may alter the price and market. Cf. *monopoly; perfect (pure) monopoly.*

partial payment: a payment that is not equal to the full amount owed and is not intended to constitute the full payment.

participating bond: see *bond, participating.*

participating-dividend performance: the right of preferred shareholders to receive equal distributions of dividends on a proportionate basis with common shareholders.

participating insurance: insurance or reinsurance that contributes proportionately with other insurance on the same risk.

participating preferred: a preferred stock that is entitled to its stated dividend and also to additional dividends on a specified basis (i.e., with respect to the plan participated in) on payment of dividends on the common stock.

participation loan: a loan having two or more banks as creditors. Laws prohibit banks from lending more than a fixed percentage of their capital and surplus to any one borrower. Thus banks invite other banks to participate in making large loans.

participative-democratic leadership style: a basic leadership style in which management has complete confidence and trust in the subordinates and in which decision making is highly decentralized. Cf. *Caesar management.*

participative management: process where subordinates share a significant degree of decision-making power with their immediate superiors.

particular average: damage or loss less than the total value; partial loss. Cf. *incurably depreciated.*

particular lien: a right to keep something valuable that belongs to another person as compensation for labor, supplies, or money spent in his or her behalf. Synonymous with *special lien.* Cf. *artisan's lien; factor's lien; general lien; mechanic's lien.*

partnership: a contractual relationship between two or more people in a joint enterprise who agree to share, not necessarily equally, in the profits and losses of the organization. Cf. *joint venture; syndicate.*

part-time employees: workers who work less than a full day or full week.

party at interest: an individual or group of individuals that has a vested interest in a commercial enterprise.

par value: face value. The par value of stocks on the date of issuance is the principal. Synonymous with *face value.*

passbook: a book record prepared by a bank for a depositor, listing date and amount of deposits, with an initial or an identifying symbol indicating the teller who received the deposit. For savings accounts, the passbook lists deposits, withdrawals, interest paid by the bank, dates of all transactions, each new balance, and the initial or identifying symbol of the teller handling each transaction. The passbook also shows the depositor's name or names and account number. Cf. *no-passbook savings.*

passed dividend: a regular or scheduled dividend that has been omitted.

passing title: the handing over of title to a new owner. Synonymous with *closing title.*

passive bond: see *bond, passive.*

passive trade balance: an unfavorable balance of trade.

passive trust: a trust whose trustee has no tasks to perform but merely retains title to the trust property.

pass-through: the tax advantage of a limited partnership, which permits income, profit, loss, and deductions to pass through the legal structure for the benefit of the individuals involved in the partnership rather than their organization. Synonymous with *flow-through.*

past-due item: any note, acceptance, or other time instrument of indebtedness that has not been paid on the due date.

patent: a right, assigned for 17 years to the inventor of a device or process, to exclude others from making, using, or selling the invention without permission. Cf. *copyright; trademark.*

patent pool: assigning a patent to a trade association or corporation so that a number of participants can use it.

paternal, aggressive company: an organization that aggressively attempts to achieve various objectives and liberally rewards good performance. Cf. *impersonal, aggressive management.*

paternal, passive company: an organization that does not aggressively pursue various objectives and treats its workers in a rather protective manner. Cf. *impersonal, passive management.*

paternalism: used in a negative sense to describe the "fatherly" interest of an employer in "his" workers.

patronage discount: a discount permitted on the basis of the amount of business done with one company.

path-goal theory of leadership: a leadership theory that views the leader's function as clarifying the subordinates' paths to work-goal attainment and increasing opportunities for personal satisfaction.

patronage motives: the reasons that customers shop in a particular retail outlet.

patronize: to frequent a store; to be a regular customer.

pattern bargaining: see *multiemployer bargaining.*

patternitis: the assumption that wage settlements in an industry should follow the pattern of settlement negotiated by any one of the companies in that industry.

pawn:

(1) **finance:** the pledge to pay a debt.

(2) **human resources:** an individual who is easily manipulated by another.

pay:

(1) to give money, as a form of compensation.

(2) to give to a person what is due, as for goods received, services rendered, etc.

payback period: the period of time that passes before the incoming cash equals the outgoing cash on a specific project, order, or other effort.

pay dues: (slang) to take on menial tasks while working one's way toward a specific opportunity.

payee: the legal entity named in an instrument as the recipient of the amount shown on the instrument.

pay equity: an employee's perception that compensation received is equal to the value of the work performed.

payer: the party primarily responsible for payment of an amount owed, as evidenced by a negotiable instrument.

pay grade: a number of similar jobs grouped together to simplify the job-pricing process.

pay level: relationship between an organizations rate of cash compensation and the general level for comparable jobs in the labor market.

payment date: the date on which dividends are paid by a corporation to its shareholders.

payment for honor: payment of a bill by someone other than the one on whom it is drawn when the latter has defaulted, to save the reputation or credit of the original drawee.

payments deficit: the excess of the value of a nation's imports over its exports.

payments surplus: the excess of the value of a nation's exports over its imports.

payments system: an approach (involving people, machines, and procedures) used to transfer value from one party to another.

payola: (slang) a gift or other valuable item offered to people who have the potential for using their influence in the promotion or sale of a product or service.

payout plan: a projection into the future that shows funds available, funds spent, and the resulting economic profit for a proposed marketing program.

payroll:

(1) the wages or salary earned by a firm's employees for a certain period of time. Various deductions for withholding tax, health benefits insurance, and so on, are identified on the employee's record affixed to the payroll check.

(2) a list of employees receiving pay during a wage period.

payroll deductions: sums withheld from an employee's gross pay for federal and state income taxes, Social Security, or other governmental levies. They may include, on authorization of employees, deductions for union dues and assessments, premiums for group insurance, contributions to pension plans, and so on.

payroll tax: a tax used to finance an employer's contribution to the Social Security program; a tax levied on a company's payroll. See *Federal Insurance Contributions Act.*

pay secrecy: a management policy of maintaining silence or secrecy about individual employee salaries.

pay structure: relative values and pay ranges for each job in an organization.

p/e: see *price-earnings ratio.*

peak: an exceptionally busy period in a business.

peak capacity: the sum of employee productivity, working at the fastest speed and with no regard for efficiency. The primary consideration is output rather than quality. Cf. *ideal capacity; practical capacity; production capacity.*

peak season: the period of days or months in which an item is in greatest customer demand (e.g., charcoal for barbecuing during the summer months).

peculation: the embezzlement of funds or goods, especially public funds or goods, by an individual in whose care they have been entrusted. Cf. *defalcation.*

pecuniary exchange: any trade that uses money.

peddler: a person who travels and sells small quantities of merchandise.

peer appraisal: performance appraisal done by one's fellow employees, generally on forms that are compiled into a single profile for use in the performance interview conducted by the employee's manager.

peg (pegging): to fix or stabilize the price of something (e.g., stock, currency, commodity) by manipulating or regulating the market. For example, the government may peg the price of gold by purchasing all that is available at a stated price. See *adjustable peg; crawling peg.*

peg point: the pay rate for a major task that becomes the base from which rates of pay for other related tasks are derived.

penal bond: see *bond, penal.*

penalty: see *liquidated damages.*

pencil pusher: (slang) an officer worker.

penetration pricing: an approach in which the price of an item is set low in order to enter the market quickly.

penny stocks: low-priced issues, often highly speculative, that sell at less than $1 a share. This is frequently a term of disparagement, although a few penny stocks have developed into investment-caliber issues.

Pension Benefit Guaranty Corporation: established in 1974, guarantees payment of nonforfeitable pension benefits. See *Employee Retirement Income Security Act.*

pension plan: a method used by a firm or union to pay annuities or pensions to retired and/or disabled employees. Sections 401 and 404 of the Internal Revenue Code identify conditions enabling an organization to establish a pension plan. See *Employee Retirement Income Security Act; trust agreement.*

peon: a common laborer or a person who performs work that is primarily unskilled.

people's capitalism: the full range of the income levels in the population of a community being represented in the ownership of the business. Cf. *private enterprise.*

per annum: by the year.

per capita income: average income per person in a country; total income divided by the number of individuals. Per capita income can be adjusted to reflect changes in prices or purchasing power over a stated time period to show real per capita income.

per capita output: the gross national product of a nation divided by its population. This is often used to identify a country's standard of living.

per capita tax:

    (1) **general:** a tax based on the result of dividing stated sums of

money by a specified number of people to show the amount to be paid by each person.

(2) **labor relations:** a stated periodic payment by a union, on the basis of membership, to a parent union or to local, district, and state councils. It is also the amount paid by a national union to a federation or other affiliate body.

perceived equitable rewards: the rewards people feel they should receive as the result of their performance.

perceived risk: the hazards a customer believes to be related to the buying of a specific item (e.g., difficulty of obtaining servicing; cost of servicing; lifetime of the item; obsolescence of the item).

percentage of sales method: a method of setting a marketing budget based on a forecast of sales.

percentage order: either a market or limited price order to buy (or sell) a stated amount of a specified stock after a fixed number of shares of such stock have traded.

per contra item: a balance in one account that is offset by a balance from another account.

per diem: for each day.

perfect competition: an industry or market unit consisting of a large number of purchasers and sellers, all involved in the buying and selling of a homogeneous good, with awareness of prices and volume, no discrimination in buying and selling, and a mobility of resources.

perfect (pure) monopoly: a situation in which one person or organization has total control over the manufacture and marketing of an item. Cf. *monopoly; oligopoly.*

performance: what a person does when faced with a task.

performance appraisal: a methodical review of an employee's performance on the job to evaluate the effectiveness or adequacy of the person's work. Cf. leveling.

performance bond: see *bond, performance.*

performance gap: the difference between the predicted or expected level of performance and the actual level.

performance plan: an understanding between an employee and a manager concerning what and how a job is to be done such that both parties know what is expected and how success in defined and measured.

performance standards: utilizing tests, interviews or other means to review an employee's performance on the job; to determine the quality and effectiveness of his or her work.

peril: the cause of a loss insured found in an insurance policy (e.g.. fire. windstorm, explosion).

peril point: the greatest reduction in U.S. import duty that could be made for a stated item without creating a major hardship to domestic manufacturers or to makers of a closely related item. Cf. *open door policy*.

period cost: synonymous with *fixed cost*.

period expense: an expenditure that cannot be associated with or assigned to a product and so is reported as an expense in the period in which it is incurred. Cf. *product costing*.

periodic stock control: a unit control system in which stock is identified and recorded periodically and sales for intervening time slots are calculated. See *inventory control; out of stock*.

period of digestion: a time immediately following the release of a new or large security offering during which sales are made primarily to regular investment customers.

perishable goods: items that are subject to rapid decay unless given proper storage (e.g., meat, dairy products). See *cobweb chart*.

perks: (slang) synonymous with *perquisites*.

permanent accounts: synonymous with *real accounts*.

permanent disability benefits: periodic compensation, usually weekly, for a disability that renders any employment impossible. Such compensation may be limited by a maximum time or a maximum amount. If unlimited, it may run for the lifetime of the insured.

permanent income: a worker's average income level throughout his or her working life. Actual current income varies around this long-term expected average because of transitory changes in income due to overtime work or layoffs, for example.

permissive leadership: leadership characterized by the attitude or practice of permitting or encouraging subordinates to solve or make decisions concerning work-related issues according to their own judgment. See *democratic leadership*.

permit bond: see *bond, permit*.

perpetual inventory: a book inventory identifying the stock on hand by means of a detailed record, enabling the firm to know the composition of its inventory at any point in time. See *book inventory*. Cf. *inventory*.

perpetual inventory control: a unit control system whereby orders, receipts, and sales are identified as they occur and inventory is computed.

perpetuity:

(1) **finance:** removal of anything that is from the ordinary channel of commerce by limiting its capacity to be sold for a period longer than that of a life or lives in being and 21 years thereafter, plus the period of development. See *consol*.

(2) **general:** endlessness; the quality of going on forever (e.g., an estate willed in perpetuity).

perquisites: additional compensation furnished by management, usually in goods or services, over and above the general payment of wages. Synonymous with *perks*.

perseverance: the tendency to continue with an activity despite difficulties.

personal check: a check drawn by someone as an individual (i.e., not acting as an employer or in a fiduciary capacity).

personal consumption expenditures: the funds spent by households for consumer items. Disposable personal income minus savings equals personal consumption expenditures.

personal distribution of income: the distribution of natural income among individuals or households.

personal finance company: a business that lends small sums of money to people, usually for personal needs, at relatively high interest rates. Most states require that these organizations be licensed.

personal income: national income less various kinds of income not actually received by individuals, nonprofit institutions, and so on (e.g., undistributed corporate profits, corporate taxes, employer contributions for social insurance), plus certain receipts that do not arise from production (i.e., transfer payments and government interest).

personal installment loan: funds borrowed by an individual for personal needs that are repaid in regular monthly installments over a specified period.

personal loan: a type of loan generally obtained by individual borrowers in small amounts, usually less than $1,000. A personal loan is often secured for consolidating debts or paying taxes, insurance premiums, or hospital bills. Synonymous with *installment loan*.

personal saving: the difference between disposable personal income and personal consumption expenditures, including the changes in cash and deposits, security holdings, indebtedness, reserves of life insurance companies and mutual savings institutions, the net investment of unincorporated enterprises, and the acquisition of real property net of depreciation.

personal selling: a promotion method involving interpersonal communication between individuals; verbal presentation to a prospective customer for the purpose of making a sale.

personal space: the physical area surrounding an employee that is assigned to him or her for use in carrying out his or her work.

personnel: a major activity performed within organizations, which includes such functions as personnel planning, recruitment, selection, training and development, compensation, health and safety, employee and labor relations, and personnel research. Synonymous with *human resources.*

personnel administration: a well-planned, properly executed, and efficiently evaluated approach to manpower recruitment, screening, usage, and development. See *process principles.*

personnel audit: an evaluation of the personnel activities in a company.

personnel demand analysis: a method of determining the number and type of employees required to achieve a firm's objectives. Synonymous with *workload analysis.*

personnel department: the department of an organization responsible for recruiting, hiring, testing, training, counseling, and promoting employees, as well as handling industrial relations and other functions dealing with employee activities, as stated by management.

personnel management: the study of how employers obtain, develop, utilize, evaluate, maintain, and retain the right numbers and types of workers.

personnel manager: a manager who normally acts in an advisory or staff capacity and is primarily responsible for coordinating a firm's human resources management activities.

personnel planning: the analysis of future personnel requirements for accomplishing a firm's objectives.

personnel psychology: a subdivision of applied psychology that treats an individual's psychological qualities in relation to his or her job. It deals with employment procedures, selection, placement, training, promotion, supervision, morale, and other personal aspects of job attitude and behavior. Cf. *applied psychology.*

persuasion: the act of influencing an individual or group to work for a desired objective.

PERT: see *program evaluation and review technique.*

PERT/COST: a modified PERT system that, in addition to time, deadlines, and schedules, includes all cost considerations. Cf. *program evaluation and review technique.*

Peter Principle: the dictum of Dr. Lawrence J. Peter that "in a hierarchy, every employee tends to rise to his level of incompetence."

petition in bankruptcy: the form used for declaring voluntary bankruptcy. See *bankruptcy.*

petrodollars: huge sums of money from oil-producing nations other than the United States or Great Britain. These funds are initially converted into Eurocurrency and deposited with international banks to be used for future investment and for paying debts. These banks traditionally set limits on the sums they will accept from any one country. See *Organization of Petroleum Exporting Countries.*

petty cash: see *imprest fund.*

phantom: (slang) an individual who is on a firm's payroll under an assumed name.

phantom freight: freight charges paid by the purchaser that were never absorbed by the seller.

phantom stock: in executive compensation programs, a number of shares of the company granted to an executive. Each share entitles the executive to the amount, if any, by which the market price of the stock at some future time exceeds the current market price.

phased retirement: a system whereby a person is gradually provided additional leisure time as he or she approaches the planned retirement age.

physical distribution: movement of merchandise from manufacturer to consumer.

physical hazard: characteristics of an insurance risk (e.g., material, structural, or operational).

physical inventory: inventory calculation obtained by making an actual listing of stock on hand.

physical product: the actual physical entity or service that is offered to consumers.

physical quantity budget: a budget expressed in physical units rather than dollar amounts (e.g., the number of labor hours needed for completion of a project).

picketing: publicizing the existence of a labor dispute by patrolling near the firm involved in the dispute. When large numbers of employees on strike assemble, it is called mass picketing. Organizational or recognition picketing (partially limited by the Taft-Hartley and Landrum Griffin Acts) is an attempt by a union to force acceptance of the union by the employer or to convince unorganized workers to join the union. Cross-picketing applies when there are two or more rival unions, each one claiming to represent the workers. Secondary picketing is picketing of locations that are not directly involved in the dispute. See *chain picketing; consumer picketing; pink tea picketing; situs picketing.* Cf. *strike.*

pie-card: synonymous with *labor skate.*

piece rate (wage): the amount of money received for each unit of output. When wages are so determined, an incentive wage system is in operation.

piece work: tasks performed for wages based on unit output. See *pace setter.*

Pigou effect concept: when a lowering of the overall price level creates higher consumption of time and services. Cf. *inflationary spiral.*

pilferage: taking of another's property while such goods are in transit or being stored. See *inventory shortage.*

pilot plant scale production: production of a modest number of units in small facilities designed to prove methods that may be used in full-scale plants.

PIMS: profit impact of marketing strategy.

pinch:
(1) **general:** a bind or tight situation.
(2) **finance:** a sudden, unanticipated rise in prices. When money rates go up suddenly, it is called a money pinch.

pink slip: (slang) a discharged worker.

pink tea picketing: picketing by a small group of peaceful demonstrators.

pinochle season: (slang) in the garment industry, the off- season.

pioneering stage: the first stage in the product life cycle. Emphasis is placed on achieving a demand for sale of the item.

PIPS: see *paperless item processing system.*

pit: a circular area in the middle of the floor of a stock exchange. Steps lead down into the pit, giving greater visibility to the trading action occurring there. Synonymous with *ring.* See *floor; open order; outcry market.*

P.I.T.I.: common abbreviation for "principal, interest, taxes, and insurance," used when describing the monthly carrying charges on a mortgage.

placement:
(1) **human resources:** the assignment of a worker to a job for which he or she is judged fitted.

(2) **securities:** negotiating for the sale of a new securities issue or arranging for a long-term loan.

place utility: the additional value in having a product where it is utilized or consumed.

plain bond: see *bond, plain.*

planholder: a pension plan shareholder.

planned change: change activities that are intentional and goal-oriented.

planned gap: the difference between a forecast and a plan; the difference between what will occur assuming that no changes are made (forecast) and a projection of what the organization wants to accomplish (plan).

planned obsolescence: an approach of consciously making an item out of fashion in the eyes of the consumer by repeatedly bringing out new models or products featuring improvements that are promoted as being superior or beneficial. There is a question of the value to the consumer of these systematic changes. The weakest-link theory claims that the least durable component in a product will determine its useful life. See *weakest-link theory.* Cf. *product obsolescence.*

planned (canned) presentation: a preplanned, organized statement in which major selling points are memorized for word-by-word presentation.

planning: an organizational activity that requires establishment of a predetermined course of action, beginning with a statement of goals. See *organizational analysis and planning.*

planning function: all managerial activities that lead to the definition of goals and to the determination of appropriate means to achieve those goals.

planning-programming-budgeting (PPB): mainly in government accounting, a system of administration for federal agencies. Its concepts include (1) long- and short-range planning of objectives and end products; (2) realistic cost estimates; (3) a search for greater efficiency; (4) budgetary projections of outputs in terms of goods and services; and (5) reports on current and prospective outlays, designed to service management controls and to supply information on budgetary administration for all levels of government.

plant: an establishment that manufactures or distributes items and services.

plant turnover ratio: the relationship between an organization's sales income and the cost of operating its physical plant. It gives the sales volume generated for each dollar invested in physical facilities.

play around: (slang) to go after a job or business venture with minimal interest or intent.

Plc.: abbreviation used in the United Kingdom to indicate a publicly held, limited liability company.

pledging: the offering by a borrower of his or her assets as security for the repayment of a debt. Cf. *hypothecation.*

plow back: to put earnings from sales back into the business operation.

plug:
   (1) **general:** to work hard and steadily.
   (2) **packaging:** a type of closure made to be inserted into the opening of a container.
   (3) **advertising:** a testimonial that is received without charge.

plunger: an individual speculator who takes great risks, resulting in substantial profits or losses.

plural executives: committees that have the authority to order that their recommendations be implemented.

pluralism: synonymous with *deconglomeration.*

plus tick: synonymous with *up tick.*

p.m.: see *push money.*

PML: see *probable maximum loss.*

P/N: see *promissory note.*

point: in shares of stock, a term that means $1.

point factor method: job evaluation approach in which points are assigned to jobs on the basis of the degree to which the jobs contain selected compensable factors.

point of equilibrium: the point at which supply equals demand.

point of ideal proportion: in a production process, the point at which the most profitable relative amount of the forces of production (land, labor, capital, and management) are used. Cf. *diminishing returns.*

point of indifference: in production, the point at which the cost of an added increment of land, labor, capital, or management merely equals the money return of the additional item made because of that increase. Cf. *diminishing returns; diseconomies of scale.*

point of origin: the location at which goods are received for transportation.

point-of-purchase advertising: see *POP advertising.*

point-of-sale terminal (POST): a communication and data-capture terminal located where payment is made for goods or services.

point system: a form of job evaluation that assesses the relative importance of each job's key factors in order to arrive at the relative worth of jobs. See *job evaluation*.

poison pill: a defense that makes the takeover so expensive that the predator gives up the quest. The target firm, for example, might give shareholders securities that could be turned in for cash if the unwanted takeover succeeds.

poisson distribution: a statistical distribution used in inventory control to forecast the probable number of orders that will be received, not the total quantity of demand that will be received.

policy:
(1) **insurance:** a written contract of insurance.
(2) **administration:** a plan of action.

policyholder: a person or company that is protected by an insurance contract.

policyholders' surplus: the sum remaining in a policy after all liabilities have been deducted from all assets. Sums such as paid-in capital and special voluntary reserves are also included. This surplus is an additional financial protection for policyholders in the event of unexpected or catastrophic losses.

policy keyboard: the full range of policy considerations open to an executive who makes final policy decisions.

policy loan: funds borrowed from a life insurance organization, usually at low interest rates, using as security the cash value of the holder's policy.

policy register: a record maintained by an insurance company for noting the issuance of and thus accounting for all its policies. Cf. *daily reports*.

policy reserves: see *reserve*.

policy rights: in purchasing, the authority granted managers to set procurement goals.

policy value: the amount of money available to the insured upon the maturity of the policy.

policy year experience: an aggregate record of all transactions on contracts becoming effective during a given 12-month period (the policy year).

political risk: the probability of occurrence of some political event that will change the profitability of a given investment.

political strategies: the general approaches used by firms in dealing with important and powerful components in the environment.

political system: the components in a business firm's environment that can influence its decisions, its survival, or its growth.

polygraph testing: a machine for reading physiological characteristics, i.e., pulse rate. Often erroneously called lie-detector, as there is minimal evidence that "lies" can be detected.

polyspecialist: a manager who is neither a generalist nor a specialist but has knowledge in a variety of areas.

Ponzi scheme: a confidence game in which the swindler lures money from investors with promises of high returns, without actually investing in anything, and simply absconds with the money.

pool:

(1) **finance:** an agreement between two or more companies to curtail output, divide sales areas, or in any other way avoid competition.

(2) **administration:** a combination of resources of funds, for some common purpose or benefit. See *supplementary unemployment benefits.*

(3) **insurance:** firms joined to share business over a fixed time. See *assigned risk.*

(4) **securities:** a combination of persons (brokers, traders) organized for the purpose of exploiting stocks. The SEC prohibits pool operations. See *SEC.*

pooled interdependence: the relationships between units of an organization such that their separate products can be added together to form the total final product.

POP advertising: promotional material placed at the point of purchase, such as interior displays, printed material at store counters, or window displays.

pork-chopper: (slang) a full-time union employee. Cf. *rank and file.*

port:

(1) the left side of a ship, barge, or airplane.

(2) a ship's place of entry; anywhere a ship goes where federal customs officials are able to inspect cargo and levy duties.

portability:

(1) **finance:** a characteristic of valuables that allows them to be carried easily (e.g., diamonds or stamps are more portable than bullion).

(2) **human resources:** a characteristic of pension plans that allows an employee to carry whatever pension credits he or she has earned from one position to another or from one industry to another. See *multi-employer pension plans.*

portable pensions: pension plans that increase the mobility of employees by allowing them to transfer earned pension credits from one employer to another.

portal-to-portal pay: pay for time traveling getting to and from the job, so called because it was originally pay for time spent going from the mine entrance to the actual place of excavation and return. Synonymous with *travel time.*

portfolio: holdings of securities by an individual or institution. A portfolio may contain bonds, preferred stocks, and common stocks of enterprises of various types.

portfolio investment: an ownership interest in a foreign firm without managerial involvement.

POSDCORB: the seven functions of administration: planning, organizing, staffing, directing, coordinating, reporting, and budgeting.

position:

(1) **securities:** an individual's stake in the market. See *technical position.*

(2) **human resources:** a job; an employment situation.

positional power: power that comes from one's formal position in the organization. It usually includes the right to reward and punish.

position-based influence: the ability to influence or affect the behavior of others that is based on the position a person holds in the organizational hierarchy.

position classification: a process of categorizing positions on the basis of similarity of duties, functions, responsibilities, or qualifications. See *job classification.*

positioning: the projection of an item as possessing a desired image, to make it attractive to a part of the market for that type of merchandise (e.g., a low-priced sports car that looks like an expensive model). See *market outline; market target.*

positive economics: the study of economics that does not depend on the value judgments of the economist. Cf. *normative economics.*

positive file: an authorization system file that contains information about every account holder and is capable of providing a variety of data to be evaluated in responding to a request for authorization of credit, check cashing, or other privileges. See *ratio of accounts payable to purchases.* Cf. *negative file.*

positive reinforcement: the administration of positive rewards, contingent on good performance, that strengthen desired behavior in the future.

POST: see *point-of-sale terminal.*

post:

(1) to record onto detailed subsidiary records (ledgers) amounts that were recorded in chronological records of original entry.

(2) to enter a unit of information on a record.

post audit: an audit of the financial records of an organization at some point after all the transactions have been properly recorded or have been approved for recording by the internal auditor or certified public accountants. See *audit*.

postdated check: a check bearing a date that has not yet arrived. Such a check cannot be paid by a bank before the date shown and must be returned to the maker or to the person attempting to use it. If presented on or after the date shown, the same check will be honored if the account contains sufficient funds.

posting: the practice of announcing the availability of positions, promotions, or transfers. Posting is usually guaranteed in a union contract. See *post*.

Postmodern organizations: flexible organizations that are decentralized, computer linked, and less hierarchical than bureaucracies.

potential demand: demand that can be expected to become effective at a future date (e.g., when purchasing power is increased). Cf. *overall market capability*.

potential market saturation: the maximum number of potential users (or buyers) during a specified period. Cf. *overall market capability*.

potentially dilutive: see *dilution*.

power: the ability to control others in an organization, utilizing personal persuasion and other personal characteristics, various approaches for reward and punishment, position title, and level of competence and experience. See *autocratic; Caesar management; laissez-faire; Machiavellian manager*.

power of appointment: the equivalent of total ownership of part or all of a trust, since the individual having this power can identify the ultimate recipients of the trust's assets.

power of attorney: a written instrument, usually acknowledged before a public officer or witness, in which one person grants to another the rights of utilization, tenancy, transfer, or disposal of assets owned by the first person as though he himself were exercising these rights. A power of attorney has the force of law; it may be limited with respect to the assets listed in the power of attorney, or it may give full power over all assets owned. Cf. *proxy; stock power*.

power structure: the positions of influence within an organization. Positions in the power structure exist because of formal authority, informal power, or some combination of the two.

PPBS: *programming, planning, and budgeting systems.* See *planning-programming-budgeting.*

PPF: see *production possibility frontier.*

practical capacity: the maximum level at which a plant or department can economically operate most efficiently. Cf. *peak capacity.*

practical school of management thought: traditional approach to international management, which holds that effective managerial behavior is universal; a successful manager in one location will be effective in any other location of the world.

pragmatic value orientation: an individual's tendency to respond to highly important concepts as "successful."

preapproach: the step in the sales process of finding critical data about a potential customer prior to contact. Synonymous with *territory screening.*

prearrival stage: period of learning that occurs before a new employee joins the organization.

preaudit: the examination of a creditor's invoices, payrolls, claims, and expected reimbursements before actual payment, or the verification of sales transactions before delivery.

preauthorized payment: a banking service that enables a debtor to request that funds be transferred from his or her deposit account to the account of a creditor.

precautionary demand for money: money that is held in excess of that required for day-to-day transactions, because of fear of unexpected contingencies.

precautionary motive: a rationale used by firms and consumers for retaining a portion of their assets in cash, to ensure their ability to satisfy unexpected demands easily.

preclusive purchasing:

(1) **finance:** buying materials with the expectation of denying their use to a competitor.

(2) **international business:** the activity of a belligerent country, aimed at preventing neutrals from selling the items purchased to an enemy. Cf. *blockade.*

predatory pricing: cutting prices with the objective of harming one's competitors. See *rate war.*

predetermined motion times system: a listing of all movements that a person can or will perform accomplishing a stated task, and a standard performance time for making each of the motions. See *time and motion study.*

predictive research: the category on the level-of-outcome dimension when the outcome of a research effort is to predict the future.

preemptive right: the privilege of a stockholder to buy a portion of a new issue of stock equal to his or her existing percentage holding.

prefabricate: to manufacture standardized components of a larger unit in a factory, thus making possible the assembling of the item elsewhere (e.g., the buyer's home) without production facilities.

preference as to assets: in the event of dissolution of a firm, before disbursement of a declared dividend, the right of stockholders holding preferred shares to claim payments before payments are made to common stockholders.

preference bond: see *bond, preference.*

preference item: a consumer's choice of a particular item even when similar items are less costly (e.g., insisting on Coca Cola, although a chain grocery store's cola-type soft drink is cheaper).

preferences about goals: the degree of agreement or disagreement between two or more managers as to the goals that should be pursued.

preferential rehiring: a contract provision calling for reemployment of workers after layoffs on the basis of seniority. See *bumping.*

preferential shop: a firm in which management has agreed to hire union members so long as they are available. Cf. *union shop.*

preferred debt: a debt that takes precedence over others.

preferred position: any advertisement position (e.g., island position) for which the advertiser pays a premium when specifically requested. Cf. *split run.*

preferred stock: corporate stock whose owners have some preference as to assets, earnings, and so on, that is not granted to the owners of common stock of the same corporation. See *adjustment preferred securities; cumulative preferred; effective par; guaranteed stock; privilege issue; voting right.*

preliminary expenses: expenses incurred in the establishment of an organization (e.g., costs for developing and circulating a prospectus).

premising: forecasting what is likely to happen inside and outside of an organization.

premium:

(1) **securities:** the amount by which a preferred stock or bond may sell above its par value. In the case of a new issue of bonds or stocks, a premium is the amount the market price rises over the original selling price.

(2) **securities:** a charge sometimes made when a stock is borrowed to make delivery on a short sale.

(3) **securities:** the redemption price of a bond or preferred stock if this price is higher than face value.

(4) **insurance:** the sum paid for a policy (not to be confused with *premiums*). An earned premium is the portion of the written premium covering the part of the policy term that is included in the time period. A pure premium, found by dividing losses by a hazard or contingency, is one to which no operating expenses of the firm have been added (e.g., commission). Synonymous with *consideration*. Cf. *rate*.

(5) **retailing:** an offer of merchandise, at a minimal cost or at no charge, as an inducement to the customer to purchase a given item.

(6) **finance:** the amount by which one form of funds exceeds another in buying power.

premium audit: an examination by a representative of the insurer of the insured's records, insofar as they relate to the policies or coverages under consideration. See *audit*.

premium bond: see *bond, premium*.

premium finance: a facility that allows an insured to finance his or her payment over a specified period within the term of the policy.

premium on stock: the excess of the insurance (market) price of stock over its par or stated value.

premium pay: a wage rate higher than straight time, that is payable for overtime work, work on holidays or scheduled days off, or work on evening shifts.

premiums (net written): premium income retained by insurance companies directly or through reinsurance, less payments made for business reinsured. See *loading*.

premium servicing fee: synonymous with *loan fee*.

prepackaging:

(1) **general:** packaging of fresh foods (meats, vegetables, cheeses) in consumer units for self-service sales.

(2) **merchandising:** to avoid repackaging by the retailer, packaging of merchandise such as chinaware and furniture by the manufacturer so that it may be sold directly to the consumer without opening.

prepaid: a term indicating that shipping charges have already been paid or are to be paid at the point of delivery. See *franco delivery.*

prepaid expenses: payment for items not yet received; a charge deferred for a period of time until the benefit for which payment has been made occurs (e.g., rent paid for future months). Cf. *accrued liabilities.*

prepak: synonymous with *prepackaging.*

prepay: to pay before or in advance of receipt of goods or services.

prepayment: payment of a debt before it actually becomes due.

prepayment clause: the privilege of repaying part or all of a loan in advance of date or dates stated in a contract.

prerefunding: refunding in which securities eligible for conversion mature in no more than one year.

preretailing: assignment by the retailer of retail prices to goods at the time an order is made, thus allowing the determination of retail values of items on order. This practice also speeds up the checking and marking procedures when merchandise arrives.

prescientific management: the time period from the beginning of cooperative efforts to the first attempts, in about 1880, to approach the study of management scientifically. Cf. *scientific management.*

present value: the discounted value of a certain sum that is due and payable at a specified future date.

present value of expected cash flow: the net cash that a company expects to realize or pay out from holding an asset or liability, discounted by an appropriate rate of interest. Cf. *expected exit value.*

president: the highest ranking executive responsible for the policy decisions of an organization. The president reports to a board of directors.

Presidential Task Force on Market Mechanisms: synonymous with *Brady Commission.*

prestige card: a plastic identification card issued by savings and loan associations to their customers to be used in electronic funds-transfer systems.

prestige pricing: increasing the price of an item to establish a quality image of the product or the seller.

pretest: a test given to determine an individual's performance in some area in advance of training, education, or some other condition that is expected to improve performance.

preventive discipline: action take to encourage employees to follow the standards and rules so that infractions are prevented. Cf. *corrective discipline.*

previous work experience: an influence on the decision to create an entrepreneurial venture, such as losing one's job, dissatisfaction with one's current job, etc.

price: the amount of money a seller receives for goods or services at the factory or place of business. Price is not what the seller asks for the product but what is actually received.

price analysis: the investigation by a buyer of a supplier's costs to make an item, with the goal of aiding the buyer to negotiate a price closely parallel with the supplier's cost to produce.

price control:

(1) **merchandising:** the result of the demand by a manufacturer that the buyer for resale not be able to determine a resale price for the goods. See *fair trade price.*

(2) **general:** regulation of the prices of goods and services with the intent to reduce increases in the cost of living. See *valorization.*

price cutting: offering goods or services for sale at a price below that recognized as typical or appropriate by buyers and sellers. See *underselling.*

price determination: a provision for price changes in contracts for purchasing or selling items.

price discretion: reflected in the decision of a sales representative to alter the price of an item for purposes of making a sale.

price discrimination: the practice of charging different prices to different buyers for the same quality and quantity of merchandise. Should this practice result in reducing competition, it is illegal under the antitrust laws. See *Robinson-Patman Act of 1936.* Cf. *functional discount; rate discrimination.*

price-earnings (p/e) ratio: the price of a share of stock divided by its earnings per share for a 12-month period. For example, a stock selling for $50 a share and earning $5 a share is said to be selling at a price earnings ratio of 10:1.

price elasticity: reflected in a reduction in sales when the price of an item is raised.

price fixing: an agreement by competing organizations to avoid competitive pricing by charging identical prices or by changing prices at the same time. Price fixing is in violation of the Sherman Antitrust Act. Cf. *conscious parallel action; price stabilization.*

price index: a measure to illustrate the changes in the average level of prices. See *purchasing power of the dollar; wholesale price index.*

price inelasticity: a change in price that yields a disproportionately small change in demand.

price leadership: a situation in which prices can be determined by one major manufacturer in an industry, thus influencing others to accept the prices as determined. See *administered price.*

price level: the value of money in comparison with a specified base period.

price lining: placing several items of varying costs together and selling them all at the same price. This practice is used frequently in retailing.

price loco: the price at the place where a purchase occurs.

price out of the market: items that have been made so expensive that they are no longer purchased in their usual market (e.g., vendors of $12 ice cream cones would find themselves priced out of the juvenile market). Cf. *inelastic demand.*

price rigidity: a long-term lack of concern for prices of raw or produced items in relation to the inflationary aspects of a depression or recession.

price-specie flow theory: a theory stating that imports of precious metals increase the supply of funds and therefore advance the price level of items that use these metals.

price spreading: the simultaneous purchase and sale of options in the same class with the same expiration date but with different striking prices.

price stabilization: keeping prices at a stated level. This is primarily a government strategy, especially during wartime or periods of rapid inflation, but it is illegal when practiced by private companies. See *Sherman Antitrust Act of 1890.* Cf. *price fixing.*

price system: the market system of resource allocation.

price takers: firms that have no market power over price. Therefore, the market dictates price for them.

primacy of planning: the principle that, at least initially, planning precedes all other managerial functions.

primary demand: demand for a product type.

primary deposits: cash deposits in a bank.

primary distribution: the original sale of a company's securities. Synonymous with *primary offering.*

primary insurance: insurance coverage up to a specified amount or against specific perils. See *excess insurance.*

primary offering: synonymous with *primary distribution.* .

primary organization: an organization that claims the complete personal and emotional involvement of its members. It is characterized by personal, direct, spontaneous, face-to-face relationships.

primary reserves: a bank's legal reserves of cash and demand deposits with the Federal Reserve Bank and other banks.

prime cost: the sum of direct labor expenditures plus direct material costs that are identified with a product. See *loading*.

prime interest (rate): the rate of interest charged by a commercial bank for large loans made to its most credit-worthy business and industrial customers. It is the lowest interest rate charged by the bank. The prime rate level is determined by how much banks have to pay for the supply of money from which they make loans. In an inflated economy, banks pay increasingly higher rates for funds, and the prime rate rises. When inflation subsides, the prime rate usually drops. The Federal Reserve Bank's charge for negotiable business instruments, which is publicly established, influences the rate for all other business interest payments. Cf. *inflation*.

prime maker: the party (or parties) signing a negotiable instrument and becoming the original party responsible for its ultimate payment. See *liabilities*.

prime rate: see *prime interest (rate)*.

principal:

(1) **finance:** the face value of an instrument, which becomes the obligation of the maker or drawee to pay to a holder in due course. Interest is charged on the principal amount.

(2) **securities:** the person for whom a broker executes an order, or a dealer who is buying or selling for his or her own account.

(3) **general:** one of the major parties to a transaction, either the seller or purchaser.

(4) **banking:** the original amount of a deposit, loan, or other amount of money on which interest is earned or paid. See *billed principal*.

principal sum: the amount specified under an accident policy, (e.g., with the death benefit).

principle of selectivity: the principle that in any series of elements to be controlled, a small number of elements always accounts for a large portion of the results.

principles of organization: in general, the division of work, authority, responsibility and accountability, span of control, lines and units of communication and command, legitimacy, and coordination.

prior deductions method: an improper method of determining bond interest or preferred dividend coverage in which the requirements of senior obligations are first deducted from earnings and the balance is applied to the requirements of the junior issue.

prioritize: to set in order of preference or priority the attributes or needs of an organization. Assignments are made from this list of priorities.

prior-lien bond: see *bond, prior-lien.*

prior-period adjustments: adjustments made directly to retained earnings that are required to correct errors in the financial statements of prior periods.

prior preferred (stock): a preferred issue that ranks ahead of another preferred issue of the same company.

private bank: a bank chartered by the state in which it operates, subject to state laws and regulations, and subject to examinations by the state banking authorities. The principal distinction between private banks and other state banks is that a private bank may arise from a partnership, with no capital stock.

private brand: a middleman-owned brand name or trademark (e.g., Sears Roebuck owns the Kenmore brand).

private carrier: a transportation line that is not a common carrier.

private corporation: corporation created either wholly or in part for private benefits.

private cost: the cost of a specific item to an individual.

private enterprise: an organization of production in which the business is owned and operated by people who take risks and are motivated by the wish to make a profit. See *capitalist.* Cf. *people's capitalism.*

private lender: an individual who lends money from institutional funds (insurance companies, banks, etc.).

private placement agencies: private, for-profit firms that help job seekers find employment. Cf. *search firms.*

private rate of return:

(1) **general:** the financial rate of return anticipated by businessmen prior to investing their monies.

(2) **finance:** the expected net profit after taxes and all costs, including depreciation, expressed as a percentage annual return on the total cost of an effort or the net worth of the stockholder owners. See *ROI.*

private sector: the segment of the total economy composed of businesses and households but excluding government. Cf. *public sector.*

privatization:
(1) where state-owned organizations are sold to private business people.
(2) selling a nationalized industry to private owners.

privileged bond: see *bond, privileged.*

privilege issue: a preferred stock or bond that has a conversion or participating right or that has a stock purchase warrant on it.

proactive change: type of change that occurs when an organization's managers conclude that a change would be desirable, as opposed to being necessary.

proactive management: a management style in which decision makers anticipate problems and take affirmative steps to minimize those problems, rather than waiting until a problem occurs before taking action.

probable maximum loss (PML): the maximum insurance loss that can be expected under normal circumstances. Extraordinary circumstances, such as delayed alarm or insufficient water supply, can result in a loss exceeding the PML. Cf. *maximum foreseeable loss.*

probationary employee: a newly hired worker who is subject to a trial period, usually several months. This worker can be terminated without any penalty to the employer.

procedural justice: perceived fairness of the process used to determine the distribution of rewards.

proceeds:
(1) **finance:** the actual amount of funds given to a borrower, following deductions for interest charges, fees, and so on.
(2) **economics:** the funds received by a seller after deductions for the payment of commissions (e.g., proceeds from a sale).

process analysis: the study of the approaches used for producing a part or a product for purposes of yielding the lowest cost and most efficient process that will produce items of adequate quality.

process control: a monitoring method to assure that the production system is functioning properly.

process costing: a method of product costing whereby costs are accumulated by process or work centers and averaged over all products manufactured in those centers for a specified period. Cf. *job-order costing.*

process departmentation: grouping jobs into subunits based on the sequential processes involved in an organization's operations. This is common in one-product plants, such as oil refineries. Cf. *functional departmentation; geographical departmentation; matrix departmentation; product departmentation.*

process effects: the increase in consumer spending and private investment as a result of the spending on public works projects.

process inspection: inspection at intervals during or between production operations. Cf. *quality control.*

process principles: organizational principles, defined by Henri Fayol,
that describe the desirable behavior of managers as they deal with
workers. Cf. *situational theory of leadership.*

process value analysis: determination to what degree each organizational process adds value to the organization's distinctive competencies.

procuration: the authority given to another to sign instruments and to
act on behalf of the person granting the authority.

procurement: the purchase of goods for resale to a store's customers.
Cf. *purchasing agent.*

produce exchange: a market for perishable agricultural products.

producer:
　(1) **general:** an individual who manufactures goods and services.
　(2) **insurance:** the individual—either an agent or a broker—who has
　solicited insurance business from the buyer and is placing it with the
　company.

producer commodity cartel: an organization of producers of a key raw
material commodity in world trade (e.g., the Organization of
Petroleum Exporting Countries).

producer-controlled brands: brands owned or controlled by firms that
are primarily in the manufacturing business.

producer goods: items intended to be used and worn out in the course
of producing other items in the future (e.g., ink in newspaper printing).

product:
　(1) goods and services made available to consumers.
　(2) the total of benefits offered.

product assortment: the brands and types of items in a product class
available to consumers.

product class: a group of items that are treated as natural substitutes
and/or complements by most consumers.

product costing: the assignment of manufacturing costs to products in
order to determine the cost of finished goods. See *absorption costing;
variable cost.* Cf. *period expense.*

product departmentation: grouping jobs into subunits based on the
different products or programs of the organization. Cf. *functional*

departmentation; geographical departmentation; matrix departmentation; process departmentation.

product development: the generation of new ideas for new or improved goods to be added to or to replace existing items. Cf. *functional obsolescence.*

product differentiation: a marketing approach based on the creation and promotion of differences among similar items.

product differentiation: an operating strategy under which the firm or small-business unit attempts to compete based on nonprice factors such as quality, service, and other product characteristics.

production:

(1) **economics:** any form of activity that adds value to goods and services, including creation, transportation, and warehousing until used.

(2) **administration:** criterion of effectiveness that refers to an organization's ability to provide the outputs demanded of it by the environment.

production bonus: a type of incentive system that provides workers with additional compensation when they surpass stated production goals. See *bonus.*

production budget: a schedule of production requirements for a budget period.

production capacity: the maximum quantity of units that can be made in a stated period with available equipment. Cf. *peak capacity; scheduled production.*

production control: the planning, routing, scheduling, dispatching, and inspection of operations of a given item being manufactured. The goals are to improve efficiency, cut costs, and evolve a quality product. See *requisition.* Cf. *quality control.*

production costs: factory costs plus administrative expenses.

production-dominated strategy: the focus of key decision makers on manufacturing and processing know-how.

production-efficiency-oriented production: production in a foreign country because of lower factory costs or special incentives such as lower taxes.

production fit: the compatibility of a new product with established manufacturing equipment and processes.

production possibility frontier (PPF): the limits of the combinations of items that can be made by an entire economy. This boundary is a function of the scarcity of resources and the availability of existing technology. Cf. *consumption possibility frontier.*

production sharing: a situation in which a product is manufactured in one country, assembled in another, and marketed in a third. See *duty drawback*. Cf. *multinational corporation; reexport*.

production workers: employees engaged directly in manufacturing or operating processes, as distinct from maintenance forces, supervisors, clerical workers, stock room attendants, and so on. See *direct labor*. Cf. *indirect labor costs*.

productive efficiency: a situation that exists when there is no possibility of increasing the yield of one item without decreasing the yield of another item. Cf. *efficiency*.

productivity: a measurement of the efficiency of production; a ratio of output to input (e.g., 10 units per man-hour).

productivity factor: a union contract provision calling for periodic pay increases, apart from negotiations, to compensate for continued increases in man-hour output by workers.

product liability: liability imposed for damages caused by accident and arising out of goods or products manufactured, sold, handled, or distributed by the insured or by others trading under his or her name. The accident must have occurred after possession of goods had been relinquished to others and away from premises owned, rented, or controlled by the insured. In the case of food products, however, the accident does not have to occur away from the premises (e.g., a restaurant).

product lifecycle: the six stages of market acceptance of any goods: pioneering, growth, maturity, saturation, decline, and abandonment.

product line: the assortment of items presented by a firm, or a group of items that are closely related because they either satisfy a need, are used with each other, are sold to the same consumer, are marketed within the same outlets, or are within similar price ranges. Cf. *line*.

product manager: an executive responsible for marketing approaches, such as promotion, pricing, distribution, and establishing product characteristics. The product manager deals more with the planning aspects than with actual selling to the consumer. Cf. *sales manager*.

product markets: markets in which firms sell the outputs that they produce.

product mix: the composite of items offered for sale by one company.

product obsolescence: the effect on items that become less attractive to the consumer because of the introduction of newly improved items that do the job less expensively or better or perhaps both. Cf. *planned obsolescence*.

product pattern: an organizational pattern whereby jobs and activities are grouped on the basis of types of products or services.

product planning: the process leading to the identification of goals and procedures as well as the precise nature of the merchandise to be marketed. See *market research*.

product portfolio: a group of products marketed by the same company.

product positioning: the way in which a product is characterized to attract consumer interest and purchase. A product may be positioned in a variety of ways, such as economical, durable, stylish, safe, convenient, and so forth.

product reliability: the probability that a product will perform a stated function under specific conditions for a specified period without failure. See *guarantee*.

Product Safety and Liability Commission: a five-member commission that prescribes safety standards for more than 10,000 products; identifies products considered substantial hazards and, where appropriate, will request the manufacturer to take corrective action.

product/service lifecycle: the market phases for most products and services.

products market equilibrium: a situation in which aggregate demand equals aggregate supply. See *aggregate demand; aggregate supply*.

profile analysis: a method for appraising individual uniqueness and characteristics that consists of a search for patterns of behavior displayed by an individual.

profit:

(1) **marketing:** the excess of the selling price over all costs and expenses incurred in making a sale. See *PIMS*.

(2) **finance:** the reward to the entrepreneur for the risks assumed by him or her in the establishment, operation, and management of a given enterprise or undertaking. See *uncertainty theory*.

(3) **accounting:** the monies remaining after a business has paid all its bills. See *contribution profit*.

profitability: a firm's ability to earn a profit and its potential for future earnings.

profitability measures: the ratios of net profit to capital, to total assets, and to sales.

profit and loss (operating) statement (P/L): the summary listing of a firm's total revenues and expenses within a specified time period. Synonymous with *income and expense statement*.

profit budget: a budget that includes expenses and revenue budgets in a single statement.

profit center: a segment of a business that is responsible for both revenues and expenses. Cf. *investment center.*

profit margin: sales less all operating expenses divided by the number of sales.

profit-maximizing management: a theory of business management based solely on the objective of profit maximization.

profit objective: the profit goal of a profit-seeking organization, which is achieved by efficient use of scarce resources. See *profit.*

profit sharing: an arrangement whereby employees share in company profits, based on company successes, according to a plan. This compensation is paid in addition to wages. There are cash plans (giving a share of profits in cash) and deferred plans (setting up a trust for payment upon retirement, death, or disability). See *employee stock ownership plans; Lincoln incentive management plan.*

profit squeeze: profit shrinkage resulting from stable prices and increasing costs.

profits tax: a tax on business profits, excluding income taxes.

profit taking: the sale of stock that has appreciated in value since purchase, in order to realize the profit that has been made possible. This activity is often cited to explain a downturn in the market following a period of rising prices. Cf. *unloading.*

pro forma invoice: a preliminary invoice indicating the value of the items listed and informing the recipient that all have been sent. It is not a demand for money.

program budgeting: a long-range approach to budgetary decision making that relates future expenditures to broadly defined objectives of the organization.

program evaluation and review technique (PERT): a method to facilitate planning and to give management tools for the control of specific programs. Original PERT programs were developed by the U.S. Navy. Cf. *critical path method; PERT/COST.*

programmed conflict: encourages different opinions without protecting management's personal feelings.

programmed decisions: responses to repetitive and routine problems according to a standard procedure that has been developed by management.

program merchandising: combined efforts of a retailer and a key source to make merchandising and promotion plans for a store.

progressive discipline: a system of management stressing that disciplinary action should make penalties appropriate to the violation (or accumulated violations).

progressive tax: an income tax that rises as income increases. The rate of increase varies. See *ability to pay; degressive taxation; graduated tax*. Cf. *regressive taxes.*

prohibited issue: an issue that cannot be bargained over in management-labor discussions.

prohibited risk: a line that an insurance company will not insure under any condition.

project authority: authority exercised by project managers over personnel assigned to them for a project. This authority, which flows horizontally, contrasts with functional authority.

projection: attributing one's own characteristics to other people.

project organization: an organization that is created for the attainment of a particular objective and is disbanded on completion of the project.

promissory note (P/N): a written promise to pay; a negotiable instrument that is evidence of a debt contracted by a borrower from a creditor (a lender of funds). If the instrument does not have all the qualities of a negotiable instrument, it cannot legally be transferred. See *accommodation paper; note.*

promotability: the qualities of a worker that indicate inherent potential for performance of more complex and more responsible duties.

promoter: an individual who brings together those forming a business venture and those interested in backing the enterprise. Cf. *backer.*

promotion:

(1) **retailing:** stimulating the demand for goods by advertising, publicity, and events to attract attention and create interest among consumers.

(2) **human resources:** advancement to a position of higher rank, responsibility, or prestige. See *horizontal promotion; vertical promotion.*

promotional allowance: payments given to a middleman by a manufacturer to pay for the middleman's promotion of goods. Cf. *advertising allowance.*

promotional fit: the compatibility of a new product with existing advertising approaches.

promotional mix: the combined promotional efforts of advertising, publicity, sales promotion, and personal selling as they attempt to communicate with customers to sell a product.

promotion from within: a policy whereby management positions are filled by people who are already employees of the organization.

Prompt Payments Act: federal law requiring that small businesses doing work for the federal government be paid within 30 days with an additional 15-day grace period; otherwise, interest penalty charges become retroactive from the 30-day point.

proof of loss: a formal statement made by an insured to the insurance company regarding a claim that serves the company as a basis for determining its liability under the policy or bond.

property:
(1) **economics:** the exclusive right or interest of a person in his or her belongings.
(2) **business law:** that which is legally owned by a person or persons and may be used and disposed of as the owner(s) sees fit.

property, personal:
(1) chattels, choses in possession.
(2) everything that is owned except real estate.

property, public: real and personal property held by the government for eventual use or benefit of its population. Cf. *public domain.*

property damage liability insurance: protection against liability for damage to the property of another that is not in the care, custody, and control of the insured-as distinguished from liability for bodily injury.

property dividend: distributions to shareholders of assets other than cash or company stock.

property, plant, and equipment: tangible, long-term assets acquired for use in a business rather than for resale.

proportional law: the relationship between factors of production and the results of production; the desirable relationship among production factors that will yield maximum returns. Cf. *law of increasing costs.*

proportional tax: a tax whose percentage rate stays constant as the tax base increases, resulting in the amount of paid tax being proportional to the tax base (e.g., property tax).

proprietary company: a nonfunctioning parent company or a non-functioning controlling company formed for the purpose of investing in the securities of other companies and for controlling these companies through such holdings. Synonymous with *holding company; parent company.*

proprietor: a person who has an exclusive right or interest in property or in a business.

proprietorship: a business that is owned by one person. The individual owner has the rights to all profits from the business as well as all liabilities and losses. Synonymous with *individual proprietorship.*

proprietorship certificate: a certificate filed with a bank showing the ownership of a privately owned business enterprise.

proprietory accounts: accounts showing the actual assets and liabilities of an organization.

pro rata: "according to the rate" (*Latin*); in proportion to a total amount. For example, if a contract is terminated before the end of the period for which payment has been given, a pro rata return of the payment is made in proportion to the unused period of time remaining.

pro rata cancellation: the termination of an insurance contract or bond, with the premium charge being adjusted in proportion to the exact time the protection has been in force. Cf. *flat cancellation; short-rate cancellation.* See *unearned premium.*

pro rata distribution clause: a clause providing for the distribution of an insurance amount over the several locations or objects covered, in proportion to their value; or, if several policies are involved, the proportionate distribution of the liability among them. See *double insurance.*

prorate: to redistribute a portion of a cost to a department or product in accordance with an agreed upon formula.

prospect: a potential customer. See *qualified prospect.*

prospecting: searching for an individual or concern that needs a product or service and possesses the ability to purchase it.

prospector strategy: business-level strategy that involves innovation through seeking out new opportunities, taking risks, and expanding.

prospectus:
(1) **general:** a plan for a proposed enterprise.
(2) **securities:** a written offer to sell a security. It provides information about the quality of the stock as regulated by the U.S. Securities and Exchange Commission. Cf. *open prospectus; red herring.*

prosperity: the uppermost phase of a business cycle. Cf. *depression.*

protected classes: individuals of a minority race, women, older persons, and those with disabilities who are covered by federal laws on equal employment opportunity.

protected groups: classes of people who are protected from employment discrimination under one or more laws. See *concentration in employment; underutilization.*

protection:

(1) **insurance:** synonymous with *coverage.*

(2) **general:** the imposition of high (i.e., protective) tariffs on imports that are presumed to compete with domestic items, with the objective of giving the domestic manufacturer an advantage. See *infant industry argument.*

protectionists: people who favor high tariffs and other import restrictions to enable domestic items to compete more favorably with foreign items.

protective injunction: a court order prohibiting a strike or boycott. See *injunction.*

protective tariff: a tax on imported goods designed to give domestic manufacturers an economic shield against price competition from abroad. Cf. *revenue tariffs.*

Protestant ethic: theory that there is more economic growth when work is viewed as a means of salvation and when people prefer to transform productivity gains into additional output rather than into additional leisure.

protest jacket: synonymous with *notice of dishonor.*

protocols: standard set of rules and procedures for the control of communications in a network.

proximate cause:

(1) **general:** a cause that leads to other causes; the factor responsible for any harm.

(2) **insurance:** an unbroken chain of causes and effects between the occurrence of an insured peril and damage to property or persons (e.g., fire is the proximate cause of damage done by the water used to extinguish it).

proximate damages: damages that are direct, immediate, and the result of negligence or wrong, and that might have been expected. Cf. *consequential loss.*

proximo: "in the following month" (*Latin*). Cf. *instant.*

proxy: a power of attorney given by a stockholder to an individual or individuals to exercise the stockholder's rights to vote at corporate meetings. Cf. *power of attorney.*

proxy statement: printed information required by the Securities and Exchange Commission to be given to potential holders of securities traded on a national exchange, supplying minimum descriptions of the stock, timing of the proposed sale, and so on.

prudent investment-cost standard: a means of defining the value of an organization by subtracting the costs of unwise, inappropriate, or wasteful investments from the original costs of the assets.

prudent man rule: an investment standard. In some states, the law requires that a fiduciary, such as a trustee, may invest the fund's money only in a list of securities designated by the state–the so-called legal list. In other states, the trustee may invest in a security if it is one that would be bought by a prudent person of discretion and intelligence who is seeking a reasonable income and preservation of capital.

P-star: a Federal Reserve predictor of the nation's long-term inflation rate. The formula is $P = M2 \times V\star$ divided by $Q\star$, where: $P\star$ is the general level of future prices; M2 is one of the official measures of the money in the economy; $V\star$ is a constant, representing the velocity of M2 over the past 33 years. Velocity is the rate at which money in the economy changes hands; $Q\star$ is an estimate for the value of the nation's gross national product in the future, assuming the economy grows at 2.5 percent a year. Federal economists believe that it is the fastest that the economy can grow without increasing inflation.

psychic income: nonmonetary income regarded by an individual as desirable to fulfill his or her needs, wants, and psychological demands. Power, control, independence, and actualization are examples of psychic income. Synonymous with *intangible rewards.*

psychological contract: the sum total of what the individual expects to get from the organization and what the organization expects to get from the individual.

psychological pricing: synonymous with *odd pricing.*

psychological product: the physical product along with its warranties, services, and psychological overtones.

public bond: see *bond, public.*

public consumption monopoly: a governmental monopoly created to regulate the consumption of specific items that are considered harmful. Cf. *sumptuary laws.*

public corporation: a corporation created by and for a government agency to assist in the discharge of a public service (e.g., a port authority).

public debt transaction: see *backdoor financing.*

public domain: federally owned land. Cf. *property, public.*

public finance: see *finance*.

public interest:

(1) a moral imperative based on the assumption that there exists some collective, overarching community or national good and that this good, the public interest, should be served.

(2) the result of group struggles.

(3) the accommodation of a multiplicity of competing interests.

publicity: any event or communication, through established media or otherwise, free or paid, solicited or not, that attracts attention to a product.

Public Law 94-455: synonymous with *Tax Reform Act of 1976*.

public member: the member of a tripartite fact-finding or other group who is not directly connected with the union or the employer. Cf. *observer*.

public policy:

(1) any conduct that affects the public good.

(2) an official position in regard to a national concern or public interest that may lead to legislation and other changes in activity.

public property: see *property, public*.

public relations: any communication or activity created or performed primarily to enhance prestige or goodwill for an individual or an organization.

public responsibility: the responsibilities of individuals or groups that are presumed to reflect the broader and more pervasive needs of the entire community, state, or nation.

public revenue: income received by a government agency (taxes, tariffs, customs, etc.).

public sale: a sale of property at a public auction.

public sector: the segment of the total economy that includes all levels of government and excludes businesses and households. Cf. *private sector*.

public service advertising: advertising related not to the marketing of products but to social betterment goals (e.g., preventing forest fires, promoting traffic safety, securing blood donations).

public utility: a private corporation that sells services to the public (e.g., gas and water supplies). Such organizations are government regulated and are usually given a monopoly to operate in a community. See *fair rate of return; rate regulation; utility; utility expenditures*.

Public Utility Holding Company Act of 1935: federal legislation forbidding pyramiding of holding companies in the public utilities industry.

publisher's representative: an independent organization or person that sells advertising space for a publication.

punishment:

(1) method of making desired responses less likely because the undesired behavior is followed by a distinctly undesirable consequence.

(2) the application of negative consequences to stop or correct improper behavior.

(3) a behavioral modification option that applies penalties for the undesired behavior to reduce the possibility that it will recur.

punt: (slang) shares that will rarely turn out to be profitable.

purchase allowance: a lowering of the price of an item when the merchandise as requested does not meet the expectations as identified on the invoice. Cf. *on consignment; returns to vendor.*

purchase contract: an agreement between a buyer and a seller that itemizes items and services to be bought and sold, respectively.

purchase discount: a reduction in the price of an order that has been paid promptly.

purchase money: monies paid to obtain ownership of property.

purchase order: a statement permitting a vendor to deliver merchandise or materials at an agreed-upon price.

purchase price: the amount for which any item is bought.

purchaser: a buyer; a person who obtains title to or an interest in property by the act of purchase.

purchase returns and allowances: a contra-purchases account in which the returns of or allowances for previously purchased merchandise are recorded.

purchasing agent: an individual who buys products for store maintenance and daily operation, not for resale to customers. Cf. *procurement.*

purchasing power: the value of money measured by the items it can buy. Cf. *money; real value of money.*

purchasing power of the dollar: a measurement of the quantity of goods and services that a dollar will buy in a specified market, compared with the amount it could buy in some base period. It is obtained by taking the reciprocal of an appropriate price index. See *money; wage.*

pure competition: a situation in which there are many sellers and buyers of a standardized product with free entrance to the market and no collusion.

pure economic discrimination: a condition that exists when, in considering two workers with the same skills and training, an employer prefers one worker over the other on the basis of race, ethnic background, or some other criterion that is not directly related to the worker's ability to perform his or her job.

pure interest: the price paid for the use of capital, not including monies for risk or all other costs incurred because of the loan. Synonymous with *net interest; true interest.* Cf. *interest.*

pure market economy: a competitive economic system of numerous buyers and sellers, in which prices are determined by the free interaction of supply and demand. See *free enterprise.*

pure monopoly: see *perfect (pure) monopoly.*

pure premium: a premium, arrived at by dividing losses by exposure, to which no loading has been added for commissions, taxes, and expenses.

pure profit: synonymous with *economic profit.*

push a pen: (slang) to perform clerical or other office work.

push money (p.m.): a commission for retail clerks who are successful in selling specified goods. This is a type of incentive system.

push-pull strategy: the balance between a firm's attempts to stimulate the demand for its products by pushing them forward through the channels through efforts aimed at the middleman and pulling the goods through the channels to the consumer through promotional efforts aimed directly at the market.

puts: option contracts that entitle the holder to sell a number of shares of the underlying stock at a stated price on or before a fixed expiration date. See *puts and calls.*

puts and calls: options that give the right to buy or sell a fixed amount of certain stock at a specified price within a specified time. A put gives the holder the right to sell the stock; a call conveys the right to buy the stock. Puts are purchased by those who think a stock may go down. A put obligates the seller of the contract, commonly known as the option writer, to take delivery of the stock and to pay the specified price to the owner of the option within the time limit of the contract. The price specified in a put or call is usually close to the market price of the stock at the time the contract is made. Calls are purchased by those who think a stock may rise. A call gives the holder the right to buy the stock from the writer at the specified price within a fixed period of time. Put and call contracts may be written for 30, 60, or 90 days, or longer. Six months and ten days is the most common term. If the purchaser of a put or call does not wish to exercise the option, the price paid for the option becomes a loss. See *spread; Tax Reform Act of 1976.*

putting-out system: the second stage in the evolution of a materially productive civilization, initially characterized by an entrepreneur's agreement to take all the output an individual (or family) can produce at a fixed price. This stage eventually progressed to the stage at which the entrepreneur provided the workers with the raw materials and paid them on a piece-rate basis for finished goods.

pryamider: see *pyramid selling.*

pyramiding: employing profits of open or unliquidated positions to add to the holder's original position. See *Public Utility Holding Company Act of 1935.*

pyramid ratio: a tool used in the analysis of management and income to determine the relationship of profits and capital.

pyramid selling (schemes): business opportunity frauds, usually promoted through advertisements for job opportunities guaranteed to yield enormous or quick profits, requiring little education or demanding a minimal personal investment. There are government regulations against certain pyramid schemes. The pyramider induces many people to buy his products, which they are to resell at a higher price. For example, if 10 people buy 50 units each but can sell only 15 each, the pyramider is still ahead, because he has sold 500 units. See *fraud.*

Q

qualification check: a formal or informal method of verifying and recording information about the skill, knowledge, experience, character, or related factors required of a candidate for employment that cannot be accurately measured by interview or examination.

qualified endorsement: an endorsement asserting that the limits of liability of an endorser release him or her of all responsibility in the event of nonpayment or non-acceptance of an instrument. A qualified endorsement is often stated on a document as "without recourse."

qualified handicapped: handicapped people who can perform jobs with reasonable employer accommodation.

qualified opinion: an audit opinion by a CPA stating that some specified aspect of the audit prevents an unqualified opinion.

qualified prospect: a potential customer who is able to buy a product and has the authority to make a decision to purchase. This conclusion is often arrived at following a check on the individual's credit.

qualified stock option plan: a compensation plan where options to purchase stock are granted to workers and where the implicit compensation is neither tax deductible as an expense by the employer nor as taxable income to the worker. See *Tax Reform Act of 1986*.

qualifying period: see *waiting period*.

quality assurance: method of assuring that products or services meet customer expectations.

quality circles: voluntary groups of operative employees who periodically brainstorm on how to increase the firm's output.

quality control: the attempt to ensure the presence of qualitative factors in a product or standards of performance in a service. Cf. *material control; process inspection; production control.*

quality improvement teams: small groups of employees who work on solving specific problems related to quality and productivity, often with stated targets for improvement.

quality market: a market in which quality is more important than price.

quality marks: in strategic planning, businesses in high-growth industries, but with low relative market shares.

quantitative school: a modern school of management thought consisting of theories on management as a system of mathematical models and processes. Advocates of this school are greatly concerned with decision making. This school is the genesis of scientific management.

quantity demanded: amount which would be purchased at a particular price, at a moment of time.

quantity discount: a reduction that is given for volume buying.

quantity theory: a theory stating that a special relationship exists between the quantity of money and money income and that people spend excess money holdings irrespective of the interest rate and the manner in which the new money holdings were received. Cf. *Gresham's law; Keynesian economics; liquidity trap; marginal propensity to invest; marginal propensity to save.*

quantity variance: the standard price for a given resource, multiplied by the difference between the actual quantity used and the total standard quantity allowed for the number of units produced.

quantum meruit: "as much as is merited" (*Latin*); a principle of business law providing that when a service is given without a written estimate of price, there is an implied promise by the purchaser of the service to pay for the work as much as it is worth. See *lien.*

quarter stock: stock with a par value of $25 for each share.

quasi: as if; that which resembles.

quasi corporation: any political subdivision of an organization or group (e.g., an unincorporated town).

quasi-public company: a privately operated corporation in which the public has a special interest (e.g., eleemosynary institutions).

quasi reorganization: a restructuring that does not lead to the formation of a new company; undertaken for purposes of absorbing a deficit, avoiding bankruptcy, and affording an opportunity to begin again. Cf. reorganization.

queuing theory: see *waiting line theory.*

quick assets:

(1) **general:** assets that will be converted into cash within a reasonably short time in the ordinary course of business.

(2) **finance:** assets that can be readily converted into cash without appreciable loss. See *liquidity.*

quick ratio: the ratio between existing liabilities and quick assets, showing a firm's ability to pay off its liabilities rapidly with available funds.

quid pro quo: "something for something" (*Latin*); a mutual consideration; an advantage or a concession received in return for a similar favor.

quiescing: a process of bringing a device or a system to a halt by rejecting new requests for work.

quiet title suit: a legal action to remove a defect or any questionable claim against the title to property.

quota: the amount of production expected from the average employee in order to receive the specified base pay. See *sales quota*.

quota rule: a union regulation in a labor-management contract establishing the number of workers to be hired for a particular job within the union's jurisdiction.

quota-share reinsurance: an agreement by which the reinsurer accepts a stated percentage of a risk written by an insurance company. See *reinsurance; retained risk*.

quotation (quote): the highest bid to buy and the lowest offer to sell a security in a given market at a given time. For example, if you ask a broker for a "quote" on a stock, the reply may be something like "45-1/4 to 45-1/2." This means that $45.25 is the highest price any buyer wanted to pay at the time the quote was given on the floor of a stock exchange, and $45.50 was the lowest price any seller would take at the same time. See *bid and asked*.

quoted price: the stated price of a security or commodity.

quote sheet: an analysis of costs used as a basis for determining selling prices.

R

rabble hypothesis: the belief that workers are a disorganized group of individuals, each acting out of personal interest.

rack: in the rack department, sorts, distributes, and proves items in the commercial operations of a bank.

racketeering: the practice of unethical and extortionate use of power or violence to obtain an advantage; any dishonest scheme for obtaining money.

Racketeer Influenced and Corrupt Organizations Act (RICO): 1970 federal legislation to fight organized crime and to protect legitimate businesses from invasions by organized crime.

rack jobber: a wholesaler who maintains stocks of convenience-type merchandise, primarily in supermarkets, drugstores, and other related retail operations.

radial movement: movement either toward or away from an organization's central core of power.

Radiation Control for Health and Safety Act of 1968: federal legislation establishing performance standards and limits of radiation that may be emitted from consumer items (television sets, microwave ovens, etc.).

radiation selling: using a specific sale as a starting point for future related sales, based on the first sale as the example of need (e.g., selling the camera that will lead to sales of film and film processing services).

rag business (trade): the sentimental name given to the fashion apparel industry.

raid:

(1) **securities:** a deliberate attempt by professional traders and others to depress the market price of a stock.

(2) **labor relations:** the attempt by a union to enroll members from another union (local, regional, or national), thereby encroaching on the second union's jurisdiction. See *no-raiding agreements; rival unionism.*

rainmakers: (slang) law firm partners who bring in business, sometimes because they have held high government positions.

raise:

(1) **economics:** an increase in value or amount (e.g., wages, prices).

(2) **securities:** a fraudulent increase in the face value of a negotiable instrument.

raised check: a check on which the amount has been illegally increased.

rally: a brisk rise following a decline in the general price level of the market or of an individual stock.

Rand formula: a system whereby an employee who does not wish to become a union member pays his or her monthly union dues but is not listed as a union participant. Cf. *free rider; union shop.*

random demand: a change in market demand that has no pattern and cannot be forecast.

rank:
(1) **general:** to arrange in an ascending or descending series according to importance.
(2) **administration:** a title or position in an organization.
(3) **securities:** see *restricted shares.*

rank and file:
(1) **human resources:** employees of an organization who do not participate in management activities.
(2) **labor relations:** members of a union who are not full-time paid officials (e.g., members of a shop committee, officers of a local union). Cf. *pork-chopper.*

ranking: a type of performance appraisal in which the rater ranks his or her subordinates from highest to lowest, based on some criterion.

rapport: the relationship, accord, and balance between a sales representative and a potential customer.

rate:
(1) **general:** to categorize and rank in terms of special qualities or properties.
(2) **insurance:** the cost of a unit of insurance. Cf. *premium.*
(3) **finance:** a charge, fee, or price.

rate cutting: a unilateral wage rate reduction by an employer in the absence of changes in job content.

rate discrimination: charging different prices for almost identical services. When this action tends to lessen competition, it may be illegal under antitrust laws. Cf. *price discrimination.*

rate of basic compensation: compensation fixed by law or administrative action for the position held by a worker.

rate of exchange: the amount of funds of one nation that can be bought on a specific date for a sum of currency of another country. Rates fluctuate often because of economic, political, and other forces.

rate of inflation: the average percentage rate of increase of the price of money, weighted and stated in annual terms.

rate of interest: the charge for borrowing money.

rate of return on investment (capital): see *ROI*.

rate regulation: the determination by a commission or public service agency of the maximum (and at times the minimum) charge that public utility corporations may demand for their services. See *fair rate of return; public utility; utility.*

rate setting: the establishment of rates by agreement between labor and management or by an employer alone.

rate variance: in accounting procedures, the difference between actual wages paid and the standard wage rate, multiplied by the total actual hours of direct labor used.

rate war: a negative form of competition in which sellers drop their prices below their costs for purposes of putting the competition out of business. See *predatory pricing, underselling.*

ratify: to confirm or approve.

rating: a traditional method of performance appraisal in which a judge evaluates performance in terms of a value or index that is used in some standard way. It traditionally involves global rating scales.

rating, merit: see *merit rating.*

rating bureaus: organizations that develop suggested rates for a substantial proportion of the fire insurance business. Rates are based on loss and expense experience of all fire insurance companies. Individual insurers are permitted to deviate, within limits, from bureau rates. See *experience rating.*

ratio:

   (1) **general:** a number relationship between two things (e.g., ratio of births to deaths).

   (2) **accounting:** any relationship that can be used in measuring the rating or financial position of a firm (e.g., the relationship of a company's earnings to the firm's market price for its stock).

   (3) **finance:** one of the various analyses made by a money-lending or credit agency of the financial statements of an individual, company, or other business enterprise seeking credit, to determine the desirability of granting the requested credit.

   (4) **finance:** the relative values of silver and gold in a monetary system that is based on both. See *bimetallism.*

ratio (acid-test): see *acid-test ratio.*

ratio analysis: analysis of financial statements through a comparison of one figure, such as net profit, to another, such as sales or total investment.

rational buying motives: all costs of money, use, labor, and profit that affect a purchaser. Cf. *motivation, unconscious.*

rational goal model: model of assessing organizational effectiveness that is concerned with organizational development and promotion.

rationalization: what managers use in justifying questionable conduct.

rational-legal authority: an authority structure based on law (e.g., a supervisor is obeyed because of his or her position in the organization's hierarchy).

ratio of accounts payable to purchases: a ratio, determined for the present period and compared with a similar ratio for previous periods, that indicates the trend toward or away from prompt payment of current obligations.

ratio of capital to fixed assets: a ratio that is usually determined for a number of years to ascertain whether there is a trend toward converting the investment of the owners into fixed assets, thereby indicating a possible reliance on creditors for furnishing the required working capital.

ratio of finished goods inventory to the cost of goods sold: a ratio determined by dividing the cost of goods sold by the average finished goods inventory. The resulting figure is the number of times the investment in the finished-goods inventory has turned over during the period under consideration. The present ratio is compared with a similar ratio for several previous periods, since it portrays the stability and trend of sales or a possibly overstated or expanded inventory.

ratio of fixed assets to fixed liabilities: a ratio that indicates the margin of safety to the present mortgage and bond holders, if any. Failure of the ratio to meet the minimum requirement frequently suggests that additional funds should be raised from the owners rather than by mortgaging fixed assets.

ratio of notes payable to accounts payable: a ratio whose desirability is determined by consideration of three quantitative factors: (1) notes issued in payment of merchandise; (2) notes issued to banks and brokers; and (3) notes issued to others. If a relatively large number of the outstanding notes were issued to merchandise creditors, this might indicate that the firm is unable to take advantage of the cash discounts offered in the trade and that other lending agencies might consider the firm's credit unfavorably.

ratio of notes receivable to accounts receivable: a ratio that, if large as compared with other firms in a similar line of business, indicates that the firm with the high ratio may have a lax credit policy or may be extending credit to customers whose ability to pay promptly is dubious.

ratio of owned capital to borrowed capital: a ratio considered to be important in determining the advisability of extending additional long-term credit to an applicant. If this ratio is not considered favorable, it frequently suggests that the funds desired should be raised from the owners of the business (i.e., the applicants themselves) rather than through additional pledging of any assets.

ratio of raw-materials inventory to cost of manufacture: a ratio determined by dividing the cost of goods manufactured by the average raw-materials inventory. The resulting figure is the number of times the investment in the raw-materials inventory has turned over during the period under consideration. When the present ratio is compared with a similar ratio for previous periods, it portrays the trend and steadiness of production or indicates a possibly overstated or overexpanded inventory.

ratio reinforcement: a schedule of rewards that ties reinforcements directly to acts or behavior. It can be fixed or variable.

rat race: (slang) an occupation or style of living in which personal satisfaction is considered a less important goal than competition, climbing the organizational ladder, material acquisition, and the like.

raw material: nonprocessed resources utilized in producing an item. The act of production results in an alteration in the form of the original material.

raw-materials inventory: items purchased by a manufacturing firm to be used in production.

razorback: (slang) manual worker.

RBO: see *relationship by objective.*

reach: the total audience a medium actually gets to, in unduplicated persons.

reaction: a drop in securities prices following a sustained period of increasing prices.

reactive management: a management style in which decision makers respond to problems rather than anticipating problems before they occur.

reactor: a coalition strategy entailing a shifting emphasis for the firm.

readership: the total audience of a publication. Cf. *circulation*.

Reaganomics: the economic program of President Ronald Reagan. Beginning in 1981, it consisted of tax cuts to stimulate economic productivity, reduction in government spending, deregulation to reduce government involvement, and a tight money policy for curbing inflation. Cf. *supply-side economics*.

real accounts: the accounts appearing on the balance sheet that are not closed to a zero balance at the end of each accounting period. Synonymous with *permanent accounts*.

real earnings: earnings adjusted to exclude the effects of price change.

real estate: tangible land and all physical property, including all physical substances below, upon, or attached to land. Thus, houses, trees, and fences are classified as real estate; all else is personal property.

real estate bond: see *bond, real estate*.

real income: the sum total of the purchasing power of a nation or individual.

real interest rate: the rate at which a person earns future purchasing power on monetary assets. It equals the money rate minus the rate of inflation.

real investment: an expenditure that establishes a new capital asset, thus creating a new capital formation.

realistic job previews (RJP): the practice of providing realistic information to new employees to avoid creating expectations that cannot be realized.

reality shock syndrome: an individual's reaction to the difference between high job expectations and the frustrating day-to-day realities of the workplace.

realization (realize):
    (1) **finance:** the act or process of converting into cash an asset or the total assets of an individual or business.
    (2) **securities:** receiving a profit from selling a security following an increase in its price.

reallocation: allocation of the costs of operating the service departments to the various production departments in proportion to the relative benefits or services received by each production department. Synonymous with *reapportionment*.

real money: money containing one or more metals that have intrinsic value, as distinguished from representative money, such as currency issued by a realm and checks, drafts, and so on, issued by legal entities. See *bimetallism; monometallism*. Cf. *fiat money*.

real price: the price of goods and services measured by the quantity of manpower needed to earn sufficient money to purchase the goods or services.

real value of money: the price of money measured in terms of goods. Cf. *purchasing power.*

real wages: the cost of items and services that can be purchased with money wages. It is useful for comparing changes in the standard of living by eliminating the effect of changes in the general price level. See *money wages.*

reapportionment: allocation of the costs of operating the service departments to the various production departments in proportion to the relative benefits or services received by each production unit. Synonymous with *reallocation.*

reappraisal: when property is appraised a second time.

reasonable accommodation: attempt by employers to adjust, without undue hardship, the working conditions or schedules of employees with disabilities or religious preferences.

reassignment: a change of an employee from one job, position, or office to another, without promotion or demotion, while serving continuously within the same department, unit, or organization.

rebate:
(1) **finance:** unearned interest that may be returned to a borrower if the loan is paid off before the maturity date.
(2) **sales:** any deduction made from a payment or charge. In contrast to a discount, a rebate is not deducted in advance but is returned to the consumer following payment of the full amount (e.g., a GE appliance costs $24, with a rebate of $5 after the consumer has mailed in a coupon from the appliance package). Cf. *discount.*

rebating: the illegal and unethical practice of selling a policy at less than the legal rate, allowing the insured a refund of the premium, or giving him or her goods of any value, thus avoiding payment of the full legal premium.

rebuild strategy: investment and marketing efforts designed to increase or exceed sales, profits, or market share levels that were held at an earlier time.

recall:
(1) **human resources:** the return to work of laid-off workers, usually on a seniority basis. See *bumping.*
(2) **manufacturing:** the return of a distributed product for purposes of adjustment, repair, or other necessary work.

recapitalization: altering the capital structure of a firm by increasing or decreasing its capital stock.

receipt: written acknowledgment of value received.

receipt-of-goods dating: see *ROG dating.*

receivables: accounts receivable owned by a business. These may be pledged as collateral for a loan secured from a bank or other financial institution.

receiver: a court-appointed, neutral party named to handle property under litigation or the affairs of a bankrupt person. The receiver is required to maintain the property and its assets for the benefit of those having equity in it until a court decision as to its disposition is made. See *sequestered account.*

receivership: the state of being under the care of administration of a receiver.

receiving apron: a statement used in the receiving department of a store that contains all pertinent data concerning an incoming shipment. The form is used to identify the shipment for purposes of accounting and control. See *financial statement; pro forma invoice.*

recency effect: a rater bias that occurs when the rater allows recent employee performance to sway the overall evaluation of the worker's performance.

recession:
(1) occurs when the gross national product shrinks for six consecutive months.
(2) a recurring period of decline in total output, income, employment, and trade, usually lasting from six months to a year and marked by widespread contractions in many sectors of the economy.

recessionary: pertaining to or causing recession, especially economic recession.

reciprocal causation: the process in which a leader influences the behavior and attitudes of subordinates while the subordinates simultaneously influence the leader's behavior and attitudes.

reciprocal holdings: where firm A owns stock of firm B and firm B owns stock of firm A.

reciprocal interdependence: where groups exchange inputs and outputs.

reciprocal trade agreement: an international agreement between two or more countries to establish mutual trade concessions that are expected to be of equal value. Cf. *free trade agreement.*

reciprocity: the purchasing of goods by one firm from another on a preferential basis, with the expectation that the second firm will preferentially buy the goods of the first.

reclamation:

(1) **general:** the act of obtaining useful materials from waste products. Cf. *recycling.*

(2) **banking:** a sum of money due or owing by a bank, resulting from an error in the listing of the amount of a check on a clearinghouse balance.

recognition:

(1) **advertising:** acceptance of an agency by a medium. A recognized agency receives standard agency discounts.

(2) **labor relations:** an agreement by an employer to accept a given union as the collective-bargaining agent of that firm's employees.

recompense: a payment or award made to anyone to make amends for a loss or damage. See *compensation.*

reconciliation:

(1) **accounting:** a process for determining the differences between two items of an account (e.g., a bank statement and an up-to-date checkbook)so as to bring them into agreement. See *adjustment.*

(2) **labor relations:** bringing harmony to a labor dispute; settling a labor-management conflict.

reconsignment: any alteration, including a route change, made in a consignment before the items have arrived at their billed destination.

record date: the date on which a person must be registered as a shareholder on the stock book of a company in order to receive a declared dividend or, among other things, to vote on company affairs. Cf. *ex-dividend.*

recourse: the right to seek payment on a discounted note from the payee if the maker defaults.

recovery:

(1) **economics:** the period of the business cycle that follows a depression.

(2) **insurance:** following a loss, the money received by an insurance company from a reinsurer by subrogation or from salvage.

(3) **securities:** a rise in stock prices following a period of declining prices. Synonymous with *expansion (economics).*

Recovery Act: see *Economic Recovery Tax Act of 1981.*

recruiting: personnel department activity involving the search for employees to meet the specific needs of an organization. In addition, the company may utilize the services of outside recruiting firms. See *headhunter; special events recruiting.*

recruitment: the attempt to attract compatible individuals to a firm as potential employees.

recurring payoff: further income from a sound investment paid back to the investor with interest paid in addition to the original investment; a repeated return on a single investment.

recycling: the conversion of waste products (i.e., empty beer cans) to usable material for the purpose of reducing pollution, saving money, and/or conserving resources. Cf. *reclamation.*

red apple: (slang) a nonunion worker, usually an individual who plays up to a boss by deciding not to join the union.

red-circle rates: wages or salaries that are inappropriate for a given job according to a job evaluation plan.

redeemable stock: a preferred stock that can be called in at the option of the issuing company. See *redemption price.*

redemption: the liquidation of an indebtedness on or before maturity (e.g., the retirement of a bond issue prior to its maturity date).

redemption bond: see *bond, redemption.*

redemption fund: a fund created for the purpose of retiring an obligation.

redemption price: the price (usually par value) at which a bond may be redeemed before maturity when it is retired at the option of the issuing company; the amount a company must pay to call in certain types of preferred stock.

redeployment: reassignment and accompanying training of employees, resulting from changing technology or equipment or from business decisions requiring new skills. Cf. *labor-saving equipment.*

red herring: a financial prospectus with a cautionary statement on the first page, printed in red. It is informational and not intended as an offer to sell the securities described. Cf. *open prospectus.*

rediscount:

(1) **banking:** a negotiable instrument that has been discounted by a bank and subsequently discounted a second time by a Federal Reserve Bank or another bank for the benefit of the bank that originally discounted the instrument. See *bank credit.*

(2) **finance:** to discount for the second time.

rediscount rate: the rate set by a Federal Reserve Bank for discounting a second time monies offered by their district member banks; the interest rate charged for discounting a negotiable instrument that has already been discounted.

red one: (slang) a successful business day.

red tape: (slang) the delay caused by inefficient and/or bureaucratic routine.

reduced rate average: see *coinsurance.*

redundancy: (British usage) cause for dismissal of a worker when his or her job ceases to exist.

reemployment: bringing a laid-off employee back to work. See *recall.*

reengineering: reconsiders how work would be done and the organization structured if they were being created from scratch.

reexport: to export already imported items, without duty charges, in basically similar form to a third country. Cf. *production sharing.*

reference check: a procedure used to verify the accuracy of information contained in an application form and/or to increase knowledge about the applicant.

reference cycle: the sequence of expansion and contraction in the general business activity. Cf. *business cycle.*

referendum: a vote by the rank and file to choose nominees in a national union office election, to decide on dues or assessment increases, to ratify a proposed contract, or to address other issues.

referent power: the influence exerted on a subordinate who identifies with his or her superior's style and personality. A powerful superior who is admired acquires a certain amount of power over the admirer.

referral leads: names of potential customers given to a sales representative, usually by satisfied customers.

referral risks: risks beyond the underwriting authority of an office that must be referred to a supervisory office for a decision on acceptance. See *overline; substandard.*

refinance: to revise a payment timetable and, frequently, to modify interest charges on the obligation.

refinanced loan: a loan that has had an addition to the principal balance. Such increases are usually for property improvements such as an added room. Normally, the term and/or the payment amount is also affected.

refinancing: synonymous with *refunding (finance).*

reflation: upon recovering from a depression or a recession, the period during which prices are returned to the level they had attained during a period of prosperity by lowering the purchasing power of money.

refundable interest: the unearned portion of interest previously charged that will be returned to the debtor (maker of a note) if the indebtedness is liquidated prior to maturity.

refund check:

(1) **general:** a check or other instrument of currency that is repayment of money for any reason. See *rebate*.

(2) **merchandising:** a statement for a customer's purchase that is returned.

(3) **taxes**: a check from a government tax bureau for overpayment of taxes.

refunding:

(1) **securities:** replacing an older bond issue with a new issue, either before or at maturity of the older one. It is often done to change the interest rate on the debt.

(2) **finance:** the act of returning a portion of money to the giver from an amount already paid out. See *debt*.

refunding bond: see *bond, refunding*.

refusal to sell: the right of a seller to choose the dealers that will handle his or her merchandise. Invoking this right, which is recognized by law, a seller may refuse to deal with firms that do not meet certain standards or qualifications. Cf. *franchise*.

regiocentric: management philosophy oriented toward larger areas, including the global marketplace.

regional bargaining: see *multiemployer bargaining*.

regional differential: among broad geographical subdivisions, the difference in prevailing wages for equal work.

regional economic integration: expansion of commercial and financial ties among countries in a regional group, leaving the rest of the world outside of the group; ranges from free trade agreements to full economic and political unions.

regional store: a branch store, usually located far from the central store, that functions under the name of the parent store. In most cases a regional store operates as an autonomous unit. Cf. *branch store*.

register:

(1) **general:** to make a permanent record of events.

(2) **transportation:** a written document prepared by a customs official that allows a ship to engage in foreign trade.

register(ed) check: a check prepared by a teller, using funds recorded and placed aside in a special register, for the convenience of a purchaser who may wish to make a payment by check but does not maintain a checking account. The check has two stubs; one is for the purchaser and the other is used by the bank for record keeping. It is actually a money order, prepared in the form of a check. The bank usually charges a small fee for each registered check sold.

registered bond: see *bond, registered.*

registered check: see *register(ed) check.*

registered representative (trader): or "customer's man"; a full-time employee of a stock exchange member organization who has met the requirements of the exchange with respect to background and knowledge of the securities business. Synonymous with *account executive; customer's broker.*

registrar: an agency, usually a trust company or a bank, charged with the responsibility for preventing the issuance of more stock than has been authorized by a company. The registrar's primary function is to authenticate the issuing of securities. See *overissue.*

registration: filing of a statement with the SEC by the issuer before a public offering may be made of new securities by a company or of outstanding securities by controlling stockholders. The securities must be registered under the Securities Act of 1933. The registration statement discloses pertinent information relating to the company's operations, securities, management, and purpose of the public offering. On security offerings involving less than $300,000, the information required is less detailed.

regressive supply: the situation in which, when the price of an item drops, a greater quantity of the item is offered.

regressive taxes: rates in a tax system that decrease as the base amount taxed increases (a rate of 500, 4 percent applied to a base of $2,000, etc.). A sales tax is a regressive tax. Cf. *progressive tax.*

regular dating: terms of a sale under which the period for discount and the date on which payment is required are determined from the date of the invoice. Cf. *ROG dating.*

regulated investment company: an investment company that can avoid income tax on its ordinary income and capital gains by distributing profits as dividends and by conforming to other statutory rules. Cf. *investment company.*

Regulation Q: as established by the Federal Reserve Board, a formula it uses to determine the maximum interest that can be paid by commercial banks to their customers on time deposits.

Regulation T: the Federal Reserve Board criterion governing the amount of credit that may be advanced by brokers and dealers to customers for the purchase of securities. See *margin.*

Regulation U: the Federal Reserve Board criterion governing the amount of credit that may be advanced by a bank to its customers for the purchase of listed stocks.

Rehabilitation Act of 1973: legislation that prohibits discrimination against those who are handicapped but qualified to perform work. It applies to employers who receive federal monies and to federal agencies of the executive branch. See *qualified handicapped.*

reinforcement theory: behavior is a function of its consequences.

reinstatement:

(1) **insurance:** when payment of a claim reduces the principal amount of a policy by the amount of the claim, a provision that is usually made for reestablishing the policy to an original amount. Depending on policy conditions, it may be done automatically, either with or without premium consideration, or at the request of the insured. See *waiver of restoration premium.*

(2) **human resources:** restoration of a worker to a former position without loss of seniority or benefits. See *make whole.*

reinsurance: assumption by one insurance company of all or part of a risk undertaken by another insurance company. Cf. *quota-share reinsurance; retained risk.* See *excess of loss reinsurance.*

reinsurance broker: an organization that places (brokers) reinsurance through a reinsurance underwriter; not to be confused with a broker of insurance.

reinvestment: use of retained earnings to replace depreciated assets or to add to the existing stock of capital.

reinvestment privilege: the automatic investment of dividends from holdings in a mutual fund in additional shares of the fund, sometimes without a sales charge.

related diversification: strategy of expanding into other industries or markets related to a company's current business lines.

relationship by objective (RBO): a group dynamics approach, used primarily in labor-management relations, in which an atmosphere is developed that allows all sides to speak out freely and to attempt to develop mutual goals and the means of attaining them. Mediators work largely with union committeemen and key supervisors from the shop.

relationship enterprises: networks of strategic alliances among big companies, spanning different industries and countries.

relationship-motivated leadership: the leadership style shown by a leader who is motivated to form or join other groups or organizations.

relative income concept: the hypothesis that spending is a function of a family's relative place in the income distribution of similar family units (i.e., people who earn the same amount tend to spend the same amount of money).

relaxation training: popular methods, developed and researched by Harvard Medical School's Herb Benson, M.D., including mediation and biofeedback, by which individuals learn to control muscle tension and ease the experience of stress.

release:

(1) **business law:** the cancellation or resolution of a claim against another person.

(2) **insurance:** the written statement of a claim's settlement.

(3) **human resources:** dismissal of a worker for proper cause.

relevant range: the band of activity in which budgeted sales and expense relationships will be valid.

reliability engineering: a structure technique for achieving maximum product reliability through systematic gathering of management, engineering, mathematical, and statistical elements and concepts.

relocation services: services provided to an employee who is transferred to a new location, which might include help in moving, in selling a home, in orienting to a new culture, or in learning a new language.

remargining: placing added margin against a loan. Remargining is one option for brokers who require additional cash or collateral when their securities have lost some of their value.

remise: to give or grant back; to discharge or release.

remittance: funds forwarded from one person to another as payment for purchased items or services.

remonetization: the reinstatement of a coin as standard money after it has been demonetized.

remote delivery: sending goods from a central warehouse to customers via area delivery stations located in the suburbs or by truck.

removal: separation of a worker from his or her office or position for cause.

remunerations: wages and other financial benefits received from employment.

renege: to go back on a promise; to pull out of an agreement. See *repudiation*.

renegotiation: process by which international companies and governments decide on a change in terms for operations.

renewal: extending the maturity of an existing loan obligation or other document of relationship. Cf. *novation*.

renewal certificate: a certificate issued to renew an insurance policy rather than writing out a new policy. The certificate refers to the policy but does not enumerate all its items.

reopener clause: a provision calling for the reopening of a current contract at a specified time for negotiations on stated subjects (e.g., wage increases, pensions, health and welfare). Cf. *contract bar; zipper clause.*

reorganization: an alteration of a firm's capital structure, often resulting from a merger, that affects the rights and responsibilities of the owners. The objectives of a reorganization are to eliminate the cause of failure, settle with creditors, and allow the firm to remain in business. See *National Bankruptcy Act of 1898*. Cf. *quasi reorganization.*

reorganization bond: see *bond, reorganization.*

rep:
  (1) **general:** short for representative.
  (2) **advertising:** short for representative; the person who sells space or time for an advertising medium.

repatriation: the liquidation of overseas investments and the return of the proceeds to the country of the investor.

repeat demand: the demand created for items that are frequently requested and bought.

repertory grid: a marketing technique for ascertaining the characteristics of product similarities and differences under varied use contexts.

replacement charts: graphic representations of who will replace whom in the organization when a job opening occurs. See *replacement summaries.*

replacement-cost insurance: insurance that provides for replacement of the damaged property without deduction for depreciation. The usual replacement-cost form requires that the property actually be replaced before the insured can collect a claim under it. It is primarily available only for buildings, with a few exceptions, and is subject to a coinsurance requirement.

replacement-cost standard: the cost of replacing equipment with new equipment for tasks identical to those performed by worn or obsolete equipment. It provides a way of determining a firm's value.

replacement demand: capital goods or consumer items that are in demand because of depreciation or obsolescence.

replacement summaries: lists of likely replacements for each job and their relative strengths and weaknesses. See *replacement charts.*

reporting form: an insurance policy designed for use when values of the insured property fluctuate during the policy term. Usually, an adequate limit of liability is set; then the insured reports the values actually on hand on a given day of each month. At the end of the year or the policy term, these reported values are averaged and the premium is adjusted.

reporting pay: the minimum wage that is guaranteed under union contract when an employee who is scheduled to work arrives at the assigned place for activity and finds no work opportunity. Synonymous with *call-in pay.*

repossession: the reclaiming or taking back of items that were bought on an installment sales contract on which the buyer has fallen behind in payments.

representation: the statements made by an insured person to his or her insurance company, enabling the firm to establish a policy and set the proper risk amounts and fee charges. See *declaration; warranty (insurance).*

representation election: a vote conducted by the National Labor Relations Board to determine whether a majority of the workers in a previously established unit want to be represented by a given union. See *appropriate unit; Wagner-Connery Act.* Cf. *consent election; run-off election.*

representative money:
(1) **finance:** paper money secured by monetary metal (i.e., gold or silver certificates) deposited in the treasury of a country.
(2) **commodities:** funds that are backed in full by a commodity.

representative participation: workers participate in organizational decision making through a small group of representative employees.

repressive tax: a tax that discourages production. Its effect is to lower potential taxable income.

reproducible capital: productive assets that can themselves be produced (e.g., equipment and buildings).

repudiation: intentional and willful refusal to pay a debt in whole or in part; usually refers to the willful act of a government or a subdivision thereof. Cf. *nullification of agreement.*

repurchase agreement: an agreement between a seller and a buyer that the seller will buy back the note, security, or other property at the expiration of a stated period or upon completion of certain conditions, or both.

required activities: the formally assigned tasks that a group must perform.

required interaction: the condition that occurs when a person's activity follows or is influenced by the activity of another. Such interaction can be verbal or nonverbal.

required reserves: liquid assets that state-chartered banks must hold in accordance with regulations of state banking agencies and Federal Reserve officials.

required return: the lowest return or profit needed to justify an investment.

requisition: a written demand from a department to its purchasing department to release on a specific date materials to be used in a production process or other activity of consumption within an organization. See *excess materials requisitions.*

resale: the selling of goods or services that have been bought by the seller from another person in essentially the same form.

resale price maintenance: a supplier's control over the selling price of his or her goods at various stages of distribution by means of contractual arrangement under fair trade laws or other means.

rescission: making void or annulling (e.g., rescission of a law or judgment). See *right of rescission.*

research and development (R & D):
(1) **general:** applying the findings of science and technology in creating a firm's products or services. Cf. *applied research.*
(2) **securities:** the dollar amount spent on company-sponsored research and development for the year, as reported to the SEC. The total excludes any expenditures for research and development performed under contract for others, such as U.S. government agencies.

reseller markets: firms and individuals who buy products in order to resell them to others.

reservation price: the highest offered price at which a seller will continue to hold back from selling. The seller will sell, however, at any offer above the reservation price. Cf. *upset price.*

reserve:

(1) **accounting:** a portion of the profits allocated to various reserve accounts to protect any depreciation in asset values. The reserves are taken from profits before any declaration of dividends by the board of directors.

(2) **insurance:** funds earmarked for specific purposes (e.g., reserves for unearned premiums, reserves for losses in process of adjustment). Cf. *legal reserve.*

(3) **banking:** assets in the form of cash maintained in a bank's own vault. See *reserve ratio.*

reserved rights: concept that management's authority is supreme in all matters except those it has expressly conceded to the union in the collective agreement.

reserve ratio (requirement): the relationship of the amount of money that must be held in a reserve account, as declared by the Federal Reserve Bank, to the total demand deposits of a member bank.

reserve requisition control: periodic stock count control whereby all the goods in the forward stock are considered as sold and counts are made on the reserve stock that is not on the selling floor. As forward stock diminishes, additional items are requested from the reserve. Sales are determined by adding up the requisitions made in a specified time period. Cf. *forward stock.*

reserves: see *reserve.*

reserve stock control: a technique for earmarking appropriate stock for the maintenance of business until new merchandise is purchased.

resident buyer: any person or firm located in a market area who aids retailers in making market contacts and assists in their purchasing. Cf. *merchandise mart.*

residual income: the net income of a profit center or investment center, less the imputed interest on the net assets used by the center.

residual interest: the owners' equity in an entity's assets after deducting liabilities and any other claims that have a higher priority.

residual value: the predicted disposal value of a long-lived asset.

resignation: a step taken by an employee to terminate his or her relationship with an employer. Notice is usually given, and the date on which the resignation will take effect is specified.

Resolution Trust Corporation (RTC): its function, between August 1989 and August 1992, was to take over 400 to 500 insolvent savings associations with assets of almost $300 billion, to find buyers for the "sick" institutions, and to liquidate those for which there are no buyers. Eventually RTC had to liquidate almost $150 billion in troubled assets that it cannot sell. Its charter expired in 1996. See *RTC Oversight Board*.

resource:

(1) **general:** anything a country uses to produce goods and services (manpower, minerals, oil, etc.). See *nonrenewable natural resources*.

(2) **merchandising:** a producer or wholesaler from whom a merchant buys goods for resale.

resource allocator role: the function of a manager in deciding who will get what resources in the unit. The resources can include time, money, material, equipment, people, and the unit's reputation.

resource-augmenting technical change: a technical change that has the same effect on output as if the quantity of natural resources had been increased. Cf. *labor-augmenting technical change*.

resource budget: a budget based on establishing limitations for each cost element (e.g., labor hours, materials).

resource dependence: an approach to controls that argues that managers need to consider controls mainly in areas in which they depend on others for resources necessary to reach organizational goals.

resource deployment: internal distribution of an organization's resources, including how much money it will spend in pursuit of its goals.

resource-oriented production: production of raw materials, minerals, or components in a foreign country for shipment to a multinational corporation's home country or other component unit.

respondentia: under conditions of hypothecation, the security offered against a loan (e.g., the goods on a truck).

responsible global capitalism: a concept of Professor John Dunning, the efficient and socially acceptable production, exchange, and distribution of goods and services, as determined by the institutions of global capitalism, within a framework of social democracy, an acceptable degree of national autonomy, and a persuasive and virtuous moral order.

responsibility accounting: a system under which someone is held responsible for each activity that occurs in a particular area of a firm.

responsibility center: an organizational unit in which the manager has control over and is accountable for costs, costs and revenues, and investments. See *investment center, profit center*.

resting order: an order that can remain open or good until canceled when (1) an order to purchase securities is limited to a price lower than the market or (2) an order to sell is limited to a price above the market. Cf. *good 'til canceled order.*

restitution: the enforced payment of money, or its equivalent, to its rightful owner, as established by law.

restoration premium: the premium charged to restore a policy or bond to its original value after payment of a loss.

restraining order: a court order in aid of a suit to maintain the status quo until all parties can be heard from. See *injunction.*

restraint of trade: the effect of any contract, combination, or agreement (e.g., a monopoly) that impedes free competition. See *Robinson-Patman Act of 1936; Sherman Antitrust Act of 1890.*

restricted shares: common stock released under an arrangement whereby the shares do not rank for dividends until some event has taken place, usually the attainment of a certain level of earnings.

restrictive license: an agreement under whose terms an owner of a patented item allows a licensee to sell the patented good under certain limited conditions.

restructuring: method of increasing organizational efficiency and effectiveness that involves making a major change in organization structure and often includes reducing management levels and changing components of the organization through divestiture and/or acquisitions, as well as shrinking the size of the work force.

results orientation: the understanding by sales representatives that they will be judged, and therefore their destiny with the organization determined, by individual selling ability.

retailer: a merchant whose primary activity is to sell directly to consumers.

retailing: the activity of purchasing for resale to a customer.

retail inventory method: see *retail method of inventory.*

retail method of inventory: an accounting technique for recording all inventory inputs, including sales, purchases, markdowns, and so on, at their retail values. Purchased items are recorded at cost.

retail outlet: a store that sells directly to the customer.

retail price: the price at which goods are identified for sale or are sold.

retail price maintenance: allowing a manufacturer, under protection of state law, to set retail prices for his products. This is in accord with the terms of the fair trade acts. See *fair trade acts.*

retained earnings: corporate monies retained after taxes and distribution of dividends to stockholders. Synonymous with *undistributed profits.*

retained risk: the insurance for a stated risk or property that is covered by an insurance firm on its own account after some of the coverage has been reinsured. See *quota-share reinsurance; reinsurance.*

retainer: payment to cover future services and advice, submitted in advance to the individual who is expected to render the services.

retaliatory duty: a differential duty designed to penalize foreign nations for alleged discriminatory commerce activity or to force them into making trade concessions. See *tariff war.* Cf. *most-favored nation status.*

retention:
(1) **insurance:** the amount of liability retained by a company on a given risk. It consists of the gross line less reinsurance.
(2) **human resources:** extent to which a firm is able to retain its employees.

Retiree Benefit Bankruptcy Protection Act: 1988 federal legislation that makes it difficult for companies under the protection of bankruptcy laws to reduce or eliminate medical benefits.

retirement:
(1) **human resources:** voluntary or forced termination of employment because of age, disability, or illness. Contracts usually define the age of retirement, which facilitates establishment of a retirement allowance or pension.
(2) **finance:** the paying off of a debt prior to or at maturity.

retirement fund: monies set aside by an organization in a fund that builds up value over the year to provide income for employees who are eligible to retire and receive income from it.

retirement income: a stipulated amount of income starting at a selected retirement age. This is derived by exercising one of the settlement options available against the policy or annuity cash value. See *individual retirement accounts.*

retiring a bill: paying a bill of exchange on its due date or before, at a discount.

retraining: a technique for preparing employees already within an organization for new skills requirements that are created by various internal (organizational) or external (economic, social, technological, etc.) changes.

retrenchment: reduction of the size or scope of a firm's activities.

retroactive extension: extending the terms (except amount) of present coverage into the period of prior insurance. This is used, for example, in errors and omissions insurance to provide coverage against prior undiscovered losses.

retroactive pay: a delayed wage payment for work done when employees were being paid at a lower rate for the same work. A new contract may provide a wage increase for work that was completed before the agreement goes into effect.

retroactive restoration: a provision in a policy or bond whereby, after payment of a loss, the original amount of coverage is automatically restored to take care of prior undiscovered losses as well as future losses.

retrocession: a reinsuring organization ceding (i.e., reinsuring) a portion of a reinsurance transaction.

retrogression: a procedure in some union contracts permitting a worker who, because of accident, impairment, and sometimes incapacity due to age, has become less productive to return to a position that makes less onerous demands on the individual and still allows the person to hold a job, seniority, and rights.

return: a statement of financial and related information required by government tax agencies (e.g., a tax return). See *yield.*

return item: a negotiable instrument, usually a check, that has been sent to one bank by another for collection and payment and is returned unpaid to the sending bank.

return on investment: see *ROI.*

return on net worth: the ratio of an organization's net profit following taxes to its net worth, providing a measure of the rate of return on a shareholder's investment.

return on stockholders' equity: a measure of performance from a stockholders' viewpoint, computed by dividing net income by average stockholders' equity.

return on total assets: the ratio of an organization's net profit following taxes to its total assets, providing a measure of the rate of return on, or productivity of, total assets.

return premium: the amount due the insured if a policy is reduced in rate, reduced in amount, or canceled, or—if it is subject to audit—if the audit yields a finding of less exposure(s) than the original estimate(s).

returns to vendor: goods sent back to the vendor by a store for various reasons (e.g., damaged merchandise, lateness of delivery). See *vendor charge-backs.* Cf. *purchase allowance.*

revaluation (revalorization): restoration of the value of a depreciated national currency that has previously been devalued by lowering the request for or raising the supply of foreign currencies by restricting imports and promoting exports.

revenue: the grand total of all resources received from the sale of a firm's product or service during a stated period; not to be confused with *general revenue*. Cf. *gross revenue*. See *government revenue*.

Revenue Act of 1962: federal legislation that provided an investment tax credit of 7 percent on new and used property other than buildings. See *Revenue Act of 1964; Revenue Act of 1971; Revenue Act of 1978*.

Revenue Act of 1964: federal legislation that provided for a two-stage cut in personal income tax liabilities and corporate profits tax liabilities in 1964 and 1965. See *Revenue Act of 1962; Revenue Act of 1971; Revenue Act of 1978*.

Revenue Act of 1971: federal legislation that accelerated by one year scheduled increases in personal exemptions and standard deductions. It repealed excise taxes on automobiles retroactive to August 15, 1971, and on small trucks and buses to September 22, 1971. It also reinstated the 7 percent investment tax credit and incorporated depreciation range guidelines. See also *Revenue Act of 1962; Revenue Act of 1964; Revenue Act of 1978*.

Revenue Act of 1978: federal legislation that reduced taxes for individuals and businesses. It contained some elements of tax reform and extended several temporary provisions of the Tax Reduction and Simplification Act of 1977. See *Revenue Act of 1962; Revenue Act of 1964; Revenue Act of 1971; Tax Reduction and Simplification Act of 1977*.

Revenue Adjustment Act of 1975: federal legislation that provided tax reductions for the first six months of 1976. It extended corporate rate reductions enacted in the Tax Reduction Act of 1975 and reduced individual taxes in order to maintain withholding rates that applied during the last eight months of 1975. See *Tax Reduction Act of 1975*.

Revenue and Expenditure Control Act of 1968: federal legislation that levied a 10 percent surtax on personal income taxes, effective April 1, 1968, and on corporate taxes, effective January 1, 1968. It postponed a reduction in excise tax rates on automobiles and telephone service.

revenue bond: see *bond, revenue*.

revenue from own sources: total revenue from taxes, charges, and miscellaneous revenue, and revenue from utilities, liquor stores (where applicable), and insurance trusts.

revenue recognition principle: the concept that revenues should be recorded when the earnings process has been substantially completed and an exchange has taken place.

revenue sharing: the return by a larger unit of government, which has greater taxing powers, of a part of its revenue to a smaller component of government. See *intergovernmental expenditures.* Cf. *grants-in-aid; shared revenue.*

revenue tariffs: duties placed on imports with the goal of increasing revenues rather than protecting domestic industries. Cf. *protective tariff.*

revenue waybill: a written description showing a shipment's charges and goods.

reverse discrimination: the selection of minority persons or women for jobs or education in place of better-qualified whites or men.

reverse stock split: a reduction in the number of outstanding shares. Synonymous with *stock split down.*

reversionary interest: a claim or interest that an individual can keep to property or income that has been assigned to someone else.

revolving fund: money that is renewed as it is used, either by additional appropriations or by income from the programs it finances. Thus the fund retains a balance at all times.

revolving letter of credit: a letter of credit issued for a specific amount that is automatically renewed for the same amount over a given period. Usually the unused renewable portion of the credit is cumulative, so long as drafts are drawn before the expiration of the credit.

revolving loan: a loan that is automatically renewed (upon maturity) without additional negotiation.

reward bases: the various methods for distributing rewards in an organization (e.g., equity, equality, power, and need). A problem arises for management when bases conflict in reward policy.

reward power: the opposite of *coercive power.* It exists when a subordinate perceives that compliance with the wishes of his or her superior will result in positive rewards and recognition, either monetary or psychological.

rhochrematics: the method of managing an entire system of material flow, involving as an integrated system the basic functions of producing and marketing in a selection of the most efficient combination of activities to achieve goals.

RICO: see *Racketeer Influenced and Corrupt Organizations Act.*

riders: in insurance, forms of special provisions that are not contained in the basic policy contract. In bonding and in personal accident insurance, such added clauses are called riders rather than endorsements. See *family income rider.*

rifle technique: the sales practice of concentrating on selling only a few items, using a carefully prepared style of presentation that will lead to a rapid decision. Cf. *shotgun approach.*

rigged market: the situation that exists when purchases and sales are manipulated to distort a normal supply and demand price.

right of rescission: the privilege, guaranteed by the Truth in Lending Act, of canceling a contract under certain circumstances within three business days, without penalty and with full refund of all deposits that have been submitted. See *voidable contract.*

rights: when a company that wants to raise more funds by issuing additional securities gives its stockholders the opportunity, ahead of others, to buy the new securities in proportion to the number of shares each owns, the piece of paper evidencing this privilege. Because the additional stock is usually offered to stockholders below the current market price, rights ordinarily have a market value of their own and are actively traded. In most cases they must be exercised within a relatively short period. Failure to exercise or sell rights may result in actual loss to the holder. See *cum right; sliding scale.*

rights of arbitration: arbitration over interpretation of the meaning of contract terms or employee work grievances.

rights of consumers: a doctrine enunciated by President John F. Kennedy, stating that consumers have the right to be safe, to be informed, to choose, and to be heard.

right-to-work laws: state laws that make it illegal for a collective agreement to contain provisions for union shops, maintenance of membership, preferential hiring, or any other clauses calling for compulsory union membership. State legislatures are empowered under the rule of the Taft-Hartley Act to pass laws that are more restrictive than the union security provisions of federal law (i.e., the Wagner-Connery Act). The courts have also granted the states authority to enforce the law. Some states have amended their constitutions to prohibit enactment of union security provisions within their states.

ring: synonymous with *pit.*

ripening cost: the cost of waiting for an investment to provide a return (e.g., the cost of waiting for land to increase in value or become suitable for development).

risk:
  (1) **general:** any chance of loss.
  (2) **insurance:** the insured or the peril insured against.
risk capital:
  (1) **general:** capitalization that is not secured by a lien.
  (2) **finance:** long-term loans or capital invested in high-risk business activities.
  (3) **securities:** common stock from a new enterprise.
risk decisions: decision situations in which managers do not know for certain the probability of occurrence of the state of nature or of competitive actions but have some past experience and/or data upon which they can develop probabilities. These probabilities are used with conditional values to determine expected values.
risk experience program: the procedure of keeping a listing of premiums and losses on larger risks for the underwriter's reference.
risk management: an approach of management that is concerned with the preservation of the assets and earning power of the business against risks of accidental loss.
risk propensity: a personality characteristic involving a person's like or dislike for taking chances.
risk taker: one who is willing to take chances and may aggressively seek out chancy situations that offer the possibility of significant payoffs.
risky shift phenomenon: the concept that the action of people as individuals is often radically different from their group behavior and thus that the shift away from conformity can be risky.
rival unionism: competition between two or more unions for members and recognition in a company and/ or industry. See *raid*.
RJP: see *realistic job previews*.
Robinson-Patman Act of 1936: federal legislation, amending the Clayton Antitrust Act of 1914, in which price discrimination practices are more clearly identified. Quantity discounts in excess of the cost savings realized by selling in such quantities are declared illegal, as are false brokerage deals. Promotional allowances must be made to all buyers on a proportionately equal basis, and price discrimination is acceptable if it is done to meet a proper low price of a competitor and if the price does not restrict competition.
rock bottom: (slang) the lowest level that will be entertained in a business transaction (e.g., the rock bottom price is the lowest price at which a seller will agree to sell his or her goods).

ROG dating: receipt-of-goods dating. Under this condition of sales, the date for payment and the discount period are determined from the date the buyer obtains shipment, rather than from the invoice date. This procedure is primarily employed when great shipping distances are involved. Cf. *regular dating.*

ROI: return on investment. The amount earned in direct proportion to the capital invested. See *private rate of return.*

role ambiguity: lack of clarity about what or how a person is to do a job.

role analysis team building: a process designed to clarify role expectations and responsibilities of team members. This clarification can be brought about by group meeting and discussion.

role conflict: a situation in which an individual faces two or more role requirements simultaneously and the performance of one role would prevent the fulfillment of the other. See *approach-approach conflict; avoidance-avoidance conflict.*

role perception: an individual's view of how he or she is supposed to act in a given situation.

rolling stock: the physical property of a railroad that performs on rails on the railroad's own wheels (locomotives, passenger cars, etc.).

rollover: see *refunding.*

ropes, know the: (slang) to be completely familiar with the details of a task or business venture.

roping: the machinations of management spies, who bring a worker among them and offer a bribe in return for information about the activities of a union. Synonymous with *hooking.*

Rorabaugh reports: quarterly statements on spot advertising expenditures in television that are released by a private advertising consultant every three months.

rotating shift: changing of crews, usually done to distribute day and night work on an equal basis.

roundabout process: a process that utilizes less direct but more efficient means of production, although investment in equipment must be made to initiate the modification.

round lot: a unit of trading or a multiple thereof. It is usually a unit of trading of 100 shares in stocks or $1,000 par value in bonds. The unit of trading in some inactive stocks is 10 shares. Cf. *odd-lot orders.* Synonymous with *full lot.*

round-table interview: an interview that consists of a discussion of a stated topic by several candidates for employment under the leadership of a discussor. The discussion is observed and evaluated by several executives or other officers who, although present, do not participate in any way.

round turn: the completion of an order to purchase a futures contract and later sell it, or the reverse.

routing: the selection of a path and steps in the operations performed on materials during the manufacturing process. Cf. *traffic.*

royalty: compensation for the use of a person's property, based on an agreed percentage of the income arising from its use (e.g., to an author on sales of his or her book; to a manufacturer for use of his machinery in another manufacturer's factory; to a composer or a performer). It is a payment reserved by a grantor of a patent, lease, or similar right, whereas a residual payment is often made on properties that have not been patented or are not patentable. See *syndicate.*

RTC: see *Resolution Trust Corporation.*

RTC Oversight Board: the arms of the Executive Branch responsible for setting broad policies for RTC. Is ultimately held accountable for fraud and other mismanagement problems at RTC. Oversees the work of the RTC, to set general policy guidelines for RTC management and to dispense funds for S&L closings. See *Resolution Trust Corporation.*

rubber check: (slang), a bad check returned by a bank because of lack of funds in the account against which it is drawn.

rubricated account: any earmarked account.

Rucker plan: a group incentive program that uses day-to-day employee participation and broad coverage to determine where cost reductions can be made and to improve company profits. Productivity advances are measured in terms of money, not physical components.

run:

(1) **general:** an action of a large number of people (e.g., a run on a bank occurs when a great many customers make massive withdrawals of funds).

(2) **transportation:** a work assignment.

runaway: the condition in which part of a system undergoes a sudden or undesirable and often destructive increase in activity.

runaway inflation: synonymous with *galloping inflation.*

runaway shop: a company or plant that moves its facilities to another state; among other reasons, to avoid existing state labor laws, the activities of a particular union, or a union contract that it has agreed on.

runner: a best-selling item, especially one that is continually kept in stock because of its heavy sales volume. Cf. *sleeper.*

running costs: direct or indirect costs that result from keeping an operation and/or machinery functioning. These costs include wages, rent, and taxes.

running days: consecutive days, including Sundays, as distinguished from working days, which exclude Sundays.

run-off election: a procedure used by the National Labor Relations Board when no single union receives a first-poll majority in a representation election. A second election is called for, in which participants are to select between the two unions receiving the highest votes. Cf. *representation election.*

run on a bank: see *run.*

run sizes: the number of items manufactured at one time in a given lot.

S

sabbatical leave: a leave granted at intervals, usually to a teacher for study or travel. It is increasingly used by organizations awarded to promising employees.

sabotage, industrial: a deliberate attempt to slow down production by workers who believe they have a grievance against their employer. It may take the form of wasting time, making equipment unworkable, or, at an extreme, the actual destruction of machinery. See *Luddites*.

sack: (slang) to discharge a worker.

sacrifice: to make a sale at a loss for purposes of raising cash, with the awareness that the profit will be lowered.

safety factor: the ratio of the interest on a funded debt to the net income after the payment of the interest.

safety stock: a minimum inventory, that provides a cushion against reasonably expected maximum demand and against variations in lead time.

sag: a minimal drop or price weakness of shares, usually resulting from a weak demand for the securities.

SAIF: see *Savings Association Insurance Fund*.

salary: compensation received by an employee for services rendered during a specified period. See *wage*. Synonymous with *stipend*.

salary administration: policies and procedures created for the compensation of white-collar employees and executives.

salary compression: a wage and salary program whereby salaries for one employee group slowly move up toward those for higher-classification jobs. It often stifles enthusiasm for promotions, boosts turnover, and increases personnel costs.

salary reduction plan: a scheme that permits workers to defer a percentage of their salary each year and place that money into a company profit-sharing or savings plan, where the funds accumulate tax-free until they are withdrawn when the worker quits, retires, or reaches the age of 59-1/2 years.

salary review: the examination of an employee's wage rate in terms of his or her performance and cost of living or other economic factors.

salary standardization: the process of integrating rates of pay with the duties and responsibilities performed by employees. The result is equal pay for equal work.

sale: the transfer of title to an item or items or the agreement to perform a service in return for cash or the expectation of cash payment.

sales:

(1) **merchandising:** final sales plus producer item sales.

(2) **marketing:** synonymous with *net sales.*

(3) **finance:** revenue received from the sale of goods.

(4) **accounting:** the sum of the income received when goods and services are sold.

(5) see *selling.*

sales agent: a middleman who undertakes to sell the entire output of items of a business that he or she represents.

sales allowance: a lowering of the price on an item when merchandise delivered is not exactly what was ordered by a buyer.

sales analysis: an aspect of market research involving the systematic study and comparison of sales information.

sales anchors: concepts and statements used by sales representatives when attempting to overcome customer resistance.

sales aptitude: the capability to achieve success in the sales field, as acknowledged by a sales department and measured by means of interviews and recommendations.

sales branch: a producer's outlet that maintains inventory and delivers to buyers from that stock.

sales budget: a budget based on forecasted sales for a coming period.

sales discount: a reduction in the sales price that is allowed if payment is received within a specified period. Synonymous with *cash discount.*

sales engineer: a person who sells products that require technical knowledge and training.

sales finance company: a financial organization that purchases installment contracts from dealers and finances dealers' inventories.

sales force: canvassers and sales representatives who contact potential purchasers of goods and attempt to persuade them that they should buy the items being sold.

sales forecast: a dollar or unit sales estimate made for a specified period in a marketing campaign.

sales forecast opportunity variance: a measure of the differential between scheduled capacity and the master budget sales forecast capacity, usually expressed in dollars.

sales journal: a book in which records of sales are entered.

sales manager: an executive responsible for planning, directing, and controlling the activities of sales personnel. Cf. *product manager.*

salesmanship: the art of selling goods or services by creating a demand or need for a particular item and realizing an actual order.

sales manual: a book describing the product, merchandise, or service to be sold and suggesting approaches for selling to a customer.

sales mix: a combination of the various company products leading to a firm's total sales.

sales office: a facility for taking orders and handling adjustments that serves as a contact point for suppliers and customers. No inventory is maintained at the office. Cf. *merchandise mart*.

sales pitch: a strong statement aimed at persuading a potential customer to buy the salesman's product or service.

sales plan: a merchandise budget that contains a detailed projection of sales for a given period, specifying the purchases, inventory, and so on, needed to achieve this goal.

sales presentation: the total selling process of describing to a potential customer the product or service, including the attempt to place an order. See *trial close*.

sales promotion: see *promotion (retailing)*.

sales quota: a projected goal for sales of a product. Usually the quota is established as part of a marketing campaign.

sales returns and allowances: a contra-sales account in which the returns of or allowances for previously sold merchandise are recorded.

sales tax: a tax levied by a state or municipality on items at the time of their purchase. It may be a tax on the sale of an item every time it changes hands or only upon its transfer of ownership at one specific time. The sales of manufacturers are taxed when the items are considered to be completed goods; the sales of wholesalers are taxed when their goods are sold to retailers; and retail sales are taxed when the goods are purchased by consumers. See *tax*.

sales trainee: a recently hired sales representative who is engaged in learning the basic concepts of selling. Usually the trainee receives a small salary during this period.

salvage:

(1) **general:** equipment or property that is no longer used for its initial purpose.

(2) **insurance:** damaged property taken over by an insurance firm following payment of a claim; in marine insurance, the cost of saving property that is exposed to a peril. See *recovery; salvage value*.

(3) **merchandising:** goods that are soiled beyond reclamation for pur-

poses of sale and thus usually disposed of by other means.

salvage value:
(1) **accounting:** the expected worth of a depreciable item at the end of its service life.
(2) **insurance:** the value remaining in property or goods that have been damaged by a peril. See *salvage.*

sanction:
(1) **business law:** a penalty for the breach of a rule of law.
(2) **international business:** a coercive measure, usually undertaken by several nations, to force another country to cease violation of a treaty or an international agreement. See *embargo.*

Sarbanes-Oxley Act: executive certification of financial results was made a permanent accounting reform legislative package signed by President Bush in July 2002; requires CEOs and CFOs for all 15,000 publicly traded companies in the U.S., including foreign companies quoted in New York, to file statements each quarter swearing to the accuracy and completeness of their major financial filings. Executives who make false statements could be prosecuted and imprisoned. Also bans subsidized personal loans to top executives and requires prompt disclosure of share dealings to repay company loans. See *Corporate Accountability Act of 2002.*

SARs: see *stock-appreciation rights.*

satisfaction: a criterion of effectiveness that refers to an organization's ability to gratify the needs of its employees. Synonymous with *morale.*

satisficing: decision-making behavior in which the manager selects an alternative that is good enough, (i.e., one that will yield a satisfactory return to the organization).

Satisfiers: in F. Herzberg's theory of satisfiers and dissatisfiers, the activities in a job that bring satisfaction to the worker (e.g., the work itself, the quality of supervision). See *job enrichment.* Cf. *dissatisfiers; organizational climate.*

saturation: the phase of the product lifecycle in which an item is no longer able to be sold because most consumers who are likely to be interested in it have already purchased it. See *product life cycle.*

saturation campaign: intensive use of radio or television advertising to promote or sell a product in a market. There are usually special low rates for saturation-level advertising. See *flight saturation.*

Saturday night special: (slang) a direct tender offer, made without any forewarning, that expires in one week. Such offerings were made possible by the Williams Act of 1968, which permits tender offers to run as short as seven days and does not require the bidder give advance notification.

saving: the amount of existing income that is not spent on consumption. Cf. *overseeing*.

savings account: money that is deposited in a bank, usually in small amounts periodically over a long period, and is not subject to withdrawal by check. Savings accounts usually bear interest, and some banks levy a service charge for excess withdrawal activity on an account. Synonymous with *thrift account*.

savings and investment theory: the concept developed by John Maynard Keynes and D. H. Robertson that business cycles occur because people save either more or less than the amounts invested in new capital. Cf. *veil of money theory*.

savings and loan association: a mutual, cooperative, quasi-public financial institution that is owned by its members (depositors) and chartered by a state or by the federal government. The association receives the savings of its members and uses these funds to finance long-term amortized mortgage loans to its members and to the general public. Such an association may also be organized as a corporation owned by stockholders. See *Cincotta-Conklin Bill of 1976; Savings Association Insurance Fund*.

Savings Association Insurance Fund (SAIF): formerly the Federal Savings and Loan Insurance Corporation, which insures deposits up to $100,000 at thrift institutions and has been depleted by massive failures. Higher premiums from S&Ls will be put toward replenishing this fund. SAIF replaces the now insolvent FSLIC. See *Savings Industry Bill*.

savings bank: a banking association whose purpose is to promote thrift and savings habits in a community. It may be either a stock organization (a bank with a capital stock structure) or a mutual savings bank. Until passage of the Cincotta-Conklin Act in New York State and other similar bills, a savings bank had no power to perform commercial functions except specialized interest-bearing savings accounts, investing these savings in long-term bonds, mortgage loans, and other investment opportunities for the benefit of all depositors. Now, in many states, a savings bank may offer checking account privileges to its customers.

Savings Bond: see *Bond, Savings (U.S.)*.

Savings Industry Bill: law signed by President George Bush on August 9, 1989, under which hundreds of savings and loan associations over time were permanently closed; others merged, and still others reopened under stricter federal security. The independent regulatory apparatus of the Federal Home Loan Bank Board was subsumed by a new Treasury Department entity called the Office of Thrift Supervision. Responsibility for insuring the deposits of savings and loan associations moved to the Federal Deposit Insurance Corporation, and to a new body called the Resolution Trust Corporation. The law called for outlays of some $166 billion over 10 years to close and merge insolvent institutions, and many more billions after that, representing the largest federal rescue on record. That represented $50 billion to shut the savings institutions that were insolvent, $40 billion to cover the costs of rescues undertaken in 1988, $33 billion to cover future failures of savings institutions, and $43 billion in interest payments. Over 30 years, including interest, the cost is estimated at nearly $300 billion, with taxpayers paying about $225 billion and the healthy portion of the industry paying the rest. The fund insuring savings and loan deposits, the Federal Savings and Loan Insurance Corporation, moved to the Federal Deposit Insurance Corporation. The Savings Association Insurance Fund (SAIF) replaced the FSLIC. The Resolution Trust Corporation was created to sell more than $300 billion in real estate owned by bankrupt savings and loans.

savings rate: the ratio of income saved to income earned.

SBA: see *Small Business Administration.*

SBUs: see *strategic business units.*

scab: (slang) a worker in a struck plant who continues on the job during a strike; more specifically, one who fills the job of a striker. Synonymous with *blackleg; boll weevil.*

scalar chain principle: an organizational concept wherein the graded chain of authority is created through the delegation process.

scale order: an order to buy (or sell) a security that specifies the total amount to be bought (or sold) and the amount to be bought (or sold) at specified price variations.

scaling: trading in securities by placing orders for purchase or sale at intervals of price instead of giving the order in full at the market price or at a stated price.

scalper: a speculator who constantly sells his or her shares at fractional profit or at one or two points profit per share.

Scanlon plan: a management incentive scheme designed by Joseph Scanlon of MIT to achieve increased productivity with improved efficiency by distributing accrued savings among the employees.

scarcity value: an increase in value caused by a demand for an item whose supply cannot be increased (e.g., works of art from the nineteenth century).

scare purchasing: purchasing to hoard; unusually heavy buying of items in short supply.

schedule:

(1) **insurance:** a type of individual risk rating that measures, based on physical characteristics of the risk, the extent to which a particular risk deviates from the average of its class. This deviation is reflected in the scheduled rate for the risk.

(2) **advertising:** a list of ads, by stated media, giving dates of appearance, space, time, and so on.

(3) **administration:** a systematic plan for future operations over a given period.

schedule bond: see *bond, schedule.*

scheduled maintenance: maintenance carried out in accordance with an established plan. It is often used as a preventive measure to assure efficiency in the operation of equipment (e.g., replacement of tubes, lubrication of moving parts).

scheduled production: the rate of activity assigned for the production of a given item in a specified period. Cf. *production capacity.*

schedule of insurance: a list of individual items covered under one policy (e.g., various buildings, animals, and other property in farm insurance; rings and bracelets insured under a jewelry floater).

schedule of variance: the difference between actual production and scheduled production.

scheduling:

(1) **marketing:** the organization and control of the time needed to carry out a sales effort.

(2) **human resources:** determining which employee will work when and at which machine or in which department; and determining the work itself.

scientific management: popularized in the work of Frederick W. Taylor that includes approaches to increased efficiency, cost reductions, and maximum utilization of human and material resources. Cf. *prescientific management.*

scientific tariff: a duty to cover foreign and domestic manufacturing costs.

scouting: a recruiting technique used to obtain the best-qualified persons in the nation. Scouting is carried out more actively in a tight labor market.

scrambled merchandising: an approach by retail outlets of maintaining types of goods not normally found in those stores (e.g., clothing and large appliances sold in a drugstore).

scratch daily report: a copy of the daily report completed by the underwriter or rater, or both, for use by the policy writer in preparing the policy. Cf. *daily reports.*

scratch endorsement: a copy of an endorsement completed by the underwriter or rater, or both, for use by the policy writer in incorporating the endorsement into the policy. Cf. *endorsement.*

screening controls: forms of concurrent control by which managers often try to identify critical "go, no go" stages of organizational activity.

scrip: a temporary document that entitles the holder or bearer to receive stock or a fractional share of stock in a corporation, cash, or some other article of value on demand or at some specified future date. Some industries issue scrip to their employees as a supplement to salary, for use in company-owned stores.

scrip dividend: a type of dividend issued by a corporation to its stockholders, entitling the holder or bearer to receive cash, stock, or a fractional share of stock, or one or more units of the product manufactured upon presentation or at a specified future date.

SCT: see *service counter terminal.*

SDRs: see *special drawing rights.*

sealing:
(1) **advertising:** reducing or enlarging an illustration or ad.
(2) **securities:** concealed bids that are simultaneously revealed. The most attractive one is accepted on the spot, without further bidding.

search: the process of recruiting executive talent for a specific organization.

search firms: private, for-profit organizations that exist to help employers locate hard-to-find applicants. Cf. *private placement agencies.*

seasonal appointment: a temporary appointment.

seasonal discount: a price reduction given for purchases made out of season (e.g., ski equipment can usually be bought at a discount in the spring). Cf. *static inventory problem.*

seasonal employee: a worker who is employed for limited periods of activity (e.g., for harvesting during the fall).

seasonal fluctuations: regular and predictable shifts in business activity created by changes in the season (e.g., housing construction increases during the spring).

seasonal forecast: changes in market demand that depend primarily on the time of year.

seasonal industry: an industry that has high peaks of employment at specified times of the year and down periods during other seasons.

seasonal unemployment: joblessness due to seasonality of the work. Teachers who do not work during the summer months are representative of the seasonally unemployed.

seasoned issues: securities from well-established corporations that have been favorably known to the investment population over time, including good and bad periods.

seasoned security: a security possessing a fine performance record in the paying of dividends or interest; one that has been listed for a considerable period of time and sells at a relatively stable price.

seat on the exchange: a traditional figure of speech designating membership on an exchange. Price and admission requirements vary.

SEC (Securities and Exchange Commission): established by Congress to protect investors. The SEC administers the Securities Act of 1933, the Securities Exchange Act of 1934, the Trust Indenture Act, the Investment Company Act, the Investment Advisers Act, and the Public Utility Holding Company Act. The principal provisions of these acts are (1) that the Securities and Exchange Commission, created in 1934, administers the federal laws applying to securities; (2) that corporations issuing securities and investment bankers selling them must make full disclosure of the character of the securities (i.e., they must state all relevant facts in registration statements to the SEC and in prospectuses submitted to the public); see also *waiting period;* (3) that any omission of fact or insertion of false information makes all persons (bankers, lawyers, accountants, etc.) whose names appear on the prospectus and the registration statement liable to the purchasers of the securities for any losses suffered; (4) that organization of people (brokers, traders, etc.) to manipulate the prices of securities is forbidden; see *pool;* (5) that dealings by corporation officers in securities of their own corporations are restricted; and (6) that the Board of Governors of the Federal Reserve System is given power to fix margin requirements on loans secured by bonds and stocks. See *National Association of Securities Dealers; pool; waiting period.*

secondary boycott: see *boycott.*

secondary distribution: the redistribution of a block of stock some time after it has been sold by the issuing company. The sale is handled off the exchange by a securities firm or group of firms, and the shares are usually offered at a fixed price that is related to the current market price of the stock. Cf. *distribution.* Synonymous with *secondary offering.*

secondary employment: synonymous with *moonlighting.*

secondary offering: the selling by a large stockholder of a large block of shares. Such a sale is frequently made on an exchange, to minimize the impact on the general market. Synonymous with *secondary distribution.*

secondary picketing: see *picketing.*

secondary reserves: assets other than primary reserves retained by banks and capable of being rapidly converted into cash. Government bonds are a prime example.

secondary strike: a strike called against an employer doing business with another company whose workers are on strike.

secondary worker: a person who is part of a household that has a major earner and who can therefore choose whether or not to work, depending on wage and unemployment conditions. Secondary workers include children, retired persons, and spouses.

second-level outcome: the effect brought about by a first-level outcome, such as a promotion (second-level outcome) brought about by increased productivity (first-level outcome).

second-mortgage bond: see *bond, second-mortgage.*

seconds: goods bearing defects that have possible effects on wearability and appearance. See *bargain store.* Cf. *firsts.*

second sale: a sale achieved by building on a customer's receptive mood following an initial purchase; an additional sale to the same person.

secret partner: an active partner in an organization whose capacity as a partner is not known to the public. Cf. *silent partner.*

secular inflation: the most serious economic problem of the late 1960s and the 1970s. In contrast to cyclical inflation, which moves in and out of the economic system roughly every two years, secular inflation is primarily a long-term social phenomenon. Cf. *cyclical inflation.*

secular stagnation: a low level of economic movement measured over an extended time period.

secular trend: a tendency of values in a time series to move upward or downward over a number of years.

secular unemployment: unemployment resulting from changes in the economic system whose long-run effect is a decline in employment. See *technological unemployment.*

secured bond: see *bond, secured.*

secured creditor: a creditor whose obligation is made safe or backed by a pledge or collateral. See *collateral.*

secured debt: any debt for which some form of acceptable collateral has been pledged.

secured loan: a loan that is made safe, or backed, by marketable securities or other marketable values.

securities: documents that identify legal ownership of a physical commodity or legal claims to another's wealth.

Securities and Exchange Commission: see *SEC.*

Securities Exchange Act: see *SEC.*

securities firm: an organization that relies for its income on other firms' securities, which it retains for investment. It may also issue stocks and bonds of its own. Synonymous with *investment company.* See *holding company.*

securities trading:

(1) selling or buying securities through recognized channels.

(2) the operations of brokers in the various exchanges.

security:

(1) **general:** property pledged as collateral.

(2) **insurance:** protection against risk.

(3) **business law:** any evidence of debt or right to a property.

(4) **business law:** an individual who agrees to make good the failure of another to pay.

(5) **securities:** stocks and bonds placed by a debtor with a creditor, with authority to sell for the creditor's account if the debt is not paid.

security agreement: the agreement between a seller and a buyer that the seller shall have an interest in the goods. The security agreement must be signed by the buyer and must describe the goods.

security anchor: need for stability in one's career, either by remaining with the same company or by staying in a particular geographic area.

security capital: low-risk capital (e.g., government bonds; mortgages).

security needs: Maslow's second set of human needs, which reflects the desire to keep free from physical harm. See *hierarchy of needs.*

segmentation research: a form of marketing research that uncovers new bases for market segmentation.

segregation: separating from an operating or holding firm one or more of its subsidiaries or operating divisions, effected by distributing stock of the subsidiary to the parent company's shareholders.

selection: the process of choosing from a number of job applicants the one individual to be offered a position and/or advancement.

selection ratio: a ratio expressed as the number of individuals hired to fill a particular job divided by the number of applicants.

selective blend situation: strategy situation entailing major changes in organizational strategy that blends both outsiders and insiders to perform corrective measures.

selective demand: demand for a particular brand.

selective distribution (selling): choosing retail outlets that will be permitted to receive one's merchandise for sale.

self-actualization: drive to become what one is capable of becoming.

self-appraisal: performance appraisal done by the employee being evaluated, generally on an appraisal form completed by the employee prior to the performance interview.

self-concept theory: the notion that two factors influencing an individual's purchasing behavior are how the person perceives himself or herself, and how he or she wishes to be perceived by others. Cf. *motivation, unconscious.*

self-employed: the gainfully occupied part of the workforce whose members work for themselves, as opposed to salaried or commissioned workers who are the employees of others.

self-esteem: individual's degree of liking or disliking for themselves.

self-insurance: a system whereby a firm or individual, by setting aside an amount of money, provides for the occurrence of any losses that could ordinarily be covered under an insurance program. The monies that would normally be used for premium payments are added to this special fund for payment of losses incurred. See *service excess.*

self-leadership: ability of workers to motivate themselves to perform both tasks that are naturally rewarding and those that are necessary but not appealing.

self-liquidating: an asset that can be converted into cash or is subject to total recovery of invested money over a period of time.

self-liquidating loan: a short-term commercial loan, usually supported by a lien on a given product or on sale of the product or commodities.

self-mailer: a direct-mail piece that can be sent through the mail without using an envelope or wrap.

self-managed work teams: groups of 10 to 15 people who take on responsibilities of their former supervisors.

self-management: learning techniques that allow individuals to manage their own behavior so that less external management control is necessary.

self-reducing clause: a life insurance statement that has the effect of lowering an obligation or mortgage. The amount of insurance automatically drops during the term of the policy, matching the lowering amount of the debt involved.

self-selection selling: a merchandising approach that allows customers to make their choices without the initial assistance of sales help.

self-service: a sales outlet or store in which the customer chooses the items to be purchased, removes them from the shelves, carries them to a checkout counter for completion of the transaction, and carries or sends them to the place of use.

seller's lien: the seller's privilege of holding onto certain items until the buyer has delivered payment. See *general lien.* Cf. *carrier's lien; vendor's lien.*

sellers' market: a market in which demand is greater than supply, resulting in sellers setting the prices and terms of sale. It is a market characterized by rising or high prices.

seller's option: a special transaction on an exchange whereby the seller holding the option can deliver the stocks or bonds at any time within a specified period, ranging from not less than six business days to not more than 60 days. seller's seven sale: an agreed-upon delay of seven or more days for the delivery of a security. See *settlement day.*

seller's surplus: the difference between the price a seller actually receives and the lowest price that he or she would accept.

selling: the process of assisting and/ or persuading a potential customer to buy merchandise or services.

selling costs: marketing costs (e.g., advertising, sales promotion) necessary to attract a potential buyer to an item or service.

selling group: syndicated dealers of an underwriting company that operate in the public sale of an issue of securities.

selling price: the cash price that a customer must pay for purchased items.

selling short: a trading technique employed when a drop in the market price of a security is expected. A temporarily borrowed stock is sold to effect delivery. If the price drops, the trader can purchase the security for less than he or she sold it, pay the borrowing cost, and clear a profit. See *bear position; loaned flat.*

sell out:

(1) **general:** to betray a person, organization, or cause, usually for profit or special treatment.

(2) **securities:** to close out a customer's account by selling held securities or commodities.

(3) **business:** to dispose of an entire stock or set of products.

(4) **labor relations:** pertaining to a union leader, to conclude a negotiation that is unpopular with the membership. This may imply that the leader is believed to have received personal gain from the settlement.

semi-autonomous teams: work groups that have considerable input into managing the activities in their own work area but are still headed by a supervisor.

semiskilled labor: a worker's level of performance between skilled and unskilled. It is often applied to workers who have had some training and perform routine tasks.

semivariable costs: synonymous with *mixed costs.*

send money: funds set aside to commence an activity.

senior bond: see *bond, senior.*

senior issue: see *junior issue.*

seniority: an employee's length of service, used as a factor in determining salary, benefits, and promotion priorities. See *bumping.*

sensitive market: a market characterized by fluctuations determined by the announcement of favorable or unfavorable news.

sensitivity training: a form of educational experience, conducted in small classes called T-groups, that stresses the emotional dynamics of self-development training. The training may be highly structured or highly unstructured, to permit the participants to learn more about their strengths and weaknesses. See *critical incident; situational theory of leadership.*

separation: conflict resolution technique in which parties on opposite sides of a conflict are kept apart until they agree to a solution.

separation rate: the average number of persons dropped from a payroll per 100 employees. See *turnover (human resources).* Cf. *accession rate.*

September 11, 2001: terrorists destroy the World Trade Towers in New York City and a portion of the Pentagon in Washington, D.C., with a significant loss of lives and negative impact on the U.S. economy. See *Black Tuesday*.

sequential interdependence: the relationship between units of an organization such that the product of one is passed along to the next in order, after which the final product results.

sequestered account: an account that has been impounded under due process of law. Since disbursement of such an account is subject to court order, the account is usually set up in a separate control. See *frozen account; receiver*.

serial bond: see *bond, serial*.

serial organization: a type of organization in which the entire process of accomplishing a job is assigned to one specific department, division, or unit.

SERP: see *Supplementary Employee Retirement Plan*.

service charge: a payment by a financial institution against an individual or organization for services rendered.

service costs: the operating costs of service departments that are usually allocated to production departments.

service counter terminal (SCT): a device for handling information, located in retail stores and similar places, through which individuals can obtain access to funds and possibly credit at their disposal, for purposes of making deposits and withdrawals and potentially for making third-party payments. See *electronic funds-transfer system*.

service department: an organizational unit that does not directly produce goods but serves other departments.

service excess: a special program for large risks wherein claims within a large-deductible or self-insured retention are serviced by the insurer for a fee. Excess insurance is then written by the company to cover the losses above the insured's retention. Cf. *excess insurance*.

service life: the anticipated time of usefulness of an asset.

service salesperson: a person who sells intangibles, such as insurance and advertising.

setback: a reversal or partial loss in an activity.

settlement day: the deadline by which a purchaser of stock must pay for what has been bought and the seller must deliver the certificates for the securities that have been sold. The settlement day is usually the fifth business day following the execution of an order. Cf. *shave (securities)*.

settlement options: provisions in a life policy or annuity contract for alternative methods of settlement in place of lump-sum payments.

settling down: time period when most people begin working hard to establish the groundwork for their career advancement.

setup: the time or costs needed before production of an item can commence. See *lead time*.

severance pay: synonymous with *dismissal pay*.

severity rate: a formula used to compute the number of days lost because of accidents per million people-hours worked.

sex differential: differences in rates for work of comparable quality and quantity that are based on the worker's sex. It is now generally forbidden by federal law. See *Civil Rights Act of 1964; Equal Pay Act of 1963; equal pay for equal work*.

sexual harassment: unwelcome advances, requests for sexual favors, and other verbal or physical conduct of a sexual nature.

shading: giving a small reduction in a price or terms of a sale.

shakeout:

(1) **securities:** shift inactivity that forces speculators to sell their shares.

(2) **finance:** a trend or shift in an industry that forces weaker members toward bankruptcy.

shapeup: a lineup of men seeking work in the maritime industry, from which steamship or stevedoring companies select the workers they want. Cf. *hiring hall*.

share: a unit of stock that names the holder and indicates ownership in a corporation.

shared management agreement: management arrangement in which each partner in a strategic alliance fully and actively participates in managing the alliance.

share draft: an order by a credit union member to pay to a third party against funds on deposit with the credit union and cleared through a commercial bank.

shared revenue: payments to the states and localities of a portion of the proceeds from the sale of certain federal property, products, and services, and payments to the territories of certain federal tax collections derived within their boundaries or from transactions affecting them. Synonymous with *intergovernmental revenue*. Cf. *revenue sharing*.

shareholder: the possessor of shares or stocks in an organization (company, corporation, etc.).

share loan: a simple interest loan secured by funds on deposit at a credit union or a savings and loan institution. One purpose of a share loan is to preserve dividends due on deposits by not withdrawing the funds until the dividend payment date.

share of advertising method: a method of setting the advertising budget based on a share of the total advertising expenditures in a specific field.

share of audience: the percentage of radio or television sets in use or households watching a particular program. Cf. *audience flow; Hooperating; Nielsen rating.*

share of the market: the ratio or percentage of an advertiser's sales to the total industry sales, based on an actual or potential standard.

shares outstanding: the shares issued by a corporation, excluding treasury stock.

share-the-work: retention of jobs by shortening the work week for the entire employee group rather than laying off some of the workers. See *work sharing.*

shark repellent: (slang) a state statute that demands strict notification and disclosure of tender offers for companies incorporated or transacting business within its boundaries.

shave:

(1) **finance:** a charge higher than the accepted rate that is made for handling a note or other instrument of low quality or for which the seller will take a smaller amount for any reason.

(2) **securities:** the additional charge (premium) made for the right to extend the delivery time on a security. Cf. *settlement day.*

shelf registration: a Securities and Exchange Commission ruling effective March 1983 permitting an issuer to register one big issue of bonds with the SEC. Instead of selling the bonds all at once, issuers will put at least some of them aside—on the shelf—to be sold piecemeal whenever they see a need for funds, find favorable market conditions, or receive a call from a trader or institution offering attractive terms.

shelf-sitters: (slang) upwardly immobile managers who block promotion channels.

shell firm: an organization that is incorporated but does not function or produce any goods or services.

Sherman Antitrust Act of 1890: federal legislation aimed at preventing business monopoly. Some courts, however, applied the sanctions of the law against strikes, and unions were fined triple damages for acts that were considered to be in restraint of trade. New legislation was required to protect the unions against further misinterpretations, since, in the absence of legislative action, antiunion rulings would continue to be sustained under the principle of res adjudicata.

shift: the part of a 24-hour work day comprising a working schedule (e.g., the 8:00 A.M. to 4:00 P.M. shift).

shift differential: additional pay for working more than one shift.

shifting tax: a tax whose burden is transferred from the original tax-payer (individual or organization) to another.

shift premium: extra compensation given to a shift worker for the inconvenience of altering his or her daily working hours. See *shift differential.*

shinplaster:
(1) **general:** any money made worthless either by inflation or by inadequate security.
(2) **banking:** a pre–Civil War term used to depreciate the value of paper money.
(3) **finance:** paper money, usually of less than one dollar face value, once used by some private banks.

shipment:
(1) **general:** delivery and transport of items by a carrier.
(2) **transportation:** a collection of items that are transported as a unit.
(3) **marketing:** merchandise sent to a manufacturer to be processed, or items sent from the manufacturer to a wholesaler or retailer. See *drop shipper; middleman.*

shock loss: a loss larger than expected.

shop chairman: the principal union spokesperson in a work place, usually a worker who is selected by his or her coworkers. Cf. *shop steward.*

shop committee: a group of union members named to speak for the whole union on grievances, negotiations, and other labor-management issues.

shop merchandising: establishing certain locations in a store for serving buyers with special interests (e.g., tennis shop; teen-age corner).

shopping goods: consumer goods that are purchased only after the buyer compares the offerings of more than one store.

shop steward: a union official who represents a specific group of members and the union in grievance matters and other employment conditions. Sometimes called a committeeman. Stewards are usually part of the work force they represent. Cf. *business agent; shop chairman.*

shortage: an excess of quantity demanded over quantity supplied, indicating that price is below equilibrium.

short bill: a bill of exchange that is payable upon request, at sight, or within a brief period, usually less than 10 days.

short covering: buying a stock to return stock previously borrowed to make delivery on a short sale.

shortfall: spending, usually in a governmental agency, that falls sharply below projections, thus contributing to economic sluggishness. Cf. *overage.*

short interest: the sum of the short sales outstanding in a security or commodity or on an exchange stock.

short merchandise:

(1) **general:** goods bought in small quantities, usually in extreme sizes, to complete an assortment.

(2) **merchandising:** purchased goods that were not included in a shipment. See *over, short, and damaged.*

short of destination: prior to reaching the final port, warehouse, or destination.

short of exchange: the position of a foreign exchange trader who has sold more foreign bills than the quantity of bills he or she has in possession to cover the sales.

short position: stocks sold short and not covered as of a particular date. On an exchange, a tabulation is usually issued once a month, listing all issues on the exchange in which there was a short position of 5,000 or more shares and issues in which the short position had changed by 2,000 or more shares in the preceding month. The term is also used for the total amount of stock an individual has sold short and has covered as of a particular date.

short purchase: buying a stock to cover an earlier short sale of the same stock.

short rate: the higher rate an advertiser pays when he or she fails to use the space or time contracted for.

short-rate cancellation: the charge required for insurance or bonds taken for less than one year. In some cases, it denotes the earned premium for insurance or bonds canceled by the insured before the end of the policy period or term of bond. Cf. *pro rata cancellation.*

short run:

(1) **general:** a one-time job.

(2) **finance:** the time during which a firm can alter the price or out-

put of its goods but not change the size of its plant or close down operations.

short sale: a transaction made by a person who believes a stock will decline and places a sell order, although he or she does not own any of the shares. Stock exchange and federal regulations govern and limit the conditions under which a short sale may be made.

short selling: selling a stock and purchasing it at a lower price to receive a profit.

short-tail: (slang) a nonunion worker.

short-term capital flows: investments, such as purchases of stock, deposits of funds in U.S. banks, and investments in Treasury bills and other money market securities, that are expected to remain in a foreign country for less than one year.

short-term capital movements: an item in the balance-of-payments accounts indicating financial obligations due or payable within a year.

short-term debt: an obligation that is usually due within the year.

short-term funds: money borrowed for from 30 days to one year.

short-term investment: an expenditure for nonoperating assets that a business enterprise intends to hold for only a short period of time, usually less than a year.

short ton: 2,000 pounds. Cf. *long ton.*

shotgun approach: a disorganized approach to selling or advertising, aimed at reaching a large number of potential customers without expecting to making sales to all. Cf. *rifle technique.*

shrinkage: see *inventory shortage (shrinkage).*

Shunto: spring wave offensive, in Japan characterized by coordinating collective bargaining by enterprise unions seeking wage increases that mainly pertain to cost-of-living and industry productivity concerns.

shutdown: a stoppage of production due to installation or breakdown of equipment, shortage of work orders, lack of materials or skilled labor, and so on.

SIC: see *Standard Industrial Classification System.*

sick leave: contractually provided conditions under which employees are paid during illness. The individual retains all job rights, including seniority and other privileges.

sick pay: compensation given an employee because of illness, accident, or some other incapacity. The worker retains his or her job rights, including seniority, during the period of receiving sick pay.

side car: see *circuit breakers.*

sideline stores: stores whose primary interest is other than retailing (e.g., a wholesaler who also sells to the consumer as an accommodation).

sight bill of exchange: a bill of exchange that becomes due and payable when presented by the holder to the party on whom it is drawn. See *short bill.*

sight draft: a draft payable upon delivery and presentation to the drawee, or upon sight.

silent partner: an individual who gives funds for a business partnership but takes no part in the management of the firm. This is not to be confused with *secret partner.*

silver handshake: an early-retirement incentive in the form of increased pension benefits for several years or a cash bonus.

simple interest: interest calculated on a principal sum and not on any interest that has been earned by that sum. Cf. *compound interest.*

simple structure: structure characterized by a low degree of departmentalization, wide spans of control, authority centralized in a single person, and little formalization.

simultaneous inflation and unemployment (inflump): a situation calling for a value judgment of whether inflation or unemployment is the more serious problem and whether the economy is moving toward worse inflation or worse unemployment. Cf. *inflation.*

sinecure: a position of limited or nonexistent responsibility that demands little or no labor service.

Single Act: synonymous with *Single European Act.*

single-digit: a percentage smaller than 10, especially with reference to rates below that level.

single entry: a bookkeeping approach in which each transaction is entered only once on the account books. The single-entry system is used primarily by small businesses. Cf. *double entry.*

Single European Act: a major amendment to the Treaty of Rome; to facilitate the adoption of the White Paper measures within its timeframe; adapted the European Community's procedures for decision making and increased the scope for a type of majority (as opposed to unanimous) voting in the Council of Ministers; effective July 1, 1987; ratified by the Parliaments of all 12 member states; improved significantly the institutional system and set new objectives for the Community, notably the completion of the internal market "an area without internal frontiers in which the free movement of goods, persons, services, and capital is ensured in accordance with provisions of this Treaty" by 1992 and the strengthening of economic and social cohesion, without internal frontiers. Synonymous with *Single Act*. See *internal market; White Paper*.

single-line store: a store that carries a wide variety of one type of goods.

single-payment loan: a loan whose entire principal is due on one maturity date.

single proprietorship: ownership of a business by one person.

single rate: a wage rate that is identical for all employees working in the same job or classification.

single-use plans: plans that are used only once or a few times because they focus on organizational situations that do not occur repeatedly.

sinking fund: a fund used to accumulate the cash needed to pay off a bond or other security. By accumulating cash in a sinking fund, the firm is in a better position to pay its securities when due, and the risk is therefore reduced to the security holder. Cf. *contingency fund*.

sinking fund bonds: see *bond, sinking fund*.

sinking fund depreciation: a system for calculating depreciation whereby the yearly amount is presumed to be deposited in a sinking fund that will also increase as a result of earnings from the fund investment.

sit-down strike: a work stoppage in which employees report for work but remain idle at the job. This form of strike is forbidden by law. Cf. *blacking*.

situational analysis: an assessment of the marketing environment; key part of the marketing plan, often referred to as the market review.

situational design theory: the concept that there is no single best way to design an organization. Cf. *organizational analysis and planning; universal design theory*.

situational interview: an interview in which an applicant is given a hypothetical incident and asked how he or she would respond to it. Cf. *structured interview*.

situational theory of leadership: the concept that, before selecting a leadership style, leaders must understand their own behavior, that of their subordinates, and the demands of the tasks. Such understanding requires diagnostic skills in human behavior. See *organic structure; process principles; sensitivity training*.

situs picketing: picketing a subcontractor at a construction site. Under the Taft–Hartley Act, this is a secondary boycott and therefore an illegal practice. See *Taft-Hartley Act*.

skill: an inherent or learned ability to apply one's knowledge and/or experience to one's job, vocation, or profession.

skill-based pay: pay levels based on how many skills employees have or how many jobs they can do.

skills inventories: summaries of each worker's skills and abilities, usually used for nonmanagement workers. See *management inventories*.

skill variety: the degree to which a person must perform several different activities to complete a job, involving the use of a number of skills and talents.

skimming prices: use of a high introductory price followed by a series of price reductions, designed to get all the trade the market will bear at one price level before lowering the price and also to appeal to the more price-conscious consumer.

skim-the-cream pricing: the pricing technique of establishing price at the upper limit of the range.

skip: a customer who moves from a known address without paying the bill of a business or utility.

skippy strike: (slang) an employee's way of showing annoyance with working conditions by disregarding some of the work assignment.

skunkworks: a highly innovative enterprise that uses groups functioning outside traditional lines of authority.

slack:
(1) **production:** the time in which a minor operation can be completed in advance of the next major operation that depends on it.
(2) **business:** dull or inactive business period (e.g., a slack season).

sleeper: a fast-selling item that has the potential to become a runner. Cf. *runner*.

slide: a posting error by which an amount is wrongly recorded by a bookkeeper who unintentionally places the decimal one or more digits to the right or left of the true decimal position.

sliding scale: a reason for increasing or decreasing charges to a customer in relation to the volume of activity or usage over a stated time (e.g., a gas company may charge for gas on a sliding scale, with lower rates for greater consumption).

slippage: lost time.

slow asset: an asset that can be converted into cash, near its book value, only after a lengthy passage of time.

slowdown: lessening of work effort, by concerted agreement among employees, to force, management concessions. A slowdown is sometimes used as an alternative to a strike. Cf. *blacking.*

slump: a short-lived decline in the activity of a business or economy.

small business: an independently owned and managed profit-seeking enterprise with fewer than 100 employees.

Small Business Administration (SBA): a federal agency established in 1953 solely to advise and assist the nation's small businesses. The SBA provides loans, loan guarantees, and other financial assistance, and offers loans to victims of floods, riots, and other catastrophes and to those who have suffered economic harm as a result of federal programs. It also conducts economic research on conditions that affect small businesses.

smart money: experienced and professional security traders who exploit inside information to make profits at the expense of other investors.

smoke damage insurance: insurance against damage caused by smoke from the sudden, unusual, and faulty operation of a heating or cooking unit, but only when such a unit is connected to a chimney by a smoke pipe and while it is on the premises described in the policy. Smoke damage from fireplaces and industrial operations is usually excluded. Cf. *fire insurance.*

smoothing over: in conflict management, the act of diminishing or avoiding a conflict issue.

snake system: an international agreement between Belgium, the Netherlands, Luxembourg, Denmark, Sweden, Norway, and West Germany, linking the currencies of these countries in an exchange rate system. The signatories have agreed to limit fluctuations in exchange rates among their currencies to 2.25 percent above or below set median rates. The snake was designed to be the first stage in forming a uniform Common Market currency. Members maintain fairly even exchange rates among themselves by buying or selling their currencies when the rates threaten to drop or rise beyond the 2.25 percent limits. See *European Economic Community; European Free Trade Association; swap.*

snap strike: a stoppage of work by employees without authorization of the union. See *illegal strike.*

social audit: an identification and evaluation of organizational activities that are believed to have a positive social impact.

social benefit: the value to a society resulting from a specific act or action (e.g., the discovery of penicillin; the invention of the automobile).

social contract: a model conceptualizing the relationship between a firm and society as a whole, whereby the organization is granted freedom to exist and is obligated to function in the public interest.

social (opportunity) cost: the price paid by citizens for the side effects of economic performance (e.g., pollution, destruction of forests). See *comparative advantage*.

social infrastructure expenditures: expenditures for public projects that are established for the good of the community (e.g., highway construction; health care programs).

socialist economy: an economy in which the means of production are owned by the state and economic activity is coordinated by plan.

social marketing: the use of marketing philosophy and techniques in the dissemination of societally useful ideas. The concept was propounded by Phillip Kotler and Gerald Zaltman in the 1970s. See *responsible global capitalism*.

social mobility: ability of individuals to move from one stratum of society to another.

social responsibility: the expectation that companies should act in the public interest and contribute to the solution of social and ecological problems.

social responsiveness approach: an approach to meeting social obligations that considers business to have societal and economic goals as well as the obligation to anticipate upcoming social problems and work actively to prevent their appearance.

social security: the combination of social insurance plans sponsored by the federal government, including old age and survivors' insurance and unemployment insurance. Wage and payroll deductions are made to finance these programs. Federal employees are exempt from contributing to the costs of such coverage.

Social Security Act of 1935: legislation that resulted in a national social insurance program to provide old age and survivors' benefits; public assistance to the aged, the blind, and needy children; unemployment insurance; and disability benefits.

Social Security taxes (FICA): the Federal Insurance Contributions Act taxes imposed on employees and employers, used mainly to provide retirement benefits.

societal environment: forces external to an organization that influence what happens internally. Among these forces are political, regulatory, resource, economic, and technological factors.

sociogram: diagram that graphically maps the preferred social interactions obtained from interviews or questionnaires. See *sociometry*.

sociometry: a technique developed by J. L. Moreno for attempting to match individuals to tasks based on their preferences for coworkers.

sociotechnical systems: an organizational development technique that seeks to obtain a good fit between the organization's technical system and its social system.

soft currency: the funds of a country that are controlled by exchange procedures, thereby having limited convertibility into gold and other currencies.

soft goods: ready-to-wear clothing, piece goods, linens, towels, and small fashion accessories.

soft loan: a loan whose terms of repayment are generous and sometimes have a low rate of interest.

soft money: paper currency, as contrasted with coinage. See *hard money*.

soft sell: a selling technique that is convincing, subtle, and indirect. Cf. *hard sell*.

SOH: stock on hand.

soldiering: the act of loafing on the job or otherwise reducing productivity. See *blacking*.

sole proprietorship: business owned and operated by one person.

solvency: the condition that exists when liabilities, other than those of ownership, amount to less than total assets; the ability to pay debts.

solvent: the condition of an individual who is able to pay his or her debts.

sound value: the value of property for fire insurance purposes. See *actual cash value*.

sourcing strategy: strategy that a company pursues in purchasing materials, components, and final products; can be from domestic and foreign locations and from inside and outside the company.

space buyer: an advertising agency executive who assists in the planning of printed media campaigns and chooses and purchases space in the media. Cf. *time buyer*.

spam: (slang), unwanted e-mail messages, including advertisements. See *spammers*.

spammers: people who send out spams to the public, with little or no regard for privacy. See *spam*.

span of control: the extent of a supervisor's responsibility, usually identified in the organizational chart by lines of authority. See *chain of command; Lockheed model.*

special assessment: the process, by an assessor, court, or board of review, of making formal and official estimation of the value of a property as a basis for levying taxes for raising revenue for special purposes.

special assessment bond: see *bond, special assessment.*

special audit: an audit that is selected to cover a particular phase of activity of a specified time period.

special bid: a method of filling an order to buy a large block of stock on the exchange floor. The bidder for the block of stock pays a special commission to the broker who represents him or her in making the purchase. The seller does not pay a commission. The special bid is made on the floor of the exchange at a fixed price, which may not be below the last sale of the security or the current bid in the regular market, whichever is higher. Member firms may sell this stock for customers directly to the buyer's broker during trading hours.

special drawing rights (SDRs): the amount by which each country is permitted to have its international checking account with the International Monetary Fund go negative before the nation must ask for additional loans. SDRs were established at the Rio de Janeiro conference of 1967.

special events recruiting: an effort on the part of a single employer or group of employers to attract a large number of applicants for interviews by use of job fairs, open houses, and the like. See re*cruiting.*

special interest account: used by commercial banks to describe a savings account. Some states do not permit a commercial bank to accept savings accounts. In such cases, deposits may be accepted on which interest is paid under the same interest-bearing rates as a savings bank, but another name, such as special interest accounts, must be used. Synonymous with *thrift account.*

special issues: securities issued by the Treasury for investment of reserves of government trust funds and for certain payments to veterans.

specialist: a member of an exchange who has two functions: to maintain an orderly market, insofar as is reasonably practicable, in the stocks in which he is registered by an exchange as a specialist; and to act as a broker's broker. Cf. *stock broker.*

specialization: reducing an operation or task into separate simplified, individual activities. See *therbligs.*

special lien: synonymous with *particular lien*.

special offering: a large block of stock that becomes available for sale but requires special handling because of its size and the market in that particular issue. A notice is printed on the ticker tape announcing that the stock will be offered for sale on the exchange floor at a fixed price. Member firms may buy this stock for customers directly from the seller's broker during trading hours. The price is usually based on the last transaction in the regular auction market. Only the seller pays a commission on a special offering. Special offerings must be approved by the SEC.

special order: an order that may be priced below the normal price in order to utilize excess capacity and thereby contribute to company profits.

special-purpose funds: mutual funds that invest exclusively in securities from one industry. See *investment company*.

specialty merchandise: consumer goods that have special features for which buyers are willing to make a major purchasing effort (e.g., imported foods, hi-fi equipment, cameras).

specialty stores: retail outlets that maintain a large selection in a limited line of merchandise (e.g., men's apparel stores).

specie: money in coin.

specification: a written identification of the work to be done and materials to be used in the completion of a task.

specific identification: a method of valuing inventory and determining cost of goods sold whereby the actual costs of specific inventory items are assigned to those items of inventory on hand and to those that have been sold.

specific insurance: coverage that applies to separate and specifically named objects or locations, as distinguished from blanket insurance. Cf. *blanket policy*.

specific subsidy: the per-unit subsidy on a commodity.

specific tariff: a tariff based on a fixed amount charged per unit of the goods imported. **specific tax:** the per-unit tax on a commodity.

speculation: the employment of funds by a speculator. Safety of principal is a factor secondary to increasing capital. See *letter stock*. Cf. *defensive investment; inflation*.

speculative demand for money: a demand for liquidity generated by the expectation that changes in interest rates and bond prices will make it profitable to temporarily hold cash rather than income earning assets.

speculative purchasing: buying items when prices appear lowest, with the expectation that there will be a future price increase that will make possible a profit.

speculator: one who is willing to assume a relatively large risk in the hope of gain. The speculator's principal concern is to increase capital rather than dividend income. Speculators may buy and sell the same day or may invest in enterprises that they do not expect to be profitable for years. Cf. *investor.*

speed-up: a management-directed attempt to increase production without any increase in pay. A worker slow-down may follow as a reaction against a speed-up. Cf. *incentive pay; stretch-out.*

spendable earnings: net earnings after deductions for taxes, or the amount available for spending. Synonymous with *take-home pay.*

spillovers: external benefits or costs of efforts for which there is no compensation. Synonymous with *externalities.*

spin-off organization: company now operating almost independently of the parent organization because its activities do not fit easily with the parent's existing competencies.

spiral career concept: career concept by which individuals motivated by personal growth perform well enough to advance in status and rank.

split: the division of the outstanding shares of a corporation into a larger number of shares. A 3-for-1 split by a company with 1 million shares outstanding would result in 3 million shares outstanding. Each holder of 100 shares before the 3-for-1 split would have 300 shares. Of course, the shareholder's proportionate equity in the company would remain the same, since 100 parts of 1 million is the equivalent of 300 parts of 3 million. Ordinarily, a split must be voted by directors and approved by shareholders. Such action by a corporation does not alter the total contributed capital but merely increases the number of shares issued and outstanding and the par value per share. Cf. *stock split down.*

split investment company: a closed end investment firm that issues two types of capital stock. The first (income shares) receives dividends from investments; the second (capital shares) receives dividends from the appreciation of investments. Synonymous with *dual-purpose fund.* Cf. *investment company.*

split-off point: see *joint production costs.*

split order: a large order that is separated into smaller units that are sold over a period of time. When purchasing or selling a security or commodity, a very large transaction could cause substantial price fluctuation, and the splitting is supposed to prevent this.

split run: two or more ads of equal size with the identical position in different copies of the same publication issue. This affords a means of determining the impact of differing versions of an advertisement, and it allows an advertiser to feature different products in regional printings of a national publication. Cf. *preferred position.*

split shift: the daily working time of an employee that is divided into two or more working periods, to meet peak needs (e.g., bus drivers who work in morning and afternoon transportation rush hours). Synonymous with *broken time.*

split up: the issuance of two or more stock shares to replace each outstanding share, used for financial and tax purposes. This increase, although lowering the value per share, does not alter the total liability of the issuing firm for the outstanding capital stock. See *split.*

spokesperson role: a manager's role in speaking for the unit and representing it to others. A key concept of the spokesperson role is that of representation; the manager must act as an advocate for subordinates.

sponsor: upper-level managers involved in the major decision-making activities of the organization.

spot:
(1) **finance:** the ready delivery of commodities and foreign exchange that are usually delivered less rapidly.
(2) **media:** a place or position in a listing or schedule (e.g., having a spot on television).

spot advertising: a campaign wherein advertisers choose specific stations to be used. This contrasts with network or local advertising. See *flight saturation.*

spot announcement: a brief commercial, usually one minute long or less, inserted between portions of a radio or television program.

spot delivery: immediate delivery.

spot market: a market in which commodities are sold for cash and delivered quickly. See *fixing the price.* Cf. *commodity.*

spot price: the selling price of a physical commodity.

spread:
(1) **securities:** two different options, a put (price below the prevailing market) and a call (price above the prevailing market), with both

options pertaining to the same stock and expiring on the same day. Thus the trader is guaranteed a sale at a price not lower than the put price if the market drops and a buy at a price not higher than the call price if the market increases. See *butterfly spread, straddle.*

(2) **securities:** the differences between the bid and asked prices of securities.

(3) **securities:** two prices given instead of one.

(4) **finance:** the difference between two prices.

spread effect: the positive impact of international trade on the domestic economies of the trading countries.

spreader: a trader in commodities who attempts to gain from differences in the futures prices of the same commodities on different commodity exchanges by purchasing on one and selling on another.

spreadsheet: in accounting, a work sheet arranged in the manner of a mathematical matrix and containing a multicolumn analysis of related entries and accounts for easy access on a single sheet.

SRDS: Standard Rate and Data Service, Inc., an organization that releases up-to-date data on advertising rates, standards, and so on, of various media. SRDS is considered the prime source of advertising media information.

stability situation: strategy situation in which good past performance and the minor nature of needed change make insiders the best choice for implementing.

stabilization policy: the efforts of government to use fiscal and monetary means to eliminate inflation, unemployment, or both. See *wage stabilization.*

stable money: currency that remains constant in terms of the items and services it can purchase.

staff: employees who advise and assist line managers and employees but are not directly engaged in the production of the final good or service.

staff authority: see *line and staff authority*

staff department: a department that provides assistance and support to line departments in attaining basic objectives of the organization. In a manufacturing firm, purchasing and accounting would be staff departments.

staff function: service, advisory, or otherwise supportive activities performed by staff units in line and staff organizations.

staffing table: a list of anticipated employment openings for each type of job.

staff managers: managers who support line managers but who are not directly involved in the production of goods or services.

staff organization: an administrative concept by which planning, research, organizing, fact-finding, and advisory assistance is provided to the line (command) through departments, units, or individual officers who are specifically created and maintained for such purposes, usually with limited functional authority and control.

stag: an individual speculator who rapidly buys and then sells shares for profit, having had no intention of retaining the securities for any length of time. Cf. *digested securities.*

stagflation: inflation coexisting with economic stagnation. Prices for goods and services continue to increase during a period of minimal capital investment in equipment, research and development, and so on. Cf. *hesiflation; inflation.*

staggering of hours: a procedure for adjusting hours of employment in order to schedule work more evenly.

stagnation: conditions of minimal growth rate, or growth that is increasing at a lower rate than expected.

stakeholders: persons whom the organization is dedicated to serve.

stale check: any check dated 90 days prior to presentation for payment.

stamp tax: a government tax collected through the sale of stamps that are affixed to certain products (e.g., liquor, tobacco, stock certificates, title deeds). See *transfer tax.*

Standard & Poor's 500 Stock Average: an index of stock prices composed of 425 industrials, 50 utilities, and 25 railroads. Cf. *Dow-Jones Averages.*

standard costs: an estimate of what actual costs should be under projected conditions.

standard hour plan: a method of incentive compensation that uses time allowances rather than piece rates.

Standard Industrial Classification System (SIC): a numerical system developed by the U.S. Bureau of the Budget to classify establishments by type of activity for purposes of facilitating the collection, tabulation, presentation, and analysis of data relating to such establishments and for promoting uniformity within U.S. agencies. Cf. *Dictionary of Occupational Titles.*

standardization:

(1) **general:** the determination of basic limits or grade ranges in the form of specifications to which produced items should conform.

(2) **manufacturing:** establishing specific criteria levels (size, quality, weight, etc.).

standard of living: the level of material affluence of a nation as measured by per capita output. See *per capita output.*

Standard Rate and Data Service, Inc.: see *SRDS.*

standing committee: a committee, often advisory in nature, that exists for an indefinite period of time.

standing order: an authority given by a customer for the bank to regularly pay funds, usually a fixed dollar amount, from his or her demand deposit account.

standing plan: an established set of decisions, used by managers to deal with recurring or organizational activities, major types of policies, procedures, and rules.

standstill agreement: an arrangement between a debtor and a creditor under which new limits and conditions for the loan are established. Typically, a postponement of obligation payment is the result. Cf. *novation.*

staple stock: goods on hand that are in continuous demand.

state bank: a bank that is organized according to the laws of a state and is chartered by the state in which it is located to operate as a banking business. The various states have different laws governing the operation of banks.

state capitalism: condition where some developed countries, such as Japan and Korea, have intervened in the economy to direct the allocation and control of resources.

stated capital: the sum of capital amounts contributed by stockholders.

state disability plan: a plan of some states that involves short-term insurance to replace income lost by eligible persons employed in that state. Cf. *disability income; workers' compensation.*

stated value: a nominal value assigned to no-par stock by the board of directors of a corporation.

statement:

(1) **banking:** a record prepared by a bank for a depositor, listing all checks drawn and deposits made together with the new balance after each posting.

(2) **accounting:** a summary of transactions between a creditor and his or her debts or a presentation of names and amounts of accounts to show a financial condition (e.g., an IRS statement).

static inventory problem: the tendency of items bought for a specific selling season to lose value, either partly or completely, because of changes in the market at the season's end.

static model: a concept for studying economic events without reference to time and without relation to preceding or succeeding events. Time is not permitted to alter analysis in any way to affect conclusions.

station:

(1) **securities:** the place where a specialist on an exchange transacts orders.

(2) **transportation:** a place at which trains stop to pick up or discharge passengers or freight.

(3) **human resources:** a worker's assigned post or place of activity.

statism: any indication of increased government intervention in a nation's economic activity, with primary focus on movement toward greater control over major industries. See *controlled economy*. Cf. *laissez-faire*.

statistical accounting: the application of probability theory and statistical sampling approaches to the evolution of prime accounting information and/or verification, authentication, and audit of accounting data prepared by other means.

statistics: the mathematics of gathering data and the approaches used in describing and analyzing numerical information.

status consensus: the agreement of group members about the relative status of members of the group. Synonymous with *status consequence*.

status consequence: synonymous with *status consensus*.

status quo: the existing state of affairs.

statute of limitations: see *limitations of actions*.

steady-state career concept: career concept by which an individual chooses a field but, even though improving professionally and financially, does not seek to move up the organizational hierarchy.

steering controls: controls in which results are predicted and corrective action is taken while the operation or task is being performed.

stepped costs: costs that climb by increments with increased volumes of activity.

step-review system: system for reviewing employee complaints and disputes by successively higher levels of management.

step-up: an automatic wage increase based on length of service. Cf. *incentive pay*.

sterling: the currency basis of Great Britain, the unit of which is the pound sterling. It may also represent bills of exchange that are drawn in terms of British currency. Sterling silver is silver of at least 222 parts pure silver out of 240 and no more than 18 parts of an alloy.

steward: see *shop steward.*

sticker: an employee who is unwilling to accept an offer for promotion.

stipend: synonymous with *salary.*

stock:

(1) **merchandising:** merchandise held for sale (e.g., inventory).

(2) **securities:** the legal capital of a corporation divided into shares. See *assented securities; authorized stock; blue chip; callable; capital stock; common stock; convertibles; cumulative preferred; deferred stock; float; growth stock; guaranteed stock; inactive stock; issue; listed securities; nonassessable stock; noncumulative; no par value stock; ordinary stock; outstanding; over-the-counter securities; paid-up stock; participating preferred; par value; penny stocks; preferred stock; prior preferred; redeemable stock; treasury stock; unissued stock; unlisted securities;, voting right; watered stock.*

stock ahead:

(1) **merchandising:** to maintain sufficient quantities of goods in inventory to cover an anticipated surge in future demand for the items.

(2) **securities:** a situation when an investor who has entered an order to buy or sell a stock at a certain price sees transactions at that price reported on the ticker tape before his or her own order has been executed. This may have occurred because other buy and sell orders at the same price came in to a trading specialist earlier and had priority.

stock-appreciation rights (SARs): privileges that can be attached to a nonqualified option. With an SAR, an executive can ignore the option and take a bonus equal to the value of the stock's appreciation over a span of time. An SEC rule permits an SAR bonus to be paid in cash, rather than in company shares. The SAR can be acted on at any time during the 10-year term of the attached nonqualified stock option.

stock broker: an individual who acts as a middleman between buyers and sellers of stock. Cf. *specialist.*

stock certificate: written evidence of ownership of a company's shares, indicating the number of shares registered in the name of the owner, the corporation issuing the capital stock, and whether the stock is a par value or a no par-value stock.

Stock Clearing Corporation: the New York Stock Exchange's clearinghouse. Its major responsibilities include the clearing and settling of money balances between members, the clearing of purchases and sales transactions, and the delivery of stock.

stock dividend: a portion of the net earnings of a corporation, payable (in shares of fractional shares of designated stock of a given corporation) to the stockholders of record of corporation. It is paid in securities rather than cash, and it may be additional shares of the issuing company or shares of another company held by the corporation.

stock exchanges: organizations that provide a market for the trading of bonds and stocks. Regulations for the admission of securities for trading on the stock exchanges are very stringent.

stockholder of record: a stockholder whose name is registered on the books of the issuing corporation. See *voting right.*

stockholders' equity: synonymous with *owners' equity.*

stock-index arbitrage: purchasing or selling baskets of stocks while at the same time executing offsetting trades in stock-index futures or options. Traders profit by trying to capture fleeting price discrepancies between stocks and the index futures or options. Should stocks become temporarily cheaper than futures, for example, an arbitrager will purchase stocks and sell futures. Cf. *stock-index futures; stock-index options.*

stock-index futures: contracts to purchase or sell the cash value of a stock-index by a specified date. The cash value is determined by multiplying the index number by a specified amount. The most common program-trading vehicles are futures contracts on Standard & Poor's 500 stock index (traded on the Chicago Mercantile Exchange); the Major Market Index, a 20-stock index that is similar to the Dow Jones Industrial Average (traded on the Chicago Board of Trade); and the S&P 100 options (traded on the Chicago Board Options Exchange, and based on 100 stocks selected from the S&P 500). Cf. *stock-index arbitrage; stock-index options.*

stock-index options: options which give holders the right, but not the obligation, to buy (a call) or sell (a put) a specified amount of an underlying investment by a given date at a preset price, known as the strike price. For stock indexes, the underlying investment may be a stock-index futures contract or the cash value of a stock index. For example, there are options on the S&P 500 futures contract and on the S&P 100 index. Cf. *stock-index arbitrage; stock-index futures.*

stocking allowance: a special allowance by a manufacturer to encourage distributor organizations to carry a particular product.

stock in trade:
   (1) **general:** the business activity that is usually carried on by a firm.
   (2) **securities:** the quantity of securities held.

stock jobbing: irresponsible or dishonest manipulation of the price of securities.

stock levels: the inventory carried by a business firm.

stock market: the buying and selling of stock for the purpose of profit for both buyers and sellers of the security. See *market.*

stock option: an arrangement for compensating top management, in addition to salary, with an opportunity to buy a certain amount of company stock, often at a price under the market price. See *Tax Reform Act of 1976.*

stockout: a condition that occurs when all inventory has been used or sold. *Stockouts* are very costly, as other inputs must then be utilized.

stockpiling: government purchases of various agricultural commodities and raw materials for storage, to support the prices of these products. Cf. *hoarding; subsidy.*

stock power: a power of attorney permitting a person other than the owner of stock to legally transfer the title of ownership to a third party. Stock powers are usually given when stock is pledged as collateral to loans. Cf. *power of attorney.*

stock purchase plan: a company plan for the purchase of stock by employees, with or without a contribution from the employer, at terms usually below the market price.

stock-sales ratio: the inventory retail value at the beginning of a given month, divided by sales for that month. This relationship is used to control the sales and inventory balance.

stock shortage: a condition that occurs when the dollar value of the real inventory in stock is less than that which is shown on the inventory books.

stock split: see *split.*

stock split down: the reverse of a stock split, whereby the total number of shares outstanding is lowered, without reducing the total value of the issue, by issuing a new stock share to replace each of two or more shares presently in circulation. The motivation is to increase the market price of a stock. Synonymous with *reverse stock split.*

stock transfer: the act of canceling a stock certificate submitted for transfer, issuing a new certificate in the name of the designated transferee, and recording the change in ownership on the records of a corporation's stock transfer book. See *stock transfer tax.*

stock transfer tax: a tax levied by some states on the transfer of securities from one owner to another, either when purchased or given as a gift. See *stock transfer.*

stock turnover: see *turnover.*

stock watering: see *watered stock.*

stopgo: a British concept of fiscal policy, shifting between economic growth and slowdown. Synonymous with *go-stop.*

stop limit order: a stop order that becomes a limit order after the specified stop price has been reached.

stop loss: a guarantee from one company (the reinsurer) to another (the reinsured) that losses over and above an agreed-upon amount will be paid by the reinsuring company.

stop order: an order to buy at a price above or to sell at a price below the current market. Stop buy orders are generally used to limit loss or to protect unrealized profits on a short sale. Stop sell orders are generally used to protect unrealized profits or to limit loss on a holding. A stop order becomes a market order when the stock sells at or beyond the specified price and thus may not necessarily be executed at that price.

stoppage in transit (in transitu): under certain conditions, a shipper's right to halt delivery of a shipment that is already in transit, when payment has not been made. Cf. *carrier's lien.*

stop payment: the order given to a bank by a depositor who wishes to prevent payment on a check he or she has issued. The depositor requests in writing that the bank stop payment or telephones the instructions and confirms them in writing.

stop price: the price at which a customer's stop order to his broker becomes a market order.

store: any place where merchandise, goods, or services can be purchased, or a place for storage.

store audit: a count of the merchandise carried and sold in a retail outlet.

store count distribution: a measure of distribution based on the number of stores. A product sold in 90 percent of all grocery stores would have 90 percent store count distribution.

straddle: an option that allows the trader to buy or sell securities at an agreed-upon price within a given period. See *butterfly spread; spread.* Cf. *options.*

straight bill of lading: a bill of lading that cannot be negotiated, identifying the individual who is to receive goods.

straight investment: a preferred stock or bond, limited in interest or dividend rate, that is bought because of its income return and not for expectation of any rise in value. See *investment*.

straight-line depreciation: the simplest method of depreciation, whereby capital cost is amortized in uniform periodic amounts over the anticipated life of the asset.

straight-line interest amortization: a method of systematically writing off a bond premium or discount in equal amounts each period until maturity. Cf. *effective-interest amortization*.

straight loan: a loan to an individual or other legal entity in which the basis for granting credit is the debtor's general ability to pay, unsupported by any form of collateral security.

straight piecework plan: a method of compensation whereby a predetermined amount of money is paid or each unit produced. It is an alternative to the hourly rate.

straight time: the wage rate paid for hours worked during the normal period prescribed by a union contract or by law. Cf. time-*and-a-half pay*.

strategic alliances: any agreement between potential and actual competitors to achieve common objectives.

strategic business units (SBUs): divisions composed of key businesses within multiproduct companies, with specific managers, resources, objectives, and competitors. SBUs may encompass a division, a product line, or a single product.

strategic constituencies approach: assessing an organization's effectiveness by evaluating the degree to which the needs of the organization's constituents have been satisfied.

strategic goals: broadly defined targets or future end results set by top management.

strategic groups: work groups whose jobs are mostly individual operations requiring high skill levels. They experience a high degree of internal unity and relatively good production records over the long run.

strategic intervention: organization development applications aimed at effecting a suitable fit among a firm's strategy, structure, culture, and external environment.

strategic planning: a basic type of planning by which a firm formulates its long-range goals and selects activities for achieving those goals.

strategic planning gap: the difference between the present position of a company and its desired future position.

strategic posture: the actual relationship between a firm and its environment.

strategic resource monopoly: an organization that has a monopoly by virtue of controlling a vital input to a production process (e.g., DeBeers of South Africa owns most of the world's diamond mines). Cf. *monopoly*.

strategy: guidelines for making directional decisions that influence an organization's long-run performance.

straw boss: a group leader or assistant foreman, often one who has no formal title or permanent status. Synonymous with *foreman; gang boss*.

Street: the New York financial community; the lower Manhattan (i.e., Wall Street) area.

street broker: an over-the-counter broker, as distinguished from a broker who is a member of an exchange.

street name: a stock certificate in the name of a broker who trades in securities and is a member of an exchange. This stock is never considered to be part of the broker's personal wealth.

stretch-out:

(1) **administration:** a management concept for malingering.

(2) **human resources:** an increase in work without comparable pay increases. Cf. *speed-up*.

strike: a concerted work stoppage designed to pressure management into agreeing on contract terms, to correct an unsettled grievance, or to recognize a union as a collective-bargaining agent. A general strike is an action by all or most organized workers (rare in this country). A quickie strike is a spontaneously organized strike, triggered by some incident on the job and occurring without authorization of the union. A wildcat strike is a nonspontaneous strike organized and carried out by the members without union authorization and in violation of the contract. A sympathy strike is a strike by workers who are not directly involved in the labor dispute but wish to display solidarity with the strikers. An economic strike is a strike because of wages, hours, or other conditions, usually resulting from a strike vote of the union membership taken when an existing labor agreement is about to expire. Cf. *boycott; downer; picketing*. See *illegal strike; jurisdictional strike; secondary strike; work stoppages*. Synonymous with *walkout*.

strike authorization: a strike vote that invests a designated group with the right to call a strike on a given issue without further consultation with the union membership.

strike benefits: payments by the union to members who are on strike in the form of a flat sum or graduated according to family needs. Cf. *out-of-work benefits.*

strikebreaker: a person who accepts employment in place of a striker or organizes a back-to-work movement. See *scab.*

strike fund: funds taken from union dues and held by the union to cover the costs of approved programs (e.g., benefits, printing of union literature, picket signs). See *strike pay.*

strike notice: a formal notice to an employer, to the Federal Mediation and Conciliation Service, or to a state labor-management relations agency that a union has rejected the company's latest offer and that a strike is impending.

strike pay: monies paid by the union to members of a union to compensate for income lost during a strike. See *strike fund.* Cf. *out-of-work benefits.*

striking price: synonymous with *exercise price.*

stringency: a money market condition of hard-to-obtain credit, accompanied by an increase in the rates of interest.

strong market: a market that has a greater demand for purchasing than for selling.

struck work: goods produced by strikebreakers, or goods produced by a firm that is not on strike, for the use or relief of a struck company. Cf. *unfair goods.*

structural change approaches: changes that are brought about through new formal guidelines, procedures, policies, and organizational rearrangements.

structural inflation: increasing prices caused by an uneven upward demand or cost pressures in a key industry, even when total demand remains in balance with total supply for the economy as a whole.

structural intervention: changing the structure of an organization so that people can develop new approaches for dealing with others on the job. See *group dynamics.*

structural principles: principles that assist a manager in designing the formal task and authority relationships in the organization. See *classical design theory; task orientation.*

structural unemployment: unemployment resulting from a mismatch between the skills that available workers have to offer and the skills that potential employers are seeking.

structured interview: an interview in which a set of standardized questions having an established set of answers is used. Cf. *situational interview; unstructured interview.*

stub shift: a work shift that has fewer hours than the regular shift. See *shift.*

SUB: see *supplementary unemployment benefits.*

Subchapter S corporation: a company that is legally organized as a corporation in which income or loss is passed through and taxed to individual stockholders.

subcontracting: work given out to another employer. If done to evade bargaining with a union, subcontracting is an unfair practice under the Taft–Hartley Act.

subenvironment: characteristics of people and their tasks that affect the performance of employees in their work and their relationships with each other. Cf. *differentiation.*

subject bid: a bid that is negotiable, rather than firm.

submarginal: yielding less than enough to cover the cost of production.

submittal notice: a broker's notification to a property owner that the owner's property has been offered for sale. The offering price and prospect's name and address are included in the notice.

suboptimization: operating at a less than optimal level in one segment of a firm in order to optimize the functioning of the organization as a whole. See *optimization.*

subpartner: person who is not a member of a partnership but who contracts with one of the partners to participate in the interest of that partner in the firm's operations.

subrogation:

(1) **business law:** substitution of one person for another, either as a creditor or as the owner of any lawful right, so that the substituted individual succeeds to the rights, remedies, or proceeds of the claim.

(2) **insurance:** the legal process by which an insurance company seeks recovery of the amount paid to the policyholder from a third party who has caused the loss.

subscriber: one who agrees in writing to purchase a certain offering (e.g., a certain number of shares of designated stock of a given corporation; a certain number of bonds of a stipulated face value).

subscription: an agreement to purchase a security; a solicitation of subscribers.

subsidiary: an organization whose voting stock is more than 50 percent owned by another firm. Synonymous with *underlying company.*

subsidy: federal payments to an individual or organization for which the government receives no products or services. The primary objective of a subsidy is to allow for production of the goods at prices that will attract buyers. Cf. *stockpiling.*

subsistence law of wages: synonymous with *iron law of wages.*

subsistence theory of wages: an economic theory of the late eighteenth and early nineteenth centuries claiming that wages per employee tend to equal what the worker needs to maintain himself and his family. See *standard of living.*

substandard: conditions that make a risk less desirable than normal for its class. See *referral risks.*

substandard rate: a wage rate that is below established plant or occupational minimum, federal or state minimum laws, or prevailing levels. Cf. *minimum wage.*

substitute goods: items that can easily replace one another either in production or in consumption (e.g., natural and synthetic fibers; strawberries and raspberries). An increase in the price of one substitute good encourages purchase of the other(s).

substitution: see *subrogation.*

substitution law: the economic statement that if one product or service can be a replacement for another, the prices of the two must be very close to each other.

succession:

(1) **business law:** the transfer of all rights and obligations of a deceased person to those who are entitled to inherit.

(2) **administration:** following another in an office, an estate, and so on.

succession planning: process of identifying, developing, and tracking key individuals for executive positions.

suggestion box: a designated place in an organization where workers deposit suggestions concerning policies, procedures, activities, or methods.

suggestion programs: specific procedures designed to encourage workers to recommend improvements.

suggestive selling: the strategy of suggesting to a potential purchaser that he or she might have an additional need related to what has already been purchased (e.g., it might be suggested that a woman who has bought a dress also select appropriate shoes or a sweater). See *complementary products.* Cf. *derived demand.*

suitable employment: a provision of unemployment compensation that recipients are not required to accept any available job but are required only to accept jobs for which they are suited by training, education, or experience.

summary of international transactions: a revised version of the balance-of-payments accounts, adopted in 1976, that purports to deemphasize the concept of balances and to encourage more detailed assessment of international transactions.

summary powers: powers possessed by executives to act promptly in certain matters that are considered to be of prime importance.

sumptuary laws: laws that attempt to minimize the consumption of items that are believed to be harmful to individuals or to society in general. Cf. *public consumption monopoly.*

sunk cost: a cost that has already been incurred and is now irrelevant to the decision-making process.

sunset: to lower costs to U.S. treasury, the prevention by lawmakers to assure that features of a tax act will not quickly expire. See *Tax Act of 2003.*

sunset industry: any business, such as steel making, having declining growth caused by technological change.

sunshine trading: a strategy of investing requiring big players to announce the extent of their buy and sell orders rather than hide their actions by feeding orders into the marketplace piecemeal.

superior goods: commodities and services that are demanded in larger quantities as incomes rise (e.g., expensive cars; caviar; fur coats).

superleadership: occurs when a leader gradually and purposefully turns over power, responsibility, and control to a self-managing work group.

superordinate goals: goals for all subordinate persons or departments that can best be achieved through cooperation.

supershares: based on slicing up two conventional funds. By starting with two conventional funds—an index fund owning stocks in the S.& P. 500 and a money market fund. One security gives the holder the right to all dividends and to all price appreciation during three years, up to 25 percent. The other security would get all the price appreciation above that. In effect, it would be a long-term call option on the entire stock market.

superstructure: division of activities at the top of the organizational hierarchy, providing the primary structural form of the organization.

supervisor: any individual who has management responsibilities, usually including the right to hire and fire or to recommend such action.

supervisory managers: managers who directly oversee the efforts of those who actually perform the work.

supplemental monthly budget: a budgetary approach in which a firm determines a minimum operational budget and, prior to the beginning of each month, provides the units with additional funds to supplement this minimum.

Supplementary Employee Retirement Plan (SERP): unlike a standard qualified plan in which an employer puts aside money in an employee's name, a SERP is not prefunded. It is just an agreement between an employer and employee where the promises are only as good as the company's ability to pay and its willingness to pay. With a SERP, a firm promises to pay employees out of general operating profits when they retire. Contributions to the plan are not tax-deductible, nor guaranteed by the Government's Pension Benefit Guaranty Corporation.

Supplementary Security Income (SSI): a federal program of income assistance to the aged, blind, and disabled.

supplementary unemployment benefits (SUB): a company provision for benefits to laid-off workers, in addition to unemployment insurance. Funds may come from individual employee contributions made over the years or from contributions made to a pool of funds. See *pool (administration)*.

supply chain: interrelationships with other businesses needed to build and sell a product make up a network of business relationships. See *supply chain management*.

supply chain management: management concept that integrates the management of supply chain process. The goals are to cut costs, increase profits, improve performance in relationships with customers and suppliers, and develop value-added services that give a company a competitive edge. Major objectives are to get the right product to the right place at the least cost, keep inventory as low as possible, and reduce cycle time.

supply price: the lowest price needed to produce a specified output. It is the lowest price a seller will accept for the act of supplying a given quantity of a commodity.

supply schedule: a table of prices and corresponding quantities offered for sale in a given period.

supply-side economics: a school of economic thought of cutting marginal tax rates giving individuals incentive to work, save, and invest. The government role in the economy should be kept to an absolute minimum. Cf. *Reagonomics.*

supply-sider: a person, especially an economist, who advocates or promotes supply-side economics or its policy.

supporting the market: placing purchasing orders at or somewhat below the prevailing market level in order to maintain and balance existing prices and to encourage a price rise.

supportive approach to supervision: an approach whereby employees are given opportunities for self-direction, participation in decision making, and some freedom in their work. Cf. *collegial approach to supervision; custodial approach to supervision.*

support level: the point at which demand for a product or service is reached. It is the moment when the resistance level is overcome.

supramarginal: yielding more than the cost of production.

supreme court of finance: synonymous with *Federal Reserve Board.*

surcharge: an added charge to a tax or other cost or account.

surety:

(1) **business law:** an individual who agrees, usually in writing, to be responsible for the performance of another person on a contract or for a certain debt or debts of the other individual.

(2) **insurance:** a bond, guaranty, or other security that protects a person, corporation, or other legal entity in cases of another's default in the payment of a given obligation, improper performance of a given contract, malfeasance of office, and so on.

surety bond: see *bond, surety.*

surface changes: shifts in consumer preferences and interests that direct spending patterns from one activity to another without signaling a basic change in fundamental cultural values.

surface value: objective meaning or worth of a reward to an employee.

surplus:

(1) **general:** anything remaining or left over.

(2) **accounting:** an excess of assets over the total of liabilities and capital.

surrender value: designating the amount of the total life insurance in force that will be paid to the policyholder, after a certain stipulated number of premiums have been paid, if the policyholder elects to surrender the policy and receive such proportionate part. The cash surrender value of a policy is also the amount used to determine how much will be loaned against the policy.

surtax: the extra tax applied to corporations when their net taxable income has exceeded a certain amount. For example, a surtax is demanded at the rate of 26 percent for all corporate income over $25,000. See *Tax Reform Act of 1969*.

suspended trading: a binding stock exchange decision to cease trading that results from an unusual occurrence, such as an unexpected jump in buy or sell orders on all or several securities. Sometimes suspended trading may be brought about by equipment failure or other unexpected emergencies.

suspension:

(1) **human resources:** a disciplinary layoff of a worker without pay.

(2) **administration:** termination of a business.

(3) **banking:** a temporary closing of a bank.

(4) **securities:** a decision made by a stock exchange board of directors prohibiting a securities firm or broker from conducting business for a period. See *under the rule*.

(5) **labor relations:** an employer's disciplinary action against an employee. It is less critical than a discharge. See *trusteeship*.

sustainable competitive advantage: advantage over competitors that can be sustained over time.

swap:

(1) **general:** to exchange or barter.

(2) **banking:** an arrangement between the central banks or two countries for standby credit to facilitate the exchange of each other's currencies. See *credit*.

sweatshop: a place of work considered to be far below acceptable standards of working conditions.

sweetheart agreement: a secret deal with management by a corrupt union agent for an inferior contract, made without the knowledge of the membership and without genuine collective bargaining; denounced by the AFL-CIO in its Code of Ethical Practices.

swing shift: in a factory under continuous production, a systematic rotation of crews among work shifts to provide for days off.

switch (contingent) order: an order for the purchase (sale) of one stock and the sale (purchase) of another stock at a stipulated price difference.

switching customers: bringing in a sales specialist when the salesperson who originally served a customer is unable to close a sale.

switch selling: an unethical practice of using high-pressure tactics to sell an item that is more expensive than one advertised at a lower price. See *bait and switch*.

symbolic management: process in which managers attempt to influence deep cultural norms and values by shaping the surface cultural elements that organization members use to express and transmit cultural understandings.

symbolic pricing: using price to create an impression about a product or a brand in the minds of consumers.

symmetry problem: the problem of devising an international monetary system that will produce equal pressure on countries to revalue or devalue to correct balance-of-payments surpluses or deficits.

sympathy strike: see *strike*.

syndicalism: an economic concept whereby workers exert control over the industries that employ them.

syndicate:

(1) **general:** the association of two or more individuals, established to carry out a business activity. Members share in all profits or losses in proportion to their contribution to the resources of the syndicate. Cf. *joint venture; partnership.*

(2) **publishing:** an organization that distributes material of writers, artists, and others to newspapers, magazines, periodicals, and so on, with the contributor receiving either a stated fee or a royalty.

(3) **finance:** a group of investment bankers and securities dealers who, by agreement among themselves, have joined together for the purpose of distributing a new issue of securities for a corporation.

synergism: the concept of putting diverse business enterprises together in order to yield greater and quicker growth than the sum of their individual parts.

synthetic stocks: complex hybrids of all kinds of securities, customized to perform in a way that is predictable based on previous market behavior. They may be a blend of a dozen or more investment vehicles, including stock-index futures, zero-coupon bonds, and currency options. Another use for synthetic stocks is to hedge existing stock portfolios for which no conventional hedging vehicles exist.

System Four: a form of organization development, designed by Rensis Likert, that emphasizes participative, employee-centered leadership, open communication, and group decision making and goal setting.

systems theory: view of management based on the notion that organizations can be visualized as systems.

systems-type leadership: a leadership style in which all corporate activities are directed toward the achievement of specified objectives.

T

tactical plans: plans that show how top management's plans are to be carried out at the departmental, short-term level.

Taft-Hartley Act: the Labor-Management Relations Act of 1947, amending the Wagner-Connery Act of 1935. Its major provisions are (1) that the closed shop is forbidden; (2) that the government is authorized to seek an injunction preventing any work stoppage for 80 days when a strike threatens the nation's welfare and health; (3) that unions cannot use union monies in connection with national elections; (4) that officers of unions must swear that they are not members of the Communist party before the union can be certified (amended by the Landrum-Griffin Act); (5) that unions must file financial reports with the U.S. Department of Labor, along with a membership list; and (6) that the states are permitted to pass right-to-work laws. Certain unfair labor practices are also identified in the act. See *COPE; Hatch Act; jurisdictional strike.*

tag:

(1) **broadcasting:** an addition to a commercial broadcast (e.g., a voice-over message following a transcribed statement, an announcement or insertion of music serving as a conclusion).

(2) **merchandising:** see *Kimball tags.*

take:

(1) **general:** (slang) any profit from a business activity, usually one of a suspicious nature.

(2) **business law:** to lay hold of, seize, or have in possession.

take a bath: (slang) to have a substantial financial loss.

take-home pay: synonymous with *spendable earnings.*

take-out loan: the permanent financing that replaces an interim or construction loan.

takeover: the acquisition of an ongoing organization by another through purchase of the firm and/or exchange of capital stock. Cf. *consolidation; merger.*

takeover time: the time required in marketing for a superior new product to go from 10 to 90 percent displacement of an inferior older product.

take stock: to make an inventory of items on hand.

taking inventory: the procedure of counting all inventory on hand at a time set aside for this purpose. Cf. *unit control.*

talent management: an approach to sourcing strategy, developing and promoting the top executives and those likely to replace them; includes a number of human resources processes including hiring, retention, succession planning, development, assessment, coaching, and mentoring. See *sourcing strategy.*

tall organization structure: an organizational structure in which there is a narrow span of control within a large number of levels in the hierarchy. Cf. *flat organization.*

tall pyramid structure: an organizational structure that fosters narrow spans of control, a large number of management levels, and more centralized decision making.

talon:

(1) **general**: a special coupon (e.g., a voucher stub).

(2) **finance:** the part of a debt instrument remaining on an unmatured bond after the interest coupons that were formerly attached have been presented. Cf. *coupon.*

tandem increase: a pay increase given to certain groups in a factory (usually office workers) as the result of a raise negotiated by the production workers.

tangible assets: physical and material (perceptible to touch) assets, as distinguished from intangible assets, which are imperceptible to touch (e.g., cash, land, buildings).

tangible, personal, depreciable business property: property used in a business that is not considered to be real estate.

tangible property: property in physical form that can be touched, such as a house or land.

target customers: the people who are the objects of a store's total efforts to attract business. Cf. *market target.*

target elements of change: components of an organization that may be changed.

target market: see *market target.*

target net income: a desired profit level that is predetermined by management.

target pricing: a technique of establishing prices to reach a profit objective.

target risk:

(1) **insurance:** a policyholder or prospect for insurance whose business develops large premiums and who is considered to be a target for competing insurance producers.

(2) **insurance:** a risk of large value or limits; a severe hazard that is difficult to insure or have reinsured.

tariff:

(1) **general:** a schedule of taxes on items imported or exported. In the United States, tariffs are imposed on imported goods only. Cf. *customs.*
(2) **finance:** any list of prices, charges, duties, and so on.

tariff rate: the charge rate or schedule established by the rating organization that has jurisdiction over a given class and territory (e.g., a schedule of freight rates for transporting different items to various cities).

tariff war: a form of competition between nations as evidenced by tariff discrimination of various forms. See *retaliatory duty.*

task: a unit of work assigned to an employee or a group of workers.

task accomplishment activities: activities aimed at helping a group accomplish its goals.

task analysis: process of determining what the content of a training program should be on the basis of a study of the task or duties involved in the job.

task and bonus system: a compensation approach that guarantees the employee a fixed daily wage for efforts to finish a given assignment and a bonus when the employee exceeds the task.

task behaviors: such actions as giving suggestions, providing information, analyzing problems, evaluating alternatives, and making decisions.

task characteristics theories: seeks to identify task characteristics of jobs, how these characteristics are combined to form different jobs, and their relationship to employee motivation, satisfaction, and performance.

task demands: stress associated with the specific job a person performs.

task dependency: the situation in which one group or individual must rely on another group or individual for services, information, or goods.

task environment: all the factors and forces external to the organization that are important to managerial decision making.

task force: a team of individuals, often representing various departments or interests, that has responsibility for coordinating a study or other efforts that involve a number of organizational units.

task group: a group of employees working as a unit to complete a project or task.

task identity: the opportunity to do an entire piece of work, which enables an employee to have a sense of responsibility and pride.

task interdependency: the extent to which two or more groups or individuals rely on each other for service, information, and goods to accomplish their own goals.

task-motivated leadership: a leadership style in which the manager tends to describe his or her least preferred coworker in an unfavorable light. Such a leader is primarily involved in task controlling and managing and is less concerned with the human relations aspects of the job.

task orientation: a dimension of leadership behavior that focuses on organizational structure, task assignments, specification of the ways in which tasks are to be completed, and clarification of schedules. See *structural principles.*

task significance: the degree to which a job has a substantial impact on the lives or work of others in the company.

task structure: the extent to which a task is simple (routine) or complex (nonroutine).

task uncertainty: the extent to which internal or external events create a state of uncertainty with respect to job predictability.

tax: a charge levied by a government against the income of an individual, corporation, or other profit-making center of activity. In addition to federal income taxes, other types of taxes include state, city, sales, excise, etc. .

tax abatement: a decrease or rebate of a tax or burden that was improperly levied. Sometimes a tax abatement may only reflect an acknowledgment of a changed situation.

taxable income: the amount of income remaining after all permitted deductions and exemptions have been subtracted, thus the income that is subject to taxation

Tax Act of 1981: see *Economic Recovery Tax Act of 1981.*

Tax Act of 2003: a tax bill of $320 billion tax savings over 10 years. Over a decade the Treasury cost in lost revenue stands to be over $800 billion; signed into law on May 29, 2003, by President George W. Bush. Key provisions of the law include:
Capital Gains: top rate falls to 15% from 20%, and for lower-income taxpayers to 5% from 10%, effective May 6, 2003. For low-income taxpayers, tax is phased out in 2008; expires December 31, 2008.
Dividends: top rate falls to 15% from 38.6%, retroactive to January 1,

2003. For low-income taxpayers, tax disappears in 2008; expires December 31, 2008. *Income Taxes*: accelerates to 2003 and next across-the-board cuts currently scheduled for 2004 through 2006; would be permanent. *Child credit*: raises the credit to $1,000 from $600; expires December 31, 2004. *Marriage tax breaks*: increases standard deduction and expands 15% bracket for married couples; expires December 31, 2004. *Alternative minimum tax*: raises exemption to $58,000 for married couples and $42,250 for unmarried taxpayers; expires December 31, 2004. *Business bonus depreciation*: expands write-off bonus to 50% from current 30%, effective May 5, 2003; expires December 31, 2004. *Small-business expensing*: increases minimum to $100,000 from $25,000; expires December 31, 2005. See *Economic Growth and Tax Relief Reconciliation Act of 2001; sunset*. Synonymous with *Jobs and Growth Tax Relief Reconciliation Act of 2003*.

tax anticipation note: a short-term, interest-bearing obligation created to be bought by businesses with monies assembled as a reserve in order to pay taxes. These notes are sold by government agencies to increase revenue.

tax avoidance: taking advantage of deductions and other provisions of tax law to reduce one's taxes. See *tax shelter*. Cf. *tax dodge*.

tax base:

(1) the commodity, income, or service on which a tax is levied.

(2) the part of the value of an item that can be taxed.

tax-based income policy (TIP): a surcharge placed on the corporate income tax if the firm grants its employees wage increases in excess of some government-set standard. Likewise, by holding its average wage increases below the standards, a company becomes eligible for a government tax reduction.

tax credit: a direct reduction in tax liability, usually granted to encourage a particular action or to provide tax relief for certain classes of taxpayers.

tax-deferred annuity (tax-sheltered annuity): an annuity available to public school teachers and employees of certain nonprofit organizations that enables the employee to contribute monies toward retirement. Accumulations of these funds are not taxed at the time of contribution in that federal income taxes are not paid until monies are withdrawn from the plan. See *exclusion allowance*.

tax dodge: an activity that constitutes an illegal attempt to avoid paying taxes (e.g., moving out of the country). Cf. *tax avoidance*.

Tax Equity and Fiscal Responsibility Act of 1982 (TEFRA): aside from the fundamental objective of increasing government revenues, TEFRA is intended to curtail perceived abuses and unintended benefits in the present tax system, assure better compliance with existing tax laws, and impose increased excise taxes on selected products and services.

tax evasion: unlawful attempts to avoid payment of a tax (e.g., not properly reporting all earned income).

tax-exempt bond: see *bond, tax exempt.*

tax-exempt corporation: a legal entity that is chartered by a state for scientific, religious, educational, charitable, or similar purposes.

tax exemption: a right, secured by law, permitting freedom from a charge of taxes (e.g., on income that constitutes primary support of a child).

tax haven: a nation that offers low tax rates and other incentives for corporations of other countries. See *flight of capital.*

tax limit: a legislative decision that limits the tax ceiling that can be imposed by an appropriate authority.

tax preference items: in federal income tax liability, transactions receiving special treatment by lowering taxable income. See *Tax Reform Act of 1986.*

tax ratables: public revenues derived from private properties which are ratable for tax.

tax rate: the amount of tax applied per unit of tax base, expressed as a percentage (e.g., a tax of $5 on a base of $100 represents a tax rate of 5 percent).

Tax Reduction Act of 1975: federal legislation that provided for a 10 percent rebate on 1974 taxes up to a maximum of $200 for individuals and provided tax cuts retroactive to January 1975 for both individuals and corporations. For individuals, the reduction was in the form of increased standard deductions, a $30 exemption credit, and an earned income credit for low-income families. The act also reduced corporate income tax, increased the investment surtax exemption, and increased the investment tax credit to 10 percent. See *Revenue Adjustment Act of 1975; Tax Reform Act of 1986.*

Tax Reduction and Simplification Act of 1977: legislation signed by President Carter for a $34 billion tax cut, giving credit to industry to create jobs and attempting to simplify tax filing procedures.

Tax Reform Act of 1969: federal legislation removing major benefits from controlled corporations. See *Tax Reform Act of 1976; Tax Reform Act of 1986.*

Tax Reform Act of 1976: federal legislation revising tax rates, exemptions, and deductions in various areas (e.g., capital gains and losses; tax shelters; estate and gift taxes). Synonymous with *Public Law 94-455*. See *Tax Reform Act of 1986*.

Tax Reform Act of 1986 (HR-3838): federal legislation signed by President Reagan on October 22, 1986. Among the regulations dealing with individuals the law:

(1) compressed the 14 current tax brackets (15 for single taxpayers) into only 2-15 percent and 28 percent. The 15 percent rate applies to all taxable income of as much as $29,750 for married couples; the 28 percent rate applies above that. (2) raised the standard deduction and the personal exemption. (3) phased out the benefits of the 15 percent rate and the personal exemption for high-income taxpayers. The effect was to place a 5 percent surtax on some income. (4) eliminated deductions for contributions to individual retirements accounts by families whose adjusted gross income before IRA deductions exceeded $50,000 ($35,000 for singles), and who were covered by employers' pension plans. It retained the full $2,000 deduction for all families whose income was less than $40,000 ($25,000 for individuals), and for all workers not covered by employer pensions. The spousal IRA deduction remained at $250. (5) ended the special tax treatment of long-term capital gains. Capital gains are taxed at the same rate as other income, so the top rate for individuals became 28 percent. The new rate went into effect for gains on assets sold after December 31, 1986. In 1987, the top capital gains rate was held to 28 percent. (6) eliminated many tax preferences for individuals, such as deductions for consumer interest on such items as credit cards, auto loans, and student loans. Interest paid on loans used to finance investments are only now deductible to the extent of the taxpayer's investment income. The interest restrictions are to be phased in over five years. (7) retained the most popular deductions used by individuals, including the deduction for mortgage interest payments on first and second homes, for charitable contributions, and for state and local income and property taxes. The sales tax deduction was repealed. (8) prevented taxpayers from using paper losses generated by tax shelters to reduce tax liability. (9) cut the amount of income that could be deferred under so-called 401(k) retirement savings plans provided by employers. Annual deferrals under 401(k) plans are limited to $7,000, down from $30,000. (10) repealed the special deduction of as much

as $3,000 for married couples who both work.

Among the regulations dealing chiefly with business, the law: (1) changed the top corporate tax rate to 34 percent from 46 percent, occurring in mid-1987. The Act continued to allow lower rates for small businesses. (2) repealed the lower tax rate for corporate net capital gains. Gains are now taxed at the new ordinary rate of 34 percent. (3) eliminated the 6 percent or 10 percent investment tax credits effective for property placed in service after January 1, 1986. The Act also reduced by 35 percent the value of any credits carried over from previous years. (4) reduced depreciation allowances somewhat. (5) limited deductions for business meals and entertainment to 80 percent of their value. (6) made slight reductions in oil and gas, mining and timber preferences. See *Technical and Miscellaneous Revenue Act of 1988*.

Tax Relief and Reconciliation Act of 2001: see *Economic Growth and Tax Relief Reconciliation Act of 2001; Tax Act of 2003.*

tax roll: an official statement describing taxed property, including the names of the taxpayers and the amounts of their taxes.

tax-saving retirement plan: see *Keogh plan.*

tax sharing: see *revenue sharing; shared revenue.*

tax shelter: a means of legal avoidance of paying a portion of one's income taxes by careful interpretation of tax regulations and adjustment of one's finances to take advantage of IRS rulings. The Tax Reform Act of 1976 placed new restrictions on tax shelters.

tax shield: the amount of depreciation charged against income, thus protecting that amount from tax (e.g., a depreciation deduction of $10,000 produces a tax shield of $3,600 when the tax rate is 36 percent).

Taylorism: the work of Frederick W. Taylor (1856–1915), who outlined the concepts of scientific management and work efficiency.

team appraisal: performance appraisal that recognizes team accomplishment rather than individual performance.

team-based pay: linking pay to teamwork behavior and/or team results.

team building: a conscious effort to develop effective work groups throughout an organization.

tear sheet: a page bearing advertising to appear in a publication that is sent to the advertiser for purposes of proofing.

teaser: an ad that purports to increase curiosity by holding back the name of the advertiser or the product but pledging additional data in future statements.

Technical and Miscellaneous Revenue Act of 1988: federal legislation that increases a variety of business taxes, cuts some taxes on individuals, and makes extensive technical corrections in the Tax Reform Act of 1986; also established a Taxpayer Bill of Rights. In addition to correcting flaws in the 1986 law and raising $4.1 billion in new revenues, the bill extended several minor tax provisions scheduled to expire, and bestowed minor tax breaks on dozens of interest groups. The legislation also exempts from income taxes the interest on United States savings bonds cashed in to pay for college expenses. See *Tax Reform Act of 1986*.

technical core: zone in which managers have directed responsibility for producing and delivering an organization's goods and/or services.

technical position: applied to various internal factors affecting the market, as opposed to external forces such as earnings, dividends, and general economic conditions. Some internal factors are the size of the short-term interest; whether the market has had a sustained advance or decline without interruption; and the amount of credit in use in the market.

technical skill: the skill of working with the resources and knowledge in a specific area. Such skill is most important to first-level managers.

technical specialists: group members who show a great deal of concern with task-related problems and use their expertise to solve them.

technological assessment: a technique for evaluating the impact of technological change on society. Cf. *technological forecasting.*

technological forecasting: predicting changes in technology and their organizational and societal implications. See *public policy.* Cf. *technological assessment.*

technological unemployment: unemployment resulting from the introduction of new methods of production and/or operations. See *labor-augmenting technical change; redeployment; secular unemployment.* Cf. *labor-saving equipment.*

technology: industrial science, especially when applied to the replacement of skilled labor by advanced equipment; applied scientific knowledge utilized in the resolution of practical issues and problems, in the evolution of new products and new processes of manufacture, and in the introduction of major changes in techniques of physical distribution.

technology absorbing capacity: ability of the recipient to work effectively with technology, particularly in relation to the need for training and equity in the recipient in order to effect a transfer.

technology transfer: transfer, often to another country, of systematic knowledge for the manufacturing of a product, for the application of a process, or for the rendering of a service; does not extend to the mere sales or lease of goods.

TEFRA: see *Tax Equity and Fiscal Responsibility Act of 1982*.

telecommunications:
(1) the electronic transmission of data, text, graphics, voice (audio), or image (video) over literally any distance.
(2) the exchange of information in any form over computer-based networks.

telecommuting: where employees do their work at home on a computer that is linked to their office.

teleconferencing: conducting or participating in discussions by telephone or videophone.

telemarketing: use of telephone communications to directly contact and sell merchandise to consumers.

Teller Act: synonymous with *Welfare and Pension Plans Disclosure Act of 1958*.

temporary bond: see *bond, temporary*.

temporary disability benefits: the weekly benefits payable (out of company pension plans) to employees for nonoccupational accidents and sickness. Cf. *workers' compensation*.

temporary employees: nonpermanent members of an organization's work force, often hired to do clerical work.

temporary investments: investments in marketable securities that an owner expects to sell within a short time, usually one year, and that thereby are classified as current assets.

temporary total disability benefits: the weekly benefit payable to an employee, as prescribed by a workers' compensation law, when he or she is temporarily unable to perform any job duties because of an accident or sickness sustained during and arising out of his or her employment. Cf. *workers' compensation*.

tender:
(1) **business law:** to offer money in satisfaction of a debt by producing the money and stating to the creditor a desire to pay.
(2) **securities:** a corporation's offer of securities by asking for bids for them, at prices above a minimum.

ten-forty: a United States bond that is redeemable after 10 years and due and payable after 40 years.

10-K: the financial report that is filed annually with the SEC by firms with securities traded on a national exchange or in the over-the-counter market.

tenor: the period between the formation of a debt and the date of expected payment.

10-Q: a quarterly report filed with the SEC that is usually unaudited.

tenure: assuming satisfactory performance, the period of time an employee may expect to serve under his or her current appointment without fear of arbitrary dismissal.

term: the prescribed time a person has to make installment or other payments as identified in a loan or credit contract.

term bond: see *bond, term.*

terminal market: a market (e.g., a commodity market) that deals in futures.

terminal positions: jobs in an organization that do not offer any possibilities for advancement. Cf. *upgrading.*

termination: voluntary or involuntary separation from employment.

termination pay: synonymous with *dismissal pay.*

term life insurance: life insurance protection during a certain number of years, usually expiring without policy cash value if the insured survives the stated period. See *extended term insurance; family income rider.* Cf. *term policy.*

term loan: usually a long-term loan running up to 10 years. Such loans generally are made by the larger commercial banks and insurance companies to large, well-established business enterprises for capital expenditures such as plant improvements and purchases of equipment.

term policy: usually a fire or casualty policy written for more than one year; not to be confused with *term life insurance.*

terms: the details, specifications, and conditions of a loan.

terms of sale: identification of a vendor's given time to pay an invoice, any discounts offered, and other conditions of the sale.

terms of trade: the number of units of items that must be surrendered for one unit of goods obtained by a group or nation that is a party to a transaction.

territorial departmentalization: organization of a department according to geographic location (e.g., a company with four major divisions: eastern, midwestern, western, and foreign).

territory screening: examining a list of buyers or potential customers to determine the priorities of opportunity, and profitability. Synonymous with *canvass*. Cf. *cold canvassing; preapproach*.

testing: examining human resources for qualities that are relevant to performance of available jobs.

test marketing: trial distribution of a new product in a small market to determine its likely acceptance in the total market. Cf. *market fit*.

TF: see *till forbid*.

T-groups: see *sensitivity training*.

theme: the major idea of an advertising campaign.

Theory X and Theory Y: concept presented by Douglas McGregor in *The Human Side of Enterprise*. Theory X describes a worker who is lazy and money oriented and produces only because of the presence of an authoritarian supervisor. Theory Y describes a worker who is eager to work, is motivated by various means, and requires a flexible, human-relations style of leadership. See *autocratic; mirror principle; organic structure*. Cf. *Theory Z*.

Theory Z: belief that a high degree of mutual responsibility, loyalty, and consideration between companies and their employees will result in higher productivity and improved welfare. Cf. *Theory X and Theory Y*.

therbligs: motions of the body, classified by Frank G. Gilbreth, that are needed to carry out any form of work. In all, there are 17 basic types of movement. Therblig is an anagram of Gilbreth. Cf. *motion study; three-position plan*.

thin corporation: a corporation that owes a large number of debts relative to its equity position.

think tank: an organization purporting to examine issues of society, science, technology, and business.

thin market: a market in which there are comparatively few bids to buy or offers to sell, or both; may apply to a single security or to the entire stock market. In a thin market, price fluctuations between transactions are usually larger than they are when the market is liquid. A thin market in a particular stock may reflect a lack of interest or a lack of demand for stock.

third market: listed stocks that are not traded on a securities exchange; over-the-counter trading in listed securities.

third-party insurance: generally, coverage that protects the insured against his or her liability arising out of bodily injury to others or damage to their property.

third-party transaction: a three-way business activity involving a buyer, a seller, and a source of consumer credit.

thirds: goods of extremely poor quality, lower in grade than seconds.

third shift: synonymous with *midnight shift*.

third wave of change: changes that are now occurring as a result of recent developments in such areas as technology, information handling, the world of work, organizational loyalty, organizational structures, redefinition of organizational purpose, and multinational corporations.

thirty-three: (slang) a potential customer who refuses to make a purchase from one salesman and is then turned over to another.

three-dimensional leadership model: a model developed by William J. Reddin that stresses the importance of three factors: task orientation, relationships orientation, and effectiveness.

three-ply company: an organization that has the primary managerial levels: top, middle, and lower.

three-position plan: scientific management concept developed by Frank and Lillian Gilbreth in which each worker would simultaneously do his or her job, prepare for the next job, and train his or her future replacement. Cf. *therbligs*.

three-sheet: (slang) an advertising circular, brochure, or handbill.

threshold companies: companies that are on the threshold of corporate maturity in that they are not yet managed by professionals but are run intuitively by a handful of entrepreneurs. The concept was developed by Donald Clifford, Jr.

thrift account: synonymous with *savings account; special interest account.*

through bill of lading: a bill of lading covering items that are moving from the origin point to a final location, even if they are moved from one carrier to another.

ticker: an instrument that prints prices and volume of security transactions in cities and towns throughout the United States and Canada within minutes of each trade on any listed exchange.

tickler file: a follow-up diary or folder containing memos, letters, and so on, ordered by future dates and pulled periodically for review and action. Cf. *deferred premium file*.

tie-in sales: sales that are limited so that a buyer cannot purchase one product or service without purchasing something else from the same manufacturer. The Clayton Antitrust Act of 1914 made this practice illegal in interstate commerce. See *tying arrangement*.

tight credit: synonymous with *tight money.*

tight money: high interest rates demanded in the borrowing of money. Synonymous with *tight credit.*

TIGR: see *Treasury Investment Growth Receipt.*

till forbid (TF): instructions to continue using an advertisement until told otherwise.

till money: funds kept at a front desk or register, as distinguished from monies held in a bank.

time-adjusted rate of return: the rate of interest at which the existing value of anticipated cash inflows from a particular project equals the present value of expected cash outflow of the same activity.

time-and-a-half pay: compensation at the rate of one and one half times the worker's regular pay. The Fair Labor Standards Act of 1938 made this rate mandatory for work performed beyond 40 hours a week by workers employed by firms engaged in interstate commerce. Cf. *straight time.*

time and motion study: an approach for studying the time used and the motions made by an employee to perform a specified task, or a portion thereof, so as to identify job standards. Cf. *job analysis; micromotion study; motion study; predetermined motion times system; time study.* Synonymous with *methods analysis.*

time bargain: an agreement between a seller and a purchaser of securities to exchange a specific stock at a stated price at a stated future time.

time buyer: an executive in an advertising agency who assists in the planning of media campaigns and chooses and buys radio and television time. Cf. *space buyer.*

time deposit (open account): funds deposited under agreement that bear interest from the date of deposit, although the agreement usually requires that such funds remain on deposit for at least 30 days. The agreement stipulates a fixed maturity date or number of days after which payment will be made, or it is stipulated that payment will be made after a given period following notice by the depositor of intention to withdraw. See *Regulation Q.*

time discount: a reduction in an advertising rate determined by the frequency of appearance of an ad. Cf. *transient rate.*

time-event analyses: control techniques that permit the manager to monitor and evaluate elapsed time and attained progress on an undertaking.

time loan: a loan made for a specified period. The maturity date generally is 30, 60, 90, or 120 days after the date of the loan. Interest is usually collected in advance, at the time the loan is made, in the form of a discount.

time management: managing your time effectively by focusing on the areas most important in accomplishing the goal.

time order: an order that becomes a market or limited price order at a specified time.

time scarcity: lack of time, and the difficulty in allocating time for planning in the face of continual day-to-day operating problems.

time-sharing priority: a ranking within the group of tasks associated with a single user, used to determine their precedence for the allocation of system resources.

time standard: the period an average employee needs to complete a task or job under normal conditions of work. Cf. *normal time*.

time study: a procedure by which the actual elapsed time for performing an operation or subdivisions or elements thereof is determined by use of a suitable timing device and recorded. The procedure usually includes adjustment of the actual time according to performance rating to derive the time that should be required to perform the task at a standard pace. Synonymous with *work measurement*. Cf. *time and motion study*.

time ticket: a record of each production employee's hour-by-hour activities, kept so that labor costs can be allocated to the proper jobs or products.

tinge: *(slang)* a salesperson who specializes in the sale of undesirable merchandise that earns him or her bonus payments.

tin parachutes: a plan to protect workers following a takeover; ensures cash payments of up to two and a half times an employee's annual compensation. A form of poison pill, it serves to make a takeover prohibitively expensive. See *poison pill*.

TIP: see *tax-based income policy*.

tips:

(1) **general:** monies offered to encourage or ensure promptness; monies given for services rendered (e.g., 15 percent of a restaurant bill constitutes the waiter's tip).

(2) **securities:** supposedly inside information on corporation affairs; a subjective recommendation to buy or sell a particular stock.

title flows: the path of the title to or ownership of products as they flow through channels of distribution.

Title VII: see *Civil Rights Act of 1964.*

titlewave: (slang) a shakeup in the hierarchy of an organization.

tokenism: as applied to equal employment, the gesture of hiring a few minority group members in an attempt to satisfy government affirmative action requirements or the demands of pressure groups.

token money: an object, usually coins, whose value as money is greater than the market value of the materials of which it is composed.

token order:

(1) a small order placed to test the acceptability of the item.

(2) a small order placed as the simplest way of getting rid of an overly persistent salesperson.

Tokyo Round: a long series of global negotiations for the purpose of mutually removing obstacles to international trade entered into among member nations of the General Agreement on Tariffs and Trade between 1973 and 1979. Cf. *Kennedy Round; Uruguay Round.* See *General Agreement on Tariffs and Trade.*

tolerance: the standard or limit within which a measurement should fall.

toll: originally, a tax for permission to produce something; currently, a charge for permission to utilize a public facility or service (e.g., a bridge, highway, ferry, long-distance telephone system).

top credit: ready credit.

top-down approach: an approach to strategy whereby the major decisions are made at the top levels of the organization and transmitted to the bottom levels.

top leader: a person who heads the multiple command system of an organization.

top management: the top level of an administrative hierarchy. Managers at this level coordinate the work of other managers but do not report to a manager.

top out: the peak period of demand for a product or service, after which demand decreases.

total cost: the sum of a firm's total fixed costs and total variable costs.

total debt: all long-term obligations of the government and its agencies and all interest-bearing short-term credit obligations. Long-term obligations are those that are repayable more than one year after issue.

total fixed costs: the costs that do not change with an organization's output (e.g., payments on rent, property taxes).

total loss: items that have been so badly damaged that they are not considered to be worth repairing (e.g., a car that has suffered a head-on collision with a truck; merchandise that is partly destroyed by fire). See *incurably depreciated*.

total overhead variance: the extent to which actual overhead varies from the amount included in work-in-process inventory; the difference between actual and applied overhead.

total quality management: philosophy of management that is driven by the constant attainment of customer satisfaction through the continuous improvement of all organizational processes.

total revenue: total receipts of a company. It is equal to the price per unit times the number of units sold.

total variable costs: costs that change directly with the firm's output, increasing as output rises over the total range of production (e.g., labor, fuel).

Toxic Substances Control Act of 1976: federal legislation requiring chemical manufacturers to give the Environmental Protection Agency at least three months' notice before beginning commercial production of a new chemical or before marketing an existing chemical for a new use. If the EPA sees no risks, the firm may proceed.

trace:

(1) **general:** the record of a series of events.

(2) **insurance***:* to record a policy holder's record of premium payments.

traceable costs: costs that are directly associated with and assigned to specific responsibility centers.

trade: see *Trade Bill of 1988*.

trade association: a nonprofit organization that purports to serve the common interest of its membership. Usually, members work in closely related industries.

Trade Bill of 1988: signed by President Reagan in August 1988; establishing new guidelines in critical areas: (1) unfair trade: investigation of countries with "pervasive" unfair trade practices. Retaliation if their barriers are not eliminated. *(2)* trade relief: some protection for industries seriously injured by imports if willing to make "positive adjustment" to foreign competition. (3) foreign corruption: clarification of the *Foreign Corrupt Practices Act* to specify what kind of knowledge makes American corporate officials liable if their foreign employees or agents are involved in bribery. (4) worker assistance: expansion of programs for workers displaced by imports. Creation of a $1 billion retraining program, with most of the money going to states. (5) agriculture loans: a marketing loan provision for grains and oilseeds that would be activated in 1990 by a stalemate in trade liberalization talks. Farmers pay such loans at market rates, thus protecting their income while releasing crops to the market. (6) securities: a ban against foreign companies serving as primary dealers in U.S. government securities unless their homeland lets American firms compete against domestic firms. (7) negotiating authority: President given special authority to complete international trade negotiations aimed at increasing markets for banking, insurance, etc., liberalizing rules of investment, and slashing tariffs up to 50 percent.

trade deficit: a negative trade balance.

trade discount: a deduction from the agreed price, usually expressed as a percentage or a series of percentages, that is used in commerce to encourage prompt payment of bills. Trade discount should not be entered in the books of account, nor should it be considered to be a type of earnings.

trade diversion: situation in which exports shift to a less efficient producing country because of preferential trade barriers.

Trade Expansion Act of 1962: federal legislation permitting the president to negotiate additional tariff reductions, eliminate or reduce tariffs on items of the European Common Market, reduce tariffs on the basis of reciprocal trade agreements, and grant technical and financial assistance to employers whose business is adversely affected by tariff reductions.

trade in invisibles: British term denoting *trade in services*.

trademark:

(1) **production:** a word or symbol affixed to goods or their package to identify the manufacturer or place or origin.

(2) **business law:** a distinctive identification of a manufactured product or of a service in the form of a name, logo, motto, and so on. A trademarked brand has legal protection, and only the owner can use the mark. Organizations that file an application at the U.S. Patent Office and use the brand for five years may be granted a trademark. A firm may lose a trademark that has become generic. Generic names are those that consumers use to identify the product, rather than to specify a particular brand (e.g., escalator, aspirin, nylon). Cf. *patent*.

trade name: the name under which an organization conducts business or by which the business or its goods and services are identified. It may or may not be registered as a *trademark*.

trader:
   (1) **general:** anyone who is engaged in trade or commerce.
   (2) **securities:** one who buys and sells for his or her own account for short-term profit.

trade reference: a person or firm to which a seller is referred for credit data on a potential customer.

trade union: workers organized into a voluntary association to further their mutual interests with respect to wages, hours, and working conditions.

trading area: the area surrounding an economic institution from which it derives most of its business.

trading difference: a difference of a fraction of a point in the charged price for securities bought and sold in an odd-lot transaction that is in excess of the price at which the security would be traded in traditional round lots.

trading down: attempting to increase the market of a store or item with an established reputation by lowering price or quality or by changing promotional strategy to appeal to a larger potential market, which is frequently in a lower socioeconomic level. By trading down, the image of the item is often sacrificed for gains in profit. See *nonprice competition; trading up; wheel of retailing.*

trading floor: see *floor.*

trading post: one of many trading locations on the floor of stock exchanges at which stocks assigned to that location are bought and sold. See *floor; specialist.*

trading stamp: a promotional device; a stamp given to customers that is worth a small percentage of the total amount paid for purchases. When a large number of stamps have been accumulated, they can be redeemed at the store or at a warehouse for merchandise.

trading up: attempting to improve the image of a store or item by increasing prices or quality or by altering advertisement approaches, usually to appeal to a market in a higher socioeconomic level. See *wheel of retailing.* Cf. *nonprice competition; trading down.*

Trading-with-the-Enemy Act: U.S. government law that forbids U.S. firms from doing business with countries that are from time to time listed as enemies, for example, North Korea and Cuba.

traditional corporation: the corporation viewed as an instrumentality of a single group—the shareholders—and as having one clear cut purpose: conducting business for maximal profit. This view recognizes no public responsibilities except legal ones and leaves the public interest to the care of the state. Cf. *metrocorporation; well-tempered corporation.*

traditional managers: motivated primarily by promotion and typical corporate rewards; tend to adhere strictly to established hierarchical structures, to be less risk-oriented, and to emphasize short-term results.

traffic:

(1) **merchandising:** the flow of people who are exposed to a store's goods. Measurement of traffic (i.e., counting the people) is usually done as customers enter and leave the store's premises.

(2) **transportation:** business done by a transportation or communications company.

traffic department: the department that schedules the work responsibilities of other units in an advertising agency and has primary responsibility for ensuring that deadlines are met.

training: process of altering employee behavior and attitudes in a way that increases the probability of goal attainment.

training, blitz: rapid training, accomplished during a short period, that attempts to bring personnel to the highest skill level possible under such pressure conditions.

training, cold storage: a form of training that is offered to prepare employees for positions that they may fill at some future date. Synonymous with *training, reserve.*

training, reserve: synonymous with *training, cold storage.*

training, vestibule: training provided in an area that is removed from the factory floor, where similar equipment is available and teachers can function without disturbing the other workers. Cf. *on-the-job training.*

training groups: see *sensitivity training.*

training laboratory: an organized and controlled social situation or setting that is used for the training and development of managers, executives, or officers in various related leadership positions. See *sensitivity training.*

trait theory of leadership: identification of the physical, mental, and personality characteristics believed to be linked to successful leadership.

transaction: any agreement between two or more parties that establishes a legal obligation.

transactional leaders: leaders who guide or motivate their followers in the direction of established goals by clarifying role and task requirements.

transaction analysis: the procedures for analyzing, recording, summarizing, and reporting the transactions of an entity.

transactions demand for money: the demand for cash to finance regular expenses. Transactions demand depends on the frequency with which income payments are received and expenses must be paid.

transactions motive: the holding, by consumers and businessmen, of some of their assets in liquid form to make possible participation in day-to-day spending activities.

transfer:

(1) **human resources:** to shift an employee from one job to another within the same organization.

(2) **securities:** see *stock transfer.*

transfer agent: an agent who keeps a record of the name of each registered shareowner, his or her address, and the number of shares owned. It is the agent's responsibility to see that certificates presented to the office for transfer are properly canceled and that new certificates are issued in the name of the transferee.

transfer costs: the costs that a department accepts for items supplied by other departments. See *transfer price.*

transference: the applicability of training to actual job situations, as evaluated by how readily the trainee can transfer the learning to his or her job.

transfer of training: effective application of principles learned to what is required on the job.

transfer price: the price charged by one segment of an organization for a product or service it supplies to another part of the same firm. See *transfer costs.*

transfer tax: a tax imposed by the federal government and some state governments when a security is sold or transferred from one person to another. The tax is paid by the seller. There is no tax on transfers of bonds. The transfer tax is usually collected as a stamp tax.

transformation process: see *black box concept.*

transient rate: the one-time rate for ads, without quantity or frequency reductions. Cf. *time discount.*

transition management: process of systematically planning, organizing, and implementing change.

transition period: when people evaluate their career progress and sometimes, if things are not going according to their plan, move to another organization.

transnational company: futuristic model of a global, decentralized network with no distinct national identity.

transshipping:
(1) **transportation:** the transfer of items from one carrier to another.
(2) **sales:** the shipment of merchandise by a dealer or distributor to another dealer or distributor beyond the usual selling.

travel and entertainment credit card (T & E card): a credit card issued for use primarily for the purchase of meals, lodging, and transportation.

traveler's letter of credit: a letter of credit issued by a bank to a customer who is preparing for an extended trip. The customer pays for the letter of credit, which is issued for a specified period of time in the amount purchased. The bank furnishes a list of correspondent banks at which drafts drawn against the letter of credit will be honored. See *guaranteed letters of credit; letter of indication.* Cf. *letter of credit.*

traveling sales representative: a salesperson who travels considerably to obtain orders.

travel time: the period required to report from a designated point to the place of work, compensated at negotiated rates of pay. Synonymous with *portal-to-portal pay.*

treasureship: the functions of management that are responsible for the custody and investment of money, the granting of credit and collection of accounts, capital provision, maintenance of a market for the firm's securities, and so on.

Treasury bill: a U.S. government short-term security, sold to the public each week and maturing in 91 to 182 days.

Treasury bond: see *bond, Treasury.*

Treasury certificates: U.S. government short-term securities, sold to the public and maturing in one year.

Treasury deposits: federal government tax receipts that the U.S. Treasury keeps on deposit in Federal Reserve Banks.

Treasury Investment Growth Receipt (TIGR): a right to a U.S. Treasury bond, which matures at a stated time. TIGRs are sold by a brokerage house. The certificate is in effect a discounted bond on which no coupons are paid and which is redeemed at face value upon maturity.

Treasury note: a U.S. government long-term security, sold to the public and maturing in one to five years.

Treasury obligations: see *bond, Treasury; Treasury bill; Treasury certificates; Treasury note.*

treasury stock: the title to previously issued stock of a corporation that has been reacquired by that corporation by purchase, gift, donation, inheritance, or other means. The value of such stock should be considered to be a deduction from the value of outstanding stock of similar type, rather than as an asset of the issuing corporation.

treaty: a reinsurance contract between companies.

Treaty of Paris: see *European Community.*

Treaty of Rome: see *European Community.*

trend forecast: the long-term changes in market demand.

trend-projection technique: method of forecasting employment needs that involves trying to tie employment needs to one or more casual factors.

trial:

(1) **business law:** a proceeding by authorized officials to examine the evidence for the purpose of determining an issue presented according to proper rules of law.

(2) **marketing:** in the adoption process of a consumer, the period when a product is first used. This is a critical point in determining the continued acceptance of the item by consumers.

trial and error pricing: selling an item at varying prices in different locations and then assessing the response to each of the prices.

trial balance: a listing of all account balances that provides a means of testing whether debits equal credits for the total of all accounts.

trial close: an attempt, based on perpetual clues, to zero in on the close of a sale before the natural termination of the sales presentation.

trial period: see *probationary employee.*

triangular trade: trade among three countries in which an attempt is made to create a favorable balance for each.

trickle-down: the process by which federal funds flowing into the national economy stimulate growth by being distributed into organizations, as opposed to stimulating growth by direct payments (e.g., welfare).

trigger points: events that are designated to set a contingency plan in action.

trigger-price system: a federal system for identifying cut-rate steel that is dumped in the United States. It sets minimum prices below which imported steel cannot be sold in this country without triggering an investigation by the Treasury Department. If the agency determines that the steel has been sold at unfairly low prices, bonds and, ultimately antidumping duties can be imposed on the products.

trough: the lowest point of economic activity.

true interest: synonymous with *pure interest*.

trunk show: the display of a vendor's total line of merchandise before an audience that is gathered for the purpose of inspecting the wares.

trust:

(1) **general:** a feeling of confidence in an individual or group.

(2) **securities:** a combination of corporations, usually in the same industry. Stockholders relinquish their stock to a board of trustees, which then issues certificates and dividends. The purposes of creating a trust include controlling costs of production, increasing profits, and reducing competition. See *monopoly*.

trust, corporate: the division of a bank that handles the trust and agency business of corporations.

trust agreement (trust instrument): an agreement between an employer and a trustee that is used in connection with a pension plan. It defines the trustee's powers and duties and states how the funds of the pension plan shall be invested and how payments shall be made to those who benefit under the plan. A trust agreement is usually used in connection with self-administered pension plans and individual policy pension plans.

trust company: an institution, usually state supervised, that engages in the trust business and, usually, in all commercial banking activities.

trustee: a person to whom the title to property has been conveyed for the benefit of another.

trustee in bankruptcy: the individual appointed by a court or by creditors to carry out the responsibilities of trust in a bankruptcy proceeding.

trustee management: a management system whereby managers are responsible for and to the claims of stockholders, the broader community, employees, suppliers, and customers, in addition to being responsible for making a profit.

trusteeship: suspension by an international union of the officers of a local union, with the international taking over control and administration of the local. The Landrum Griffin Act of 1959 established controls over the creation and administration of trusteeships.

trust fund: the funds held by a trustee for the benefit of another person.

trust funds, federal: trust funds established to account for receipts that are held in trust by the government for use in carrying out specific purposes and programs in accordance with a trust agreement or a statute.

trust indenture: a written instrument that contains: a description of all property originally placed in a trust; the agreement with respect to the duties of the trustee in administering the property; the rights of all beneficiaries named and their proportionate shares in the trust; the duration of the trusteeship; the distribution of income from the trust principal to the life tenants; and the distribution of the trust property to the remainder-men at the termination of the trust.

trust instrument: see *trust agreement*.

trustor: an individual who establishes a trust.

Truth in Lending Act of 1968: officially, the Consumer Credit Protection Act of 1968, which requires that most categories of lenders disclose the true annual interest rate on virtually all types of loans and credit sales as well as the total dollar cost and other terms of a loan. See *Fair Credit Billing Act; right of rescission*.

turn:

(1) **general:** (slang) to earn money by performing a task.

(2) **securities:** a description of the full cycle in the buying and selling of a security or a commodity.

(3) **merchandising:** a turnover of merchandise in an inventory.

turnaround:

(1) the return to profitability of an ailing company.

(2) movement by a freight carrier in which the driver returns to the point of origin following the unloading and reloading of cargo.

turnkey: a contractual agreement between a customer and an organization to provide full services or a complete product.

turnover:

(1) **human resources:** the rate at which workers move into and out of employment, usually expressed as the number of accessions and separations during a fixed period for every 100 employees. The Bureau of Labor Statistics computes monthly turnover rates by industry.

(2) **retailing:** the frequency with which an inventory is sold and replaced over a stated period, usually determined by dividing the net sales for the period by the average retail value of the inventory during that period.

(3) **securities:** the volume of business in a security or in the entire market. If turnover on the exchange is reported at 15 million shares on a particular day, this means that 15 million shares changed hands. Odd-lot turnover is tabulated separately and ordinarily is not included in reported volume.

turnover ratio: a measure of capital activity or another factor of business (e.g., when the portfolio of securities is altered, or turned over, within one year). See *operating profit ratio.*

turn over the cover: to investigate both sides of a proposal, idea, proposition, and the like.

twenty-first (21st) century managing: management approach to the rapidly changing business work that emphasizes responsiveness and effective leadership.

twisting: the practice of inducing a policyholder to lapse or cancel a policy for the purpose of replacing it with another, to the detriment of the policyholder. This practice is both unethical and illegal.

two-boss manager: person who is at the point of intersection of two or more of an organization's multiple structures and, thus, is directly responsible to more than one boss.

two-dimensional leadership model: a model that addresses the importance of two factors: task orientation and relationship orientation.

two-dollar brokers: members on the floor of the exchange who execute orders for other brokers who have more business at that time than they can handle themselves or for firms that do not have their exchange member on the floor; recalls the time when these independent brokers received $2 per hundred shares for executing such orders. See *give-up.*

two faces of power: a concept of power in which the negative face involves personal domination of others and the positive face involves power that is exercised not for personal advancement or benefit but for the good of the organization or society.

two-factor theory: a concept developed by Frederick Herzberg that job motivation has two independent sources: hygiene factors and motivators. See *dissatisfiers; satisfiers.*

two-name paper: a short-term negotiable instrument wherein two people guarantee payment.

two-tier gold system: a system devised in 1968 to keep the world's monetary gold from being depleted by speculation and hoarding. International Monetary Fund member nations agreed to keep their present gold reserves for use in settlement of international trade balances only. All gold that was not part of this official tier supply and all newly minted gold would be traded in the open market. The open market gold no longer had any potential monetary value, since all IMF members had promised not to buy any of it for their reserves.

See *International Monetary Fund*.

two-tier wage system: wage system where newly hired employees performing the same jobs as senior employees receive lower rates of pay.

tying arrangement: an agreement in which a purchaser agrees to buy one good from a supplier in order to obtain supplies of another good. Tying arrangements were outlawed by the Clayton Act. See *tie-in sales*.

tying contract: see *tie-in sales*.

type A: people who are extremely competitive, highly committed to work, and have a strong sense of time urgency. Cf. *type B; type Z*.

type B: people who are less competitive, less committed to work, and have a weaker sense of time urgency. Cf. *type A; type Z*.

type Z: type of firm committed to retaining employees; evaluates worker performance based on both qualitative and quantitative information; emphasizes broad career paths, exercises control through informal, implicit mechanisms; requires that decision making occur in groups and based on full-information sharing and consensus; expects individuals to take responsibility for decisions; and emphasizes concern for people. Cf. *type A; type B*.

U

ultimate consumer: the individual who actually uses the bought merchandise.

ultra vires: "beyond power" (*Latin*); describing acts of a corporation when they exceed the power or capability of the corporation as granted by the state in its charter.

umbrella liability: a form of insurance protection against losses in excess of amounts covered by other liability insurance policies. It also protects the insured in many situations that are not covered by the usual liability policies. Such insurance is usually written for sums in the $1 million range for professionals, executives, and businessmen who may be liable to malpractice suits and other large liability claims. Cf. *liability limits.*

umpire: an individual who is called in to decide a controversy. Synonymous with *arbitrator.*

unadjusted rate of return: an expression of the utility of a given project as the ratio of the increase in future average annual net income to the initial increase in needed investment.

unaffiliated union: a local or national union that is not affiliated with the parent labor organization, the AFL–CIO.

unamortized bond discount: the portion of the original bond discount that has not been charged off against earnings.

unappropriated profits: the portion of a firm's profit which has not been paid out in dividends or allocated for any special purpose.

unauthorized strike: a strike that does not have the authorization of the union. See *illegal strike; snap strike; strike.*

unbalanced growth: capital investment that grows at different rates in different areas of an economy.

unbilled revenue: fees earned in a given period for which bills have not yet been sent to the customers.

unbundle:

(1) **general:** to separate the charges for related products and services usually offered in a single transaction at one all–inclusive price, as in computer or financial services.

(2) **insurance:** where a policyholder pays one amount for insurance coverage (including the agent's typically high commission) and, for a small additional fee, places a substantially greater amount of money in a savings fund, where it can earn a high, tax–free yield.

unbundled stock units (USUs): units break down into three pieces: a bond; a share of preferred stock; and an equity appreciation certificate (EAC). The pieces can be traded as a unit or separately. The trio of securities could be worth more than the common share of stock they replace. Corporations buy back shares with USUs, the package of securities that include bonds and two new securities whose value will be based on the firm's dividends and share prices.

uncalled capital: the portion of the issued share capital of a corporation that has not yet been called up.

uncertainty theory: the theory that profit arises from uncertainties due to innovations, changes in taste, price fluctuations, and the vagaries of competition.

unclaimed balances: the balances of the accounts for funds on deposit that have remained inactive for a period designated by the bank. Eventually these unclaimed balances are handed over to the U.S. Comptroller of the Currency.

uncollected funds: a portion of a deposit balance that has not yet been collected by the depository bank; that is, sufficient time has not elapsed to permit checks drawn on other banks to have been returned for nonpayment. See *float*.

uncontrollable factors: factors beyond the direct control of the manager (e.g., competitors' activities, international developments, economic conditions).

underapplied overhead: the excess of factory overhead incurred over factory overhead applied. In practice, this means that the actual cost of overhead incurred was more than the amount charged to the manufacturing process during the year.

under bond: see *warehouse, U.S. Customs bonded*.

undercharge: to charge less than the legal amount.

undercontrol: granting of autonomy to an employee to such a point that the organization loses its ability to direct the individual's efforts toward achieving organizational goals.

underdeveloped country: a nation in which per capita real income is proportionately low in comparison to the per capita real income of nations where industry flourishes. See *less-developed country; vent for surplus*. Cf. *mature economy*.

underemployed: an individual who is working on a job at a lower level than that for which he or she was trained or is experienced to handle. Total skills are untapped, and the employee is often frustrated and/or angry with the job situation.

underemployment: result of taking a job that requires less education, training, or skills than possessed by the worker.

underinsurance: a situation in which not enough insurance is being carried to cover the value of the property or to satisfy a coinsurance clause.

underloading: stress caused when a worker does not have enough work to do, resulting in boredom and monotony.

underlying bond: see *bond, underlying.*

underlying company: synonymous with *subsidiary.*

underselling: selling at a price lower than that listed by a competitor. See *rate war.*

under the rule: an action of selling or buying by stock exchange offi-cers to complete a transaction entered into by a delinquent member of the exchange, who is charged with any difference in price that occurs.

underutilization: a situation in which a department or employer has a smaller proportion of members of a protected class than are found in the employer's labor market. See *concentration in employment.*

underwriter:
(1) **general:** an individual or organization that assumes a risk for a fee
(2) **insurance:** an individual in the insurance business who has the responsibility of accepting risks and determining the amount of insurance the company will write on each acceptable risk.
(3) **securities:** an individual or party that agrees to underwrite a secu-rities issue. See *letter stock.*

undigested securities: securities that are issued beyond the need or ability of the public to absorb them. See *overissue.* Cf. *float; oversub-scribed.*

undistributed profits: the profits of a partnership, syndicate, or joint venture prior to division among the individuals concerned. Synonymous with *retained earnings.*

unearned discount: interest that is received but not yet earned.

unearned income: income that has been collected in advance of the performance of a contract; income derived from investment divi-dends, property rentals, and other sources that do not involve the individual's personal efforts. Cf. *earned income.*

unearned increment: the increase in the value of property that can be attributed to changing social or economic conditions beyond the control of the title holder, as distinguished from an increase in value that can be attributed to the improvements made or additions made by the labor or investment of the title holder.

unearned premium: the portion of the original premium that has not yet been earned by the company because the policy still has some time to run before expiration. A fire or casualty insurance company must carry all unearned premiums as a liability in its financial statement, for if the policy were cancelled, the company would have to pay back part of the premium. See *pro rata cancellation*.

unearned revenues: amounts that are received before they have been earned.

unemployable: a person who is unable to find work; refers to an individual who is too sick, too young, too old, or too badly impaired in mind or body, or to anyone who attempts to avoid work or is a criminal. Cf. *hard-core unemployed*.

unemployment: a condition of not being employed; according to the U.S. government, the condition of a member of the labor force who seeks work but does not find it. Unemployment may be caused by numerous changes in business activity. See *chronic unemployment; cyclical unemployment; frictional unemployment; technological unemployment*.

unemployment compensation: a system of insuring workers against hardship during periods of unemployment. The Unemployment Insurance Act of 1935, as part of the social security program, is administered by the states individually, allowing for variations in rates, duration of payments, and eligibility. Costs are borne by the employers, who get allowances in the form of tax credits. See *supplementary unemployment benefits*.

unexpired cost: any asset.

unfair competition: practices employed by a seller to increase profit by means of misleading advertising; selling below cost or dumping; obtaining rebates from suppliers; or utilizing other devices that unfairly take advantage of a competing firm. Cf. *competition (business)*.

unfair goods: products or items that are not produced by members of a union. See *hot cargo; hot cargo provisions*. Cf. *struck work*.

unfair labor practices: illegal antiunion behavior or illegal union behavior as determined by the National Labor Relations Board, subject to court appeal. For unfair labor practices on the part of management, see *Wagner-Connery Act*. For unfair labor practices on the part of unions, see *Taft-Hartley Act*.

unfair labor practice strike: a strike that is provoked by the employer. This strategy is considered an unfair labor practice under federal and state labor laws.

unfair list: a list of firms that are considered to be unfair to labor, distributed by unions to reduce patronage or otherwise exert pressure.

unfair practices acts: state regulations establishing minimum resale prices. Such laws stipulate that goods must be sold for cost plus some nominal percentage. In practice, there is little enforcement of these rulings.

unfreezing: change efforts to overcome the pressures of both individual resistance and group conformity.

unfunded: a pension fund for which there has been no advance funding and from which payments are made when actual needs arise to pay the pensioners. It is a pay-as-you-go plan.

uniform cash flows: cash flows that are the same for every year.

Uniform Commercial Code: a set of statutes purporting to provide some consistency among states' commercial laws. It includes uniform laws dealing with bills of lading, negotiable instruments, sales, stock transfers, trust receipts, and warehouse receipts.

uniform delivered price: a pricing method whereby all the products are sold at the same delivery price in a stated area, without regard for delivery costs.

Uniform Negotiable Instruments Act: see *negotiable instrument.*

uniform plant loading: establishing monthly production plans and strictly adhering to them so that wide swings in production levels are minimized.

unifunctionalism: a process of combining related organizational functions or activities under a few large departments or units.

unilateral strategy: an organizational development approach that precludes participation by employees. The management hierarchy exercises authority to determine the development program. See *classical design theory.* Cf. *human relations theory; multiple management.*

unilateral transfers: international transfers of resources that involve no exchange or return. They are gifts.

union: a worker's organization whose major objective is representation of its members in bargaining with employers.

union rate: the minimum hourly wage rate accepted by a union for a specific type of activity. It is employed in negotiations.

union recognition: acceptance by an employer of a union as the collective-bargaining representative of his or her workers.

union security clauses: negotiated contract clauses providing for a union shop, maintenance-of-membership, agency shop, or payroll deduction of union dues. These clauses protect the institutional life of the union.

union shop: a contract clause requiring that all members of a bargaining unit retain union membership as a condition of employment, and further requiring that new employees join the union after a stated period, usually 60 to 90 days after being hired. See *union security clauses.* Cf. *preferential shop; modified union shop; Rand formula; union shop.*

union steward: see *shop steward.*

unissued stock: part of the authorized capital stock of a corporation that is not issued or outstanding. It is not part of the corporation's capital stock and receives no dividends. It must be shown on the firm's balance sheet, even though it is neither an asset nor a liability. See *when issued.*

unitary elasticity: the concept that a change in price will be compensated by a corresponding change in demand, so that total income will remain the same.

unit billing: a list of all purchases by a customer, prepared on a single statement.

unit contribution margin: the excess of the sales price of one unit over its variable costs.

unit control: an approach for listing the quantity of goods bought, sold, in stock, and on order, with additional breakdowns as needed. Cf. *taking inventory.*

unit cost: the cost of producing or distributing one unit of a processed item.

United States Employment Service (USES): a federal-state system for helping the jobless to find work or for giving advice on opportunities to workers who seek better jobs.

unit labor cost: the cost of an employee needed to produce one unit of output, determined by dividing compensation by output.

unit pricing: the quotation of prices given in terms of a standard of measurement (by weight, length, count, etc.).

unit-production: production of individual goods or services that are tailored to a customer's specifications.

unit-small batch technology: custom manufacturing of individual items.

unit technology: the approach of a company that spends a large amount of capital on labor relative to its investment in machinery.

unit trust: a British term for mutual investment; a mutual fund.

unity of command: the concept in classical management that a subordinate must be responsible to only one superior. Cf. *chain of command*.

unity of direction: synonymous with *unity of management*.

unity of management: one of Henri Fayol's classic principles, calling for one manager and one plan for all operations that have the same objectives. Synonymous with *unity of direction*.

universal design theory: the concept that there is a single best way to design an organization. Cf. *organizational analysis and planning; situational design theory*.

university-related incubators: an incubator that is a spin-off of an academic research project, and whose major goal is to transfer the findings of basic research and development into a new product or technology.

unlimited accounts: large or reputable businesses that are eligible for any amount of credit.

unlimited tax bond: see *bond, unlimited tax*.

unlisted securities: securities that are not listed on a stock exchange See also *discontinuous market*. Synonymous with *over-the-counter stock*.

unloading:
(1) **merchandising:** selling merchandise at a relatively low price. Synonymous with *dumping*.
(2) **securities:** the sale of stocks and commodities to avoid a loss during a period of a falling market. Cf. *profit taking*.

unpaid balance: on a credit purchase, the difference between the purchase price and the down payment or the value of a trade-in; on a cash loan, the difference between the total loan and the amount that is still owed.

unpaid dividend: a dividend that is declared but not yet distributed.

unrealized profits: paper profits that are not made actual until the firm's securities have been sold.

unrecorded expenses and accrued liabilities: expenses that have not previously been recognized, and companion payable accounts that were incurred during a period but were not paid for by the end of that period.

unrecorded revenues and accrued assets: revenues that have not previously been recognized, and companion receivable accounts that were earned during a period but were not received by the end of that period.

unsecured bond: see *bond, debenture.*

unsecured debt: a debt for which no collateral has been pledged.

unsecured loan: a loan made by a bank based on credit information about the borrower and his or her ability to repay the obligation. The loan is not secured by collateral but is made on the signature of the borrower and sometimes his or her spouse. See *comaker, debenture.*

unskilled worker: a person who can perform only simple manual operations that are easily learned and require no complex skills. Synonymous with *common laborer.*

unsought goods: goods that consumers neither currently need nor seek, such as encyclopedias and cemetery plots.

unstable market: a market in which forces of disequilibrium are reinforced so that movements away from equilibrium are not reversible.

unstructured interview: an interview in which the interviewer asks whatever seems appropriate and adapts the discussion to the responses, choosing those areas where further questions appear warranted and ignoring those where additional discussion seems fruitless. Cf. *structured interview.*

upgrading:

(1) **administration:** a well-defined approach for training and advancement of qualified workers in an organization. Cf. *terminal positions.*

(2) **retailing:** offering superior goods and a greater assortment to customers.

upkeep: the cost of maintaining property or machinery in sound, workable condition. **upper turning point:** a short period during which an upswing ends and a downswing begins. Cf. *lower turning point.*

upscale: people and households of well above average income and education.

upset price: the minimal price at which a seller is willing to sell; the beginning price asked at an auction prior to public bidding. See *marginal seller.* Cf. *knocked-down price; negotiated pric;, reservation price.*

up tick: a transaction made at a price higher than the preceding transaction. A stock may be sold short only on an up tick or on a zero-plus tick (i.e., a transaction at the same price as the preceding trade but higher than the preceding different price). Synonymous with *plus tick.*

upward communication: the flow of communication from lower levels in an organization's hierarchy to employees on higher levels. This is the primary source of feedback in an organization. Cf. *downward communication*.

upward feedback: when subordinates evaluate their boss.

Uruguay Round: On April 8, 1989, 105 nations agreed on greater liberalization of trade in goods and agriculture, as well as extending the General Agreement on Tariffs and Trade's authority to such new areas as trade in services and trade-related intellectual property rights. This marked the halfway point to the scheduled completion of the Round—the GATT seventh—at the end of 1990. By mid-1992 the Uruguay Round was still being negotiated. See *General Agreement on Tariffs and Trade*. Cf. *Kennedy Round; Tokyo Round*.

usance:

(1) **economics:** employment.

(2) **finance:** interest or income.

(3) **finance:** the period allowed for payment of a foreign obligation.

useless quality: goods created with quality, dependability, and/or performance that is superior to that demanded by the public.

user calls: callbacks made by a sales representative to a customer who has already made a purchase from him or her or from the organization.

user expectation: a sales forecast that is construed after a consumer survey or some other form of consumer research has been conducted. Cf. *callback*.

USES: see *United States Employment Services*.

use tax: a tax levied on the initial use of an item rather than on the merchandise when it is sold.

U.S. Savings Bond: see *Bond, Savings (U.S.)*.

usurious: a contract for a loan of money that is made at a rate of interest in excess of that authorized by the statute.

usury: a rate of interest paid for the use of another's money, or for credit extended, that exceeds the legal limit allowed for that type of transaction by the state whose laws govern the legality of the transaction. Cf. *legal interest*.

USUs: see *unbundled stock units*.

utility:

(1) **general:** the capability or power of an item to satisfy a need, as determined by the satisfaction one receives from consuming something.

(2) **economics:** a publicly owned facility (e.g., an electric power plant).

utility expenditures: expenditures for construction or acquisition of publicly owned utility facilities or equipment, for production and distribution of utility commodities and services, and for interest on debt.

utter: to put out or pass off (e.g., to utter a check is to give it to another in payment of an obligation).

V

vacation pay: compensation received for a specified vacation period, which usually varies in time with the employee's length of service.

valence: a person's preference for a first-level outcome. See *expectancy theory of motivation; first-level outcome.*

validity: how well a test or selection procedure measures a person's attributes.

valorization: government action leading to the establishment of a price or value for an item or service.

valuation:
  (1) **general:** synonymous with *appraise.*
  (2) **finance:** setting a value for anything.

valuation reserves:
  (1) reserves established to provide for a drop in the existing value of the assets to which they pertain.
  (2) reserves established to provide for a reasonably probable failure to achieve full value.

value: the worth of property, goods, services, and so on; purchasing power. See *book value.*

value added: the part of the value of produced goods that is developed in a company. It is determined by subtracting from sales the costs of materials and supplies, energy, contract work, and so on, and it includes labor expenses, administrative and sales costs, and other operating profits.

value-added tax (VAT): a government tax on the value added; a tax on the selling price of manufactured items less the cost of the materials and expenses used in their production.

value analysis: a purchasing strategy of asking the buyer's engineers to project the cost of goods in an attempt to keep the vendor's prices low.

value approach: including ethical and value judgments in the decision-making process to effect change in an organization.

value attainment: extent to which a job allows fulfillment of one's work values.

value-based hiring: practice of screening and hiring people whose values are consistent with those of the company, rather than looking just at an applicant's job-related skills.

value compensated: a purchase or sale of foreign exchange to be executed by cable. The purchaser reimburses the seller for the earlier value on the data of actual payment abroad of the foreign currency, theoretically resulting in no loss of interest to either party.

value date: the date on which a bank deposit becomes effective. The date fixed is based on the time required to collect a payment on the item deposited from another bank. See *collection*.

value engineering: the systematic use of tools that identify the required function, establish a value for that function, and ultimately provide the function at the lowest overall cost.

value in use: the value of goods to the individual who uses them.

variable annuity: an annuity contract providing lifetime retirement payments that vary in amount with the results of investment in a separate account portfolio. See *annuity accumulation unit*.

variable budget: a budget that divides expenses into fixed costs and variable costs. The latter are allowed to vary on a predetermined basis with differing levels of output.

variable cost: a cost that is uniform per unit but changes in total in direct proportion to changes in the related total activity or volume.

variable expenses: expenses that vary with the level of factory output or plant capacity (e.g., the expenses of power, oils, and lubricants vary with the number of machines in operation; the expense of compensation insurance varies with the number of employees in the department). Generally, variable expenses are controllable.

variable inspection: a method of quality control in which measurements are used to determine the deviation from standards.

variable-pay programs: portion of an employee's pay is based on some individual and/or organizational measure of performance.

variance:

(1) **general:** a disagreement between two sets of figures or facts.

(2) **administration:** the difference between budgeted expectations and actual results; a means for reporting on management by exception. A variance may be positive or negative, depending on the relationship between budget and actual results.

(3) **accounting:** the difference between expected and actual production costs.

variety of skill: the degree to which a job calls for activities that involve different talents and skills.

variety store: a retail operation that carries limited quantities of apparel and accessories for the family as well as other goods, with prices set somewhat lower than in retail stores.

VAT: see *value-added tax*.

vault: a large room or rooms in a bank or financial institution where the cash on hand is stored and safe deposit boxes are located.

veil of money theory: the theory that money is neutral and does not reflect a nation's true economic condition but is merely a cosmetic for other social and financial forces and activity. Cf. *savings and investment theory*.

velocity of circulation: the rate at which money supply is spent for a stated time period, usually one year.

vend: to offer to sell something.

vendor: a manufacturer, wholesaler, or importer from whom goods are purchased.

vendor charge-backs: the return of goods to a vendor, accompanied by an adjusted invoice. Proof of delivery to the vendor is usually provided.

vendor performance index: an index of the percentage of purchasing agents reporting slower deliveries from suppliers.

vendor point rating system: a method of evaluating vendor performance where points are assigned to how well the vendor performed on several factors, such as quality, delivery, and price.

vendor reliability: the capability of the seller to meet the conditions of the contract.

vendor's lien: an unpaid seller's right to take possession of property until the purchase price has been recovered. See *general lien*. Cf. *seller's lien*.

vent for surplus: the hypothesis that economic progress spreads from developing industrial locations to less-developed geographic locations by means of the increasing demand for items in former areas.

venture: a business activity or undertaking that involves some or considerable risk.

venture capital:
  (1) **securities:** funds available from the issue of new stock.
  (2) **finance:** reinvested monies from stockholders.
  (3) **finance:** funds invested in enterprises that do not usually have access to conventional sources of capital (banks, stock market, etc.).

venture capital funds: mutual funds invested in securities of firms that are little known and often are not yet registered with the SEC.

venture capitalist: an individual who provides a full range of financial service for new or growing ventures, such as capital for startups and expansions, marketing research, management consulting, assistance in negotiating technical agreements, and assistance in employee recruitment and development of employee agreements.

venture team: small group of people who operate as a semi-autonomous unit to create and develop a new idea.

verbal communication: the sharing of ideas through words.

vertical communication: any communication that moves up or down the chain of command.

vertical coordination: linking the activities at the top of the organization with those at the middle and lower levels in order to achieve organizational goals.

vertical dyad: two persons who are related hierarchically, such as supervisor-subordinate pair.

vertical equity: the principle that those who are different should be treated in correspondingly different ways.

vertical integration: see *integration, vertical.*

vertical job enrichment: type of work design based on the idea that giving jobholders the discretion to choose job activities and outcomes will improve their satisfaction.

vertically combined (integrated): a business firm that performs all the various stages of production of a single finished item.

vertical merger: the joining of firms that are responsible for different production stages of a particular product so that more of the entire process, from raw material to retail sales, is under the control of a single management.

vertical mobility: see *labor mobility.*

vertical promotion: a form of advancement that increases employee opportunities, provides for additional training, increases responsibility, and in most cases is accompanied by additional pay.

vertical specialization: factors in the division of labor that involve degrees of power, influence, and decision making. Cf. *horizontal specialization.*

vertical strain: the competition that exists between different hierarchical levels in a company.

vertical union: synonymous with *industrial union.*

vested rights: provisions in a pension program ensuring that if a worker leaves the firm for any reason, he or she can retain the pension rights acquired while employed by the company offering the plan. See *fully vested; instant vesting.*

vestibule school: see *training, vestibule.*

vesting: the right of an employee under a retirement plan to retain part or all of the annuities purchased by the employer's contributions on his or her behalf; or, in some plans, the right to receive a cash payment of equivalent value on termination of employment after certain qualifying conditions have been met.

vicarious liability: the principle that an employer is legally responsible for the actions of his or her employees while they are on the job. See *liability.*

video conferencing: live television exchange between people in different locations. Synonymous with *video teleconferencing.*

Videodex: a research firm that supplies indices of television program popularity, employing the diary technique to obtain information. See *diary method.*

video teleconferencing: synonymous with *video conferencing.*

vintage capital: a measure of capital stock that assumes that newly produced capital goods are more productive than older ones.

visible trade: the portion of commerce between nations that is shown by records of transactions involving the exchange of tangible items.

vitalist theory: a concept that it is more important to plan in terms of the total economic system and then integrate the full system relative to its individual smaller parts.

VLCC: very large crude carrier.

vocation: a person's business, profession, or occupation.

Vocational Rehabilitation Act of 1973: a federal law prohibiting discrimination against physically or mentally handicapped workers who are employed by organizations with government contracts of $2,500 or more.

voidable contract: an agreement that can be rescinded by either of the parties in the event of fraud, incompetence, or other sufficient cause.

voluntary bankruptcy: see *bankruptcy.*

voluntary chain: a wholesaling organization established by independent retailers or wholesalers to gather increased purchasing power.

voluntary issue: an issue that may be raised in collective bargaining, although neither side may insist that it be bargained over.

vostro account: an account maintained with a depository bank by a bank in a foreign country. Cf. *nostro account.*

voting right: a stockholder's right to vote his or her stock in the affairs of the company. Most common shares have one vote each. Preferred stock usually carries the right to vote when preferred dividends are in default for a specified period. The right to vote is usually delegated by proxy of the stockholder to another person.

voting trust: an agreement whereby stockholders turn over their voting rights to a small group of people, who are called voting trustees.

voucher: a written statement that bears witness or vouches for something (e.g. a voucher showing that services have been rendered or goods bought).

voucher check: a form of check to which a voucher is attached. The voucher portion of the check is used to describe or otherwise designate the purpose for which the check is drawn. When a voucher check is received from a buyer by a seller, the seller detaches the voucher from the check before presenting the check for payment. The voucher is then used as the posting medium to credit the accounts receivable ledger, thereby showing payment received from the buyer. Many businesses use copies of *voucher checks* as their record of invoices paid.

vouching: the auditing method of tracing a transaction back to its documentary support.

Vroom-Yetton model: a contingency model of leadership that focuses on the degree of participation leaders should use in reaching a decision. The diagnosis of situational factors determines the degree of participation required.

vulture capital: partnerships that aim to buy busted properties at distressed prices, turn them around and sell them later for big profits.

vulture funds: funds formed to purchase distressed properties at bargain prices, turn them around, and then sell them at a substantial profit.

W

wage: compensation of employees who receive a stated sum per piece, hour, day, or any other unit or period; usually refers to all compensation paid, including salaries. Cf. *earnings; payroll; rate variance.*

wage and salary administration: a well-defined approach for establishing wages and salaries according to an organization's rules and policies and in line with the practice of other companies in the same industry and/or area of work.

wage bracket (range): the range of salary payment for a specific occupation.

wage compression: the condition that occurs when the difference between wages for the top and the lowest jobs is narrowed. This usually results from giving larger pay increases to lower-paid jobs than to higher-paid jobs.

wage control: centralized control and stabilization of wages, usually during national crises.

wage curve: a graphic representation of a smooth progression between pay grades.

wage floor: a minimum wage, established by contract, below which an employee cannot be hired, or the legal minimum defined by the Fair Labor Standards Act or state labor laws.

wage freeze: a limit on salary increases, usually imposed by a government.

wage incentive plan: see *incentive pay*

wage minimum: see *minimum wage.*

wage-price spiral: see *inflationary spiral.*

wage rate: the amount of pay for a given period (hour, day, week, etc.). See *rate variance, wage scale.*

wage-rate compression: compression of differentials between job classes, particularly the differential between hourly workers and their managers.

wage scale: a wage rate structure covering all employees in a department, division, plant, or office. In most cases, the scale is based on the employer's judgment of a task's value.

wages fund theory: a theory proposed by John Stuart Mill in 1848, stating that manufacturers should put aside a portion of their capital funds for the purpose of hiring workers needed for production.

wage stabilization: a governmental program to keep wages for a particular industry or location from rapidly increasing beyond existing levels. See *inflationary spiral; stabilization policy.*

wage stop: a practice of not permitting an unemployed worker to receive more public monies than he or she would earn while working. See *workfare.*

Wagner Act: the National Labor Relations Act of 1935. Synonymous with *Wagner-Connery Act.*

Wagner-Connery Act: federal legislation that guarantees the right of workers to organize and bargain collectively for a contract and declares specific employer actions to be unfair labor practices. The law created the National Labor Relations Board to administer its functions. See *Baby Wagner Acts; bargaining agent; blacklist; discriminatory discharge; employer interference; subcontracting; unfair labor practices.* Synonymous with *Wagner Act*, its popular name.

waiting line theory: an approach to maximizing the efficient servicing of arrivals at a service facility by balancing the costs associated with waiting time and idle time; the application of queuing theory to practical problems.

waiting period:

(1) **insurance:** the time specified in certain policies that insure against loss of use, or against disability, that must pass before payment will begin.

(2) **administration:** the time between filing a claim for unemployment benefits or workers' compensation and the beginning of such benefit payments.

(3) **securities:** the time, usually 20 days, that must pass between the application for listing a new security with the SEC and the date when the securities can be offered to the public.

wait order: a request to a medium to hold an advertisement and not release it until a date in the future is named.

wait state: the condition of a specific task that is dependent on one or more events before it can enter the ready condition.

waiver of premium: a life insurance clause providing that if the insured becomes totally and permanently disabled, his or her insurance policy will be continued in full force and the company will exempt the insured from paying further premiums during disability.

waiver of protest: a statement, signed by the endorser of a note, indicating that he or she will remain liable even if he or she is not notified that the note has not been paid when due.

waiver of restoration premium: a provision in many contracts whereby the company agrees not to charge an additional premium for reinstating the amount of the contract after loss has occurred.

walking delegate: a local union's officer who is responsible for the union's financial, administrative, or labor relations activities. Synonymous with *business agent*.

walk-ins: job seekers who arrive at the personnel department in search of a position without any prior referrals and not in response to a specific ad or request.

walkout: synonymous with *strike*.

Wall Street: popular name for the New York City business and financial district.

want ads: ads that describe an available job and its benefits, identify the employer, and tell those who are interested how to apply.

want slips: written statements submitted to buyers by salespersons indicating items not in stock that have been requested by customers.

warehouse: a structure where goods are stored prior to distribution.

warehouse, bonded: see *bonded*.

warehouse, bulk: a warehouse for the tank storage of liquids and open, dry products (e.g., coal, sand, stone).

warehouse, captive: synonymous with *warehouse, private*.

warehouse, commodity: a warehouse that stores commodity goods (cotton, wool, tobacco, and other grown items). See *godown*.

warehouse, company: synonymous with *warehouse, private*.

warehouse, private: a warehouse operated by an owner, which holds his goods. Synonymous with *warehouse, captive; warehouse, company*. See *locker stocks*.

warehouse, public: a warehouse that is rented out by the owner as a facility for storing goods.

warehouse, state bonded: a public warehouse, under government supervision, that has been licensed by a state prior to operation. Merchandise is stored there without payment of duties or taxes until it is withdrawn from the warehouse.

warehouse, U.S. Customs bonded: a federal warehouse where goods remain until duty has been collected from the importer. Goods under bond are also kept there.

warehouse, U.S. Internal Revenue: a public warehouse in which the owner of goods has posted a bond guaranteeing payment of internal revenue tax on U.S.-produced items.

warehouse receipt: an instrument listing the goods or commodities deposited in a warehouse. It is a receipt for the commodities listed, for which the warehouse is the bailee. Warehouse receipts may be either nonnegotiable or negotiable.

warehouse stock: goods held in quantity in a warehouse for reasons of economy.

wares: items or commodities that are offered for sale.

WARN: see *Worker Adjustment and Retraining Notification Act.*

warrant: a certificate giving the holder the right to purchase securities at a stipulated price within a specified time limit or at any time. Sometimes a warrant is offered with securities as an inducement to buy.

warranty:

(1) **sales:** a promise by a seller that the product or property that is being sold is as he or she has represented it. Usually a warranty is presented with the sold goods. See *caveat emptor; express warranty.*

(2) **insurance:** a statement in a policy of the existence of a fact or a condition of the subject of insurance that, if found to be untrue by misrepresentation, will void the policy.

wash sale: a spurious sale in which the seller becomes the purchaser of what he sells. The purpose is to create activity in the item or to establish a market price. A wash sale is prohibited by law.

waste circulation: advertising that is done in a location where there is no distribution for the advertised product.

wasting assets: assets whose value is depleted and will eventually be exhausted by the continued operations of an extractive business (e.g., oil wells, mining claims). See *depletion allowance.*

watch filing: a procedure by which losses on small risks are referred to the underwriter for attention.

watered stock: corporate stock issued by a corporation for property at an overvaluation, or stock released for which the corporation receives nothing in payment.

waybill: a statement identifying a shipment, showing the shipper, consignee, routing, rate, and weights. It is used by the carrier as an internal record.

weakest-link theory: the concept that the least durable component in a product will control its useful life. According to this theory, all components should be built so that their life span will be equal in all units of similar function and price. See *functional obsolescence.*

weak market: a situation characterized by a greater demand for selling than for purchasing.

wealth: an economic term designating the value of a person's total possessions and rights in property. Cf. *national wealth.*

wealth effect: see *Pigou effect concept.*

wealth tax: an annual tax on a person's assets above a stated minimum, even if these assets do not yield any income.

weight breaks: the levels at which the charges per 100 pounds decrease as the shipment increases in weight.

weighted application blank: a technique used to differentiate between successful and less successful employees through the use of application blank factors.

weighted average: a periodic inventory cost flow assumption whereby the cost of goods sold and the ending inventory are determined to be a weighted-average cost of all merchandise available for sale during the period.

Welfare and Pension Plans Disclosure Act of 1958: a federal law covering all nongovernmental welfare and pension plans that affect more than 25 employees. Administrators must file annual reports to the Secretary of Labor, describing annual financial statements. Synonymous with *Teller Act.*

welfare economics: a branch of economic theory that deals with the evolution of principles for maximizing social welfare.

wellhead tax: a government proposal to tax domestic oil as it leaves the well. The amount of the tax is the difference between its current controlled price and the world market price imposed by the OPEC cartel.

wellness programs: organizationally supported programs that focus on the employee's total physical and mental condition.

well-tempered corporation: the corporation viewed as lying between the two extremes of the traditional corporation and the metrocorporation. This type of corporation takes public expectations into account, but with full regard for management's responsibilities to the stockholders. Its supporters hold that the claims of stockholders and creditors will more likely be met if a firm develops a position as a socially responsible company. Cf. *metrocorporation; traditional corporation.*

wet goods: liquids.

wharfage: a charge levied against a vessel resting at a wharf. Synonymous with *dockage and moorage.*

wheel of retailing: the theory that, when entering the market, new forms of retailing first emphasize lower prices but as time passes the prices rise, making the merchandise subject to competition from newer organizations, which commence operations with lower prices. See *trading down; trading up.*

when issued: a short form of "when, as, and if issued," a term that indicates a conditional transaction in a security authorized for issuance but not yet actually issued. All "when-issued" transactions are on a conditional basis, to be settled if and when the actual security is issued and the exchange or the National Association of Securities Dealers rules that the transactions are to be settled.

whipsawed: to have experienced a substantial loss at both ends of a securities transaction.

whistle-blowers: individuals who report unethical practices by their employers to authorities inside and/or outside the organization.

white-collar: workers in offices and other nonproduction phases of industry. During the 1960s, white-collar personnel for the first time came to outnumber blue-collar workers.

white elephant: property that is so costly to maintain that it is virtually impossible to operate it at a profit; or property with respect to which a loss is certain.

white goods: appliances of substantial size and cost (e.g., refrigerators, freezers, washing machines, stoves).

white knight: in order to encourage a successful company takeover by another firm, a friendly bidder who is brought in to put down another bidder. Cf. *gray knight; white squires.*

White Paper: published in June 1985, the European Commission's program for "Completing the Internal Market," which listed over 300 legislative proposals and a timetable for their adoption. Its aim was to weld together the 12 separate national economies into a single market by 1992. It was approved by the European Community Heads of State or Government and given a constitutional basis by the Single European Act of 1986. See *Single European Act.*

white squires: like corporate white knights that rescue firms from hostile takeovers, they only make friendly investments, usually stopping short of taking total control of firms in which they invest. Instead, they agree to hold a stake, usually more than 15 percent, for several years, frequently with a voice in running the company. Cf. *white knight.*

whole coverage: any type of insurance that provides for payment from all losses without any deductions.

whole life: synonymous with *ordinary life.*

wholesale: to sell goods in gross to retailers, who then sell the merchandise to customers.

wholesale price: the price for a good that is paid by retailers to suppliers.

wholesale price index: a measure compiled by the U.S. Bureau of Labor Statistics, showing the average change in the price of approximately 2,200 commodities at the primary market level (usually the level at which the commodity is first sold commercially in substantial volume) compared to the average level in selected base years.

wholesaler: an individual who buys and sells goods to retailers and other users but does not sell in significant amounts to the consumer. Cf. *merchant wholesaler.* See *full-service wholesaler.*

wholesaling: selling merchandise to firms that purchase in the bid and asked prices at the beginning of the market day.

wider environment: the aspects of an organization's environment that are outside the task environment.

wide span of control: span of control in which a large number of people, often between eight and 15, report to a superior.

wildcat strike: see *strike.*

Williams Act of 1968: see *Saturday night special.*

windfall profit: an unexpected profit arising from causes that were not controlled by the recipient.

winding up: the process of liquidating a company.

window dressing: statements that appear to be more positive than warranted; statements that make something appear better than it is. See *painting the bus.*

wire house: a member firm of an exchange that maintains a communications network either linking its own branch offices to offices of correspondent firms or linking some combination of such offices.

with all faults: without a guarantee of the absence of imperfections, usually in real estate transactions; as is.

withholding tax: federal, state, or city taxes that are withheld by employers from the salaries of employees and paid directly to the taxing agency.

without dividend: synonymous with *ex-dividend,.*

without recourse:
    (1) **finance:** used in endorsing a negotiable instrument when the

endorser of a note is no longer responsible, should the obligation not be paid. See *qualified endorsement.*

(2) **sales:** an agreement that the purchaser accepts all risks in the transaction and gives up all rights of recourse. See *caveat emptor.*

with recourse:

(1) **finance:** used in endorsing a negotiable instrument when the endorser of a note continues to be responsible, should the obligation not be paid.

(2) **sales:** an agreement that if the seller is unable to meet his or her obligations, the purchaser has the right to endorse a claim against the seller for sustained damages.

wolf: an experienced and often crafty speculator.

Women's Business Opportunity Act: federal law to establish programs and initiate efforts to assist the development of women-owned businesses.

work agenda: loosely connected set of tentative goals and tasks that a manager is attempting to accomplish.

workaholic: an individual who desires to work constantly.

work audit: synonymous with *desk audit.*

work centrality: importance of work in an individual's life relative to other areas of interest.

Worker Adjustment and Retraining Notification Act (WARN): federal legislation, taking effect on February 4, 1989, requiring firms that close factories to give workers and the government a 60-day advance notice.

work ethic: a belief in the inherent value of work in a society.

workfare: a recently introduced concept authorizing state and local officials to require that welfare recipients perform any kind of work assigned to them as a condition of getting welfare checks. See *wage stop.*

work low: the sequence of jobs in an organization needed to produce the firm's goods or services.

work force: see *labor force.*

work force diversity: increasingly heterogeneity of organizations with the inclusion of different groups.

work group: the group of employees formally assigned to perform a specific task or function.

working capital: the excess of current assets over current liabilities, representing the capital immediately available for the continued operation of a business.

working capital turnover: a measure of the amount of working capital used in sustaining the sales of a period, computed by dividing net sales by average working capital.

working control: theoretically, ownership of 51 percent of a company's voting stock, thus a controlling interest. In practice, however—and this is particularly true in the case of a large corporation—effective (i.e., working) control sometimes can be exerted through ownership, individually or by a group acting in concert, of less than 50 percent of the stock. Cf. *controlled company.*

work-in-process inventory: all products that have begun the manufacturing process but have not been completed. Work-in-process inventory is the cost of partially completed production. Cf. *finished-goods inventory; inventory.*

work-in-progress: see *work-in-process inventory.*

workload: a quantitative measure of the amount of work performed, measured by the hour or by day.

workload analysis: synonymous with *personnel demand analysis.*

work measurement: synonymous with *time study.*

workers' compensation: a system for compensating workers who are injured or disabled on the job; programs are established by state law and differ widely. Typically, benefits are paid under private insurance policies, but awards are determined by state boards. Cf. *state disability plan; temporary disability benefit; temporary total disability benefits.* See *average weekly benefits.* Also referred to as *workmen's compensation.*

workmen's compensation: see *workers' compensation.*

work overload: a situation in which someone has too much to do (quantitative overload) or someone does not have the necessary skills to perform the job (qualitative overload). Cf. *work underload.*

workplace politics: organization members intentionally seeking selfish goals that conflict with those of others in the organization.

work rules: usually part of a union contract, rules that regulate on-the-job working conditions, to protect employees from arbitrary employer action, ensure decent conditions and health standards, and often prescribe a code of conduct for the workers.

work sharing: distribution of work evenly among employees to prevent layoffs during slack periods. See *share-the-work.*

work simplification: a reorganization of methods, equipment, resources, and working conditions to minimize worker fatigue and increase worker efficiency and output.

work specialization: degree to which tasks in the organization are subdivided into separate jobs.

work stoppages: strikes or lockouts that involve six or more workers and extend to a full work shift or longer.

work title: a distinctive, designative, but usually unofficial name or title given to a work activity, process, or operation.

work underload: a situation in which someone has too little to do (quantitative underload) or someone has many more skills than are necessary to perform the job (qualitative underload). Cf. *work overload.*

work unit: the smallest subdivision of a job or operation.

workweek: the scheduled number of working hours for a week or for any seven-day period of work.

World Bank: see *International Bank for Reconstruction and Development.*

World Trade Organization (WTO): replaced GATT in 1995 as an international organization that facilitates the implementation of trade agreements reached in various rounds. By 2003, more than 145 nations were brought together under one institutional umbrella. China became a WTO member in December 2002.

worldwide coverage: insurance coverage of all goods (e.g., jewelry, furs) throughout the world.

worldwide product division: a structure in which each product unit is given international responsibilities.

worth: the total value of something, including an investment in a business. See *net worth.*

wrap account: a special brokerage account for wealthy investors who want to shift the burden of stock-pricing decisions to an outside money manager. In return for a flat annual fee, the brokerage house helps the investor select a money manager, pays the manager's fee, executes whatever trades the manager orders, and monitors performance.

write:

(1) **insurance:** to insure or to underwrite.

(2) **insurance:** sometimes, to sell insurance.

write-down: the book value to which an asset has been reduced to adjust for the capital that has been lost on a decline of the asset's value.

write-off: an asset that has been determined to be uncollectible and therefore has been charged off as a loss. Sometimes it is the debt itself. Cf. *charge off; written-down value.*

writer: the seller of an option contract.

write-up:
(1) **accounting:** an increase in an asset's book value that does not result from added costs, or an adjustment of an asset account to correspond to an appraisal value.

(2) **sales:** documentation of the making of a sale.

written-down value: in accounting, the valuation or cost of any asset minus the written-off depreciation. Cf. *write-off*.

X

XD: a symbol in a newspaper listing of stock prices indicating that a stock is ex dividend.

x-off: transmitter off.

x-on: transmitter on.

Y

Yankee bond market: issues floated in the United States, in dollars, by foreign governments and corporations.

yellow-dog contract: an individual agreement between an employer and an employee that, as a condition of employment, the latter will not join a union.

yes-man: (slang) an employee who constantly agrees with his superior.

yes-no controls: controls that allow for a screening process point at which specific approval is needed to permit the activity to continue.

yield:

(1) **general:** the profit or income created through an investment in property.

(2) **finance:** to give up possession; to pay.

(3) **economics:** the net return of a tax.

(4) **finance:** the rate of return received from an investment in a specific security or a specific piece of property, most commonly expressed in terms that designate the annual rate of return on the investment. Synonymous with *return*. See *ROI*.

yield ratio: percentage of applicants from a recruitment source that made it to the next
phase of the selection process.

yield to maturity: the rate of return on an investment when it is retained until maturity, given as a percentage.

youth market: people under 25 years of age, who are often interested in goods and services that are different, unusual, or suggest values other than those held by older people.

yo-yo stocks: highly volatile securities. These stocks are high-priced specialty issues that fluctuate greatly in price.

Z

ZBB: see *zero-base budgeting.*

zero balance: see *balance of account.*

zero-balance account: a practice, currently illegal, involving the establishment by commercial banks of a demand deposit account and a savings account for the same customer, with the understanding that funds would not be allowed to remain idle in the demand deposit account. Deposits to the demand account would be transferred into the savings account, and funds would be transferred (for a service charge) automatically by the bank from the savings account to the demand account to cover checks written on the demand account.

zero-base budgeting (ZBB):

(1) **accounting and budgeting:** a financial management technique to redirect funds from lower-priority current programs to higher ones to pinpoint opportunities for improved efficiency and effectiveness, to reduce budgets while raising operating performance, and to improve profitability. See *planning-programming-budgeting.*

(2) **economics:** the approach of justifying the budget and its program for each year or two, instead of studying funding increases or decreases in the programs separately as the need arises.

zero-base media planning: a media selection process that involves (1) listing and ranking media objectives in order of importance; (2) examining and ranking possible media components in terms of their compatibility with the stated media objectives; (3) forming decision packages (i.e., plans consisting of one or more of these components); (4) comparing the decision packages with other packages that are retained and compatible with objectives; and (5) reviewing, making tradeoffs, and arriving at resolution of the plan.

zero-coupon bond: see *bond, zero-coupon.*

zero defects: an approach to reward employees who make no mistakes and waste no resources while discharging their function over a given period.

zero floor limit: see *floor limit.*

zero-plus tick: see *up tick.*

zero proof: a mechanical method of posting records in a manner serving to prove that the previous balance on each line of posting was made correctly.

zero-sum situation: a competitive situation in which resources are fixed so that when one group succeeds, the other group must fail.

zipper clause: a standard clause in a negotiated contract that represents an attempt to preclude any discussion of contract conditions during the life of the agreement. The clause states that the agreement is the sole and complete instrument between the two parties. Cf. *reopener clause*.

zone of indifference: a category of subordinates' attitudes toward authority in which certain orders are accepted without question.

zoning price: the result of a policy of separating a total marketing area into areas (zones) for which different prices are established. All buyers in a zone pay the same price. See *market segmentation*.